A HISTORY OF
KOREAN LITERATURE

This is a comprehensive narrative history of Korean literature from
its inception and the establishment of a royal Confucian academy in
the seventh century, through a period during which most literature
in Korea was written in Chinese and the subsequent invention of
the Korean alphabet in 1443–1444, to the present day. It provides a
wealth of information for scholars, students, and lovers of literature.
Combining both history and criticism, the study reflects the latest
scholarship and offers a systematic account of the development of
all genres. Consisting of twenty-five chapters, it covers twentieth-
century poetry, fiction by women, and the literature of North Korea.
Other topics include the canon, ideology, and further critical issues
central to an understanding of Korean literary history. This is a major
contribution to the field and a study that will stand for many years as
the primary resource for studying Korean literature.

A HISTORY OF
KOREAN LITERATURE

EDITED BY

PETER H. LEE

CAMBRIDGE
UNIVERSITY PRESS

CAMBRIDGE UNIVERSITY PRESS
Cambridge, New York, Melbourne, Madrid, Cape Town, Singapore, São Paulo, Delhi

Cambridge University Press
The Edinburgh Building, Cambridge CB2 8RU, UK

Published in the United States of America by Cambridge University Press, New York

www.cambridge.org
Information on this title: www.cambridge.org/9780521828581

First published 2003
This digitally printed version 2008

A catalogue record for this publication is available from the British Library

ISBN 978-0-521-82858-1 hardback
ISBN 978-0-521-10065-6 paperback

The generous contribution of the Korea Foundation in support of
this volume is gratefully acknowledged.

To our fellow students of Korean literature

Contents

Contents

Illustrations

Contributors

HO-MIN SOHN is Professor of Korean Linguistics at the University of Hawaii at Manoa. He is the author of numerous books, including *The Korean Language* (1999).

KIM CHŎNGNAN is Professor of French at Sangji University; she is the author of three volumes of poetry, two volumes of criticism, and translator of French literary works into Korean.

KIM HŬNGGYU is Professor of Korean Literature and Director of the Institute of Korean Culture at Korea University. He is the author of a number of books on traditional and modern Korean literature.

PETER H. LEE is Professor of Korean and Comparative Literature at the University of California, Los Angeles. He is the author of numerous books on Korean literature and civilization, including the two-volume *Sourcebook of Korean Civilization* (1993–1996), *The Columbia Anthology of Traditional Korean Poetry* (2002), and *Myths of Korea* (2000).

CAROLYN SO holds a Ph.D. from UCLA, and she specializes in modern Korean women writers.

KWŎN YŎNGMIN is Professor of Modern Korean Literature at Seoul National University. He is a foremost critic of twentieth-century Korean literature and the author of some dozen major critical studies.

CH'OE YUN is Professor of French Literature at Sogang University. She is the author of prize-winning works of fiction, including "You Are No Longer You" (1991), "There a Petal Silently Falls" (1988), and "The Gray Snowman" (1992), and a collection of essays. She has translated a number of modern Korean works of fiction into French.

Preface

A History of Korean Literature has been written to meet the needs of students and general readers who wish to know the main outline of Korean literature. It reflects the latest scholarship on all genres and periods and traces the development of Korean literature – encompassing literary works written in the *hyangch'al* system, literary Chinese, and the vernacular after the invention of the Korean alphabet in the mid fifteenth century. Unlike Chinese and Japanese literature, however, a large number of Korean classical works are not yet available in translation. Thus, translations presented here are mostly my own. Unlike other literary histories, we have avoided current jargon or theory because we want this history to be useful for more than a decade. When contemporary theory and criticism are useful in reading a text, however, we have employed it. Throughout, we are mindful that this is a narrative history of Korean literature, combining both history and criticism, addressed to the English-speaking reader. Topics in the general introduction include canon and ideology, traditional generic hierarchy, and other critical issues central to an understanding of Korean literary history. We have allotted more space to twentieth-century literature, but here the names swarm and the treatment is inevitably cursory. Minor figures are omitted so that attention may be focused on major writers and their representative works, the ones most likely to be read. Although there is no such thing as an innocent eye, we have tried to steer clear of ideological readings – nationalist, populist, or leftist.

Generally, chapters on traditional literary genres tend to be shorter than those on twentieth-century literature, because they aim simply to provide basic information on the main authors, works, schools, and movements of the period, genre, or form. What the student and the general reader need is accurate data – not always provided by books in Korean published in Korea and books in English published in the English-speaking countries. Proportionally, treatments of twentieth-century literature tend to be long for at least two reasons. The Korean literature written in the twentieth century exceeds in volume all the Korean literature in the vernacular since the invention of the Korean alphabet in the mid fifteenth century. To date, however, there is no accurate and reliable account of either poetry or fiction in Korean. Another reason for assigning more space to contemporary literature has to do with the demand of students. Most graduate students are especially interested in twentieth-century literature. All but one of my graduate students, for example, specialize in the subject – and the same is true in other East Asian literature departments in the West. The reasons are not far to seek: the study of classical Korean literature requires many years of rigorous training in literary Chinese and Middle Korean as well as thorough knowledge of Korean language and literature, Korean historical and other indigenous culture, Korean reception of Confucian canonical texts, Chinese histories and literature, at least one other literature besides Korean, and, finally, literary theory, Korean as well as Western.

As in Chinese literature, most known authors in Korea are male. Women known by name include exceptional female entertainers (such as Hwang Chini who wrote both in literary Chinese and in Korean) or middle- or upper-class women dating mostly from the eighteenth century. Only one Silla song is attributed to a woman. Clear signs of the lyric persona and the abundant use of honorific verbal endings in Koryŏ songs, however, indicate that not only the lyric speaker but also the performer was female. Some portions of anonymous *sijo* and *kasa*, moreover, are probably by women. We wish to recover neglected works by women writers and reexamine the criteria of a traditionally male canon. Gender is a factor in certain genres, as women writers chose *sijo*, *kasa*, letters, prose essays, and stories as their favored forms of expression in late Chosŏn. To present the literary achievement of women writers in the present objectively, we have assigned separate chapters to women scholars of the subject (Chapters 20, 22, and 24). Their contributions demonstrate considerable variation in approach, scope, and style, but as teachers of Korean literature they have sought to share their perspectives and knowledge with the reader.

A word should be said on collaboration. Given our essential agreement on matters of literary theory and methodology, Professor Kim Hŭnggyu and I first decided to collaborate on the project. Chapters are undertaken on the basis of research interest and previous publications. Later, Professors Ch'oe Yun, Kim Chŏngnan, Kwŏn Yŏngmin, Carolyn So, and Ho-min Sohn agreed to join in our endeavor. I contributed the introduction, part of Chapter 1, and Chapters 2 to 11, part of Chapter 14, and Chapters 17, 18, and 21; Kim Hŭnggyu wrote Chapters 12–13, 15–16, and part of Chapter 14;

Ch'oe Yun, Chapter 24; Kim Chŏngnan, Chapter 22; Kwŏn Yŏngmin, Chapters 19, 23, and 25; Carolyn So, Chapter 20; and Ho-min Sohn, the introductory essay on the Korean language in Chapter 1.

Kim Hŭnggyu and Kim Uch'ang first suggested the project. I would like to thank my collaborators for their contributions, which offer such a variety of viewpoints, and the translators of chapters originally written in Korean: Chŏng Chinbae, Mickey Hong, Jennifer Lee, Julie Park, Youngju Ryu, and Peter Yun. It was my good fortune to have been encouraged by several colleagues and friends and to have had the chance of learning from the students I have taught. Kim Hŭnggyu, Kwŏn Yŏngmin, and Paek Nakch'ŏng obtained books for me.

A glossary, with sinographs, provides information on Chinese literary genres used by Korean writers as well as authors, works, and technical terms that will be useful to the reader. Those who wish access to the important primary texts concerning the sociopolitical, intellectual, and cultural background may turn to Peter H. Lee (ed.), *Sourcebook of Korean Civilization*, 2 vols. (New York: Columbia University Press, 1993–1996), also available now in Italian: *Fonti per lo Studio della Civiltá Coreana*, 3 vols. (Milan: O barra O, 2000–2002); Peter H. Lee et al. (eds.), *Sources of Korean Tradition*, 2 vols. (New York: Columbia University Press, 1997–2001); and Ki-baik Lee, *A New History of Korea* (Cambridge, Mass.: Harvard University Press, 1984).

Linda Bree of Cambridge University Press furthered and followed the progress of my work. I owe special thanks to anonymous readers of the text for their helpful suggestions and to my editor, Don Yoder, who encouraged me in a difficult time and offered many tactical suggestions.

This history was written over a period of time during which I received generous support from the UCLA Academic Senate and the Korea Research Foundation. I record my profound thanks to both.

PETER H. LEE

Note on the text

For complete author's name, title, and publishing details of the works cited in short form, see the Bibliography. The romanization of Korean names follows the McCune-Reischauer system and certain suggestions made in *Korean Studies* 4 (1980):111–125. The apostrophe to mark two separate sounds (as in the word *han'gŭl*) has been omitted throughout. Dates for rulers of China and Korea are reign dates without *r*. They are preceded by birth and death dates if required. All Korean dates are converted to the Western calendar.

Works cited frequently in the notes have been abbreviated according to the following list. All Korean-language texts were published in Seoul unless otherwise indicated:

ACKS	*Akchang kasa* (Words for songs and music). In *Wŏnbon Hanguk kojŏn ch'ongsŏ*. Taejegak, 1972
AHKB	Sŏng Hyŏn, *Akhak kwebŏm* (Canon of music). Yŏnse taehakkyo Inmun kwahak yŏnguso, 1968
CHKY	Hwang Suyŏng, ed., *Chŭngbo Hanguk kŭmsŏk yumun* (Augmented epigraphic remains of Korea). Ilchisa, 1978
CKK	Chōsen kosho kankōkai (Old Korean Books Publication Society)
CN	Nam Hyoon, *Ch'ugang naenghwa* (Literary miscellany of Nam Hyoon). *CKK*, 1909
CWS	Kuksa p'yŏnch'an wiwŏnhoe, ed., *Chosŏn wangjo sillok* (Veritable records of the Chosŏn dynasty [an annalistic history compiled by a royal committee after the death of a king]). 48 vols. 1955–1958
CY	Yi Sugwang, *Chibong yusŏl* (Literary miscellany of Yi Sugwang). *CKK*, 1915
HHS	Fan Ye et al., *Hou Hanshu* (History of the Later Han). 12 vols. Peking: Zhonghua shuju, 1963

HHST	*Hanguk hyŏndae simunhak taegye* (Modern Korean Poetry Series). Chisik sanŏpsa ed.
HKMT	*Hanguk kojŏn munhak taegye* (Classic Korean Literature Series)
JKS	*Journal of Korean Studies*
KJ	*Korea Journal*
KMC	*Koryŏ myŏnghyŏn chip* (Collected works of renowned worthies of the Koryŏ dynasty). Taedong munhwa yŏnguwŏn
KRS	Chŏng Inji et al., *Koryŏ sa* (History of Koryŏ). 3 vols. Tongbanghak yŏnguso, 1955–1961
KS	*Korean Studies*
KT	*Koryŏ taejanggyŏng*, 48 vols. Tongguk taehakkyo, 1957–1976
KYS	Sim Chaewan, ed., *Kyobon yŏktae sijo chŏnsŏ* (Variorum edition of the complete *sijo* canon). Sejong munhwasa, 1972
NP	Yi Chehyŏn, *Nagong pisŏl* (or *Yŏgong p'aesŏl*) (Lowly jottings by old man "Oak"). (*KMC* 2:1973)
PaC	Yi Illo, *P'ahan chip* (Jottings to break up idleness) (*KMC* 2:1973)
PoC	Ch'oe Cha, *Pohan chip* (*KMC* 2:1973)
PS	Yi Kyubo, *Paegun sosŏl* (Jottings by the retired gentleman White Cloud) (*KMC* 1:1973)
SGSG	Kim Pusik, *Samguk sagi* (Historical records of the Three Kingdoms), ed. Yi Pyŏngdo. 1977
SGYS	Iryŏn, *Samguk yusa*, (Memorabilia of the Three Kingdoms), ed. Ch'oe Namsŏn. Minjung sŏgwan, 1954
SGZ	Chen Shou, *Sanguo zhi* (History of the Three Kingdoms). 5 vols. Peking: Zhonghua shuju
SH	*Siyong hyangak po* (Notations for Korean music in contemporary use). In *Wŏnbon Hanguk kojŏn ch'ongsŏ*. Taejegak, 1972
SJK	*Seoul Journal of Korean Studies*
SL	Peter H. Lee, ed., *The Silence of Love: Twentieth-Century Korean Poetry*. Honolulu: University Press of Hawaii, 1980
SPK	Hŏ Kyun, *Sŏngso pokpu ko*. In *Hŏ Kyun chŏnjip* (Collected works of Hŏ Kyun). Taedong munhwa yŏnguwŏn, 1972
TMS	Sŏ Kŏjŏng, *Tong munsŏn* (Anthology of Korean literature in Chinese). 3 vols. Kyŏnghŭi ch'ulp'ansa, 1966–1967
TS	Sŏ Kŏjŏng, *Tongin sihwa* (Remarks on poetry by a man from the East), ed. Chang Hongjae. Hagusa, 1980

TYC   Yi Kyubo, *Tongguk Yi-sangguk chip* (Collected works of
             Minister Yi of Korea). Tongguk munhwasa, 1958
YMC   *Yijo myŏnghyŏn chip* (Collected works of renowned worthies
             of the Yi dynasty). 4 vols. Taedong munhwa yŏnguwŏn,
             1984–1986

Korean dynasties

Old Chosŏn (2333–194 BC)
Wiman Chosŏn (194–108 BC)
Puyŏ (?–346)
Pon Kaya (42–532)
Koguryŏ (37 BC – AD 668)
Paekche (18 BC – AD 660)
Silla (57 BC – AD 935)
Parhae (698–926)
Koryŏ (918–1392)
Chosŏn (1392–1910)
1. T'aejo (1335–1408; r. 1392–1398)
2. Chŏngjong (1357–1419; r. 1398–1400)
3. T'aejong (1367–1422; r. 1400–1418)
4. Sejong (1397–1450; r. 1418–1450)
5. Munjong (1414–1452; r. 1450–1452)
6. Tanjong (1441–1457; r. 1452–1455)
7. Sejo (1417–1468; r. 1455–1468)
8. Yejong (1450–1469; r. 1468–1469)
9. Sŏngjong (1456–1494; r. 1469–1494)
10. Yŏnsangun (1476–1506; r. 1494–1506)
11. Chungjong (1488–1544; r. 1506–1544)
12. Injong (1515–1545; r. 1544–1545)
13. Myŏngjong (1534–1567; r. 1545–1567)
14. Sŏnjo (1552–1608; r. 1567–1608)
15. Kwanghaegun (1575–1641; r. 1608–1623)
16. Injo (1595–1649; r. 1623–1649)
17. Hyojong (1619–1659; r. 1649–1659)
18. Hyŏnjong (1641–1674; r. 1659–1674)
19. Sukchong (1661–1720; r. 1674–1720)
20. Kyŏngjong (1688–1724; r. 1720–1724)

21. Yŏngjo (1694–1776; r. 1724–1776)
22. Chŏngjo (1752–1800; r. 1776–1800)
23. Sunjo (1790–1834; r. 1800–1834)
24. Hŏnjong (1827–1849; r. 1834–1849)
25. Ch'ŏlchong (1831–1864; r. 1849–1864)
26. Kojong (1853–1907; r. 1864–1907)
27. Sunjong (1874–1926; r. 1907–1910)

Glossary

Akchang kasa 樂章歌詞 (Words for songs and music). Anonymous compilation of song texts dating from Koryŏ and early Chosŏn.

Amitāyus 無量壽佛. Buddha of Infinite Life, or Amitābha 無量光明佛, the Boddha of Infinite Light who presides over the Western Paradise.

Analects (*Lunyu* 論語). Confucian canonical text memorized by students in China and Korea in the past. Consisting of 20 chapters divided into 497 sections, it is a collection of statements made by Confucius and his disciples.

An Chohwan 安肇煥 (or Chowŏn, fl. 1777–1800). Author of *Manŏn sa* 萬言詞 (An exile's life).

An Chŏnggi 안정기 (n.d.). North Korean writer of verse.

An Ch'uk 安軸 (1282–1348). Author of two *kyŏnggi-ch'e* songs: "Kwandong pyŏlgok" 關東別曲 (Song of Diamond Mountains, c. 1328 or 1330) in 8 stanzas, and "Chukkye pyŏlgok" 竹溪別曲 (Song of the bamboo stream, 1348) in 5 stanzas – both in *idu* and Chinese.

An Hamgwang 安含光 (1910–82). North Korean writer of fiction who wrote *Chosŏn munhak sa* (History of Korean literature, 1956).

An Hoenam 安懷南 (1910–66). Writer of fiction who was drafted to work in a coal mine in Kyushu by the Japanese. Returning to Korea after the liberation, he went north and was purged in 1966.

aniri 아니리. Spoken passages in *p'ansori*.

An Kuksŏn 安國善 (1854–1928). Author of *Kŭmsu hoeŭi rok* 禽獸會議錄 (Proceedings of the council of birds and beasts, 1908) who published Korea's first collection of stories in the twentieth century.

An Minyŏng 安玟英 (1816–86?). Professional singer of *sijo* and coeditor of *Kagok wŏllyu* 歌曲源流 (Sourcebook of songs, 1876). He addressed 10 *sijo* to plum blossoms.

An Sŏkkyŏng 安錫儆 (1718–74). Author of *Sapkyo mallok* 霅橋漫錄 (Random records at Sapkyo).

An Sugil 安壽吉 (1911–77). Writer of fiction including *Pukkando* 北間島 (North Jiandao, 1959), which celebrates the Korean farmers' attachment to land in their diasporic settlement in northern Manchuria.

Arai Hakuseki 新井白石 (1657–1725). Japanese scholar, historian, and poet in Chinese.

Avalokiteśvara 觀世音. "One who observes the sounds of the world," bodhisattva 菩薩 of compassion.

Ban Gu 班固 (32–92). Compiler of *Qian Hanshu* 前漢書 (History of the Former Han).

Bodhisattva. One who arouses the thought of supreme perfect enlightenment and is intent on achieving buddhahood by practicing the six (sometimes ten) perfections: donation, morality, patience, vigor, meditation, and wisdom.

Bo Juyi 白居易 (772–846). Tang poet widely read in Korea and Japan, especially his "Changhen ge" 長恨歌 (Song of everlasting sorrow, 806) and "Pipa xing" 琵琶行 (Song of the lute, 816).

Book of Changes (*Yijing* 易經 or *Zhouyi* 周易). Divination manual with a list of 64 hexagrams composed of 6 lines, unbroken or broken once in the middle, and a number of later speculations.

Book of Documents (*Shujing* 書經 or *Shangshu* 尚書). Confucian canonical text consisting mostly of speeches attributed to kings and ministers in laconic language.

Book of Filial Piety (*Xiaojing* 孝經). One of the 13 Confucian canonical texts, it takes the form of a colloquy between Confucius and his disciple Zeng Shen 曾參 (505–436 BC) on filial devotion as the cornerstone of all moral action.

Book of Songs (*Shijing* 詩經). China's oldest anthology of poetry and one of the Confucia canonical texts. The 305 songs are divided into airs (*feng* 風), 1–160; lesser odes (*xiaoya* 小雅), 161–234; greater odes (*daya* 大雅), 235–65; and encomia (*sung* 頌), 266–305.

Cao Pi 曹丕 (187–226). Eldest son of Cao Cao and first ruler of the Wei. Wrote verse and "Lun wen" 論文 (Discourse on literature), included in *Wenxuan* 文選.

Ch'ae Chegong 蔡濟恭 (1720–99). Chosŏn statesman and writer who opposed suppression of Catholics.

Ch'ae Mansik 蔡萬植 (1902–50). Writer of fiction such as *T'angnyu* (Muddy currents, 1937) and *T'aep'yŏng ch'ŏnha* (Peace under heaven, 1938), a satirical portrayal of how tradition clashes with the new materialism.

Chang Chiyŏn 張志淵 (1864–1921). Journalist and anti-Japanese writer of a biographical fiction, *Aeguk puin chŏn* 愛國婦人傳 (Life of a patriotic woman, 1907), on Joan of Arc who was burned at the stake on 30 May 1431 at age 19.

Changhwa Hongnyŏn chŏn 薔花紅蓮傳 (Tale of Rose Flower and Pink Lotus). Popular traditional narrative story about an evil stepmother and two stepdaughters.

Ch'angjak kwa pip'yŏng 創作과批評 (Creation and criticism). Influential quarterly begun in January 1966 under the direction of Paek Nakch'ŏng with the intent of strengthening the social function of literature; later became an organ of nationalist and committed writers.

Ch'angjo 創造 (Creation, February 1919 – May 1921). Korea's first literary coterie journal published by Korean students studying in Japan, first in Tokyo then in Seoul; published stories of naturalistic realism and romantic poems such as Chu Yohan's "Pullori" (Fireworks).

Changkki chŏn 장끼傳 (Tale of a pheasant cock). Anonymous traditional narrative story, a fictionalized version of "Ballad of the Pheasant Cock," already current in middle to late eighteenth century.

Changkki t'aryŏng 장끼打令 (Ballad of the pheasant cock). One of the 12 *p'ansori* pieces but no longer extant. Its content might have been the same as the narrative story.

Chang Kyŏngse 張經世 (1547–1615). Scholar and poet who passed the 1589 examination and wrote a *sijo* sequence of 12 songs.

Chang Manyŏng 張萬榮 (1914–77). Imagist poet known for pictorial quality.

Chang P'ungun chŏn 張風雲傳 (Tale of Chang P'ungun). Anonymous traditional narrative story in Korean about the protagonist Chang's tribulations; separated from his parents, he ultimately finds his father.

Chang Tŏkcho 張德祚 (b. 1914). Woman writer of fiction including historical fiction.

Chang Yonghak 張龍鶴 (b. 1912). Writer drafted into the Japanese army during the Second World War. His story "Yohan sijip" (Poems of John the Baptist, 1955) is said to have been influenced by Sartre's *La Nausée* (1938). His full-length fiction, *Wŏnhyŏng ŭi chŏnsŏl* (Legend of a circle, 1962), concerns the tragic nature of the postwar human condition in Korea.

Chang Yu 張維 (1587–1638). Passed the 1609 examination and was known for his Chinese prose in the Tang and Song style; collected works published as *Kyegok chip* 谿谷集.

chapka 雜歌 (miscellaneous songs). Songs sung by roving actors and professional singers, usually to the accompaniment of music, such as "Sipchang ka" 十杖歌 (Song of ten strokes); less refined than *kagok* and *sijo* songs.

chapki 雜記 (literary miscellany). Korean counterpart of the Chinese *biji* 筆記 and the Japanese *zuihitsu* 隨筆 written in plain-style Chinese about current events, along with prose portraits, and literary criticism.

Chi Haryŏn 池河連 (pen name of Yi Hyŏnuk, 1912–60). Woman writer, Im Hwa's second wife, who delved into the hypocrisy of patriarchy and investigated woman's selfhood. She went north in 1947.

chingol 眞骨 (True Bone). The highest stratum of Silla aristocracy.

chinsa 進士 (literary licentiate). Candidates for civil-service examination who were required to compose one rhymeprose and one old-style poem, each based on the topic and rhyme provided; 100 successful candidates qualified to enroll in the Royal Confucian Academy.

Cho Chihun 趙芝薰 (1920–68). Poet and critic who made his debut in 1939 with polished and ornate poems; later wrote social poetry.

Cho Chŏngnae 趙廷來 (b. 1943). Writer of fiction who focused on the reality of Korea's division and tried to trace its origin in a 10-volume historical fiction, *T'aebaek sanmaek* (T'aebaek mountain range, 1983–89).

Cho Chonsŏng 趙存性 (1554–1628). Writer of a *sijo* sequence of 4 songs, "Hoa kok" 呼兒曲 (Calling a boy).

Cho Chun 趙浚 (d. 1405). Supporter of General Yi Sŏnggye, who founded the state of Chosŏn; 2 *sijo* are attributed to him.

Ch'oe Cha 崔滋 (1188–1260). Author of *Pohan chip* 補閑集 (Supplementary jottings in idleness, 1254), a collection of anecdotes and poetry criticism.

Ch'oe Ch'ansik 崔瓚植 (1881–1951). Early twentieth-century writer of fiction – for example, *Ch'uwŏl saek* 秋月色 (Color of the autumn moon, 1912).

Ch'oe Ch'iwŏn 崔致遠 (b. 857). Silla writer who passed the Tang examination for foreigners in 874 at age 18 and served as secretary to Gao Bian at the time of the Huang Qiao 黃巢 rebellion (874). After returning to Korea he led a retired life. His collected works, *Kyewŏn p'ilgyŏng [chip]* 桂苑筆耕 [集] (Plowing the laurel grove with a writing brush), preface dated 886, are included in the Chinese collectanea *Sibu congkan* 四部叢刊.

Ch'oe Chŏnghŭi 崔貞熙 (1912–90). Woman writer of fiction who declared she was a "woman with the lamp of her heart always lit."

Ch'oe Hae 崔瀣 (1287–1340). Koryŏ writer who wrote "Yesan ŭnja chŏn" 猊山隱者傳 (Life of the hermit Yesan), an autobiographical narrative in the third person.

Ch'oe Haenggwi 崔行歸 (late tenth century). Translator of Great Master Kyunyŏ's 均如 (923–73) 11 Buddhist songs into Chinese in 967.

Ch'oe Haksu 최학수 (n.d.). North Korean writer of fiction.

Ch'oe Harim 崔夏林 (b. 1935). Poet who wrote internalized poetry of engagement.

Ch'oe Inho 崔仁浩 (b. 1945). Writer of bestsellers and serious fiction concerned with the world's discord and falsity disguised by the ruling ideology.

Ch'oe Inhun 崔仁勳 (b. 1936). Writer of fiction and drama who prefers the dramatization of ideas and the inner life to chronological realism. His characters are often faceless abstractions – sometimes only a voice.

Ch'oe Kyŏngch'ang 崔慶昌 (1539–83). Poet, statesman, and addressee of one *sijo* by Hong Nang 洪娘.

Ch'oe Malli 崔萬理 (fl. 1419–44). Opposed use of the new Korean alphabet invented by King Sejong.

Ch'oe Myŏnghŭi 崔明熙 (1945–98). Woman writer of fiction known especially for her major multi-volume work, *Honppul* (Soul fire, 1983–96).

Ch'oe Myŏngik 崔明翊 (b. 1908). Writer of fiction who went north and has written such historical fiction as *Sŏsan taesa* (Great Master Sŏsan, 1956) about the great monk who organized monk soldiers during the Japanese invasion of Korea.

Ch'oe Namsŏn 崔南善 (1890–1957). Historian and poet who wrote Korea's first example of free verse, "Hae egesŏ sonyŏn ege" (From the sea to boys, 1908), and *sijo*; also compiled an anthology of *sijo* (1928).

Ch'oe Pyŏngdu t'aryŏng 崔병두타령 (Ballad of Ch'oe Pyŏngdu). *P'ansori* work that narrates an incident in Wŏnju, Kangwŏn province, concerning a corrupt magistrate Chŏng who extorted the wealth of Ch'oe Pyŏngdu (or Pyŏngdo). Ch'oe's tragic story comprises two-thirds of Yi Injik's fiction *Ŭnsegye* 銀世界 (A silvery world, 1908). A dramatized version is performed at Wŏngaksa theatre.

Ch'oe Sŏhae 崔曙海 (1901–37). Writer of class-conscious fiction.

Ch'oe Sŏktu 崔石斗 (1917–51). North Korean writer of poetry.

Ch'oe Sŭngja 崔勝子 (b. 1952). Woman writer, translator, and critic known for feminist poetry with her consciousness at its center.

Ch'oe Yŏng 崔瑩 (1316–88). Famous Koryŏ general killed by the pro-Yi-Sŏnggye party; 2 *sijo* are attributed to him.

Ch'oe Yun 崔胤 (b. 1953). Woman writer of postmodernist fiction, critic, and professor of French literature at Sogang University.

Chogwang 朝光 (Morning light or Korea's light, November 1935 – December 1944). Monthly omnibus magazine published by *Chosŏn Daily*; altogether 110 numbers.

Cho Hŭibaek 趙熙百 (late nineteenth century). Author of "Tohae ka" 渡海歌 (Song of crossing the sea, 1875) concerning his trip from Chŏlla to Kanghwa Island.

Cho Kich'ŏn 趙基天 (1913–51). Farmer's son who studied in Russia and wrote such narrative verses as *Paektusan* (Mount Paektu, 1948), *Uri ŭi kil* (Our road, 1949), and *Chosŏn ŭn ssaunda* (Korea fights, 1951).

Chŏkpyŏk ka 赤壁歌 (Song of Red Cliff). A *p'ansori* work based on an episode in the *Romance of the Three Kingdoms* 三國志演義.

Cho Kwangjo 趙光祖 (1482–1519). Upright Confucian minister who introduced social and cultural reforms but became the envy of the entrenched bureaucracy and a victim of the 1519 literati purge; later enshrined in the Confucian Temple.

Cho Myŏnghŭi 趙明熙 (1894–1942). Writer of class-conscious fiction.

Chŏngbi chŏn 鄭妃傳 (Tale of Princess Chŏng). Anonymous traditional narrative fiction in Korean concerning a crown princess who saves her father and the crown prince from an evil minister's rebellion.

Chŏng Chisang 鄭知常 (d. 1135). Koryŏ poet known especially for "Taedong kang" (Taedong River) or "Songin" (Sending off a friend); later executed by his poetic rival Kim Pusik for alleged involvement in a rebellion.

Chŏng Chiyong 鄭芝溶 (1903–50?). Successful prewar poet, known for inventive use of polished language, who wrote some 120 poems between 1925 and 1941. Also served as poetry editor of *K'at'ollik ch'ŏngnyŏn* 카톨릭青年 (Catholic youth, 1933–36) and *Munjang* 文章 (Literature, 1939–41). After 1945 he was unproductive and is presumed to have been killed during the Korean War.

Chŏng Ch'ŏl 鄭澈 (1537–94). Poet, statesman, scholar, and author of 5 *kasa* and 79 *sijo* included in the *Songgang kasa* 松江歌詞 (Pine River anthology).

Ch'ŏnggu yadam 青邱野談 (Unofficial stories from the green hills). Late nineteenth-century collection of 178 stories in Chinese with realistic depiction.

Ch'ŏnggu yŏngŏn 青丘永言 (Songs of green hills, 1728). First anthology of *sijo* compiled by Kim Ch'ŏnt'aek; the number of *sijo* varies according to the edition.

Chŏng Hagyu 丁學遊 (1786–1855). Writer of a 518-line *kasa*, *Nongga wŏllyŏng ka* 農家月令歌 (The farmer's works and days).

Chŏng Hwajin 정화진 (b. 1959). Contemporary woman writer of feminist poetry.

Chŏng Hyŏnjong 鄭玄宗 (b. 1938). Contemporary poet who initially explored the questions of death and life's emptiness. Later he wrote witty, more accessible poems about the unity of humans and nature and merging the self into the cosmos through transformation and participation. He is professor of modern Korean literature at Yonsei University.

Chŏng Inji 鄭麟趾 (1396–1478). Scholar and statesman of early Chosŏn who helped King Sejong in his linguistic research that led to the invention of the Korean alphabet and compilation of such literary works as *Yongbi ŏch'ŏn ka* 龍飛御天歌 (*Songs of Flying Dragons*, 1445–47).

Chŏng Io 鄭以吾 (1354–1434). Writer of "Yŏlbu Ch'oe-ssi chŏn" 烈婦崔氏傳 (Life of Lady Ch'oe of Chŏlla), whose subject died c. 1379.

Chŏng Kihwa 鄭琦和 (1686–1740). Writer of *Ch'ŏngun pongi* 天君本紀 (Basic annals of the human mind; also called *Simsa* 心史 [History of the mind]) in Chinese.

Chŏng Kŭgin 丁克仁 (1401–81). Writer of the *kasa* "Sangch'un kok" 賞春曲 (In praise of spring).

Chŏng Mongju 鄭夢周 (1337–92). Koryŏ loyalist and scholar widely revered by posterity; 1 *sijo* is attributed to him.

Chŏng Munhyang 정문향 (1919–89). North Korean writer of poetry.

Chŏng Naegyo 鄭來僑 (1681–1757). Writer of a preface to *Ch'ŏnggu yŏngŏn* 青丘永言 (Songs of green hills, 1728); left 2 *sijo*.

Ch'ŏngnyŏn hoesim kok 青年悔心曲 (Song of a youth's repentance). Anonymous traditional narrative in Korean set in the time of King Injo (1623–79). The *kasa* quoted in the story warns of the dangerous allure of female entertainers.

"Chŏngsan pyŏlgok" 青山別曲 (Song of green mountain). Koryŏ popular song consisting of eight 4-line stanzas with the same refrain at the end of each stanza.

Chŏng Sŏ 鄭敍 (fl. 1151–70). Composed the 10-line song "Chŏng Kwajŏng" 鄭瓜亭 (Regret, c. 1156) at the place of his exile in Tongnae.

"Chŏngsŏk ka" 鄭石歌 (Song of the gong and chimes). Anonymous Koryŏ ceremonial song with a 3-line introduction, followed by 5 6-line stanzas.

Chŏng Sujŏng chŏn 鄭秀(喬)貞傳 (Tale of Chŏng Sujŏng). Anonymous traditional narrative about the military prowess of the woman general Chŏng, in some 10 editions. Also called *Yŏ changgun chŏn* 女將軍傳 (Tale of a woman general).

Chŏng T'aeje 鄭泰齊 (1612–69). Author of *Ch'ŏngun yŏnŭi* 天君演義 (Romance of the human mind) in Chinese.

Chŏng Tojŏn 鄭道傳 (d. 1398). Architect of Chosŏn dynasty institutions and author of eulogies praising Yi Sŏnggye's military exploits and the new capital Seoul.

"Chŏngŭp-kun millansi yŏhang ch'ŏngyo" 井邑郡民亂時閭巷聽謠 (Song heard during a rebellion in Chŏngŭp). Anonymous *kasa* about corrupt administration during the late seventeenth century.

Chŏng Yagyong 丁若鏞 (1762–1836). Great Practical Learning scholar and writer of poems about farming and the misery of the people.

Chŏn Kwangyong 全光鏞 (1919–88). Writer of fiction and professor of modern Korean literature at Seoul National University; awarded the Tongin prize for a short story "Kapitan Lee" (1962).

Chŏn Pyŏngsun 田炳淳 (b. 1929). Woman writer of fiction.

Chŏn Sangguk 全相國 (b. 1940). Writer of fiction dealing with Korea's division, the problem of evil, and the meaning of education. Strong fathers play central roles in his work.

Ch'ŏn Sebong 千世鳳 (1915–86). North Korean writer of fiction including *Chosŏn ŭi pom* (Spring in Korea, 1991).

Ch'ŏnsusŏk 泉水石 (Stones in the spring water). Anonymous 9-volume traditional fiction in Korean existing only in manuscript. Set in late Tang China, it concerns the life of the protagonist Wi Pohyŏng. The edited version was published in 1972.

Ch'ŏn Yanghŭi 千良姬 (b. 1942). Woman writer of feminist poetry and essays.

Chŏn Yŏngt'aek 田榮澤 (1894–1967). Writer of fiction who was active in Christian education.

Cho Pyŏgam 趙碧岩 (1908–85). Poet who went north and was active there.

Cho Pyŏngsŏk 조병석 (n.d.). North Korean writer of poetry.

"Chŏryŏng sinhwa" 絕纓新話 (New funny story that loosens the hat strings). Story in the form of conversation between a scholar going to market and a scatterbrain going to Seoul that ridicules the changing social situation of the 1900s; serialized in *Taehan minbo* 大韓民報 (Korea People's Press, 14 October to 23 November 1909), signed by "An Idiot" 白痴生.

Cho Sehŭi 趙世熙 (b. 1942). Writer of fiction known for a group of stories dealing with the urban proletariat during Korea's industrialization in the 1960s and 1970s. In the story *Nanjangi ka ssoaollin chagŭn kong* (Dwarf launches a little bowl, 1976) Cho analyzes, through many voices, the realities of labor and the hypocrisy of society as dislocated workers oscillate between their anguish and fantasies of flight.

"Chosin" 調信. Story of a caretaker who falls in love with a magistrate's daughter in a dream allegory in the *Memorabilia of the Three Kingdoms*. This story shares the same motif with such Tang tales of wonder as "The Prefect of South Branch" and "The World Inside a Pillow" and, later, records of a dream journey. The theme concerns the ultimate vanity of striving for worldly renown.

Chosŏn 朝鮮 (1392–1910). Dynasty ruled by the Yi house.

Chosŏn Daily 朝鮮日報. Korean-language daily from 6 March 1920 to 10 August 1940 when Japanese colonial authorities banned publication; resumed on 23 November 1945.

Cho Sŏnggi 趙聖期 (1638–89). Author of the vernacular fiction *Ch'angsŏn kamŭi rok* 彰善感義錄 (Showing goodness and stirred by righteousness), written to entertain his mother.

Cho Sŏnggwan 조성관 (n.d.). North Korean writer of fiction.

Chosŏn mundan 朝鮮文壇 (Korean literary circle). First full-scale literary journal in Korea; ran from October 1924 to June 1936, twice interrupted in 1927 and 1935. Published new tendency and naturalist works but later leaned toward anticlass and nationalist works.

Chosŏn p'ŭroret'aria yesul tongmaeng조선프로레타리아예술동맹(Korea Artista Proleta Federatio in Esperanto, KAPF). Formed on 23 August 1925 by 19 members and dissolved on 20 May 1935.

Cho Uin 曹友仁 (1561–1625). Writer of 3 *kasa* including "Ch'ulsae kok" 出塞曲 (Song of going out the pass, c. 1617).

Cho Ung chŏn 趙雄傳 (Tale of Cho Ung). Anonymous traditional military tale in Korean set in Song China.

Cho Wi 曹偉 (1454–1503). Writer of a *kasa*, "Manbun ka" 萬憤歌 (Song of fury), riddled with allusion.

Cho Wihan 趙緯韓 (1558–1649). Writer of *Ch'oe Ch'ŏk chŏn* 崔陟傳 (Tale of Ch'oe Ch'ŏk) in Chinese on the vicissitudes of the Ch'oe family during the Japanese invasion.

"Ch'ŏyong ka" 處容歌 (Song of Ch'ŏyong). 8 lines Silla song attributed to Ch'ŏyong, son of the dragon king. Also a Koryŏ dramatic song of 45 lines consisting of 6 parts, to expel evil spirits.

chuanqi 傳奇 (tale of wonder). Tales written in literary Chinese from Tang and thereafter. Features include liberal use of incidental poems, didactic commentary at the end, and a narrator who is also witness to the event. Korean examples present variations in form and style, with supernatural elements. Kim Sisŭp's *Kŭmo sinhwa* 金鰲新話 (New tales from Gold Turtle Mountain) is an early Korean example.

Chu Hŭich'ŏl 주희철 (n.d.). North Korean writer of poetry.

Chumong 朱蒙 (37–19 BC). Founder of Koguryŏ 高句麗 whose exploits are celebrated in 東明王篇 "Lay of King Tongmyŏng" by Yi Kyubo (1169–1241). The grandson of Haemosu 解慕漱 and a daughter of the River Earl, he was born from an egg.

Chungang 中央 (Center, November 1933 – September 1936). Monthly omnibus magazine published by *Chosŏn Chungang Daily* 朝鮮中央日報, altogether 35 numbers.

Ch'ungdam, Master 忠談師 (c. 742–65). Writer of 2 10-line *hyangga*, "Ch'an Kip'arang ka" 讚耆婆郎歌 (Ode to Knight Kip'a) and "Anmin ka" 安民歌 (Statesmanship, 765).

chungin 中人 ("middle people"). Holders of government positions who served in the technical posts – physicians, translators, interpreters, astronomer-meteorologists, accountants, law clerks, scribes, government artists – and took the examination for these fields on a hereditary basis. Mostly secondary sons, they formed the technical specialist class. They were among the first to espouse Catholicism and proposed an enlightened reform of government administration. Poets of this class compiled three anthologies of poetry in literary Chinese. Discrimination against secondary sons was formally ended in 1894.

Ch'unhyang chŏn 春香傳 (Tale of Ch'unhyang). *P'ansori* fiction stemming from the sung version. The story exists in woodblock and printed editions.

Ch'unhyang ka 春香歌 (Song of Ch'unhyang). One of the 12 *p'ansori* redacted by Sin Chaehyo.

Ch'up'ung kambyŏl kok 秋風感別曲 (Song of longing in the autumn wind). Anonymous traditional narrative fiction of love in Korean between the commoners Kim Ch'aebong and Kang P'ilsŏng set in late Chosŏn when political corruption was rampant. The story contains a *kasa*, "Kambyŏl kok," hence the title.

Chu Sebung 周世鵬 (1495–1554). Writer of "Oryun ka" 五倫歌 (Songs of five relations) and other didactic *sijo*.

Chu Ŭisik 朱義植 (1675–1720). Graduate of the military examination who served as a magistrate, painted plum blossoms well, and left 14 *sijo*.

Chu Yohan 朱耀翰 (1900–79). Twentieth-century poet who advocated a truly Korean poetic form based on a study of folk songs.

Chu Yosŏp 朱耀燮 (1902–72). Writer of short stories and longer fiction who studied in Shanghai and Stanford and taught at Furen University in Peking (1934–45).

Ch'wibari 취발이. Old bachelor or prodigal – archetype of the lively young merchant in Pongsan mask dance play and Yangju *pyŏlsandae* mask dance play.

ci 詞 (song words or lyric meters). Chinese song form characterized by prescribed rhyme and tonal sequence and the use of lines of varying length. Originally *ci* were lyrics written to tunes imported from Central Asia, but eventually they became a poetic form without music. The form flourished in China in the tenth and eleventh centuries.

Daoxuan 道宣 (596–667). Tang monk and author of *Shijia shipu* 釋迦世譜 (Life of the Buddha).

Diamond Scripture 金剛經 (*Vajrachedikā prajñāpāramitā sūtra*). Sutra setting forth the doctrines of emptiness (*śunyatā*) and intuitive wisdom (*prajñā*). There are 6 Chinese translations.

Doctrine of the Mean (*Zhongyong* 中庸). A metaphysical chapter in the *Record of Rites* included by Zhu Xi 朱熹 in his Four Books (along with *Analects*, *Mencius*, and *Great Learning*).

Du Fu 杜甫 (710–70). China's great poet – widely read, studied, and translated in traditional Korea.

Fan Ye 范曄 (398–445). Compiler of *Hou Hanshu* 後漢書 (History of the Later Han).

Five Classics 五經. Five Confucian canonical texts: *Book of Changes, Book of Documents, Book of Songs, Record of Rites,* and *Spring and Autumn Annals.* See Michael Nylan, *The Five "Confucian" Classics* (New Haven, 2001).

Four Books 四書. *Analects, Great Learning, Doctrine of the Mean,* and *Mencius.*

fu 賦 (rhymeprose or rhapsody). Chinese poetic form consisting of a combination of prose and rhymed verse of unspecified length. Descriptive or philosophical, it is often quite long and ornate, the monosyllable *xi* appears within or at the end of a line; end rhyme occurs.

Fujii Sadamoto 藤井貞幹 (?1732–97). Japanese historical researcher.

Great Learning, The (*Daxue* 大學). A chapter on sociopolitical matters in the *Record of Rites* included by Zhu Xi in his Four Books.

gushi 古詩 (old-style verse). Chinese verse genre that emerged in the second century. A poem consists of tetra-, penta- or heptasyllabic lines of uniform length; rhyme and parallelism occur, but without the rules of tonal parallelism.

Haebang kinyŏm sijip 解放記念詩集 (Collection in celebration of liberation, 1945). Anthology of 24 pieces.

Haedong kayo 海東歌謠 (Songs of Korea, 1763, 1775). Anthology of *sijo* chronologically arranged by Kim Sujang 金壽長. Two editions exist: the first contains 568 pieces; the second, 638.

"Haega" 海歌 (Song of the sea). Song sung by the people when Lady Suro 水路夫人, wife of Lord Sunjŏng 純貞公, was kidnapped by the sea dragon.

Hahoe *pyŏlsin* shamanist ritual 河回別神굿. Mask play held as village ritual at the New Year in Hahoe-dong, Andong county, North Kyŏngsang province. Consists of 12 acts (*kŏri*) and contains religious elements. Topics include poverty of commoners and satire of apostate monks and the gentleman class (*yangban*). The dialogue is not transmitted, but the ritual itself is considered the oldest and best of extant rites.

Ha Kŭnch'an 河瑾燦 (b. 1931). Writer of fiction whose topics include the effects of war on rural people and how Japanese and Western civilizations destroyed communal values and customs.

"Hallim pyŏlgok" 翰林別曲 (Song of Confucian scholars, c. 1216). The refrain *kŭi ŏttŏhaniikko*? 긔 엇더하니잇고 (How about that?) recurs in the fourth and sixth lines of each of 8 stanzas in Chinese and particles and refrains in Korean, whose text is preserved in *Words for Songs and Music*.

Han Chŏngim 한정임 (b. 1964). Contemporary woman writer of fiction.

Han Malsuk 韓末淑 (b. 1931). Woman writer of fiction.

Han Musuk 韓戊淑 (1918–93). Woman writer of fiction whose *Mannam* (1986) has been translated as *Encounter: A Novel of Nineteenth-Century Korea*.

Hansan kŏsa 漢山居士 (Retired gentleman of Hansan, n.d.). Writer of a 762-line *kasa*, *Hanyang ka* (Song of Seoul, 1844).

Han Sŏrya 韓雪野 (1901–63). Writer of fiction who was also active in the North.

Han-ssi samdae rok 韓氏三代錄 (Three-generation record of the Han clan). Anonymous traditional *roman-fleuve* in Korean.

Hanu 寒雨 ("Cold Rain," n.d.). Female entertainer known to have exchanged *sijo* with Im Che 林悌 (1549–87).

Han Yongun 韓龍雲 (1879–1944). Buddhist monk, nationalist, and author of *Nim ŭi ch'immuk* (The silence of love, 1926) – 88 poems plus a foreword and note to the reader. Han is considered one of the great modern Korean poets.

Han Yu 韓愈 (768–824). Tang poet, prose master, and author of a pseudo-biography, "Mao ying zhuan" 毛穎傳 (Biography of a writing brush).

"Hapkangjŏng ka" 合江亭歌 (Song of Hapkang arbor, c. 1792). Anonymous *kasa* about the social ills of the eighteenth century, especially extortion of the people by local magistrates.

Hŏ Chun 許俊 (n.d.). Writer of fiction who went north in 1945.

"*Hŏdu ka*" 虛頭歌 (or *tanga*). Introductory piece such as "Kwangdae ka" 廣大歌 (Song of the singer) delivered by the *p'ansori* singer before the main work to relax his voice.

Hŏ Kyun 許筠 (1569–1618). Poet, critic, and writer of prose fiction to whom *Hong Kiltong chŏn* 홍길동전 (Tale of Hong Kiltong) is attributed. He was executed for involvement in a seditious plot.

Hŏ Nansŏrhŏn 許蘭雪軒 (Hŏ Ch'ohŭi, 1563–89). Writer of Chinese and Korean verse and 1 *kasa*, "Kyuwŏn ka" 閨怨歌 (A woman's sorrow).

Hong Chikp'il 洪直弼 (1776–1852). Chosŏn writer of prose who excelled in literary style.

Hong Hŭibok 洪羲福 (1794–1859). Translator of Li Ruzhen's *Jinghua yuan* 鏡花緣 (Flowers in the mirror, 1828) as *Cheil kiŏn* 第一奇諺 (The greatest tale of wonder, 1835–48).

Hongjang 紅粧 (late fourteenth century). Female entertainer from Kangnŭng who befriended Pak Sin 朴信 (1362–1444) and left a single *sijo*. Her beauty and talent were mentioned by such writers as Sŏ Kŏjŏng 徐居正 (1420–89) and Chŏng Ch'ŏl 鄭澈 (1573–93).

Hong Kyŏngnae silgi 洪景來實記 (True record of Hong Kyŏngnae). Hong Kyŏngnae (1780–1812), leader of a peasant rebellion in North P'yŏngan, led a force of 2,000 but government troops took his fortress by storm and killed him.

Hong Manjong 洪萬宗 (1643–1725). Critic of poetry in Chinese and prose fiction who compiled *Sihwa ch'ongnim* 詩話叢林 (Collection of remarks on poetry), selections from 22 writers.

Hong Myŏnghŭi 洪命熹 (1888–1968). Writer of fiction known for his long historical work *Im Kkŏkchŏng* 林巨正. Based on a mid-sixteenth-century bandit chief, the work was first serialized in *Chosŏn Daily* 朝鮮日報 (1928–39) and published in book form in 1948, the year he went north. It is rich in vocabulary and description of customs during the Chosŏn dynasty.

Hong Nang 洪娘 (fl. 1567–1600). Official female entertainer in Hongwŏn, South Hamgyŏng, who sent a *sijo* to Minister Ch'oe Kyŏngch'ang (1539–83), a well-known poet in Chinese, at their parting.

Hong Set'ae 洪世泰 (1653–1725). Poet of commoner origin – a secondary son who passed the interpreters' examination in 1675. Hong compiled *Haedong yuju* 海東遺珠 (Remaining gems of Korea, 1712), a collection of poetry in Chinese by writers of the middle people. He also wrote 3 biographical sketches, among them "Kim Yŏngch'ŏl chŏn" 金英哲傳 (Life of Kim Yŏngch'ŏl). His collected works in 14 chapters were published in 1731.

Hong Sŏkchu 洪奭周 (1774–1842). Writer who excelled in old-style prose. His collected works are in *Yŏnch'ŏn chip* 淵泉集.

Hong Sŏkchung 홍석중 (b. 1941). Grandson of Hong Myŏnghŭi and North Korean writer of fiction including *Nopsae param* (Northeastern wind, 1983–91).

Hong Sunhak 洪淳學 (1842–92). Writer of the *kasa*, *Yŏnhaeng ka* 燕行歌 (Song of a trip to Peking, 1866).

Hong Tongji 洪同知. Nephew of Pak Ch'ŏmji in the puppet play, he has a naked body in red and even reveals an erect member – a satirical and humorous character.

Hong Yangho 洪良浩 (1724–1802). Writer of *Puksae kiryak* 北塞記略 (Record of the northern pass) in which he used Chinese graphs for their sound to record the dialect of Kongju (Kyŏnghŭng in North Hamgyŏng).

"Hŏnhwa ka" 獻花歌 (Dedication of the flowers, c. 702–37). A 4-line *hyangga* supposedly composed by an old herdsman.

Hŏ Sugyŏng 허수경 (b. 1964). Contemporary woman writer of feminist poetry.

Huang Tingjian 黃庭堅 (1045–1105). Song poet whose poetry of allusion was admired by Korean poets until the sixteenth century.

Hubangi Tonginhoe 後半期同人會. Group of young poets who called themselves "Sin Siron" ("New poetics") group but changed the name to "Hubangi Tonginhoe" ("Hubangi coterie") in 1949. Active in Pusan, the wartime capital, they attempted to register modern consciousness as splintered and fragmentary.

Hŭimyŏng 希明 (c. 762–65). Putative author of the 10-line *hyangga*, "To Ch'ŏnsu Kwanŭm ka" 禱千手觀音歌 (Hymn to the thousand-eyed bodhisattva who observes the sounds of the world).

Hŭmhŭmja 흠흠자. Pen name of the author of *Kŭmsu chaep'an* 禽獸裁判 (Trials of birds and beasts, 1910) in Korean.

Hŭngbo ka 興甫歌 (Song of Hŭngbo). Also called *Pak t'aryŏng* (Ballad of the gourd), a *p'ansori* work redacted by Sin Chaehyo (1812–84).

Hŭngbu chŏn 興夫傳 (Tale of Hŭngbu). *P'ansori* fiction about the good younger brother who was rewarded by heaven.

Hunmin chŏngŭm 訓民正音 (Correct sounds for teaching the people, *hangŭl*). Korean alphabet promulgated by King Sejong 世宗 (1418–50) on 9 October 1446.

"Hwajŏn ka" 花煎歌 (Song of the flower-adorned cake). Song bewailing the lot of a woman who became a widow 5 times.

Hwang Chini 黃眞伊 (fl. 1506–44). Under the professional name "Myŏngwŏl" 明月 ("Bright Moon"), she studied the Confucian canon and excelled in poetry in Chinese, calligraphy, music, and *sijo*. Said to have written a *sijo* to Pyŏkkyesu 碧溪水, a royal kinsman, and another to the philosopher Sŏ Kyŏngdŏk 徐敬德 (1499–1546). Her 4 *sijo* in *Ch'ŏnggu yŏngŏn* (Songs of green hills) affect the reader by infusing desire for her lovers with an exquisite sense of her own subjectivity.

Hwang Chiu 黃芝雨 (b. 1952). Postmodern poet with social conscience and irony who indicts the dehumanization of capitalist civilization and has practiced a poetry of open form.

Hwang Hŭi 黃喜 (1363–1452). Graduate of the 1389 examination who served King Sejong as chief state counselor for 18 years and was known as an incorruptible and beneficent minister. Several *sijo* are attributed to him.

Hwang Insuk 黃仁淑 (b. 1958). Contemporary woman writer of feminist poetry.

Hwang Kŏn 黃鍵(健) (1918–91). North Korean writer of fiction.

Hwangok 還穀 (grain loan system). One of the three prime sources of government revenue during the Chosŏn dynasty. Loans were made to poor peasants from government stores in the lean spring months to be repaid at harvest time with a wastage charge of 10% – a pretext for charging interest that ruined many farmers.

Hwang Sŏgyŏng 黃皙暎 (b. 1943). Writer of such fiction works as *Kaekchi* (Strange land, 1974) and *Chang Kilsan* (1984), a 10-volume historical fiction about Chang, actor, robber, and son of a slave in the mid seventeenth century.

Hwang Sunwŏn 黃順元 (1915–2000). Master of the short-story form and writer of longer fiction. His twelve stories are translated in *The Stars and Other Korean Stories*.

Hwang Tonggyu 黃東奎 (b. 1938). Writer of modern and committed poetry as well as a poetry sequence *P'ungjang* (Wind burial, 1982–95) consisting of 70 poems in which the speaker confronts death in order to explore the meaning of life. Hwang is currently professor of English at Seoul National University.

hwarang 花郎. Silla's unique social group organized at the village or clan level. From the early sixth century, the *hwarang* members, now a semiofficial body at the national level, came into being as an organization dedicated to nurturing talent. The group comprised several hundred men headed by a youth from the True Bone aristocracy and several eminent monks (such as Wŏngwang 圓光 542–640). Vowing to serve in times of national need, they rendered great service to the unification of the Three Kingdoms by Silla. Famous members include Kwanch'ang 官昌 (d. 660), Kim Hŭmun 金歆運 (d. 655), and Kim Yusin 金庾信 (595–673).

hyangch'al 鄉札. Orthographic system invented by Silla people to transcribe sentences with Chinese graphs for both their phonetic and logographic values. Considered by the Japanese scholar Konishi Jin'ichi to be a precursor of the *Man'yōgana* used in the Japanese anthology *Man'yōshū* (Collection of ten thousand leaves, c. 759).

hyangga 鄉歌 (native songs). Some 25 extant songs dating from Silla and early Koryŏ recorded in *hyangch'al* orthography. Of the 3 variant forms, the most polished and popular consisted of 2 stanzas of 4 lines plus a conclusion of 2 lines.

Hyesim 慧諶 (1178–1234). Writer of two pseudobiographies on bamboo and ice.

Hyŏn Chingŏn 玄鎮健 (1900–43). Writer of short stories and full-length fiction – *Muyŏngt'ap* (Shadowless stūpa, 1938–39) and *Chŏkto* (Equator, 1939).

Hyŏndae munhak 現代文學 (Contemporary literature). Monthly literary journal beginning in January 1955. Through its recommendation system it brought out new writers of poetry, fiction, drama, and literary criticism.

Hyŏn-ssi yangung ssangnin ki 玄氏兩雄雙麟記 (Tale of the Hyŏn brothers). Anonymous traditional clan fiction in Korean that exists in 2 manuscript editions (10 vols.) and a printed edition (1919). The first of 4 stories by several writers that explores the fortunes of the Hyŏn clan in Song China.

Hyŏn Sumun chŏn 玄秀文傳 (Tale of Hyŏn Sumun). Anonymous traditional narrative fiction in Korean consisting of 23 chapters. Set in Song China, the story presents the protagonist's heroic prowess.

Hyŏn Sŭnggŏl 현승걸 (b. 1937). North Korean writer of fiction.

idu 吏讀 (clerk reading). Sinographs used for sound and sense to indicate Korean particles and verbal endings in order to decipher Chinese sentences. Mostly used in administrative papers and public documents.

Illakchŏng ki 一樂亭記 (Record of the pleasant pavilion, 1809). Anonymous traditional family fiction in Chinese, set in Ming China, by "Old Manwa." Subtexts are *Sa-ssi namjŏng ki* (Record of Lady Sa's journey south) and *Ch'angsŏn kamŭi rok* (Showing goodness and stirred by righteousness).

Illyŏmhong 一捻紅 (Love story of Lady Hong and Bachelor Yi, 1906). Work of fiction written in popular Chinese and serialized in *Taehan ilbo* 大韓日報, 23 January – 18 February 1906.

Im Che 林悌 (1549–87). Graduate of the 1577 examination who scorned factious politics and led a retired life. Tradition says he composed a *sijo* when he visited the tomb of Hwang Chini to pay tribute to her memory.

Im Ch'un 林椿 (d. 1170). Writer of two pseudobiographies on wine and a square-holed coin.

Im Hoŭn chŏn 林虎隱傳 (Tale of Im Hoŭn). Anonymous traditional narrative story in Korean. Im descends from heaven, learns military arts from a Daoist master, and marries six beauties, but an evil minister exiles him. Then the Manchus invade, and Im saves the son of heaven.

Im Hwa 林和 (pen name of Im Insik 林仁植, 1908–53). Writer who took over the leadership of KAPF in 1931 and wrote narrative verse about the proletariat – for example, "Uri oppa wa hwaro" (My older brother and a brazier). He went north but was accused of being an American spy and executed.

Imjin nok 壬辰綠 (Record of the black dragon year). Popular traditional narrative tale about the Japanese invasion of Korea in 1592–8; some 40 versions exist.

Im Kyŏngŏp chŏn 林慶業傳 (Tale of Im Kyŏngŏp). Popular narrative tale about the Manchu invasion in Chinese and Korean versions. It is close to the true history of Im (1594–1646).

Im Ogin 林玉仁 (1915–95). Woman writer of fiction who dealt with husband – wife relations and unconventional women.

Im Pangul 林芳蔚 (1904–61). Master singer of *p'ansori* who was designated a Human Cultural Asset.

Im Yuhu 任有後 (1601–73). Writer of the *kasa* "Moktong mundap ka" 牧童問答歌 (Song of the cowherd).

Inmun p'yŏngnon 人文評論 (Criticism of humanity, October 1939 – April 1941). Journal sponsored by the colonial government and edited by Ch'oe Chaesŏ (1908–64).

Iryŏn 一然 (1206–89). Monk of the Meditation school and compiler of *Samguk yusa* 三國遺事 (Memorabilia of the Three Kingdoms, 1285), which records the texts of 14 *hyangga* in *hyangch'al* orthography.

"Isang kok" 履霜曲 (Treading frost). Anonymous Koryŏ love song of 13 lines with no stanzaic division and a refrain in line 3 spoken by a woman.

Jin Ping Mei 金瓶梅 (The plum in the golden vase, or Gold Vase Plum). A major anonymous full-length Chinese fiction of manners published around 1617. The protagonist is Ximen Qing and the action takes place between 1112 and 1127.

jintishi 今體詩 (modern-style verse). Any poetic form such as regulated verse, cut-off lines, or *pailü* 排律 that observes the rules of tonal parallelism.

jueju 絕句 (cut-off lines or quatrains). Chinese verse form consisting of 4 penta- or heptasyllabic lines. The third line tends to introduce a critical turn. A single rhyme is used, nearly always in the level tone in the even-numbered lines. The distribution of level tones and deflected tones follows a fixed pattern.

Kaebyŏk 開闢 (The beginning, June 1920 – August 1926). Periodical sponsored by Ch'ŏndogyo (the Heavenly Way religion) that issued 72 numbers and was closed down by the Japanese censors; republished from November 1934 to February 1935 and again from January 1946 to March 1949. It published Kim Sowŏl's "Chindallaekkot" (Azaleas) and Yi Sanghwa's "Ppaeakkin t̆uredo pomŭn onŭnga" (Does spring come to the stolen fields?).

kagok 歌曲. Type of traditional vocal music in Korea: a vocal solo accompanied by a chamber ensemble of string, wind, and percussion instruments, or a musical tune or its lyrics. Today *kagok* is divided into male and female voice or alternate singing between a man and women. The text for male voice is always for solo, but that for female voice is usually to be sung in unison. *Sijo* lyrics can be sung to the *kagok* tune.

Kakhun 覺訓 (n.d.). Koryŏ monk and compiler of *Haedong kosŭng chŏn* 海東高僧傳 (Lives of eminent Korean monks, 1215).

"Kammin ka" 甲民歌 (Song of the Kapsan people). Anonymous *kasa* in dialogue form. Produced in Kapsan, Hamgyŏng province, and recorded in *Songs of Korea* 海東歌謠, it concerns military service exacted by an oppressive government that forces people to flee.

kana 假名 (temporary or pseudoscript). Japanese phonetic script based on simplified Chinese graphs (*kana*); opposed to Chinese graphs called true script (*mana* 眞名).

Kang Ich'ŏn 姜彛天 (1769–1801). Author of the poem "Namsŏng kwanhŭija" 南城觀戲子 (Upon seeing a play at South Gate).

Kang Kyŏngae 姜敬愛 (1907–43). Socially committed woman writer of fiction who dealt with the plight of marginalized and impoverished farmers and factory workers in *Ingan munje* (Human problems, 1934) and "Chiha ch'on" (Underground village, 1936).

Kangnŭng Maehwa t'aryŏng 江陵梅花打令 (Ballad of Maehwa of Kangnŭng). Considered to have been a popular *p'ansori* piece in the mid eighteenth century to warn men of the captivating charms of women, but the text is no longer extant.

Kang Sinjae 康信哉 (b. 1924). Woman writer of fiction who dealt with the destiny of women in love, as well as divorce and changes in the modes of life caused by war. Her hope seems reserved for the young.

Kang Sŏkkyŏng 姜石景 (b. 1951). Contemporary woman writer of fiction.

Kangsu 强首 (d. 692). Silla writer of Chinese prose.

Kang Sŭnghan 姜承翰 (1918–50). North Korean writer of plays and poetry including such narrative verse as *Hallasan* (Mount Halla, 1948) about the communist rebellion on Cheju Island in 1948. During the Korean War he was caught by UN soldiers and executed.

Kang Ŭngyo 姜恩喬 (b. 1945). Woman writer of feminist poetry and criticism on a wide range of topics from the absurdity of existence to communal values and dreams.

kasa 歌詞. One of 4 poetic forms of traditional Korea. Originating as song lyrics written to a prevailing *kasa* tune, it is characterized by a lack of stanzaic division and variable length, a tendency toward description and exposition, and, at times, also lyricism and the use of balanced parallel phrases, verbal and syntactical. Often likened to the Chinese *fu*, it emerged as a new genre toward the middle of the fifteenth century.

"Kasiri" 가시리 (Will you go?). Anonymous Koryŏ love song, spoken by a woman, consisting of 4 2-line stanzas with a refrain at the end of each stanza.

Kihwa, Monk 己和 (1376–1433). Writer of 5 devotional songs in *kyŏnggi-ch'e* form.

Kim Ch'aewŏn 金采原 (b. 1965). Contemporary woman writer of fiction.

Kim Ch'anghyŏp 金昌協 (1651–1708). Master of old-style Chinese prose.

Kim Chiha 金芝河 (b. 1941). Poet and activist who wrote a number of satirical verses beginning with "Ojŏk" (Five outlaws, 1970). His current project, *Taesŏl Nam* (Big story south), began in 1982.

Kim Chinhyŏng 金鎭衡 (1801–65). Author of the *kasa* "Pukch'ŏn ka" 北遷歌 (Song of a northern exile, 1854).

Kim Chiwŏn 金知原 (b. 1943). Contemporary woman writer of fiction who has been living in New York since the 1970s.

Kim Chiyŏn 金芝娟 (b. 1942). Contemporary woman writer of fiction.

Kim Chogyu 김조규 (b. 1914). North Korean writer of poetry.

Kim Chŏng 김정 (n.d.). North Korean writer of fiction.

Kim Chongjik 金宗直 (1431–92). Scholar and writer who nurtured a number of renowned pupils; master of the Human Nature and Principle learning (a branch of Neo-Confucianism devoted to metaphysical inquiry into human nature and moral self-cultivation); compiler of *Ch'ŏnggu p'unga* 青邱風雅, an annotated anthology of poems in Chinese by Koreans from the Three Kingdoms to Koryŏ.

Kim Ch'ŏngmyŏng 金陟明 (fl. 1010–83). Putative compiler of *Sui chŏn* 殊異傳 (Tales of the extraordinary).

Kim Chŏngnan 김정란 (b. 1953). Contemporary feminist poet, critic, and professor of French at Sangji University in Wŏnju.

Kim Ch'ŏnt'aek 金天澤 (b. 1685). Policeman, singer of *sijo*, author of 79 *sijo*, and compiler of *Ch'ŏnggu yŏngŏn* (Songs of green hills, 1728).

Kim Ch'unsu 金春洙 (b. 1922). Modernist who has advocated a "poem of no meaning" – descriptive imagery without meaning, a display of free associations and momentary fantasies.

Kim Ch'unt'aek 金春澤 (1670–1717). Great-grandson of Kim Manjung; scholar and poet of the *kasa* "Pyŏl sa miin kok" 別思美人曲 (Separate hymn of constancy), written in exile on Cheju Island, whose subtext is Chŏng Ch'ŏl's "Sa miin kok" 思美人曲 (Hymn of constancy).

Kim Chuyŏng 金周榮 (b. 1939). Writer of satirical and historical fiction. *Kaekchu* (The inn, 10 vols., 1981), about an inn where traveling merchants meet, offers a panoramic view of the lives of people of all strata as well as a rich hoard of folk and indigenous words of the time.

Kim Hŭigyŏng chŏn 金喜慶傳 (Tale of Kim Hŭigyŏng). Anonymous traditional narrative story in Korean of the woman Chang Sŏryŏng's hardships.

Kim Hyangsuk 金香淑 (b. 1951). Contemporary woman writer of fiction.

Kim Hyesun 김혜순 (b. 1955). Feminist poet whose work dazzles with its variety, wit, and range of affections; also wrote a critical study of the poetry of Kim Suyŏng (1921–68).

Kim Hyŏnggyŏng 김형경 (b. 1960). Contemporary woman writer of fiction.

Kim Ilsŏng 金日成 (Kim Il Sung, 1912–94). North Korean leader. *Pulmyŏl ŭi yŏksa* (Imperishable history) is a collection of tributes to his revolutionary struggle for Korea's independence by different writers.

Kim Ingyŏm 金仁謙 (1707–72). Author of the narrative *kasa, Iltong changyu ka* 日東壯遊歌 (Song of a grand trip to Japan, 1764).

Kim Kagi 金可紀 (d. 859). Silla national who passed the Tang examination for foreigners and spent his life in China as a Daoist recluse.

Kim Kijin 金基鎮 (1903–85). Translated the debate between Henri Barbusse (1874–1935) and Romain Rolland (1866–1944) and proposed that literature should not be used as a vehicle of politics and that short narrative verse is the best form for proletarian poetry.

Kim Kirim 金起林 (b. 1919). Modernist poet, critic, and author of *Kisangdo* (The weather chart, 1936), whose subtext is Eliot's *Waste Land* (1922).

Kim Ku 金絿 (1488–1534). Statesman who wrote a *sijo* addressed to King Chungjong 中宗 (1506–1544).

Kim Kuyong 金九容 (1338–84). Koryŏ scholar who specialized in Cheng-Zhu philosophy and died in China as an envoy sent to the Ming.

Kim Kwanggyun 金光均 (1914–93). Imagist poet who stressed poetry's pictorial and auditory quality – for example, comparing the sounds of snowfall to the swishing of a woman undressing.

Kim Kwanguk 金光煜 (1574–1656). Passed the 1606 examination, held high office, and wrote *Yulli yugok* 栗里遺曲 (Remaining songs of Chestnut Village), a *sijo* sequence of 14 songs.

Kim Kyoje 金敎濟 (fl. 1911–23). Writer of "new fiction" who completed Yi Injik's *Ch'iaksan* (Mount Pheasant, 1911) and several other works.

Kim Kyŏngnin 金璟麟 (b. 1919). Member of the Hubangi coterie who experimented with language and proposed the use of intellectual imagery, existential philosophy, and positive confrontation with actuality.

Kim Kyudong 金奎東 (b. 1925). Modernist poet active in the 1950s espousing Pound's logopoeia.

Kim Kyuyŏp 김규엽 (1919–86). Writer who was born in Seoul but went north during the Korean War, and wrote fiction about farming villages, including *Saebom* (New spring, 1978), considered his typical work.

Kim Malbong 金末峰 (1901–61). Woman writer of fiction who dealt directly with the women's movement in *Hwaryŏhan chiok* (A splendid hell, 1952).

Kim Manjung 金萬重 (1637–92). Scholar, statesman, and acute critic of the current literary situation, and author of *Kuun mong* 九雲夢 (Dream of nine clouds) and *Sa-ssi namjŏng ki* 謝氏南征記 (Record of Lady Sa's journey south).

Kim Minsuk 金玟熟 (b. 1948). Contemporary woman writer of fiction.

Kim Myŏngsun 金明淳 (1896–1951?). Woman writer of verse, fiction, and essays who died in a mental asylum.

Kim Namch'ŏn 金南天 (1911–53). Writer of fiction and critic who went north and was purged.

Kim Ŏk 金億 (b. 1895). Early translator of symbolist poetry who published *Onoe ŭi mudo* (Dance of anguish, March 1921), the first volume of Western poetry in Korean translation. Also published *Haep'ari ŭi norae* (Songs of jellyfish, June 1923), the first volume of new verse by a single poet imbued with symbolist languor. He also wrote a handbook of Esperanto.

Kim P'ilsu 김필수 (n.d.). Writer of *Kyŏngsejong* (A bell warning the public, 1908), a new satirical fiction in which animals speak about the ugliness of the human world.

Kim Pusik 金富軾 (1075–1151). Koryŏ historian and compiler of *Samguk sagi* 三國史記 (Historical records of the Three Kingdoms, 1146).

Kim Sisŭp 金時習 (1453–93). Scholar, writer of verse and prose, and author of *Kŭmo sinhwa* 金鰲新話 (New tales from Gold Turtle Mountain) in Chinese, comprising 5 tales of wonder.

Kim Sohaeng 金紹行 (1765–1859). Author of *Samhan sŭbyu* 三韓拾遺 (Remains of the Three Han, 1814), also called *Hyangnang chŏn* 香娘傳 (Tale of Hyangnang), a fiction in Chinese about Hyangnang's suicide in Sŏnsan in 1702 (*Sukchong sillok* 39:50a–b). Kim transfers the setting to Silla. The heroine appeals to the Jade Emperor and returns to life, marries, and helps unify the Three Kingdoms by her military prowess. There are battle scenes between heavenly soldiers and devils.

Kim Sŏnggi 金聖器 (c. 1724–76). Professional singer of *sijo* and friend of Kim Ch'ŏnt'aek who left 8 *sijo* songs.

Kim Sŏnggwan 김성관 (n.d.). North Korean writer of fiction.

Kim Sŏnghan 金聲翰 (b. 1919). Writer of fiction, including a three-part historical fiction *Yi Sŏnggye* (1966).

Kim Sŏngwŏn 金成遠 (1525–98). Friend of Chŏng Ch'ŏl praised in his "Sŏngsan pyŏlgok" 星山別曲 (Little odes to Mount Star, c. 1578) for his elegant life in South Chŏlla.

Kim Sowŏl 金素月 (1902–34). Early twentieth-century folk-song-style poet with only one collection, *Chindallaekkot* (Azaleas, 1925), comprising 127 pieces. Kim committed suicide in 1934.

Kim Sujang 金壽長 (1690–1769). *Sijo* poet and singer of common origin who left 129 *sijo*.

Kim Sŭnghŭi 金勝熙 (b. 1952). Feminist poet, critic, and professor of Korean literature at Sogang University in Seoul.

Kim Sŭngok 金承鈺 (b. 1941). Writer of fiction and spokesman for the student revolution in 1960 who attempted to form new values and introduce a new era in fiction. Kim's characters explore desolation and weariness with everyday affairs in search of a more vigorous and honest life. Kim's efforts to innovate language and renovate sensibility have often been successful. He has not been active since the 1980s.

Kim Suon 金守溫 (1409–81). Writer who passed the 1438 and 1441 examinations and worked in the Hall of Worthies. He wrote sinewy poetry and prose and took part in the translation projects of Confucian canonical texts and Buddhist scriptures.

Kim Suyŏng 金洙暎 (1921–68). Modernist writer of committed poetry about the sorrows of the disenfranchised petite bourgeoisie as well as resistance poetry for political reform – all in free verse.

Kim Tonghwan 金東煥 (b. 1901). Early modern poet who wrote narrative verse.

Kim Tongin 金東仁 (1900–51). Author of short stories and full-length fiction (including historical fiction, some in the naturalistic realistic style) and a critic in whose honor the journal *Sasanggye* established the Tongin Literary Prize in 1955.

Kim Tongni 金東里 (1913–95). A defender of humanism whose earlier works concern the crumbling of traditional society and the family, its nucleus. His characters are people controlled by fatalism and nihilism who solve their relations with others by precedent and custom. When tradition is gone, Kim says, we should seek our true bearings in a timeless mythic age, especially in Korea's indigenous beliefs. He also wrote about the political division, however, and a fiction based on biblical stories.

Kim Tŏngnyŏng 金德齡 (1567–96). A military man of obscure origin who plays an important role as general during the Japanese invasion. In *Imjin nok* 壬辰錄 (Record of the Black Dragon year), he is portrayed as a wronged hero.

Kim Tŭgyŏn 金得研 (1555–1637). Poet who wrote a sequence of 49 *sijo* and another sequence of 6.

Kim Tŭksin 金得臣 (1604–84). Graduate of the 1662 examination known for his poetry in Chinese.

Kim Ugyu 金友奎 (b. 1691). Clerk under Sukchong's reign who wrote 18 *sijo*.

Kim Ungyŏng 金雲卿 (fl. 821–41). Silla national who passed the Tang examination for foreigners in 821 and returned to Silla in 841.

Kim Uong 金宇顒 (1540–1603). Writer of *Ch'ŏngun chŏn* 天君傳 (Tale of the human mind) in Chinese.

Kim Wŏnil 金源一 (b. 1942). Writer of fiction concerned deeply about the national division, the activities of leftists in the South before the war, and traumatic experiences ensuing from ideological conflict. His works include the *roman-fleuve Nŭl p'urŭn sonamu* (The evergreen pine, 9 vols., 1993).

Kim Wŏnju 金元周 (Buddhist name Iryŏp 一葉, 1896–1971). Champion of the women's movement who organized the women's group Ch'ŏngdaphoe (Bluestockings, 1919) and launched the women's journal *Sinyŏja* (New women, 1920); later became a Buddhist nun.

Kim Yŏ 金鑢 (1765–1821). Author of "Ka sujae chŏn" 賈秀才傳 (Tale of the recluse Ka) about an anti-Confucian and anti-Buddhist salesman of dried fish.

Kim Yŏnggŭn 김영근 (n.d.). North Korean writer of fiction.

Kim Yŏngnang 金永郞 (1903–50). Poet who searched for beauty with a sense of music and prose rhythm; later wrote works confronting reality and death.

Kim Yugi 金裕器 (d. 1788?). *Sijo* poet and singer of common origin who left 10 *sijo*.

Kim Yujŏng 金裕貞 (1908–37). Writer of humorous and ironic short stories (with deep pathos beneath the surface) about urban laborers and poor farmers who sell their wives.

Kim Yusin 金庾信 (595–673), Silla general who joined the *hwarang* order in 609 and rendered meritorious service in unifying the Three Kingdoms.

King Kwanggaet'o stele 廣開土王碑 (414). Stele recording the military prowess of the nineteenth Koguryŏ king Kwanggaaet'o (391–413) in Tonggou 通溝, Manchuria; discovered in 1875, it consists of about 1,800 Chinese graphs written in 44 lines.

kisaeng 妓生. Korean female entertainers trained in poetry, music, dancing, and polite conversation – an important part of entertainment at royal banquets, receptions for foreign envoys, and other ceremonies. Official *kisaeng* were registered at court. Some such as Hwang Chini were accomplished poets in both Chinese and Korean. Some were known in China for their beauty and accomplishments and were eagerly sought by Chinese envoys.

"Kiŭm norae" 기음노래 (Song of weeding). *Kasa* concerning the farmer's life.

Kkoktu kaksi [*norŭm*] 꼭두각시 [노름]. Puppet play also called *Tŏlmi, Pak Ch'ŏmji norŭm*, or *Hong Tongji norŭm*. Roving actors staged this play in which the interlocutor (*sanbaji* 산받이), who faces the stage, carries on dialogue with puppets and the character Pak explains the plot and tells what is to come. Other main characters include Pak's wife Kkoktu kaksi, an apostate monk, and the governor of P'yŏngan. Consisting of 7 scenes and taking up to 2 hours, it contains a satire on the apostate monk, the oppressive governor, and prevailing morality. *Ch'ŏmji* and *tongji* are prestige titles without actual function or power. This play was designated an Intangible Cultural Asset in 1964.

"Kŏbu ohae" 車夫誤解 (Misunderstanding of rickshaw men, 1906). A satirical story, serialized in *Korea Daily News* 大韓每日新報 that takes the form of a conversation between rickshaw pullers and attacks political change and social transformation.

Ko Chŏnghŭi 高靜熙 (1948–91). Feminist critic, journalist, and writer of poetry.

Kogŭm kagok 古今歌曲 (Ancient and modern songs). Anthology of *sijo*, topically arranged, and *kasa*; compiler unknown.

Kong Chiyŏng 공지영 (b. 1963). Contemporary woman writer of fiction.

"Konghu in" 箜篌引 (Medley for the harp). A *yuefu*-style song written by the wife of a madman or Yŏok, the wife of a ferryman. Also known as "Kong mudoha ka" 公無渡河歌 (Milord, don't cross the river).

Kong Sŏnok 공선옥 (b. 1963). Contemporary woman writer of fiction.

Korean Language Society (Chosŏnŏ hakhoe 朝鮮語學會). Originally Chosŏnŏ yŏnguhoe 朝鮮語研究會 until November 1931; it became Hangŭl hakhoe 한글학회 in 1949.

Koryŏ 高麗 (918–1392). Dynasty ruled by the Wang house.

Koryŏ Kang sijung chŏn 高麗姜侍中傳 (Life of the Koryŏ minister Kang Kamch'an 姜邯贊, 1908). Story by U Kisŏn about the life of Kang (948–1031) who repulsed the Khitans, and published by Hyŏn Kongnyŏm, owner of the publisher Taech'ang Sŏwŏn.

Koryŏ songs (*Yŏyo* 麗謠, or *sogyo* 俗謠). Typical Koryŏ songs – chain verses with no set number of stanzas – are characterized by a recurrent refrain either in the middle or at the end of each stanza. The theme of most of these anonymous songs is love.

Ko Sugwan 高壽寬 (n.d.). Late Chosŏn master singer of *p'ansori* especially known for "Song of Love" from *Song of Ch'unhyang*. The poet Sin Wi 申緯 (1769–1845) invited him to his home several times.

Ko Ŭn 高銀 (b. 1933). Former Buddhist monk, prolific activist poet, and author of *Paektusan* (Mount Paektu, 7 vols., 1987–94), a long narrative verse about Korean history from the 1900s to 1940, and *Manin po* (Ten thousand lives, 15 vols., 1986–97).

Ko Ŭngch'ŏk 高應陟 (1531–1605). Poet of Chinese poetry and *sijo*.

Ku Hyegyŏng 구혜경 (b. 1931). Woman writer of fiction.

"Kuji ka" 龜旨歌 (Song of Kuji, AD 42). Song sung by some 300 people who climbed Mount Kuji; also known as "Yŏng singun ka" 迎神君歌 (Song of welcoming the divine lord).

Kŭmsŏng 金星 (Venus, 1923–24). Poetry journal issued by Korean students attending Waseda University in Tokyo that folded after 3 issues in January 1924; included original works and translations from Western poetry.

Kungmin munhak 國民文學 (National literature, November 1941 to February 1945). Japanese-sponsored journal edited by Ch'oe Chaesŏ and published both in Korean and Japanese at first, but after 1942 only in Japanese (as *Kokumin bungaku*). Some Korean writers published their works in Korean and Japanese.

Kunjŏng 軍政 (military service tax). Levy of one bolt of cloth demanded from each able-bodied male and, at times, on behalf of family members who had died.

"Kunma taewang" 軍馬大王 (Great king of the warhorse). Anonymous Koryŏ song consisting of 7 lines of meaningless sounds.

Ku samguk sa 舊三國史 (Old history of the Three Kingdoms). Book consulted by both Kim Pusik and Yi Kyubo but now lost.

kut 굿. Shamanist ritual, or any spectacle worth seeing.

Kuun ki 九雲記 (Record of nine clouds). Revised and expanded version of *Dream of Nine Clouds* in Chinese.

"Kwabu ka" 과부가 (Song of a widow). Anonymous *kasa* in Korean about a 14-year-old girl who loses her husband 15 days after marriage and spends her life in loneliness and sorrow.

Kwak Yŏ 郭輿 (1058–1130). Koryŏ writer who befriended Yejong when he was heir apparent; after he became king, Yejong often visited Kwak so they could enjoy poetry together.

Kwanch'ang 官昌 (d. 660). Silla warrior killed in battle against Paekche in 660.

"Kwandŭng ka" 觀燈歌 (Song of the lantern festival). Anonymous calendrical *kasa*, one of the Twelve Kasa, probably composed before 1728. The extant version covers only the events from the first to the fifth lunar months.

kwangdae 廣大. Public performer or professional actor and singer including those in mask dance plays, puppet plays, and *p'ansori*. They belonged to the lowest class and traveled all over the country. *KRS* defines the *kwangdae* as "one who wears a mask and dances."

Kwangdŏk 廣德 (fl. 661–81). Writer of the 10-line *hyangga* "Wŏn wangsaeng ka" 顧往生歌 (Prayer to Amitāyus).

Kwŏn Che 權踶 (1387–1445). Son of Kwŏn Kŭn and graduate of the 1429 examination who, with others, drafted *Songs of Flying Dragons* and presented it to King Sejong in 1445.

Kwŏn Chŏngung 權正雄 (b. 1925). North Korean writer of fiction including *Paegilhong* (Crape myrtle, 1961) on socialist nation building.

Kwŏn Homun 權好文 (1532–87). Writer of the *sijo* sequence "Hangŏ sipp'al kok" 閑居十八曲 (Eighteen songs of idle life) and another cycle, "Tongnak p'algok" 獨樂八曲 (Eight songs of solitary enjoyment), in *kyŏnggi-ch'e* form.

Kwŏn Hwan 權煥 (1903–54). Writer of proletarian poetry.

Kwŏn Kŭn 權近 (1352–1409). Statesman and philosopher who also wrote biographical sketches of 3 people and the eulogy "Sangdae pŏlgok" 霜臺別曲 (Song of the censorate, c. 1399–1409).

Kwŏn P'il 權韠 (1569–1612). Poet who did not take the examination because he had no interest in a worldly career. At one time, urged by poet friends, he exchanged poems with a Ming envoy to Korea – meriting the highest recognition and honor. Kwŏn also wrote *Chusaeng chŏn* 周生傳 (Tale of Chu Hoe), a love story in Chinese that includes song lyrics (*ci*).

Kwŏn Samdŭk 權三得 (1771–1841). Master singer of *p'ansori* mentioned in Sin Chaehyo's "Kwangdae ka" (Song of the singer), he was especially known for his interpretation and singing of the swallow's song in *Song of Hŭngbo*.

Kwŏn Sŏp 權燮 (1671–1759). Poet who left 79 *sijo*, including one about shamanist music.

Kyerang 桂娘 (Laurel lady, Yi Hyanggŭm 李香今, 1513–50). Famous entertainer from Puan, North Chŏlla, versed in poetry, who left some 70 pieces in Korean and Chinese under the pen name Maech'ang 梅窓 (Plum Window). But her collected works are no longer extant.

Kyewŏrhyang 桂月香 (also Wŏlsŏn 月仙) (n.d.). Female entertainer in P'yŏngyang who helped the Korean general Kim Ŭngsŏ 金應瑞 to kill a

Japanese commander in the popular narrative fiction *Imjin nok* (Record of the Black Dragon year).

Kye Yongmuk 桂鎔默 (1904–61). Writer of fiction such as "Paekch'i Adada" (Adada the Idiot, 1935) and essays.

kyŏnggi-ch'e song 景幾體歌. Koryŏ and Chosŏn songs with a refrain that begins *kŭi ŏttŏhaniikko* 긔 엇더하니잇고 (How about that?) in *idu* and recurs in the fourth and sixth lines of each stanza in Koryŏ examples. In Koryŏ a line consists of 3 or 4 metric segments with 3 or 4 syllables in each segment: 3 3 4 / 3 3 4 / 4 4 4/ wi (Ah!) 3 3 4 / 4 4 4 4 / wi (Ah!) 3 3 4. The form underwent changes in Chosŏn.

Kyunyŏ, Great Master 均如大師 (923–73). Buddhist exegete and poet who wrote 11 devotional songs after the 10 vows of the Bodhisattva Samanta-bhadra: *Bhadra-cari-praṇīdhāna* (Vows on the practices of the bodhisattva).

"Kyusu sangsa kok" 규수상사곡 (Song of a lovestruck man). Anonymous *kasa* about a bachelor's love for a married woman.

Li Bo 李白 (701–62). Famous Tang poet known for his poems on wine and the moon.

Li Gongzuo 李公佐 (c. 770–848). Author of "Nanke taishou zhuan" 南柯太守傳 (Prefect of south branch), a Tang *chuanqi* 傳奇 (tale of wonder).

Li Ruzhen 李汝珍 (c. 1763–1830), author of *Jinghua yuan* 鏡花緣 (Flowers in the mirror, 1828) – a 100-chapter piece of vernacular fiction about a Daoist transcendent's fall from grace and her subsequent efforts in the mundane world to regain her immortality; also read as an allegory of the vicissitudes of human consciousness caught between appearance and reality, the temporal and the eternal.

Liu Ling 劉伶 (c. 225–80). One of the Seven Worthies of the Bamboo Grove. His "Jiude song" 酒德頌 (Hymn to the virtue of wine) survives.

Liu Zongyuan 柳宗元 (773–819). Tang poet and prose writer.

Li Zicheng 李自成 (1605–45). Bandit leader of the Ming who took Peking in 1644.

Lu Kai 陸凱 (fifth century). Chinese poet of the Liu-Song dynasty (420–79) in the South.

lüshi 律詩 (regulated verse). Chinese verse form in 8 penta- or heptasyllabic lines observing the rules of tonal parallelism. A single rhyme appears at the end of the second, fourth, sixth, and eighth lines, and optionally at the end of the first. The rhyme is generally in the level tone. Verbal parallelism is required in the second and third couplets.

Maeng Sasŏng 孟思誠 (1360–1438). Author of the first *sijo* sequence: "Kangho sasi ka" 江湖四時歌 (Four seasons by rivers and lakes).

Malttugi 말뚝이. Satirical and humorous character in Pongsan mask dance play and Yangju *pyŏlsandae* mask dance play. The servant of a gentleman, he figures also in other *ogwangdae* plays.

"Manjŏnch'un" 滿殿春 (Spring overflows the pavilion). Anonymous Koryŏ love song of 18 or 26 lines.

Mansŏkchung 만석중. Puppet play performed on the eighth of the fourth lunar month, Buddha's birthday, ostensibly to mock the great master of meditation Chijŏk, who broke his vows because of the famous female entertainer Hwang Chini (c. 1504–44).

Matsuo, Bashō 松尾芭蕉 (1644–94). *Haikai* poet canonized as one of Japan's great writers.

Mei Yaochen 梅堯臣 (1002–60). Song poet.

Mencius 孟子 (Mengzi, 371–290 BC). One of the Four Books compiled by his disciples, it consists of 7 chapters, each divided into 2 parts. Mencius was a professional teacher who advocated humane government and held a view that human nature is basically good.

Min Pyŏnggyun 민병균 (n.d.). North Korean poet who wrote the narrative verse *Ŏrŏri pŏl* (The plains of Ŏrŏri, 1952) about a peasant woman who joins a guerrilla unit.

Miyal halmi 미얄할미(old woman). Character in the Yangju *pyŏlsandae* mask dance play.

Mo Hŭnggap 牟興甲 (fl. 1834–49). Master singer of *p'ansori*.

Mŏkchung 먹중. Stubborn junior monk in the mask dance play.

Mo Yunsuk 毛允淑 (1910–90). Woman writer of poetry active in the 1930s–1950s and publisher of the monthly literary journal *Munye* 文藝 from 1949 to 1954.

Mu, King 武王 (600–41). Thirtieth king of Paekche and author of "Sŏdong yo" 薯童謠 (Song of Sŏdong, c. 600).

Much'ŏn 舞天 (Dancing to heaven). State assembly of Ye 濊 held in the tenth month.

Mun Chŏnghŭi 文貞熙 (b. 1947). Contemporary woman writer of poetry.

Munhak kwa chisŏng 文學과 知性 (Literature and intellect). Literary quarterly from August 1970 that introduced Western literary and theoretical works, espoused liberalism, and emphasized formal aesthetics. The name changed to *Munhak kwa sahoe* 文學과 社會 (Literature and society) in spring 1988.

Munhak yesul 文學藝術 (Literature and art, or Literary art). Fortnightly journal in tabloid form (1925–58) active in introducing Western literature and discovering new writers.

munkwa 文科 (final [higher] civil service examination). Examination in three stages (provincial, metropolitan, and palace) taken by holders of classics and literary licentiates who wished to qualify for appointment to major state offices. At the provincial level it consisted of 3 parts: (1) two essays as in the classics licentiate examination (the first to elucidate a passage from the Five Classics 五經, the second on the controversial reading of a passage or passages from the Four Books 四書) and a third essay in the form of disquisition (*non* 論); (2) one composition from rhymeprose, eulogy, inscription, admonition, or memorandum and another for the memorial (*p'yo* 表) or a report (*chŏn* 箋); (3) a problem essay (*ch'aek* 策). A total of 240 successful candidates from provinces, Seoul, and the Royal Confucian Academy 成均館 assembled for the metropolitan examination (*poksi* 覆試 or *hoesi* 會試). At the time of registration they were tested on their knowledge of *Kyŏngguk taejŏn* 經國大典 (National code) and *Zhuzi jiali* 朱子家禮 (Family rites of Zhu Xi). Then came a three-part examination corresponding to the preliminary examination except that candidates were now tested on the Four Books and the Three Classics 三經 orally to determine their ability to repeat the texts from memory and demonstrate their comprehension. Only 33 successful candidates were chosen to compete in the final examination to determine respective rankings. At this palace examination, candidates were tested in one essay in a form selected by the king. They were then presented to the king who personally conferred the degree on each candidate.

Munye 文藝 (Literary art). Monthly literary journal published by Mo Yunsuk from August 1949 to March 1954 (21 issues) and then from October 1954 to August 1960 (8 issues).

Muryŏng, King 武寧王 (462–523, r. 501–23). Twenty-fifth king of Paekche. His tombstone, consisting of 6 lines and a total of 52 graphs, was discovered in 1971.

Musugi t'aryŏng 武叔이打令 (Ballad of Musugi). A *p'ansori* work whose text (no longer extant) is conjectured to have dealt with the pleasure-seeker's life in Seoul.

Myŏngju powŏlbing 明珠寶月聘 (Tribulations of the three clans). A long clan fiction in Korean comprising 235 chapters in manuscript.

Myŏngok 明玉 (Bright Jade) (n.d.). Chosŏn female entertainer from Suwŏn who left 1 *sijo*.

"Naedang" 內堂 (The inner hall). An 11-line Koryŏ shamanist song riddled with textual cruxes.

Na Hŭidŏk 나희덕 (b. 1966). Contemporary woman writer of feminist poetry and prose.

Na Hyesŏk 羅蕙錫 (1896–1946). First Korean woman to study Western oil painting in Tokyo and Paris and a pioneer of the women's movement.

Nakch'ŏn tŭngun 落泉登雲 (Rise and fall of general and statesman Wang). Anonymous traditional narrative fiction in Korean dealing with life in the brothel and the role of a pimp who lures young unmarried women from impoverished families into prostitution.

Nam Hyojae 남효재 (n.d.). North Korean writer of fiction including *Chosŏn ŭi ŏmŏni* (Mother of Korea, 1970).

Nam Hyoon 南孝溫 (1454–92). Disciple of Kim Chongjik, friend of Kim Sisŭp and Kim Koengp'il, and author of *Ch'ugang chip* 秋江集, a literary miscellany.

Nam I 南怡 (1441–68). Graduate of the 1457 military examination who rendered meritorious service and became minister of war until the envious Yu Chagwang 柳子光 (d. 1512) slandered him and had him executed.

Nam Kon 南袞 (1471–1527). Powerful minister and instigator of the 1519 literati purge.

Nam Kuman 南九萬 (1629–1711). High minister who nurtured many pupils and left 1 *sijo*.

Nam Yongik 南龍翼 (1628–91). Scholar and writer known for his prose in Chinese and calligraphy. Nam compiled *Kia* 箕雅, an anthology of Chinese poetry with emphasis on regulated verse, and also *Hogok sihwa* 壺谷詩話 (Remarks on poetry by Hogok), which discussed 79 poets from Koryŏ to Chosŏn.

Nam Yŏngno 南永魯 (1810–57). Writer of *Ongnu mong* 玉樓夢 (Dream of the jade tower, c. 1835–40), a traditional narrative fiction in 64 chapters in both Chinese and Korean, known for its literary quality and popularity. The story concerns polygamy and an aristocrat's pursuit of fame.

Naong, Master 懶翁 (Hyegŭn 慧勤, 1320–76). Koryŏ monk of the Meditation school who introduced the notion of observing the critical phrase (*kanhwa* 看話) and the practice of meditation through invoking the Buddha's name. His "Sŏwang ka" 西往歌 (Song of the Pure Land) was transmitted orally until the eighteenth century.

"Narye ka" 儺禮歌 (Song of exorcism). Koryŏ song in 5 lines.

Na Tohyang 羅稻香 (1902–27). Writer whose stories deal with desire, fear, hatred, revenge – the romantic portrayal of tragic love, and dreams of material success.

No Ch'ŏnmyŏng 盧天命 (1913–57). Early modern woman poet who published her first collection *Sanhorim* (A coral forest) in 1938.

"Noch'ŏnyŏ ka" 老處女歌 (Song of a spinster). Anonymous *kasa*.

No Hyangnim 盧香林 (b. 1942). Woman writer of feminist poetry.

No Hyegyŏng 노혜경 (b. 1958). Woman writer of feminist poetry.

"Noin ka" 老人歌 (Song of old age). Anonymous *kasa* lamenting the sorrows of old age.

No Myŏnghŭm 盧命欽 (1713–75). Writer of *Tongp'ae naksong* 東稗洛誦 (Storyteller's collection from the east), anthology of 56 stories in Chinese.

Nongae 論介 (d. 1592). Female entertainer who was born into an upper-class family but lost her parents early and became a government entertainer. When the Japanese celebrated the fall of Chinju fortress, she enticed their drunken commander and threw herself with him into the river below. In 1740 a shrine was built and sacrifices are offered every spring and fall.

O Cham 吳潛 (c. 1274–1308). Sycophant of the twenty-fifth Koryŏ king Ch'ungnyŏl 忠烈王 (1236–1308; 1275–1308), the putative author of "Ssanghwajŏm" 雙花店 (The Turkish bakery).

O Changhwan 吳章煥 (1918–51). Poet who went north.

O Chŏnghŭi 吳貞熙 (b. 1947). Accomplished woman writer of fiction concerned with family life.

Ogi 五技 (Five plays). *Kŭmhwan, Wŏlchŏn, Taemyŏn, Soktok,* and *Sanye,* mentioned by Ch'oe Ch'iwŏn (b. 857) and recorded in *SGSG* 32:319.

ogwangdae 五廣大. Mask dance play, popular along the Naktong River in Kyŏngsang province, said to have originated at Pammari in Hapch'ŏn. In this 5-act play, played by 5 actors, the target of satirical attack is a gentleman whose servant Malttugi, wearing the largest mask, jokes and dances to musical accompaniment. Designated an Intangible Cultural Asset in 1970.

Ogwŏn chaehap kiyŏn 玉鴛再合奇緣 (Rare reunion of a couple). Anonymous traditional narrative fiction on love in 21 chapters in Korean; several editions exist.

Oksŏn mong 玉仙夢 (Dream of Hŏ Kŏt'ong). Anonymous traditional narrative fiction in Chinese that resembles *Kuun mong* (Dream of Nine Clouds) in plot.

Ondal 溫達 (d. 590). Koguryŏ general who, originally a foolish woodcutter, is said to have married a princess and rendered meritorious service to his country.

Ong Kojip chŏn 雍固執傳 (Tale of the miser Ong Kojip). A work in the *p'ansori* repertory now lost.

Ongnin mong 玉麟夢 (Dream of Ongnin). Traditional long narrative fiction in Chinese and Korean, attributed to Yi Chŏngjak 李庭綽 (1678–1758), about the conflict between two women.

Ongnu mong 玉樓夢 (Dream of the jade tower). Anonymous traditional fiction in 64 chapters in Chinese and Korean known for its tight structure.

ŏrŭm 어름. Tightrope walking.

"Oryun ka" 五倫歌 (Songs of five relations). Anonymous *kyŏnggi-ch'e* song of the five relations composed in early fifteenth century and recorded in

Akchang kasa 樂章歌詞 (Words for songs and music). Chu Sebung 周世鵬 (5 songs), Pak Illo 朴仁老 (22 songs), and Kim Sangyong 金尙容 (6 songs) wrote similar sequences on the same topic.

Ŏ Sukkwŏn 魚叔權 (fl. 1515–54). A secondary son of Ŏ Meangnyŏm (n.d.) who studied under Ch'oe Sejin (1473–1542) and, after passing the examination in documentary style, became an instructor. He went to Ming at least 7 times as an interpreter. He is remembered for his 2 books, *Kosa ch'waryo* 攷事撮要 (Selected essentials on verified facts, 1554) and *P'aegwan chapki* 稗官雜記 (A storyteller's miscellany, n.d.).

Ouyang Xiu 歐陽修 (1007–72). Song poet, critic, and compiler (with Song Qi 宋祁, 988–1061) of *Xin Tangshu* 新唐書 (New history of the Tang) and *Xin Wudaishi* 新五代史 (New history of the five dynasties).

O Yŏngjae 오영재 (n.d.). North Korean writer of fiction.

O Yŏngsu 吳永壽 (1914–79). Writer of short fiction who began with "Nami wa yŏtchangsu" (Nami and the taffyman, 1949) and wrote more than 100 short stories on the common people. Discovering pathos and humor in common incidents, he showed how to live in harmony with nature.

O Yuran chŏn 烏有蘭傳 (Tale of the female entertainer O Yuran). Anonymous humorous narrative fiction of manners in Chinese about the seduction of someone pretending to be a righteous gentleman.

Paekcho 白潮 (White tide, January 1922 – September 1923). Short-lived literary journal associated with the Romantic poetry movement.

Paek Haksŏn chŏn 白鶴扇傳 (Tale of the white crane fan). Anonymous traditional love story in Korean that exists in 11 editions.

Paek Injun 백인준 (b. 1919). North Korean writer of verse including *Ŏlgurŭl pulk'ira amerik'a yŏ* (Blush in shame, America), which condemns US participation in the Korean War.

Paek Kwanghong 白光弘 (1522–56). Author of the *kasa* "Kwansŏ pyŏlgok" 關西別曲 (Song of the northwest, 1555).

Paek Kwanghun 白光勳 (1537–82). One of the Three Tang-Style Poets and a writer of prose in Chinese.

Paek Sinae 白信愛 (1910–39). Socially committed woman writer of fiction.

Paek Ŭnp'al 백은팔 (n.d.). North Korean writer of fiction.

Paengmin 白民 (White-clad people, December 1945 – May 1950). Omnibus (later literary) journal edited by Kim Song (b. 1909) that published 22 issues emphasizing an autonomous spirit for literature.

Pae pijang chŏn 裵裨將傳 (Tale of subcommander Pae). Anonymous traditional satirical narrative fiction based on a *p'ansori* piece. Pae accompanies the magistrate Kim to Cheju Island where he disgraces himself with the female entertainer Aerang.

Pae pijang t'aryŏng 裴裨將打令 (Ballad of subcommander Pae). One of 12 *p'ansori* works whose song text is lost.

Pae Sua 배수아 (b. 1965). Contemporary woman writer of fiction.

pailü 排律. Regulated couplets of unlimited length.

Pak Chega 朴齊家 (1750–1805). Secondary son born of a concubine; a scholar of Practical Learning, who wrote realistic poetry.

Pak Chiwŏn 朴趾源 (1737–1805). Practical Learning scholar and author of satirical stories in Chinese on the hypocrisy of the scholar class.

Pak Ch'ŏmji 朴僉知. The most important character in the puppet play of the same name. For more see *Kkoktu kaksi.*

Pak Chonghwa 朴鍾和 (1901–81). Poet and writer of historical fiction on the sixteenth-century Japanese invasion of Korea (1955) and Great King Sejong (1977).

Pak Hwasŏng 朴花城 (1904–88). Socially committed woman writer of fiction.

Pak Hyŏn 박현 (n.d.). North Korean writer of fiction.

Pak Illo 朴仁老 (1561–1643). Soldier and poet who wrote 68 *sijo* and 7 *kasa.*

Pak Illyang 朴寅亮 (c. 1069). Koryŏ writer and putative compiler of *Sui chŏn* 殊異傳 (Tales of the extraordinary).

Pak Inhwan 朴寅煥 (1926–56). Member of the Hubangi coterie and poet who wrote on spiritual anguish but was criticized for uncritical acceptance of Western poetry.

Pak Kyŏngni 朴景利 (b. 1927). Writer of short and long fiction known especially for her major work *T'oji* (Land) in 13 volumes (1993). Often praised for her insights into human nature and a vernacular rivaling that of Hong Myŏnghŭi.

Pak Mogwŏl 朴木月 (1917–78). Poet whose early poems, written in folk-song rhythms, recreated the local color of the South. From the late 1950s he turned to open forms and looser measures and a plain, often powerful, diction. The poetry he finds in daily urban life is sometimes precarious and marginal, but his more successful poems transform incidental experiences into flashes of discovery.

Pak Nayŏn 박나연 (b. 1951). Contemporary woman writer of fiction.

Pak Nogap 朴魯甲 (1905–51). Writer of fiction who dealt deftly with everyday life and the workings of the human mind.

Pak P'aengnyŏn 朴彭年 (1417–56). One of the 6 martyred ministers of King Tanjong 端宗 (1442–57; r. 1452–55) and the author of 2 *sijo.*

Pak P'aryang 朴八陽 (b. 1906). Writer of proletarian poetry who went north.

Pak Sangch'ung 朴尙衷 (1331–75). Koryŏ poet.

Pak Seyŏng 朴世永 (1902–89). Writer of poetry who went north.

Pak Sijŏng 박시정 (b. 1942). Contemporary woman writer of fiction.

Pak Sŏwŏn 박서원 (b. 1960). Contemporary woman writer of poetry.

Pak-ssi chŏn 朴氏傳 (Tale of Lady Pak). Anonymous traditional narrative tale in Korean set during the Manchu invasion. Lady Pak, the wife of Yi Sibaek, humiliates the invaders with Daoist magic.

Pak Sunnyŏ 朴順女 (b. 1928). Woman writer of fiction about the Korean War, national division, and the lifestyle of women in a school dormitory.

Pak T'aewŏn 朴泰遠 (1909–86). Modernist writer of fiction including *Ch'ŏnbyŏn p'unggyŏng* (Scenes on the riverside, 1936). In the North he wrote the 3-part *Kabo nongmin chŏnjaeng* (Peasant war of the year kabo, 1977–86) dealing with the Tonghak peasant uprising in 1894.

Pak Tujin 朴斗鎭 (1916–98). Poet who praised the simple marvels of earth, mountain, sky, and sea. To Pak nature is "the source of God's love, light, truth, goodness, and beauty," and his Blakean innocence became imbued with a moral vision as he came to view the world in terms of moral conflict. From the mid-1960s he revealed a strong historical and cultural consciousness bearing testimony to contemporary reality.

Pak Ŭijung 朴宜中 (fl. 1388–92). Scholar versed in the Human Nature and Principle learning.

Pak Ŭnsik 朴殷植 (1859–1926). Historian and author of a dream journey (1911) intended to arouse an independent spirit in Koreans.

Pak Wansŏ 朴婉緒 (b. 1931). Prolific and popular woman writer of fiction whose themes include the disintegration of family, national division, criticism of materialistic society, middle-class avarice and hypocrisy, and equality of women. Her seamless narrative is able to summon in a single paragraph a person you surely know.

Pak Yongch'ŏl 朴龍喆 (1904–38). Early modern lyric poet who translated A. E. Housman's *The Name and Nature of Poetry* in 1933.

Pak Yŏngjun 朴榮濬 (b. 1911). Writer of fiction, short and long, who dealt with the plight of farmers and city dwellers. He also taught at Yonsei University.

Pak Yuhak 박유학 (n.d.). North Korean writer of fiction.

Pak Yujŏn 朴裕全 (c. 1834–1900). Founder of the western school of *p'ansori* singing.

palt'al 발탈 (foot mask). Mask play in which an actor lies down behind a black curtain and controls a scarecrow mask on the sole of his foot. The puppet wears a jacket and bamboo hands are connected to it by strings controlled by the puppeteer. Only the upper part of the puppet's body is shown. The play consists of a witty talk between the puppeteer and an interlocutor. Designated an Intangible Cultural Asset in 1982.

p'ansori 판소리. Korean oral narrative sung by a professional singer accompanied by a single drummer. Flourishing from the late eighteenth to the end of the nineteenth century, its repertory consisted of 12 pieces of which only 5 are extant.

pŏna 버나. Dish spinning.

Pongsan mask dance play 鳳山탈춤. Supported by merchants and performed by clerks and servants, presented on the town's busiest street on the evening of the 5th of the fifth month. It consists of 7 acts not always clearly divided. The text quotes Chinese poems and is rich in parody. Designated an Intangible Cultural Asset in 1967.

Poŭn kiu rok 報恩奇遇錄 (Record of rare encounters and requital of kindness). Anonymous traditional family fiction in 18 chapters in Korean. Set in Ming China with the protagonist Wi Yŏnch'ŏng, the story concerns a conflict in consciousness between the conservative elite and the merchant class.

Practical Learning 實學. Late Chosŏn reform Confucianism, emphasizing administrative and economic renovation and evidential learning.

p'ungmul 풍물. Farmers' music and instruments used in it – conical oboe, small and large gongs, as well as hourglass, barrel and handdrums.

"P'ungyo" 風謠 (Ode to Yangji). Anonymous 4-line Silla *hyangga* composed c. 635 to praise the virtue of Yangji.

Puyong sangsa kok 芙蓉相思曲 (Lotus' song of love). Anonymous traditional narrative tale in Korean concerning turbulent love between Kim Yusŏng and the female entertainer Puyong (Lotus) in P'yŏngyang. Lotus sends a *kasa*, "Sangsa kok" (Song of longing), to Kim in Seoul – hence the title.

P'yehŏ 廢墟 (Ruins, July 1920 – January 1921). Short-lived coterie literary journal.

Pyŏngin kanch'inhoe nok 病人懇親會錄 (Record of a reunion of the sick). Satirical story that points out the hardship caused by moral failings and corruption; first published in *Korea People's Press* 大韓民報 (19 August to 12 October 1909).

Pyŏn kangsoe ka 변강쇠가 (or *Karujigi t'aryŏng* 가루지기打令). One of the 6 *p'ansori* pieces redacted by Sin Chaehyo but not transmitted as sung text. The *p'ansori* fiction *Pyŏn Kangsoe chŏn* concerns a dissolute fellow, Pyŏn from Chŏlla, who marries Ongnyŏ from P'yŏngyang. When Pyŏn destroys a totem pole, he meets sudden death, but his wife cannot dispose of his corpse until a shamanist ritual is performed. The story offers a rich picture of the life of the lower classes.

Pyŏn Kyeryang 卞季良 (1369–1430). Author of "Hwasan pyŏlgok" 華山別曲 (Song of Mount Hwa, 1425).

Qu You 瞿佑 (1341–1427). Author of *Jiandeng xinhua* 剪燈新話 (New tales written while trimming the wick; preface dated 1378). The extant version containing 22 stories (*chuanqi*) on romance, ghosts, and unusual encounters was popular in Korea and Japan.

Qu Yuan 屈原 (340–278 BC). Loyal minister to King Huai 懷王 (r. 328–299 BC) of Chu 楚 who was rewarded with slander and banishment and ultimately drowned himself in the Miluo River. His most famous poem is *Lisao* 離騷 (Encountering sorrow), comprising 374 lines.

Rai Sanyō 賴山陽 (1780–1832). Late-Edo scholar, historian, and perhaps the best Japanese poet to write in Chinese.

Record of Rites (*Liji* 禮記). Book of instructions on such practical topics as cooking, offering sacrificial rites, funerals and mourning, education and music.

Ri Chongnyŏl 리종렬 (n.d.). North Korean writer of fiction.

Ri Kyŏngsuk 리경숙 (n.d.). North Korean writer of fiction including *Haengjin kok* (A march, 1988) about the Kwangju Uprising (May 1980).

Ri Myŏnggyun 리명균 (b. 1935). North Korean writer of fiction who wrote about the labor movement led by college students.

Ri Myŏnghun 리명훈 (n.d.). North Korean writer of fiction.

Ri Pungmyŏng 李北鳴 (b. 1910). North Korean writer of fiction.

Ri Taesang 리대상 (n.d.). North Korean writer of fiction.

Ri Tonghu 리동후 (n.d.). North Korean writer of poetry who wrote about the Kwangju Uprising (May 1980).

Sadaham 斯多含. Member of the *hwarang* corps who distinguished himself in a war against Great Kaya in 562.

saengwŏn 生員 (classics licentiate). Candidates for civil examination were tested in the Chinese classics by two essays – the first to elucidate a passage from the Five Classics, the second on the controversial reading of a passage or passages from the Four Books; 100 successful candidates (*saengwŏn*) received the white diploma and were qualified to enroll at the Royal Confucian Academy.

Saikaku 西鶴 (1642–93). Haikai poet and writer of fiction about townspeople and deep human feelings.

salp'an 살판 (tumbling).

Samdaemok 三代目 (Collection of three periods, 888). Anthology of *hyangga*, now lost, compiled by monk Taegu 大矩和尚 and prime minister Wihong 魏弘.

"Samo kok" 思母曲 (Maternal love). Anonymous Koryŏ song of 5 lines.

"Samsŏng taewang" 三城大王 (Great king of the three walled cities). A 7-line shamanist song praying for the elimination of pestilential vapors.

Samsŏn ki 三仙記 (Record of three transcendents). Anonymous traditional narrative story in Korean that presents a satirical portrait of a Neo-Confucian moralist infatuated with the two women Hong and Yu – hence "three" in the title.

sandae plays 山臺劇/戲. First mentioned in the sixth century, these plays were performed on a raised stage, decorated with colored fabrics, when the P'algwanhoe (Assembly of the eight prohibitions, a rite for native gods) and lantern festival were held in Silla and Koryŏ or on festive occasions and when receiving the Chinese envoy (Koryŏ and Chosŏn). Many spectacles were performed – tightrope walking, fire swalloing and spitting, tumbling, Ch'ŏyong dance, humorous plays, and one comic actor (without a mask) answering his own questions. The *sandae* play is also associated with the exorcism of evil spirits (*narye* 儺禮). Confucianists banned it in 1634 for its costly extravagance, and it disappeared toward the end of the eighteenth century. Consisting of dance, mime, song, and dialogue, today it is performed only at Yangju and Songp'a on the eighth day of the fourth month, fifth day of the fifth, and the fifteenth day of the eighth. Masks are more true to life than those used in Pongsan mask dance play. The *sandae* play was designated an Intangible Cultural Asset in 1964.

"Sangjŏ ka" 相杵歌 (Song of the pestle). A 4-line song dating from Koryŏ.

Sanguozhi yanyi 三國志演義 (Romance of the three kingdoms). Historical romance in vernacular Chinese attributed to Luo Guanzhong 羅貫中 (c. 1330–1400). The most popular Chinese fiction in Korea since the seventeenth century with a number of translations and adaptations. The earliest extant edition is dated 1522, with a preface dated 1494.

Sasanggye 思想界 (World of thought). Monthly omnibus educational journal, first edited by Chang Chunha (April 1953 – September 1970), that initiated the recommendation system to discover new writers and established the Tongin Literary Prize to encourage rising writers of fiction. At its height it sold up to 40,000 copies.

sasŏl sijo 辭說時調. Longer *sijo* form in which more than 2 metric segments in each line except for the first in line 3 are added. Some 540 examples are extant.

"Sat'aek chijŏk pi" 沙宅智積碑. Stele erected in 654 by Sat'aek at the time of his retirement to make vows espousing Buddhism.

se 瑟. A stringed zither.

Sejong, King 世宗 (1397–1450; 1418–50). Chosŏn king, inventor of the Korean alphabet, and author of *Wŏrin ch'ŏngang chigok* (Songs of the moon's reflections on a thousand rivers), completed before the end of 1446.

Sengyou 僧佑 (435–518). Author of *Shijia pu* 釋迦譜 in 5 chapters.

shi 詩 (poetry). In Korea and Japan, a graph reserved only for poetry written in literary Chinese.

Shuihu zhuan 水滸傳 (Water margin). One of the great Chinese works of fiction; the earliest known edition dates from the early sixteenth century. There are at least three English translations (1933, 1937, 1981) and one French (1978).

Sigyŏngam 息影庵 (fl. 1270–1350). Writer of a pseudobiography on bamboo cane.

sijo 時調. The most popular, elastic, and mnemonic poetic form of Korea. Dating from the fifteenth century, this 3-line poem/song was sung and orally transmitted until texts were written down from about the beginning of the eighteenth century. Even today it is an oral art for both the lettered and unlettered. Also known as *sijŏl kajo* 時節歌調, *tanga* 短歌, *sinsŏng* 新聲, *sinjo* 新調, *tanyo* 短謠, *tanch'ang* 短唱, *sogok* 小曲, *sinbŏn* 新翻(飜), or *singok* 新曲.

Silla 新羅 (57 BC – AD 935). Early Korean kingdom ruled by three royal houses.

Sima Qian 司馬遷 (?145–86 BC). Compiler of the *Shiji* 史記 (Historical records, or Records of the historian) in 130 chapters between 104 and 87 BC. *Shiji* covers the history of China from earliest times to 95 BC: basic annals (12 chs.), tables (10 chs.), treatises (8 chs.), hereditary families (30 chs.) and biographies (70 chs.).

Sim Ch'ŏng chŏn 沈清傳 (Tale of Sim Ch'ŏng). Anonymous traditional Korean narrative fiction concerning Sim Ch'ŏng's filial devotion to her blind father. She offers herself as a human sacrifice to the sea god so that her father may regain his sight.

Sim Ch'ŏng ka 沈清歌. *P'ansori* piece existing in at least 6 versions.

Sim Hun 沈熏 (1904–37). Fiction writer and scriptwriter for films who wrote *Sangnoksu* (Evergreen, 1936) about the rural education movement in the early 1930s. He also wrote a poem, "Kŭnari omyŏn" (When that day comes).

Sim Nŭngsuk 沈能淑 (1782–1840). Writer of *Oksu ki* 玉樹記 (Record of the jade tree, c. 1835–40), a traditional narrative tale, set in Ming China in Chinese (14 chs.), but translated into Korean by Min Ŭngsik 閔應植 (b. 1844) in 1888 (9 chs.). This work concerns love and marriage of the members of the four clans.

Simunhak 詩文學 (Poetic literature, March 1930 – October 1931). Coterie journal funded by Pak Yongch'ŏl that espoused anti-ideological purity, love for the language, and a harmony of sound and structure in poetry.

Sim Ŭi 沈義 (fl. 1475–1507). Author of "Taegwanjae mongyu rok" 大觀齋夢遊錄 (Record of a dream journey at Great Observation Study) in Chinese.

Sin Ch'aeho 申采浩 (1880–1936). Historian, nationalist, anarchist, writer of fiction and biographer of Ŭlchi Mundŏk (1908), Yi Sunsin (1908), and Ch'oe Yŏng (1909).

Sin Chaehyo 申在孝 (1812–84). The first known *p'ansori* redactor and teacher; from the middle-level people, he lived in Koch'ang county in North Chŏlla.

Sinch'ung 信忠 (fl. 737–42). Author of the 8-line *hyangga*, "Wŏnga" 怨歌 (Regret, 737), that reproaches King Hyosŏng 孝成王 for breaking a promise.

"Sindan kongan" 神斷公案 (Swift decision on a public case). Anonymous story in popular Chinese serialized in *Capital Gazette* from 19 May to 31 December 1906.

"Sindo ka" 新都歌 (Song of the new capital, 1394). Song written by Chŏng Tojŏn in praise of the new capital Seoul.

Sindonga 新東亞 (New East Asia). Monthly omnibus magazine published by *Tonga Daily* 東亞日報 from November 1931 to June 1936; shut down by Japanese colonial authorities after 59 numbers; resumed from September 1964.

Sin Hŭm 申欽 (1566–1628). Master of Chinese prose and writer of *sijo*.

Sin Kwanghan 申光漢 (1484–1555). Grandson of Sin Sukchu and author of *Kijae kii* 企齋記異 (Strange tales by Kijae, 1553), in Chinese, containing 4 stories of strange encounters, a dream journey, and a visit to the Dragon Palace.

Sin Kwangsu 申光洙 (1712–74). Chosŏn poet in Chinese whose *Kwansŏ akpu* 關西樂府 consisting of 108 poems is well known.

Sin Kyŏngjun 申景濬 (1712–81). Author of *Sich'ik* 詩則 (Principles of poetry, 1734) about poetry in Chinese.

Sin Kyŏngnim 申庚林 (b. 1936). Agrarian and activist poet who wrote about the plight of farmers marginalized by rapid industrialization. *Nam Hangang* (South Han River, 1987), some 4,000 lines long, traces the history of the Korean people's tribulations from the 1910s to 1940s.

Sin Kyŏngsuk 신경숙 (b. 1963). Contemporary woman writer of fiction about the impossibility of fulfilled love.

Sin Sŏkchŏng 辛夕汀 (1907–74). Twentieth-century lyric poet known for celebrating harmony between humans and nature.

Sin Sukchu 申叔舟 (1417–75). Scholar and writer who took part in King Sejong's philological research.

Sin Tongyŏp 申東曄 (1930–69). Activist poet who wrote about loss of innocence and a harmonious agrarian society crushed by imperialist powers. His narrative poem *Kŭmgang* (Kŭm River, 1967) concerns the Tonghak peasant uprising of 1894.

Sin Wi 申緯 (1769–1845). Known for poetry in Chinese, calligraphy, and painting, Sin translated 40 popular *sijo* into heptasyllabic quatrains (*jueju* 絶句).

Sinyŏja 新女子 (New women, March – May 1920). Omnibus magazine for women edited by Kim Wŏnju.

Sinyŏsŏng 新女性 (New women, October 1923 – April 1934). First commercially successful women's magazine.

Siyong hyangak po 時用郷樂譜 (Notations for Korean music in contemporary use). Anonymous music book dating from early sixteenth century that existed only in a single copy until Yonsei University published a photolithographic edition in 1954. Contains musical notations and texts of 26 titles, of which 19 are found nowhere else.

Sŏ Chŏngju 徐廷柱 (1915–2000). Popular and respected poet – often considered the most Korean of contemporary poets. His poems have been widely translated.

Soch'unp'ung 笑春風 (Chuckling spring breeze, c. 1469–94). Female entertainer in Yŏnghŭng who is said to have written a *sijo* to King Sŏngjong 成宗.

"Sogyŏng kwa anjŭmbangi mundap" 소경과안즘방이문답 (Questions and answers between a blind man and a cripple, 1905). Satirical story about corrupt government officials, perfunctory reforms, and foreign threats; serialized in *Korea Daily News*.

"Sŏgyŏng pyŏlgok" 西京別曲 (Song of P'yŏngyang). Anonymous Koryŏ love song, spoken by a woman, consisting of 14 3-line stanzas, with a refrain in line 3 of each stanza.

So Hyŏnsŏng nok 蘇玄成錄 (Tale of So Hyŏnsŏng). Anonymous traditional narrative fiction in Korean, set in Song China, concerning a posthumous son Hyŏnsŏng.

Sŏ Kiwŏn 徐基源 (b. 1930). Fiction writer who has deftly portrayed student soldiers in a war that fails to inspire dedication and a postwar society that is fraught with contradiction and absurdity. Life devoid of dreams and hopes and the landscape of the mind's wilderness have been recurrent themes. He has also written historical fiction on the Tonghak peasant uprising (1965) and on Kim Okkyun (1967–68).

Sŏ Kŏjŏng 徐居正 (1420–88). Prolific writer of poetry, fiction, and criticism (1474), a literary miscellany (1487), humorous tales; editor of *Tong munsŏn* 東文選 (Anthology of Korean literature in Chinese, 1478) and the arbiter of literary taste for more than 20 years.

Sŏkpo sangjŏl 釋譜詳節 (Detailed contents of the life history of Śākyamuni, published September 1447). Originally consisted of 24 chapters; now only chs. 3, 6, 9, 11, 13, 19, 21, 23, 24 are extant.

Sŏk Yugyun 석유균 (n.d.). North Korean writer of poetry and fiction on the Kwangju Uprising of May 1980.

Sŏk Yungi 석윤기 (1929–89). Farmer's son from North Kyŏngsang who wrote works of long fiction and was awarded the Kim Ilsŏng Medal in 1988.

Sŏl Ch'ong 薛聰 (c. 660–730). Author of "Hwawang kye" 花王戒 (Admonition to the king of flowers), a didactic prose piece.

Sŏl Chŏngsik 薛貞植 (1912–53). Writer of poetry who went north and was executed as a spy.

Sŏl-ssi samdae rok 薛氏三代錄 (Three-generation record of the Sŏl clan).

Son Ch'angsŏp 孫昌涉 (b. 1922). Writer of fiction and relentless researcher into the conscience of a lost generation. His characters are mostly the handicapped who view others as selfish, hypocritical enemies and indulge in sardonic self-mockery and cynical self-abandonment. Their lives are caricatures – as the titles of some of his stories suggest – "Naksŏjok" (Chalk mark tribe) and "Ingan tongmurwŏn ch'o" (Human Zoo). Spiritual ruin brought about by disintegration of values and dehumanization of society has been his major concern.

Song, Lady, of Ŭnjin 恩津宋氏. Author of a *kasa* on her trip to Kongju (1845).

Song Hŭngnok 宋興祿 (n.d.). Founder of the eastern school of *p'ansori* singing.

"Sŏnghwang pan" 城隍飯 (Food for Sŏnghwang gods). A 9-line shamanist song with onomatopoetic sounds in lines 5–7.

Sŏng Hyŏn 成俔 (1439–1504). Author of *Akhak kwebŏm* 樂學軌範 (Canon of music, 1493) and *Yongjae ch'onghwa* 慵齋叢話 (Literary miscellany of Sŏng Hyŏn, 1525); also wrote the poem, "Kwan koeroe chaphŭi si" 觀傀儡雜戲詩 (On seeing puppet plays).

Sŏngjong, King 成宗 (1456–94; 1469–94). Ninth king of Chosŏn; wrote a *sijo* to his favorite courtier Yu Hoin 兪好仁 (1445–94).

Song Kyŏnga 송경아 (b. 1971). Contemporary woman writer of fiction.

Song Mangap 宋萬甲 (1865–1939). Master singer of *p'ansori* who excelled in *Song of Ch'unhyang*, *Song of Sim Ch'ŏng*, and *Song of Red Cliff*.

Song Manjae 宋晚載 (1788–1851). Author of the poem "Kwan uhǔi" 觀優戲 (On seeing the plays of actors) consisting of 50 poems in Chinese.

Sǒng Sammun 成三問 (1418–56). One of the 6 martyred ministers of Tanjong; statesman, scholar, and writer active in helping King Sejong's research and works of compilation. One *sijo* is attributed to him.

Song Sun 宋純 (1493–1583). Author of the *kasa* "Myǒnangjǒng ka" 俛仰亭歌 (Song of Myǒnang arbor).

Sǒng Yǒhak 成汝學 (late sixteenth century). Writer of poetry in Chinese who is said to have passed the examination in his fifties.

Song Yǒng 宋影 (1903–79). Writer of fiction who went north.

Son Sohǔi 孫素熙 (1917–87). Woman writer of short and long fiction.

Sǒnu Hwi 鮮于煇 (1922–98). Writer who expressed a historical and cultural awareness hitherto dormant in postwar fiction – for example, in *Pulkkot* (Flowers of fire, 1957). Known for his ability to discover beauty in the weak and ruined. His subjects include national consciousness, brotherly love that transcends political ideology, and those who are sacrificed to politics and society.

sosǒl 小說 (*xiaoshuo, shōsetsu*). Literally "small talk," a pejorative term used to designate imaginative fiction in traditional East Asia. The term is still used for Western-inspired realistic fiction – indeed for all kinds of fiction.

So-ssi samdae rok 蘇氏三代錄 (Three-generation record of the So clan).

So Taesǒng chǒn 蘇大成傳 (Tale of So Taesǒng). Anonymous traditional narrative fiction in Korean, set in Ming China, concerning So's military exploits. There are at least 33 editions.

Sǒ Yǒngǔn 徐英恩 (b. 1943). Contemporary woman writer of fiction.

Sǒ Yuyǒng 徐有英 (1801–74). Author of *Yungmidang ki* 六美堂記 (Record of six beauties, 1863) – also known as *Kim t'aeja chǒn* 金太子傳 or *Pot'a kimun* 普陀奇聞 – a 16-chapter story of love and war with Silla king Sosǒng's crown prince Sosǒn as protagonist. One version in Korean, another in Chinese.

Spring and Autumn (*Annals*) (*Chunqiu* 春秋). Chronicle of events in the state of Lu 魯 from 722 to 481 BC in laconic style, compiled by Confucius. Among the three commentaries, the *Zuo Commentary* 左傳 (third century BC) contains lengthy narrative on the history of the period – the longest and most important historical text of the Zhou 周 period.

Sugyǒng nangja chǒn 淑英娘子傳 (Tales of Sugyǒng). Anonymous traditional narrative tale in Korean and Chinese in 6 chapters. Set in the time of King Sejong, the story shows how two Daoist transcendents solve a public case.

Sui chŏn 殊異傳 (Tales of the extraordinary). Anthology of folktales compiled between late Silla and early Koryŏ and variously attributed to Ch'oe Ch'iwŏn 崔致遠, Pak Illyang 朴寅亮, and Kim Ch'ŏngmyŏng 金陟明.

Sukhyang chŏn 淑香傳 (Tale of Sukhyang). Anonymous traditional narrative tale in Korean and Chinese, already popular by 1754, concerning the tribulations of Sukhyang and Yi Sŏn until their marriage.

Su Shi 蘇軾 (Su Dongpo 蘇東坡, 1037–1101). Song-dynasty poet, critic, and prose writer whose "Chibi fu" 赤壁賦 (Rhymeprose on Red Cliff) in two pieces is universally known to the educated.

"Taeguk" 大國 (The large country). Shamanist song in 3 stanzas read as a song of offering to shamanist gods.

Taegwanjae mongyu rok 大觀齋夢遊錄 (Record of a dream journey at Great Observation Study). Sim Ŭi 沈義 (b. 1475), pen name Taegwanjae, tells of his journey to an ideal kingdom where the Silla writer Ch'oe Ch'iwŏn is the son of heaven served by famous writers of the past.

taejabi (*son*) 대잡이 (손). Main controller of puppets in puppet plays.

"Taewang pan" 大王飯 (Food for the great king). A 6-line shamanist song whose meaning is unclear.

Taiping guangji 太平廣記 (Extensive gleanings of the reign of Great Tranquility, 981). Collection of stories compiled by Li Fang 李昉 (925–96); the single most important compendium of early Chinese fiction, widely read and partially translated into Korean.

Tangun Wanggŏm 檀君王儉. Mythological founder of Korea who established Tangun Chosŏn, with its capital at Asadal (P'yŏngyang), and called his country Chosŏn in 2333 BC. The myth seems to have emerged in the late thirteenth century. A shrine was built to honor him under King Sejong. Annually 3 October is celebrated in Korea as Foundation Day (Kaech'ŏnjŏl). He is worshiped as a deity by believers of Taejonggyo, a sect founded in 1909.

"Tanjang ka (sa)" 斷腸歌/詞 (Song of heartrending grief). *Kasa* on a married man's love for another woman.

Tao Qian 陶潛 (Tao Yuanming 陶淵明, 365–427). Important pre-Tang poet who wrote some 120 pieces including "Kui qulai ci" 歸去來辭 (The Return) and "Taohua yuan ji" 桃花源記 (Peach Blossom Spring), a literary Utopia that is widely read and cited.

Thirteen Classics 十三經. *Book of Changes* (*Yijing* or *Zhouyi*; K. *Yŏkkyŏng* or *Chuyŏk*), *Book of Documents* (*Shujing* or *Shangshu*; K. *Sŏgyŏng* or *Sangsŏ*), *Book of Songs* (*Shijing*; K. *Sigyŏng*), *Institutes of Zhou* (*Zhouli* 周禮; K. *Churye*), *Book of Ceremonial* (*Yili* 儀禮; K. *Ŭirye*), *Record of Rites* (*Liji*; K. *Yegi*), *Spring and Autumn Annals* (*Chunqiu*; K. *Ch'unch'u*) and *Zuo*

Commentary (*Zuozhuan*; K. *Chwajŏn*), *Commentary of Gongyang* 公羊傳 (*Gongyang zhuan*; K. *Kongyang chŏn*), *Commentary of Guliang* 穀梁傳 (*Guliang zhuan*; K. *Kongnyang chŏn*), *Analects* (*Lunyu*; K. *Nonŏ*), *Book of Filial Piety* (*Xiaojing*; K. *Hyogyŏng*), *Erya* 爾雅 (K. *Ia*), and *Mencius* (*Mengzi*; K. *Maengja*). *The Great Learning* (*Daxue*; K. *Taehak*) and *Doctrine of the Mean* (*Zhongyong*; K. *Chungyong*) are both short chapters of the *Record of Rites*.

"Tigusyŏng miraemong" 地球星未來夢 (Dream of the earth's future, 1909). Anonymous story serialized in *Korea Daily News* from 15 July to 10 August 1909.

T'obyŏl ka 兔鼈歌 (Song of the rabbit and the turtle, or *Sugung ka* 水宮歌 [Song of the water palace]). *P'ansori* piece redacted by Sin Chaehyo (1812–84).

T'okki chŏn 토끼전 (Tale of a rabbit). Fable turned into *p'ansori* and *p'ansori* fiction in both Chinese and Korean. A turtle lures a rabbit to get its liver to cure the dragon king's illness, but the rabbit outwits the dragon king and returns safely to land.

tŏlmi 덜미 (puppet play). Also called *tŏtpoegi* 덧뵈기, *tŏt* meaning "mask."

Tomi 都彌. Righteous man of Paekche with a beautiful chaste wife. When King Kaeru (128–66) wished to violate her, she devised a stratagem and escaped. The king then had Tomi's eyes gouged out and set him adrift on a skiff. Ultimately husband and wife were reunited.

Tonga Daily 東亞日報. Korean daily from 1 August 1920 to 10 August 1940 when it was shut down by the colonial government. It resumed publication in 1945.

"Tongdong" 動動 (Ode to the seasons). Koryŏ calendrical song with an introduction followed by 12 stanzas to the 12 lunar months.

Tongmaeng 東盟 (Dawn). Koguryŏ's national assembly held in the tenth month.

Tongya hwijip 東野彙輯 (Assorted collection from the eastern field). Collection of 242 unofficial stories in Chinese arranged topically by Yi Wŏnmyŏng 李源命 (b. 1807).

"T'ŏnorae" 터노래 ("Tosol ka" 兜率歌, "Tonnorae," or "Turinnorae"; song of peace and repose). Popular composition made in AD 28 by the grateful people of Silla.

Tŭgo 得烏 (Tŭkkok or Siro). Writer of the 8-line *hyangga* "Mo Chukchirang ka" 慕竹旨郞歌 (Ode to knight Chukchi).

Tukkŏp chŏn 두껍전 (Tale of a toad). Anonymous traditional narrative tale, in Korean, of uncertain date; a fable featuring a toad and a fox, in dialogue form.

Twelve *kasa* 十二歌詞. Sung *kasa* shorter than the regular *kasa* in length, for example, "Paekku sa" 白鷗詞 (Song of the white gull).

"Ubu ka" 愚夫歌 (Song of a foolish man). Anonymous *kasa*.

Ŭlchi Mundŏk 乙支文德 (fl. 612). Koguryŏ general who sent a quatrain in Chinese to Sui general Yu Zhongwen 于仲文 in 612.

Ŭn Hŭigyŏng 은희경 (b. 1959). Contemporary woman writer of fiction.

Unyŏng chŏn 雲英傳 (Tale of Unyŏng). Anonymous traditional narrative tale in Korean and Chinese about the tragic love between Scholar Kim and Unyŏng, a lady attached to the court of Prince Anp'yŏng (1418–53).

U T'ak 禹倬 (1263–1342). Studied Neo-Confucianism of the Cheng-Zhu school and was versed in the *Book of Documents*; 2 *sijo* are attributed to him.

waka 和歌. Broadly all Japanese poetry as opposed to poetry in Chinese; in a restricted sense, a Japanese poetic type but often synonymous with *tanka* 短歌 (short poem consisting of 5-7-5-7-7 syllables).

Waltcha t'aryŏng 曰者打令 (Ballad of military officials; also called *Musugi t'aryŏng*). *P'ansori* piece no longer extant.

Wanwŏrhoe maengyŏn 玩月會盟宴 (Pledge banquet at the moon viewing party). Longest narrative fiction in Korean consisting of 180 chapters in 180 volumes; exists only in manuscript. Set in Song China, it concerns the conflicts arising from polygamy.

Wenxuan 文選 (Selections of refined literature). Anthology compiled by Xiao Tong 蕭統 (501–31) – the most widely studied book in Korea until the nineteenth century.

Western Regions 西域. Han-dynasty term for the area west of Yumenguan (Jade gate pass), including what is now Xinjiang and parts of Central Asia.

Wiman Chosŏn 衛滿朝鮮. Kingdom that fell in 108 BC to Han Chinese forces.

Wi Paekkyu 魏伯珪 (1727–98). Scholar and writer who retired to Mount Kyehang and wrote a *sijo* sequence of 9 songs about the farm.

Wŏlmyŏng, Master 月明師 (c. 762–65). Writer of 2 *hyangga*: "Turinnorae" 두릿노래 (Song of Tuṣita Heaven, 760) to remove two suns that appeared in the sky and "Che mangmae ka" 祭亡妹歌 (Requiem for a dead sister).

Wŏn Ch'ŏnsŏk 元天錫 (fl. 1401–10). Tutor of Yi Pangwŏn, the future king of Chosŏn; 2 *sijo* are attributed to him.

Wŏngaksa 圓覺社. A round red brick theater that opened in Seoul in 1908 and closed down in 1910 where *p'ansori* and new plays were performed to an audience of 500 or 600.

Wŏngwang 圓光 (542–640). Eminent Silla monk who served as chaplain and adviser to the *hwarang* corps and wrote "Sesok ogye" 世俗五戒 (Five commandments for laymen).

Wŏnhyo 元曉 (617–86). Silla monk considered the most original of Buddhist thinkers in Korea.

Xie Lingyun 謝靈運 (385–433). First great landscape poet of China.

Xiyouji 西遊記 (Journey to the west, or Monkey). Popular Chinese fiction based loosely on the experience of the Tang monk Xuanzang 玄奘 (596–664), who took 17 years to journey to India for Buddhist scriptures. Attributed to Wu Chengen 吳承恩 (c. 1500–82). Its earlier version was known in Korea in the mid fifteenth century.

yadam 野談. Historical episode/anecdote, well-structured fictional story, or a mixture of the two narrated in a realistic style with a variety of characters. Usually composed by impoverished literati or their equivalents who personally experienced the urban atmosphere of late Chosŏn. Translated as unofficial story/anecdote.

Yangju *pyŏlsandae* mask dance play 楊州別山臺놀이. *Sandae* play still performed in Kyŏnggi province (also in Songp'a). When the *sandae* play was abolished as an official national event, actors began mask dance plays. This play is said to be patterned after a play performed in Sajikkol (western part of Seoul) – hence "pyŏl," meaning not native to Yangju, a place of commercial importance. The play is performed on the eighth day of the fourth month, fifth day of the fifth month, and the full moon of the eighth month. The masks are more realistic than those in Pongsan mask dance play. Yangju *pyŏlsandae* is said to consist of 8 acts, but actors do not divide them formally. Designated an Intangible Cultural Asset in 1964.

Yang Kison chŏn 楊己孫傳 (Tale of Yang Kison). Anonymous traditional narrative fiction in Korean dealing with the conflict between wife and concubine.

Yang Kwija 楊貴子 (b. 1955). Contemporary feminist writer of fiction.

Yang Sajun 楊士俊 (fl. 1546). Younger brother of Yang Saŏn (1517–84), author of the *kasa* "Namjŏng ka" 南征歌 (Song of the southern expedition, 1555) concerning his participation in repulsing the Japanese pirates' incursion into Chŏlla in 1555.

Yang Saŏn 楊士彦 (1517–84). Author of the *kasa* "Miin pyŏlgok" 美人別曲 (Song of a beautiful woman).

Yan Guang 嚴光 (37 BC – AD 43). Friend and adviser of Emperor Guangwu 光武帝 who lived as a fisherman in modern Zhejiang because he wished to refuse the emperor's offer of a high post.

Yan Yu 嚴羽 (fl. 1180–1235). Song critic who wrote *Canglang sihua* 滄浪詩話 (Canglang's remarks on poetry), the most famous and influential work in the genre "remarks on poetry."

Yejong, King 睿宗 (1079–1122; 1105–22). Sixteenth ruler of Koryŏ; wrote an 8-line song, "To ijang ka" 悼二將歌 (Dirge for two generals, 1120), to commemorate Sin Sunggyŏm (d. 917) and Kim Nak (d. 917), who saved the life of Wang Kŏn, founder of Koryŏ, when he was surrounded by the enemy.

Yesul Chosŏn 藝術朝鮮 (Korean art). Literary journal edited by Yun Kyŏngsŏp in 1957 that closed after 3 numbers.

Yi, Lady of Yŏnan 延安李氏. Wife of Yu Sach'un who wrote a congratulatory *kasa* on her son's and nephew's passing of the examination (1794) and a travel *kasa* on her visit to her son (1800).

Yi Chae 李縡 (1680–1748). Scholar who was versed in the Human Nature and Principle learning and supported the theory of the philosopher Yi Kan 李柬 (1677–1727).

Yi Chahyŏn 李資玄 (1061–1125). Koryŏ scholar and writer who retired to Mount Ch'ŏngp'yŏng in Ch'unch'ŏn, built a cloister and hall, and spent his life studying the Meditation school of Buddhism. He was respected by Kings Yejong 睿宗 and Injong 仁宗.

Yi Ch'an 이찬 (b. 1910). North Korean writer of poetry.

Yi Chehyŏn 李齊賢 (1287–1367). Koryŏ scholar, poet, and writer of prose who visited China at least 6 times and traveled widely there. He translated 9 contemporary folk songs into Chinese (*So akpu*) and wrote *Nagong pisŏl* 櫟翁稗說 (or *Yŏgong p'aesŏl*; Lowly jottings by old man "Oak," 1342), a literary miscellany.

Yi Chinmyŏng 이진명 (b. 1955). Contemporary woman writer of poetry who refuses to demonize the family and the male sex.

Yi Chinyu 李眞儒 (1669–1730). Author of the *kasa* "Sok samiin kok" 續思美人曲 (Continued hymn of constancy, c. 1725–27).

Yi Ch'ŏm 李詹 (1345–1405). Writer of a pseudobiography on paper and a biographical sketch of Susŏn in Chinese.

Yi Chŏngbo 李鼎輔 (1693–1766). Poet who wrote verse in Chinese and left 78 *sijo*.

Yi Chŏnggu 이정구 (n.d.). North Korean writer of poetry.

Yi Ch'ŏngjun 李淸俊 (b. 1937). Writer of fiction, long and short, whose concerns include the decline of traditional arts in modern society, people's incapacity to survive the contradictions of life in postwar Korea, and the psychological effect of political violence. *Tangsindŭre ch'ŏnguk* (This paradise of yours, 1976), set in a leper colony, for example, inquires into the human yearning to construct an earthly paradise as well as the impediments to its realization.

Yi Chŏnyŏn 李兆年 (1269–1343). Graduate of the 1294 examination who accompanied King Ch'unghye (r. 1330–32, 1339–44) to Yuan China and often admonished him for his debauchery. There is 1 *sijo* attributed to him.

Yi Ch'unp'ung chŏn 李春風傳 (Tale of profligate Yi). Anonymous traditional narrative story of manners in Korean with realistic and humorous elements. Yi is infatuated with the female entertainer Ch'uwŏl, but his wife teaches him a lesson.

Yi Haejo 李海朝 (1869–1927). Writer of 5 works of "new fiction" such as *Chayujong* 自由鐘 (Liberty bell, 1910), in which women discuss their rights and education, national independence, and social reform.

Yi Haeng 李荇 (1478–1534). Scholar and writer who edited the *Tongguk yŏji sŭngnam* 東國輿地勝覽 (Korean gazetteer, 1530); versed in Chinese prose, calligraphy, and painting.

Yi Hangbok 李恒福 (1556–1618). Statesman active during the Japanese invasion of 1592–98 and the writer of "Yu Yŏn chŏn" 柳淵傳 (Tale of Yu Yŏn, 1607).

Yi Hoch'ŏl 李浩哲 (b. 1932). Writer of fiction whose concerns include Korea's political division, corrupt public officials, and satirical portrayal of manners. A typical work is his *Sosimin* (The petit bourgeois, 1964–65), set in Pusan, Korea's wartime capital.

Yi Hŭijun 李羲準 (1775–1842). Author of *Kyesŏ yadam* 溪西野談 (Unofficial stories compiled by Kyesŏ, c. 1833–42), a collection of 312 stories in Chinese, mostly on historical personages.

Yi Hwang 李滉 (1501–71). Celebrated Neo-Confucian philosopher and writer of the *sijo* sequence *Tosan sibi kok* 陶山十二曲 (Twelve songs of Tosan).

Yi Hyangji 이향지 (b. 1942). Contemporary woman writer of poetry.

Yi Hyŏnbo 李賢輔 (1467–1555). Author of "Ŏbu tanga ojang" 漁夫短歌五章 (Five fisherman's songs), Yi shortened a 12-song cycle to 9, and shortened another cycle of 10 songs to 5.

Yi Hyosŏk 李孝石 (1907–42). Writer of fiction, long and short, who became disillusioned by socialism after a brief plunge into a proletarian literary movement. His later stories, which represent flights from civilization, promote nature and sex as escapes from the insoluble contradictions of society and self. A fusion of lyrical style and local color produced stories like "Memulkkot p'il muryŏp" (When the buckwheat blooms, 1936).

Yi I 李珥 (1536–84). Celebrated Neo-Confucian philosopher and writer of a *sijo* sequence, *Kosan kugok ka* 高山九曲歌 (Nine songs of Mount Ko), that covers the 4 seasons and 9 scenes on Mount Suyang in Haeju.

Yi Ik 李瀷 (1681–1763). Scholar of Practical Learning and author of *Kwagu rok* 藿憂錄 (Record of concern for the underprivileged).

Yi Illo 李仁老 (1152–1220). Scholar, poet, critic, and writer of the first literary miscellany in Korea: *P'ahan chip* 破閑集 (Jottings to break up idleness, pub. 1260).

Yi Injik 李仁稙 (1862–1919). Writer of "new fiction," such as *Hyŏl ŭi nu* (Tears of blood, 1906).

Yi Isun 李頤淳 (1754–1832). Writer of fiction and critic who expressed his views on the nature and function of fiction.

Yi Kae 李塏 (1417–56). Great-grandson of Yi Saek and one of the 6 martyred ministers of King Tanjong; 2 *sijo* are attributed to him.

Yi Kiyŏng 李箕永 (1895–1984). Writer of ideological fiction and agrarian fiction such as *Kohyang* (Hometown, 1933–34) who went north and wrote *Tuman kang* (Tumen River, 1961).

Yi Kok 李穀 (1298–1351). Writer of a pseudobiography on the bamboo cushion and a biographical sketch of Lady Cho.

Yi Kwangsu 李光洙 (b. 1892). Writer of the first "modern novel," *Mujŏng* (Heartless, 1917), wrote didactic and historical fiction, but his collaboration with the Japanese colonial government stained his reputation.

Yi Kyŏngja 이경자 (b. 1948). Contemporary woman writer of fiction.

Yi Kyŏngnim 이경림 (b. 1947). Contemporary woman writer of poetry.

Yi Kyubo 李奎報 (1169–1214). Koryŏ poet and critic who wrote pseudobiographies on wine and the turtle, biographical sketches, narrative poetry on King Tongmyŏng of Koguryŏ, and poems on an old shaman and on a puppet play.

Yi Kyugyŏng 李圭景 (b. 1788). Scholar of Practical Learning with encyclopedic knowledge who left a monumental work of 60 chapters on 1,400 subjects (astronomy, the calendar, the seasons, mathematics, history, institutions, geography, economics, literature, phonetics, Western learning, medicine, metallurgy, trees and plants, fish, insects).

Yi Mungu 李文求 (1941–2003). Writer of fiction known for his satiric or sympathetic portrayal of agrarian life, as in *Kwanch'on sup'il* (Essays on Kwanch'on, 1977). The incalculable effects of modernization on farming include the dissolution of family and community, corruption of moral sensibility, and disintegration of human relationships. Exploited by local officials, ineffectual government policies, and consumerism, the farmer cannot withstand the brutal impact of the industrialized world.

Yi Munnyŏl 李文烈 (b. 1948). Writer of fiction who has dealt with oppression, ideology, and political division. His historical fiction *Siin* has been translated as *The Poet*, a fictionalized life of Kim Pyŏngyŏn (1807–63); *Uridŭrŭi ilgŭrŏjin yŏngung* has been translated as *Our Twisted Hero.*

Yi Ok 李鈺 (1760–1812). Poet of urban life and vicissitudes of women's lives and writer of biographical sketches of 23 people including a deaf-mute, blind man, slave, monk, soldier, and swindler ("Yi Hong chŏn" 李泓傳).

Yi Ŏnjŏk 李彦迪 (1491–1553). Writer of philosophical poems in Chinese.

Yi Pangwŏn 李芳遠 (1367–1422; 1400–18). The third ruler of Chosŏn; a *sijo* is attributed to him.

Yi Pŏmsŏn 李範宣 (b. 1920). Writer of fiction who experimented with lyrical, social, and denunciatory styles. Yi is especially concerned with the transformation of decent people into insolent, vain, stingy creatures. He also wrote on postwar refugee life ("Obalt'an" [A stray bullet, 1961]), the hypocrisy of religion, and the survival of the weak.

Yi Pyŏngju 李炳注 (b. 1921). Writer of fiction and essays whose *Chirisan* (Mount Chiri, 1972–78) concerns activities of leftist guerrillas before and after the Korean War.

Yi Saek 李穡 (1328–96). Statesman, scholar, and poet who left some 6,000 poems in Chinese, wrote biographical sketches of his friends and others, and composed a heptasyllabic old-style poem, "Kuna haeng" 驅儺行 (On seeing the exorcism rite), and a group of poems on annual events and popular customs.

Yi Sang 李箱 (pen name of Kim Haegyŏng 金海卿, 1910–37). Modernist writer with a punkish sneer who was anxious to register a modernist rupture with the past by writing versions of surrealist/Dadaist poems. He also wrote short stories and essays. He died of consumption in Tokyo.

Yi Sanghŭi 이상희 (b. 1960). Contemporary woman writer of feminist poetry.

Yi Sanghwa 李相和 (1900–43). Lyric poet who wrote "Ppaeakkin tŭredo pomŭn onŭnga" (Does spring come to stolen fields? 1926).

Yi Sebo 李世輔 (1832–95). Writer of 458 *sijo.*

Yi Sech'un 李世春 (n.d.). Professional singer of *sijo* who, in the early eighteenth century, composed the new tune called *sijo* to earlier song texts.

Yi Sik 李植 (1584–1647). Renowned writer of Chinese prose who annotated and commented on Du Fu's poetry in 26 chapters.

Yi Sŏgu 李書九 (1754–1825). Writer of realistic poetry in Chinese.

Yi Sŏkpong 李石峰 (b. 1928). Woman writer of fiction who investigated women's selfhood and the battle between the sexes.

Yi Sŏngbu 李盛夫 (b. 1942). Writer of committed and nationalist poetry.

Yi Sugwang 李晬光 (1563–1628). Pioneer of Practical Learning who introduced Matteo Ricci's (1552–1610) *True Significance of the Lord of Heaven* and wrote a literary miscellany.

Yi Sungin 李崇仁 (1349–92). Writer of biographical sketches including accounts of praiseworthy women.

Yi Sunsin 李舜臣 (1545–98). Famous Korean admiral whose "turtle ship" defeated the Japanese navy during their invasion of 1592–98.

Yi T'aejun 李泰俊 (b. 1904). Master of the modern short-story form and a literary stylist of refinement who depicted the lives of those who retain their humanity even in bad times. Fastidious in his sense of the writer's vocation, his narrative is engrossing because of its exquisite flow. He went north.

Yi Tal 李達 (1539–1612). Together with two other poets he was known as one of the Three Tang-Style Poets who emulated the poetry of High Tang.

Yi Tŏgil 李德一 (1561–1622). Passed the military examination, served under Admiral Yi Sunsin, and wrote 28 *sijo*.

Yi Tŏkhyŏng 李德馨 (1561–1613). Went to Ming China requesting a relief army to repulse the Japanese invaders and left 4 *sijo*.

Yi Tongbaek 李東伯 (1867–1950). Master singer of *p'ansori* who performed for King Kojong (1864–1907) in 1900 and held a farewell performance before retirement in 1939. Known especially for his interpretation of *Song of Ch'unhyang* and *Song of Red Cliff*.

Yi Tonggyu 이동규 (1913–51). Writer of fiction who went north.

Yi Tŏngmu 李德懋 (1739–93). Secondary son born of a concubine; a scholar of Practical Learning, known for his wide knowledge, who wrote realistic poetry and went to Peking in 1778 and befriended Qing scholars.

Yi Ujun 李遇駿 (1801–67). His *Mongyu yadam* 夢遊野談 (Unofficial stories gathered during a dream journey) defends fiction by citing the examples of *Dream of Nine Clouds*, *Record of Lady Sa's Journey South*, and *Showing Goodness and Stirred by Righteousness*.

Yi Yango 李養吾 (1737–1811). Scholar in Ulsan who failed the examination but wrote detailed evaluations of such works as *Dream of Nine Clouds*, in heptasyllabic 30-line verse, and *Record of Lady Sa's Journey South*, in prose.

Yi Yong 李溶. Military man who wrote the *kasa* "Pukchŏng ka" 北征歌 (A trip to the north, 1776) on what he witnessed as a military chief in Hamgyŏng province.

Yi Yongak 李庸岳 (1914–71). Poet of engagement who went north and continued to write such works as *P'ibalsŏn saehae* (Bloodshot new year) to justify the Korean War.

Yi Yŏnju 이연주 (1953–92). Feminist poet who burned sorrow like fuel but ultimately committed suicide.

Yi Yuksa 李陸史 (1904–44). Nationalist, activist, and poet especially productive from 1936 to 1941, when he produced some 30 poems.

Yŏm Kyedal 廉啓達 (fl. 1834–49). Master singer of *p'ansori* who performed before King Hŏnjong 憲宗 (1834–49).

Yŏm Sangsŏp 廉想涉 (1897–1963). Master of realistic fiction who advocated accumulation of detail and defended the sovereign impartiality and invisibility of the narrator. The breadth and scope of his social compass produced such works as *Samdae* (Three generations, 1931).

Yongbi ŏch'ŏn ka 龍飛御天歌 (Songs of flying dragons, 1445–47). Great eulogy cycle consisting of 125 cantos comprising 248 poems praising the founding of the Chosŏn dynasty by General Yi Sŏnggye. The *Songs* were the first experimental use in verse of the Korean alphabet, invented in 1443–44.

"Yongbu ka" 庸婦歌 (Song of a simple life). Anonymous *kasa*.

Yŏnggo 迎鼓 (Welcoming drums). National assembly of Puyŏ 扶餘.

Yŏngjae, Monk 永才 (c. 785–98). Author of the 10-line *hyangga* "Ujŏk ka" 遇賊歌 (Meeting with bandits) who believed in poetry's power to touch the heart. In this song he transcends the moment to find a truth that he and the bandits can share.

Yu Ch'ihwan 柳致環 (1908–67). Writer of poetry known for his masculine diction and imagery. Determined to overcome sorrow and hardship, he denounces social injustice and corruption.

Yu Chinhan 柳振漢 (1711–91). Writer of *Ch'unhyang ka* (Song of Ch'unhyang, 1754), a heptasyllabic verse in 200 lines in Chinese.

Yu Chino 俞鎭午 (1906–87). Writer of fiction, scholar of law, and educator, he was president of Korea University (1952–65).

Yu Ch'ungnyŏl chŏn 劉忠烈傳 (Tale of Yu Ch'ungnyŏl). Anonymous traditional military narrative story in Korean, set in Ming China, concerning Yu's heroic prowess against the Manchus and evil ministers.

yuefu 樂府 (Music Bureau). Title of a government office in Han times that collected folk songs; later the songs themselves, which are irregular in form using penta- or heptasyllabic lines of varying lengths. Themes include love and the hard life of farmers and soldiers on border duty.

"Yugu kok" 維鳩曲 (Song of the pigeon). A 7-line Koryŏ song considered a variation on "Pŏlgokcho" 伐谷鳥 (The cuckoo) attributed to King Yejong.

Yu Kilchun 俞吉濬 (1856–1914). Politician and modernization advocate who studied at Keiō Gijuku (1881) and Boston University (1893), toured

Europe (1895) and wrote *Sŏyu kyŏnmun* 西遊見聞 (Observations on a journey west, 1895) and a book of Korean grammar (1909).

Yu Mongin 柳夢寅 (1559–1623). Writer of *Ŏu yadam* 於于野談 (Ŏu's unofficial stories) consisting of 138 anecdotes in Chinese.

Yun Chigyŏng chŏn 尹知敬傳 (Tale of Yun Chigyŏng). Anonymous traditional narrative story of love and family in Korean and Chinese set in early sixteenth-century Korea; exists in manuscript.

Yun Chŏngmo 윤정모 (b. 1946). Contemporary woman writer of fiction.

Yungch'ŏn, Master 融天師 (c. 579–632). Writer of the 10-line *hyangga*, "Hyesŏng ka" 彗星歌 (Song of the comet, 594), to make a comet disappear.

Yun Hŭnggil 尹興吉 (b. 1942). Writer of fiction dealing with the conflict between individual and society, family breakdowns because of the Korean War, and characters torn between personal consciousness and freedom in the 1970s. Other works delve into folklore and shamanism, as in *Changma* (The rainy spell, 1973). Yun's work is marked by a disciplined observation of gesture and expression and an artistic distance achieved by means of irony.

Yun Kyesŏn 尹繼善 (1577–1604). Author of "Talch'ŏn mongyu rok" 達川夢遊錄 (Record of a dream journey to Talch'ŏn, 1600) in Chinese.

Yun Sejung 尹世重 (1912–65). North Korean writer of fiction.

Yun Sŏndo 尹善道 (1587–1671). Accomplished poet of the *sijo* form who spent 14 years in exile. Yun left 75 *sijo* including a *sijo* sequence of 40 songs, *Ŏbu sasi sa* 漁夫四時詞 (The angler's calendar, 1651).

Yun Tongju 尹東柱 (1917–45). Modern poet of inner anguish and spiritual desolation who perished in Fukuoka prison suspected of anti-Japanese activity while a student at Dōshisha University in Kyoto.

Yuri, King 儒理王 (19 BC – AD 18). Second king of Koguryŏ and putative author of "Hwangjo ka" 黃鳥歌 (Song of orioles), extant as a quatrain in Chinese.

yut 윷. Popular Korean game played with 4 sticks thrown in the air, the score depending on how they land.

Yu Tŭkkong 柳得恭 (1748–1807). Secondary son, scholar of Practical Learning, and prose master who wrote realistic verse and *Kyŏngdo chapchi* 京都雜志 (Capital miscellany), a book of annual events whose modern edition dates from 1911.

Yu Wŏnp'yo 劉元杓. Writer of a dream journey record, "Monggyŏn Chegal Ryang" 夢見諸葛亮 (Dreaming of Zhuge Liang, 1908), about his visit with China's most famous strategist, Zhuge Liang (181–234).

Zeng Xi 曾皙. Favorite disciple of Confucius famed for uttering one of the most beautiful passages in the *Analects* (11:25).

Zhang Han 張翰 (c. 258–319). Took office with Prince Jing of Qi but resigned because "he could not do without the salad and bream of the Song River."

Zhong Rong 鍾嶸 (469?–518). Author of *Shipin* 詩品 (Classes of poetry, c. 513–17).

Zhou Dunyi 周敦頤 (1017–73). Song-dynasty pioneer of Neo-Confucianism.

zhu 筑. Bamboo zither.

Zhu Xi 朱熹 (1130–1200). Song-dynasty synthesizer of Neo-Confucian philosophy who influenced the thought of Korea and Japan.

Zuo Commentary 左傳. One of 13 Confucian canonical texts and a commentary on the *Spring and Autumn Annals* compiled by Confucius. This chronicle of events in the feudal states, arranged after the chronology of Lu covering the years 722–463 BC, contains direct speeches, dialogues, legend, romance, and proverbs – a handbook of moral cause and effect rich in rhetorical devices and intertextuality.

Map 1. East Asia

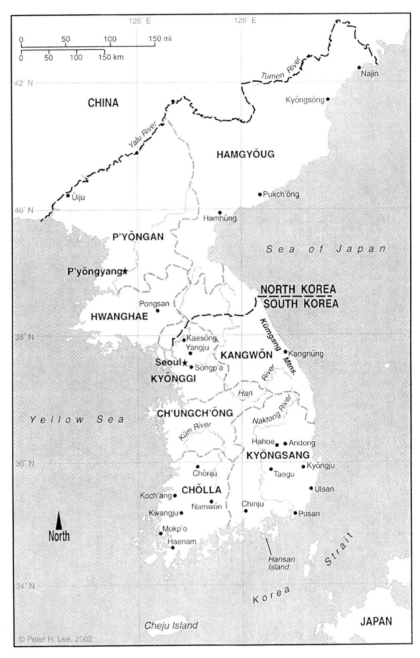

Map 2. Principal places in works discussed

Introduction

Peter H. Lee

EDUCATION AND EXAMINATION

In 682, the Silla dynasty (57 BC–AD 935) established a royal Confucian academy. Its core curriculum consisted of the *Analects* and *Book of Filial Piety* as well as specialization in one of the following: the *Book of Songs, Book of Documents, Record of Rites, Zuo Commentary,* and *Selections of Refined Literature.* Students ranged in age from fifteen to thirty and studied for nine years. In 788, a state examination system was instituted whereby students were categorized into three classes, but the system lasted only briefly.

Under the Koryŏ dynasty (918–1392), the civil service examination system began in 958, and the fixed number of 300 students was enrolled in the national academy (Kukchagam) from 992. The students studied the Confucian canonical texts for from a minimum of three to as many as nine years. The qualifying examination for entrance to the national academy included composition in poetry (*shi*) and rhymeprose (*fu*). The biennial final examination in literary composition, consisting of three sessions, tested students in the classics, poetry (old-style poetry, quatrain, regulated verse, and regulated couplets [*pailü*]) and rhymeprose, and a problem essay. The classics examination, again in three sessions, tested them on from five to nine classics. The literary composition examination was considered more prestigious, however, and the classics examination was held less frequently. In 425 years of Koryŏ history, some 251 examinations were held with 6,671 graduates in literary composition and 415 in the classics.

In the Chosŏn dynasty (1392–1910), the classics licentiate (*saengwŏn*) and literary licentiate (*chinsa*) examinations were held triennially. At the first stage, candidates were chosen from among county schools in the provinces (*hyangsi*)and the capital city (*Hansŏngsi*). The metropolitan examination – the second stage – was administered by the Ministry of Rites: the first day for the literary licentiate and the third day (one day's interval given) for the classics licentiate. The classics examination tested students in the

Four Books and Five Classics – initially one question based on one of the Four Books and one of the Five Classics. In the 502 years from 1392 to 1894 when the examination was abolished, the triennial examination in the licentiate was held 230 times, which selected 48,000 licentiates. The two-session final examination (*munkwa*) tested the candidates in the classics, literary composition (poetry, rhymeprose, eulogy, admonition, treatise, memorial, or edict), and a problem essay. The final examination was held 744 times and chose 14,606 candidates. The initially triennial final examination chose thirty-three civil officials and twenty-eight military officials, but its frequency and the number of passers increased as time went on.

In the early period of Chosŏn, some licentiates were appointed to lower-ranking positions, but the number decreased in later times. That is, the classics and literary licentiate examinations were not directly related to employment, but were still a requirement for – and an essential part of – the final examination. Some, however, proceeded directly to the final examination without taking the licentiates, and this trend increased as time went on, and toward the end of the dynasty, only 10% of the final examination passers had the licentiates in hand. The frequency of examinations and the increase in the number of passers is shown during the reign of Kojong (1864–1907), for example, when the examinations were held seventeen times within thirty years, with 7,000 licentiates, of whom only 4% proceeded to the final examination, in contrast to before the seventeenth century, when 25% of the licentiates sat for the final examination. Thus the nature of the licentiate examinations changed in late Chosŏn, but both the government and the educated seemed to feel the need for their continuation, underscoring the fervent aspiration of parents and their sons for a white certificate as a badge of prestige. True, candidates studied for the examination and read specific texts as preparation, but the primary function of the examination was to recruit the main body of officials who constituted and administered the government machinery. Most of education, however, was carried out outside of the examination system.

The three highest-ranking graduates (the first called *changwŏn*, the second *pangan*, and the third *t'amhwa*) received a certificate in red paper with the royal seal; the graduate who was placed first achieved the greatest glory.[1] They were feasted by the government and went to the Confucian Temple to report the news to the master and his disciples enshrined there.

---

[1] This information is based on Yi Sŏngmu, *Kaejŏng chŭngbo Hanguk ŭi kwagŏ chedo* (Chimmundang, 1994); Pak Yongun, *Koryŏ sidae ŭmsŏje wa kwagŏje yŏngu* (Ilchisa, 1990), and *Koryŏ sidae sa*, 2 vols. (Ilchisa, 1989), 1:144–157 and 366–382; Kuksa p'yŏnch'an wiwŏnhoe, ed., *Hanguk sa* 13 (1993):367–440 and 23 (1994):279–368; and Song Chunho, "Chosŏn hugi ŭi kwagŏ chedo," *Kuksagwan nonch'ong* 63 (1995):37–47. I am grateful to Professor Martina Deuchler for the last reference.

Together with other passers, they would entertain relatives, friends, and examiners and would parade through the streets on horseback, followed by musicians and actors. The Office of Royal Decrees compiled a roster of successful graduates, together with examination questions, and published it for wider circulation. (More than 700 of these lists remain from the Chosŏn dynasty.) From 958 to 1894, when the examination was finally abolished, the examination was the only route by which the government recruited qualified persons for officialdom.

THE WRITER

Candidates for the examination usually began their study at the age of four with the *Thousand Sinograph Primer* (*Ch'ŏnjamun*), progressed to other primers, then to the Four Books and Five Classics. They were required to be proficient in these texts and commit them to memory by reading the same passages and chapters at least a hundred times aloud. In addition, they also read Chinese histories – such as the *Historical Records* of Sima Qian (?145–86 BC), *History of the Former Han* by Ban Gu (32–92), and *History of the Later Han* by Fan Ye (398–445) – and major Chinese philosophers as well as Chinese poets and prose writers.

The students learned the following number of graphs in the classics by heart:

Analects:	11,705
Mencius:	34,685
Book of Changes:	24,107
Book of Documents:	25,700
Book of Songs:	39,234
Record of Rites:	99,010
Zuo Commentary:	196,845

In all, a student had to learn 431,286 graphs. As the *Great Learning* and *Doctrine of the Mean* are included in the *Record of Rites*, they were not counted separately. As Miyazaki Ichisada comments, "memorizing textual material amounting to more than 400,000 [graphs] is enough to make one reel."[2]

Among Koryŏ writers, Yi Illo (1152–1220) won the literary licentiate at age 28 (1180); Yi Kyubo (1169–1241), at 21 (1190); Yi Chehyŏn (1287–1367) at 14 (1301); and Yi Saek (1328–1396) at 13 (1341). Among Chosŏn writers, Sŏ Kŏjŏng (1420–1489) passed it at age 18 (1438) and passed the final examination at 24 (1444); Chŏng Ch'ŏl (1537–1594) passed it at 24

---

[2] Ichisada Miyazaki, *China's Examination Hell*, trans. Conrad Shirokauer (New Haven: Yale University Press, 1981), p. 16.

(1561) and the final examination at 25 (1562). Yun Sŏndo (1587–1671) passed it at 25 (1612). Among Neo-Confucian philosophers, Yi Hwang (1501–1571) passed it at age 27 (1528) and the final examination at 31 (1532); Yi I (1536–1584) passed both the classics and the literary licentiates one after the other in two days at age 28 (1564).

Most Korean writers went through the training described here. For them the civil service examination determined their mode of life. From childhood, virtually all aspirants to public service were trained in the same, primarily Chinese, works. Upon passing the examination, the lucky candidate would receive a political appointment that carried immense social prestige. He was lucky because at times some 90% of classics and literary licentiates were unemployed. From early in life he learned that the arts of statesmanship and literature went hand in hand. The predominance of writers at court provided the courtier with constant encouragement, though it was commonly a source of rivalry as well. Certainly it afforded him an opportunity to observe a variety of men who had achieved distinction in politics and literature – thereby affording him also some insight into human nature. Those at court could exchange erudite views concerning every major event. Apart from time spent on courtly functions and official duties, they found the opportunity to write verse and prose. Poems were produced on every conceivable courtly and social occasion; the courtiers must have dreamed and thought in verse. In fact, numerous poems were indeed inspired by dreams.

In such a setting, none could dispute the place of literature in society and culture. The typical writer had a circle of close friends among whom manuscripts (or transcriptions) were circulated. Intractable allusions, quotations, puns on people's names, numerous poems of friendship, commendatory verse, prefaces, epilogues, appreciations of individual collections – all attest to the intimate nature of the group. The reader, who was himself a writer, was presumed to be just as knowledgeable as the writer and was expected to catch all allusions and quotations. An appointment did not always guarantee uninterrupted literary activity, but this was irrelevant. Poetic talent was presumed to ensure political advancement, and most of the literati combined writing with their official duties. The relative lack of mercenary flattery or fawning – as compared, for example, with Elizabethan England – is refreshing.[3] This may explain why so few works were dedicated

---

[3] Phoebe Sheavyn, *The Literary Profession in the Elizabethan Age* (Manchester: Manchester University Press), ch. 1; Edwin H. Miller, *The Professional Writer in Elizabethan England* (Cambridge, Mass.: Harvard University Press, 1964), ch. 4; and J. W. Saunders, *The Profession of English Letters* (London: Routledge, 1964), p. 28.

to patrons (although dedication was no proof of patronage). No one wrote for pecuniary gain, and no one made a living by writing (ghost writing excepted). Yet few forsook literature.

It is essential to understand the distinction between what were considered the primary and secondary genres in the traditional canon, the relations between literature written in Chinese and in the vernacular, and the generic hierarchy in the official and unofficial canons. The first higher civilization adopted by Korea and Japan was Chinese. When Chinese civilization with its Chinese writing system arrived, neither Korea nor Japan had a script of its own. Even after the appearance of the Japanese syllabary in the ninth century and the invention of the Korean alphabet in the mid fifteenth century, the Chinese graphs were accorded deferential status. The Japanese syllabary was called *kana* (temporary, or borrowed, script) as opposed to the Chinese *mana* (true script), for example; and the Korean alphabet (1443–1444) was called *ŏnmun* (common script), though its official name was "Correct Sounds for Teaching the People" (*Hunmin chŏngŭm*, now called *hangŭl* in South Korea). If these terms smack of ideological bias, it was an ideology of the literati, who espoused the Confucian and official Chinese canon and, through their alliance with the government and the ruling class, exercised power in Japan and Korea respectively.

The major texts that Koreans and Japanese studied after the formation of their states were the Confucian canon (first five, then eleven, and finally thirteen texts). In Korea these texts formed not only the basic curriculum of education for almost 1,000 years, but the foundation for the civil service examination for 900 years (even when Buddhism was the state religion for more than seven centuries).[4] The employment of Confucian scholars at court, the establishment of a royal academy, and the recruitment of officials through the civil service examination helped in the victory of Confucianism and the hegemony of the Confucian canon. As the *sine qua non* of the educated and ruling class, knowledge of the canon was the subject of serious and sustained study. As the repository of a cultural grammar, these texts constituted the interpretive community of those with an orthodox education in East Asia.

---

[4] For the rise of Confucian learning in Japan see Yukio Hisaki, *Daigakuryō to kodai jukyō* (Tokyo: Saimaru, 1968), and Robert Borgen, *Sugawara no Michizane and the Early Heian Court* (Cambridge, Mass.: Harvard University Press, 1986), pp. 71–88.

In China, the canon's formation coincided with the expansion of the Chinese empire and the consolidation of bureaucracy. Confucianism and the Confucian canon came to Korea and Japan at a time when both countries were in the process of consolidating monarchical power in the early history of their unified states. Administrative and penal codes, cosmology and rituals, the recruitment and education of officials, inculcation of social virtues, historiography in Korea and Japan – all were influenced by the Confucian canon and its ideology.

Although the normative values of the canon were considered immutable, its functions were diverse. Certain historical moments – such as dynastic changes, a restoration of the ancient (utopian) order, the initiation of institutional or social reforms, or the rise of nationalism – invoked the canon and its ideology for support and justification. The canon served also as an ideology by which the ruling class rationalized the political order or curbed despotic power, anti-establishment scholars censured bureaucratic corruption, censors impeached the ruler and his officials, reformers advocated their cause, and Confucian martyrs vindicated their innocence.

The influence of the Confucian political, historiographic, and moral tradition on East Asian literature was pervasive. The tradition provided rhetorical commonplaces, inspired the "mirror for princes" literature and other prose narratives – both official and popular – and allegorical exegesis. In such Confucian-inspired works, the distinction between history and literature is often vague. These works use epideictic formulas, the end of which was didactic. The use of mythological and historical personages from Chinese classics and histories was the common device of comparison and amplification in all genres, primary and secondary.

The hegemony of the Confucian canon in East Asian culture and literature was long and strong. From their inception, the Confucian classics were treated as canonical by the literati (the ruling class in China and Korea and occasionally in Japan)[5] in their roles as scholars, officials, and writers. Accepted as binding texts in politics and morals, they defined the nature and function of the literati. As translators of morality into action, the literati enjoyed authority, power, and prestige. Because they were also influential writers of their times, they played a major role in forming the canon of refined literature.

The importance of the Confucian canon in traditional Korean literature is underlined here because most extant literary works were produced in the

---

[5] Japan adopted certain standards of the canon but not its political apparatus. See Hisaki, *Daigakuryō to kodai jukyō*, pp. 218–235.

Chosŏn dynasty (1392–1910), a period in Korean history strongly influenced by Confucianism and Neo-Confucianism. The literati that constituted the dominant social class in Korea wrote almost exclusively in Chinese, the main source of their prestige and power. This class, which controlled the canon of traditional Korean literature and critical discourse, adopted as official the genres of Chinese poetry and prose. The *Wenxuan* (*Selections of Refined Literature*), the most widely read and influential anthology, exercised a lasting influence in the formation of the canon.[6] The official canon includes most genres of poetry and prose in the *Selections of Refined Literature*. Of these, poetry was paramount in the generic hierarchy, as attested by anthologies and collected works of individual writers. Of the sixty chapters in the *Selections of Refined Literature*, the first thirty-five are assigned to poetry. In collected works of individual authors, poetry is presented first – even in the works of such Neo-Confucian philosophers as Zhu Xi (1130–1200) in China and Yi Hwang (1501–1571) in Korea. No single writer tried all prose forms – the *Selections* lists some thirty – but such forms as memorials, letters, admonitions, tomb inscriptions, treatises, and accounts of conduct enjoyed a lasting place in the generic paradigm.

Three secondary genres in Korea (as in China) include prose fiction, random jottings, and drama. The East Asian term for fiction (*xiaoshuo, shōsetsu,* or *sosŏl*) does not denote the Western novel. The East Asian term was used derogatively to designate all traditional prose fiction which created a world other than that sanctioned by the establishment and which offered alternative views of reality. The tyranny of historiography and the Confucian insistence on historicity exercised considerable influence in the development of fiction. Viewed with suspicion and contempt by the authorities, fiction was considered to be outside the literary canon. Some encyclopedias may include certain fictional works under various headings, but such compilations, often undertaken for political reasons to keep the literati out of trouble, were regarded as miscellaneous compendia. The literary miscellany, or random jottings (*biji, zuihitsu, chapki*) is an anti-genre that flaunts the prescriptive conventions of the formal prose genres, with their stilted rhetoric. It disregards the hierarchy of subjects but values the activity of the author's inquiring mind. It includes the reportorial, biographical, and autobiographical (and sometimes fictional) narrative and poetry criticism. Studied nonchalance and self-disparagement found expression in the title, which usually contains the East Asian equivalent of the Latin *sylvae*

---

[6] The Japanese anthology patterned after the *Wenxuan, Honchō monzui* (14 chapters) was compiled in 1011. The Korean anthology *TMS* (156 chapters) was compiled in 1478 and 1571.

(Ben Jonson entitled his collections *The Forest* or *The Underwoods*). The fact that the literary miscellany was excluded from a writer's collected works, even in the case of a high state minister, demonstrates its low status in the hierarchy of prose genres. Korean literati seldom attempted drama, which was regarded as mere entertainment or pastime.

Any canon that labels certain literary genres as secondary – outside the mainstream and unofficial – is ideological. Indeed, since the ideology of prestige and power grounded in the dominant class radically changed the course of development of Korean literature, ideology is clearly a constituent aspect of its literary history. By ideology I mean a system of ideas, beliefs, and assumptions characteristic of a particular group or class by which it seeks to defend and promote itself.[7] The ideal of the literati was ostensibly a benevolent government that rules by virtue and example in order to maintain a hierarchical and harmonious society. To maintain the order considered vital to the preservation of society, they used ideology to veil repression. The same ideology found expression in literary forms, content, and style, in acts of canonization, and much else. Gramsci's notion of ideological hegemony as a totality "which is lived at such a depth, which saturates the society to such an extent" that it "even constitutes the limit of common sense for most people under its sway"[8] might apply here.

To be sure, some Korean writers wrote in both Chinese and Korean. They knew that vernacular poetry or prose seldom brought prestige. They also knew that such pieces might not be included in their collected works. In fact, only a handful of their collected works include vernacular poetry, usually as an appendix. The reason is simple: as in the primary canon, poetry was the highest of native literary types, but was not part of the official curriculum and education. Some writers, including kings, wrote in Korean, but no one was censured for doing so. The place of prose fiction in the native canon was humble. As in Japan, vernacular fiction was considered primarily as recreational writing for women, although it enjoyed popularity from the eighteenth century among the literati and women of upper and middle classes. Korea had mask and puppet plays, but actors – as in China and Japan – occupied the lowest of the lower social strata.

The difference between Japan and Korea in the early development of vernacular poetry is that in Japan the court, which espoused the value system of China, also came to be associated with native poetry. The new canon

---

[7] For a convenient bibliography on ideology see Sacvan Bercovitch and Myra Jehlen, eds., *Ideology and Classic American Literature* (Cambridge: Cambridge University Press, 1986), pp. 443–446.
[8] Ibid., p. 127.

of native poetry as culturally esteemed and the compilation of twenty-one anthologies of the 31-syllable *waka* is exceptional.[9] Yet the reigning monarchs and noble houses that were responsible for the growth of the *waka* did not accord the same patronage to prose fiction and drama. In Japan and Korea, therefore, poetry was the highest genre regardless of the linguistic medium used. All other writings except for Chinese prose and history, again regardless of the linguistic medium, remained low in status. Saikaku (1642–1693) and Bashō (1644–1694), for example, now considered great masters of Japanese vernacular literature, were rated lower than Rai Sanyō (1780–1832), a writer of history and poetry in Chinese in the Tokugawa period when Chinese was the official written language. One Chinese prince was a playwright;[10] a Korean king was the inventor of the Korean alphabet and a writer of vernacular poetry. Neither, however, could effect a lasting change in the tastes of the entrenched literati or combat the official ideology, "an instrument of class domination, legitimation, and social mystification."[11]

We can guess what happened in modern Japan and Korea to the prestige and power associated with the ruling class and China and the literature written in Chinese. The desire for the recovery of popular literature as embodying national identity brought about a reactionary movement to belittle all writings in Chinese, which in Korea comprised more than two-thirds of the extant literature and in Japan less than one-third. It is in the nature of the canon to change, as it is in the nature of literature and knowledge. It is also in the nature of the canon to resurrect neglected works, including underground and X-rated writings, if not to confer immortality on them. Today a new canon governs literary study and instruction not only in Japan and South Korea but in the West as well.

THE TASK OF A NEW LITERARY HISTORY

There is now a powerful literary-historical consensus that a new history of Korean literature should accord priority to the vernacular literature

---

[9] Earl Miner, "The Collective and the Individual: Literary Practice and Its Social Implications," in *Principles of Classical Japanese Literature*, ed. Earl Miner (Princeton: Princeton University Press, 1985), pp. 17–62.

[10] Zhu Yudun (1379–1439), the eldest son of Zhu Su, the fifth son of the founder of Ming. He wrote thirty-one *zaju*. See Yagisawa Hajime, *Mindai gekisakka kenkyū*, pp. 50–108; see also William H. Nienhauser, Jr., ed., *Indiana Companion to Traditional Chinese Literature* (Bloomington: Indiana University Press, 1986), pp. 344–346.

[11] Fredric Jameson, *The Political Unconscious: Narrative as a Socially Symbolic Act* (Ithaca: Cornell University Press), p. 282.

that constitutes a distinct tradition – distinct, some argue, because it is a repository of native beliefs and values that speaks for the common people, as contrasted to elite literature in Chinese devoid of popular concerns. Dichotomy can be multiplied to include language, class, gender, and the nature and function of literature. The ideology of a new canon and new history is not always so simplistically presented, but there is an inherent danger of conceiving it as an ideological project from an adversarial standpoint. The historian's task is to evaluate not only native (and popular) works neglected in the past but also to examine works in Chinese once considered canonical but now neglected. The historian must consider both text and context, author and cultural history, because it was the business of literature in China and Korea to engage society and culture at all points. Literature can, it was believed, change the world. No work was considered autonomous or intransitive; literature refracts, not supplants, historical reality. Every work of worth is inscribed by historical and cultural forces. Artistic consciousness, however, was not incompatible with political and social participation.

Modern literary historians deploy an array of strategies to resurrect and reevaluate neglected areas in a traditional canon: a systematic study of Korean myths, legends, and other forms of prose narrative; a study of popular literary genres of folk origin; and a reevaluation of dissent literature. Shamanist beliefs and popular customs of ancient Korea were first written down when they were viewed by the ruling class as no longer functional. Therefore, old myth forms were emptied of their primal grandeur and colored by Confucian and Buddhist worldviews of later times. Yet, in the portrayal of heroes in history and literature, both official and unofficial, we discern a set of motifs and patterns: the same categories and elements found in myths and folklore elsewhere. The extent of expurgation of the more primitive aspects in these tales may be difficult to assess, but older materials may still remain embedded in them. In the study of archetypal patterns and symbols in traditional narrative, official history and gazetteers have been ransacked to cull folk narrative embedded in foundation myths, tales of heroes and heroines, mythological and historical materials, local traditions, etiological stories, animal tales, and the like. Heroes tend to share common biographical patterns and conform to certain types. Structural analyses of narrative have been undertaken – including folkloristic structure as the underlying framework of narrative discourse. Such recurring heroes and heroines in popular tales as the loyal minister, the filial son and daughter, the chaste wife, and the honest younger brother embody the official Confucian virtues and exemplify the society's values in a subtle way.

Study has been extended to oral poetry, including shamanist chants, and to folk narrative and drama. Oral narratives have been recorded and their types and motifs classified according to the Aarne-Thompson system. Happily, few have claimed oral poetry as the collective creation of the spirit of the folk, and the latter as unconscious anonymous creations. Folk dramas such as mask and puppet plays were closely associated with shamanism and Buddhism. Folk songs and dances formed the basis of the plays with musical accompaniment. The mask play is usually performed on a makeshift stage in open air in the village square on festive occasions. The targets of exaggerated humor and satire in both are the literati and Buddhist monks. Bakhtin's notion of the "dialogic" as a "carnivalesque dispersal of the hegemonic order of a dominant culture"[12] might be relevant here. Of these forms, the most valuable research concerns the *p'ansori*, a narrative verse form that flourished in the eighteenth and nineteenth centuries. It is performed by a single professional singer (*kwangdae*), who both narrates and assumes the roles of his characters, accompanied by a single drummer.

Finally, dissent literature has been recovered for its social and cultural criticism of the status quo. The context of dissent literature is both the dominant culture and the adversarial culture – those who keenly felt the contradictions of dominant culture, and those alienated and marginalized victims of the established order. A literature of dissent exists both in Chinese and in Korean, written by both the dominant and the repressed classes.

Texts by outsiders – secondary sons, Buddhist monks, servants, and slaves – became subjects of literary inquiry as well. In their poems and fictional narratives, they attempted to fashion a world of their own to wage a personal revolt against society. Some withdrew from history to lament the moral disruption caused by political upheavals such as usurpation of the throne or the butchering of upright officials. Without regular employment, some roamed the countryside and others subsisted as tenant farmers or on charity. Dedicated to subverting the ideological foundation of the ruling class, they neither saw their works (except those on nonpolitical subjects) published in their time, nor had a definite readership. Works by exceptional writers of dissent were recorded later from memory by members of the lettered class.

Among the socially discriminated against, secondary sons fared better because of their technical knowledge and skill (as interpreters, physicians, librarians, editors, and artisans). Unlike amongst the literati in Tang or

---

[12] Ibid., p. 285. See also M. M. Bakhtin, *Rabelais and His World*, trans. Helene Isowolsky (Bloomington: Indiana University Press, 1984), pp. 256, 426; and Bakhtin, *The Dialogic Imagination*, ed. Michael Holquist (Austin: University of Texas Press, 1989).

Ming China (or indeed in earlier periods of Korean history), children born to concubines of the literati were discriminated against in the Chosŏn dynasty. In line with a rigid interpretation of Neo-Confucian morality, the distinction between high and low was upheld to the letter. Unable to qualify for the final civil service examination – the only path to high officialdom – and deprived of their inheritance rights, even the learned and talented sons of concubines were victimized until 1894, when discrimination against them was finally abolished. Only during the reigns of Chungjong (1506–1544) and Chŏngjo (1776–1800) were such men employed: as interpreters, drafters of diplomatic papers, and editors in the royal library. They wrote poetry and poetry criticism, literary miscellany, history and historical criticism. Some of their works are scattered in the literary miscellany; others are gathered in later collections.

Such writers adopted their culture's values in order to stress the discrepancy between theory and practice, vision and actuality, not as individuals separated from society but as men better qualified to see from below the contradictions imposed from above. In an unfree society without real choice, none of them thought that they could overcome repression and discrimination. Although their criticism of society was often termed subversive, we see their complicity in the culture they wished to repudiate. Ultimately their dissent is but an affirmation of cultural values.

In the name of impartiality, objectivity, inclusiveness, the historian attempts to historicize the excluded and valorize the subversive. The formation of a new canon is explicitly ideological – denouncing the old canon as ideological, hegemonic, and elitist. Before making claims for a text, however, the historian's task is to demonstrate its sociohistorical density: the extent of its engagement with culture in its time. Like other texts produced by the same culture, it must withstand a literary analysis. These areas, hitherto neglected, are now revalued as essential subjects of Korean literary history. Thus recent studies have not only broadened the scope of Korean literature but have provided a more balanced understanding of it. They have not yet fully explored the relation between popular and official literary genres, however, or offered a methodology that can establish a meaningful relation between literatures written in two languages. The historian's treatment of an author writing in one language cannot be the same as that of another who writes in two different languages. The sheer bulk of poetry written in Chinese demands from the historian considerable knowledge of the development of poetry in China; otherwise the historian cannot evaluate a poet's invention and originality or merits and demerits. It is the same with prose. Knowledge of the principal forms, conventions, styles, and precedents is a prerequisite for literary analysis. If the same writer wrote in both the florid parallel prose and the plain style, the historian must ask why. Prose fiction sometimes existed in two languages or in several versions. Here I have broadened the scope of dissent literature to encompass the ruling and the ruled. Dissent is not a monopoly of the oppressed.

The reconstitution of literary history requires of the historian a viable methodology grounded on literary theory. East Asian literature – and Korean literature in particular – cannot be separated from society and culture. Literature was seldom conceived as discontinuous from life or freed from history – hence the East Asian insistence on the nonfictionality of literature in order to escape the censure of having it denounced as a lie or an artifice. Likewise, the fact that most official prose forms are nonfiction seems to reflect the Chinese view that literature is not mimetic. Prose fiction was seldom considered as belonging to the class of refined writing (*wen*), as the convention of titling all works of secondary genres seems to indicate.[13] Yet the meaning of a work is never exhausted by the intention of its author. The alterity of a text does not necessarily make it accessible to the latecomer. He should ask living questions of it and be ready to be interrogated by it. Although the text does not have a single stable meaning, not all reading is misreading. Chastened by the historicity of interpretation as shown by series of misreadings, historians should make clear their own convictions, allegiances, and prejudice[14] and be aware of the ideological components of their own – and others' – critical standpoint.

Western critical theories have limitations when applied to East Asian literature: almost none of them, for example, takes into account the East Asian literary experience. One cannot build a theory without knowing the works that compose a tradition. Only after reading extensively and developing standards by which to evaluate the works can one begin to acquire a new sense of tradition. Other matters deserving caution include the use of Western critical terms already steeped in the judgment of value ("epic," "tragic," "lyric," for example, none of which can be found in East Asia) and the imposition of Western cultural and literary standards. One should not allow Western theory to dictate the manner of presenting Korean literature. Although we have to impose taxonomies of Western origin, we must not be led to believe that they correspond to historical realities of Korea.[15]

---

[13] Harry Levin, "The Title as a Literary Genre," *Modern Language Review* 72 (1977):xxiii–xxvi.

[14] See Hans-Georg Gadamer, *Wahrheit und Methode: Grundzüge einer philosophischen Hermeneutik* (Tübingen: Mohr, 1965), p. 283.

[15] David Perkins, ed., *Theoretical Issues in Literary History* (Cambridge, Mass.: Harvard University Press, 1991), p. 252.

We need both traditional commentary and Western critical methodology, however, and only those who have both can do justice to traditional Korean literature. Finally, because no reader exists independent of time and we live in a pluralistic society, any literary canon is bound to change.[16]

[16] Harold H. Kolb, Jr., "Defining the Canon," in *Redefining American Literary History*, ed. A. La Vonne Brown Ruoff and Jerry W. Ward, Jr. (New York: Modern Language Association, 1990), pp. 39–40.

CHAPTER I

Language, forms, prosody, and themes

Ho-Min Sohn and Peter H. Lee

THE KOREAN LANGUAGE

Korean is spoken on the Korean peninsula as the sole native language and overseas as a second or foreign language. The current population of South Korea is over 45 million and that of North Korea around 23 million. Some 5.6 million Koreans reside outside the Korean peninsula. The major countries with a significant Korean population are China (2 million), the United States (2 million), Japan (700,000), and the former Soviet Union (500,000). Due to constant immigration, Koreans in the United States have become the fastest-growing segment of the overseas Korean population.

GENETIC AFFILIATION

There is no denying that Korean and Japanese are sister languages, although they are not mutually intelligible and their relationship is much more distant than that between, say, English and French. A sizeable number of cognates, partially attested sound correspondences, and many uniquely shared grammatical properties support the existence of a genetic relationship. The common origin of Korean and Japanese has been proposed by a number of scholars since Arai Hakuseki (1657–1725), a Tokugawa Confucian, in 1717, and Fujii Sadamoto (?1732–1797), a pioneer of modern archaeology in Japan, in 1781, first brought up the issue.[1] Samuel Martin systematically compares 320 sets of seeming cognates in Korean (K) and Japanese (J).[2]

The grammatical similarities between Korean and Japanese are conspicuous. Both are typical subject-object-verb (SOV) word-order languages.

---

[1] Roy A. Miller, *The Japanese Language* (Chicago: University of Chicago Press, 1967), pp. 61–62.

[2] S. E. Martin, "Lexical Evidence Relating Korean to Japanese," *Language* 42 (1966): 185–251. Martin used modern and available Middle Korean (fifteenth-century) forms and modern or slightly antiquated Japanese forms. See J. B. Whitman, "The Phonological Basis for the Comparison of Japanese and Korean" (Ph.D. dissertation, Harvard University, 1985), for a further study on the same subject.

Thus all predicates (verbs and adjectives) come at the end of a sentence or a clause; all modifiers (adjectives, adverbs, pronouns, numerals, genitive phrases, relative or conjunctive clauses, and so forth) precede their modified elements; and all particles follow their associated nominals as postpositions. Both languages have productive multiple-subject constructions (K *kkoch' ŭn changmi ka yeppŏyo* vs. J *hana wa bara ga kirei*: "[As for] flowers, roses are pretty"). Both languages allow situationally or contextually understood elements (subject, object, and so forth) to be omitted in speech. Both are pitch-accent languages, although in Korean only two of seven dialects (Kyŏngsang and Hamgyŏng) remain so. In both languages, intricate human relationships are encoded in the linguistic structure in terms of referent honorifics and speech levels.

Based on certain shared linguistic patterns, numerous historical-comparative linguists have proposed that Korean and Japanese are genetically related to the Altaic languages.[3] This Altaic hypothesis is quite persuasive given the available data and methodological refinements. It assigns Korean and Japanese to the Altaic family, which is composed mainly of Turkic, Mongolian, and Manchu-Tungus groups that range widely in the regions west and north of China. Original Altaic is thought to have been a linguistic unity spoken sometime during the Neolithic period, and its original homeland is assumed to be somewhere in northern or north-central Eurasia.[4]

Suggestions have also been made for a genetic affiliation of Korean and Japanese to Austronesian languages, on the one hand,[5] and to Dravidian languages on the other.[6] While an Austronesian stratum is quite dense in Japanese, any hypothesis linking Korean to Austronesian is premature in view of the lack of useful evidence.[7] The Dravidian hypothesis, however, merits our attention. For instance, M. E. Clippinger proposes a Korean–Dravidian (especially Tamil) connection by presenting 408 putative

[3] See Shiratori Kurakichi, "Chōsen-go to Ural-Altai go tono hikaku kenkyū," in *Shiratori Kurakichi zenshū* (Tokyo: Iwanami) 3 (1972):1–280; G. J. Ramstedt, *Studies in Korean Etymology* (Helsinki: Suomalis-Ugrilanen Seura, 1949); Yi Kimun, *Kaejŏng kugŏsa kaesŏl* (Minjung sŏgwan, 1976); and Baeg-in Sung "The Present State of Problems of Genealogical Studies of Korean," *KJ* 37 (1997):166–225.

[4] Roy A. Miller, *Japanese Language*, p. 341.

[5] See Susumu Ohno, *The Origin of the Japanese Language* (Tokyo: Kokusai bunka shinkōkai, 1970), and Shichiro Murayama, "The Malayo-Polynesian Component in the Japanese Language," *Journal of Japanese Studies* 2:2 (1976):413–436.

[6] See, for example, H. B. Hulbert, *A Comparative Grammar of the Korean Language and the Dravidian Languages of India* (Seoul: Methodist Publishing House, 1905); Susumo Ohno, *Origin of the Japanese Language*; and M. E. Clippinger, "Korean and Dravidian: Lexical Evidence for an Old Theory," *Korean Studies* 8 (1984) 1–57.

[7] Unlike Korean, Japanese shares obvious phonological and lexical similarities with Oceanic languages: open syllables, lack of consonant clusters, and quite a few putative cognate sets.

cognates. He further points out various grammatical similarities between Korean and Dravidian, including the SOV word-order.

HISTORICAL DEVELOPMENT

Written historical data on early forms of the Korean language are scarce and cannot be traced far back. A few old language fragments are available in the literature dating from the eleventh century, such as *Kyunyŏ chŏn* (*Life of the Great Master Kyunyŏ*, 1075) by Hyŏngnyŏn Chŏng, *Kyerim yusa* (*Things on Korea*, 1103–1104) by the Song scholar Sun Mu, *Samguk sagi* (*Historical Records of the Three Kingdoms*, 1146) by Kim Pusik, and *Samyuk yusa* (*Memorabilia of the Three Kingdoms*, 1285) by the monk Iryŏn, all written in Chinese graphs. Moreover, much of the earlier vocabulary has been either irretrievably lost or obscured by succeeding waves of linguistic contact, including a massive influx of Chinese words. Thus our knowledge of the evolution of Korean during the Old Korean period (prehistory to the tenth century) is seriously limited. The few fragmentary records in *Weiji* (*Records of Wei*, written by Chen Shou in 285–297), *Hou Hanshu* (*History of Later Han*, by Fan Ye in 398–445), and *Zhoushu* (*History of Zhou*, c. 629), as well as some extant linguistic fragments, enable us to speculate that the Koguryŏ language was Tungusic, as were with the languages of Puyŏ, Okchŏ, and Yemaek; that the languages of the Three Han states were merely dialects of each other; and that the languages of Silla and Paekche, which absorbed the Three Han states, were much closer to each other than they were to the Koguryŏ language.[8] The period of Old Korean was the initial stage of the influx of sinograph words. In the sixth century, the titles of the kings were changed from pure Korean to Sino-Korean forms using the term *wang* (king). In the middle of the eighth century – during the Unified Silla period – native place-names were altered and modeled after the Chinese tradition so that they consisted of two Chinese graphs as they do now.

The form of Middle Korean (eleventh to sixteenth centuries) is much better known than that of Old Korean thanks to the invention of *hangŭl*, the Korean alphabet, by King Sejong in 1443–1444. Since abundant textual materials are available from the fifteenth century on, the development of Korean over the past 500 years has been captured in a systematic manner. Also, solid knowledge of fifteenth-century Korean has enabled scholars to reconstruct earlier forms, especially Early Middle Korean.

The Middle Korean period may be characterized by, among other things, the influx of a huge number of Chinese words into the Korean vocabulary.

---

[8] Yi Kimun, *Kaejŏng kugŏsa kaesŏl*, is an in-depth study of the history of Korean.

Before this period, Chinese words were limited, in general, to the names of places, people, and government ranks. Starting with the Koryŏ dynasty (918–1392), however, Chinese words began to pervade the spoken language, as well as being used exclusively in writing.

Modern Korean (seventeenth to nineteenth centuries) and Contemporary Korean (twentieth century on) differ sharply from Middle Korean as a result of accumulated changes during the Middle Korean period. Modern Korean underwent further changes – probably expedited by the social and political disorder in the wake of the seven-year Japanese invasion that started in 1592, the popularization of vernacular literature, contact with foreign languages, and the importation of Western civilization.

Contemporary Korean has undergone an unprecedentedly complex history: the entry of missionaries, the collision between foreign powers in Korea, Japanese domination of Korea for thirty-five years, liberation from Japanese rule, division into North and South Korea, wide international contacts, the Korean War, rapid economic and technological growth, especially in South Korea, and social transformation in recent decades. All these events have had various effects on the language, especially the vocabulary. Thousands of newly coined words based on native elements in North Korea and thousands of recent loanwords from English in South Korea attest to this impact.

DIALECTAL VARIATIONS

Although the Korean language is relatively homogeneous – there is mutual intelligibility among speakers from different areas – there are minor but distinct dialectal differences. The Korean peninsula, both North and South Korea, may be divided into seven dialectal zones that correspond by and large to administrative districts:[9]

Hamgyŏng Zone: North and South Hamgyŏng, extending to the north of Ch'ŏngp'yŏng, and Huch'ang in North P'yŏngan
P'yŏngan Zone: North and South P'yŏngan (excluding Huch'ang)
Central Zone: Kyŏnggi, Kangwŏn, Hwanghae, and South Hamgyŏng extending to Yŏnghŭng to the north
Ch'ungch'ŏng Zone: North and South Ch'ungch'ŏng and Kŭmsan and Muju in North Chŏlla
Kyŏngsang Zone: North and South Kyŏngsang
Chŏlla Zone: North and South Chŏlla (other than Kŭmsan and Muju)
Cheju Zone: Cheju

---

[9] Kim Hyŏnggyu, *Hanguk pangŏn yŏngu*. Although Seoul is a separate administrative unit, it is regarded as part of Kyŏnggi province.

The dialect used by the Korean community in the Yanbian Autonomous Prefecture of China in Manchuria can be included in the Hamgyŏng Zone because it has evolved as part of the Hamgyŏng dialect due to the early immigration of Hamgyŏng people to that area and their subsequent linguistic contacts. The dialects spoken by Koreans in the other areas of China and other countries around the globe also reflect the seven dialectal zones, depending on where the speakers originally migrated from.

The major cause of the formation of the dialectal zones has been geographic, but historical and political factors have also played important roles. The characteristics of the Cheju dialect, for instance, have been shaped by its isolation from the mainland. Moreover, the two neighboring areas, Kyŏngsang and Chŏlla, manifest great differences since, in the past, there was no major transport network connecting the two zones. Historically, too, these two zones were under two different dynasties, Kyŏngsang under the Silla kingdom and Chŏlla under Paekche. Another historical factor explains the demarcation between the Hamgyŏng dialect and the Central dialect, where there is no natural barrier. During the Koryŏ and Chosŏn dynasties, the area between Chŏngp'yŏng in the Hamgyŏng Zone and Yŏnghŭng in the Central Zone was the site of constant battling between the Manchu tribes called Jurchens in the north and the Koreans in the south. After the Manchu tribes were driven north during the Chosŏn dynasty, P'yŏngan province was inhabited by people from neighboring Hwanghae and Hamgyŏng was settled mainly by people from Kyŏngsang in the south. This explains the similarity between the P'yŏngan dialect and the Central dialect, on the one hand, and between the Hamgyŏng dialect and the Kyŏngsang dialect on the other. While influencing one another, the two northern dialects have also been affected by foreign languages such as Chinese, Tungus, Jurchen, and Russian, a fact responsible for the maturation of the P'yŏngan and Hamgyŏng dialects.

Many characteristics are unique either to each dialectal zone or to only a few zones. The general intonation patterns, utterance tempo, and sound qualities are quite different from one dialect to another. Vocabulary, word structure, sentence structure, and usage too are all slightly dissimilar.[10]

LINGUISTIC DIVERGENCE IN SOUTH AND NORTH

Apart from the geographically based dialectal differences discussed thus far, there is a superordinate bifurcation between North and South Korea. Linguistic divergence between the two Koreas since 1945 has been

---

[10] Ho-min Sohn, *The Korean Language* (Cambridge: Cambridge University Press, 1999), for details.

accelerated mainly by three interrelated factors: complete physical insulation for over fifty years; polarized political, ideological, and social distinctions (with socialism in the North and capitalism in the South); and the different language policies implemented by the two governments, culminating in North Korea's institution of the P'yŏngyang-based Cultured Language (*munhwaŏ*) as their standard speech as opposed to the traditional Seoul-based Standard Language (*p'yojun mal*) of South Korea.

The areas of major linguistic divergence between Cultured Language (CL) and Standard Language (SL) include pronunciations, *hangŭl* spelling conventions, lexicon, meanings, and styles. Thus many words manifest phonological differences – the most conspicuous one appearing in the word-initial *r* in Sino-Korean words. In CL, *r* occurs freely in this position, whereas in SL it is omitted before *i* and *y* and replaced by *n* otherwise – as in CL *ri-ron* vs. SL *i-ron* (theory); CL *rye* vs. SL *ye* (example); CL *rag-wŏn* vs. SL *nag-wŏn* (paradise). Another difference appears in the presence in CL and absence in SL of the word-initial *n* before *i* and *y* – as in CL *nilgop* vs. SL *ilkop* (seven) and CL *nyŏ-sŏng* vs. SL *yŏ-sŏng* (female). Pronunciation of loanwords differs considerably between CL and SL – as in CL *minusu* vs. SL *mainŏsŭ* (minus); CL *rajio* vs. SL *radio* (radio); CL *ttangk'ŭ* vs. SL *t'aengk'ŭ* (tank); CL *wenggŭria* vs. SL *hŏnggari* (Hungary); and CL *mehikko* vs. SL *meksik'o* (Mexico).[11]

Considerable spelling disparities exist as well.[12] The differences can be traced to several causes. First, as a result of the emergence of two standards of speech, widening disparity in the two systems of spelling became inevitable – as in CL *tal.kal* vs. SL *tal.kyal* (egg) and CL *rae.il* vs. SL *nae.il* (tomorrow). Second, identical or similar phenomena are analyzed differently in determining affixes and words – as in CL *toe.yŏss.ta* vs. SL *toe.ŏss.ta* (became); CL *kal.ka?* vs. SL *kal.kka?* (shall [we] go?); and CL *nŏp.chŏk.k'o* vs. SL *nŏlp.chŏk.k'o* (flat nose). Third, while sharing the basic principle that spaces should be placed between words, South Korea observes this principle rather narrowly and North Korea's convention is, in many cases, to spell two or more words without spacing, giving them compound status – as in CL *segae* vs. SL *se kae* (three items) and CL *i.pak.sa* vs. SL *i pak.sa* (Dr. Lee). Fourth, the two systems adopt different conventions in regularizing forms

---

[11] Chŏn Sut'ae and Ch'oe Hoch'ŏl, *NambukHan ŏnŏ pigyo* (Nokchin, 1989), pp. 258–270.
[12] These disparities are systematically analyzed in Ho-min Sohn, "Orthographic Divergence in South and North Korea: Toward a Unified Spelling System," in Young-Key Kim-Renaud, ed., *The Korean Alphabet: Its History and Structure* (Honolulu: University of Hawaii Press, 1997), based on a comparison of two currently used *hangŭl* spelling systems: South Korea's *Hangŭl match'um pŏp* and North Korea's *Kaejŏnghan Chosŏnmal kyubŏm chip*.

and concepts, breaking with tradition to different degrees. North Korea's system appears to have broken with tradition more frequently and pursues more formal uniformity. South Korea follows the tradition allowing both horizontal and vertical writing, for instance, whereas North Korea stipulates that horizontal writing be used in principle. Only North Korea has changed the traditional names of the three letters *ki.yŏk*, *ti.gŭt*, and *si.os* to *ki.ŭk*, *ti.ŭt*, and *si.ŭt* to conform to the other consonants. For double consonants, South Korea uses the traditional Sino-Korean term *ssang* (twin) whereas North Korea uses the new term *toen* (hard, tense). The so-called epenthetic *s* is spelled in South Korea only when the preceding noun root ends in a vowel in native compounds and a few Sino-Korean compounds and is left out otherwise, whereas it is left out after every noun root in North Korea (since 1966) – as in CL *nae.ka* vs. SL *naes.ka* (riverside); and CL *se.cip* vs. SL *ses.cip* (house for rent). Furthermore, the alphabetical orders used for dictionary entries do not agree.

Divergence is particularly great in the lexicon. North Korea has enforced policies to standardize the language normatively in accordance with their communist ideology. In North Korea, both the abolition of Chinese graphs and the initiation of Cultured Language have been tied to a strong language purification movement. Thus North Korea has coined some 5,000 lexical items either by nativizing Sino-Korean words or by creating new words based on native roots, affixes, obsolete forms, and dialectal elements, while maximally limiting the importation of new loanwords. South Korea has been relatively generous in increasing the number of Sino-Korean words by creating new ones or importing Sino-Japanese words. In addition, nearly 20,000 English-based loanwords have been imported. Some examples of lexical divergence: CL *k'ŭn.gol* vs. SL *tae.noe* (the cerebrum); CL *ŏmun.il.kun* vs. SL *ŏn.ŏ.hak.cha* (linguist); CL *al.gok* vs. SL *yang.gok* (grains); CL *cik.sŭng.gi* vs. SL *hel.gi* (helicopter); and CL: *son-gich'ŏk* vs. SL *nok'ŭ* (knock).

While meanings and styles of words and phrases in South Korea are largely neutral, many expressions in North Korea have metaphorical connotations orienting the people toward socialism. Thus denotational or connotational meaning differences have been developed in certain words of daily usage. For instance, *inmin* (people) in North Korea refers to all the people who take a positive role in the development of a socialist country. Due to this ideological connotation, South Korea does not use the term but favors *kungmin* (people). Similarly, *rodong* (CL) / *nodong* (SL) (labor) has a different meaning in the two Koreas. In the North, it denotes a purposive action by means of political or physical effort that is beneficial to society; in the South, it simply refers to physical work. The word *ilkun* (CL) / *ilkkun* (SL) refers to a person who is engaged in either physical or mental work in the North, but in the South it refers in general to a person engaged in hard manual labor.

KOREAN VOCABULARY

Due to its long and frequent historical contact with China and Japan and rapid modernization in all walks of life, Korea has come to have a rich vocabulary. Some 450,000 lexical items are entered in *Urimal k'ŭn sajŏn* (*Great Dictionary of the Korean language*, 1991). The contemporary South Korean lexicon consists of approximately 35% native, 60% Sino-Korean, and 5% loan elements. Native words (*koyuŏ*) include not only the vocabulary essential to the maintenance of basic human life but also items unique to the time-honored culture of traditional Korea. Thus body parts, natural objects, flora and fauna, kinship terms, basic color terms, personal pronouns, simple numbers, basic actions, physical and psychological states, items relating to essential food, clothing, and shelter, terms for agriculture and fishery, honorific expressions, and onomatopoeia are all symbolized by native words, although many of the content words coexist with Sino-Korean (SK) counterparts. Basic grammatical relations are represented only by native particles or suffixes.

Rice, for instance, is a Korean staple food represented by many different native words: *mo* (rice seedling), *pyŏ/narak* (rice plant, unhusked rice), *ssal* (husked rice), *ssaragi* (broken bits of husked rice), *pap* (cooked rice), *nwi* (unhusked rice in husked rice), *olbyŏ* (early ripening rice plant or its unhusked rice), *ipssal* (white husked rice), *ch'apssal* (glutinous husked rice), *mepssal* (nonglutinous husked rice). Tradition is also reflected in the verbs of "wearing" and "carrying," which are differentiated depending on what parts of the body are involved. These include *ch'ada* (to wear [a watch, a sword, a decoration]), *chida* (to carry an inanimate object on the back), *ŏpta* (to carry an animate object on the back), *ida* (to carry on the head), *ipta* (to wear a dress), and *turŭda* (to wear a shawl).

Of the several thousand sound-symbolic or ideophonic words, most belong to the native stock. Examples are *p'adak* vs. *p'ŏdŏk* (flapping, flopping, splashing), *norat'a* vs. *nurŏt'a* (to be yellow), *kosohada* vs. *kusuhada* (to taste or smell like sesame or rice tea), and *tonggŭrat'a* vs. *tunggŭrŏt'a* (to be round).

The traditional borrowing was mainly from China. Although borrowings from spoken Chinese ceased long ago, Chinese graphs and the concepts they represent have been used expediently and productively to coin thousands of new words. All Koreanized words based on Chinese graphs – whether ancient borrowings directly from China, reborrowings indirectly from Sino-Japanese, or coinages in Korea – are called SK words or *hanchaŏ* (sinograph words) for two reasons: because Chinese culture and learning permeated all facets of Korean life in the past and because, due to the logographic and monosyllabic nature of the graphs, Sino-Korean forms facilitate new word formation much more efficiently than native forms to represent the new concepts and products that continuously appear as civilization progresses. Thus nearly all terms in academic fields, politics, occupations, economy, law, society, and other cultural domains, as well as personal, place, and institutional names, are Sino-Korean words. Numerals, months, days of the week, color terms, and a large number of kinship terms and classifier nouns are also in Sino-Korean. The majority of these terms were coined in Japan as Sino-Japanese and then introduced to Korea, as well as to China, since Japan was the first nation in East Asia to import Western civilization and culture during the Meiji Restoration. The difference between Sino-Japanese and Sino-Korean words is primarily in pronunciation.

When were Chinese words and Chinese graphs first introduced into Korea? This question remains unanswered due to the lack of historical data. The only deduction we can make is that they must have been used in Korea as early as the first century BC, when Han China colonized the western and northern parts of the Korean peninsula and established its four commanderies there. One historical record shows that a Paekche national named Wang In went to Japan with many Chinese books around AD 400 – suggesting that Chinese culture and graphs had achieved considerable popularity in the Three Kingdoms period. With the unification of the Korean peninsula by the Silla dynasty in 677, the use of Chinese graphs in Korea gained more popularity as Silla's unification was achieved with Tang China's military support and subsequently contact between the two countries became frequent. Earlier, in 503, the name of the country and the title of the king were changed from native forms to Sino-Korean terms. In 682, a government organization in charge of national education (*kukhak*) was established and many Chinese classics began to be taught. In 757, native place-names were changed to two-graph Sino-Korean; in 759, all official titles were Sino-Koreanized as well. Personal names of the elite began to be Sino-Koreanized during the Silla period.

Native words began to be overwhelmed by Sino-Korean words in the Koryŏ dynasty. This was particularly the case after King Kwangjong adopted, in 958, the Chinese system of civil service examinations based on the Chinese classics. In this period, government officials and the elite, as well as scholars and literary men, used native words in speaking but Sino-Korean words in writing. The Chosŏn dynasty observed the all-out infiltration of Chinese graphs into every facet of Korean culture and society – chiefly because of the dynasty's adoption of Confucianism as the state political and moral philosophy and, as a result, the popular admiration of everything Chinese.

As for the origin of Sino-Korean sounds, it is generally assumed that the pronunciation of Chinese graphs used in the northern part of China during the Sui and Tang dynasties around the seventh to eighth centuries constituted their basis. This was during the Unified Silla period when innumerable written materials on Chinese civilization were imported from China. Thus pronunciations of contemporary Chinese words in Korean are similar to those of Middle Chinese, although independent vowel and consonant changes as well as the loss of tones have occurred in Korea.

As noted earlier, there are three layers of Sino-Korean words: Sino-Korean words from Chinese such as *chayŏn* (nature), *ch'ŏnji* (heaven and earth), *haksaeng* (student), and *hyoja* (filial son); Sino-Korean words from Sino-Japanese such as *chango* (deposit balance), *chŏnsŏn* (electricity cord), *chwadam* (table talk), and *ipku* (entrance); Sino-Korean words coined in Korea such as *chŏndap* (paddies and dry fields), *ch'onggak* (bachelor), *chujŏnja* (tea-kettle), *oesang* (on credit). The first of the three layers has the most members. The Sino-Korean words in this layer were introduced mainly through Confucian classics, history, and literary books, as well as Chinese works written in colloquial Chinese. Sino-Japanese coinages abound in Korean. Words like *pihaenggi* (airplane), *yŏnghwa* (movie), *kongjang* (factory), *ch'ukku* (football), *pul* (dollar), and other words coined by Japanese are used only in Japan and Korea, not in China.

Some Sino-Korean words were borrowed from written Chinese in ancient times and have undergone change either in form alone or in both form and meaning. Moreover, a few words were introduced from spoken Chinese. Examples are *paech'u* (Chinese cabbage; SK *paekch'ae* [white vegetable]); *mŏk* (inkstone; SK *muk*); *siwŏl* (ten-moon [October]; SK *sipwŏl*); *ka* (edge; SK *kye*; Ancient Chinese *kai*); *kage* (store; SK *kaga* [false house]); *kanan* (poverty; SK *kannan* [hardship]).[13]

Loanwords are abundant in Korean. The modern borrowing has been predominantly from the scientifically and technologically advanced United

[13] See Sim Chaegi, *Kugŏ ŏhwi non* (Chimmundang, 1983); Jeon Jae-Ho, *Kugŏ ŏhwisa yŏngu* (Taegu: Kyŏngbuk University Press, 1992); and Kim Chong-taek, *Kugŏ ŏhwi ron* (Tower, 1993).

States and Europe. These non-Sino-Korean loanwords are called *oeraeŏ* (words from abroad). Up until 1945 when Korea was liberated from thirty-five years of Japanese domination, loanwords were introduced into Korean exclusively through Japanese with spelling and pronunciation adjustments in accordance with Korean sound patterns. Only since 1945 has direct importation from English been prevalent. A number of English words have been introduced as new loanwords and many existing loanwords from other languages have been replaced by English loans. As a result, the total number of current loanwords is estimated at more than 20,000, of which English accounts for over 90%. In fact, most borrowings in South Korea since 1945 are words from English ranging over all aspects of life including clothing, food and drink, electricity and electronics, automobiles, sports, arts, social activities, politics, and economy. Random examples are *aisŭ-k'ŭrim* (ice cream), *allibai* (alibi), *heding* (heading in soccer), *hint'ŭ* (hint), *k'alla* (collar), *k'aemp'ŏsŭ* (campus), and *k'ŭredit k'adŭ* (credit card).

Both Sino-Korean and loanwords are an integral part of the Korean vocabulary. The impact of such non-native words on the Korean language is considerable. One effect is the proliferation of a number of synonymous expressions. The SK word *sŭngganggi* has long been used to denote an elevator, for instance, but is gradually being replaced by the loanword *el-libeit'ŏ*. The SK word *t'ajagi* and the loanword *t'aip'urait'ŏ* for a typewriter and the SK word *chŏnch'a* and the loanword *t'aengk'ŭ* (tank) are used with about equal frequency. Many SK words are still used exclusively: *sŏnp'unggi* (electric fan), *chadongch'a* (car), *chŏnhwa* (telephone), and *naengjanggo* (refrigerator), for example.

Frequently, synonymous words are associated with different shades of meaning and stylistic or social values, thus enriching the Korean vocabulary. When synonyms exist, native words usually represent traditional culture, both conceptual and physical, whereas Sino-Korean words, conveying more formality, tend to denote more sophisticated objects and more formal, abstract, and sometimes more socially prestigious concepts than their native counterparts do. Loanwords are, in general, associated with modern and stylish objects and concepts. For instance, the native word *karak* (rhythm) is usually used with reference to traditional Korean folk songs, the SK word *unyul* in formal or academic situations, and the loanword *ridŭm* for some sort of Western flavor. The triplet *ch'um* (native), *muyong* (SK), and *taensŭ* (loan) for "dance" has similar connotational differences. The native word *chip* is used when referring to one's own house or a house of a social inferior, but the SK word *taek* is used when referring to a socially superior adult's house. While there is no native term for a hotel, the SK word *yŏgwan* refers to inexpensive Korean-style inns whereas the loanword *hot'el* refers to expensive Western-style hotels where beds are provided.

Although some Sino-Korean words and loanwords have been adapted to the sound patterns of native Korean, native sound patterns are sometimes affected by non-native words. For instance, fifteenth-century Korean had (and the Kyŏngsang and Hamgyŏng dialects still have) lexical tones that may be due to the prolonged influx of Chinese words. Loanwords where word-initial *r* appears – such as *rak'et* (racket), *radio* (radio), *rait'ŏ* (lighter), and *rotte hot'el* (Hotel Lotte) – have been disrupting the original sound pattern where no native words begin with an initial *r* sound, a characteristic shared by Altaic languages. Furthermore, Sino-Korean words where no vowel harmony is observed have contributed to the collapse of vowel harmony in native words.

As a consequence, many native words have been lost in the battle with Sino-Korean and loanwords and disappeared from usage long ago, frequently irrecoverably. While Chinese graphs in Japanese are read in both Sino-Japanese pronunciation and the pronunciation of corresponding native words, thereby contributing to the maintenance of the latter, Chinese graphs in Korea are read only in Sino-Korean pronunciation, contributing to the atrophy of native words. Sino-Korean *san* (mountain), *kang* (river), *ch'inch'ŏk* (relative), *paek* (100), and *ch'ŏn* (1,000), for example, have completely replaced the native *moe, karam, aam, on*, and *chŭmŭn*, respectively.

THE KOREAN ALPHABET: *HANGŬL*

At present, the Korean alphabet called *hangŭl* is the main writing system used by all Koreans to represent native, Sino-Korean, and loanwords. (Chinese graphs are optionally used to represent only Sino-Korean words.) Before the nineteenth century when Western cultures began to permeate East Asia, China had long been the center of East Asian civilization. Chinese civilization was propagated to neighboring countries mainly through written Chinese based on Chinese graphs. Thus the Chinese script has long been an integral part of the writing systems of Koreans and indeed was the only system before the creation of *hangŭl* in 1443–1444. Before *hangŭl*, since Chinese graphs were used mostly by the elite, commoners had no means of written communication. The ruling class of Korea devoted their entire lives to the study of classical Chinese, written in graphs, because it was the main goal of education, the official means of government affairs, and the medium of civil service examinations.

In an effort to remedy this predicament, early scholars devised writing systems using Chinese graphs for the pronunciation and transcription of native Korean affixes, words, and sentences. A few varieties of this writing were subsumed under the term *idu* (clerk reading) and were used during all three ancient kingdoms (Silla, Paekche, and Koguryŏ) and also later during the Koryŏ and Chosŏn dynasties. The *idu* script was used to record Korean expressions by means of Chinese graphs borrowed in their Chinese meaning but read as the corresponding Korean sounds (glossograms) or by means of Chinese graphs borrowed in their Chinese sounds only (phonograms). This script allowed people to record personal names, place-names, and vernacular songs and poems. This writing was also used to clarify government documents and other books written in Chinese. The King Kwanggaet'o stele of Koguryŏ contains many phonetic transcriptions written in the *idu* script, as do early Silla inscriptions. Moreover, a number of Chinese graphs in the *idu* script are found in the *Historical Records of the Three Kingdoms* and *Memorabilia of the Three Kingdoms*. Because this writing was inadequate as a means of written communication, the *hyangch'al* system was invented to transcribe entire sentences into Chinese graphs for sound and sense.

It was under these circumstances that *hangŭl* was created – a phonetic writing system completely disengaged from the Chinese script. This indigenous phonetic alphabet is one of the most remarkable writing systems ever devised.[14] For the design of the *hangŭl* alphabet, King Sejong (1397–1450) and the scholars of the Hall of Worthies studied the rich Chinese linguistic tradition, such as the concepts of consonants (initials), syllables, and tones, as well as their philosophical background. The orthographic design of *hangŭl* – based on a rigorous analysis of Korean and Sino-Korean sound – was completed in 1443. To test the new writing system, the king ordered the composition of *Yongbi ŏch'ŏn ka* (*Songs of Flying Dragons*, 1445–1447), a eulogy cycle in 125 cantos with 248 poems, in the new alphabet with translations in Chinese graphs.[15]

---

[14] This alphabet was named *hangŭl* by Chu Sigyŏng (1876–1914), a pioneer linguist of Korean. Formerly it was popularly called *ŏnmun* (vernacular writing, vulgar script). There are many works on the study of *hangŭl*. In English see Gari K. Ledyard, "The Korean Language Reform of 1446: The Origin, Background and Early History of the Korean Alphabet" (Ph.D. dissertation, University of California, Berkeley, 1966); Cheong-Ho Lee, *Haesŏl yŏkchu Hunmin chŏngŭm. Translated and Annotated Hunmin Chŏngŭm* (Korean Library Science Research Institute, 1972); Kim-Renaud, ed., *The Korean Alphabet*; and Sek Yen Kim-Cho, *The Korean Alphabet of 1446* (Seoul: Asia Culture Press, and Amherst, N.Y.: Humanity Books, 2002). The present survey owes to Ledyard's dissertation.

[15] See Peter H. Lee, *Songs of Flying Dragons: A Critical Reading* (Cambridge, Mass.: Harvard University Press, 1975), for an extensive discussion of this cycle.

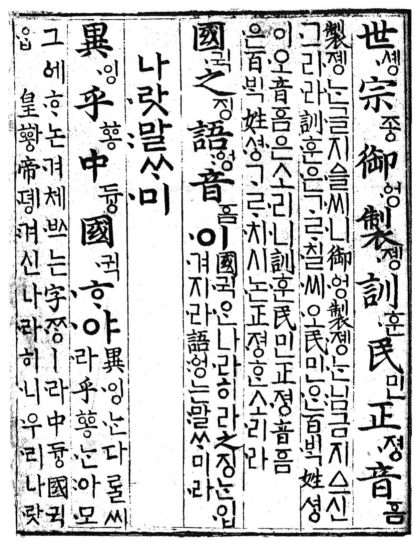

Example 1.   King Sejong (1397–1450), beginning of *Correct Sounds for Teaching the People* (1459).

King Sejong promulgated *hangŭl* on 9 October 1446 under the name *Hunmin chŏngŭm* (*Correct Sounds for Teaching the People*). Written by Sejong himself, the alphabet was accompanied by *Hunmin chŏngŭm haerye* (*Explanations and Examples of the Correct Sounds*), compiled by a group of scholars commissioned by the king. These two documents were published as a single book. The text of *Hunmin chŏngŭm* consists of three parts: preface, pronunciation of the letters, and rules for combining letters. The preface briefly summarizes Sejong's motives for inventing *hangŭl*: "The speech sounds of Korea are distinct from those of China and thus are not communicable with Chinese graphs. Hence many people having something to put into words are unable to express their feelings. To overcome such distressing circumstances, I have newly devised twenty-eight letters that everyone can learn with ease and use with convenience in daily life." In the second part, the sound values of the newly devised twenty-eight letters (seventeen consonants and eleven vowels) are explained in Chinese graphs; the third part presents rules regarding the use of *hangŭl* letters and other symbols in syllable blocks. *Hunmin chŏngŭm haerye* explains and illustrates the contents of *Hunmin chŏngŭm* in detail. It consists of seven parts: design of the letters, syllable-initial sounds, syllable-medial sounds, syllable-final sounds, combinations of letters, use of the letters, and a postface by Chŏng Inji (1397–1478).

After its creation, *hangŭl* underwent several major ordeals in the course of its diffusion in the face of the long tradition of the use of Chinese graphs by the nobility and officials during the Chosŏn period. Although King Sejong's invention of *hangŭl* was a great cultural achievement, a group of scholar-officials led by Ch'oe Malli (fl. 1419–1444), then associate academician of the Hall of Worthies, opposed the common use of the alphabet and presented an anti-*hangŭl* memorial to the throne in 1444. Their main argument was that Korea had long emulated Chinese ideas and institutions and that adoption of Korea's own writing system would make it impossible to identify Korean civilization with that of China but instead would identify Korea with barbarians such as Mongols, Tanguts, Jurchens, Japanese, and Tibetans who had their own scripts. This appeal had little effect on Sejong's determination.

After Sejong's death, the opposition to *hangŭl* continued until Sejo (1455–1468), the seventh king, propagated *hangŭl* with Buddhism. Still, literary Chinese and *idu* were predominant while *hangŭl* served as an aid for the study of literary Chinese and was used mostly by women. Not until the Kabo Reform of 1894 did *hangŭl* come to be used in official documents. King Kojong's decree of 21 November 1894 stipulated that all regulations and royal decrees be written in the alphabet. Exclusive use of *hangŭl* in government documents was rather exceptional, however, and a host of government regulations were written in the alphabet mixed with Chinese graphs. Indeed, mixed use of the two scripts became a common practice among the general public, as it is today.

During the Japanese occupation of Korea (1910–1945), the use of Korean, including *hangŭl*, was suppressed and the Korean people were forced to use Japanese. When Korea was liberated from Japan in 1945, use of the Korean language and alphabet was restored in both South and North Korea and became a symbol of independence and the reawakening of national consciousness.

The Korean consonants, which correspond to nineteen *hangŭl* letters, are *p/b, p', pp; t/d, t', tt; ch/j, ch', tch; k/g, k', kk; s, ss; h; m, n, ng*; and *l/r*. Korean has eight vowels (*i, e, ae, ŭ, ŏ, a, u, o*), two semivowels (*w, y*), and a number of diphthongs. Some dialectal zones lack a few of these consonants, vowels, and diphthongs.

In the speech of older Koreans (aged fifty and older as of the year 2000), vowel length is significant in differentiating meanings. Vowel length (:) is not indicated in *hangŭl* orthography – as in *chong* [chong] (bell) vs. *chong* [cho:ng] (servant), *mal* [mal] (horse) vs. *mal* [ma:l] (language), *nun* [nun] (eye) vs. *nun* [nu:n] (snow), and *pae* [pae] (ship/pear/stomach) vs. *pae* [pae:] (double). Younger speakers do not make such vowel length distinctions.

In Korean there is a difference between written (here boldface) and spoken (here italic) syllables in that the former allow consonant clusters in the syllable-final position (**kaps** [price]) while the latter do not allow more than one consonant in that position (*kap* [price]). Korean spoken syllables have a simple internal structure. One vowel must be present as the nucleus. It may be preceded by a consonant, a semivowel, or both, and may be followed by a consonant – as in **i** *i* (two), **na** *na* (I), **ip'** *ip* (leaf), **hyŏ** *hyŏ* (tongue), **talk** *tak* (chicken), **salm** *sam* (life), **pu.ok'** *pu.ŏk* (kitchen), where boldface is written and italics are spoken forms and the dot (.) stands for a syllable boundary.

Speech sounds alternate in different environments without changing meanings. For instance, **ch'** in the written form **kkoch'** (flower) shows the following sound alternations: *ch'* as in **kkoch' i** → *kko.ch'i* (flower [subject] – before a vowel), *t* as in **kkoch'** → *kkot* (flower) and **kkoch'-to** → *kkot.to* ("flower" also – pronounced independently or before a non-nasal consonant), and *n* as in **kkoch'-namu** → *kkon.na.mu* (flower tree – before a nasal consonant). Note that the consonants alternate in these examples without changing the meaning "flower." There are some two dozen sound-alternation rules in Korean.

Sound symbolism (mimesis) is widespread in Korean, which has several thousand sound-symbolic words. Sound symbolism is reflected in both vowels and consonants. As for vowels, bright (*yang*) vowels *a, ae, o* tend to connote brightness, sharpness, lightness, smallness, thinness, and quickness, whereas dark (*ŭm*) vowels *e, u, ŏ* indicate darkness, heaviness, dullness, slowness, deepness, and thickness. In pairs such as *p'adak* vs. *p'ŏdŏk* (flapping), *norat'a* vs. *nurŏt'a* (yellow), *hwanhada* vs. *hwŏnhada* (open, clear), for instance, the first word contains a bright vowel *a* or *o* while the second has a dark vowel *ŏ* or *u*, causing bright and dark connotational differences. As for consonants, sound-symbolic words show differences among plain, aspirated, and tensed consonants. A plain consonant tends to connote slowness, gentleness, heaviness, and bigness; an aspirated consonant flexibility, elasticity, crispness, and swiftness; and a tensed consonant compactness, tightness, hardness, smallness, and extra swiftness. For instance, *chul-jul, ch'ul-ch'ul*, and *tchul-tchul* (trickling, flowing persistently) denote, among other things, an increasingly smaller quantity of liquid but faster action. Similarly, in *ping-ping, p'ing-p'ing*, and *pping-pping* (round and round – spinning, turning, whirling), the manner of turning is gradually faster. Thus a plane whirls in the sky in a *ping-ping* manner, a top turns in a *p'ing-p'ing* manner, and a rotary press spins in a *pping-pping* manner.

WORD STRUCTURE

Korean is a typical agglutinative language in that one or more affixes with constant form and meaning may be attached to various stems. In *po-i-si-ŏt-kes-sŭm-ni-da* ([a respectable person] may have been seen), for instance, the passive verb stem *po-i* (be seen) consists of the verb stem *po* (see) and the passive suffix *-i*. The remaining suffixes indicate various grammatical functions of the stem *po-i*: the subject honorific *-si*, the past tense *-ŏt*, the modal *-kes* (may), the addressee honorific *-sŭm*, the indicative *-ni*, and the declarative ending *-da*. Many Korean suffixes either do not have counterparts or correspond to independent words in nonagglutinative languages such as English and Chinese. For instance, some English conjunctive words are equivalent to Korean suffixes – as in *ka-go* (go and) and *ka-myŏn* (if one goes) where *-ko* (and) and *-myŏn* (if) are suffixes.

Many words are formed by compounding two or more noun roots or predicate stems. For instance, the expression *annyŏnghaseyo?* (how are you?) consists of SK roots *an* and *nyŏng* (safety) and native adjective stem *ha* (to be), followed by the subject honorific suffix *-se* and the courtesy ending *-yo*. The two roots *an* and *nyŏng* constitute a compound noun that in turn compounds with *ha* – resulting in a compound adjective stem *annyŏngha* (peaceful). The meanings of compound words may be idiomatized to varying degrees from complete fusion – as in *nun-chit* (eye

behavior – wink), *ttang-gŏmi* (earth-black – dusk), *kŏ-rae* (go-come – trans-
action), and *p'ung-wŏl* (wind-moon – poetry) – to relatively transparent
association as in *pam-nat* (day and night), *ma-so* (horses and oxen), *chip-
chip* (houses), *hyo-ja* (filial son), and *mi-in* (pretty person, pretty woman).
In general, a native element combines with a native element and an SK
element with an SK element – as in native *sŏk-tal* and SK *sam-gae-wŏl*,
both meaning "three months."

Of all types of compounds, compound nouns are the most numerous and
varied. Examples of compound verbs are *am-mot-poda* (front-unable-see –
be blind), *maŭm-mŏkta* (mind-eat – intend, plan), *son-boda* (hand-see – fix),
and *tol-boda* (go around-see – take good care of). Examples of compound
adjectives are *hŏmul-ŏpta* (fault-lack – be on friendly terms), *him-dŭlda*
(power-enter – be strenuous), *nun-mŏlda* (eye-far – be blind), and *sil-ŏpta*
(substance-lack – be insincere).

Numerous words are formed through derivational affixation (prefixing
and suffixing). Affixes are from both the native and the SK stocks. Loan
affixes are rare. In general, a native affix occurs with a native root or stem, and
an SK affix with an SK root or stem. There are several hundred derivational
affixes (boldface here) in Korean. They occur predominantly in nouns,
verbs, and adjectives – **maen**-*bal* (bare-foot – barefoot), **hor**-*abi* (single-
father – widower), **mad**-*adŭl* (first-son – the eldest son), and **chŏn**-*sege*
(entire-world – whole world). Derived verbs include **cit**-*papta* (randomly-
step on – overrun), **pi**-*utta* (twisted-laugh – scorn), **pin**-*nagada* (aslant-go
out – go astray), **sŏl**-*ikta* (insufficiently-ripe – be half-cooked/half-ripe),
and *chungŏl*-**daeda** (mutter-repeat – mutter repeatedly). Derived verbs also
include causative or passive ones – as in *po*-**ida** (see-cause/be – show, be
seen), *chop*-**hida** (narrow-cause – make narrow), *mut*-**hida** (bury-be – be
buried), and *mul*-**lida** (bite-cause/be – cause someone to bite, be bitten).
Examples of derived adjectives are **sae**-*kkamat'a*/**si**-*kkŏmŏt'a* (vivid-black –
be deep black), *nop*-**tarat'a** (high-rather – rather high), *nunmul*-**gyŏpta**
(tears-full – be touching), and *hyanggi*-**ropta** (aroma-characterized by – be
fragrant).

SENTENCE STRUCTURE

Korean sentences are predicate-final – sharing the grammatical properties
of other predicate-final languages such as Japanese, Altaic, and Dravidian –
and are very different from sentences of, for example, English, French,
Chinese, and Austronesian. In normal speech, the predicate (verb or adjective) comes at the end of a sentence or a clause. All other elements,
including the subject and object, must appear before the predicate – as

illustrated here, where SB = subject, RL = relative clause suffix, OB = object, SH = subject honorific suffix, and PL = polite-level ending:

[*Nae ka hakkyo esŏ **manna**]-n pun   i   hangugŏ rŭl **karŭch'i-seyo**.*
I   SB school at   meet-RL   person SB Korean OB teach-SH-PL
"The person I met at school teaches Korean."

Notice that the verb *manna* (meet) occurs at the end of the relative clause and the verb *karŭch'ida* (teach) at the end of the whole sentence.

In Korean all modifiers – whether adjectives, adverbs, numerals, relative clauses, subordinate or coordinate clauses, determiners, or genitive constructions – must precede the element they modify. In *Pusan kkaji aju ppalli talli-nŭn kich'a* (the train which runs very fast to Pusan), for example, *Pusan kkaji* (to Pusan) and *aju ppalli* (very fast) modify their head verb *tallida* (run); *aju* (very) modifies its head *ppalli* (fast); and the whole relative clause *Pusan kkaji aju ppalli talli-nŭn* (which runs very fast to Pusan) modifies *kich'a* (train). Note also that the relative-clause suffix *-nŭn* functions like an English relative pronoun.

As observed in many of the preceding examples, particles (boldface) are postpositional, occurring after a nominal – as in *Nae **ka**, hakkyo **esŏ**, pun **i**, hangugŏ **rŭl**,* and *Pusan **kkaji**.* Titles follow names – as in *Kim paksa-nim* (Dr. Kim). Grammatical functions such as subject and addressee honorification, past tense, mood, and sentence types are expressed in the form of suffixes occurring after predicate stems, as already noted earlier under "Word structure." Also, unlike English, there is no inversion of any element in question sentences.

The comparative expression takes the order: standard + comparative particle + degree adverb + adjective, as in *Mirani nŭn Mia poda tŏ yeppŭ-ta* (Miran is prettier than Mia), where *Mia* is a standard, *poda* is a comparative particle, *tŏ* is a degree adverb, and *yeppŭ-ta* is an adjective.

Particles are responsible for various grammatical and semantic functions. Particles may be agglutinated to each other after a relevant nominal – as in *Miguk ŭro-put'ŏ-ŭi sosik* (news from the United States). Note that the particles such as directional *ŭro*, source *put'ŏ*, and possessive *ŭi* occur in sequence after *Miguk*.

Although the subject tends to appear first in a sentence, it and other nominal elements can be scrambled for emphatic or other figurative purposes:

Na nŭn   ŏje   san   esŏ kkwŏng ŭl   chab-ass-ŏyo.
I   as for yesterday mountain on pheasant OB catch-PAST-PL
"I caught a pheasant on the mountain yesterday."

Korean is often called a situation-oriented or discourse-oriented language in that contextually or situationally understood elements (including subject and object) are left unexpressed more frequently than not. Thus, for instance, in *ŏdi ka-se-yo?* (where-go? – Where are you going?), the subject "you" does not appear. Using a word denoting "you" in such expressions would sound awkward in normal contexts, unless "you" is emphasized or contrasted with someone else – as in "as for you."

Korean is a "macro-to-micro" language in that the universe is represented in the order of a set (macro) and then its members (micro). Thus, for instance, Koreans say the family name first and then the given name followed by a title; say an address in the order of country, province, city, street, house number, and personal name; and refer to time with year first and seconds last.

While nouns occur freely by themselves, verbs and adjectives cannot function without an ending. For this reason the dummy suffix *-ta/-da* is attached to a stem for citation or dictionary entries. For instance, the verb stem *po* (see) and the adjective stem *choh* (be good) are entered in the dictionary as *poda* and *chot'a*, respectively.

There are four major sentence types characterized by sentence endings: declarative (statement), interrogative (question), propositive (proposal), and imperative (command) – as in *cha-nda* (declarative: [He] sleeps), *cha-ni?* (interrogative: Does [he] sleep?), *cha-ra* (imperative: Go to sleep!), and *cha-ja* (propositive: Let's sleep). These four types are interwoven with six speech levels.

LINGUISTIC COURTESY

Language has two important tasks: transmitting information (transactional function) and maintaining human relationships (interactional function). It is the interactional function that is relevant to linguistic courtesy. Although courtesy expressions are ubiquitous across all languages, their forms and functions differ from language to language – conditioned by respective linguistic structures and usage as well as by the cultural perspectives (attitudes, beliefs, values) of the speaker. For instance, compare English and Korean in expressing "Good night" by son and father: [English] "Good night, Dad" (by son) and "Good night, John" (by father) vs. [Korean] "Abŏji, annyŏnghi chumu-se-yo" ("Dad, sleep well") (by son) and "nŏdo chal cha-ra" ("You too sleep well") (by father). Note that in English son and father use the same expression except for the address terms: a kinship term by the son and a given name by the father. In Korean, by contrast, they use entirely different utterances. Not a single element is shared. Under no circumstances may the son use any part of his father's utterance in expressing "good night" to his father and vice versa. Both the son's and the father's utterances are appropriate and polite. They must always be used in that way.

There are two types of linguistic courtesy, normative and strategic. The function of normative politeness is social indexing; that of strategic politeness is saving face. In general, expression of normative politeness is bound by the cultural norms of a society whereas expression of strategic politeness is controlled by interlocutors in interactive situations in performing their communicative goals. Thus while the former is largely culture-bound, the latter is universal to a great extent. Both types of courtesy expressions normally occur together in the same discourse. By and large, normative politeness in Korean is expressed by time-honored grammatical forms of courtesy, which are called honorifics, whereas strategic politeness is expressed by various assertion-softening or assertion-reinforcing measures – phatic expressions, conversational formulas, hedges, intonation, and direct or indirect speech acts – as well as praise, approval, sympathy, seeking agreement, and giving options to the addressee.

Korean has an elaborate honorific system.[16] Sentences cannot be uttered without the speaker's approximate knowledge of his social relationship with the addressee or referent in terms of age category (adult, adolescent, or child), social status, kinship, and in- and out-groupness. Korean honorifics include speech levels, personal pronouns, address-reference terms, content words and particles, and subject- and addressee-honorific suffixes.

Speech levels

Korean has six speech levels marked by sentence endings, illustrated here with *po-* (see):

	Declarative	Interrogative	Imperative	Propositive
plain	*po-nda*	*po-ni?/po-nŭnya?*	*po-ara/pora*	*po-ja*
intimate	*po-a*	*po-a?*	*po-a*	*po-a*
familiar	*po-ne*	*po-na?*	*po-ge*	*po-se*
blunt	*po-o*	*po-o?*	*po-o*	*po-psida*
polite	*po-ayo*	*po-ayo?*	*po-ayo*	*po-ayo*
deferential	*po-mnida*	*po-mnikka?*	*po-si-psio*	*po-si-psida*

Speakers use different levels based on whom they are talking to. The plain level is used by any speaker to any child, to one's own siblings, children, or grandchildren regardless of age, to one's daughter-in-law, or between

---

[16] The honorific system of Korean is one of the most systematic of all known languages. In this respect, Korean may be called an honorific language.

intimate adult friends whose friendship started in childhood. The intimate level (polite-level form minus -*yo*), also called a half-talk style, is used by an adult to an adult junior such as a student, by a child of preschool age to his or her family members including parents, or between close friends whose friendship began in childhood or adolescence; this level is frequently intermixed with the plain or familiar level in the same discourse with the same person. The familiar level is typically used by a male adult to an adult inferior or adolescent such as a high school or college student or to one's son-in-law or to an old friend. The blunt level, sometimes used by a boss to his subordinates, is disappearing from daily usage (probably due to its blunt connotation). Most young speakers use only the plain, intimate, polite, and deferential levels.

The most popular level toward an adult is the polite one, which is an informal counterpart of the deferential level. This level is widely used by both males and females in casual conversation. While females predominantly use this level in all conversations, males use both the polite and deferential levels to address an equal or superior adult. Even in a formal conversational situation, the deferential and polite levels are intermixed by the same interlocutors in the same discourse. In formal situations such as news reports and public lectures, only the deferential style is used.

Personal pronouns

There are person, number, and speech-level distinctions also. Here *D* stands for a demonstrative *i* (this), *kŭ* (that), and *chŏ* (that over there):

		Singular	Plural
1st person:	Plain	*na*	*uri(-tŭl)*
	Humble	*chŏ*	*chŏ-hŭi(-dŭl)*
2nd person:	Plain	*nŏ*	*nŏ-hui(-dŭl)*
	Familiar	*chane*	*chane-dŭl*
	Intimate	*chagi*	*chagi-dŭl*
	Blunt	*tangsin*	*tangsin-dŭl*
		taek	*taek-tŭl*
	Deferential	*ŏrŭsin*	*ŏrŭsin-dŭl*
3rd person:	Thing	*D-kŏt*	*D-kŏt-tŭl*
	Child	*D-ae*	*D-ay-dŭl*
	Adult-familiar	*D-saram*	*D-saram-dŭl*
	Adult-blunt	*D-i*	*D-i-dŭl*
	Adult-polite	*D-bun*	*D-bun-dŭl*

3rd-person	Plain	*chŏ(-jasin)*	*chŏ(-jasin)-dŭl*
reflexive (self):	Neutral	*chagi(-jasin)*	*chagi(-jasin)-dŭl*
	Deferential	*tangsin(-jasin)*	*tangsin(-jasin)-dŭl*

Address-reference terms

An extensive set of highly stratified address-reference terms is used – here given in the order of decreasing deference and distance: *Kim paksa-nim* (Hon. Dr. Kim), *Kim paksa* (Dr. Kim), *Kim Minho ssi* (Mr. Minho Kim), *Minho ssi* (Mr. Minho), *Kim ssi* (Mr. Kim), *Kim (Minho) kun* (Mr. [Minho] Kim), *Minho kun* (Mr. Minho), *Minho* (Minho!), and *Minho ya* (Minho!). While English honorific titles such as "Mr.," "Mrs.," "Miss," and "Ms." are used primarily to indicate gender roles and marital status, Korean honorific titles are hierarchical. The honorific suffix *-nim* is used for one's superiors or distant adult equals, *ssi* for colleagues or subordinates, and *kun/yang* for much younger inferiors or subordinates.[17] Personal names with the vocative particle (*i* or null) are used to address one's intimate adult friends or one's adult or adolescent students, while those with the particle *(y)a* are for addressing children.

Kinship terms used as address-reference terms are highly diversified. They include terms for older siblings such as *oppa* (female's older brother), *hyŏng* (male's older brother; rarely, female's older sister), *nunim* (male's older sister), and *ŏnni* (female's older sister). Furthermore, kinship terms are extensively used to non-kin.

Content words and particles

Korean has a small set of nouns and predicates to refer to a superior or distant adult's family member, possession, and action, as well as a few humble predicates to refer to one's own or an inferior person's action in reference to a superior person – as in *sŏngham* (hon.) vs. *irŭm* (plain) (name), *taek* (hon.) vs. *chip* (plain) (house), *chinji* (hon.) vs. *pap* (plain) (meal), and *yŏnse* vs. *nai* (plain) (age). In addition, two particles have neutral and honorific forms, as in the subject particle *kkesŏ* (hon.) vs. *kal i* (neutral) and the dative/locative/goal particle *kke* (hon.) vs. *egel hant'e* (neutral). While the neutral forms are used for both children and adults, the honorific forms are used for adults to indicate special deference.

---

[17] Noteworthy is the fact that a married woman uses *abŏnim* (father) and *ŏmŏnim* (mother) to address or refer to her parents-in-law and *abŏji* and *ŏmŏni* or *appa* and *ŏmma* for her own parents.

Subject- and addressee-honorific suffixes

Korean has a suffixal device for subject honorification: employing the suffix -*(ŭ)si*/-*(ŭ)se* immediately after a predicate stem when the subject referent deserves the speaker's deference – as in *kyosu-nim i ka-**si**-n-da* (the professor is going). Korean also has the addressee-honorific suffix -*(sŭ)p* (-*sŭp* after a consonant; -*p*/-*m* after a vowel). This suffix appears only with the deferential speech level – as in *i kŭrim ŭn chos-**sŭp**-ni-da* (this picture is good) and *chŏ nŭn ka-**m**-ni-da* (I am going). In *Kim sŏnsaeng-nim ŭn ka-**si**-ŏs-**sŭm**-ni-kka?* (did Professor Kim go?), both the subject referent and the addressee are honored.

Strategic politeness

In addition to honorifics, courtesy is expressed in many strategic ways. If a speech act is performed for the benefit of the addressee, the utterance is usually direct, often utilizing the imperative sentence type, as strong assertion is frequently needed for politeness. Examples are *ŏsŏ o-si-psio* (welcome; literally "come quickly") and *annyŏnghi chumuse-yo* (good night; "sleep peacefully"). If a speech act is not for the benefit of the addressee but for the speaker or somebody else, indirect speech acts are felicitous because direct speech acts are often face-threatening to the addressee's positive self-esteem or to his freedom from imposition. Indirect utterances are used especially when the addressee is a senior or a distant equal or the utterances in question are made for the benefit of the speaker. Note the decreasing degrees of indirectness denoting decreasing degrees of courtesy in both Korean and English:

1. *Sillyeha-mnida man, mun chom yŏrŏ chu-si-gessŏyo?* (Excuse me, but would you please open the door for me?)
2. *Mun chom yŏrŏ chu-si-gessŏ yo?* (Would you please open the door for me?)
3. *Mun chom yŏrŏ chu-se-yo.* (Please open the door for me.)
4. *Mun yŏrŏ chu-se-yo.* (Open the door for me.)
5. *Mun yŏ-se-yo.* (Open the door.)

All these sentences are at the polite speech level and thus may be uttered to an adult. Sentence 5, however, is a sheer command in both Korean and English and thus impolite unless the act of opening the door is for the sake of the addressee. In general, the longer a sentence is, the more indirect and therefore the more polite it is, since more hedges are included. In sentence 1, several hedging devices are involved: the request-introducing formula *sillyeha-mnida man* (excuse me but); the diminutive *chom* (just; a little; please); the benefactive auxiliary verb *chuda* (to do for); the modal (conjectural) suffix *-ket* (would); and the interrogative sentence type with rising intonation. As in English, use of interrogative sentences for requests has become quite widespread recently.

Many indirect speech acts are idiomatized. One such case is to pose a question to a social superior about his or her name, age, and such. The formula is: *ŏttŏ-k'e toe-se-yo?* (What is . . . ?; literally "How does it become?") – as in the plain form *irŭm i mwŏ yeyo?* (to a child or junior adult) (What is your name?) vs. the polite form *sŏngham i ŏttŏ k'e toe-se-yo?* (to a senior or distant adult) (May I ask your name? – literally "How does your name become?"). Also noteworthy is the productive use of the phrase *kŏt kat'-ayo* (it seems that . . .) in daily interactions – as in *chŏ nŭn mot kal kŏt kat'-ayo* (I may not be able to go) instead of the intended expression *chŏnŭn mot ka-yo* (I am unable to go.) This is a speaker's politeness strategy to tone down the assertion.

Despite the strong contemporary trend toward democratization in all walks of life, Koreans still value traditional hierarchism to a great extent in personal interactions. Moreover, as alluded to in the use of kinship terms to non-kin, honorifics and politeness strategies are also governed by Koreans' collectivistic value orientation. Thus the structure and use of courtesy expressions cannot be properly grasped without understanding Koreans' deep-rooted hierarchical and collectivistic consciousness in contrast to, say, English-speakers' egalitarian and individualistic consciousness.[18]

FORMS, PROSODY, AND THEMES

Korean literature includes works written in literary Chinese and those written in the vernacular. Because of the absence of a writing system of native origin till the mid fifteenth century when the Korean alphabet was invented, the extant poetry from early times was either transcribed in Chinese for

---

[18] For more discussion of Korean politeness and honorifics see Juck-Ryoon Hwang, "Role of Sociolinguistics in Foreign Language Education with Reference to Korean and English terms of Address and Levels of Deference" (Ph.D. dissertation, University of Texas at Austin, 1975); Choon-hak Cho, *A Study of Korean Pragmatics: Deixis and Politeness* (Hanshin, 1982); Ho-min Sohn, *Linguistic Expeditions* (Hanshin, 1986); Woo-kyu Lee, "Honorifics and Politeness in Korean" (Ph.D. dissertation, University of Wisconsin, Madison, 1991); and Suh Cheong-soo, *Kugŏ munpŏp* (Hanyang taehakkyo ch'ulp'anbu, 1996). Further readings on various structural aspects of Korean include Hyun Bok Lee, *Korean Grammar* (Oxford: Oxford University Press, 1989); Samuel E. Martin, *A Reference Grammar of Korean* (Rutland: Tuttle, 1992); Suk-Jin Chang, *Korean* (Amsterdam: Benjamins, 1996); and Sohn, *The Korean Language*.

both its sound and sense (*hyangga*), or in the new alphabet (Koryŏ songs). The linguistic and literary evidence indicates that early in their history Koreans learned to read and write the Chinese script. The bulk of verse and prose was written directly in Chinese in the Chinese literary forms. Almost every Chosŏn-dynasty scholar-official of importance left behind collected works containing verse and prose in Chinese. Some wrote in both Chinese and Korean from the fifteenth century.

POETRY

In traditional Korea, every educated man and woman wrote poetry in literary Chinese – and judging from the extant collected works of individual writers, the amount of poetry they wrote is staggering. The Chinese verse forms include *gushi* (old-style verse), *lüshi* (regulated eight-line verse) – including *pailü* (regulated couplets of unlimited length) – *fu* (rhymeprose), and *ci* (a synonym for *fu* or *sao* [elegy]), with fewer examples of the *ci* (song words or lyric meter) and *yuefu* ballads. The first 22 out of a total of 133 chapters (chs. 23 to 133 cover prose genres) in the *Tong munsŏn* (*Anthology of Korean Literature in Chinese*, 1478) are assigned to poetry:

I	*Ci* (ten examples) and rhymeprose
2–3	Rhymeprose (thirty-five examples)
4–5	Pentasyllabic old-style verse
6–8	Heptasyllabic old-style verse
9–11	Pentasyllabic regulated verse
12–17	Heptasyllabic regulated verse
18	Heptasyllabic regulated couplets
19	Penta- and heptasyllabic quatrain (*jueju*, cut-off lines)
20–21	Heptasyllabic quatrain
22	Heptasyllabic quatrain and hexasyllabic verse (three examples)

OLD-STYLE VERSE

Praised by Yi Kyubo (1168–1241) as possessing remarkable classic purity (without being refined or effete) and evincing a heroic spirit no weakling could approach, the Koguryŏ general Ŭlchi Mundŏk is said to have sent the following to the invading Sui general in 612:

	a b c d e
Your divine plans have plumbed the heavens;	1. 神策究天文
Your subtle reckoning has spanned the earth.	2. 妙算窮地理
You win every battle, your military merit is great.	3. 戰勝功旣高
Why then not be content and stop the war?	4. 知足願云止

Lines 1 and 2 show a syntactic parallelism – a parallel couplet. Lines 3 and 4 do not parallel syntactically (grammatical particles in 3d and 4d). The poet makes use of intertextual strategies – lines 1–2 allude to a passage in the *Book of Changes*: "Looking upward, we contemplate with its help the signs in the heavens; looking down, we examine the lines of the earth."[19] Line 4a–b alludes to *Daodejing* 44 (see Chapter 4). This poem, as in old-style verse, does not observe the rules of tonal parallelism. Rhyme occurs at the end of each couplet, in lines 2 and 4 in deflected tone, and there is a caesura between the second and third syllables. This poem is an old-style verse, because tones at 1b and 2b are both deflected rather than in opposition as we expect in a regulated verse form.

REGULATED VERSE: QUATRAIN

The following pentasyllabic quatrain, "On a Rainy Autumn Night," is by Ch'oe Ch'iwŏn, who returned to Silla in 874 after twelve years of study and sojourn in Tang China (see Chapter 4). The poem was probably written in his late teens while he was preparing for the Tang civil service examination:

		a b c d e
I only chant painfully in the autumn wind,	1.	秋風惟苦吟
For I have few friends in the wide world.	2.	世路少知音
At third watch, it rains outside.	3.	窓外三更雨
By the lamp my heart flies myriad miles away.	4.	燈前萬里心

While lines 1 and 2 do not match, lines 3 and 4 match grammatically and syntactically. One notes a contrast between outside and inside: outside the window and inside by the lamp; the third watch and a myriad tricents (translated as miles); and the rain outside and his heart inside. Graph 1d in deflected tone sounds important because of its position in the line. "Friends" in line 2d–e (*chiŭm*) refers to Zhong Ziqi (sixth century BC), who could tell the thoughts of Boya playing the zither. After Zhong died, Boya laid aside his zither and never played it again, for he had lost the one true friend who understood his music. A single rhyme occurs at the end of lines 1, 2, and 4 in the level tone. Parallelism in the second couplet engenders a rhetorical rhythm – a rhythm of thought. Despite the highly structured form with complex tonal pattern, the speaker skillfully expresses his innermost feelings by blending emotion and scenery.

The next poem, "Sending Off a Friend" by Chŏng Chisang (d. 1135), is an example of the heptasyllabic quatrain. Lines 1 and 2 do not match, and line 3 introduces a turn by posing a startling question. At first it appears unrelated to the first couplet, but line 4 reveals why this rhetorical question must be

---

[19] Richard Wilhelm, *The I Ching or Book of Changes*, trans. Cary F. Baynes, 2 vols. (New York: Pantheon Books, 1950) 1:316.

asked. Couched in terms of impossibility, it does not serve as a closure, but increases tension, especially because the line ends in the deflected tone. The purpose of the question is to pour out the enormity of the speaker's sorrow. Friendship transcends distance and vicissitudes, but the speaker must register the pain of separation. The poem observes the rule in second, fourth, and sixth positions (1–4b, d, f) as well as rhyme positions in lines 2 and 4. A departure from the rule in the first, third, and fifth positions is not considered a violation. End rhyme occurs in lines 1, 2, and 4 in the level tone (aaba):

a b c d e f g

After a rain on the long dike, grasses are thick.   1. 雨歇長堤草色多
With a sad song I send you off to South Cove.   2. 送君南浦動悲歌
When will Taedong River cease to flow?   3. 大同江水何時盡
Year after year my tears will swell the green waves.   4. 別淚年年添綠波

Both quatrains discussed here observe the standard tonal pattern of Tang "modern-style" poetry.

CI (ELEGY)

Yi Illo's (1152–1220) *ci* "Hwa kwigŏrae sa" harmonizing with Tao Qian's (365–427) "The Return" uses a line of from four to seven syllables that is broken twice in the middle and four times at the end of a line by the insertion of the meaningless particle pronounced in modern Chinese as *xi*.[20] The diction is dense with allusion – for example, to "Li Sao" ("Encountering Sorrow") by Qu Yuan (c. 340–278 BC), *Zhuangzi*, and *Liezi*. "Sanjung sa" ("In the Mountain") by Yi Saek (1328–1396) uses a line of six to eleven syllables, *xi* within or at the end of a line, and alliterating compounds.[21] In "Ae ch'usŏk sa" ("A Lament for an Autumn Evening"), Yi Sungin (1349–1392) uses a line of six to eight syllables with *xi* in the middle or at the end of a line.[22] In this lament the speaker holds an imaginary dialogue with the Jade Emperor and discusses the art of living according to his aspiration.

RHYMEPROSE

Thirty-five examples in the *Anthology* use lines of varying length, some with a prose preface. The diction is florid with extensive use of parallelism and antithesis, allusion, alliteration, assonance, repetition with slight variation, rhyme in every other line. It is descriptive, subjective, or philosophical. The speaker (the poet appears in the third person) in Yi Illo's "Oktang

[20] *TMS* 1:1a.   [21] *TMS* 1:1a–2a.   [22] *TMS* 1:7b–8b.

paek pu" ("Rhymeprose on the Cypress by the Hallim Academy") holds an imaginary dialogue with the tree.[23] In "Pangsŏn pu" ("Freeing the Cicada") by Yi Kyubo, the speaker again holds an imaginary dialogue with a passerby who blames him for starving the spider by freeing the cicada caught in the web.[24] The speaker retorts by saying that the spider is by nature covetous whereas the cicada feeding on dewdrops is clean – and ends with advice to the latter on the art of survival.

SONG WORDS (*CI*)

Because most Korean poets did not speak Chinese and either memorized the rhyme words or relied on the rhyming dictionary they carried in their sleeves, few ventured to write song words to intricate musical patterns. Dating from the eighth century in China and flourishing in the tenth and eleventh centuries, the form's features include prescribed rhyme, tonal sequence, and the use of varying length. "Yanggun kyŏn hwaujak" ("Again Harmonizing with My Two Friends") by Yi Kyubo is written to the tune "Ripples Sifting Sand" (*Langtaosha*).[25] Yi Chehyŏn (1287–1367), who knew spoken Chinese well, wrote "Ŭm maekchu" ("Drinking Barley Wine") to the tune "Partridge Sky" (*Zhugetian*) and composed "Songdo p'algyŏng" ("Eight Scenes of Kaesŏng") to the tune "A Stretch of Cloud over Mount Wu" (*Wushan yiduan yun*).[26]

YUEFU (MUSIC BUREAU) SONGS

The Music Bureau was a government office set up around 120 BC in Han China to collect anonymous folk songs, and gradually the term also began to designate the songs themselves. Later examples written by the literati in the style of such songs were also called music bureau songs, or ballads. These songs are often irregular in form with lines of varying length. The oldest examples were transmitted orally, and the form kept its musical origins with a simple diction free from allusion. Consider, for example, the four-line song the divine person asked the nine chiefs to sing in AD 42 to pray for the appearance of King Suro of Karak, "Song of Kuji" (see Chapter 2), or "Kong mudoha ka" ("Milord, Don't Cross the River") (also called "Konghu in" ['A Medley for the Harp']) attributed to the wife of a madman who drowned. Based on folk songs current in his day, Yi Chehyŏn wrote nine music bureau songs in heptasyllabic quatrain (see Chapter 6). Kim

[23] *TMS* 2:9a–10a. [24] *TMS* 1:5a–b. [25] *TYC* hujip (later collection) 5:4a.
[26] Yi Chehyon, *Ikchae nango* 10:2a–b and 10a–12a, in *Ikchae chip* (*KMC* 2).

Chongjik (1431–1492) wrote several ballads based on the oral narratives popular in the Kyŏngju area and was followed by such writers as Sim Kwangse (1577–1624), Im Ch'angt'aek (1683–1723), Yi Ik (1681–1763), and others.

FORMS AND PROSODY OF VERNACULAR POETRY

There are four major vernacular poetic forms in traditional Korea: *hyangga* (Silla songs; sixth to tenth centuries); *yŏyo* (Koryŏ songs, also called *sogyo*; eleventh to fourteenth centuries); *sijo* (fifteenth century to the present); and *kasa* (fifteenth to nineteenth centuries). Other poetic forms that flourished briefly include *kyŏnggi-ch'e* songs (fourteenth and fifteenth centuries; see Chapter 4), and the *akchang* (eulogies; fifteenth century). The most important *akchang* is the *Songs of Flying Dragons* (see Chapter 7). Most vernacular lyric is primarily addressed to the ear as song.

Hyangga

It is difficult to generalize the forms and prosody of Silla songs on the basis of extant examples. The four-line "P'ungyo" ("Ode to Yangji," c. 635) is in trimeter lines: 2/2/2; 2/2/2; 2/2/2; 2/3/2. "Ch'ŏyong ka" (Song of Ch'ŏyong, 879) scans as follows: 2/2/2; 3/4; 3/4; 3/4//2/4; 2/4; /2/5; and 3/5. The ten-line song "Ch'an Kip'arang ka" ("Ode to Knight Kip'a," c. 742–765) goes: 3; 3/2; 3/2/6; 4/4//5/3; 2/2/3; 2/5; 3/2/4//2 (interjection)/3/2; 5/3. This song, like all ten-line songs, begins the ninth line with an interjection. The syllable count and meter vary according to how one deciphers the text in *hyangch'al* orthography. Silla songs usually come with prose settings provided by the compiler Iryŏn, but at times he tries to imagine the context in which a song is composed or sung.

Koryŏ songs

Generally two forms are recognized in Koryŏ songs:[27]
Form 1:
1. Each metric segment in a line has two to four syllables, but commonly three.
2. Each line consists of three metric segments, but four segments are possible.
3. There is no set number of stanzas in a song.
4. The refrain occurs either in the middle or at the end of each stanza.

---

[27] Chŏng Pyŏnguk, *Chŭngbop'an Hanguk kojŏn siganon* (Singu munhwasa, 1999), pp. 110–111.

5. A song consists of several stanzas.

Form 2:

1. Each metric segment has two or three syllables, but mostly four.
2. Each line consists of either three or four segments, but four segments occur frequently.
3. There is no set number of stanzas in a song.
4. The refrain tends to disappear.
5. A song consists of several stanzas.

The refrains in some songs are meaningless onomatopoeia of the sounds of musical instruments or nonsense jingles: "au tongdong tari" in "Tongdong" ("Ode to the Seasons") and "yalli yalli yallasyŏng yallari yalla" in "Ch'ŏngsan pyŏlgok" ("Song of Green Mountain").

Sijo

Dating from the end of the fourteenth century, the regular or standard *sijo* is a three-line song generally said to have the following metric pattern:

$$3/4 \quad 4 \quad 3/4 \quad 4$$
$$3/4 \quad 4 \quad 3/4 \quad 4$$
$$3 \quad 5 \quad 4 \quad 3/4$$

Each line consists of four rhythmic groups, with a varying number of syllables in each group. In this book I shall call each rhythmic unit a metric segment, with a minor pause at the end of the second segment and a major pause at the end of the fourth. A deliberate twist or turn is introduced in the first metric segment in the third line. Yun Sŏndo, in his *sijo* sequence *Ŏbu sasisa* (*The Angler's Calendar*, 1651), introduces a different form (see Chapter 10). There are two other kinds of *sijo*: *ŏt sijo* has one or more syllables in all metric segments except for the first metric segment in the third line (an extra syllable to any metric segments in the third line is rare); *sasŏl sijo* is a form in which more than two metric segments in each line, except for the first in the third line, are added (see Chapter 10). The three-line *sijo* in the original is usually translated as a six-line poem – either all six lines flush left or the even-numbered lines indented to indicate that indented lines continue the nonindented line representing one line in the original (a matter of personal preference). In the past, however, all poetry whether in Chinese or in the vernacular was written or printed in vertical lines from top to bottom without punctuation. One can scan Chinese poetry by following the rhyme marking the line ends and by reading aloud the *sijo* following its prosody.

Kasa

Appearing in the fourteenth century, *kasa*'s features include a lack of stanzaic division, a tendency toward description and exposition (at times also lyricism), and the use of parallel phrases both verbal and syntactic. Its norm consists of two four-syllable words, or alternating three and four syllables, that form a unit and are repeated in parallel form. "Sangch'un kok" ("In Praise of Spring") by Chŏng Kŭgin (1401–1481) begins with a line of 3, 4, 4, and 4 metric segments and ends with a line of 3, 5, 4, and 4. (For more on different prosody used in the woman's and commoner's *kasa* see Chapter 11.)

FIGURATIVE LANGUAGE

On the level of sound, Korean poetry makes use of consonance, alliteration, and onomatopoeia, but not rhyme. Onomatopoeia includes phonomimes that mimic natural sounds, such as *tchiktchik* to depict the chirp of a bird, phenomimes that depict manners of the external world, such as *salsal* (gently), referring to the soft wind, and psychomimes depicting mental conditions or states, such as *mesŭkmesŭk* (feel sick). There are at least 4,000 examples of sound symbolism (ideophones), mostly used in reduplicated form, that function syntactically as adverbs.[28] Simile (stated comparison) and metaphor (implied comparison) function in Korean poetry as they do in Chinese and Japanese poetry. Examples of metaphoric transfer are: "Knight, you are the towering pine, / That scorns frost and ignores snow" in "Ode to Knight Kip'a," and "The mind is a moonlit autumn field" ("Eleven Devotional Songs," song 6 by Great Master Kyunyŏ). More explicit comparisons use "like" or "as": "I who have yearned for you and wept / Am like a bird in the hills" (by Chŏng Sŏ between 1151 and 1170), and "On a June day I am like / A comb cast from a cliff" ("Ode to the Seasons"). *Kasa* tends to make more use of stated comparison. In "Snowflakes flutter – butterflies chase flowers; / Ants float – my wine is thick" (Kim Yŏng, fl. 1776–1800), an implicit connection is drawn between two adjacent objects in a line, as in Li Bo's (701–762) "The moon descends, a flying heavenly mirror" ("Crossing at Jingmen: A Farewell"). Such connections seem to be based more on metonymic contiguity than true metaphoric substitution. In this sense, "truly extended tropes of comparison or substitution"[29] are rare in Korean poetry, and indeed in other East Asian poetry. When the Knight

---

[28] Ho-min Sohn, *The Korean Language*, pp. 96–102.
[29] Pauline Yu, "Metaphor and Chinese Poetry," *CLEAR* 3:2 (1981):217.

Kip'a is identified as a "towering pine," the pine is "an icon in a shared cultural code, an icon whose significance has already been established by tradition"[30] (see Chapters 3 and 7). Korean poetry draws its significance from its emblematic imagery, formulas, topics, and other rhetorical devices. Like Chinese and Japanese poets, the Korean poet usually sought out existing analogies and affirmed whatever correlations there were rather than striving to create new ones.

The interaction of speaker and audience is a characteristic of the *sijo* and other poetic genres. Sometimes the lyric speaker addresses a fictional character – like Petrarch's Laura. The role and ethos the speaker assumes is defined by convention, and recurring rhetorical situations often elicit standardized expectations and responses from the audience. The recurrence of certain topics, images, and themes indicates not only the poet's awareness of immediate concerns and audience preferences but also the mode of his composition. In an age that was intent upon the more perfect expression of what had been said before, originality was a confession of poverty, not a sign of wealth. While using the resources of other poets to reaffirm cultural values that engage the lively concerns of their audience, successful poets were able to find their own voice by a skillful use of poetic techniques at their disposal.

FAVORED TOPICS

Spring and autumn seem to have been the favored poetic seasons. Nature's spontaneous profusion, with a catalogue of seasonal images, is often the subject of spring poems – peach, plum, apricot, pear, green willows, and graceful birds flirting and singing. Cherry blossoms, so prominent in classic Japanese poetry as an ideal seasonal image, are absent. Autumn poems suggest the beauty of the season of dying as it lingers, passes, and finally gives way to the season of desolation and death. Nature is evoked for its metaphorical power to intensify a contrast or a parallel: bright moon, autumn wind, cold river, sleeping fish set against the sadness of absence and longing; a brief moment of worldly glory set against the autumnal beauty; the cry of a cricket or a goose as a symbol of the speaker's state of mind; a melancholy dusk; a lone traveler spending a sleepless night in a moonlit garden. Some identify autumn with the onset of old age and decay. The prevalence of autumn as the favorite season – as a mood and subject of

---

[30] Ibid., 219. Also see Michelle Yeh, "Metaphor and Bi: Western and Chinese Poetics," *Comparative Literature* 39:3 (1987):237–254.

poetry – and the deliberate cultivation of the dark and mysterious, the sad and veiled, the fleeting and intangible as the highest aesthetic ideals were responsible for autumn poems that fuse the "now" of summer's warmth and glory with the "then" of winter's cold and desolation in order to capture the "evanescence of a treasured now," the awful transition between being and nothingness.[31] There are few happy spring or autumn poems, however, because in spring we are reminded that our spring will never return and in autumn we are reminded of impending death. Some seasonal images that develop into topics in East Asian poetry seem to have grown on tradition rather than in nature.

There are, as well, poems on the happiness of rural retirement in both Chinese and Korean. Topics range from modest sufficiency (which appears metonymically in the form of a simple dwelling, vegetarian diet, homespun clothes, and uncomfortable bedding) to the cultivation of the True ("Can you fathom my joy?"), to the pleasant place remote in time and space (such as the first Chinese literary *locus amoenus*, Peach Blossom Spring), to mountains as positive images and the fisherman as sage. A conjunction of such images as the gentle breeze, aimless clouds, homing bird, flowing spring, trees and plants in the courtyard – especially pine, bamboo, and chrysanthemum – and a thatched roof girt with hills and waters – like grass, shade, and water in the topos of *locus amoenus* beginning with the seventh idyll of Theocritus – became the favorite device for indicating withdrawal from the active world, either in panegyrics to innocence, simplicity, and contentment or in polemical-satiric attacks on the hypocrisy of the court. It signals the acceptance of solitude as the only dramatic resolution of the perennial conflict between society and individual and as a fit metaphor of the landscape of the poet's regenerated mind. The retired scholar or poet-recluse is content to live in obscurity and poverty, the *sine qua non* of contemplative life. Poetry of praise addressed to a solitary recluse, Daoist or Buddhist, commends the subject for his rejection of worldly values in favor of a life of repose and contemplation in nature and final attainment of a complete harmony with nature – he is invisible, vanishing behind clouds and mist, occasionally leaving behind a footprint on a rock or the moss. Such homage, considered the highest praise, transmutes the subject into a symbol, a fragrance, and radiance. This topic seems to be better suited to poems in Chinese than in the vernacular. The poet's commitment to nature demands a commitment to the finality of death. Usually, however, the poet

---

[31] Peter H. Lee, *Celebration of Continuity: Themes in Classic East Asian Poetry* (Cambridge, Mass.: Harvard University Press, 1979), p. 59.

accepts the terror of discontinuity as "the ultimate homecoming," a return to the infinite flux. Whether our criterion is that of the distance between human beings and nature or that of people's willingness to adapt themselves to the natural world, Korean nature poetry allied with the discovery of the individual seeks to understand life in relation to the patterns of nature and the final acceptance of the human condition.

The tone of most love lyrics is retrospective. As a result, the pathos of separation and pangs of desertion rather than the pursuit of passion in the present – fulfillment and ecstasy – are recurrent themes. Such topics as courtship, the ladder of love, *carpe diem*, and *carpe florem* are almost neglected. The social position of women – and the Confucian morality in which passion is disruptive and unworthy of serious concern in refined literature – had a lasting impact on the development of love poetry in China and Korea. This explains, as well, the relative absence of praise of the woman's body (*blason*) and the elevation of the beloved's beauty as the manifestation of an inner perfection (hence no eternizing conceit). Seldom is love presented as ennobling or purifying; nor is it advanced as a mode of knowledge, spiritual development, or an analogue of divine love.[32] Most poets adopt an indirect, retrospective stance with an emphasis on parting, desertion, and neglect, and the resulting physical and mental anguish and dilemma ("odi et amo" [I hate and I love]; Catullus, song 85). Dream visions and metamorphoses are recurrent topics. Moving love lyrics were, however, produced by anonymous poets or women. Unlike the ladies in Latin love elegies and English sonnet sequences, in Korea it was women who conferred lasting fame on themselves. Time and again the speaker drives home the disjunction between peace in nature and turmoil in the heart. Indeed, the sadness of separation was thought to be more poetic than the satisfaction of fulfillment.

A number of poems on the topic of friendship can be found in Chinese. All learned men in Korea (as in China) aspired to official careers and were subjected to changes of fortune and policy. The speaker in propemptic poems either sends his friend off or himself takes leave of his friend on account of a new appointment, exile, withdrawal, or retirement – all characteristic patterns of the life of a civil servant. Such image clusters as flowing water, a solitary boat, lonely clouds, the setting sun, a long wind, the willow tree, and a cup of wine, with an emphasis on distance, gain resonance in a society where the moral, intellectual, and aesthetic values of friendship had a

---

[32] For a different view see Patrick M. Thomas, "The Troubadour, the Shaman, and the Palace Lady: The Crosscurrents of Desire," *Comparative Criticism* 18 (1996):127–153.

cultural force. Moreover, the vagaries of court life often led officials to return home as a gesture of moral protest, a renunciation of a worldly career,
or a return to nature. Parting, longing for the absent friend, dream visions,
and the joy of music and wine to celebrate a reunion are recurrent themes as
well. Called a "care-dispelling thing" that exorcises all our concerns, wine is
a symbol of release from anxiety, fear, change, chilly winds, or signs of snow.
Beautiful scenes of nature or feelings of zest call for wine and friends also.
The archetype of Korean drinkers is Li Bo and occasionally Liu Ling (c.
225–280) and Su Shi (1037–1101). The associated images of moon, flowers,
wine, music, and friend recall the Horatian ingredients of a banquet: wine,
rose blossoms, and perfume (*Odes* 3:3:13–16). Seasonal imagery plays an
important role in poems of parting and longing. In such poems, the "I will
follow you to the end of the world" topic is usually absent. The speaker,
however, in an effort to compliment his friend, sends him a painting of
autumn sound, a handful of moonlight, or nature itself.

Korean images of time are drawn mostly from nature – either to compare
the transient nature of human existence with the cycle of the seasons or
to drive home an ironic contrast between linear human existence and the
cyclical patterns of nature. Of these perhaps the most common emblem
is the dying flower that underscores the ephemeral character of all existence. The concept of time as transience also occurs through the images
of an unstable state of active life ruled by time, the ruins of monuments,
or the irreparable past. Time's relentless movement is represented by the
metaphor of the river – both as the context and condition of existence and
in its utter indifference to human enterprise. Such time imagery reflects
the Korean poet's conception of mortality in the world of temporality,
whether it is ruled by a Confucian heaven that controls cosmic order, human history, and personal events, by the Daoist's naturalistic Way, or by the
Buddhist's karmic retribution. The persistent mood is one of calm acceptance, but there is neither contempt for this world nor espousal of the other
world.

Nature offered moving metaphors not only of transience but of perma-
nence. Poets found consolation in contemplating the virtues of the pine
and chrysanthemum or the "four gentlemen": plum, orchid, bamboo, and
chrysanthemum, all of which figure prominently in East Asian poetry and
painting. Armed with the Daoist philosophy of nondiscrimination and the
utility of inutility (nonaction), poets were happiest when they contemplated harmony with nature or enjoyed the good life with friends. Friends
and wine can drive away care, northern winds, frost, and snow. A man
is not old if he can still enjoy flowers, laugh with friends, and exchange

cups. Indeed, what counts is the quality of life, the moments of experience, how one accepts change and embraces death. Above all, poets transcend time by their acts of celebration and by their faith in poetry. When a poet contemplates and communicates with the tradition, he places himself in a vital relation to past and future. His fidelity to the art, his allegiance to the tradition, is an act of transcending imperious time. Indeed, the poetic contemplation of the past is a means of combating oblivion, for the names and events of the past unsung will be lost and forgotten. As poets succeed poets and reaffirm the place of poetry in life, what they celebrate is the hope of poetry, a denial of mortality and change.

CHAPTER 2

From oral to written literature

Peter H. Lee

Korea too has a Paleolithic period. Indeed, some thirty Paleolithic excavations indicate that Stone Age people lived throughout the Korean peninsula. Whether the Korean people of today are ethnic descendants of these forest foragers (500,000–10,000 BC) is uncertain. These people lived in cave dwellings, hunted, fished, and gathered vegetation. That they used fire we know from the remains of a hearth found at a late Paleolithic site in midwestern Korea. They made hand axes, choppers, points, scrapers, and gravers by chipping stone, and sometimes they also used bone and horn. Late Paleolithic people made crude figurines as well, and carved decorations of dogs or fish.

The era characterized by simple undecorated pottery (6000 BC) and villages with semisubterranean dwellings has been called the Neolithic, or Early Villages, period (6000–2000 BC). Then came the pointed-bottom or rounded-base gray combware period (around 4000 BC) – incised pottery decorated on the exterior with geometric patterns – followed by flat-bottomed pottery, often with wave and thunderbolt designs.[1] The Early Villages people are not the former Paleolithic foragers but a new group of pottery producers from the north. Located mainly on river terraces or on the coast of the Eastern Sea and Yellow Sea in clusters, village sites contain pottery and chipped stone tools in or near semisubterranean dwellings heated by central hearths. At this time the major land animals were deer, boar, and antelope in the north and boar and dog in the south. These people lived by hunting, fishing, and shellfish gathering.[2] The village sites discovered on sandy riverbanks, spaced a few kilometers apart, are interpreted as agricultural villages with the clan as the basic unit rather than as simple hunting and fishing camps.[3] Excavated articles include stone hoes, stone sickles, stone mortars, pestles, grinding stones, and boar's-tusk sickles,

---

[1] Sarah M. Nelson, *The Archaeology of Korea* (Cambridge: Cambridge University Press, 1993), p. 58.
[2] Ibid., p. 98.   [3] Ibid., p. 103.

together with kernels of grain, mostly millet. The Early Villages practiced exogamy and chose their leaders from village chiefs.

The appearance of dolmens – above-ground constructions of large unmarked stones – and other megalithic monuments, together with coarse pottery ranging in color from buff to brown and ashy gray in a variety of shapes, began about 2000 BC. Now living mostly on hillsides, the Megalithic people cultivated foxtail millet, barley, sorghum, and rice (grains have been dated to 2400–2100 BC), and used semilunar stone knives to cut rice stalks. Villages and dolmens are usually found together.[4] Such bronze artifacts as daggers (some with geometric decoration), halberds, spearheads, and mirrors seem to indicate continuity between the combware people and Early Villages cultures.

Dolmen tombs were the burial sites of those who wielded power and authority in a stratified society and could mobilize large numbers of people to build hill forts and form small walled town-states, the earliest form of state structure in Korea. Items found in stone cist tombs and pit graves include stone artifacts and decorated spoons (in the north), burnished red vessels, tubular jades, bronze daggers, halberds, mirrors, socketed axes, some shamans' paraphernalia of bronze artifacts, beads for necklaces, comma-shaped beads, geometric twin-knobbed mirrors – all suggesting the existence of craft specialists. Pit graves in Choyangdong, Kyŏngju, yielded a glass bead "with a face on it from the Western world," pointing to long-distance trade.[5] Menhirs, or single standing megaliths, are sometimes arranged in a circle or in a shape like the Big Dipper. Round capstones and rectangular dolmen stones may symbolize heaven and earth respectively. Large panels of pecked rock drawings in southeastern Korea date from this period. Near Taegong-ni, such geometric patterns as spirals, circles, and lozenges decorate a large smooth rock, along with deer, reindeer, tigers, goats, wild boars, dogs, and cats as well as whales and dolphins. Several men in a boat or with weapons also appear.[6]

The iron culture of China and a bronze culture of Scytho-Siberian origins (as evinced in animal-shaped belt buckles) came to the Taedong River basin. An above-ground house would have required iron tools to make the planks for its ondol floors.[7] By the fourth century BC Old Chosŏn, which originally rose in the basins of the Liao and Taedong rivers, combined with other walled town-states and formed a single confederation with a king at its head. Old Chosŏn as a confederate kingdom coincided with the advent of the Iron Age by 400 BC, or earlier. Early leaders of Old Chosŏn were

---

[4] Ibid., pp. 38–159.   [5] Ibid., p. 198.   [6] Ibid., p. 154.   [7] Ibid., p. 164.

called Tangun Wanggŏm, both tribal chief and shaman, and claimed to be descendants of the Heavenly Ruler.

During the Early Villages period, the Dongyi tribes who lived in an area stretching from the Huai River, Shandong peninsula, southern Manchuria to the Gulf of Bohai, and the Korean peninsula were recipients of the Shang and Scytho-Siberian civilization – the latter influence arriving from Central Asia through northern China. The tribes' close ties with these civilizations helped them to form their own Bronze Age. In addition, those along the Huai and on the Shandong peninsula were in contact with civilization south of the Yangzi. Among the Dongyi were the Yemaek and Han tribes that constituted the original nucleus of the Korean people. In their eastward migration, these tribes absorbed or pushed out societies distinguished by their production of combware pottery and became the core of the undecorated pottery culture. Linguistically they are thought to have been a branch of the Tungusic tribes and thus to belong to the Altaic family. With agriculture as their economic basis, they absorbed the red pottery and black pottery cultures, thus building a broad foundation for their own civilization. With the fall of the Shang and the rise of the Zhou to the west, tribes migrated from along the Huai River and Shandong peninsula to southern Manchuria and the Korean peninsula. Those who reached the Taedong River basin merged with the inhabitants there and formed Old Chosŏn.

Those under Chinese control continued to have their tribal groups and maintained their bases until the end of the Warring States period (403–221 BC). The illustrations on the stone slabs in the Wu family shrine in Jiaxiang xian in Shandong, built in 147 BC, depict the content of the Tangun legend as recorded in the *Samguk yusa* (*Memorabilia of the Three Kingdoms*, 1285).[8] The superior bronze culture tribes of Old Chosŏn ruled over those who were still in the Early Villages state and tried to assert the authority of their tradition and elevate their own heritage. Consequently, the natives' worship of the gods of wind, rain, and clouds, together with their totemic belief in the bear and the tiger, gave way to the worship of the sun god. Among the oral narratives and primal songs of the peoples of ancient Korea, the Tangun legend is the oldest.

FOUNDATION MYTHS

Although they believed in the power and efficacy of language, ancient Korean singers of tales and songs wrote nothing down. Indeed, their works were not recorded until the advent of a literary culture based on written

---

[8] Chewon Kim, "Han Dynasty Mythology and the Korean Legend of Tangun," *Archives of Chinese Art Society of America* 3 (1948–1949):43–48.

Chinese. When written down, a song or a tale is subject to the writer's manipulation, distortion, and contamination according to his religious or cultural prejudice. Any Korean text that has come down to us was surely written by someone well-read in Chinese history and literature. We know little about the process by which the foundation myths and early songs were recorded. Did the singer dictate a tale or song to a scribe? Or did a scribe jot it down immediately after an oral performance? Or was it a reconstruction from memory by someone who knew something about the tradition? During the early history of Korean literature – say until the beginning of the twelfth century – more crucial than any suppression of oral traditions by a written tradition is the fact that much of what was committed to writing perished during internal disorders, dynastic wars, and foreign invasions. Later, however, with the rise of Confucianism and Neo-Confucianism in the Chosŏn dynasty, much of the oral tradition was driven underground and kept alive by shamans, peasant folk, and women.

Take, for example, the foundation myth of ancient Korea: the story of Tangun. The earliest surviving version is Great Master Iryŏn's account in his *Memorabilia of the Three Kingdoms*,[9] based on the *Weishu* (*History of Wei*), an otherwise unidentifiable text, and the *Kogi* (*Old Record*) – probably referring to the *Ku samguk sa* (*Old History of the Three Kingdoms*), now lost but read by Yi Kyubo when he composed the "Lay of King Tongmyŏng" (1193), a tale of the founding of Koguryŏ. About the compilers and the date of compilation of the *Old Record* we know nothing. Consider also another example: a tale about Suro, the founder of Karak. Because of its early demise in the sixth century, Karak (Kaya) did not leave any records of its own. Again Iryŏn quotes the oldest and most detailed extant account concerning Karak's founder from *Karakkuk ki* (*Record of the State of Karak*), compiled in the late eleventh century by a magistrate of Kŭmgwan (modern Kimhae), the principal state of the Kaya federation. Iryŏn's account, however, represents an abridged version.[10] No matter who the first scribe might have been, no matter what might have been lost in the process of translation and transmission, without men like Iryŏn throughout the history of Korean literature, writing this chapter would not have been possible.

The *Weishu* tells us that 2,000 years ago, at the time of Emperor Yao, Tangun Wanggŏm chose Asadal as his capital and founded the state of Chosŏn. Hwanung's descent betokens a migration of the people of Old Chosŏn to the Taedong River basin. He brought three heavenly seals – the symbols of the shaman-king's authority and power – that might have been bells, a sword, and a mirror, objects commonly used by the contemporary

---

[9] *SGYS* 1:33–34.   [10] *SGYS* 2:108–120.

shaman in ritual ceremony. Hwanung descended upon the tree by the divine altar: the tree of life and country that connects heaven and earth and where the gods of mountain and agriculture reside. Each clan or tribe had its own guardian deity, and the origin of such a deity was sung or narrated by a shaman, the voice and memory of the community. Tangun, the son of Hwanung and a she-bear, was the first ruler of the age of theocracy. Looked upon as a messenger between the spirit world and the material world, Tangun was a spiritual representative of his people – embodying the qualities that his people prized most – and the well-being of the social and natural orders depended on his vitality and wisdom. That the ruler of Puyŏ was either killed or replaced if the harvest was bad indicates the crucial role played by such shaman representatives.[11]

The beginning of a tribal federation on the Korean peninsula, though undeveloped, may be seen in the union of Old Chosŏn, Wiman Chosŏn (which fell in 108 BC), and the Chin state in the south. When a strong tribe rose up as a leader as in Puyŏ and Koguryŏ, federations quickly established their power, while the Ye and the Three Han, which suffered pressure from nearby Chinese colonies, were comparatively slow in development. Skilled in cattle breeding and agriculture, the peoples of Puyŏ and Koguryŏ were also horse riders with strong mobility and combat capability; the people in the south, by contrast, were sedentary. The migrants from the north at the time of the demise of Old Chosŏn stimulated the indigenous society in the south by disseminating iron culture and enlarging the economic base through active trade among tribes and the fusion of cultures. These stimulated the reorganization of clans and finally the formation of tribal federations in the south.

The foundation myth of Koguryŏ, as recorded in King Tongmyŏng's story, is not a myth of the world's creation, but one of migration, with vestiges of the tradition transmitted from Old Chosŏn. That the founders of Paekche were a group of migrants from the Puyŏ family is attested by a number of sources.[12] How the iron-culture migrants joined with the natives there to build a state is told in the story of Pak Hyŏkkŏse and Kim Alchi. The Sŏk clan arrived next, and the tribal federation comprising Pak, Sŏk, and Kim ensued.

---

[11] *SKC* 30:842.
[12] They include the letter sent to the Northern Wei by King Kaero; the name of the state, South Puyŏ, given by King Sŏng after transferring his capital to Sabi; Puyŏ as the clan name of the Paekche king; and Chinese accounts starting from the *Weishu*. The protagonist of the legends, however, varies: Onjo and Puryu in *SGSG*; Kudae in Linghou Defen, *Zhoushu*, 3 vols. (Peking: Zhonghua, 1971); Tomo in Sugano no Mamichi et al., *Shoku Nihongi*, ed. Aoki Kazuo et al., 6 vols. (Tokyo: Iwanami shoten, 1989–2000) (41). Of these, the account in *SGSG* is most detailed.

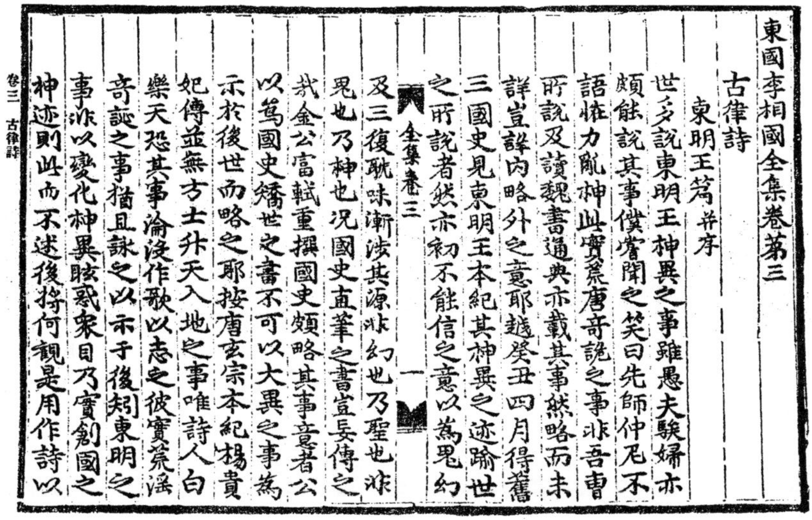
東國李相國全集卷第三
古律詩
東明王篇 并序
世多說東明王神異之事雖愚夫騃婦亦
頗能說其事僕嘗聞之笑曰先師仲尼不
語怪力亂神此實荒唐奇詭之事非吾曹
所說及讀魏書通典亦載其事然略而未
詳豈詳內略外之意耶越癸丑四月得舊
三國史見東明王本紀其神異之迹踰世
之所說者然亦初不能信之意以為鬼幻
全集卷三 一
及三復耽味漸涉其源非幻也乃聖也非
鬼也乃神也況國史直筆之書豈妄傳之
哉金公富軾重撰國史頗略其事意者公
以為國史矯世之書不可以大異之事為
示於後世而略之耶按唐玄宗本紀楊貴
妃傳並無方士升天入地之事唯詩人白
樂天恐其事淪沒作歌以志之彼實荒淫
奇誕之事猶且詠之以示于後矧東明之
事非以變化神異眩惑衆目乃實創國之
神迹則此而不述後將何觀是用作詩以
卷三 古律詩

記之欲使夫天下知我國本聖人之都耳
元氣判沌渾天皇地皇氏十三十一頭體貌多
奇異其餘聖帝王亦備載經史女節感大星乃
生大昊摯女樞生顓頊亦感瑤光暐伏羲制牲
犧燧人始鑽燧生蓂高帝祥雨粟神農瑞青天
女媧補洪水大禹理黃帝將升天胡髯龍自至
太古淳朴時靈聖難備記後世漸澆漓風俗例
汰侈聖人間或生神迹少所示漢神雀三年孟
夏斗立巳 漢神雀三年四月甲寅 海東解慕漱真是天之
子 本記云夫余王解夫婁老無子祭山川求嗣所御馬至鯤淵見大石流淚王怪之使人轉
全集卷三 二
其石有小兒金色蛙形王曰此天錫我令胤乎乃收養之名曰金蛙立為太子其相阿蘭弗曰日者天降我曰將使吾子孫立國於此汝其避之東海之濱有地號迦葉原土宜五穀可都阿蘭弗勸王移都號東夫余於舊都解慕漱為天帝子來都 初從空中下身
乘五龍軌從者百餘人騎鵠紛襂襹清樂動鏘
洋彩雲浮旖旎 漢神雀三年壬戌歲天帝遣太子降遊扶余王古都號解慕漱從天而下乘五龍車從者百餘人皆騎白鵠彩雲浮於上音樂動雲中止熊心山經十餘日始下首戴烏羽之冠腰帶龍光之劍 自古受命君何是非天賜白
日下青冥從昔所未睹朝居人世中暮反天宮
裡 朝則聽事暮即升天世謂之天王郎 吾聞於古人蒼穹之去地
二億萬八千七百八十里梯棧躡難升羽翮飛

Example 2. Yi Kyubo (1169–1214), beginning of "Lay of King Tongmyŏng." *Collected Works of Minister Yi of Korea* (1251) 3:1a–2b.

According to "The Lay of King Tongmyŏng" by Yi Kyubo (1169–1214),[13] in his travels between heaven and earth, Haemosu, the "son of the heavenly emperor," espies the three daughters of the River Earl. With a riding whip he traces the foundations and creates a bronze palace, where he flirts with Willow Flower (Yuhwa), the Earl's eldest daughter. Angrily the River Earl reprimands Haemosu for breaking the proper ritual for a union and challenges him to a duel of transmogrification. The Earl, however, loses the contest – as a carp, pheasant, and stag he is overpowered by Haemosu's transformations into an otter, eagle, and wolf – and acknowledges Haemosu's divinity. A fisherwoman spots Yuhwa abandoned by her father and reports the matter to King Kŭmwa. Kŭmwa recognizes her as Haemosu's wife and gives her a palace to live in. It is there that she is impregnated by sunlight and gives birth to an egg:

> He was born from a pottle-sized egg
> That frightened all who saw it.
> The king thought it inauspicious,
> Monstrous and inhuman,
> And put it into the horse corral,
> But the horses took care not to trample it;
> It was thrown down steep hills,
> But the wild beasts all protected it;
> Its mother retrieved it and nurtured it,
> Till the boy hatched. His first words were:
> "The flies are nibbling my eyes,
> I cannot lie and sleep in peace."
> His mother made him a bow and arrows,
> And he never missed a shot.

Puyŏ's crown prince is jealous of the valor and prowess of Chumong (the founder of Koguryŏ), forces him to tend horses, and conspires to kill him. For heaven's grandson to tend horses is "unbearable shame," but it is a trial – a test of fortitude and perseverance. Chumong resolves:

> I had rather die than live like this.
> I would go southward,
> Found a nation, build a city –
> But for my mother,
> Whom it is hard to leave.

His loving mother, however, urges him on and finds him a "beautiful bay," which becomes his trusted friend. The pursuing enemy close behind,

---

[13] *TYC* 3:2a–8a.

Chumong and his party are able to cross the Ŏm River by wondrous means:

> Gripping his bow, he struck the water:
> Fishes and turtles hurried, heads and tails together,
> To form a great bridge,
> Which the friends at once traversed.
> Suddenly pursuing troops appeared
> And mounted the bridge; but it melted away.
> A pair of doves brought barley in their bills,
> Messengers sent by his mysterious mother.

Chumong then chooses the site for his capital, becomes king of his people, and subdues the king of Piryu, Songyang.

Chumong – like Suro and T'arhae[14] – is portrayed as embodying in his own person the struggles and trials of his people. By persevering, Chumong overcomes his initial hardships and grows confident of his fate. Heaven shows its concern in his destiny and answers his prayers first by causing fishes and turtles to form a bridge – thereby reducing the tension of danger – and then by sending a flood to drown Piryu (Songyang's state). Although the introduction of the supernatural is intended as divine testimony, it can also be said to diminish the hero's valor and glory.[15]

By emphasizing the solitary nature of Chumong's task, the song chooses only the most moving and memorable events. Motifs (floating intercultural narrative elements) from traditional hero stories and folktales are fused in this and other foundation myths discussed here, but the origin of the tales is in history, and they have a religious and social basis. The quest motif is prominent – for example, Chumong founds the state of Koguryŏ and T'arhae becomes the progenitor of the Sŏk clan which produced eight rulers of Silla. Such motifs as miraculous birth, divine intervention, the exposed child, and a descent into the underworld (the trials of the bear in the myth of Tangun; T'arhae's seven-day isolation in a cave) adorn the narrative of the hero's life.

BIOGRAPHICAL PATTERNS OF HEROES

All of the ancient mythic Korean heroes are born from an egg (a source of life and a symbol of the sun, which is an emblem of royalty), and all except T'arhae can claim divine paternity. Chumong, the son of Haemosu and a

---

[14] *SGYS* 1:47–48.
[15] For the concept of fate in fiction, especially in epic, see James Redfield, *Nature and Culture in the Iliad* (Chicago: University of Chicago Press, 1975), p. 133.

daughter of the River Earl, is born from a "pottle-sized egg"; Hyŏkkŏse,[16] from a red egg in the shape of a gourd, hence his surname Pak, which means "gourd" in Korean; T'arhae from a huge egg in a casket set adrift on the waters, a recurrent motif in shamanist songs. The birth of each hero is usually celebrated by people and nature alike. The hero's size and awesome appearance, and by implication strength, are emphasized: T'arhae was nine feet seven inches in height and Suro was nine feet tall. Chumong's "form was wonderful, / His voice of mighty power." He was a supreme archer, as his name indicates (Chumong means "excellent archer" according to the Chinese source), and he could "split a jade ring." The size of his weapon is not mentioned, however, nor is there a description of his horse, the most important animal for the warrior in the heroic age. There was also a cult of Chumong (also written Ch'umo; King Tongmyŏng) and his mother Yuhwa. Their images were enshrined and worshipped with a shamanist ceremony. It is said that when Koguryŏ was destroyed by the Tang army, the image of Tongmyŏng's mother shed tears of blood for three days.[17] She was not only the goddess of earth and agriculture but the guardian of Koguryŏ as well.

KOREANS' LOVE OF SONG AND DANCE

The religious life of the peoples of Puyŏ, Koguryŏ, and Ye in the north and those of Mahan, Pyŏnhan, and Chinhan in the south is vividly recorded first in the *Weizhi* in the *Sanguozhi* (*History of the Three Kingdoms*, compiled 285–297), followed by the *Hou Hanshu* (*History of the Later Han*, compiled 398–445). The following descriptions appear in the *History of the Wei* and *History of the Later Han*:

> Puyŏ
> When, in the first month according to the Yin
> calendar, there is a great assembly in the
> state, they eat and drink, dance and sing for
> days on end. Such occasions are called *yŏnggo*
> ("Welcoming drums"). Old and young, they all sing when walking
> along the road whether it be day or night;
> all day long the sound of their voices never ceases.[18]

> Koguryŏ
> In the tenth month they sacrifice to heaven in a
> national assembly called *tongmaeng* ("Dawn").
> Their people delight in singing and dancing. In villages

[16] *SGYS* 1:43–45.　　[17] *SGSG* 21:98.　　[18] *SGZ* 30:841; also in *HHS* 85:2811.

throughout the state, men and women gather in groups at nightfall for communal singing and games.[19]

Ye
They always use the festival of the tenth month to worship heaven. Drinking, singing, and dancing day and night, they call this [assembly] *much'ŏn* ("Dancing to heaven").[20]

Mahan
In the fifth month, when the sowing has been finished, they always sacrifice to their ghosts and spirits. Coming together in groups they sing and dance; they drink wine day and night without ceasing. In their dancing, scores of men get up together and form a line; looking upward and downwards as they stomp the ground, they move hands and feet in concert with a rhythm that is similar to our Chinese bell-clapper dance. When the farmwork is finished in the tenth month they perform a similar ceremony.[21]

Pyŏnhan
By custom they take delight in singing, dancing, and drinking. They have a stringed zither (*se*) shaped like our bamboo zither (*zhu*).[22]

Chinhan
The people delight in singing, dancing, and drinking wine. They have a drum and a stringed zither (*se*).[23]

What struck the Chinese above all was the Korean peoples' love of singing and dancing. Puyŏ's *yŏnggo* in the first month, Koguryŏ's *tongmaeng* and Ye's *much'ŏn* in the tenth month, and Mahan's ceremonies in the fifth and tenth months were national assemblies when the high and low worshipped heaven, invoked gods and spirits, offered thanksgiving for a good harvest, and prayed for continued prosperity and protection. The narrative chanted or sung by a chief officiating shaman told the story of the divine origin of the founder and his extraordinary deeds in war and peace. Even today on Cheju Island a shamaness chants the origin of a village god. Recited narrative was interspersed with primal songs (*norae*) that not only welcomed, entertained, and bid farewell to gods and spirits but also seemed to set all nature dancing in harmony. In these assemblies, song, music, and dance were inseparable.

---

[19] *SGZ* 30:844; *HHS* 85:2812.   [20] *SGZ* 30:849.   [21] *SGZ* 30:852; *HHS* 85:2819.
[22] *HHS* 85:2819.   [23] *SGZ* 30:853.

POWER OF PRIMAL SONGS

The first recorded short song used as a means of incantation occurs in the first century AD. In the section on the Karak state in the *Memorabilia of the Three Kingdoms*, we are told that during the third month of the year 42, 9 chiefs and 200 or 300 people climbed Mount Kuji to greet the sovereign, dug a hole at the summit, and sang in joy the "Kuji ka" ("Song of Kuji"). The purpose of the incantation was to pray for the descent of King Suro. Iryŏn's account reads:

They [the people] and their nine chiefs heard the voice but could not see the speaker.
The voice asked, "Is anyone here?"
The chiefs replied, "Yes."
"Where is this place?"
"This is Kuji."

The voice continued:

Heaven commanded me to come here to found a country and be your king, so I have come. Dig the earth on the peak, sing this song, and dance with joy to welcome your great king:

> O turtle, O turtle.
> Show your head!
> If you do not,
> We'll roast you and eat you.[24]

"Show your head" in line 2 gave rise to the king's name, Suro, meaning "showed his head." The turtle, according to one reading, symbolizes life. A threat to roast the turtle, which usually lives in the water, was intended to urge it to make strenuous efforts to appear. The whole tone is coercive, but it worked. There is another title for this song, "Yŏng singun ka" ("Song of Welcoming the Divine Lord"). This song, or spell, was not composed in writing, but it comes to us transcribed into Chinese. Its original form can never be known. It was probably sung by a nameless and unlettered shaman, yet the present written version is also powerful, moving, and alive.

The "Song of Kuji" was probably not itself an independent song but part of a larger piece. Some fragments known as the "Song of Kuji" appear again in the "Haega" ("Song of the Sea"), this time sung by the common people when Lady Suro was abducted by a dragon in the early eighth century. The lady is the wife of Lord Sunjŏng, on his way at the time to his post as governor of Kangnŭng:

[24] *SGYS* 2:108–109.

After two days, the lord's party was again lunching at the Imhae Arbor when the sea dragon suddenly emerged and kidnapped [Lady] Suro to his underwater abode. The lord stamped his feet but could not devise any plan for her rescue. Again an old man appeared and said, "An old saying has it that many mouths can melt even iron. Even the sea monster is bound to be afraid of many mouths. Gather the people from the area, compose a song, and strike a hill with sticks. Then you will regain your wife."

The lord followed his advice, and the dragon reappeared and returned the lady. When the lord asked his wife about the bottom of the sea, she replied: "The food at the Palace of the Seven Jewels is delicious, fragrant and clean, unlike our own." Her dress exuded a strange perfume hitherto unknown in the world of men. Being of peerless beauty, Suro would find herself snatched away by divine beings whenever she traveled through deep mountains and along large lakes.

The song sung by the people goes:

> O turtle, turtle, release Suro!
> How grave the sin of taking another's wife!
> If you go against our will,
> We'll catch you in a net and roast and eat you.[25]

While the singer of the "Song of Kuji" was a shaman, the people who sang the "Song of the Sea" were not. As time passed, apparently, a song using threats to achieve one's wishes could be used by anyone on any occasion.

Judging from the primal songs sung at the great national assemblies and the example of the "Song of Kuji" recorded in writing, the quality of the earliest Korean poetry was religious or magical. Its norm was probably a few lines of simple language, often followed by a refrain. The language was incantatory, rich in its associative power and in its rhythm and melody. It exerted a binding effect not only upon men but on gods and spirits as well. It was, first of all, a means of communication between gods and mortals. The magical power of poetry was accepted to such an extent that it was supposed to please the gods, help avoid natural calamities, bring rain and stop the winds, and promote recovery from diseases. The ancient Chinese idea of poetry was essentially similar. A good example can be found in Emperor Shun's statement – supposed to have been made when he directed his master of music Kui to gather the songs in current use – that spirits and men might be brought into harmony by poetry.[26] Furthermore, Chinese sources affirm that the same view about the function of poetry was held

---

[25] *SGYS* 2:79.
[26] James Legge, *The Chinese Classics*, 5 vols. (Hong Kong: Hong Kong University Press, 1960), 3:47–49.

by ancient Koreans: Korean music, with its bright spirit, was said to have helped the growth of all relationships between heaven and earth. Thus this ancient people realized the magical power of song and treated it with reverence. Their society was tribal and patriarchal, and their life was lived in terms of communal value and significance. Poetry, music, and dance, the three vital elements in their religious service, were inseparable and indispensable. Without historical records, it is impossible to present a full and systematic picture of the earliest Korean poetry; the artistic life of ancient Koreans and their popular songs are lost. What little record we have, however, does show us that their poetry was a folk art which grew naturally from the life of the time and that it dealt mainly with communal wishes and prayers.

Two other recorded songs, however, seem to suggest certain important changes in their poetic development. The circumstances surrounding the composition of one of them, "Konghu in" ("A Medley for the Harp"), are as follows. Early one morning a ferryman witnessed a strange sight: a madman, gray hair flowing about, was crossing the river, clutching a wine bottle. His wife followed after him and tried to stop him, but he continued on his way and finally fell in halfway across and drowned. The wife then sang a song, "Milord, Don't Cross the River," to the accompaniment of the harp. Her mournful song over, she jumped into the river and died. Upon returning home, the ferryman told the story to his wife. She too sang the song, plucking the harp, and spread it among her neighbors.[27] The song laments a madman's death, and there are debates over who he was and why he died. One reading proposes that he was a shaman who drowned himself in a trance. Perhaps he had lost his shamanic powers and hence his authority. Other questions were debated as well. Was the author of the song the wife of the madman or Yŏok, the wife of the ferryman, Kwangni Chago? Is Kwangni Chago a Chinese or a Korean national (most likely from Koguryŏ)? Is the place referred to along the Taedong River or in Liaodong? In its present version, the song exists in a tetrasyllabic quatrain, recalling the anonymous folk songs in the Chinese *yuefu* (Music Bureau):

> Milord, don't cross the river,
> Milord after all crosses it.
> He falls into the river and dies.
> What can I do for Milord?

---

[27] Guo Maoqian, *Yuefu shiji* (Peking: Zhonghua, 1979), 26:377–378. For a study of this song see Yingxiong Zhou, "Lord, Do Not Cross the River," pp. 109–126.

A third song, the "Hwangjo ka" ("Song of Orioles"), supposedly composed in 17 BC, is attributed to King Yuri (19 BC – AD 18), the second king of Koguryŏ and son of King Tongmyŏng (Chumong). The circumstances of its composition are provided by the *Historical Records of the Three Kingdoms*:

> When, in the tenth month, his queen, nee Song, died, he took two women as his secondary wives: Lady Hwa, the daughter of a man of Kolch'ŏn, and Lady Ch'i, the daughter of a Chinese. The two were jealous of one another and quarreled, and so the king had two palaces, east and west, built in Yang Valley to house them. When the king went hunting on Mount Ki and did not return for seven days, the two ladies quarreled again. Lady Hwa abused Lady Ch'i, saying, "As a lowly slave from a Chinese family, your discourtesy is unbearable." Lady Ch'i, ashamed and indignant, ran away. The king whipped his horse and pursued her, but she refused to return.
>
> One day, while he was resting under a tree, the king happened to see a flock of orioles gather. He sang:
>
>> Flutter, flutter, orioles,
>> Male and female, in pairs.
>> How lonely I am;
>> With whom shall I return?[28]

It is generally accepted that the song cannot be attributed to King Yuri, who is somewhat shrouded in mystery, but is rather a song of wooing among the young men and women of the time, reminiscent of courtship lyrics in the *Book of Songs*.

These last two songs move the reader because their central concerns are universal emotions sung in literature: sorrow over the death of a loved one and the pangs of love and loneliness from separation, respectively. These songs were composed and sung by an individual. Assuming that the Chinese written version reproduced the original syntax and form faithfully, the texts' paratactic structure and symmetry indicate that the authors arranged words differently from ordinary speech. These songs can be considered literature.

---

[28] *SGSG* 13:220.

CHAPTER 3

Hyangga

Peter H. Lee

The first record of Silla songs occurs in the *Historical Records of the Three Kingdoms*, though the *Memorabilia of the Three Kingdoms* adds more information. When King Yuri (24–57), the third king of Silla, made an inspection tour of the country in the eleventh month, AD 28, he happened to see an old woman dying of hunger and cold in the open. He reproached himself saying that it was his fault if the old and the young had so little to eat and were suffering to such an extreme. After covering the old woman with his own coat and giving her food, he ordered the civil authorities to seek out those who could not provide for themselves – the widowers and widows, the destitute, the old and the sick – in order to give them food and shelter. When they heard this story, many people from the neighboring provinces came to Silla to praise the king. That year the grateful people composed the "Tosol ka."[1]

Earlier, "Tosol ka" was read as "Tonnorae" or "T'ŏnorae," but now the more plausible reading "Turinnorae" has been proposed.[2] *Turi* is a cognate of such words as "peace" (or "peaceful"), "content," "repose," and "happy"; hence the term means "song of peace and repose." To say that this is the first vernacular song and music of Silla does not mean there were no songs in Silla before this period. It merely indicates that the establishment of a new kind of song – more individual and lyrical than religious and communal – begins with the "Turinnorae." In 760, Master Wŏlmyŏng composed a song with the same title.[3] Hence the term refers to a poetic genre, although the context of Wŏlmyŏng's song enables one to render the title as the "Song of Tuṣita Heaven," for the song prays for the advent of Maitreya (the future Buddha who resides in Tuṣita Heaven) on earth.

Making reference to the same song, the *Memorabilia of the Three Kingdoms* comments that the song is in the *ch'asa sanoe* style (*kyŏk*).[4] If the

---

[1] *SGSG* 1:5.   [2] Chŏng Pyŏnguk, *Hanguk kojŏn siganon*, p. 79.   [3] *SGYS* 5:222–223.
[4] *SGYS* 1:46.

ch'asa refers to interjections, then its form resembles the ten-line *hyangga*, the ninth line of which begins with an interjection. Because, however, the song is described as the first new music accompanied by song, *ch'asa* might have been a kind of refrain used to keep time with the music. That *sanoe* is a comprehensive term covering many songs is indicated when King Kyŏngdŏk, in a conversation with Master Ch'ungdam, refers to the "Ode to Knight Kip'a," one of the ten-line *hyangga*, as a *sanoe* song.[5] Great Master Kyunyŏ (923–973) refers to his eleven devotional songs with the same term, as does the translator of his songs into Chinese, Ch'oe Haenggwi ("The songs are called *sanoe*").[6] The biographer of the Great Master Kyunyŏ also glosses *sanoe* by saying: "It is called *noe* because its meaning is more refined than its diction."[7] *Sanoe ka* means vernacular song and covers both the "Turinnorae" and twenty-five other songs transcribed in the *hyangch'al* system. The name *sanoe ka* was translated into Chinese as *hyangga* – meaning vernacular song as opposed to poetry written in literary Chinese – and it is by this name that these songs have subsequently been known.

In his preface to the Chinese translation of Great Master Kyunyŏ's devotional songs, Ch'oe Haenggwi underscores the difference between poetry written in Chinese and Korean songs written in the vernacular: "The sounds of Chinese and Korean poetry are as far apart as Orion and Antares."[8] Kyunyŏ and Ch'oe Haenggwi are aware of the linguistic differences between Chinese and Korean – the literary and the colloquial. The fundamental difference between Chinese poetry – or poetry written in literary Chinese – and Korean poetry is brought home by the way in which vernacular poetry was designated. While the Chinese graph for poetry, *shi* (*si* in Korean), was reserved for poems written in literary Chinese, poetry written in the vernacular was called *ka* (*norae*), meaning "song." The latter term emphasizes orality, the vibrant relation between poet and audience and between poetry and music. Indeed, all terms for native poetic genres in Korea (and Japan) contain the same graph for song (*ka*) and its cognate.

Like all subsequent vernacular poetic forms in Korea, the *hyangga* (native songs) were sung. The forms and styles of Korean poetry therefore reflect its melodic origins. The basis of its prosody is a line consisting of metric segments of three or four syllables, the rhythm most natural to the language. In the ten-line *hyangga*, the ninth line usually begins with an interjection that indicates heightened emotions, a change in tempo and pitch, and also the song's conclusion. Musical notations indicate that the

---

[5] *SGYS* 2:80.   [6] *Kyunyŏ chŏn*, in *SGYS*, Appendix, p. 59.   [7] Ibid.   [8] Ibid., p. 63.

musical divisions of each popular Koryŏ song, signaled by an interjection followed by a refrain, are different from its poetic (stanzaic) divisions. Later in Korean literary history, the interjection preceding a refrain in Koryŏ songs or *akchang* (eulogies) may have developed into the first word in the last line of the *sijo*, where it appears as an interjection or form of address that indicates a shift to subjectivity. Furthermore, the association – if not to say identity – of verbal and musical rhythms can be seen in the refrain of Koryŏ songs. Nonsense jingles or onomatopoetic representations of the sounds of such musical instruments as the drum, gong, or double-reed oboe attest to the refrain's musical origins and function.

The musical aspect may be cited here not so much as a categorical principle of the lyric, but as one of its structural and dramatic devices. The singer is the lyric persona, the performer, and the interpreter. If the poet happens to sing his own song, he assumes the multiple role of composer and singer, poet and persona. The distance between the poet and his persona also determines his relationship with the audience. This relationship is essentially dramatic; using masks, the singer assumes different roles, much as the poet speaks through his personae. When the speaker addresses an explicitly fictional character, his fictive interlocutor mediates between the author and the speaker on the one hand and the audience on the other, significantly affecting the audience's response. The poet or singer presents a verbal artifact – a poem – that is validated whenever it finds an audience versed in traditional norms and conventions. The making of such verbal artifacts is thus a collective enterprise involving the poet, the singer, and the audience.

Hyangga designates Korean songs, but it refers specifically to the twenty-five extant songs produced between the seventh and tenth centuries. A collection of *hyangga*, entitled *Samdaemok* (*Collection of Three Periods*), compiled in 888 by Monk Taegu and Prime Minister Wihong during the reign of Queen Chinsŏng (887–897), is now lost.[9] In the absence of a native system of writing, the Koreans devised the *idu* system to facilitate the reading of Chinese texts by providing particles and inflections. The system used in the *hyangga*, however, is the *hyangch'al* orthographic system, in which Chinese graphs are used phonetically and semantically to represent the sounds of Old Korean, much like the Japanese *Man'yōgana* system. Some graphs were used for their meaning (mostly nouns), while others transcribed verbs, particles, and inflections. While the *idu* is said to have been systematized by Sŏl Ch'ong, the son of Great Master Wŏnhyo, the

---

[9] *SGSG* 11:119.

creator of the *hyangch'al* system is not known. The transcription of *hyangga* into Chinese graphs for sound and sense preserved the extant songs but made them inaccessible to, for example, the Chinese of the time and today present great difficulties for modern philologists trying to decipher them. Ch'oe Haenggwi comments:

What is regrettable is that while talented and renowned Koreans can appreciate Chinese poetry, scholars and sages in China cannot understand our native poetry. Furthermore, while Chinese graphs lie spread out like Indra's net and are easy for Koreans to read, sinographs in the Korean style of transcription, the *hyangch'al*, run together as in a Sanskrit book and are difficult for the Chinese to decipher. Though Chinese works from the Liang and Liu Sung, as fine as round and square pieces of jade, have reached Korea, the songs of Silla, as beautiful as embroidered brocade, are seldom transmitted to China. This is regrettable indeed![10]

On the basis of the surviving songs, we may say that there are three forms: a stanza of four lines; two stanzas of four lines; and two stanzas of four lines plus a stanza of two lines. The first form is the simplest and accounts for four of the twenty-five extant works. Nursery rhymes, children's songs, and folk songs retain this simple form, which is easy to sing and memorize. The second form evinces a middle state in the *hyangga*'s structural development and occurs three times. The third is the most polished and popular form and appeared toward the end of the sixth century. It has two stanzas of four lines, that introduce and develop the main theme, and a stanza of two lines, in the form of wishes, commands, or exclamations, that summarize a thought developed in the song. This last stanza constitutes a conclusion to the song, at times in sophisticated manner, and has an epigrammatic quality that makes it memorable and quotable. Structurally the ninth line begins with an interjection that is indicated variously, but is reconstructed throughout the *hyangga* as *aya* (Ah!). (*Ayayo* occurs once and conveys the same sense.)[11]

Now a word about the difficulty of deciphering *hyangch'al* orthography. Thanks to the efforts of scholars, we can now make general sense of twenty-five song texts. Problems still exist, however. The small number of extant

[10] *Kyunyŏ chŏn*, p. 63.
[11] On the other hand, referring to the form of *hyangga*, Ch'oe Haenggwi comments: "Their [Chinese] poetry is written in Chinese in penta- and heptasyllabic lines. Our songs are written in the vernacular in three-line stanzas of six phrases each." His "three-line stanzas of six phrases [one phrase (*ku*) perhaps comprising two metric segments?] each" is a tentative reading of the original *samgu yungmyŏng*, a phrase that remains an unresolved topic of debate. Jin'ichi Konishi observes the functional resemblance between the *hugu* (the concluding stanza of *hyangga*) and the envoi to *chōka* and considers the latter a conscious imitation of the former. See his *History of Japanese Literature*, trans. Aileen Gatten and Nicholas Teele; ed. Earl Miner, vol. 1 (Princeton: Princeton University Press, 1984), p. 334.

examples, the absence of parallel texts dating from the same period, our inadequate knowledge of the phonological system of ancient Korean all constitute obstacles. From the philological research carried out since the 1920s, we have learned that generally one sound should be allocated to one Chinese graph, the same sound can be transcribed differently, and the same graph can be read both for sound and for sense – read it in its Korean pronunciation, that is, and translate it into Korean for meaning. Sometimes, the graph indicating the meaning of a Korean word is placed first, followed by other linguistic elements, which enables the reader to comprehend its meaning and its form in the context. We have also learned that the texts Iryŏn consulted at the time of his compilation of *Memorabilia of the Three Kingdoms* were already corrupted by scribal errors – to date, thirty-three such examples have been adduced to prove the fallibility of the scribe, together with missing graphs in a phrase.

Finally, the deciphering of *hyangch'al* orthographic transcription calls for a knowledge, not only of philology, but also of poetry. Early efforts relied first on the Rosetta Stone of *hyangch'al* transcription: Kyunyŏ's eleven songs, which exist both in *hyangch'al* and in Chinese translations (eight heptasyllabic lines), although the latter do not follow the imagery and meter of the original closely. A new reading, no matter how ingenious, must take into account the fact that a *hyangga* is a song performed before an audience that shared common values and beliefs. Imposition of an arbitrary reading, therefore, affects the meaning of the whole song. In an age when poets privileged speech over writing, we can imagine the role of a general audience contemporary with the *hyangga*. A performance is designed to produce in its listeners a positive effect: affective and suasive tropes are directed at them in order to evoke and transform their emotions. *Hyangga* and its reception are culturally determined, and the audience is assumed to share the same background and expectations – a play of complex interaction among song texts, traditions, and beliefs. If some parts of the texts are still impenetrable, it is because we have not yet overcome the problem of interpretation. In what follows, I have chosen a reading that is philologically accurate and, I hope, poetically adequate.

FOUR-LINE SONGS

The "Sŏdong yo" ("Song of Sŏdong," c. 600) is said to have been composed by King Mu of Paekche as part of a stratagem to win Princess Sŏnhwa, third daughter of the Silla king, Chingp'yŏng (579–632):

> Princess Sŏnhwa,
> After a secret affair,
> Steals away at night,
> With Sŏdong in her arms.[12]

An alternate reading has the princess being carried to Sŏdong's room. Perhaps the song was intended to express violation of social barriers; the boy, the offspring of a commoner and the water dragon, was a seller of Chinese yams.

The "P'ungyo" ("Ode to Yangji"; literally "a popular song," c. 635) is an anonymous song composed to praise the virtues of Yangji, an enlightened monk as well as a master painter, calligrapher, and sculptor. The song is said to have spread among the people when they helped Yangji cast the 16-foot-high statue of Buddha for Yŏngmyo Monastery. The song, Iryŏn continues, was popular even in his day and was sung when pounding rice and constructing buildings.

> We've come, have come, have come,
> How sad, we have come! –
> Sad are the living beings.
> We have come to garner merit.[13]

The sorrow expressed in the poem refers to the basic Buddhistic truth that all living beings suffer. The song implies that the way out of suffering is to accumulate merits by doing meritorious deeds.

The "Hŏnhwa ka" ("Dedication of the Flower," c. 702–737) was sung by a certain old herdsman. When Lady Suro, Lord Sunjŏng's wife, asked for an azalea blooming on a cliff, nobody except the old herdsman dared to make the perilous climb to the top. He plucked the flowers and dedicated them to her with this song:

> If you would let me leave
> The cattle tethered to the brown rock,
> And feel no shame for me,
> I would pluck and dedicate the flowers![14]

The "Turinnorae" ("Song of Tuṣita Heaven," 760) was composed by Master Wŏlmyŏng – monk, poet, and member of the *hwarang*, leaders of the knights of Silla. In 760, on the first day of the fourth month (20 April 760), two suns appeared in the sky and remained for ten days. King Kyŏngdŏk, on the suggestion of his astrologer, had an altar built to

---

[12] *SGYS* 2:98–99.   [13] *SGYS* 4:188.   [14] *SGYS* 2:78–79.

pray to the Buddha and waited for the arrival of a monk destined to perform the proper service. It is then that Master Wŏlmyŏng passed by and,
in response to a request from the king, he began the ceremony with this
song:

> O flowers strewn today
> With a song. Since you attend
> My honest mind's command,
> You serve Maitreya!

Master Wŏlmyŏng, according to *Memorabilia of the Three Kingdoms*, was
"a monk destined by karma to compose a song on the merit of scattering
flowers." Iryŏn offers the following reading of the song: "On the Dragon
Tower I sing a song of scattering flowers and send petals to the blue cloud.
In place of my sincere wish, go and welcome the Great Sage in the Tuṣita
Heaven!"[15]

EIGHT-LINE SONGS

The "Mo Chukchirang ka" ("Ode to Knight Chukchi," c. 692–702) was
written by Tŭgo to praise his master, Knight Chukchi, a member of the
hwarang:

> All living beings sorrow and lament
> Over the spring that is past;
> Your face once fair and bright
> Is about to wear deep furrows.
>
> I must glimpse you
> Even for an awesome moment.
> My fervent mind cannot rest at night
> In the mugwort-rank hollow.[16]

In the first stanza the poet compares the spring to his master and laments
that the once fair and bright face of the knight has begun to wear "deep
furrows." The last two lines of the song achieve the culmination of his
intense admiration for his dead master. Until he sees him again, even if just
for a moment, he cannot enjoy peace of mind. His longing for him will
torment him even in the hollow that is rank with mugwort.

In "Wŏnga" ("Regret," 737), Sinch'ung, a member of the nobility,
reproaches King Hyosŏng (731–741) for breaking a promise:

---

[15] *SGYS* 5:222–223.   [16] *SGYS* 2:76–78.

You said you would no more forget me
Than the densely green pine
Would wither in the fall.
That familiar face is there still.

The moon in the ancient lake
Complains of the transient tide.
I still glimpse your figure,
But how I dislike this world.[17]

The comparison of nature and humankind is introduced to emphasize the mutability of human mind. In the first stanza, the contrast is between the pine tree and a breach of promise. It is amplified in the second stanza – this time between the moon and the tide or between the moon, the tide, and the king. Although the moon "[c]omplains of the transient tide," the moon itself is changeable. Yet the speaker realizes that the moon and the tide, however changeable they may be, are renewed and renewing in their cyclic changes, whereas a man, once he has forgotten a promise, will never recall it. The nature described here symbolizes not only the speaker's deploring state of mind but also the contrast between the indifference of the universe and his own despair. Historically speaking, however, Sinch'ung began to hold high court rank in 739 and in 757 he was appointed prime minister. Later he became a monk and prayed for the soul of King Hyosŏng.[18]

The "Ch'ŏyong ka" ("Song of Ch'ŏyong," 879) is probably the most famous of all Silla songs. Its author, Ch'ŏyong, was one of the seven sons of the Dragon King of the Eastern Sea. Our source informs us that Ch'ŏyong married a beautiful woman. Seeing that she was so lovely, however, a demon of pestilence transformed himself into a man and attacked her in her room while Ch'ŏyong was away. When Ch'ŏyong returned and witnessed the scene, he calmly sang this song, which so moved the demon that it went away:

Having caroused far into the night
In the moonlit capital,
I returned home and in my bed,
Behold, four legs.

Two were mine;
Whose are the other two?
Formerly two were mine;
What shall be done now they are taken?[19]

---

[17] *SGYS* 5:232–233. The text indicates that the last two lines are lost.   [18] *SGSG* 9:90, 93.
[19] *SGYS* 2:88–89. For a stimulating reading of this song by David R. McCann, see *Early Korean Literature: Selections and Introductions* (New York: Columbia University Press, 2000), pp. 101–122.

Traditionally Ch'ŏyong has been considered a shaman, since he expelled the demon not by confrontation but by means of song and dance, thus shaming the demon into submission. His identity remains a topic of speculation, and his calm handling of the situation has been called magnanimous, fatalistic, or magical, to mention just a few of the many attributes ascribed by commentators. As for the demon that transformed itself into a man, perhaps it is symbolic of the moral sickness and political corruption destroying Silla society. Although the last two lines seem to indicate that the song accompanied a dramatic dance with two actors representing good and evil, the Ch'ŏyong dance performed at the temporary capital on Kanghwa Island during the Mongol invasion (1236) appears to be a solo dance.[20] Later, during the Chosŏn dynasty, the Ch'ŏyong dance, combined with the crane dance, became an important court pageant.

TEN-LINE SONGS

The "Hyesŏng ka" ("Song of a Comet," 594), written by Master Yungch'ŏn, who was probably an astrologer, worked a miracle: it cleared away a comet that had ominously appeared in the sky:

> There is a castle by the Eastern Sea,
> Where once a mirage used to play.
> Japanese soldiers came,
> Torches were burnt in the forest.
>
> When knights visited this mountain,
> The moon marked its westerly course
> And a star was about to sweep a path,
> Someone said, "Look, there is a comet."
>
> Ah, the moon has already departed.
> Now, where shall we look for the long-tailed star?[21]

In the second line of the first stanza, the original refers to a mirage as "the castle where Gandharva plays." The comet is variously described as "a star with a broomstick" (line 7; shortened in translation) that sweeps the path for the moon and as "the long-tailed star." Iryŏn comments that once the song was composed, "the uncanny comet disappeared and the Japanese troops withdrew, thus turning a misfortune into a blessing."

The "Wŏn wangsaeng ka" ("Prayer to Amitāyus," c. 661–681) was written either by the monk Kwangdŏk or his wife:

---

[20] *KRS* 23:31a.　[21] *SGYS* 5:228; *SGSG* 27:239 mentions the event.

O moon,
Go to the West, and
Pray to Amitāyus
And tell

That there is one who
Adores the judicial throne, and
Longs for the Pure Land,
Praying before him with folded hands.

Ah, would he leave me out
When he fulfills the forty-eight vows?[22]

In the first stanza the speaker addresses the moon and asks it to undertake a journey to the West where Amitāyus (Infinite Life) resides. The second stanza amplifies the praise of the virtues of Amitāyus. He not only possesses "infinite life" but is also wise – another name is Amitābha (Infinite Light) – and passes judgment from his "judicial throne." The last stanza presents a rhetorical question in which the speaker affirms that the flesh, which stands between the promised land and this world, must be annihilated.

The "Che mangmae ka" ("Requiem for the Dead Sister," c. 762–765) was written by Master Wŏlmyŏng in memory of his sister. The song is built on a single theme of separation through death. In the first stanza there is the image of a crossroads ("the . . . road of life and death") and in the second there is the image of the tree:

On the hard road of life and death
That is near our land,
You went, afraid,
Without words.

We know not where we go,
Leaves blown, scattered,
Though fallen from the same tree,
By the first winds of autumn.

Ah, I will polish the path
Until I meet you in the Pure Land.[23]

The chaotic state of our existence is compared here to the branches of the tree. The branches, however, come from the same source: the trunk. Leaves that grow on the branches, however, when fallen, are permanently separated from one another. We are, the poet says, like the leaves, and once we die, we must part forever from our loved ones. The theme is therefore

[22] *SGYS* 5:219–220. [23] *SGYS* 5:223.

Illustration 1.   Silla gold crown.

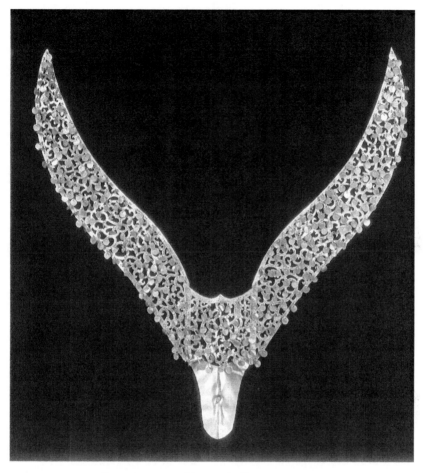

Illustration 2. Gold-winged Silla cap ornaments.

skillfully developed by the simple figure of a tree: branches growing out from the tree, leaves separated from the branch, and finally scattered leaves blown asunder. Homer, underscoring the brevity of human life, had already compared the generation of men to that of leaves (*Iliad* 6:146–150); the same simile occurs in the Parabasis of Aristophanes' *The Birds* (lines 685–689). In the last stanza of Master Wŏlmyŏng's requiem, the poet, in the speech of a devout Buddhist, hopes to meet his sister again in "the Pure Land."

The "Ch'an Kip'arang ka" ("Ode to Knight Kip'a," c. 742–765) is a eulogy by Master Ch'ungdam written to praise Knight Kip'a, a member of the *hwarang*. This song was known for its intense emotion and noble spirit, and King Kyŏngdŏk himself praised it highly. Unlike the other songs, it has no introductory note by Iryŏn.

> The moon that pushes her way
> Through the thickets of clouds,
> Is she not pursuing
> The white clouds?
>
> Knight Kip'a once stood by the water,
> Reflecting his face in the Iro.
> Henceforth I shall seek and gather
> Among pebbles the depth of his mind.
>
> Knight, you are the towering pine
> That scorns frost, ignores snow.[24]

The first and second stanzas present a thematic comparison – a symbolic equation – between the moon that pursues white clouds and the speaker seeking among pebbles the depth of his friend's mind. The pebbles themselves, however, are unstable objects, symbols of insecurity and the brevity of existence. Like the pebbles, Knight Kip'a was a prey to mutability and exists no more. The knight once stood by the water, the river of time, a continuous and irreversible flow toward death. The speaker has not denied time as illusory; rather, he accepts it on its own terms. Hence the concluding stanza introduces a correspondence between the knight and the pine which acknowledges that the knight is dead while asserting that his moral beauty endures. His integrity not only scorns mutability but imposes a sense of order on the landscape. His nobility is that of the mind. The knight represents the principle of growth and order; he is an emblem of an enduring culture.

Another poem by Ch'ungdam, the "Anmin ka" ("Statesmanship," 765), is built upon a simple metaphor: an implied comparison between the government and the family.

> The king is father,
> And his ministers are loving mothers.
> His subjects are foolish children;
> They only receive what love brings.
>
> Schooled in saving the masses,
> The king feeds and guides them.

---

[24] *SGYS* 2:79–80. The first *hyangch'al* graph for "frost" (*sŏri*) is the same as the one for "snow," but was probably intended to mean two things.

Then no one will desert this land —
This is the way to govern a country.

Ah, peace and prosperity will prevail if each —
King, minister, and subject — lives as he should.[25]

The notion that the ruler is the "father and mother of his people" is commonplace. (One finds it in Seneca and Erasmus, for example.)

The "To Ch'ŏnsu Kwanŭm ka" ("Hymn to the Thousand-Eyed Bodhisattva Who Observes the Sounds of the World", the Sound Observer, c. 762–765) by Hŭimyŏng shows another instance of a miracle brought about by the power of poetry. This time the speaker, on behalf of her son who has lost his eyesight, implores the image of the Thousand-Eyed Sound Observer painted on the north wall of Punhwang Monastery's Left Hall:

> Falling on my knees,
> Pressing my hands together,
> Thousand-Eyed Sound Observer,
> I implore thee.
>
> Yield me,
> Who lacks,
> One among your thousand eyes,
> By your mystery restore me whole.
>
> If you grant me one of your many eyes,
> O the bounty, then, of your charity.[26]

The four lines of the first stanza describe in vivid language the external bodily preparation necessary for the prayer. The actual prayer is given in the following stanzas, lines 5 to 10. The effects of calm and poise are achieved by the conditional "if" at the beginning of the ninth line. The "one" in the same line should be taken as an indefinite, rhetorical number.

The "Ujŏk ka" ("Meeting with Bandits," c. 785–798), by Master Yŏngjae, is the most difficult of all Silla songs — partly because four graphs are missing from the extant text and partly because the poet's symbolic language is polysemous. Following is both Iryŏn's introductory note and the song itself:

The monk Yŏngjae was broad-minded and humorous and unattached to riches, and he excelled in poetry. Intending to spend his last days on South Peak in retirement, he was crossing the Taehyŏn Ridge when he met sixty thieves. The bandits drew their swords and threatened him; but he showed no fear and stated

---

[25] *SGYS* 2:80.   [26] *SGYS* 3:158–159.

his name. Since the bandits had heard of his reputation as a poet, they asked him to compose an impromptu song:

> The day I did not know
> My true mind –
> Now I am awakened from ignorance
> And am going through the forest.
>
> Transgressors hiding in the bushes,
> You can turn your merits to save others.
> If I'm stabbed to death,
> Then a good day will dawn.
>
> Ah, this much good deed
> Cannot build a lofty edifice.

Moved by the song, the bandits presented him with two pieces of silk. The monk laughed and declined the gift, saying that since he knew riches were the root of evil, he was about to abandon the world and live in the mountains. When the monk threw the silk to the ground with these words, the bandits threw away their swords and spears, shaved their heads, and remained on Mount Chiri all their lives. Yŏngjae was ninety years old then. This took place during the reign of King Wŏnsŏng (785–798).

The eulogy says:

> Resolved, he goes into the hills with his staff,
> White silk and pearls cannot rule his heart.
> Thieves in the woods offered him gifts,
> But he has no cause to go to hell.[27]

The first stanza introduces the first theme: journeying. Night is not only the setting, it is a symbol of the speaker's mind in the world of illusion. After long wandering in the dark, the speaker is awakened and sets out for enlightenment. On the way he meets the bandits, who are also wandering in the forest. This act of meeting them is, on the one hand, a source of enlightenment both for himself and for the bandits. The bandits' swords finally help the speaker to comprehend the relations between illusion and enlightenment. On the other hand, it is the enlightened speaker who in turn enlightens the bandits. Thus the second stanza fully develops the theme of the polarity between illusion and enlightenment that was hinted at in the previous stanza. The last stanza describes a constant harmony with the

---

[27] *SGYS* 5:235. A reading by Kim Wanjin goes: "I cannot see / The mind's true nature. / The sun has set and birds return to roost. / As the moon rises, I go into the forest. / Even if the transgressing bandit stops me, / Would I be frightened? / You have listened to the dharma / That scorns arms. / But my good deed is nothing / Compared to the Buddha's might." See Kim Wanjin, *Hyangga haedokpŏp yŏngu* (Seoul taehakkyo ch'ulp'anbu, 1980), pp. 144–156.

living and the mind that is one with the wisdom of the Buddha. Thus the song is a revelation of the process of attaining enlightenment. It is built on the contrasts between night and day, darkness and light, and illusion and enlightenment.

Great Master Kyunyŏ (b. 20 September 923; d. 19 July 973) was a learned monk-poet who single-handedly revived the Flower Garland school in the tenth century. A voluminous commentator and an evangelist, he composed poems in the vernacular, taught them orally, and encouraged the congregation to chant and memorize. Some of his commentaries on Buddhist texts were written in the vernacular, as well, before being translated into Chinese. In his Chinese preface to the eleven devotional songs, Kyunyŏ tells us his intent in using the vernacular:

While the *sanoe* is a medium of popular entertainment, the practice of the vows is essential to the cultivation of the bodhisattva's practices. One must proceed therefore from the easy to the profound, from the near at hand to the distant. If one does not proceed according to the way of the world, one cannot lead men of inferior faculties. If one does not express oneself in common language, one cannot make known the path of universal causation. Thus I begin from the easily comprehensible and the near at hand and then lead the people to the more difficult and profound teachings of Buddhism. I have written eleven songs on the model of the ten great vows. The songs may appear disgraceful in the eyes of the people; yet they may tally with the wishes of the many buddhas. My intent may be lost and my words awry, and my songs may not conform to the wonderful teachings of our saints, but I wish to convey these teachings through poetry to plant wholesome roots among the living. Thus even those who memorize these songs laughingly may lay a basis for their salvation, and those who chant them abusingly may benefit from them. I beg to make it known that it is a matter of indifference to me whether posterity denounces or praises my songs.[28]

Ch'oe Haenggwi, who translated Kyunyŏ's songs into Chinese in 967, praises the great master in these words:

As the teacher of three thousand disciples, Kyunyŏ's influence is second only to that of Varaprabha [Wonderful Light]. As the master of eighty chapters of the *Flower Garland Scripture*, he was the head of his school and taught the masses to take refuge in the Three Jewels. As a great tree [bodhisattva] moistened by the rain of dharma, he benefited all living beings.[29]

Great Master Kyunyŏ entitled his songs after the ten vows of Bodhisattva Samantabhadra (Universal Worthy), with the exception of the eleventh song, which constitutes the conclusion. The topics of the songs are: (1) worshipping and honoring the buddhas; (2) praise of the Thus Come

---

[28] *Kyunyŏ chŏn*, pp. 59–60.   [29] Ibid., p. 63.

One; (3) wide cultivation and the making of offerings; (4) repentance for sins; (5) rejoicing in the merit of others; (6) entreaty for the turning of the dharma wheel; (7) entreaty for the buddhas to live in this world; (8) constant following of the teaching of the buddhas; (9) constant harmony with the living; (10) transfer of merit; (11) the conclusion.[30]

Although the eleven songs were inspired by the *Bhadra-cari- praṇidhāna* (*Vows on the Practices of the Bodhisattva*), the imagery is often more striking and beautiful than in the Sanskrit original or its Chinese translations. The sixth song, which asks the Buddha to turn the dharma wheel, is the most dramatic and lyrical of all his songs.

> To the majestic assembly of buddhas
> In the dharma realm,
> I go forth and pray
> For the dharma rain.
>
> Disperse the blight of affliction
> Rooted deep in the soil of ignorance,
> And wet the mind's field of living beings,
> Where good grasses struggle to grow.
>
> Ah, how happy is a moonlit autumn field,
> Ripe with the fruit of knowledge.

The song opens with a fervent prayer for the sweet dharma rain. The mind is the soil of ignorance, which suffers from "the blight of affliction." It is the dried field where the good grasses struggle to grow because of this blight, and where the temptations of ignorance pervade there cannot but be "the soil of ignorance." If "sweet dharma rain" falls over the dried, ignorant, dark soil of the mind, the blight will be dispelled, the grass will grow, and the soil will bear the golden "fruit of knowledge." This harmonious state of mind is expressed in the last stanza by the single beautiful metaphor of "a moonlit autumn field." The autumn field must be illuminated by the

---

[30] The texts of eleven poems are in ibid., pp. 60–62. Readings by Korean philologists (e.g., Yang Chudong [1942, 1968], Chi Hŏnyŏng [1948], Yi T'aek [1958], Sŏ Chegŭk [1974], Kim Chunyŏng [1979], Kim Wanjin [1980], Ch'oe Ch'ŏl [1990], Yu Ch'anggyun [1994], and Sin Chaehong [2000], to name a few) differ at a number of places. Adrian Buzo's translation in *Kyunyŏ-jŏn* offers the linear trot and misreadings, including the characteristic Buddhist metaphoric diction in meditative verse, such as the genitive metaphor in line 1 of song 1. For "I draw with the mind as my brush" read "I draw with the mind's brush [maŭm ŭi put]." There is no simile in the original. Similar devices occur at 6:8, 9:3, and 10:3. This metaphoric tradition is continued by Han Yongun in his *Silence of Love* (1926); for example *mulkkŏp'um ŭi kkot* (froth's flowers, poem 10), *saengmyŏng ŭi kkot* (life's blossoms, poem 10), and *sarang ŭi soesasŭl* (love's chain, poem 43). For a survey of *hyangga* studies, see Yi Tongyŏng, *Hanguk munhak yŏngusa* (Pusan: Pusan taehakkyo ch'ulp'anbu, 1999), pp. 426–455.

moon, since the bodhi-moon is a symbol for enlightenment. Thus the last stanza achieves a magnificent unity of tone.

BUDDHISM AND THE *HWARANG* CLASS

We have seen that eighteen of the twenty-five *hyangga* are Buddhist in inspiration and content, reflecting certain trends in Silla and early Koryŏ Buddhism. Belief in the Tuṣita Heaven of Maitreya and the Pure Land of Amitāyus ("Infinite Life") is reflected in "Prayer to Amitāyus," "Song of Tuṣita Heaven," and "Requiem for the Dead Sister"; belief in the bodhisattva Avalokiteśvara ("He Who Observes the Sounds of the World," the Sound Observer) is reflected in "Hymn to the Thousand-Eyed Sound Observer." Finally, Great Master Kyunyŏ's songs were intended to teach the people to make vows, earn merit, and rejoice in the bodhisattva path, thus stressing both faith and work.

The Maitreya cult in Silla was a product of a belief that Silla was the Buddha land of Maitreya. This version of the cult played an important role in Silla Buddhism. Not only was Maitreya ("The Friendly One") the patron saint of the *hwarang*, the elite society of Silla knights, but members of the *hwarang* class were thought to be reincarnations of Maitreya. Kim Yusin and his group were called "the band of the Dragon Flower Tree" – a reference to the bodhi tree of Maitreya on his advent to earth to save living beings. By adopting the Buddhist name Pŏbun ("Dharma Cloud"), King Chinhŭng sought to be a wheel-turning king in the land of Maitreya. Devotees prayed before an image of Maitreya, asking that the celestial bodhisattva be reborn as a *hwarang*. In his "Song of Tuṣita Heaven," Master Wŏlmyŏng enjoins flowers to serve Maitreya.

The Amitāyus cult was equally strong in Silla. In accord with a literal interpretation of the eighteenth, nineteenth, and twentieth of the forty-eight vows of Amitāyus,[31] the invocation of his name was thought to enable people to be reborn in the Pure Land, or Happy Land, of the Buddha of Infinite Light (Amitāyus). Transcending barriers of social class, it was the most appealing form of devotion. Thus the Pure Land belief became an effective ideology by which the court could unify the people and the church could popularize Buddha dharma among the masses.

The form of Buddhism that fulfilled the needs of the people was belief in the Pure Land and the Sound Observer. Belief in Maitreya's paradise was

---

[31] For the Amitāyus cult see Takakusu Junjirō, *Amitāyurdhyāna sūtra*, Sacred Books of the East 49 (Oxford: Clarendon Press, 1894), pp. 167–199.

prevalent among the nobility during the Three Kingdoms period; worship of Amitāyus was prevalent around the time of unification in the mid and late seventh century. While devotees of Amitāyus viewed this world as a sea of sorrow and sought rebirth in the future, believers in the Sound Observer stressed that the bodhisattva's mercy would save people from suffering and calamity. The spread of Amitāyus worship fostered the worship of the Sound Observer, as believers sought not only deliverance and enlightenment in the future but also rewards in this world. Stories of miracles performed by the Sound Observer were joyfully transmitted by way of mouth. Those who preached faith in the Buddha Amitāyus and the bodhisattva Sound Observer were monks, such as Hyesuk, Hyegong, Taean, and Wŏnhyo who went among the people to proselytize. Unaided by the court or the nobility, they preached on the roadside or in the marketplace, making Buddhism a popular faith for the first time in Silla.

Hyangga include songs in praise of Silla's elite corps of knights, the *hwarang*. The origin of Silla's unique social group may be traced to the "age set" organization of earlier times. Through its communal life and rites, a group, organized by young men of a certain age range, learned the society's traditional values and through military arts, poetry, and music fostered mutual understanding and friendship. Generally organized at the village or clan level, this group functioned as a basic social group to maintain a fixed social structure. From the middle of the fourth century on, however, as Silla accelerated its development toward a state, the village-based or clan-based group was increasingly hard to maintain. In the early sixth century Silla began to expand its territory and a transformation of the youth groups became inevitable. Under the new conditions, the *hwarang*, now a semi-official body at the national level, came into being as an organization dedicated to the nurturing of talent.

A *hwarang* group, comprising several hundred youths, was headed by a youth from the "true bone" (*chingol*) aristocracy and several monks. For a fixed period they lived together to learn military arts and cultivate virtue. They also toured mountains and rivers to nurture love of country, learned the beauty of order and harmony through poetry and music and prayed for the country's peace and development. Monks serving as chaplains were entrusted with their religious education and taught them universalistic Buddhism and loyalty to the king.

Wŏngwang's "Five Commandments for Laymen" best illustrates the content of their education: serve the king with loyalty; tend parents with filial piety; treat friends with sincerity; never retreat from a battlefield; be discriminate about the taking of life.[32] To the Confucian virtues were added courage required in the war for unification and the Buddhist concept of compassion. Of these, loyalty and sincerity were considered to be fundamental virtues, an indication of the times. Some *hwarang* members went on to study the Confucian classics, the *Record of Rites* and the *Zuo Commentary*.

Willing to lay down their life for their country, the *hwarang* members vowed to serve in times of national need. Such spirit nurtured during a *hwarang* member's youth continued to inspire him as he came of age and began his career as politician or soldier. With a firm foundation of national morality and spirit established, the *hwarang* became a prime source of Silla's military success against its enemies. Such exemplary members of *hwarang* as Sadaham, Kim Hŭmun, and Kwanch'ang distinguished themselves in Silla's wars: Sadaham in a war against Great Kaya in 562; Kim Hŭmun in a war against Paekche in 655;[33] and Kwanch'ang in an attack against Paekche in 660.[34] Although we have no detailed description of the battles, we do know that Kim Hŭmun maintained his personal integrity in the face of inevitable defeat and that Kwanch'ang, the sixteen-year-old adjunct general of Silla, met his death on the plain of Hwangsan.

Both Kim Hŭmun and Kwanch'ang sacrificed their lives to preserve the honor due their own persons as members of *hwarang*. People especially wept for Kwanch'ang, whose life was taken from him at such a young age.[35] These heroes mirror an ideal not only of a particular class but also of their time. We may recall that Master Ch'ungdam praised Knight Kip'a. History does not record the knight's deeds. By an implied comparison of the knight with a towering pine, however, the poet not only heightens the effect of his praise but compresses the knight's career into a single metaphor, thus conferring upon him enduring fame. The poet does even more, however. For the pine is a symbol not only of the knight and the *hwarang* order but also of Silla society and culture.

---

[32] Peter H. Lee, *Lives of Eminent Korean Monks* (Cambridge, Mass.: Harvard University Press, 1969), pp. 79–80.

[33] *SGSG* 4:40.   [34] *SGSG* 47:437–438.   [35] *SGSG* 47:437.

Extant hyangga

King Mu of Paekche	"Sŏdong yo" (c. 600)	*SGYS* 2:98
Master Yungch'ŏn	"Hyesŏng ka" (594)	*SGYS* 2:228
Anonymous	"P'ungyo" (c. 635)	*SGYS* 4:187–188
Kwangdŏk or his wife (c. 661–681)	"Wŏn wangsaeng ka"	*SGYS* 5:220
Tŭgo (c. 692–702)	"Mo Chukchirang ka"	*SGYS* 2:76–78
An Old Herdsman (c. 702–737)	"Hŏnhwa ka"	*SGYS* 2:79
Sinch'ung	"Wŏnga" (737)	*SGYS* 5:232–233
Master Wŏlmyŏng (c. 742–765)	"Turinnorae" (760)	*SGYS* 5:222
Master Wŏlmyŏng (c. 742–765)	"Che mangmae ka"	*SGYS* 5:223
Master Ch'ungdam (c. 742–765)	"Anmin ka" (765)	*SGYS* 2:79–80
Master Ch'ungdam	"Ch'an Kip'arang ka"	*SGYS* 2:80–81
Hŭimyŏng (c. 762–765)	"To Ch'ŏnsu Kwanŭm ka"	*SGYS* 3:158–159
Master Yŏngjae (c. 785–798)	"Ujŏk ka"	*SGYS* 5:235
Ch'ŏyong	"Ch'ŏyong ka" (879)	*SGYS* 2:88–89
Great Master Kyunyŏ (923–973)	"Pohyŏn sibwŏn ka"	*SGYS* Appendix 60–62

CHAPTER 4

Silla writings in Chinese

Peter H. Lee

Owing to geographic proximity, Chinese graphs and classics were introduced into the ancient Korean kingdoms as early as the second century BC.
The fact of cultural intercourse between China and the Korean states is
documented by Chinese and Korean sources alike. With the establishment
of Chinese commanderies in the peninsula, the flow of Chinese culture
increased and the Koguryŏ kingdom in the northwest commenced active
contact with Chinese immigrants.

Koguryŏ used the Chinese script from early times. Under King Sosurim
(371–384), a Chinese-style national academy was established and the learned
class studied the Five Classics, histories, and the *Wenxuan* (*Selections of
Refined Literature*).[1] There were also private schools (*kyŏngdang*) that taught
Chinese and archery.[2] The representative example of Koguryŏ writing is
the inscription to the monument erected in honor of King Kwanggaet'o,
an inscription in Korean-style calligraphy.[3]

The Paekche kingdom had erudites (*paksa*) of the Five Classics, medicine,
and the calendar, and it was they who transmitted Chinese writing to Japan.
An example of Paekche writing is the state paper sent by King Kaero (455–
475) in 472 to the Northern Wei, preserved in the *Weishu* (7A:137),[4] and
the monument of Sat'aek Chijŏk.[5] Monuments erected at the sites of King
Chinhŭng's tours of inspection show the mastery of written Chinese in
Silla. The four monuments built when King Chinhŭng inspected the newly
acquired territory include those at Mount Pukhan (555), at Ch'angnyŏng
(561), and at Hwangch'o Pass and Maun Pass (both erected in 568).[6] Another
monument, discovered in 1978 at Chŏksŏng in Tamyang (c. 550), is not
related to these tours of inspection.[7]

---

[1] *SGSG* 18:166.   [2] *Jiu Tangshu* 199A:5320; *Xin Tangshu* 220:6186.
[3] *SGYS*, Appendix, pp. 3–6.
[4] Wei Shou, *Weishu*. 7 vols. (Peking: Zhonghua, 1974) 7A:137.
[5] *CHKY*, no. 11, p. 53.   [6] *SGYS*, Appendix, pp. 9–15.   [7] *CHKY*, no. 336, pp. 455–457.

Proficiency in Chinese enabled the compilation of national histories in the Three Kingdoms: in Koguryŏ in 600, Yi Munjin edited a history of 100 chapters (*kwŏn*) into 5 chapters; Kohŭng compiled a history in Paekche (and, judging from the quotations in the *Nihon shoki* [*The Records of Japan*, 720], other historical material also existed), and Kŏch'ilpu compiled a history in Silla (545).[8] The compilation of history in Paekche and Silla coincided with their territorial expansion and may be said to reflect their national consciousness.

EARLY METHODS OF READING CHINESE

Because Chinese is an utterly foreign language belonging to a totally different linguistic family, the Koreans had to devise ways to decode it and use it in writing. The Korean ways of reading Chinese show how they assimilated a language that had a different grammar, sound system, and vocabulary. In its early phase of introduction, it is unclear whether Chinese was read with contemporary Chinese pronunciation. With the spread of Chinese and the teaching of it at educational institutions, Chinese was read in Sino-Korean pronunciation. The basic pattern of reading Chinese graphs in Korean pronunciation probably came into being in 372, when Koguryŏ established a national academy to teach Chinese classics and literature. This entailed the assimilation of Chinese into the Korean phonetic system. Koreans were not learning to speak Chinese, but to decipher the content of a given Chinese text: they read it for sense, not sound.

Because knowledge of Chinese classics and skill in writing Chinese were deemed essential by the educated, they devised several ways of reading. Examples from late Koryŏ of the use of oral formulas (口訣 *kugyŏl*) – adding grammatical elements to the Chinese text to indicate the case relationship of nouns and verb endings – are to be found in Buddhist texts such as the old translation of the *Scripture for Benevolent Kings* (discovered in 1973). The oral formula graphs (吐 *t'o*) provided to the right of a Chinese sentence are first read down as far as the return dot and then one goes back to the top to read oral formula graphs on the left – all this is to rearrange the Chinese sentence into Korean syntactic order. For this Koreans devised simplified forms of graphs, such as 亻 for 伊 (subject particle), ㄱ for 隱 (topic particle), and 厂 for 厓 (locative particle). This method of reading is called *sŏktok kugyŏl* (釋讀口訣 explanatory reading oral formulas). The oral formulas used during the Chosŏn period in reading Confucian texts or

---

[8] *SGSG* 20:182 for Koguryŏ; 24:221–222 for Paekche; and 4:37 for Silla.

primers were simpler. They were merely added to clarify the structure of a Chinese text – a method known as *ŭmdok kugyŏl* (音讀 Sino-Korean oral formulas). Explanatory formulas indicate that Koreans read some Chinese graphs into Korean reading (訓 *hun*). The graph 有, for example, followed by the graph 叱 (s), is read *it* in Korean, meaning "is" or "exists," and 復爲隱 is read *tto han* (also, likewise). Koreans read a Chinese graph in *hun* (meaning, gloss) reading as follows: the graph 天 (heaven) is read *hanŭl ch'ŏn* – *hanŭl* is the Korean word for "heaven," *ch'ŏn* its Sino-Korean pronunciation. The former method is known as *sŏk* (釋 explanation) or *hun* (gloss). Thus in Korea a native word and its Sino-Korean pronunciation are connected to every Chinese graph. Sŏl Ch'ong is said to have glossed (*hun*) and interpreted (解 *hae*) the literature of the Six Classics (*SGYS* 4:196), but the extant examples of such glosses are found mostly in Buddhist texts. Further, *hun* transcription 買忽 represents the Koguryŏ place-name, and 水城 represents its sinicized name used in late Silla and thereafter (*SGSG* 37:351). The first set transcribes the sound *maehol* and the second its meaning (water fortress). This seems to indicate that the use of meaning glosses (*hun*) probably began in Koguryŏ. It is worth noting that the Korean *hun* and the Japanese *kun* (訓) are similar in function, and the simplified Chinese graphs used by the Koreans to indicate oral formulas (including the return dot, *kaeriten* in Japanese) are similar in form to Japanese *katakana*, the square form of the Japanese syllabary. These examples indicate how the ancient Koreans experimented with reading literary Chinese in their own language. In the process of devising oral formulas they also devised simplified graphs that did not exist in China.

Next came the *idu* system, in which Chinese word order and Korean word order were mixed and the use of Chinese coverbs was influenced by Korean verb stems and particles. This seems to be evidence of the existence of a certain fixed pattern of reading Chinese. An earlier phase of *idu* in the Three Kingdoms may be detected in what is termed vulgar Chinese (俗漢文 *sok hanmun*). In the so-called *sŏgi* (誓記 oath) style, Chinese was written in Korean word order (subject-object-verb; noun followed by a particle; and so on) – as in the "Record of the Oath Made in the Year *Imsin*" (612?), a document of seventy-four graphs, in a plain style that was used by monks, village chiefs, and lower officials.[9] The *hyangch'al* 鄉札 orthographic system, which came into being after the unification of the peninsula under Silla, combines the *sŏgi* method with Korean particles. This system transcribes

---

[9] *CHKY*, no. 6, pp. 48–49. For the decoding of oral formulas see Chung Jae-young (Chŏng Chaeyŏng), "Sŏktokkugyŏl in the Koryŏ Period," *SJK* 12 (1999):29–45.

Korean in Chinese graphs for their sound and sense, but only someone who knows Chinese graphs and Chinese writing can use it. This shows how the art of studying Chinese influenced the development of transcription of Korean in Chinese.

Straight reading of Chinese text (順讀口訣 *sundok kugyŏl*), which began during Koryŏ times, read a given text straight down, with Korean particles added. This method of reading was able to keep the Chinese syntax intact while deciphering its meaning. Also good for committing a text to memory, it is probably the most widely practiced way of reading Chinese up until the present day. In this system Chinese nouns are read as loanwords in Korean. Then the suffix -*hada* is added to the Chinese verbs; -*hada*, -*rapta*, -*tapta* to the adjectives; and -*hi*, -*hyŏ*, and -*ro* to the adverbs. Through this and earlier methods of reading, the difficulties inherent in the Chinese text were overcome, and straight reading helped to bridge the chasm between the two languages.

Vulgar Chinese and *idu* were not used in literary composition but in administrative papers, the recording of the completion of buildings, statutes, and the like. Great Master Kyunyŏ's masterpiece *Wŏnt'ong ki* (*Record of Perfect Penetration*) was first written in *idu* but was later edited to conform to the normal Chinese prose style. The use of *idu* also appears in the *kyŏnggi-ch'e* songs of Koryŏ and documents dating from the Chosŏn dynasty. Such Korean elements as particles and suffixes were added only in reading; in writing, most Korean writers followed the Chinese grammar and syntax. One notes, however, certain differences in works written in Chinese by Korean writers. While the *Historical Records of the Three Kingdoms* follows an official historical narrative style, for example, the *Memorabilia of the Three Kingdoms* resembles vulgar Chinese, as Iryŏn's intent was to preserve the spoken Korean as much as possible.[10]

USE OF CHINESE IN THE THREE KINGDOMS

Chinese was used first in state archives, diplomatic papers, and inscriptions; it was also used to teach Confucian texts and Buddhist scriptures. Extant inscriptions from Koguryŏ are few. The inscription on the Chŏmsŏn monument (Yonggang, South P'yŏngan) is in the form of a prayer to a mountain god for a good harvest and an end to banditry.[11] At the Chungwŏn monument, Silla is referred to as the "Eastern Barbarians," while the inscription

[10] Hwang P'aegang et al., eds., *Hanguk munhak yŏngu immun* (Chisik sanŏpsa, 1982), pp. 171–177.
[11] *SGYS*, Appendix, pp. 1–2 (also in Chōsen sōtokufu, ed. *Chōsen kinseki sōran*, 2 vols. [1919] 1:1).

to the King Kwanggaet'o stele shows a command of Chinese prose.[12] The earliest extant poem written in Chinese is attributed to the famous Koguryŏ general Ŭlchi Mundŏk. The poem, a pentasyllabic quatrain, was sent to General Yu Zhongwen of the invading Sui army in 612 (see Chapter 1):

> Your divine plans have plumbed the heavens;
> Your subtle reckoning has spanned the earth.
> You win every battle, your military merit is great.
> Why then not be content and stop the war?[13]

An early example of Paekche writing, the tombstone of King Muryŏng (462–523; r. 501–523), discovered in Kongju in 1971, consists of six lines and a total of fifty-two graphs:

The Great General and Pacifier of the East [the title given him by the Liang in 521], King Sama [Muryŏng] of Paekche, died at the age of sixty-two on the seventh day, *imjin*, of the fifth month, *pyŏngsul*, of the fifth year, *kyemo* [5 June 523]. On the twelfth day, *kapsin*, of the eighth month, *kyeyu*, of the *ŭlsa* year [14 September 525], he was laid to rest in a great tomb with due ceremony. We have recorded as on the left [to prove that the plot was purchased from the earth god].[14]

Another example is the inscription on a monument known as the "Sat'aek Chijŏk pi," erected in 654. Only four lines, fourteen graphs to a line, remain. Sat'aek Chijŏk, a member of the Sa clan, one of the eight great clans in Paekche, held the rank of prime minister (*sangjwap'yŏng*). He retired from public life in 654. Reminiscing on the prime of his life and lamenting the approach of old age, he decided to espouse Buddhism. He had the main hall and the stupa built and had this inscription made to commemorate the occasion:

On the ninth day of the first month of the year *kabin* [1 February 654], Sat'aek Chijŏk of Naji Walled Town [Naeji-ri, Ŭnsan-myŏn, Puyŏ, South Ch'ungch'ŏng] laments the manner in which his days pass quickly and his months never return. He mined gold to build the main hall and chiseled jade to erect the jeweled reliquary. How imposing – its compassionate appearance emits a spiritual glow to dispel clouds. How lofty – its sad face bears sage brightness to . . .[15]

Extant examples of Chinese prose from early Silla include, for instance, the inscription on a monument erected on the occasion of the completion

---

[12] Chŏng Yŏngho, "Chungwŏn Koryŏ pi ŭi palgyŏn chosa wa yŏngu chŏnmang," *Sahakchi* 13 (1979): 1–19; Yi Pyŏngdo, "Chungwŏn Koryŏ pi ŭi taehayŏ," *Sahakchi* 13 (1979):21–32; and Hŏ Hŭngsik, *Hanguk kŭmsŏk chŏnmun* (Asea munhwasa, 1984), pp. 15–16.

[13] *SGSG* 44:410. The last line alludes to ch. 44 of the *Daodejing*: "Know contentment / And you will suffer no disgrace; / Know when to stop / And you will meet with no danger"; see D. C. Lau, *Tao Te Ching* (Harmondsworth: Penguin, 1963), p. 105.

[14] *CHKY*, no. 7, pp. 49–50.   [15] *CHKY*, no. 11, p. 53.

of a dike in Yŏngch'ŏn (536). Although this inscription is chipped and illegible, an inscription on the back side tells us when the dike was repaired (798).[16] The monument at Maun Pass, erected in 568, may be cited as a typical pre-unification Silla epigraph.[17] In the same monument, in order to justify Silla's territorial expansion, royal authority was expressed by means of the kingly way set forth in the *Book of Documents* and Confucian political thought in the *Analects*. The advocacy of kingly virtue, however, was also a means to curb autocratic rule. In an admonition to King Chinp'yŏng criticizing his excessive love of hunting, Kim Hujik (fl. 579–631), the erstwhile minister of war, quotes passages from the *Book of Documents* and *Laozi* to drive home his message.[18] Later, in his conversation with Prime Minister Ch'unggong in 822, Nokchin propounds how the government can be worthy of trust.[19] Lessons of history are available only to the learned. Citing of historical examples or parallels is in the interest of persuasive effect: how to resist the temptations of life and discover the importance of moral improvement. The proclamation of Confucian rule at the time of unification encouraged studies in Chinese classics and literature, and study of Confucian political and moral doctrine formed the basis of education. In 636 Queen Chindŏk had appointed scholars to teach Chinese learning. With the establishment of the national academy in 682, the core curriculum consisted of the *Analects* and the *Book of Filial Piety*, along with specialization in one of the following: the *Book of Songs*, the *Book of Changes*, the *Book of Documents*, the *Record of Rites*, the *Zuo Commentary*, and the *Selections of Refined Literature (Wenxuan).*[20]

Because of their knowledge of Chinese and contacts with monks from China and elsewhere, Silla monks were in the forefront of Chinese learning and writing – not only as royal chaplains and advisers, politicians and diplomats, but also as compilers and exegetes. Indeed, their works on Buddhist and other subjects constitute some of the earliest extant examples of writings in Chinese. Of these, Great Master Wŏnhyo (617–686), the most influential Buddhist thinker in Korea, contributed greatly to the development of a distinctively Korean style of Buddhist philosophy and practice. Abandoning a plan to study abroad, Wŏnhyo became the most original and prolific Buddhist philosopher and writer in Korea. His range of scholarly endeavors spanned the whole of East Asian Buddhist materials, and some one hundred works are attributed to him. He was a master of Chinese prose, the prefaces to his commentaries on various Mahāyāna scriptures are

---

[16] *CHKY*, no. 5, pp. 43–46.   [17] *SGYS*, Appendix, p. 14.   [18] *SGSG* 45:420.
[19] *SGSG* 45:420–421.   [20] *SGSG* 38:366–367.

known for their concision and clarity, and he had a gift for summarizing the doctrine presented in various scriptures. Consider his preface to the thematic essentials of the *Lotus Blossom Scripture*:

The grand meaning of the *Scripture of the Lotus Blossom of the Fine Dharma* is the appearance of the buddhas of the ten directions and the three time periods. The scripture is the wide gateway through which the four kinds of beings in the nine destinies all enter the one path. Its text is skillfully wrought and its meaning is profound; everything in it has attained the epitome of subtlety. Its phraseology is well arranged and its principles exalted; they proclaim every dharma. Its text and phraseology are skillfully wrought and well arranged; thus while being ornate, it is also real. Its meaning and principles are profound and exalted; thus while being real, it contains expedients. Its principle is profound and exalted; thus it is nondual and without distinctions. Its phraseology is skillfully wrought and well arranged; thus its display of expedient devices shows the real. Examples of setting forth expedient devices include the parables of the three carriages and the conjuring up of a city midway to lead travelers to a jewel cache;[21] the attainment of enlightenment under the bodhi tree is not the beginning, and achieving perfect extinction [*parinirvāṇa*] between śāla trees is not the end. Examples of demonstrating the real are: the four kinds of beings are all our children; two-vehicle adherents should all become buddhas; particles of dust are not sufficient to measure the life span of the Buddha; and the flames at the end of cosmic age cannot scorch the Buddha land. This is what is meant by "skillful and subtle." "Nondual" means that one great purpose of the scripture is to make us know and realize the knowledge and vision of the buddhas and reveal that the access to awakening is unexcelled and undifferentiated. "Without distinction" means the three kinds of equality; all vehicles and bodies are all the same principle and the world and nirvana forever leave the two extremes of eternality and annihilationism. This is what is meant by "the doctrinal truth that is profound and subtle." The truth of the scripture's sentences is ever subtle, and everything offers mysterious precepts; everything shows how the constant way is distinguished from the coarse path. Hence it is called the fine dharma. Blossoms of expedient devices are set forth, and fruits of the truth manifest themselves clearly. Hence its untainted beauty is likened to the lotus blossom.

Yet the fine dharma is finely absolute. How is it, then, that now it is three [the threefold way to salvation] and now one? The perfect man is utterly dark – who is short and who is tall? This is fascinating and hard to comprehend, and students were confused and could not grasp it easily. Thereupon the Thus Come One used

---

[21] This refers to the parables used by the Buddha to teach sentient beings. "The three carriages" refers to an expedient device used by the father to entice his children out from a burning house with such playthings as a goat-drawn, a deer-drawn, and an ox-drawn carriage. "A jewel cache" tells how the Buddha enticed weary travelers on the steep road by conjuring up a city for them to rest and the promise of a jewel cache. See Takakusu Junjirō and Watanabe Kaigyoku, eds., *Taishō shinshū daizōkyō*, 85 vols. (Tokyo: Taishō issaikyō kankōkai, 1924–1934), 9 (no. 262):12b–13c and 25c–26a; Leon Hurvitz, *Scripture of the Lotus Blossom of the Fine Dharma* (New York: Columbia University Press, 1976), pp. 58–64 and 148–155.

expedients to guide them, and in the Deer Park [Mṛgadāva] displayed a goat cart [*śrāvakayāna*] to show the crisis of a body that is dependent on existence. And yoking a white ox [Buddhayāna] on Vulture Peak [Gṛdhrakūṭa], he manifested endless long life. This is indeed to use one vehicle and break three vehicles; and when three are eliminated, even one is discarded. By borrowing the long, he drove away the short; when the short disappeared, the long too vanished.

These dharmas cannot be demonstrated. Words, which are only signs, are quiescent in them, with no basis or reliance. I do not know how to express the scripture's meaning and strain to call it the *Lotus Blossom of the Fine Dharma*. Thus seating his listeners separately, the Buddha commanded them to receive the scripture appropriate to the wheel-turning king, Indra, and Brahmā. A hearer of a single phrase will receive unexcelled enlightenment. So how much more is this the case through the merit accruing from receiving, keeping, and discoursing on the scripture – how could this be conceived by thought?

I state its grand meaning in order to clarify its title and call it the *Scripture of the Lotus Blossom of the Fine Dharma.*[22]

Dubbed "Master Strong Head" by King Muyŏl because of "a piece of bone protruding from the rear of his skull," Kangsu (d. 692) was an accomplished writer of Chinese prose who studied the *Book of Filial Piety*, the "Various Rites," the *Erya* – a lexical work – and the *Selections of Refined Literature*. In 654 he was able to interpret an edict brought by a Tang envoy and drafted a memorial of thanks to the emperor, that was praised by the historian Kim Pusik as "well wrought, and its import deep." King Munmu's remarks quoted in the *Historical Records of the Three Kingdoms* best summarize the accomplishments of Kangsu as a writer in the services of his state: "Kangsu accepted the responsibility of a scribe, conveying our wishes in letters to China, Koguryŏ, and Paekche, and succeeded in establishing friendly relations with neighboring countries. With military aid from Tang China, our former king [Muyŏl] pacified Koguryŏ and Paekche. His military feats owe also to the help given by Kangsu's literary ability. Kangsu's achievements cannot be neglected."[23] Thus, in the king's estimate, the writing brush was as mighty as the sword.

In his *Admonition to the King of Flowers* (*Hwawang kye*), an allegory told by Sŏl Ch'ong (c. 660–730) to King Sinmun at the king's request, the importance of moral cultivation is stressed again in the idea that a perfect prince who rules by example must be armed with virtue and wisdom.[24] Another inscription by Sŏl Ch'ong, however, commemorating the casting of the image of the Thus Come One of Infinite Light at Kamsan Monastery, indicates a spread of Daoism among the nobility.[25] The image was cast by

[22] *TMS* 83:1a–2a.   [23] *SGSG* 46:428–429.   [24] *SGSG* 46:431–432.
[25] Chōsen sōtokufu, ed., *Chōsen kinseki sōran* 1:36.

Kim Chisŏng (also Kim Chijŏn, died. c. 720) for the souls of his parents. Upon his retirement Kim Chisŏng, who held the rank of vice-minister of state, had two images cast – the bodhisattva Maitreya and Amitābha Tathāgata. The inscription says that upon his retirement, Kim read the *Mahāyānasaṃgraha* (*Compendium of Mahāyāna*), the *Stages of Yoga Practice*, the *Laozi*, and the "Free and Easy Wandering" chapter from the *Zhuangzi*. Kim sought freedom from conventional values and distinctions between subject and object, withdrew from the world of appearance and illusion, and resolved to undergo a bodhisattva's spiritual development.

By 640, sons of the royal family were being sent to China to study Confucian texts and attend the lectures of Kong Yingda (574–648).[26] When the central authority in Silla began to decline, the students going abroad consisted mainly of the sixth "head rank" class. The number of students, both official and private, increased, and in 837 no fewer than 216 traveled to Tang China to spend a term of ten years there; in 840, some 105 students who spent more than ten years in China were sent home by imperial order.[27] What attracted Koreans to Tang China was the civil service examination for foreigners. Until 907 when Tang was destroyed, 58 Silla nationals passed the Tang examination, beginning with Kim Ungyŏng in 821. Some returned to Silla briefly and went back to China – Kim Kagi (d. 859), for example, spent his life there as a Daoist recluse. A zeal for Chinese culture and literature among the ruling class may be measured by King Kyŏngmun's discussion with Monk Nanghye of the *Wenxin diaolong* (*The Literary Mind and the Carving of Dragons*) by Liu Xie (c. 465–532). The king himself wrote an inscription for the monument to Great Master Chingyŏng.[28]

CH'OE CH'IWŎN

Of those who studied in Tang China, perhaps the most famous is Ch'oe Ch'iwŏn (b. 857), who at age twelve went to China and passed the examination in 874 at the age of eighteen. He was appointed district defender in Liaoshui county, then secretary and censor in attendance, and received a purple pouch for a golden fish tally (*yüdai*). When the Huang Chao rebellion broke out in 874, Gao Pian, circuit field commander, appointed Ch'oe as his secretary. Ch'oe says he "did his best to expedite military missives, which in four years had come to number over ten thousand." Ch'oe befriended such writers as Ku Yun, Lo Yin (833–909), and Zhang Qiao.

[26] *SGSG* 5:47. [27] Yi Kidong, *Silla kolp'umje sahoe wa hwarangdo*, pp. 280–304.
[28] Chōsen sōtokufu, ed., *Chōsen kinseki sōran* 1:78.

Emperor Huizong (873–888) sent Ch'oe to Korea as envoy with an edict. Ch'oe then held a number of positions but criticized the central government from the perspective of Confucian political and moral philosophy. "Upon returning to Korea," history comments, "Ch'oe wished to realize his ideas; but these were decadent times and as an object of suspicion and envy, he was not accepted."[29] Why should he battle against the marauding wolves in sheep's clothing? Lamenting social disorder – especially the seven years of armed revolt that ravaged the country at the end of the ninth century – and finding the hurly-burly of politics distasteful, Ch'oe retired to Mount Kaya and, as one tradition has it, became a transcendent. Fate and fortune had frustrated his dream of success. Like a good Confucian scholar, Ch'oe wished to serve his king and people. Probably no one at the time could rival Ch'oe in learning and mastery of Chinese prose and verse, but the corrupt, squabbling court was incapable of appreciating his talent. Ch'oe was posthumously enfeoffed as the Marquis of Bright Culture in 1023.

The "Monograph on Literature" in the *New History of the Tang* says: "Ch'oe Ch'iwŏn has written a chapter of parallel prose and twenty chapters of his works called *Kyewŏn p'ilgyŏng* [*chip*] (Plowing the laurel grove with a writing brush)."[30] In his preface to the *Kyewŏn p'ilgyŏng chip*, dated 886, presented to the throne, Ch'oe says his works consist of twenty-eight chapters:

Modern style verse: five pieces in one chapter

Penta- and heptasyllabic modern-style verse: one hundred pieces in one chapter

Miscellaneous poems and rhymeprose: thirty pieces in one chapter

Chungsan pokkwe chip: five chapters

Kyewŏn p'ilgyŏng chip: twenty chapters[31]

The extant *Kyewŏn p'ilgyŏng chip* in such standard Chinese collections (*congshu*) as *Sibu congkan* consists mainly of memorials and missives, but the *Tong munsŏn* (*Anthology of Korean Literature in Chinese*) preserves 146 poems of his.

In a number of poems Ch'oe sings of loss, solitude, and suffering. True friends are rare, especially in a foreign land. When you have to part from one, however, as in "Seeing a Fellow Villager Off in Shanyang," the poet can say: "Don't think me strange gazing windward dispirited, / It's hard to

[29] *SGSG* 46:429.
[30] Ouyang Xiu and Song Qi, *Xin Tangshu*, 20 vols. (Peking: Zhonghua, 1975) 60:1617a3.
[31] *SGSG* 46:431; but see the preface to *Kyewŏn p'ilgyŏng chip* (*Sibu congkan*) 1:32.

meet a friend this far from home."[32] "At the Ugang Station" and "On a Rainy Autumn Night" also deal with privation and separation:

"At the Ugang Station"

Dismounting on the sandbar I wait for a boat.
A stretch of smoke and waves, an endless sorrow.
Only when the hills are worn flat and the waters dried up
Will there be no parting in the world of man.[33]

"On a Rainy Autumn Night"

I only chant painfully in the autumn wind,
For I have few friends in the wide world.
At third watch, it rains outside.
By the lamp my heart flies myriad miles away.[34]

Friendship was often considered vital to moral improvement, in addition to study and contemplation. Who is it that the poet longs for? Was he looking for unreserved affection and support? Are tranquility and solitude worth the suffering they entail? Ch'oe seems to think so in "Inscribed at the Study on Mount Kaya," which delights in a mountain torrent as it rushes down jumbled rocks and drowns out the cacophony of the world below. The speaker scorns distinctions, all petty disputes, for he is no longer affected by life and death, benefit and harm. Thus by nondiscrimination he has withstood the onslaught of time. He has not asked great questions but offers a Daoist solution to his problems.

Ch'oe Ch'iwŏn is also the author of four epitaphs inscribed on monuments at monasteries. All written by royal order, they were studied by the clergy as important documents for learning about the history of Silla Buddhism and esteemed by the literati as models of ornate parallel prose. Three of the four monuments were erected in honor of the Meditation (Sŏn) school of Silla Buddhism. The first of these is graced by Ch'oe Ch'iwŏn's own calligraphy and was erected in 887 in praise of the Meditation Master Chingam (Hyeso, 774–850) at Ssanggye Monastery in Hadong, South Kyŏngsang. The epitaph consists of a preface in which Ch'oe expounds the similarity between Confucianism, Buddhism, and Daoism, a biographical notice, and a eulogy. Chingam, who was in China from 804 to 830, had lived at Okch'ŏn Monastery on Mount Chiri and refused the summons of King Minae in 838.

---

[32] *TMS* 19:13a.   [33] *TMS* 19:13a.
[34] *TMS* 19:1a; Yu Sŏngjun, "*Chŏn Tangsi* sojae Sillain si," *Hanguk hanmunhak yŏngu* 3–4 (1979):101–119. Konishi notes Ch'oe's mastery of the late Tang poetic style in *A History of Japanese Literature* 2:33. For a comparison of the prose style of Ch'oe Ch'iwŏn and Kūkai (774–835), see pp. 43–46.

The second monument, at Sŏngju Monastery in Poryŏng, South Ch'ungch'ŏng, was erected in about 890 in honor of National Preceptor Muyŏm (800–888), with calligraphy by Ch'oe Ŏnwi (868–944). Muyŏm went to Tang China in about 821 and returned in 845. The founder of the Mount Sŏngju school of meditation, he was national preceptor to kings Munsŏng (839–857) and Hŏngang (875–886). The epitaph in 5,120 graphs consists of a preface, biographical notice, *non* (critical estimate), and a pentasyllabic eulogy (*myŏng*). The third meditation-inspired monument was built in 924 in honor of Great Master Tohŏn (Chijŭng, 824–882) at Pongam Monastery, Mungyŏng, North Kyŏngsang; the epitaph by Ch'oe, completed in 893, consists of a preface, a biographical notice, and a heptasyllabic eulogy.

Unlike the other monuments, erected at centers of the Meditation school, the fourth monument was located at a monastery built for the royal house. Taesŭngbok Monastery (named by King Hŏngang in 885) and the monument there stood at least until Iryŏn compiled his *Memorabilia of the Three Kingdoms*, but today they no longer exist. Only some ten fragments of Ch'oe's calligraphy are found at the site.[35]

---

[35] Ch'oe Yŏngmu, ed., *Chuhae sasan pimyŏng* (Asea munhwasa, 1987).

CHAPTER 5

Koryŏ songs

Peter H. Lee

VICISSITUDES OF TEXTUAL TRANSMISSION

The difficulty of studying vernacular poetry of the Koryŏ dynasty can be traced to several obstacles. One is the lack of a uniform system of writing during that period. Although *hyangch'al* was used by King Yejong in 1120 to write a poem (or used by a scribe recording the royal poems) it was not in general use for recording vernacular poetry. Great Master Kyunyŏ wrote his eleven songs in *hyangch'al*, but his songs are usually discussed under *hyangga* of the Silla period. In fact, most songs of popular origin were transmitted by word of mouth until they were put down in writing in the Korean alphabet as late as the early sixteenth century.

The intensive study of Chinese classics and the prestige accorded to writing in literary Chinese contributed to the dearth of material. The Koryŏ dynasty, which espoused Buddhism as the state religion, nevertheless imitated fashionable conventions of government that were traditionally Chinese and based on Confucian political and moral philosophy. With the adoption of the civil service examination system, the two-corps system of government – civil and military – became effective in 958 but only the civil officials chosen by this examination were occupied with state affairs. After seventy-five years of peace (1047–1122), Koryŏ was battered by a military coup internally and by successive invasions of the Khitans, Jurchens, Mongols, and Japanese externally. Especially after the Mongol invasion, a degenerate hedonism formed the basis of the upper-class culture that attempted to disguise its troubles by living a secluded and often luxurious life. The ruling class cared little about the growth of vernacular poetry and indeed tended to disdain it. Thus even the songs transmitted in *hyangch'al* – unless they were composed by members of the royal family or famous officials and dealt with state administration or current affairs – were not recorded in history. This is especially true of Chosŏn-dynasty historians when they compiled the monograph on the music and songs of Koryŏ:

because the popular songs were in the vernacular, they briefly gave their origins, but not their texts.

Moreover, a handful of recorded songs were either lost in the course of time or occasionally expunged by the censors of the Chosŏn dynasty as "vulgar and obscene." As soon as the national policy was formulated to adopt Confucian political and moral philosophy as the basis of government, the Chosŏn dynasty turned its attention to the poetry and music of the previous kingdom. Built on Confucian political and moral philosophy, scholars' criteria for the subjects of songs were moral and didactic. We know how Chinese scholars misread love songs in the *Book of Songs*. To censors, or ardent advocates of morality, Koryŏ songs were mostly vulgar – their frank expression of love seemed an affront to public decency. Under kings Sejong (1418–1450), Sŏngjong (1469–1494), and Chungjong (1506–1544), the Koryŏ songs and music were compiled and edited by historians, and it was during the reign of Sŏngjong that six of the existing songs were revised (1488 and 1490).[1] Discussion continued until 1537. Official compilations such as the *Koryŏ sa* (*History of Koryŏ*, 1451) or the *Akhak kwebŏm* (*Canon of Music*, 1493) omit the texts of these songs, but compilations of unknown origins (perhaps by contemporary musicians and singers) preserve them. Thus we do not know if the texts as we have them today are censored versions or not.

Our available sources are the monograph on music in the *History of Koryŏ* (chapters 70–71), the *Canon of Music*, the *Akchang kasa* (*Words for Songs and Music*), and the *Siyong hyangak po* (*Notations for Korean Music in Contemporary Use*, early sixteenth century). These sources record seventy-two titles of Koryŏ works, thirty-three with texts:

22 in Korean
1 in *hyangch'al*
3 in *idu* and Chinese
3 in Chinese
4 in Chinese with Korean connectives

The remaining thirty-nine titles, as noted, are not accompanied by texts.[2]

Songs preserved in the *Canon of Music* and *Words for Songs and Music* and performed at court gatherings deal with love. These songs were popular during late Koryŏ, when Korean kings married Mongol princesses who brought with them Mongol entertainment. Musicians and women singers who performed both for royal audiences and in town might have introduced

---

[1] Chŏng Inji and Hwangbo In, *Sejong sillok* (*CWS* 2–6), 3:1a, 65:21b; Sin Sŭngsŏn et al., *Sŏngjong sillok* (*CWS* 8–12), 215:1a, 219:4b, 240:18b; Yi Ki and Chŏng Sunmyŏng, *Chungjong sillok* (*CWS* 14–19), 32:43b–44a.
[2] Nine pieces in *ACKS*; "Song of Ch'ŏyong" duplicated. For seventy-two titles see Pak Pyŏngch'ae, *Koryŏ kayo ŭi ŏsŏk yŏngu*, pp. 20–27, and Pak Nojun, *Koryŏ kayo ŭi yŏngu*.

popular songs to the court, where most were revised to suit the place and occasion of performance. These songs reflect a relaxing of morality and weakening of central political authority – which is why they were edited by Chosŏn-dynasty censors. For example, an introductory stanza was added to "Tongdong" ("Ode to the Seasons") and "Chŏngsŏk ka" ("Song of the Gong and Chimes") to serve as a eulogy; parts with different contents were joined together to make a new text, as in the "Manjŏnch'un pyŏlsa"; and the music of "Manjŏnch'un" ("Spring Overflows the Pavilion"), "Sŏgyŏng pyŏlgok" ("Song of P'yŏngyang"), and "Ch'ŏngsan pyŏlgok" ("Song of Green Mountain") was used for other court music repertory, though their texts were rejected because their content was "love between the sexes."[3]

The Koryŏ songs, then, owe their survival to the adoption of their accompanying music for court use from the beginning of the Chosŏn dynasty. Historical sources may denounce the texts of these songs as vulgar and unworthy of preservation, but the music books preserve their musical tune, an indication that musical notations were in use for several hundred years as part of the repertory of court and official music. Because no other music was available at the time, the eulogies compiled to praise the founding of the new dynasty had to be sung to the tune of popular Koryŏ songs. This transformation, however, required the addition of Korean grammatical elements (*-haya*, *-hadŏni*, *-hani*, *-iroda*, and *-syatta*, for instance) to the original composed in classical Chinese, usually in four-word lines, inspired by the normative tetrasyllabic line of the *Book of Songs*.

Clear markings of the lyric persona and the abundance of honorific verbal endings in Koryŏ songs indicate the gender not only of the lyric speaker but also of the performer – female slaves, entertainers, shamans – as well as the place of performance: the court, often in the presence of the king. Indeed, the occasion of performance sometimes transformed the longing for the beloved in the original – note the frequency of the word *nim* (beloved) in "Song of the Gong and Chimes" and "Will You Go?" as well as *aso nimha* (O Lord: O love) in "Treading Frost" and "Maternal Love" – into that for the lord/king. Another device was to add the elements of praise to camouflage the realistic contents of Koryŏ songs to suit the occasion (as in "Ode to the Seasons").

TWENTY-TWO SONGS IN THE VERNACULAR

The "To ijang ka" ("Dirge for Two Generals") and "Chŏng Kwajŏng" ("Regret," c. 1156) represent a transitional period between the *hyangga* and

---

[3] The first was used as instrumental music; the second for the text of "Pacification of the East"; and the third for "Song of Naghachu."

Koryŏ songs: the former is an eight-line poem written in *hyangch'al*; the latter is a ten- or eleven-line poem without stanzaic division. The characteristic forms of Koryŏ songs are the *sogyo* (popular songs) and the *kyŏnggich'e ka* (*kyŏnggi*-orthographic songs). The *sogyo* is so called because of the refrain recurring at intervals, generally at the end of each stanza, which is used to achieve a certain mood in each song. These popular songs were sung to musical accompaniment and found their place wherever men and women gathered and entertained each other with songs. The refrain serves as a meaningless onomatopoeia of the sounds of musical instruments (drum, flute, or zither) or nonsense jingles to carry the tune and spirit of the songs – as in the "Ode to the Seasons," "Song of P'yŏngyang," "Song of Green Mountain," and "Treading Frost." In the "Kasiri" ("Will You Go?"), however, the refrain has clearly definable parts within itself – an interjection, an imitation of the sounds of a zither, and a poetic phrase that might have been a later addition.

The refrain in the Koryŏ songs is an indispensable element in chain verse. By means of the refrain a song consisting of several independent parts with different content is linked together. Each stanza in most Koryŏ songs can be read as an independent unit apart from the entire song. It is the refrain that links the individual units, so that each stanza in each song can play its role in fully achieving the final effect. It should be noted, however, that among the Koryŏ songs there are some that do not have stanzaic divisions. In these songs, several different units are linked together – as, for example, in the "Ch'ŏyong ka" ("Song of Ch'ŏyong"), which consists of six parts including the song written in 879.

A record on the back of the monument at Hyŏnhwa Temple relates that upon completion of the temple, built for the repose of the souls of his parents, King Hyŏnjong (1009–1031) himself wrote a *hyangga* and his subjects presented eleven songs (*sanoe ka*) to him.[4] All of the poems praise the temple's completion and the power of the Buddha. This indicates that the *hyangga*, the most polished and popular form of Korean song in Silla, continued to be written by kings and subjects alike. The sixteenth king, Yejong, who delighted in exchanging poems in Chinese with his courtiers, himself wrote a *hyangga* at the harvest festival (P'algwanhoe) held in the western capital (P'yŏngyang) in the tenth month of 1120. At the festival the king saw two horses carrying two effigies prancing around the courtyard. Upon inquiry, he learned that they were the images of two generals, Sin Sunggyŏm and Kim Nak, who had sacrificed their own lives to save the life

---

4 Chōsen Sōtokufu, ed., *Chōsen kinseki sōran* 1:251.

of Wang Kŏn (918–943), founder of the Koryŏ dynasty. Deeply moved, the king composed a song. During the founder's reign it had been customary at the harvest festival for two men wearing the two generals' masks to dance. The practice of honoring the dead with dance and song is an old tradition, therefore, and the royal song, consisting of two stanzas, says:

> Loyal hearts that saved your king
> Reach the end of heaven.
> Though your souls departed,
> You stand erect and speak.
>
> O two heroes of merit!
> I know
> The trace of your loyalty
> Endures throughout the ages.[5]

Accused of taking part in a plot to enthrone the younger brother of King Ŭijong (1146–1170), Chŏng Sŏ was banished to his birthplace Tongnae in 1151 and was released only in 1170 after a military coup. Talented but frivolous, according to historical accounts, Chŏng was King Injong's favorite courtier. At the place of his exile, Chŏng is said to have composed this poem plucking the black zither:

> I who have yearned for you and wept
> Am like a bird in the hills.
> The waning moon and dawn stars know
> That their false words were wrong.
> May my soul be there where yours resides.
> Who opposed you?
> I've committed no errors or crime.
> They are all lies.
> How sad!
> Have you already forgotten me?
> Listen to me, O Lord, and show me favor![6]

Since this song is called *samjinjak* in the *Canon of Music* and *chinjak* appears as a musical tune for other songs, the song was probably sung to the tune of *chinjak*. Although the text appears as an eleven-line poem, the eighth and ninth lines can be collapsed to yield a total of ten. Thus the song resembles a ten-line *hyangga* with one exception: an interjection that would begin the ninth line of a *hyangga* is here included in the tenth line,

---

5 Kim Tonguk, " 'To ijang ka' ŭi munhŏn minsokhakchŏk koch'al," in *Koryŏ sidae ŭi kayo munhak*, ed. Kim Yŏlgyu and Sin Tonguk (Saemunsa, 1982), pp. 116–123.

6 *KRS* 97:23b–24a; *AHKB* 5:14b (*KRS* 71:38b–39a).

"*Aso nimha.*" Chŏng laments his rejection in the manner of the speaker in the *Li sao* (*Encountering Sorrow*). Unlike poets of later times, however, he does not offer an alternative life based upon different values.

The "Song of Ch'ŏyong" is a dramatic song of forty-five lines consisting of six parts. The first part (lines 1–30) includes a prologue, a description of the great appearance of Ch'ŏyong, and a description of the making of Ch'ŏyong. The other five parts are: Ch'ŏyong's plea (31–32); the singer's threat to the demon and an inquiry to Ch'ŏyong (33–40); Ch'ŏyong's request (41–42); the plea of the demon (43–44); and the singer's conclusion (45). Originally a song accompanying a shamanist ceremony, during the Chosŏn dynasty it was performed at court as part of the exorcism (*narye*) ceremony on New Year's Eve. During the time of King Hŏngang of Silla, portents of national ruin were exorcised as diseases or natural calamities and it was believed that Ch'ŏyong could repel them. In the Koryŏ period, when the capital was transferred to Kanghwa Island during the Mongol invasion, the ceremony was performed to drive the enemy from Korean soil. The text in the *Canon of Music* is probably what King Sejong edited and entitled "Ponghwang ŭm" ("Song of the Phoenix") to from part of the court music repertory. As in Korean shamanist songs, the poem evinces a happy mingling of shamanism and Buddhism, as in the reference to Rāhu, the son of Śākyamuni.[7]

Among popular love songs of Koryŏ, only the "Ssanghwajŏm" ("The Turkish Bakery") is not a folk song: it is an original composition made in 1279 by a sycophant of King Ch'ungnyŏl (1274–1308) named O Cham.[8] In 1274, at the age of thirty-eight, the king married a Mongol princess who was only sixteen. She died in Korea in 1297.[9] The king loved entertainments, lewd songs and dances, and his sycophants did everything to satisfy his thirst for sensual pleasure. The king had a permanent stage built in the palace grounds, recruited female entertainers from the shamans and official slaves, and had them dress in male attire, a horsehair hat included. The text is enticing, but the refrains, intended for synaesthetic effect, are also said to evoke the arousing of sexual desire: *tarorŏ kŏdirŏ* (line 4); *tŏrŏ tungsyŏng tarirŏdirŏ tarirŏdirŏ tarorŏgŏdirŏ tarorŏ* (line 5); and *wi wi tarorŏ kŏdirŏ tarorŏ* (line 7).[10] The song consists of four eight-line stanzas; part of the fourth, fifth, and seventh lines are refrains. The song is in the first

[7] *ACKS* 14a–15b; *AHKB* 5:12b–13a (see also *KRS* 71:36a).

[8] *KRS* 125:17a–22a (see also 71:42a–b).

[9] *KRS* 28:1a–b, 89:1a–11b; Louis Hambis, "Notes sur l'histoire de Corée à l'époque mongole," *T'oung Pao* 45 (1957):178–193, esp. p. 179.

[10] Yŏ Chŭngdong, "'Ssanghwajŏm' norae yŏngu," in *Koryŏ sidae ŭi kayo munhak*, ed. Kim Yŏlgyu and Sin Tonguk (Saemunsa, 1982), pp. 90–103; *ACKS* 7a–8b.

person throughout and the speaker narrates her adventures in four different circumstances. She speaks directly, and her determination finds expression in the last three lines of each stanza: "I will go, yes, go to his bower: / . . . / A narrow place, sultry and dark."

> I go to the Turkish shop, buy a bun,
> An old Turk grasps me by the hand.
> If this story is spread abroad,
> *tarorŏ kŏdirŏ,* you alone are to blame, little actor!
> *tŏrŏ tungsyŏng tarirŏdirŏ tarirŏdirŏ tarorŏgŏdirŏ tarorŏ*
> I will go, yes, go to his bower:
> *wi wi tarorŏ kŏdirŏ tarorŏ*
> A narrow place, sultry and dark.
>
> (stanza 1)

The "Ode to the Seasons" is an anonymous song of sixty-five lines, consisting of a eulogy and a love complaint, and is divided into thirteen four-line stanzas with a one-line refrain, *Aŭ tongdong tari,* at the end of each stanza. The first stanza, a panegyric prologue, was perhaps added later to make the song more suitable for court performance. The prologue has more than one reading, depending on which philologist's gloss one follows. One alternative reading, for example, is:

> We offer virtue to gods,
> Happiness to the king.
> Let's come forward
> To offer virtue and happiness.

The twelve stanzas are devoted to each of the twelve months of the lunar year, making reference to monthly observances of folk origin that survive even today.

> With virtue in one hand,
> And happiness in the other,
> Come, come, you gods
> With virtue and happiness.
>
> On the feast of irises
> I brew healing herbs
> And offer you this drink –
> May you live a thousand years.
>
> In December I am like
> Chopsticks carved from pepperwood
> Placed neatly before you:
> An unknown guest holds them![11]
>
> (stanzas 1, 6, 13)

---

[11] *AHKB* 3:8a–9a.

The speaker likens herself to "a comb cast from a cliff," "a sliced berry," and "chopsticks." Born into this world to "live alone," she seems fated to her plight forever. Following the calendrical song form, she compares the stages of her love to the four seasons, but the sorrow of abandonment and loneliness dominates her emotions. It is the discord between the changeless inner turmoil and the changing seasons that is the subject of the song.

Example 3.   Anon., "Song of Green Mountain." *Words for Songs and Music* (n.d.) 3b–4a.

얄리얄라셩얄라리얄라○가티새가티새본다물
아래가티새본다잉무든장글란가지고물아래가
티새본다얄리얄라셩얄라리얄라○이링공
더링공ᄒᆞ야나즈란디내와손뎌오리도가리도업
손바므란ᄯᅩ디호리라얄리얄라셩얄라
얄라○어듸라더디턴돌코누리라마치턴돌코미
리도괴리도업시마자셔우니노라얄리얄리얄라
셩얄라리얄라○살어리살어리랏다바ᄅᆞ래살어
리랏다누ᄆᆞ자기구조개랑먹고바ᄅᆞ래살어리랏

Example 3. *(Continued)*

In the "Song of Green Mountain," an anonymous song whose text is preserved in the *Words for Songs and Music*, a lost lover takes a pessimistic view of life and tries every means to unburden himself of sorrow. The song is written in eight five-line stanzas with the same refrain at the end of each stanza: "*Yalli yalli yallasyŏng yallari yalla.*" The speaker comes to the conclusion that wine is the perfect anodyne, and the song ends with an invocation in praise of wine. By asking rhetorically at the close, "What shall I do now?" the speaker tries to excuse himself for not proceeding to the seashore but instead settling down: he is a captive of wine. In this song, ambiguous or obsolete terms present difficulties in dividing and interpreting words and phrases. The interpretation of a word often depends on one's deciphering of another word or on the context. Some commentators follow a mere hunch and hit upon novel readings – often in a waste of ingenuity. Such readings have been given to explain, for example, the stone mentioned in "I cry being hit by a stone" in the fifth stanza. One reading contends that the song refers to a game or a fight with stones implying that the speaker's state of mind is like one being attacked with stones in a fight. Another hypothesis is that the stone stands for blind fate. The seventh stanza refers to an entertainment in which a man disguised as a stag climbs up a pole and plays a two-stringed fiddle (*haegŭm*); one reading proposes that the whole stanza might refer to a miracle without which man cannot live. Moreover, *sae* (bird) in the third stanza has been read as *sarae* (furrow), and *kadŏn sae* (passing bird) as *kaldŏn sarae* (dug furrow), to support the hypothesis that the song is sung by a displaced farmer who was driven from his home by foreign invasions or internal disturbances.[12]

Let's live, let's live,	살어리 살어리랏다
Let's live in the green mountain!	靑山애 살어리랏다
With wild grapes and thyme,	멀위랑 다래랑 먹고
Let's live in the green mountain!	靑山애 살어리랏다
Yalli yalli yallasyŏng yallari yalla	얄리 얄리 얄라셩 얄라리 얄라
Cry, cry, birds,	우러라 우러라 새여
You cry after you wake.	자고 니러 우러라 새여
I've more sorrow than you	널라와 시름한 나도
And cry after I wake.	자고 니러 우니노라
Yalli yalli yallasyŏng yallari yalla	얄리 얄리 얄라셩 얄라리 얄라
I see the bird passing, bird passing,	가던새 가던새 본다
I see the passing bird on the water.	믈아래 가던새 본다
With a mossy plow	잉무든 장글란 가지고
I see the passing bird beyond the water.	믈아래 가던새 본다
Yalli yalli yallasyŏng yallari yalla	얄리 얄리 얄라셩 얄라리 얄라
I've spent the day	이링공 뎌링공 하야
This way and that.	나즈란 디내와손뎌
But where no man comes or goes,	오리도 가리도 업슨
How am I to pass the night?	바므란 또 엇디호리라
Yalli yalli yallasyŏng yallari yalla	얄리 얄리 얄라셩 얄라리 얄라

---

[12] *ACKS* 2b–4b, and *SH* 24b–25b.

At what place is this stone thrown? 어디라 더디던 돌코
At what person is this stone thrown? 누리라 마치던 돌코
Here no one to hate or love, 므 l 리도 괴리도 업시
I cry being hit by a stone. 마자셔 우니노라
Yalli yalli yallasyŏng yallari yalla 얄리 얄리 얄라셩 얄라리 얄라

(stanzas 1–5)

The "Song of P'yŏngyang" is a dramatic lyric spoken by a woman (perhaps a female entertainer), consisting of fourteen three-line stanzas. The third line in each stanza ties the text to the musical tune and goes: *Wi tuŏrŏngsyŏng tuŏrŏngsyŏng taringdiri*. The fifth through eighth stanzas have been popular in and of themselves, separately from the complete song, and recur as the final stanza of the "Song of the Gong and Chimes."

> Were the pearls to fall on the rock,
> Would the thread be broken?
> If I parted from you for a thousand years,
> Would my heart be changed?

The ninth through fourteenth stanzas are the most intense, as the speaker pleads with a boatman on the Taedong River not to allow her lover to cross over. She adds, however, that he too is in the same predicament as the speaker – the boatman's own wife is inconstant. The song was criticized by Chosŏn censors as expressing a weak sense of virtue.[13]

The "Song of the Gong and Chimes" is an anonymous song that tells of an unbroken dynastic line and prays that the life of kings may last as long as heaven and earth. The song begins with a three-line introduction and continues in ten three-line stanzas. After offering a series of impossibilities, the poem then declares that only if these ever occur shall "we part from the virtuous lord," as the refrain in the third, fourth, and fifth stanzas states. The use of the *adynata* (impossibilities) as a rhetorical device in the poetry of praise is a commonplace in Korea, as elsewhere. The virtuous lord (*yudŏkhasin nim*) could be a loved one, or one's parents, according to the occasion, in addition to referring to the king. Thus this song of compliment accompanied by the gong and chimes became a popular ceremonial song.[14]

> Ring the gong, strike the chimes!
> In this age of calm and plenty,
> Let's live and enjoy.
>
> On a brittle sandy cliff,
> On a brittle sandy cliff,
> Let's plant roasted chestnuts, five pints.

[13] *ACKS* 4b–6a. [14] *ACKS* 2b–3b; *SH* 23a–24a.

When the chestnuts shoot and sprout,
When the chestnuts shoot and sprout,
Then we'll part from the virtuous lord.
(stanzas 1–2)

"Treading Frost" is an anonymous love song of thirteen lines with no stanzaic division. The third line is a refrain: *Tarongdiusyŏ madŭksari madunŏjŭse
nŏuji*.[15] The invocation of thunderbolts and hellfire (lines 6–9) seems to
suggest that the speaker's relation with her beloved is illicit or that her
passion for him is such that it might bring down punishment upon her.
"Will You Go?" is another love song spoken by a woman. The song
consists of four two-line stanzas plus a refrain at the end of each. This
song has much literary merit; its language is simple but intense, and it is
filled with tender sentiments for the parting lover. The court adopted the
music for its attractiveness. *Nanŭn* (the pronoun "I") appears six times for
emphasis at the end of lines 1, 2, 5, 6, 10, and 11 to underscore the plight of
the lyric persona. The refrain, *wi chŭngjulka t'aep'yŏng sŏngdae* (O age of
great peace and plenty!), must have been added later to transform it into a
song of compliment appropriate for courtly performance.

Will you go away? *nanŭn*
Will you forsake me and go? *nanŭn*
wi chŭngjulka age of great peace and plenty![16]

In "Spring Overflows the Pavilion," an anonymous love song of eighteen
lines (four three-line stanzas, one five-line stanza, and a concluding line)
or twenty-six lines (five five-line stanzas and a one-line conclusion), the
speaker says the spring in her heart is dead, killed by the loved one. But
can there be another spring outside? After an imaginary coaxing dialogue
in the fourth stanza, the fifth transforms the tone of the song by having
the treacherous man express his wish for fulfillment: he will be able to
transform the icy bamboo hut into a love grotto. Indeed, the speaker's
desire for preservation of love in absence is so strong that he (actually she
in disguise) says he can transform a bamboo hut into an ideal place:

Were I to build a bamboo hut on the ice,
Were I to die of cold with him on the ice,
Were I to build a bamboo hut on the ice,
Were I to die of cold with him on the ice,
O night, run slow, run slow, till our love is spent.[17]

---

[15] *ACKS* 8a–b; *SH* 15a–21b.   [16] *ACKS* 8b–9a; *SH* 27a–28a.   [17] *ACKS* 18a–b.

In the original, the first line of the first and third stanzas, and the first two lines of the fifth stanza, are repeated. The third stanza's second line recalls the fifth line of "Regret": "May my soul be there where yours resides." Each stanza resembles in form and meter the *sijo* form and seems to indicate its germination before it came into being as a single unified poem.

"Maternal Love" is an anonymous short song of five lines in all. The song is simple in structure and compares the difference between paternal and maternal love to the difference in sharpness between a hoe and a sickle:

> Hoe too is an edged tool;
> But in sharpness sickle certainly wins.
> Father is father of man;
> But in love mother surely surpasses.
> Yes, his indeed cannot be more than hers.[18]

KYŎNGGI-CH'E SONGS

The *kyŏnggich'e ka*, or *kyŏnggi*-orthographic song, is so called because of the refrain that begins *kŭi ŏttŏhaniikko?* and recurs in the fourth and sixth lines of each stanza. The form's origin has been traced to *hyangga*, Koryŏ songs, didactic folk songs, Chinese parallel prose, or Song *ci* (lyric), but in no instance persuasively. The basic form is as follows:

	3	3	4	
	3	3	4	
	4	4	4	
wi (Ah)	3	3	4	
	4	4	4	4
wi (Ah)	3	3	4	

Three Koryŏ products include the "Hallim pyŏlgok" ("Song of Confucian Scholars," c. 1216) by a group of literati, and the "Kwandong pyŏlgok" ("Song of Diamond Mountains," c. 1328) and "Chukkye pyŏlgok" ("Song of the Bamboo Stream," 1348) by An Ch'uk (1282–1348). Texts are either in *idu* and Chinese (An Ch'uk's poems) or in Chinese with connectives and refrains written in Korean ("Song of Confucian Scholars") and are characterized by enumeration – as in the listing of esteemed Korean scholars in the first stanza of "Song of Confucian Scholars":

> Prose of Yu Wŏnsun, poetry of Yi Illo, parallel prose of Yi Kongno,
> Double rhymes and swift composition of Yi Kyubo and Chin Hwa,

---

[18] *ACKS* 6a; *SH* 10b–13b.

Problem essays of Yu Chunggi, classical exegesis of Min Kwanggyun,
shi poetry and rhymeprose of Kim Yanggyŏng,
Ah, if these took the examination, what a sight it would be!
Kim Ŭi's pupils handsome as jade shoots, Kim Ŭi's pupils handsome
　　as jade shoots,
How many can follow me?[19]

As this literal version shows, such elitist poetry is only for literati who
have studied the Chinese classics and become accomplished writers of their
times. The principal trope of enumeration suggests plenitude. Each of the
second through seventh stanzas is devoted to one category in the following
order: titles of Chinese classics and literature; styles of calligraphy; wine;
flowers; musical instruments; and scenic spots. The poem concludes with
a swing scene in the eighth stanza. These are all ingredients of the literati's
leisurely and elegant lifestyle, and it has been suggested that each of the
writers present took turns furnishing a stanza. The recent discovery of five
examples by Buddhist monks (Kihwa, 1376–1433, for example),[20] written
to praise the Buddha and spread his teaching, indicates that the literati did
not monopolize the form.

FOLK AND SHAMANIST SONGS

Among fourteen songs recorded in *Notations for Korean Music in Contemporary Use*, two are folk songs – "Yugu kok" ("Song of the Pigeon") and "Sangjŏ
ka" ("Song of the Pestle") – and twelve are said to be associated with shamanist rituals but have not been adequately studied to date.[21] The "Song of the
Pigeon"[22] is considered to be a variation on that attributed to King Yejong
called "Pŏlgokcho" ("The Cuckoo"). The king wished to learn of popular
criticism of his faults and policies. Fearing, however, that his subjects might
not voice their true feelings, he composed the song to encourage them to
speak out like the cuckoo that loves to sing whenever it feels the urge.

> The pigeon
> The pigeon
> Can coo,
> But I like
> The cuckoo better

---

[19] *ACKS* 12a–13b for the text. For *kyŏnggi-ch'e* verse see Yi Myŏnggu, *Koryŏ kayo ŭi yŏngu* (Sinasa,
　　1980), pp. 9–130, and Pak Kyŏngju, *Kyŏnggi-ch'e ka yŏngu* (Ihoe munhwasa, 1996).
[20] Cho Tongil, *Hanguk munhak t'ongsa*, 5 vols., with a separate index, 2nd edn. (Chisik sanŏpsa, 1989)
　　2:291–292.
[21] See Pak Pyŏngch'ae, *Koryŏ kayo ŭi ŏsŏk yŏngu*, pp. 340–382.　　[22] *SH* 25b–27a.

I like
The cuckoo better.

The "Song of the Pestle"[23] is a work song sung by women around the mortar pounding rice:

Let's mill grain with a rattle *hiyae*
Let's cook coarse rice *hiyae*
And offer it to father and mother *hiyahae*
If any remains I'll eat it *hiyahae*.

For convenience we can divide the twelve songs considered to be shamanist in content and function into two groups: those whose texts follow the regular syntax and have some intended meaning; and those consisting of meaningless sounds to fill the melodic lines. "Narye ka" ("Song of Exorcism")[24] is associated with the exorcism ritual held at court and private homes on New Year's Eve in the lunar calendar. At court the ceremony consisted of music, song, and dance, performed by seventy-eight members of the troupe, including twenty-four boys from age twelve to sixteen (*chinja*) wearing masks and red gowns. The ritual was held in the palace during the Koryŏ and Chosŏn dynasties for entertainment – such as the reception of Chinese envoys, the appointment of a new governor, or an outing of the king – and for religious purposes as well. In Korea, as in China, the ritual included a demon impersonator called Pangsang-ssi (Fangxiang shi: "he who searches for evil spirits in many directions"). About this figure the *Rites of Chou* comments: "In his official function, he wears [over his head] a bearskin having four eyes of gold, and is clad in a black upper garment and a red lower garment. Grasping his lance and brandishing his shield, he leads the many officials to perform the seasonal exorcism (No), searching through houses and driving out pestilences."[25] The account of the Pangsang-ssi in the *History of Koryŏ* approximates the quotation just given.[26] From the contents of its first stanza – the only text quoted in the source – the song may have been composed after viewing a shamanist ritual.

Sŏnang gods in the "Sŏnang pan" or "Sŏnghwang pan" ("Food for Sŏnghwang Gods"),[27] originally the guardian gods of the dry moat surrounding the walled city of China, were introduced to Korea sometime during the Koryŏ dynasty, mingled with shaman gods of mountains and villages, and became popular gods of folk belief. Usually placed near the

[23] *SH* 32a–34a.   [24] *SH* 21b–23a.
[25] Derk Bodde, *Festivals in Classical China* (Princeton: Princeton University Press, 1975), p. 77.
[26] *KRS* 64:38a.   [27] *SH* 45a–54a.

entrance to the village or on a hill overlooking it, the Sŏnang god protects the village and looks after the welfare of its people. The shrine and surrounding area are regarded as holy ground and kept clean. We may recall that Tangun became a mountain god in Asadal. In addition to the shrine (*tangiip*), a large tree (*tangnamu*) is said to be the god's abode, and it is believed to eliminate calamities, confer blessings, and help fulfillment of wishes. Sacrifices are offered to deliver the state from a crisis or to report victory in a battle. Sŏnang gods are enfeoffed as the "lord who guards the state" or a "count who informs the state."

> The guardian who keeps a kingdom in the east,
> The broad-eyed guardian in the west,
> I pay homage to the guardian of increase and growth in the south,
> The guardian who hears much and is versed in the northern
>   mountain,
> *tarirŏtarori romaha*
> *tirongdiri taerirŏ romaha*
> *toramdariro taroring tirŏri*
> O exorcists with four eyes of gold within and without!

The four guardians of the world are Indra's generals who dwell each on a side of Mount Meru and ward off the attacks of malicious spirits, an indication of Buddhist influence.

The first stanza of the "Naedang" ("The Inner Hall")[28] is said to have been sung by the shamans when they prayed in a small Buddhist cloister in the palace to ward off calamities, sickness, and the like. If the speaker is a woman, it is unclear in its present reading why thirteen slaves (or men) are brought in and what the verbs following them are expected to signify. It may, one commentator proposes, have been composed by a musician attached to the Bureau of Music to create a merry atmosphere at a court banquet. The subject of the "Taewang pan" ("Food for the Great King")[29] concerns a frolicking of Sŏnang gods with eight women, or a great king frolicking with eight gods and women. The "Samsŏng taewang" ("Great King of the Three Walled Cities")[30] entreats the Sŏnang gods named Samsŏng Taewang to eliminate pestilential vapors. The "Taeguk" ("The Large Country")[31] is read as a song of offering to shamanist gods, a prayer to Sŏnang gods for the peace of the country, or a plea for a life without misfortune and unforeseen

---

[28] *SH* 54b–61a.   [29] *SH* 61a–62b.   [30] *SH* 69a–70b.
[31] *SH* 73a–78b. See Pak Kyŏngsin, "Taeguk kwa pyŏlsang kut muga," in Sŏnggyungwan taehakkyo Inmun kwahak yŏnguso, ed., *Koryŏ kayo yŏngu ŭi hyŏnhwang kwa chŏnmang* (Chimmundang, 1996), pp. 303–334.

accidents. "Four hundred ailments" in the first stanza refers to 404 ailments of the body: since each of the four elements – earth, water, fire, and wind – is responsible for 101 ailments, 202 fevers are caused by earth and fire and another 202 by water and wind.

While nine songs from the first group contain refrains, the three songs in the second group consist solely of refrains, or probably a notation that presents a set of mnemonic sounds (*yukpo*) imitating the sounds for each of the following instruments: the double-reed oboe, transverse flute, black zither, large gong, barrel drum, or two-stringed fiddle. One example, "Kunma taewang" ("The Great King of the Warhorse"),[32] may illustrate the structure and sound system of a typical song:

> Rirŏru rŏrirŏru rinrŏriru
> Rŏru rorirŏru
> Rirŏruri rŏriru
> Rori rorari
> Roriru rirŏru ronrŏriru
> Rŏru rŏrirŏru
> Rirŏruri roriru

These refrains may appear repetitive and dull on the page, but sung with musical accompaniment they could well have been lovely – as, for example, in the secular Christmas carol with four fa-la-las:

> Deck the halls with boughs of holly,
> Fa la la la la la la la la

There is no increment of meaning in our example, but the repetitions and modulations must have been deemed rhythmic. In terms of groupings of sounds, the only consonant is *l/r* and the five vowels are *a, i, u, o, ŏ*. Why is this preponderance of *l/r* (as in other songs) so insistently repeated? Are they the sounds of leading, galloping, or urging on the horse? Or the sounds of the horse's neighing? Or some mysterious charm? What hidden truth are these sounds intended to convey, and what kind of attention do they demand? Finally, what is the tradition behind this and others like it – a context of other songs and singers now half-forgotten and obscured?

For a better appreciation of these songs, then, we need more research into the circumstances surrounding the composition, the circumstances in which they were delivered, the nature and wishes of the audience, and

---

[32] *SH* 70b–73a.

the emotional response they are expected to elicit.[33] Kim Wanjin, who has published a most convincing reading of the *hyangga* songs, once said that it would take at least two years of research to elucidate each word in *Notations for Korean Music in Contemporary Use* and other Koryŏ songs riddled with textual cruxes. That explains why, to date, no convincing reading has been offered. The subject, it appears, will require years of collaborative research between the philologist, musicologist, ethnologist, poet, and literary historian.

[33] For shamanist songs see Im Chaehae, "*Siyong hyangak po* sojae mugaryu siga yŏngu," *Yŏngnam ŏmunhak* 9 (1982): 155–182; Pak Kyŏngsin, " 'Taeguk' ŭi chaengchŏm kwa chakp'um ihae ŭi kibon panghyang," in *Hanguk kojŏn siga chakp'um non* (Chimmundang, 1992) 1:359–369; and Yi T'aemun, "Mugagye Koryŏ sogyo ŭi yŏksasŏng kwa sahoesŏng," in *Koryŏ kayo ŭi munhak sahoehaksŏng*, ed. Im Kijung (Kyŏngun ch'ulp'ansa, 1993), pp. 345–394. Yi Sanggyu conjectures that the sounds mimic the sound of the double reed oboe. See "*Siyong hyangak po* sojae 'Kunma taewang' ŭi kuŭmpŏp," *Onji nonch'ong* 2 (1996): 37–53.

Extant *Koryŏ* songs

King Yejong	"To ijang ka" (1120)	*P'yŏngsan Sin-ssi sebo* 1:6b.*
Chŏng Sŏ (c. 1151–1170)	"Chŏng Kwajŏng"	*AHKB* 5:14b.
Anon.	"Ch'ŏyong ka"	*ACKS* 14a–15b; *AHKB* 5:12b–13a.
O Cham (c. 1274–1308)	"Ssanghwajŏm"	*ACKS* 7a–8b.
Anon.	"Tongdong"	*AHKB* 5:8a–b.
Anon.	"Ch'ŏngsan pyŏlgok"	*ACKS* 3b–4b; *SH* 24b–25b.
Anon.	"Sŏgyŏng pyŏlgok"	*ACKS* 4b–6a; *SH* 13a–14a.
Anon.	"Chŏngsŏk ka"	*ACKS* 2b–3b; *SH* 23a–24a.
Anon.	"Isang kok"	*ACKS* 8a–b.
Anon.	"Kasiri"	*ACKS* 8b–9a; *SH* 27a–28a.
Anon.	"Manjŏnch'un"	*ACKS* 18a–b.
Anon.	"Samo kok"	*ACKS* 6a; *SH* 10b–12b.
Confucian scholars	"Hallim pyŏlgok" (c. 1216)	*ACKS* 12a–13b.
An Ch'uk (1282–1348)	"Kwandong pyŏlgok" (c. 1328)	*Kŭnjae chip* 2:7a–8b.
An Ch'uk (1282–1348)	"Chukkye pyŏlgok" (1348)	*Kŭnjae chip* 2:8b–9b.
Anon.	"Yugu kok"	*SH* 25b–27a.
Anon.	"Sangjŏ ka"	*SH* 32a–34a.
Anon.	"Chŏngŭp sa"	*AHKB* 5:10a–b.
Anon.	"Narye ka"	*SH* 21b–23a.
Anon.	"Sŏnang pan"	*SH* 45a–54a.
Anon.	"Naedang"	*SH* 54b–61a.
Anon.	"Taewang pan"	*SH* 61a–62b.
Anon.	"Chapch'ŏyong"	*SH* 63a–69a.
Anon.	"Samsŏng taewang"	*SH* 69a–70b.
Anon.	"Taeguk," 1–3	*SH* 73a–78b.
Anon.	"Kunma taewang"	*SH* 70b–73a.
Anon.	"Kuch'ŏn"	*SH* 79a–82b.
Anon.	"Pyŏltaewang"	*SH* 82b–84b.

*Sin Wan, ed., *P'yŏngsan Sin-ssi sebo*, 4 vols., (1702).

CHAPTER 6

Koryŏ writings in Chinese

Peter H. Lee

A civil service examination system, open to both hereditary aristocratic families and petty officials in the provinces, was instituted in 958 to recruit new civilian officials to staff the bureaucracy. Among the three types of examination, the first tested the candidate's ability in literary composition in *shi* (old-style poetry), *fu* (rhymeprose), *sung* (eulogy), and *ce* (problem essays); the second in the Confucian classics; and the third in miscellaneous subjects. Although knowledge of both classics and literature was recommended, more emphasis was attached to the ability to write poetry and prose in literary Chinese. By 992 the royal academy (kukchagam) was established in the capital to teach classics and such other subjects as statutes, mathematics, and calligraphy. The model of this academy was followed by schools in the provinces. Private academies for the education of the sons of the upper class arose as well, beginning with the academy established by Ch'oe Ch'ung (984–1068) and followed by eleven others. This rise of official and private centers of learning made knowledge of the classics and literature essential for the educated. The prestige attached by the lettered upper class to proficiency in literary composition during the Koryŏ dynasty is reflected in the number of successful candidates for the composition examination (over 6,000) against that for the classics examination (450).[1]

POETRY

With the examination system in place, old-style poetry and parallel prose gradually gave way to new-style poetry and old-style prose. Thus the prose of the Han and poetry of the Tang and Song began to be studied and imitated. Because poetry occupied the highest place in the hierarchy of genres, most of the energy was spent in producing poems. An elegant

---

[1] Ki-baik Lee, *A New History of Korea*, trans. Edward W. Wagner and Edward Shultz (Ilchogak, 1967) p. 138.

pastime for sovereign and subjects consisted in exchanging or harmonizing poems; for example, King Yejong (1105–1122) – whose reign was looked upon by the literati as a golden age of poetry – and his courtiers vied in writing poetry. It is through poetry that the courtier wished to be known and remembered. Many poems were written to please and impress the ruler and his entourage – indeed as a display of verbal dexterity. One of the favorite games was to compete to see how fast one could produce a poem on a given topic and rhyme within a given time. Poems produced in such a setting tended to be jejune, or ornate, and were usually prolix. Scorning such frivolous use of poetic talent by seekers of fame and favor, some withdrew from the court to the world of nature and were subsequently praised by posterity – for example, Yi Chahyŏn (1061–1125), and Kwak Yŏ (1058–1130).

The military coup in 1170 sent many talented young writers underground or to remote mountain monasteries. Some were permanently displaced and marginalized: Im Ch'un (d. 1170)[2] spent many years wandering, for example, but could not find employment and died in his fiftieth year in poverty.[3] Yi Illo and Yi Kyubo, however, recognized for their poetic talent by the military, did hold a number of court positions.

Yi Illo (1152–1220)[4] was the sixth-generation descendant of Yi Hŏgyŏm, Marquis of Sosŏng, and a great-grandson of Yi O (1050–1110), executive director of the Royal Chancellery (Munha sirang p'yŏngjangsa). Yi lost his parents in childhood and was reared by Chief of Clerics Yoil, the master of the Flower Garland school of Buddhism and the uncle of King Myŏngjong. When the coup took place in 1170, Yi escaped death by having his head shaved and becoming a monk. In 1180 he placed first in the civil service examination. Soon after, his father-in-law traveled to Song China as the New Year's felicitation envoy and Yi accompanied him as secretary. Then he served in the Academy of Letters, the Office of Historiography, the Palace Library, the Ministry of Rites, and the Secretariat-Chancellery. With six other writers who shared his artistic predilections, Yi formed a literary coterie – the Eminent Assembly in the Bamboo Grove, named after the Seven Worthies of the Bamboo Grove of Jin China. Yi did not feel at home among the military overlords and deemed it his mission to defend literature against attempts to undermine its cultural role. He stressed the importance of diction and the perfection of craft. With Su Shi (1037–1101) and Huang Tingjian (1045–1105) as his models, he wrote poems using the same rhymes or themes as the Chinese poets he admired most. Yi's poems are usually

---

[2] *KRS* 102:11a–b.   [3] *KRS* 102:10b.   [4] *KRS* 102:10a–b.

well wrought and rich in allusions that often escape the untutored modern reader.

On his way to his new post as magistrate, Yi Illo wrote the following pentasyllabic quatrain on the wall of a cloister at Ch'ŏnsu Monastery while awaiting his friend:

> I wait for a guest who does not come;
> I look for a monk who is also out.
> Only a bird beyond the grove
> Welcomes me, urging me to drink.[5]

The bird *dihu* (K *cheho*) is supposed to sing *dihu dihu*, which means to "take the pot for wine."[6] Indeed, the bird is urging the poet to pour wine into a cup and drink in a quiet and beautiful mountain setting. In his *Tongin sihwa* (*Remarks on Poetry by a Man from the East*, 1474), Sŏ Kŏjŏng (1420–1488) comments that the poem contains endless meaning, or meaning beyond words, by capturing the setting and mood of the scenery so well that readers can experience it themselves.[7] The poem "Cicada," according to Ch'oe Cha (1188–1260), evinces close observation and precise description:

> You drink wind to empty yourself,
> Imbibe dewdrops to cleanse.
> Why do you get up at autumn dawn
> And keep crying so mournfully?[8]

The same critic praises another poem, "Picking Chestnuts," as an artfully polished and lucid virtuoso piece:

> Chestnuts fallen after frost shine reddish brown,
> At dawn I gather them in the grove still wet with dew.
> I wake up children and turn up a charcoal fire;
> The jade husk burnt, a golden kernel pops out.[9]

As a poet, Yi Illo does not merely describe the scenery that has moved him but blends scenery and feeling – his poems are both expressive and descriptive. Therefore, it is hard to accept the criticism that Yi's work values diction over meaning.

Yi Kyubo (1168–1241) came from a meager background but enjoyed the highest position among men of letters during the military rule.[10] He is

---

[5] *PaC* 1:3.
[6] Burton Watson renders the bird's name as "Bring the Jug," in *Su Tung-p'o: Selections from a Sung Dynasty Poet* (New York: Columbia University Press, 1965), p. 127.
[7] *TS* 1:61 (Chang Hongjae, p. 133). Sŏ Kŏjŏng compares this poem to Han Yu's.
[8] *PoC* 2:20.   [9] *PoC* 2:16.   [10] *KRS* 102:3a–5b.

said to have composed a couplet at age eleven. At fourteen he began his formal education. He passed the examination, however, only on his fourth attempt (1189). Recognition of his talent came in 1199, when at the mansion of Ch'oe Ch'unghŏn (1149–1219) he composed, together with Yi Illo, Ham Sun, and Yi Tamji, a poem on pomegranate blossoms.[11] He then held a number of important court posts. Some criticized his long service under the military, almost as their official poet, but his intent was to win back the respect due a writer. For Yi Kyubo held the view that poetry issues from experience in the real world and must respond to the demands of the time. No matter how rhetorically satisfying it might be, a poem without meaning and substance, Yi believed, was not a good poem. Yi Kyubo was a prolific writer, and the 2,068 poems in his collected works cover a wide range of topics: his official career, friendship, history (the most valuable example being "Lay of King Tongmyŏng"), animals and plants, landscape, travel, family, poetry, and leisure.[12] Many poems in the original make satisfying reading, but only a person well read in Chinese poetry can begin to appreciate them.

Poetry was expected to make things happen, and Yi Kyubo's engagement with contemporary cultural and social issues influences the reading of his other poems. His is the privilege of a poet who belonged (or hoped to belong) to the wealthy, powerful, and sophisticated. Although we do not know whether Yi's socially relevant poems, such as those evoking the misery of agrarian life, ever succeeded in provoking real change, the following poems do make us ponder the relation between poetry and power, especially during the military dictatorship.

> Written on Behalf of the Farmer
> Exposed to rain, I weed crouching on the furrow,
> My dirty and dark figure is not that of a man.
> Princes and nobles, do not disdain me,
> Your riches, honor, and luxury all come from me.
>
> New grains, green, are still in the field,
> But county clerks are out to collect taxes.
> Tilling hard to enrich the state depends on us.
> Why do they encroach upon us and strip our skin?[13]

His autobiographical poems, the fictional representations of historical utterances, especially on women, wine, and poetry, are written in a tone and attitude of self-criticism – whimsical, witty, and ironic. The "three

---

[11] *TYC, yŏnbo* 7a–b mentions this episode; *PoC* 2:27.
[12] Kim Kyŏngsu, *Yi Kyubo simunhak yŏngu* (Asea munhwasa, 1986). [13] *TYC, hujip* 1:3a.

demons" in Yi's life, for example, include women, wine, and poetry. One may take an interest in wine and poetry, Yi says, but excessive fondness is akin to being possessed by a demon (*ma*), as in a prose piece *To Drive Away the Poetry Demon* (*Ku sima mun*), which is an imitation of the style of Han Yu's "Farewell to Poverty." In another poem, Yi calls his excessive fondness for poetry a mania (literally "sickness"), and concludes, "Alas, that sickness cannot be cured, / There is no way but to die like this." He seems to admit that he does not intend to write poetry, but without knowing he is stirred to write and a poem comes into being spontaneously. Poetry is his life, and even when he groans with sickness, he says he could not give it up.[14] "Poetry: A Chronic Sickness" (*sibyŏk*) well illustrates his stance toward poetry:

> I'm over seventy now,
> an official of the first rank;
> I know I should give up writing poetry,
> but somehow I can't.
> Mornings I sing like a cricket;
> evenings I hoot like an owl.
> I'm possessed by a devil I can't exorcise;
> night and day it follows me stealthily around.
> Once possessed, there's never a moment free;
> a pretty mess it's got me in.
> Day after day, I shrivel heart and liver
> just to write a few poems.
> Body fats and fluids depleted,
> there's nothing left but skin and grizzle.
> Bones protruding, struggling to recite,
> I strike a very foolish figure.
> I have no words to elicit wonder,
> nothing to pass on that will last a thousand years.
> I clap my hands, guffaw, and when the laughter bout subsides,
>   I begin to recite again.
> My life and death hang on poetry;
> not even a physician could cure this disease.[15]

"To My Son Editing My Poems" summarizes the predicament of a poet whose works are read only by a handful of specialists today:

[14] *TYC* 10:8a–b, 1b, 5a–b; *TYS* 20:3a–5b. Chŏn Hyŏngdae, "Yi Kyubo ŭi si yŏngu," in *Hanguk kojŏn munhak yŏngu: Paegyŏng Chŏng Pyŏnguk sŏnsaeng hwangap kinyŏm nonch'ong* (Singu munhwasa, 1983), 3:241–249.
[15] Kevin O'Rourke, *Singing Like a Cricket, Hooting Like an Owl: Selected Poems of Yi Kyu-bo* (Ithaca: Cornell East Asia Program, 1995), p. 6.

I have always feared withering sooner than grass and trees,
But I find the volumes of my poor poems worse than nothing.
Who will know, a thousand years from now,
That a man named Yi was born in a corner of Korea?[16]

Politician, diplomat, and writer, Yi Chehyŏn (1287–1367) served seven Koryŏ kings when the dynasty was under Mongol domination. One of the most widely traveled Korean diplomats, he visited China at least six times. First summoned by King Ch'ungsŏn to the Mongol capital in 1314, he accompanied the king on his trip south of the Yangzi (1319) and visited him for the last time (1323) in his place of exile, a remote place in Gansu. Enfeoffed as the great lord of Kyerim, he was chancellor under King Kongmin.

Yi is the author of a number of poems on Chinese historical sites that he visited in order to recall the past or to ruminate on the temporality of human achievements. The subjects of such poems include: Prince Bi Gan's tomb; Meng Ford, where King Wu of the Zhou assembled his host before attacking the tyrant Zhou of the Shang; Kusu Terrace, where Xi Shi resided; the bridge under which Yu Rang hid in an attempt to assassinate Zhao Xiangzi, an enemy of his lord; the grave of an old woman who fed the starving Han Xin (d. 196 BC) by the Huai River; a monument to Wang Xiang (185–269), a paragon of filial devotion; the Yellow River; Mount Emei; the shrine of Zhuge Liang (181–234) at Chengdu, following the example of Du Fu; and the grave of Tang Empress Wu.

Yi Chehyŏn is also remembered for preserving nine folk songs current in his day by adapting them into Chinese, an act of cultural legitimation. Entitled *So akpu* (*A Small Collection of Folk Songs*), the songs shed important light on the music of the Koryŏ period. One tells the story of a Munch'ung who lived below Mount Ogwan and was devoted to his mother. The more faithfully he served her, it seemed to him, the faster she seemed to age. Thereupon he is said to have composed the following song employing the topic of impossibilities (*adynata*):

> I carve a small rooster from wood
> And pick it up with chopsticks and put it on the wall.
> When this bird crows cock-a-doodle-do,
> Then my mother's face will be like the setting sun.

Another song tells of a certain woman serving a term at the state storehouse for her misdeeds. One day, a man grasped her hand. She reproached him

---

[16] The text is in *TYC*, *hujip* 1:18b; the English translation is by Kim Jong-gil, *Slow Chrysanthemums: Classical Korean Poems in Chinese* (London: Anvil Press, 1987), p. 36.

and sang a song called "Chewibo." In Yi Chehyŏn's version, however, the speaker expresses her longing for the man:

> At a wash place by the stream under a drooping willow,
> Holding the hand of a handsome youth, I whispered.
> Not even the March rain falling from the eaves
> Could wash away his lingering scent on my fingertips!

A third song, said to be sung by a wife awaiting the return of her husband from a trip, is based on the folk belief that if a magpie sings near your house or a spider descends from the ceiling, a person you long for will return:

> A magpie chatters in a flowering bough by the hedge,
> A spider spins a web above the bed.
> Knowing my heart, they announce his return –
> My beloved will be back soon.

The "Song of Ch'ŏyong" enjoyed continued popularity, and Yi Chehyŏn must have seen a performance where a dancer with the Ch'ŏyong mask exorcised evil spirits or foreign invaders:

> Long ago in Silla, Venerable Ch'ŏyong
> Is said to have emerged from the emerald sea.
> With white teeth and ruddy lips he sang in the moonlight
> And danced in a spring wind with square shoulders and purple sleeves.

Yi Chehyŏn also preserved a satirical song that mocks a politician who twice became a victim of the wheel of fortune:

> Huddled up, sparrow, what are you doing,
> Your yellow beak stuck in a net?
> Where did you keep your eyes from the start?
> Pity, you foolish bird, caught in a net![17]

The fourth Koryŏ writer known for his contributions to politics, education, and literature is Yi Saek (1328–1396). Yi traveled widely, personally pleaded Koryŏ's case to the founder of the Ming, and did his utmost to serve the last Koryŏ kings. Cantos 77 and 82 of *Songs of Flying Dragons* are meant to illustrate how General Yi Sŏnggye enjoys cordial relations with Yi Saek: the general courteously receives Yi Saek upon his return from exile (canto 82:1391) and greets him again and grants him land and grain (canto 77:1396). Here the compilers' intent is to present the general as one who not only knows how to respect scholars but also is magnanimous and merciful

---

[17] Yi Chehyŏn, *Ikchae chip* (*KMC* 2:1972) 4:12a–13a (translation in *Ikchae chip* 1:150–151).

("his mind was large as heaven and earth") and spares his political enemy. These cantos also indicate how Yi Saek was regarded as a scholar even by his political foe.[18]

After receiving the *chinsa* degree in 1341, Yi Saek studied Neo-Confucianism in the Mongol state academy (1348). In 1353 he took the examination at the Eastern Expedition field headquarters to qualify for the metropolitan and palace examinations at the Mongol capital, both of which he passed with flying colors (1354). He was then appointed to a post in the Hanlin Academy and then as a junior compiler in the Historiography Academy. Back in Korea in 1356, he held a number of court posts including the directorship of the Office of Royal Decrees and Office of State Records. A victim of political struggles at the end of Koryŏ, he was exiled more than once. As the *sijo* attributed to him suggests, he viewed that period as "the valley besieged by perilous clouds where the snow lies thick" and regarded himself as a wayworn wanderer lost in the setting sun.[19] Yi Saek was a prolific poet who left close to 6,000 poems.

Judging from his repetition of such key passages as "the poem articulates what is on the mind intently" (The Great Preface to the *Book of Songs*)[20] or Confucius' statement that "the Three Hundred poems may be summed up in one phrase: 'No evil thoughts'" (*Analects* 2:2),[21] Yi Saek accepted the canonical definition of poetry. He reiterates the social and moral functions of poetry when he says, "Moved by the correctness of human nature and emotion in poetry, the reader returns to the state of no evil thoughts,"[22] or "By singing a song, one gives the outward shape to the beauty of government, corrects the people's mind/heart, and helps the way of the age."[23] A poem, through its mood, indicates the condition of the age. If the royal way declines, the way of poetry declines as well, because the latter reflects the former. By recording current affairs and popular customs, the poet hopes to leave behind historical materials; thus Yi sends poems to the historians and adds that it is up to them to select and record them for posterity.[24]

His poems on the relation between the examiner and candidates, the examination, the activities of the royal academy, and his own duties as

---

[18] Peter H. Lee, *Songs of Flying Dragons*, pp. 227–228, 234–235.

[19] Chŏng Pyŏnguk, ed., *Sijo munhak sajŏn* (Singu munhwasa), pp. 216 and 626 for different readings.

[20] Stephen Owen, *Readings in Chinese Literary Thought* (Cambridge, Mass.: Harvard University Press, 1992), p. 26.

[21] Arthur Waley, *The Analects of Confucius* (London: Allen and Unwin, 1949), p. 88.

[22] *Mogŭn mungo* in *Yŏgye myŏnghyŏn chip* 13:3a. The following treatment is based on Yŏ Unp'il, *Yi Saek ŭi simunhak yŏngu* (T'aehaksa, 1995), pp. 206–231.

[23] *Mogŭn sigo* in *Mogŭn mungo* 11:4b.   [24] Ibid., 21:9a–b, 35:16a.

a royal lecturer convey his sense of his role as a Neo-Confucian scholar-statesman. A central concern of poetry, however, he seems to have thought, is to observe, record, and preserve the native tradition. Poetry should teach and transform; indeed, those above can transform those below, and those below can criticize those above. Yi's poems on the annual events include, for example, the custom of eating glutinous rice and viewing the moon on the fifteenth of the first lunar month. He comments: "Both these poems sing of the custom of the East [Korea], which China does not know. If my friends in China read them, they will probably laugh them away."[25] Aware that not only the languages but the customs of the two countries are different, Yi evinces his deep interest in Korea's indigenous customs: the game of *yut* played on New Year's Day;[26] the *tano* festival on the fifth day of the fifth month when the king and officials watched stone fights, with a particular view to choosing the bravest fighters as soldiers;[27] polo;[28] women playing on a swing;[29] and *yudu* on the fifteenth of the sixth month, when women wash their hair in a river flowing eastward.[30]

Yi Saek also describes the food and clothing of the common people: the glutinous rice mentioned earlier; red bean porridge with dumplings eaten on the winter solstice;[31] the men's bamboo hats;[32] women fulling clothes by pounding with two round wooden sticks while lamenting their men in service at the frontier forts and wiping tears and praying for their prompt return.[33] In a poem addressed to the Earl of Wind, Yi's farmer-speaker worries over strong winds (and rain) at harvest time:

> Blow slowly, winds, not hard.
> Don't shake our rice plants.
> May this year bring a good harvest
> And our people prolong their lives.[34]

Yi's concern extends to women tending silkworms, indicating how their labor benefits family, landlord, and king;[35] to fishermen;[36] to woodcutters[37] – indeed, those who rule must understand the people's life and work.

We also learn that the Koreans of Yi's day divined for rain and snow on the twenty-third and eighth days[38] and that a small earthenware jar or basin (*tongji*) was called *tonghae* in common parlance.[39] He shows interest in folk arts, sundry plays and games, and exorcism rites. The part describing the

---

[25] Ibid., 13:25a–b, 14:15a. [26] Ibid., 6:29b.
[27] Ibid., 23:9b–10a, 29:21b–22a. [28] Ibid., 8:14b–15a.
[29] Ibid., 8:14a–b; see also stanza 8 of *Hallim pyŏlgok*, which was an intertext.
[30] *Mogŭn sigo* 24:15b–16b. [31] Ibid., 20:20a. [32] Ibid., 23:28a. [33] Ibid., 30:19b–20a.
[34] Ibid., 25:1b. [35] Ibid., 22:32a, 16:32a–b, 29:28a–29a. [36] Ibid., 22:32b.
[37] Ibid., 22:32a. [38] Ibid., 29:13b. [39] Ibid., 22:26a–b.

Ch'ŏyong dance in the "Kuma haeng" ("Song of Driving away Evil Spirits") complements the description by Yi Chehyŏn cited earlier:

Ch'ŏyong of Silla is adorned with the seven jewels,
On the flower spray stuck on his head falls fragrant dew.
Lowering and turning his body, his long sleeves dance Great Peace,
His drunken cheeks are ruddy – he's not yet sobered up.[40]

"*Chŏngjae* (a group dance with a song performed before the king) and sundry plays," Yi comments, "properly belong to Korea and are not extant in China."[41] The *sandae* play performed on the occasion of Sin U's return to Kaesŏng from Hanyang (1383), we learn, included music, a display of fireworks, dances of "Hŏnsŏndo" ("Offering of the Immortal Peach") and Ch'ŏyong, and acrobats dancing atop a bamboo pole.[42] Thus Yi Saek the poet was able to observe the feelings of the people and "give depth to human relations, beautifully teach and transform the people [*Analects* 12:8], and change local customs [the Great Preface]."[43]

HISTORY AND BIOGRAPHY

In traditional East Asia, history was generally regarded as a mirror, an authority, and a guide for future action. Because people are the actors in history, their conduct was thought capable of illustrating moral principles and commonly held values. If the history of a dynasty is macro-history, biography is micro-history. East Asian biography generally refers the reader to a particular system of moral, political, and intellectual values. To view biography as an exemplum implies not only a past that serves as a paradigm, but also a future that will recapitulate the past.

Essentially there are two kinds of biography: official and unofficial. The official biography may be further classified as either biography that forms a part of official history and is compiled by a court-appointed committee, or biography that forms a part of the collected works of a scholar-official, compiled by his family members, friends, or colleagues. The former type of official biography commenced when a scholar-official died and his family submitted to the authorities an "account of conduct" and a tomb inscription to be buried with the coffin. The committee then compiled the subject's *vitae* on the basis of the account of conduct and the tomb inscription. Biographical information was also contained in sacrificial speeches, eulogies, and the epitaph engraved on stone tablets and erected in front of the

40 Ibid., 21:9a–b.   41 Ibid., 30:28b.   42 Ibid., 33:27a.
43 Owen, *Readings*, p. 45, and Waley, *Analects*, p. 212.

grave. From the tenth century onward, however, chronological accounts of the subject's career began to appear. This second type of biography was appended to the subject's collected works and usually included all the sub-genres mentioned above. Sometimes the chronological account and the account of conduct ran to several volumes. The exemplary biography in the Chinese tradition is that by Sima Qian (?145–86 BC) in his *Shiji* (*Historical Records*, or *Records of the Historian*). The subjects of the seventy-chapter biographical section, called the *liezhuan* (arrayed traditions or biographies), include everyone from statesmen, generals, and philosophers to fortune-tellers, assassins, humorists, eunuchs, businessmen, and local bosses. Each subject is identified by a personality type and role model, and each account is a series of anecdotes chosen according to the historiographical principle of "praise and blame." Anecdotes presented as examples (paradigms) of Confucian conduct possess added significance, therefore, as they aim to perpetuate Confucian ethical norms. Perhaps the most interesting lives are those of villains and outsiders: with no written sources at their disposal, historians had to rely on their imagination.

Unofficial biography – what I call the "prose portrait" – is unofficial because it flouts the prescriptive conventions of the formal prose genres, including the official type of biography just described. The prose portraits are usually preserved in the literary miscellany. The portrait's intent is to demonstrate what a man is like by examining what he does. The writer does not treat his subject in great detail. Rather, he touches such essential manifestations of the subject's personality as his distinctive way of speaking, his personal views, or his idiosyncrasies.

To summarize the characteristics of these two kinds of biography: one emphasizes the similarity of men, while the other emphasizes their diversity. One emphasizes the public self; the other, the private. One attempts to give the subject's career; the other, the moment. Both, however, share a number of features: relative indifference to the subject's external appearance; a lack of markedly contemporary detail; and a dearth of information about the subject's private life. Rhetorically, both types are epideictic in that an anecdote or episode is intended to imply praise or blame, even when there is no explicit moral comment.

The biography has traditionally been a means of commemorating, rather than delineating, the subject. As a result of the form's didactic intent, it is a eulogy or panegyric in which the subject appears as emblem, symbol, or cultural ideal. A biography might recount the subject's ancestry, birth, and career with an emphasis on the historicity, accuracy, and acceptability of the events described. Significant events independent of history were usually omitted. Nor did the biographer depict critical decisions in the subject's life in terms of his inner needs. Nor did he present his own vision of the subject's character or delve into his private life. This is not because the biographer lacked personal documents such as journals, letters about the subject, published works, or contemporary opinions about the subject. Rather, it is because the biographer was not responsible for writing a sustained biography in the modern sense. He knew instinctively that his culture demanded a public version of the self.

Despite his culture's insistence on historicity, the biographer enjoys the privilege of omniscience by adopting the third-person narrative accorded by the convention. Sometimes he includes scenes or events he has not witnessed. Sometimes he enters the subject's mind, attributing to him utterances that have no legitimate source or are true more in effect than in substance. Sometimes he transmits not the original utterance but his own analysis of it. Although the biographer seldom mentions how the subject maintained continuity and coherence in his personality to become an ideal exemplar of the tradition, consistency conferred on the subject is a fiction (or looks like one) because it is manipulated. Unable to reconcile the conflicting claims of history and fiction, the power of fact and the power of imagination, the biographer necessarily reflects the limits of the Confucian view of humanity: the culturally determined notion of the self. Even the official biography is a mixed form partaking of both fiction and history.

Lives of men are written in order to draw morals from them. It is an axiom of long standing that examples work more effectively on the mind than precepts. A king rules by example, and history teaches by it. The biographer's purpose is not to uncover personality or individual character, but to turn the subject into an example. To teach by example is to move people to love virtue and abhor vice. To read an example is both enjoyable and instructive. The emphasis in the didactic function of examples is on the relation between macrocosm and microcosm: the health of a state depends on the moral health of its ruler and his subjects, a moral health that is essential to the maintenance of order and harmony. Like poetry and prose, biography is essential to social cohesion and cultural continuity. An equally important function of biography stems from the impulse to record the lives of great men so that their deeds, heroic or cultural, will not be forgotten. It is our attempt to check the onslaught of time.

Kim Pusik's *Historical Records of the Three Kingdoms* (1146), patterned after Sima Qian's *Shiji*, is the earliest surviving official history of the Three Kingdoms – Silla, Koguryŏ, and Paekche. A number of sources at Kim's disposal are no longer extant. *Ku samguk sa* (*Old History of the Three Kingdoms*) is one such text, consulted by both Yi Kyubo and Kim Pusik, but the uses they made of it are radically different, as can be seen, for example, in their respective accounts of the legends of King Tongmyŏng. It is therefore difficult to determine what Kim reproduced, discarded, or suppressed. A sinocentric historian schooled in Confucian historiography, Kim believed that it was not the historian's function to dabble in myth, legend, and folk tradition, all of which are of dubious reliability. Like other historians, however, as we will see, he was inconsistent.

The organization of the *Historical Records of the Three Kingdoms* is as follows:

Basic annals (*pongi*): 28 chapters – 12 for Silla; 10 for Koguryŏ; 6 for Paekche

Chronology (*yŏnp'yo*): 3 chapters

Treatises (*chi*): 9 chapters

Biographies (*yŏlchŏn*): 10 chapters

For students of Korean literature, the most valuable section is the *yŏlchŏn*, which gives biographies of eighty-six persons – fifty-two major and thirty-four collateral. Kim tried to include exemplary figures from the high and low classes, ranging from generals, *hwarang* warriors, statesmen, and scholars to filial sons and daughters, chaste women, musicians, painters, and rebels. He assigned three entire chapters (41–43) to Kim Yusin (595–673) for his loyal service and dedication to the cause of unification. He made use of the ten-chapter "Record of Deeds" by Kim Yusin's great-grandson, omitting some tendentious parts that show excessive flights of fancy.

The biography of Kim Yusin demonstrates how Kim Pusik weaves together fiction and history. For example, it tells us that Kim Yusin's birth was heralded by prophetic dreams that came to his father and mother. His father dreamed that the planets Mars and Saturn fell upon him and his wife and that a boy clad in golden armor floated into her room on a cloud. "Soon thereafter, she was pregnant, and after twenty months gave birth to Yusin [595]." In 611, at age sixteen, Kim goes alone into a stone grotto in the central peaks where he purifies himself and swears a pledge to heaven to defeat the invading Koguryŏ and Malgal forces. After four days of prayer, he meets an old man clad in rough garments who questions him. After Kim Yusin's repeated entreaty for help in repulsing the enemy and after the old man ascertains the youth's heroic resolve, he gives Kim a secret formula and disappears. In 612, with his precious sword, Kim Yusin again goes alone into a deep valley and purifies himself and prays to heaven to send down a light: "Let a spirit descend into my precious sword." After three days and nights, "rays of light shone brightly from the Horn and the Void, and the sword appeared to quiver."[44] At another point, Kim Pusik relates that when, in the spring of 661, Koguryŏ and Malgal forces laid siege to the Silla fortress at North Han Mountain for ten days and the inhabitants were terrified, "suddenly a great star fell toward the bandit camp, followed by quaking thunder and battering rains. Filled with great apprehension, the bandits lifted the siege and took flight." Supposedly this heavenly intervention was in response to Kim Yusin's prayer at a Buddhist monastery.[45]

In the section on upright and wise ministers, a single event or episode is made to stand for the whole career of a subject, as in the following instances. Firm of purpose and full of resources, Ŭlp'aso (d. 203) worked as a farmer until King Kogugwŏn (179–197) of Koguryŏ summoned him as the state minister; consequently, Ŭlp'aso was able to bring peace to the people and security at home and abroad.[46] Prime Minister Ch'ang Chori's admonition of King Pongsang (292–300) for indulging in public works when people are exhausted and ill at ease fell on the king's deaf ears. Ch'ang then withdrew and planned with others to depose the king. Knowing that death was inevitable, the king hanged himself.[47] Contrarily, Kim Hujik of Silla was able to persuade King Chinp'yŏng (579–632) to give up his excessive love of hunting.[48]

Among the lowborn who distinguished themselves by virtue or prowess are Ondal of Koguryŏ and Tomi's wife of Paekche. The story of Ondal concerns an absurd-looking man, known as Foolish Ondal, who marries a princess whose astute help allows him to distinguish himself as a supreme horseman and brave warrior.[49] Tomi's beautiful wife defends her chastity with her life. When King Kaeru (128–166) cannot have her because of a successful ruse, he has Tomi's eyes gouged out and sets him adrift on the river. After putting off the king for the last time, the wife escapes to the shore only to find there is no boat. She cries to heaven and an empty skiff appears. She then reaches an island where she finds her husband, and both eventually reach the territory of Koguryŏ where they die.[50] These accounts are rich in fictional elements, and Kim Pusik incorporates popular narrative to exemplify specific virtues. On the one hand, therefore, Kim tried to suppress popular tradition as unreliable and baseless; on the other, however, he was compelled for didactic purposes to embellish the lives of his subjects with the same tradition.

The oldest surviving Buddhist hagiography in Korea is the *Haedong kosŭng chŏn* (*Lives of Eminent Korean Monks*, 1215), compiled on royal order

[44] *SGSG* 41:393–394.   [45] *SGSG* 42:401.   [46] *SGSG* 45:419–420.   [47] *SGSG* 49:448.
[48] *SGSG* 45:420.   [49] *SGSG* 45:425–427.   [50] *SGSG* 48:446–447.

of King Kojong by Kakhun. Kakhun was the abbot of Yŏngt'ong Monastery on Mount Ogwan and a friend of Yi Illo and Yi Kyubo; Yi Illo likened Kakhun's poetry to that of Jia Dao (779–845) in its emotion (*p'ung* 風) and expression (*kol* 骨).[51] The two extant chapters of the *Lives* contain eighteen major and seven minor biographies of eminent monks and cover a span of 500 years. The first chapter, which deals with three Koguryŏ monks, two Silla monks, and three monks of foreign origin, is the more important of the two. It throws new and often brilliant light on the development of Korean Buddhism from the time of its introduction to the seventh century. The second chapter, which deals with Silla monks who went to China or India, consists chiefly of excerpts from the *Xu gaoseng zhuan* (*Further Lives of Eminent Monks*) and the *Da-Tang xiyu qiufa gaoseng zhuan* (*Lives of Eminent Monks of the Tang who Sought the Dharma in the Western Regions*, c. 705) of Yijing (635–713), except for the life of the monk Anham, an account found nowhere else.[52]

Old Korean documents and records, a few of which are extant, are among the works cited by Kakhun. As for Chinese sources, he is most indebted for form and style to the three *Gaoseng zhuan*, from which he seems to have adopted the subordinate biography, the critical estimate (*non*, 論), and the eulogy (*ch'an*, 贊). The differences are that the *non* – which normally is found at the end of each category in Chinese biographical collections – comes only at the beginning and, moreover, the *ch'an* following the individual biography is composed not in verse but in ornate, allusion-packed prose. The *non* outlines the history of Buddhism in China and Korea from the time of its introduction to the thirteenth century.

The myths and legends engendered by Buddhist piety refer the reader to a world presided over by the Buddha with his universal dharma, by miraculous wonders and wondrous miracles, and by the relentless workings of karmic rewards and retribution. Subjects of the *Lives* – indeed, subjects of any Buddhist hagiography – therefore move in a world where they sense the hand of the Buddha working at every moment and in every corner. Not until their maturity do most of them make their appearance in history. No striking details are given about their character or personality; these must be inferred from stock phrases that suggest their behavior patterns. Some were already blessed with enlightenment at birth (Anham) or were self-enlightened (Āryavarman); but even the less fortunate ones possessed "profound understanding and broad learning" (Ŭiyŏn), "unfathomable

51 *PaC* 2:15.
52 The following paragraphs are from Peter H. Lee, *Lives of Eminent Korean Monks*.

holiness" (Kaktŏk), "extraordinary understanding" (Wŏngwang), "great wisdom and insight" (Hyŏngak), or an "otherworldly, harmonious nature" (Hyŏnyu). Less favored ones still, like Sundo, at least "vigorously practiced virtue" and were "compassionate and patient in helping living beings." About Hyŏnt'ae we are told that he was "pensive as a child and had the marks of a great man [*Mahāpurusa*]."

Since extraordinary potentialities are present in all of them from birth, their future successes are easy to prognosticate. Some of them perform miracles, cure incurable illness, or communicate with supernatural beings such as spirits, dragons, and heavenly messengers (Wŏngwang, Mālānanda). Miracles accompany their activities. Both heaven and earth tremble in announcing the advent of Ado, and wondrous flowers rain from heaven during his sermon; music fills the air and unusual fragrance is noticed at the death of Wŏngwang. After death one monk, Anham, is seen riding squarely on the green waves, joyfully heading west. Often we are told of the subjects' feats of endurance against fire, wild beasts, or sword and ax – experiences from which, having mastered the elements of nature, they always emerge intact. Should they, however, suffer death, permitted by the Buddha to glorify his religion, miracles of the most spectacular nature take place, as in the case of the martyrdom of Ich'adon (or Yŏmch'ŏk): "When he [Ich'adon] was decapitated, his head flew to Diamond Mountain, falling on its summit, and white milk gushed forth from the cut, soaring up several hundred feet. The sun darkened, wonderful flowers rained from heaven, and the earth trembled violently." Finally, Kakhun uses conventional epithets to give color and luster to his subjects. Ŭiyŏn is "a leader of both monks and laymen," "a ferry on the sea of suffering," or "the middle beam over the gate of the dharma." Chimyŏng's moral power is "as high as Mount Song or Mount Hua," his magnanimity "as deep as a wide ocean." A single epithet, "a lotus in the fire," singles out Hyŏngak from the others. Rarely is animal imagery used, but "a lion" roaming alone in the wilderness alludes to the pilgrim Hyŏnt'ae as he braves the hardships of crossing the Himalayas.

As the theme in Western hagiography from AD 400 to 1400 was the glory of God through the praise of his saints, so the theme in the *Lives* is the glory of the world of the dharma through the lives of its monks. Such generalized biography is hardly life-writing in the truest sense of the word. It does not illuminate or recreate men but deforms them into a simulacrum of life, an exemplum of the wonderful world of the dharma. The limits of the *Lives* are the limits imposed by the nature and function of the form itself.

In his *Memorabilia of the Three Kingdoms*, Iryŏn (1206–1289) combines the narrative styles of both Buddhist biography/hagiography and official history to produce an account of Buddhism in the Three Kingdoms and unified Silla. His subjects are not only monks but men and women high and low, because faith transcends the class distinctions based on blood. Iryŏn's sources include popular narrative, epigraphs, old documents, and monastery records, which he collected for more than fifty years. After a royal chronology (ch. 1), the *Memorabilia* narrates stories about the wondrous and supernatural associated with early Korean kingdoms and kings (ch. 2); transmitters of Buddhism (ch. 3); Buddhist images, stupas, relics, and bells (ch. 4); significant events in the lives of eminent monks, especially their contributions to the understanding of Buddhist doctrines (ch. 5); esoteric Buddhism (ch. 6); miracles brought about by faith (ch. 7); anchorites (ch. 8); and filial sons and daughters (ch. 9). The *Memorabilia* is an invaluable source for the religious and cultural history of the period: his characters encompass founders of ancient kingdoms (Tangun, Tongmyŏng, Hyŏkkŏse), propagators of Buddhism (Sundo, Ich'adon), eminent monks (Wŏngwang, Chajang, Wŏnhyo, Ŭisang), and commoners such as the slave girl Ungmyŏn and the destitute daughter of a blind woman. Although Iryŏn's style is plain, it is rich in concrete, visual, and evocative detail and suited to its subject. It is a treasure trove of legends concerning the names of places, persons, and monks, folk narratives about trees, marriage, loyalty, filial piety, chastity, prophecy, dreams, heroes, divine assistance, animals, origins of monasteries, appearance of Buddhist saints, and miracles performed by eminent monks. Iryŏn also records for the first time the texts of fourteen *hyangga* in the *hyangch'al* orthographic system as well as two songs in Chinese translations and the titles of nine songs without texts.[53]

Biography (*chŏn*) in collected works of individual authors includes autobiographical as well as biographical accounts of subjects considered worthy of record for posterity. Yi Kyubo's "Paegun kŏsa chŏn," written in his twenties, together with *Paegun kŏsa ŏrok*, constitutes an additive autobiography.[54] Narrated in the third person, Yi's work attributes the good qualities of the white cloud to the retired gentleman whose three companions include the black zither, wine, and poetry. In "Yesan ŭnja chŏn," Ch'oe Hae (1287–1340) offers an acute self-examination with self-scorn, again in the third person. The hermit Yesan, although aspiring to name and fame, was too

---

[53] For folk narratives see Chang Tŏksun, *Hanguk sŏrhwa munhak yŏngu* (Seoul taehakkyo ch'ulp'anbu, 1970), pp. 405–427.
[54] *TYC* 20:18b–19a, 12b–14b.

outspoken for a society that disliked one who discriminated between right and wrong and was eventually deemed unfit to serve. In late life he leased a farm attached to Sajagap Monastery.[55]

No Kŭkch'ŏng, of unknown origin, is praised by Yi Kyubo for being righteous and not greedy.[56] The subjects of five biographies by Yi Saek are all his acquaintances or friends, who had ambition but died unexpectedly and unrecognized. Song Sŏngch'ong (b. 1318), a monk who returned to the laity, was an unconventional poet who taught the fourteen-year-old Yi Saek how to write poetry.[57] O Tong, a licentiate, died too young.[58] Pak Soyang, Kim Kwangjwa's nephew, repeatedly failed the examination but went to Peking where he worked as a petty clerk and disappeared.[59] Ch'oe Rim passed the examination with Yi (1353) but on his way home from a mission to Peking was killed by bandits on the Liao River.[60] Paek In's writing was marked by a powerful style, but he died in Peking.[61] For all these subjects Yi Saek registers his personal grief. While these five seemed well-disposed to Buddhism, Chŏng Hyŏnsuk is portrayed as a good Confucian official who opposed superstition and Buddhism.[62] "Chŏngssi kajŏn" constitutes the collective lives of the Chŏng of Sŏwŏn.[63]

Yi Sungin's "Ch'ookcha chŏn" concerns Kim Chinyang (d. 1392) of Kyŏngju whom he calls his best friend and whose frugality is, in a eulogy, likened to that of Yao, Shun, and Zhuge Liang.[64] Chŏng Tojŏn heard the story of Chŏng Ch'im, the village chief of Naju, during his banishment at Kop'yŏng, Haejin (1375). On an official mission to Cheju Island, Chŏng's ship was attacked by Japanese pirates. All aboard wished to surrender except for Chŏng who after offering a bitter fight finally chose death before dishonor by jumping into the sea. This biography provided Chŏng Tojŏn with an occasion to attach a disquisition on dying for a great cause.[65] Kwŏn Kŭn (1352–1409) met Pae Sanggyŏm while banished to Hŭnghae (Yŏngil) in 1390 and contrasts the character of Sanggyŏm to that of his father Tŭgyu. The son is praised for his love of learning, the virtue of a gentleman, poor but content. Indeed, Kwŏn found the exemplars of Confucian virtue in a remote village.[66] Pak Kang is a military figure who fought against the Red Turbans (a Chinese brigand force that invaded Korea from across the Yalu) and Japanese pirates; but because of his humble origin he was never

[55] *TMS* 100:12b–13a.   [56] *TYC* 20:19a–b; *TMS* 100:10b–11a.
[57] Yi Saek, *Mogŭn mungo* 20:1a–3b.   [58] Ibid., 20:2b–3b.   [59] Ibid., 20:3b–5a.
[60] Ibid., 20:7b–8b.   [61] Ibid., 20:8b–10a.   [62] Ibid., 20:5a–7b.   [63] Ibid., 20:10a–15a.
[64] Yi Sungin, *Toŭn (mun)jip*, in *Yŏgye myŏnghyŏn chip*, ed. Sŏnggyun taehakkyo Taedong munhwa yŏnguwŏn, 5:1a–b; see also *KRS* 117:20b–27a.
[65] Chŏng Tojŏn, *Sambong chip* (Kuksa p'yŏnch'an wiwŏnhoe, 1961) 5:115–116.
[66] Kwŏn Kŭn, *Yangch'on chip* (Asea munhwasa, 1974) 21:21b–23a.

recommended for a position, nor were his deeds recorded.[67] The actor Kunman in Chinju is praised for avenging his father by killing the tiger that had snatched him away.[68]

In "Susŏn chŏn," Yi Ch'ŏm (1345–1405) portrays Susŏn who was awakened by a passage in the *Mencius* – "There are three ways of being a bad son. The most serious is to have no heir" (4A:26) – and concluded that Buddhism was nothing more than empty promise. Showing that Susŏn was moved by the teaching of the Confucian sage was the purpose of this biography.[69]

Yi Kok, Yi Sungin, and Chŏng Io (1354–1434) wrote accounts of praiseworthy women. The chaste Lady Cho lost her father, husband, and son-in-law in wars and lived fifty years as a widow by supporting herself. Her grandson-in-law passed the examination with Yi Kok. "She is seventy-seven but healthy and has a good memory," says Yi.[70] Yi Sungin presents Pae-ssi of Kyŏngsan, the wife of Yi Tonggyo, who drowned herself in the Soya River in 1380 (?) rather than be violated by Japanese pirates. Yi visited the river where Lady Pae died for her integrity.[71] Lady Ch'oe of Chŏlla, age thirty-three, the subject of Chŏng Io, also perished (1379?) at the hands of Japanese pirates.[72]

The writers' decision to exemplify such virtues as loyalty (Chŏng Ch'im, Pak Kang), filial piety (Kunman), chastity (Ladies Cho, Pae, and Ch'oe), and antiheterodoxy (Susŏn, Chŏng Hyŏnsuk) may reflect an ideological trend toward the Cheng-Zhu school of Neo-Confucianism as well as a new aspect in the history of Koryŏ literature.

PSEUDOBIOGRAPHY

A group of prose pieces known as *kajŏn* (pseudobiography) have as their subjects wine (Im Ch'un and Yi Kyubo), a square-holed coin (Im Ch'un), a turtle (Yi Kyubo), bamboo and ice (Hyesim, 1178–1234), a cane (Sigyŏngam, fl. 1270–1350), a bamboo cushion (Yi Kok, 1298–1351), and paper (Yi Ch'ŏm, 1345–1405). As Han Yu's "Mao Ying zhuan" ("Biography of Mao Ying"), about a writing brush, was sometimes considered a precursor of fiction, so too was Koryŏ pseudobiography. Commenting on Han Yu's "Biography of Mao Ying," James Hightower writes that it is "a parody leaning heavily on word-play and allusion" and points out "its playful exuberance and

[67] Ibid. 21:16b–19a.   [68] Ibid. 21:19b–21b.   [69] *TMS* 101:15b–16b.
[70] *TMS* 100:12a–13b.   [71] Yi Sungin, *Toŭn (mun) jip* 5:2a–b.
[72] *TMS* 101:20b–21b. For biographical accounts written by Koryŏ writers see Pak Hüibyŏng, *Hanguk kojŏn inmul chŏn yŏngu* (Hangilsa, 1992), pp. 9–98.

the pointless parody of a typical *Shiji* biography."⁷³ Inspired by Han Yu's prototypical work, Koryŏ products use the form of a *Shiji* biography – as the beginning of the following pieces indicate – often with the historian's judgment at the end:

Mao Ying was a native of Zhongshan. His ancestor Mingshi helped Yu govern the East. He rendered service in nourishing living things and consequently was enfeoffed in Mao.⁷⁴ (Han Yu, "Biography of Mao Ying")

The polite name of Kuk Sun ("Strong Yeast") was Chahu ("Pleasantly Drunk"). His ancestor came from Lungxi (Gansu). His ninetieth ancestor, Mo ("Barley"), rendered service by helping Lord Millet feed the people.⁷⁵ (Im Ch'un, "Biography of Kuk Sun")

Kuk Sŏng ("Sage Yeast"), whose polite name is Chungji, is from the county of Chuch'ŏn ("Wine Spring"). From his childhood he was loved by Xu Mo, who gave him his given and polite names.⁷⁶ (Yi Kyubo, "Biography of Gentleman Kuk")

The family name of this gentleman is Cho ("Paper Mulberry"), given name Paek ("White"), polite name Mujŏm ("Without Flaw"). He is from Kuaiji (Zhejiang). He is a descendant of Cai Lun.⁷⁷ (Yi Ch'ŏm, "Biography of Gentleman Cho")

Koryŏ pseudobiographies are learned finger exercises – occasions for parading knowledge about a given subject. Just as Han Yu "drags in every notable with the surname Mao" in his Mao Ying biography,⁷⁸ Im Ch'un, in his piece on wine, brings in not only Xu Mo of the Wei but such lovers of wine as Liu Ling (c. 225–280), Ruan Ji (210–263), and Shan Tao (205–283). In addition to naming characters whose graphs include the "wine" radical, Yi Kyubo also cites Liu Ling and Tao Qian.

Occasionally the historian's remark at the end contains a moral – to offer a warning to the reader, to forestall Confucian criticism for producing "misguided" writing, or both. The historian blames, for example, Kuk Sun for making the ruler dead drunk and negligent of state affairs, for bringing misfortune to his sons and disgrace to himself (Im Ch'un), or, as the ruler's favorite, for disturbing the country's laws and discipline (Yi Kyubo). The historian in Im Ch'un's "Kongbang chŏn" ("Biography of a Square-holed Coin") enumerates the crimes of the coin as harboring two minds, pursuing profit, assuming authority, forming a faction, flattering the powerful, and plotting to injure the upright.⁷⁹ In his "Biography of Kuk Sun," Im Ch'un perhaps wishes to say that it is better to live hidden and be respected than to be employed and bring disaster to one's self, one's family, and the state.

---

⁷³ James R. Hightower, "Han Yü as Humorist," *Harvard Journal of Asiatic Studies* 44 (1984): 10, 14.
⁷⁴ Ibid., 10–11.   ⁷⁵ *TMS* 100:1a–3b.   ⁷⁶ *TYC* 20:14a–b.   ⁷⁷ *TMS* 101:13a–15a.
⁷⁸ Hightower, "Han Yü as Humorist," 44, 14.   ⁷⁹ *TMS* 100:3b–6a.

The eminent monks Hyesim and Sigyŏngam (Prince Hye) introduce a number of innovations. Hyesim's "Biography of Bamboo" enumerates ten virtues of the bamboo – a symbol for an enlightened monk – and introduces dialogue between the bamboo and other characters.[80] Sigyŏngam's "Biography of the Cane" begins with someone visiting while the speaker is dozing against a cloister wall, followed by a description of the cane, and ends with a song to send the visitor off. The whole piece, which consists of a dialogue between the author in the third person and the visitor, allows the cane to narrate its origin and function and the author to praise its qualities.[81] Pseudobiography, as humorous and diverting, continued to be written throughout the Chosŏn dynasty, and indeed until the present, on such topics as a crab, a pine tree, a horse, tobacco, a cat, and a cuckoo, all in literary Chinese. Showy and often written to dazzle, pseudobiography seems to lack genuine importance to the modern reader; its scope and appeal are particularly limited.

LITERARY MISCELLANY

Prose narratives in Koryŏ include three collections of literary miscellany comprising random jottings, tales, and poetry criticism. Written in plain prose style, these have been read primarily as the Korean counterparts of Chinese *shihua* (remarks on poetry). But because they include historical, biographical, and autobiographical narratives as well, I view them as early specimens of the literary miscellany. The first such collection on poetry and current subjects in Korea is the *P'ahan chip* (*Jottings to Break Up Idleness*, published 1260) by Yi Illo (1152–1220), followed by the *Pohan chip* (*Supplementary Jottings in Idleness*, 1254) by Ch'oe Cha (1188–1260), and the *Nagong pisŏl*, also read *Yŏgong p'aesŏl* (*Lowly Jottings by old man "Oak*," 1342) by Yi Chehyŏn (1287–1367).

Yi Illo suggests that the primary condition that led him to write was leisure.[82] Leisure is the product of disengagement – the scorn for wealth and rank of a solitary, private man who "lives hidden in the mountains and forests" seeking peace of mind and his own identity within the uncompromised self.[83]

---

[80] Kim Ch'angnyong, *Hanguk kajŏn munhaksŏn* (Chŏngŭmsa, 1985), pp. 266–267.
[81] Yi Chŏngt'ak, *Hanguk uhwa munhak yŏngu* (Iu ch'ulp'ansa, 1982), pp. 108–110.
[82] *PaC*, postscript (*KMC* 2:2b).
[83] For a similar statement by Yi Chehyŏn in his preface to *Lowly Jottings by Old Man Oak*, see *NP* 2A:1 (*KMC* 2:1a). For more on the form, style, and structure of the literary miscellany see Peter H. Lee, *A Korean Storyteller's Miscellany* (Princeton: Princeton University Press, 1989), pp. 3–56.

Yi Illo was one of the most learned and talented poet-critics of the day: his precedents included examples of the *shihua* by Song writers. A typical entry debates the pros and cons of using certain words, phrases, allusions, and rhymes, as well as information about the occasion that inspired a poem's composition. In addition to poetic criticism, Yi's random jottings contain not only autobiographical information in the style of a diary or book of memoirs but also, along with biographical information on his friends and associates, their lifestyle, and their literary taste, remarks on contemporary customs and manners. For example, Yi tells us that he once supervised the making of 5,000 ink sticks and wrote a poem on the subject (ch. 1 : item 3); that at the lantern festival held on the fifteenth day of the first month of one year during the reign of King Myŏngjong, he wrote a heptasyllabic quatrain on a lantern, the first on the subject (1:9); that when Chŏng Hŭi sent Yi a bamboo painting on a folding screen, Yi tried his hand at painting the bamboo and the result was said to recall the style of Su Shi (1:11); that when the tangerine tree in the palace garden grew well when given salt water, Yi wrote an allegorical poem in twelve rhymes on how a ruler should nurture the talented (3:24); that Yi's contemporaries praised his grass-style calligraphy (1:12); that for eight generations Yi's ancestors placed first in the state examinations and Kakhun wrote a congratulatory poem about this achievement (3:10).

Examination of candidates in poetry began in the time of King Kwangjong. Later it became customary for the examinee to make a courtesy call on his former teacher. Yi informs us (1:15) that Han Ŏnguk, together with his students, visited Ch'oe Yuch'ŏng (1095–1174). We find yet more observations on poets and poetry in the *Jottings to Break Up Idleness*. We are told that Kang Iryŏng, before writing a poem on the white heron, spent days by a river to the south of Ch'ŏnsu Monastery – observing the bird's movements in order to integrate the object of contemplation into his spirit ("entering the spirit") – but was able to produce only a couplet, which Yi completed (1:21); that Kim Puŭi (1079–1136), known for his ability to write impromptu verse in Song China and for his love of learning, would wash his brush in ice water before writing (2:2); that Kim Chaŭi (fl. 1147–1170), known for his talent and fidelity, loved wine and was admonished by the king (2:7); and that, upon his wife's death, Yi Chahyŏn (1065–1125) abandoned the world at age twenty-six, entered a cloister on Mount Ch'ŏngp'yŏng, practiced meditation (*sŏn*), and befriended the eminent monks Hyejo (fl. 1106–1122) and T'anyŏn (1070–1159). Yi Chahyŏn also declined a summons from King Yejong, who granted him the posthumous title of Lord Chillak or "True Joy" (2:8); this is the same Yejong who loved his erstwhile mentor Kwak Yŏ (1058–1130) so much he bestowed a plot of land on Mount Yaktu for his retreat (2:9). Monk Hyeso, poet and calligrapher, was fond of sugar (2:11). While on a pleasure trip to the Taedong River, Yi O (1050–1110) named a tower there Pubyŏk ("Floating Emerald"), and on that occasion Kim Hwangwŏn managed to compose a heptasyllabic couplet that was considered inimitable (2:22). It is also related that both Sinjun and Im Ch'un, born out of their times, wrote poems on the cuckoo that expressed their innermost feelings, showing that, indeed, the well-spring of poetry is the human heart (3:18).

These few samples from the *Jottings to Break Up Idleness* enable us to deduce Yi Illo's view of poetry: although the poet is born with natural endowment, he must polish and refine his art, together with close observation of nature and wide reading of the ancients; only then will he be able to capture the subtlety of things and express it in words. Yi endorses the use of proper names and allusions, but he looks askance at mere imitation. He also finds fault with Huang Tingjian's idea of "changing the bone," or imitating an idea while using different words, and "evolving from the embryo," or imitating the words while using a somewhat different idea (3:20). He does not seek novelty for its own sake but emphasizes discovery, "new meaning" (*sinŭi*) to clear a space for his own voice.[84] Yi believes that a life spent writing poetry is preferable to an active life of glory, that the poet writes because he must express his emotions, and that emotions must be communicated by the right words properly arranged. Like Cao Pi (187–226) before him, Yi seems to believe that literature endures forever.

Now that we have seen the general matter and manner of a typical literary miscellany of the Koryŏ period, let us summarize some of the recurrent concerns of Koryŏ poet-critics that appear in their critical remarks. Koryŏ poets upheld individuality as the key element in literature, as demonstrated by their discussion of *ki* (*qi* 氣), individual genius based on temperament. They may have adopted this view from the *Lun wen* (*Discourse on Literature*) by Cao Pi: "In literature, the main thing is *qi*. The purity or impurity of this *qi* has substance and cannot be achieved by strenuous effort."[85] *Ki*, said Yi Kyubo, comes from heaven and cannot be attained by learning. It is also *ki*, individual genius, that determines the depth of thought expressed in literature.[86] Yi Illo thought that poets are born, not made,[87] but he did not

[84] *PaC* 3:20.
[85] James J. Y. Liu, *Chinese Theories of Literature* (Chicago: University of Chicago Press, 1975), p. 12; also in Donald Holzman, "Literary Criticism in China in the Early Third Century AD," *Asiatische Studien* 28 (1974): esp. p. 130.
[86] Yi Kyubo, *Paegun sosŏl* (*KMC* 2:1973) 26; Yu Chaeyŏng, trans. *Paegun sosŏl yŏngu* (Iri: Wŏngwang taehakkyo ch'ulp'anguk, 1979), pp. 125–129.
[87] *PaC* 3:32.

mention *ki* as the essence of poetry. To Ch'oe Cha, *ki* seemed to come not from heaven, but from one's personal nature (*sŏng* 性): meaning relies on *ki*; language issues from emotion; emotion is meaning, idea, or message; and if talent (才), which is part of one's nature, dominates emotion (*chŏng* 情), the diction will be mature, whereas if emotion dominates talent, the diction will be vulgar.[88] Ch'oe distinguished three kinds of *ki* according to age (youth, maturity, old age), probably meaning to imply that one's *ki* matures as one grows older.[89] Ch'oe's ideal poet was one who combined talent and emotion; such a poet's talent, he thought, would have no limits. This led Ch'oe to conclude that what is most important in poetry is new thought: originality.[90] Yi Illo, by contrast, believed that one's talent does have limits, but that these can be overcome by strenuous effort.[91]

Yi Kyubo held that meaning, or import (*ŭi* 意), is the essence of prose literature. According to his view, the greatest obstacle is to organize meaning; choice of diction comes next.[92] Ch'oe Cha proposed that the critic should consider first whether a poem embodies *ki* and *ŭi*; then he may examine diction and prosody. All three upheld the ideal "meaning beyond words," often illustrated by examples that have "unlimited meaning." Yi Chehyŏn (1287–1367) compared "meaning beyond words" to the inexhaustible fragrance of orchids.[93] These critics probably had in mind a passage ascribed to Confucius in the "Appended Words" section of the *Book of Changes*: "Writing cannot express words completely. Words cannot express thoughts completely"; and in the *Zhuangzi*, "We can use words to talk about the coarseness of things, and we can use our minds to visualize the fineness of things."[94]

Both Yi Illo and Yi Kyubo often opted for spontaneous creation rather than labored pieces. The poet, when moved by nature, responds to external objects and directly expresses his emotion in poetry. These critics had in mind Zhong Rong's (fl. 469?–518) preface to his *Shipin* (*Classes of Poetry*): "The vital force (*ki*) stirs objects, and objects move people; hence one's nature is agitated, and this is embodied in dancing and singing."[95] Both cited instances of having been inspired by a landscape or by contemplation of nature to compose impromptu poems, to which they often appended the phrase "without my knowledge." Such examples of spontaneous creation inspired by external stimuli were considered superior to labored pieces, for they could embody the emotion or capture the mood of the scene.

[88] *PoC* 2:6.   [89] *PoC* 2:46.   [90] *PoC* 3:5.
[91] *PaC* 1:29.   [92] *PS* 26.   [93] *NP* 1A:15, 2A:15.
[94] Wilhelm, *The I Ching or Book of Changes* 1:246; and Burton Watson, *The Complete Works of Chuang Tzu* (New York: Columbia University Press, 1968), p. 178.
[95] James J. Y. Liu, *Chinese Theories*, p. 77.

Such poems startle either the eye or the heart; the latter target is usually preferred.[96]

Despite their emphasis on individual talent, originality in thought, meaning beyond words, and spontaneous feelings, Koryŏ poets studied Tang and Song masters and imitated them – after all, they were writing in Chinese. Frequently cited Chinese poets include Tao Qian (365–427), Xie Lingyun (385–433), Li Bo (701–762), Du Fu (710–770), Po Juyi (772–846), Liu Zongyuan (773–819), Mei Yaochen (1002–1060), Ouyang Xiu (1007–1072), Su Shi, and Huang Tingjian. Yi Illo's favorite poets were Su Shi and Huang Tingjian.[97] Yi Kyubo preferred Tao Qian and Mei Yaochen and tried to emulate Bo Juyi.[98]

Six Dynasties and late Tang poetry, we recall, was in vogue at the end of Silla and early Koryŏ until Su Shi became the most studied and imitated Chinese poet from the middle period. Yi Illo first admired Du Fu but turned to Su Shi and Huang Tingjian. Indeed, Ch'oe Cha quotes Yi as saying: "Only after studying Su and Huang behind closed doors could words become strong, rhymes resonate, and I attain the samādhi [trance of concentration] in writing poetry."[99] "Students of today," says Yi Kyubo, "first learn required works for the examination and have no leisure to sing of the breeze and the moon. Upon passing the examination, however, they learn to write poetry and enjoy Su Shi. Therefore as soon as the roster of successful candidates is posted, the people would say, 'This year we have again produced thirty Su Shis.' "[100] Yi Kyubo, however, never admitted his debt to Su.

Prototypical Chinese works may be read and followed, said Yi Kyubo, but only after one has mastered their style and essence. In fact, he compared a plagiarist to a burglar: a burglar must first familiarize himself thoroughly with the gates, doors, and walls of a rich man's house before he can break into it without leaving clues. If he rummages through bags and opens boxes, he is sure to be caught. A poet wishing to imitate a master's work must first know what he intends to imitate. Even Yi, however, a staunch opponent of imitation, could not help borrowing the ideas and diction of the ancients.[101] Ch'oe Cha censured Yi Illo for repeating Su Shi's phrases, adding that one should acquire the master's style, not repeat his words.[102] Ch'oe Cha, who

---

[96] *PoC* 2:16.   [97] *PoC* 2:46.   [98] Ibid., and *PS* 15.   [99] *PoC* 2:46.
[100] *TYC* 26:5a; repeated in *TS* 1:47.
[101] *TYC* 26:4a–7b; *PS* 29 (Yu Chaeyŏng, pp. 131–137). This instance of Yi's plagiarism from Du Fu's "Autumn Meditation" (766; 8: lines 3–4) is pointed out in *TS* 1:20 (Chang, pp. 70–71); see A. C. Graham, *Poems from the Late T'ang* (Harmondsworth: Penguin, 1965), p. 55.
[102] *PoC* 2:12, 16.

esteemed new meaning in poetry following Yi Illo, nevertheless encouraged learning of the classics and histories, not only to transmit the Way, but to perfect one's art.[103] Ch'oe's curriculum for aspiring poets included the classics, histories, the *Selections of Refined Literature*, Li Bo, Du Fu, Han Yu, and Liu Zongyuan.[104]

Related to plagiarism is the use of allusions. Ch'oe Cha advised against reading the ancients with a view to showing off one's knowledge or alluding to them.[105] While admitting that skillful use of allusions is difficult, Yi Illo offered his own advice: one may use allusions, but they must be used so well that they are as good as new.[106] These critics in general, and Yi Illo in particular, recognized the need for indefatigable striving to perfect one's art.[107] Yi Kyubo advised that one should criticize one's own poem as if it were written by an enemy.[108]

How central to the poetic procedure is the use of various modes of allusions – allusions to myths, legends, history, and prior literary works? Major poets in East Asia and the West all dealt with prior texts creatively – their themes, topoi, expressions – to the great benefit of their own works. Particularly in poems on historical subjects, allusions economically summarize a historical event or the persons involved. Yi Illo has often been considered not only a master of allusion (especially by Ch'oe Cha) but also a poet so given to refining technique and form that he seems to have regarded form and content as separable in poetry. Nowhere in his work, however, did Yi Illo make statements that might corroborate Ch'oe's censure. He knew that technique is only a means to an end, "the wondrous harmony of form and content" (diction and meaning). Yi also knew that a literary text which draws nothing from its predecessors is inconceivable and that originality does not mean owing nothing to the past. To introduce something new is to return to the old. What was valued in terms of words was precedent, the purpose of which is to invest work with resonance and polysemy.

Both Yi Kyubo and Ch'oe Cha tended to espouse a didactic view of literature, stressing the conveyance of thought with poetry as a means of communication with potential appeal. Yi Illo opted for skillful use of diction and mastery of technique; Yi Chehyŏn emphasized the atmosphere (*kisang* 氣象) and the "powerful and free" mood of poetry.[109] Though familiar with Buddhism, Yi Illo and Yi Kyubo, unlike Yen Yu (fl. 1180–1235), seldom used the miraculous awakening espoused by Chan Buddhism as an analogy to poetry. These poet-critics' views on the function of poetry were at best

---

[103] *PoC* 2:46. [104] *PoC* 2:46; 3:3. [105] *PoC* 2:40. [106] *PaC* 3:4. [107] *PaC* 3:20.
[108] *PS* 28 (Yu Chaeyŏng, pp. 130–131). [109] *NP* 2B:17.

eclectic. At times they echoed the didactic view that poetry should contain "no evil thoughts." Ch'oe Cha even censured officials who emphasized literature rather than the classics. Echoing the view of Zhou Dunyi (1017–1073), Ch'oe said that poetry is "a vehicle of the Way" that the poet must manifest. Ch'oe approvingly quoted Ch'oe Yak (fl. 1116), who proposed that writers should be banished:

The ruler should discuss the classics and histories, deliberate the art of government, transform the people by virtue, and improve the customs of the people. This will leave him no time to consort with the frivolous and dissolute, who display petty skills like the carving of insects. Poetry that is not didactic will muddy the hearts of men and corrupt the people.

Ch'oe Yak was demoted by King Yejong (1106–1122), who loved literature, but Ch'oe Cha seems to have sided with Ch'oe Yak.[110] Yi Illo and Yi Chehyŏn vacillated between the expressive and the didactic views; both, for example, wrote and endorsed admonitory poems.

Until King Ch'ungnyŏl ordered scholars versed in the classics and history to teach at the royal academy, Koryŏ Confucianism was mainly literary Confucianism. An Hyang (1243–1306) proposed in 1304 to raise an educational assistance fund to promote Confucian education and propagate the teachings of Zhu Xi. Paek Ijŏng (fl. 1298–1313) studied Cheng-Zhu philosophy in the Mongol capital and upon returning taught Yi Chehyŏn and Pak Ch'ungjwa (1287–1349). U T'ak (1263–1342) studied Cheng Yi's *Yizhuan* (*Commentary on the "Book of Changes"*), and Kwŏn Po (1262–1346) had Zhu Xi's *Sishu jizhu* (*Collected Commentaries on the Four Books*) published. When, in 1367, King Kongmin rebuilt the royal academy and Yi Saek (1328–1396) became its rector, Yi appointed as instructors Kim Kuyong (1338–1384), Chŏng Mongju (1337–1392), Pak Sangch'ung (1332–1375), Pak Ŭijung (fl. 1388–1392), and Yi Sungin (1349–1392) to lecture on the *Collected Commentaries on the Four Books* and the *Commentary on the Book of Changes*. From this time on, the views of literature held by the students of Confucianism began to be more didactic – repeating, for example, Zhou Dunyi: "Literature is a vehicle of moral principles" (*Tongshu*) or "Literary expressions are art and moral principles are substance." Yi Chehyŏn tended to emphasize the civilizing aspect of literature but had not yet rejected literary arts. Yi Saek, who sought models in Han Yu and Ouyang Xiu and whose prose was praised by Kim Ch'anghyŏp (1651–1708), regarded literary

[110] *PoC* 1:17.

composition as a "minor art"[111] or a bypath[112] and held that poetry must move beyond the correctness of personal nature and emotions and reach the state of "no evil thoughts" (*Analects* 2:2).[113] Chŏng Tojŏn ascribes to Chŏng Mongju a view that literature is a trivial art[114] and himself repeats Zhou Dunyi's view, cited earlier, emphasizing literature's moral effects on the reader.

Comments on prose are fewer than those on poetry. Kim Yunsik (1835–1922), more widely read than any modern, cites Yi Chehyŏn, Yi Kok, and Yi Saek as writers of old prose.[115] Kim Pusik tried it – especially in the biography of his *Historical Records of the Three Kingdoms* – and his story of Ondal is rated highly by Kim T'aegyŏng (1850–1927), another erudite critic of the subject.[116] Yu Sŭngdan (Wŏnsun, 1168–1232), as sung in the "Song of Confucian Literati" (c. 1216), excelled in old prose; other masters were Kim Hwangwŏn (1045–1117), Hwangbo Hang (late twelfth – early thirteenth century) who is said to have revived the prose style of Western Han, and O Sejae (early thirteenth century), whose work is likened to that of Han Yu by Yi Kyubo.[117] Both Yi Chehyŏn and his pupil Yi Saek took as their models Han Yu and Ouyang Xiu, and Yi Chehyŏn was ranked by Kim T'aegyŏng as the greatest prose writer of Korea. Chŏng Mongju's prose, according to Hŏ Kyun's estimate, is characterized by "free abandon," or "aggressive extravagance" (*hobang* 豪放).[118]

In the field of practical criticism, Koryŏ and Chosŏn critics, like Chinese writers of *shihua*, resorted to two-graph compounds or four-graph phrases to describe their impressions of a poem. They not only repeated the same compounds the Chinese used, but also made up new ones of their own. These vague but evocative phrases were intended to convey the reader's impressions or describe a poem's quality. Often the catchwords were based on lines wrenched out of context and then applied without analysis to other works by the same poet. The poetry of Chŏng Chisang (d. 1135), for example, was described by the compilers of the *History of Koryŏ* as "clear and splendid" (*ch'ŏnghwa* 淸華); that of Kim Kŭkki (fl. 1170–1197) by Nam Yongik as "flowing and beautiful" (*yuryŏ* 流麗); that of Chin Hwa (fl. 1200) by Sŏ Kŏjŏng as "lucid and new" (*ch'ŏngsin* 淸新); that of Chŏng P'o (1309–1345)

---

[111] Yi Saek, *Mogŭn mungo* 31:30a. This and subsequent paragraphs are based on Min Pyŏngsu, *Hanguk hansi sa* (T'aehaksa, 1996), pp. 9–201.
[112] Yi Saek, *Mogŭn mungo*, 8:10b.   [113] Ibid., 13:3a.   [114] Chŏng Tojŏn, *Sambong chip* 3:90.
[115] Kim Yunsik, *Unyang sokchip*, 2 vols. (Asea munhwasa, 1980) 4:46b.
[116] Kim T'aegyŏng, *Kim T'aegyŏng chŏnjip* (Asea munhwasa, 1978) 8:123.
[117] *TYC* 37:1a–3a, esp. 1b.   [118] *Hŏ Kyun chŏnjip* 25:4a.

as "terse and ancient" (*kango* 簡古) and "flowing and beautiful"; that of Yi Sungin as "terse and simple" (*kangyŏl* 簡潔).[119]

In addition to remarks on poetry and accounts of personal interests, the literary miscellany also contains animal tales, tales of wonder, and prose portraits. Three tales tell how a grateful animal repays kindness or rewards the benefactor and his heirs. When a wildfire is about to engulf the drunken Kim Kaein taking a nap in a field, his dog goes to the stream to wet his body and sprinkles his master until it dies of exhaustion. When awakened, Kim realizes what has happened, buries the animal, writes a poem, and plants his staff to mark the grave.[120] Yi Chehyŏn offers two tales of grateful animals. In one, Sŏ Sinil saves a deer wounded by a hunter. That night a divine being appears in his dream and prophesies the success of his heirs. Similarly, Pak Set'ong, magistrate of T'onghae, sets free a huge turtle stranded on the beach. In a dream an old man predicts that he, his son, and his grandson will become ministers. Both prophecies come true.[121] The story in the *Supplementary Jottings in Idleness* of a monk who is a transformed tiger resembles a story in *Memorabilia of the Three Kingdoms*.[122] In the *Supplementary Jottings*, an old monk in Pyŏnsan goes to the lantern festival in Koch'ang where he sees an unusual boy and follows him. He turns out to be a tiger in metamorphosis. A voice declares that the boy is to die in a pit. The boy then asks the monk to spear him. At the pit, the tiger foretells that he will be reborn as a boy and begs the old monk to shave his head. After fifteen years the monk meets the boy again and makes him an acolyte who later becomes an abbot of Irŏm Monastery and heals the blind and revives the dead. The analogous story in *Memorabilia* concerns a certain Kim Hyŏn who, while circumambulating the stupa at Hŭngnyun Monastery, meets a girl and has an affair. Kim follows her to her thatched cottage where he finds out that she is a tigress. Then a voice declares that one of her three brother tigers is to be punished for taking a life. She volunteers to take the place of her brother, removes Kim's sword, and kills herself. Later Kim builds a monastery to pray for her soul.

The salient feature of the literary miscellany is its emphasis on portraits of others and indeed of the author himself. The penetrating observations of human conduct and motives – observations not only of what one is but what one does – set the literary miscellany apart from biographical writing of the traditional sort. Thus the portrait in the literary miscellany

---

[119] For Chŏng Chisang see *KRS* 127:36a; *PoC* 1:21. For Kim Kŭkki see Nam Yongik, *Kia* (Asea munhwasa, 1980), p. 3. For Chin Hwa see *TS* 2:3. For Chŏng P'o, see *KRS* 106:23b–24a; Nam Yongik *Kia*, p. 3. For Yi Sungin see *TS* 1:32; *KRS* 115:51b; Yi Saek. *Mogŭn mungo* 13:2b–3a.

[120] *PoC* 2:35.   [121] *NP* 1A:16.   [122] *PoC* 3:43; *SGYS* 5:225–228.

endeavors to extend beyond the conventionalized behavior of the public self and reveal the individual. In his portrait of Kim Puŭi (1079–1170), for example, Yi Illo says: "Kim would sit decorously all day and read books. He did not like to compose poems; when he did, he would never fail to wash his brush in a bottle of ice water."[123] These sparse facts, conveyed in twenty-eight graphs, are perhaps intended to evoke Kim's propriety, his love of learning, and his dedication to poetry. Yi Chehyŏn uses a similar narrative method in his treatment of Hong Ŏnbak (1309–1363): "Hong would take a bath every evening, put on his cap and gown, and worship the stars. He never neglected this custom, even during his mission to China or when supervising public works."[124] Both Kim and Hong are portrayed as if seen from without; indeed, they are treated as objects about whom certain episodes are being recounted. In his portrait of the otherworldly monk Chisik, Ch'oe Cha uses a single, direct citation introduced by the verb "to say": "When Ch'oe U (d. 1249) presented him with tea, incense, and a copy of the *Lengyen jing* [*Śuraṅgama[samādhi] sūtra; Scripture of Heroic March Concentration*], the monk refused to write a letter of acknowledgment: 'I have severed all ties with the world. How can I communicate with a letter?' he replied."[125] The quotation of speech attributed to Chisik, conveying the subjectivity of a third person, presents him more vividly to the reader.

Generally, the portraits in the miscellany, like the three simple examples cited here, rely for their effect on verbs of external action, certain observed behavioral traits, and, occasionally, direct quotations of speech. If a sparse narrative can recreate a memorable scene, an anecdote, or a clever exchange, it can also capture a special moment of feeling or thought – that is, it can tell us what a person is by what he does and says. More accomplished pieces in the Chosŏn dynasty feature precise phrasing and deftly wrought narrative and use not only verbs of external action but those of inner action as well. Conversely, by portraying the subjectivity of the third person a writer can transform his narrative from a statement of reality into a work of fiction.

---

[123] *PaC* 2:2.   [124] *NP* 1B:18.
[125] *PoC* 3:33. For an English translation see Sara Boin-Webb, *Śūraṃgamasamādhisūtra.*

CHAPTER 7

Early Chosŏn eulogies

Peter H. Lee

According to the Confucian canon, rites and music are the two indispensable means by which a virtuous ruler administers his state. Rites teach the people a patterned sense of community, of order and degree, while music cultivates their moral virtue and regulates their feelings. Rulers of Korean kingdoms, as in China, emphasized both rites and music, mainly for their didactic function. It is no wonder, then, that the Chosŏn dynasty, which rejected Buddhism and Daoism as subversive of public morality and adopted Confucianism as its official political philosophy, should reexamine the ritual and official music of the previous kingdom. New texts, called *akchang*, were composed for music that was already in use in the ancestral temple and court ceremonies. The aims of composing *akchang* were twofold: to justify the revolution and emphasize the legitimacy of the new dynasty; and to praise the virtues and merits of its founder. As might be expected, the authors were all meritorious subjects who had assisted in the revolution and framed and executed the policy of the new government. Their eulogies remained a literature of the privileged class, and most of the forms they used for their composition disappeared soon after the end of the fifteenth century.

The first compositions of this kind, the "Mong kŭmch'ŏk" ("Dream of the Golden Ruler") and "Su porok" ("Upon Receiving the Precious Prophecy"), were presented to the throne by Chŏng Tojŏn (d. 1398) on 2 September 1393.[1] The former is in irregular meters in the *chuci* style; the latter consists of fourteen tetrasyllabic lines. Both were set to Tang music to be used at court banquets. The theme of the first recurs in canto 83 of the *Songs of Flying Dragons* (1445–1447), and that of "Upon Receiving the Precious Prophecy" in canto 86:

---

[1] Ha Yun and Pyŏn Kyeryang, eds. *T'aejo sillok* (*CWS* 1) 4:2b; *AHKB* 2:28a, 4:10a–11b; Chŏng Tojŏn *Sambong chip* (Kuksa p'yŏnch'an wiwŏnhoe, 1961) 2:61.

83
He was to map the norms with a ruler;
So wishing to charge him with a good government,
Heaven sent down
A gold ruler.

86
Were it not for the old oracle
Hidden in the stone cave,
Who would notice
Heaven's will?

Chŏng Tojŏn wrote four more poems to laud the cultural accomplishments of King T'aejo and three that praise his military genius. Among the military poems, the "Napssi ka" ("Song of Naghacu," 1393)[2] has as its theme the repulse of Naghacu in 1362 while the "Chŏng tongbang kok" ("Pacification of the East")[3] deals with the return of General Yi Sŏnggye from Wihwa Island in the Yalu River in 1388. The former was sung to the tune of "Song of Green Mountain," and the latter to "Song of P'yŏngyang."

The first in a series of poems describing the beauty of Seoul, the new capital, is an eight-line poem, the "Sindo ka" ("Song of the New Capital," 1394) by Chŏng Tojŏn.[4] In 1398 Chŏng wrote another song, the "Sindo p'algyŏng si" ("Eight Scenes of the New Capital"), in four stanzas of hexametric verse.[5] Kwŏn Kŭn (1352–1409) and Ha Yun (1347–1416) joined in the praise of Seoul, but a better poem in this vein is the "Hwasan pyŏlgok" ("Song of Mount Hwa," 1425) by Pyŏn Kyeryang (1369–1430),[6] which praises the capital and the king's good government in eight stanzas, the first of which includes the following lines:

Mount Hwa in the south, River Han in the north,
Chosŏn's most beautiful place.
White jade city, golden palaces, smooth streets running
far and wide;
Phoenixes alight, dragons soar, heaven fashioned its
contours, the warp and woof, the yin and yang.

Early Chosŏn-dynasty eulogies are written either in the traditional Chinese verse forms, usually that of the *Book of Song*'s hymns (as in the

---

[2] Ha Yun and Pyŏn Kyeryang, eds., *T'aejo sillok* 4:2b–4a; *AHKB* 2:21a; *SH* 1a–2a; Chŏng Tojŏn, *Sambong chip* 2:59–60.
[3] *AHKB* 2:20b; *ACKS* 7a–b; Chŏng Tojŏn *Sambong chip* 2:60.   [4] *ACKS* 10b–11a.
[5] Ha Yun and Pyŏn Kyeryang, eds., *T'aejo sillok* 13:14a–b; No Susin et al., *Sinjŭng Tongguk yŏji sŭngnam* (Kojŏn kanhaenghoe, 1958) 3:46a–47b.
[6] Chŏng Inji and Hwangbo In, eds., *Sejong sillok* (*CWS* 2–6) 28:1b–2a; *ACKS* 18b–20a.

case of "Dream of the Golden Ruler" and "Upon Receiving the Precious Prophecy"); in penta- or heptasyllabic Chinese verse forms with Korean connectives ("Song of Naghacu" and "Ponghwang ŭm" ["Song of the Phoenix"]); or in the *kyŏnggi-ch'e* form. The most polished examples, such as "Song of Mount Hwa," "Sangdae pyŏlgok" ("Song of the Censorate," c. 1399–1409) by Kwŏn Kŭn,[7] and the anonymous "Oryun ka" ("Song of the Five Relations")[8]and "Yŏn hyŏngje kok" ("Brothers at the Feast")[9] are in the last form. The number of stanzas varies from five to eight, but two phrases in line 5 are repeated to reinforce the meaning of the repetend. Compiled in Chinese in 1420 by the Ministry of Rites as song texts for banquet music, the "Ha sŏngdŏk ka" ("Song of Sagely Virtue"), consisting of five six-line stanzas plus one four-line stanza,[10] and "Ch'uk sŏngsu" ("Long Live the King"), composed of ten two-line stanzas,[11] are also in the *kyŏnggi-ch'e* form.

These songs commemorate the dynastic founders and were presented before ancestral spirits or courtiers on festive occasions. The praise of exalted subjects calls for encomiastic hyperbole, but such exaggeration was intended to present an image of regal virtue and popular obedience to the ruler. At the same time, compilers did not hesitate to register their concerns about the potential excesses of kings, with a warning against authority without responsibility, power without piety. The subject of the "Song of the Five Relations" is the relationships between ruler and minister, father and son, husband and wife, elder brother and younger brother, and between friends. As for "Brothers at the Feast," after praising innate love, indefatigable pursuit of knowledge and virtue, deep familial ties, and mutual support, its fourth stanza recalls how a separation caused by brotherly rivalry could plunge the dynasty into chaos. This is also the theme of canto 119 of *Songs of Flying Dragons* ("If brothers are split, / A villain will enter and sow discord"). Therefore, when a brother becomes king through virtue, let him rule humbly and reverently, warns the stanza, and as his subject one must do one's best to fulfill one's duties. The "Song of the Censorate," on the other hand, celebrates the magnificence of the censorial office in the Confucian state. The censorate, stern as frost, soars skyward among drooping pines and lush cypresses. Dazzling carriages thunder along broad avenues as runners clear the way. Upon reaching the office, censors ascend the terrace and deliberate on the fine points of statutes by consulting the ancients and moderns. They remedy abuses of power and offer advice to

---

[7] *ACKS* 23a–b.   [8] *ACKS* 20b–21b.   [9] *ACKS* 21b–22b.
[10] Chŏng Inji and Hwangbo In, *Sejong sillok* 7:19a; 44:22b–23a; presented to the throne on 3 March.
[11] Ibid.

the king. After a day's work, they fling off their caps and gowns and have a feast on "boiled dragons and roasted phoenix." Drunk, they sing praises of a golden age when the wise ruler and good subject will meet to enjoy peace and happiness together.

SONGS OF FLYING DRAGONS

The most monumental work among early Chosŏn eulogies is *Songs of Flying Dragons* (1445–1447), a cycle of 125 cantos comprising 248 poems.[12] It was compiled to praise the founding by General Yi Sŏnggye (1335–1408) of the Chosŏn dynasty. Written by the foremost philologists and literary men in the Academy of Worthies, the *Songs* combine poetry and historiography to express the orthodox view of recent history. The compilers acknowledged their indebtedness to the dynastic hymns in the *Book of Songs* that praise the Zhou founders, notably poems 154 (on agriculture), 237, 241, 245 (on Lord Millet and agriculture), 270, and 303 (on Shang's genesis). The *Songs* use mostly themes of praise found in the classics and histories – stylistic devices of comparison and amplification, the fullest exploration of the device of parallelism, the hysteron-proteron arrangement of cantos, and formulas.

Preparation began in 1437 with the gathering of accounts of deeds preserved in the veritable records as well as popular traditions circulating among the people. For example:

1437	
31 August:	Governor of Hamgil province ordered to inspect the site of Chŏk Island, where Yi Sŏnggye's great-grandfather, Ikcho, escaped the Jurchens.
1442	
11 April:	The court interviews those who heard about the 1380 battle on Mount Hwang.
12 April:	King Sejong orders An Chi and Nam Sumun to collect tales of T'aejo's heroism.
1443–1444	Invention of the Korean alphabet.
1445	
11 May:	Kwŏn Che and others present the draft of Chinese verses of *Songs of Flying Dragons*.

---

[12] The discussion of *Songs of Flying Dragons* is adapted from relevant sections in Peter H. Lee, *Celebration of Continuity: Themes in Classic East Asian Poetry* (Cambridge, Mass.: Harvard University Press, 1979).

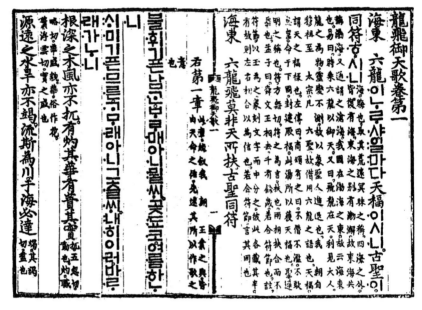

Example 4.   *Songs of Flying Dragons* (1445–1447), cantos 1–2 (1612) 1:1a–b.

3 December:	King Sejong suggests additions and improvements to the Chinese verses.
1446	
September–October	Korean alphabet promulgated.
October–March:	Korean verses completed by Ch'oe Hang (1409–1474), Pak P'aengnyŏn (1417–1456), Sin Sukchu (1417–1475), Sŏng Sammun (1418–1456), Yi Sŏllo (d. 1453), Yi Kae (1417–1456), and Kang Hŭian (1419–1464).
1447	
February–March	Ten-chapter commentary on the *Songs* completed.
17 July:	Sejong regulates the court music; the royal compositions based on the *Songs* form its nucleus.
23 November:	550 copies of the *Songs* distributed.

The first canto, which together with the second forms the proem, sets the theme, mood, and purpose of the book: praise of the four ancestors and the first and third kings of the dynasty. These six dragons flying above the land of the Eastern Sea are Mokcho (d. 1274), Ikcho, Tojo (d. 1342), Hwanjo (1315–1361), Yi Sŏnggye (1335–1408; r. 1392–1398), and Yi Pangwŏn

(1367–1422; r. 1400–1418). The central part of the book comprises cantos
3 to 124 subdivided into two sections: cantos 3–109 praise the cultural
and military accomplishments of the six dragons; cantos 110–124 consist of
admonitions to future monarchs. Canto 125 is a conclusion. Each canto,
except for cantos 1 and 125, consists of two poems, the first relating generally
the great deeds of Chinese sovereigns and the second those of the Chosŏn
kings. In the second canto, however, both poems serve as proems, and in
cantos 110–124, both poems deal with the Chosŏn kings. Cantos 86–89
are exceptions to the general scheme as well, since each poem celebrates
the deeds of the founder. Cantos 108 and 109, the only cantos assigned to
women, praise the heroic deeds of the wife of King Wen; Queen Sinhye,
wife of Wang Kŏn, the founder of Koryŏ; and Queen Wŏngyŏng (1365–
1420), wife of Yi Pangwŏn. The compilers assigned five cantos to Mokcho,
nine to Ikcho, four to Tojo, six to Hwanjo, eighty-one to Yi Sŏnggye, and
twenty-three to Yi Pangwŏn.

The stanzaic scheme characteristic of the Korean verse may be seen in
the first verse of canto 2. Each quatrain in cantos 2–124 follows the same
scheme, the total number of syllables varying from eighteen to thirty, but
most commonly twenty-four to twenty-eight. Canto 1 is a single tercet;
canto 125, a single ten-line stanza. The Chinese verses, on the other hand,
demonstrate more variety in form. While canto 1 has three irregular lines,
canto 125 has ten such lines. Cantos 2–109 consistently use four-word verses,
and cantos 110–124 introduce another form: three five-word verses.

The account of the heroic virtues of Yi Sŏnggye follows the techniques
evolved in the Chinese classics and histories, especially the biographical patterns in moral lives and eulogies of eminent men. Such works use praise or
blame to create an exemplum of virtue or vice. A portrait was usually created
through chronological narration of the subject's parentage and childhood
and idealized accounts of his heroic *facta*, especially military victories. If,
like Yi Sŏnggye, he was renowned for martial prowess, each episode was
carefully constructed to exemplify a specific martial virtue, such as fortitude, magnanimity, or constancy. If he was a universal genius, a flower of
valor and virtue, this was followed by his qualities as a leader of people,
again with episodes illustrating diverse aspects of civil virtues in action.
These topics of ancestry, nature, and character are the familiar topics of
epideictic oratory and rhetoric.

Martial valor and prowess

The posthumous epithets of heroes portrayed in histories of China and
Korea, especially dynastic founders or restorers of dwindling imperial

power, often include the graph *mu* (warrior, martial). Yi Sŏnggye was such a man as his posthumous epithets contain the formula *sinmu* (神武 august warrior or divine hero). Looked upon as an embodiment of a long native military tradition, Yi no doubt deserved such a resplendent title.

A number of cantos celebrate Yi's marksmanship (cantos 32, 43, 86, 88, and 89). The bow is his characteristic weapon:

> 86
> He shot six roebucks,
> He shot six crows,
> He flew across
> The slanting tree.

> 88
> He hit the back of forty tailed deer,
> He shot the mouths and eyes of the rebels,
> He shot down three mice from the eaves.
> Were there any like him in the past?

Like Achilles' ashen spear, Odysseus' huge bow, or Beowulf's victory-blessed blade, Yi Sŏnggye's bow was characterized by its prodigious size. He cut his own arrows made of the *hu* tree, instead of the usual bamboo, and they made a whirring noise as they flew through the air. Upon seeing the size of the bow and arrow, his own father remarked that they were not only impractical but incapable of being used by a man. Yi Sŏnggye, however, startled his father by skillfully manipulating the superhuman weapon and killing seven roebucks (canto 27).

Like so many heroes, the general's animal in peace and war was the horse. "No animal invites," Bowra comments, "so technical or so discriminating a knowledge or excites stronger affection and admiration" than the horse.[13] It is the hero's trusted friend to whom he unfailingly appeals for help. Like King Mu's eight bayards or Li Shimin's six bayards that came at the appropriate time to render service, Yi Sŏnggye had eight stalwart steeds, all of which performed miracles of one sort or another:

> 70
> Heaven gave him courage and wisdom
> Who was to bring order to the country.
> Hence eight steeds
> Appeared at the proper time.

---

[13] Maurice Bowra, *Heroic Poetry* (London: Macmillan, 1961), p. 157.

In peacetime, hunting trips, contests, or games provided him with occasions to perfect his horsemanship. In a polo match and archery contests he displayed superhuman feats of marksmanship.

> 44
> It was a polo match played by royal order –
> He hit the ball by a "sideway block."
> People on the nine state roads
> All admired his skill.[14]

> 63
> He shot pears from a hundred paces away,
> Displaying his prowess to the guests.
> They therefore
> Drank a toast.

Such contests were actually provided by heaven – or heaven induced someone to provide them – in order to manifest the general's "august power" (canto 46) as well as convince the king and the people and inspire awe (cantos 31–32, 46). Marksmanship alone, however, is not the subject of these poems: they are cited as evidence of the general's heroic virtue, indispensable for the mission he was to perform.

> 45
> Many could shoot an arrow:
> But he was aware of his heroic virtue.
> With this heroic virtue
> He saved many.

Thus the contests were also occasions for the clarification of his destiny and his recognition of the heavy burden the nation had laid on him.

With his supreme physical and spiritual qualities, Yi Sŏnggye responded to calls to bring order and peace to a nation harassed by foreign invaders. When, in 1361, the Red Turbans crossed the Yalu and seized the Koryŏ capital, he rallied his men and drove back the enemy (cantos 33–34). In 1362, as Commander of the Northeast, the general was in charge of a campaign against the Mongol minister Naghacu (cantos 35–36, 88), and in 1370 he subjugated the stronghold of the Northern Yuan in northwestern Manchuria (cantos 39–41). A final series of campaigns that brought lasting fame to Yi was against the Japanese pirates in 1377, 1380, and 1382 (cantos

[14] When the ball bounced off the goal post and came back on the horse's left, Yi Sŏnggye shook off the right stirrup and turned his body around in such a way that his right foot reached down almost to the ground. He hit the ball cleanly, then back astride his mount, he hit it again and scored. The compilers call it the "sideway block" technique.

47–52, 58–62). At such times, the enemy's strength and cruelty were a measure of his heroism.

The terror inspired by these events is augmented by strange eruptions that portend victory to Korea and disaster to the enemy, such as a red halo, a mist, or a white rainbow that suddenly fills the sky (cantos 39, 42, 50). These signs of supernatural companionship not only inspire his deeds but reinforce the consciously ethical heroic standard he represents. Nevertheless, he is also painfully aware of the suffering and loss exacted by human achievements and historical fulfillment. Although he has mastered the fear of death, in contemplating the horror of war he at once comprehends the limitations and finality of men's deeds. On his way to a decisive battle on Mount Hwang in 1380, he was overwhelmed by compassion and pity for the dead bodies covering the hills and plains and recognizes this timeless truth:

> 50
> Pitying his own people
> He passed by Changdan.
> At that time a white rainbow
> Cut across the sun.

As an embodiment of the struggles of his nation and people, Yi's career has a national and patriotic meaning that gives a unity to his struggles. As such it was fully sanctioned by Confucian orthodoxy. "When heaven is about to confer a great responsibility on a man," Mencius said, "it will exercise his mind with suffering, subject his sinews and bones to hard work, expose his body to hunger, put him to poverty, place obstacles in the paths of his deeds, so as to stimulate his mind, harden his nature, and improve wherever he is incompetent" (6B:15).[15] This is how heaven prepares men for great tasks – as was the case with the sage ruler Shun and other ideal figures of Confucian tradition. They succeeded because they were able to take obstacles as challenges necessary for their development. Through signs and portents, heaven constantly reminds them of the moral significance of their deeds, while the scope of their trials – corresponding to the adventures of the hero in the mythological cycle – is the measure of greatness. The eventual bestowal of service on his fellow men – corresponding to the return of the mythological hero – is the only justification of such trials.

Canto 41, therefore, presents Yi Sŏnggye as an emblem of humanity and justice whose purpose in war was not spoils or pillage but the restoration of order and peace. Wishing to save the dauntless Mongol general Zhao Wu,

---

[15] Wing-tsit Chan, *A Source Book in Chinese Philosophy* (Princeton: Princeton University Press, 1963), p. 78.

Yi did not use arrowheads (canto 54) but awed him into submission (in 1364). Like the English *curtana* (or *curteyn*),[16] the blunted sword of mercy and peace, Yi Sŏnggye's "wooden arrowhead" (*paktu*) manifests his refusal to wound and destroy needlessly. In accordance with the thesis of Xunzi,[17] the righteous army was followed by a mass of people in adoration of the commander's virtue – a crowd large enough to serve as a tribute to his prestige and magnificence, which also won the allegiance of the Jurchens and southern barbarians.

The general's return from Wihwa Island in 1388, in opposition to the court's planned Liaodong expedition, is singled out as an instance of chastisement in heaven's name of the crimes of the wicked Koryŏ king:

> 10
> A mad fellow was reckless and oppressive;
> They therefore awaited his banner of justice.
> With rice in baskets, wine in bottles,
> They welcomed him along the roadside.

This recent historical event is subtly compared to a similar act of King Wu of Zhou, who had been accepted by orthodox Confucian tradition as the archetype of heaven's agent and the representative of his people. This epideictic scheme enabled the compilers to interpret Yi's decision not as an act of insurrection but as a response to heaven's mandate. He is the living representative of cosmic, moral, and political processes and his allegiance to heaven's design elevates him to the level of the ideal Confucian hero with a ritualistic function consistently portrayed in the literature of praise. In spite of "a wicked plan" against him, Yi Sŏnggye, like Kings Wen and Wu, doubted heaven's bidding and continued to serve the inadequate sovereign. Only when heaven manifested its will through an auspicious dream (canto 13) and the willing allegiance of the people did he initiate a coup. Thus, the fact that his revolution was not an act of usurpation but "a gift of heaven" had finally been expounded.

Moral and kingly virtues

The heroic achievements of the Confucian soldier lie not so much in his battlefield feats as in his setting of a new standard of moral excellence. The aim of the righteous war, Xunzi reminds us, is "to put an end to violence."[18]

---

[16] Samuel C. Chew, *The Virtues Reconciled* (Toronto: University of Toronto Press, 1947), pp. 119–122.
[17] Xun Qing, *Xunzi* (Sibu congkan) 10:7b, 13b–14b; Burton Watson, *Hsün Tzu: Basic Writings* (New York: Columbia University Press, 1963), pp. 69–70.
[18] Xun Qing, *Xunzi* 10:13b (Watson, *Hsün Tzu*, p. 69).

Yi Sŏnggye fulfilled the function of a Confucian soldier by withstanding the trials, responding to the demands of destiny willed by Heaven, and by identifying his personal fate with that of the nation. The ultimate justification, however, is the preservation of order, best manifested in good government. The cantos that celebrate the statesmanship of Yi Sŏnggye and Yi Pangwŏn, therefore, explore the nature and function of kingship, the relations of power and justice, the role of mercy and remonstrance, and the importance of learning and orthodoxy, culminating in the admonitory cantos that conclude the cycle (110–125).

The rhetorical and dramatic devices are the same as those employed in the "arms" cantos. Each canto comprises parallel studies, the subjects of which are known examples from Chinese history, a universal history in the Confucian ecumene, much in the way seventeenth-century English poetry turned to sacred history for metaphorical amplification. The episodic structure and austere form required a compression of the subject's career into a few lines that enabled the compilers to achieve economy and objectivity. The use of stylistic devices for the political and moral purposes of the work was possible because the communal values to which the poems refer were familiar to every schoolboy who had read the Confucian "mirror for princes" literature. In the cantos devoted to Yi Sŏnggye, the subjects of twin studies in chronological order include: Liu Bang (founder of the Han), Liu Bei of Shu Han, Li Shimin, Guo Rong (Shizong of the Later Zhou), Zhao Kuangyin (founder of the Song), and Qubilai. They are introduced either to aggrandize Yi Sŏnggye or to demonstrate his superiority over the Chinese counterpart, as in the sustained contrast between Yi and Liu Bang (cantos 66 and 79).

The sovereign qualities of a Confucian king enumerated in the *Songs* recall the cardinal virtues of a Christian prince treated in the "mirror for princes" literature. Yi Sŏnggye possessed benevolence, justice tempered with mercy, learning, wisdom, temperance, modesty, and brotherly love. It is no accident that the great moral qualities associated with a Confucian ruler are the same as those of a Renaissance king serving as God's steward on earth. Both are asked to conform to a prototype and to perform sanctioned roles. As a defender of the moral order in the universe and a representative of his culture, the ruler's conduct becomes the cause of public order or disorder. The compilers are therefore eager to illustrate public doctrine: the special qualifications required of a ruler and the particular functions he is expected to discharge for the good of the human community. Their duty as encomiasts is to raise the real to the ideal. Their allegiance to the tradition also required them to reaffirm the public values upon which the health and destiny of the realm depended.

The dominant topic here, characteristically Confucian, is *ren* (*in* 仁) – benevolence, goodness, or love. Yi Sŏnggye's love, in its various forms, finds expression in his dealings with his subordinates, stepbrother, and rivals and enemies. He was "polite with his men, kind in words," and therefore able to steady the hearts of his subordinates (canto 66). He loved his stepbrother, even though he once rose in revolt (canto 76), for regulation of the family is necessary to public order, as is reiterated in canto 119. One who cannot set his household in order is hardly expected to act as defender of national mores and custodian of the way of the ancient sage kings. Yi Sŏnggye furthermore forgave his former rivals and enemies (canto 77) and restored them to their previous ranks. He showed a consistent concern for the welfare of meritorious subjects, as well, thus winning their lasting loyalty:

> 78
> From the start he treated them with a true heart,
> To the end his heart was true.
> Who would not
> Adore him?
>
> 79
> He was consistent from beginning to end,
> Meritorious subjects were truly loyal to him.
> He secured the throne for myriad years.
> Would his royal work ever cease?

That learning is indispensable to a prince or a gentleman is a commonplace in the tradition. The classics arm a man with precepts against every contingency, while history, which embodies the past and teaches by example, provides suitable analogies for each occasion. Both are storehouses of exempla – political and moral mirrors in which we find truth and can know ourselves. Emphasis on learning is also an affirmation of loyalty to culture, a status symbol of the ruling class that, through the civil service examination in China and Korea, manned the government. Therefore Yi Sŏnggye, like Caesar and Augustus in the West, fully accoutered in armor, read books between battles in order to learn the art of government. Regretting that his family had not yet produced a scholar, Yi Sŏnggye urged his son to pursue classical learning. Yi Sŏnggye's respect for scholarship is evidenced too in his courteous reception of Yi Saek when the latter returned from his banishment in 1391:

> 82
> Upon receiving an old scholar
> He knelt down with due politeness.

Indeed, "love of learning is akin to wisdom" (*Doctrine of the Mean* 20; *Songs of Flying Dragons* canto 122), and wisdom is among the most important qualities required of the perfect prince. The compilers went to the *Doctrine of the Mean* for inspiration. By identifying the dynastic founder as a "counterpart of heaven"[19] who "hits upon what is right without effort and apprehends without thinking,"[20] they were able to elevate Yi Sŏnggye to the level of the Confucian sage, the ultimate hyperbolic stance.

In the final section of the *Songs*, the compilers directly address King Sejong (1418–1450), their patron and the great fount of their inspiration. The principal concern in the earlier part, we recall, was the celebration of the dynastic founder's paradigmatic acts, or the virtues he exemplifies. The source of resonance was the juxtaposition – and often integration – of native and classical materials. With the final section, which consists of a series of gracious exhortations to the reigning monarch, we notice a transition to poignantly personal utterance that shifts the focus from the comparatively distant and normative to the immediate and real. This effective variation of the compilers' strategy evinces how central, by the nature and tradition of their art, was the impulse to persuade.

Stylistically and thematically, therefore, this section contains the most sententiae. These traditional commonplaces are the "vehicles for the wisdom of the ages,"[21] easily learned and memorized.

> 116
> If you are unaware of people's sorrows,
> Heaven will abandon you.

> 118
> If a king loses his inward power,
> Even his kin will rebel.

> 119
> If brothers are split,
> A villain will enter and sow discord.

> 120
> If a ruler taxes his people without measure,
> The basis of the state will crumble.

> 122
> . . . learning surpasses mere thinking.

---

[19] *The Mean* 31 (Chan, *Source Book*, p. 112).
[20] *The Mean* 20 (Chan, *Source Book*, p. 107).
[21] Martha Andresen, "Ripeness Is All: Sententiae and Commonplace in King Lear," in *Some Facets of King Lear: Essays in Prismatic Criticism*, ed. Rosalie Colie and F. T. Flahiff (Toronto: University of Toronto Press, 1974), p. 152.

125
you can secure the dynasty only
When you worship heaven and benefit the people.

These and similar "sentences" engage the audience's sympathies; they are precepts tested by history and of vital importance to the Confucian prince.

The theme of cantos 110–113 is the evils that arise from ease and luxury. Some of the royal ancestors, persecuted and humiliated, moved from place to place seeking refuge; Ikcho, for example, suffered the treachery of the Jurchen chiefs and bore hardships in a clay hut, reminiscent of Danfu. Yi Sŏnggye spent much of his life repulsing invaders and subjugating rebels and thus had little time to doff his armor or partake of food and drink at leisure. In halcyon days, however, one who is freighted with the full panoply of resplendence is likely to forget the toils of his ancestors and people. Thus the compilers plead that the king, wrapped in royal robes and girt with a belt of precious gems, should think twice when he sups "northern viands and southern dainties" and drinks "superb wine."

Cantos 114 and 115 amplify from differing viewpoints the theme that peace should breed not evil but heroic courage and resolve. When the "wolves," the Red Turbans, and the Japanese pirates wrought havoc, Yi Sŏnggye suffered wounds and scars. Thus when a ruler, protected by stately guards, rules the kingdom effortlessly with "dangling robes and folded hands," he should ask himself whether he truly deserves his royal vocation and divine sanction:

115
When you have men at your beck and call,
When you punish men and sentence men,
Remember, my lord,
His mercy and temperance.

Indeed, since the statutes of a benevolent ruler tally with the will of heaven and the people, if a ruler is truly virtuous there is no need for the statutes at all.

The perfect king is compassionate. Upon seeing the dead bodies that covered the hills and plains during the 1380 campaign against the Japanese, Yi Sŏnggye could neither sleep nor eat. He saw as compassionate heaven saw, for "he possessed a heart sensitive to the sufferings of others and manifested [it] in compassionate government" (*Mencius* 2A:6).[22] One source of suffering was taxation, and canto 73 singles out for praise Yi Sŏnggye's land reform of 1391.

[22] Lau, *Mencius* (Harmondsworth: Penguin, 1970), p. 67.

The next topic is modesty and its opposite, pride, which leads to blindness and bigotry. The compilers recognized the evil of flattery, a common theme in historical and political literature worldwide. Flatterers are also slanderers. These artisans of intrigue are at work to unleash the strong passions and irrational forces in man that threaten traditional social forms and relationships. Canto 123 emphasizes saving innocent victims from acrid tongues and treacherous designs with a warning:

> When slanderers craftily make mischief,
> When they grossly exaggerate small mistakes,
> Remember, my Lord,
> His wisdom and justice.

Canto 118 celebrates the transforming power of virtue as the bulwark of order, the only means to conquer separatism. Transformed by Yi Sŏnggye's good government, Jurchen chiefs stopped their dispute and composed their differences, just as King Wen's bright virtue caused the rulers of Yu and Rui to feel shame for their petty squabbling. Here one recalls the topic that characterizes a hero: the willing allegiance of the people – as when the people chose to follow the course of migration of Yi Sŏnggye's great-grandfather Ikcho. Hence Yi Sŏnggye is praised here as having won the support of everyone under heaven, an unmistakable sign of a great man according to *Mencius* (2B:1).[23]

> 53
> He opened the four borders,
> Men on islands had no more fear of pirates.
> Southern barbarians beyond our waters,
> How could they not come to him?

Indeed, his moral virtues prevailed to the extremities of the world, here reaching as far as Siam and Liuqiu, as earlier they did among the Mongols and Jurchens.

The final canto ends not only with a prophecy of national greatness but with an allusive rhetorical question. Again the compilers assert that the security of the throne depends entirely upon the ruler's worship of heaven and his toil for the people.

> 125
> A millennium ago,
> Heaven chose the north of the Han.
> There they accumulated goodness and founded the state.

---

[23] Ibid., p. 73.

May your sons and grandsons reign unbroken.
But you can secure the dynasty only
When you worship heaven and benefit the people.

They then evoke the figure of Tai Kang of Xia, who was sufficiently remote historically to protect them from the displeasure of the authorities. They ask:

Ah, you who will wear the crown, beware,
Could you depend upon your ancestors
When you go hunting by the waters of Luo?

On his way from a hunting trip to the south of the Luo River, Tai Kang is said to have been ambushed by Yi, who subsequently seized the throne. Tai Kang's loss of the crown by his indulging in pleasure shows how his personal conduct was the immediate source of public disorder. Probably more important in terms of the total symbolic structure is the significance of the hunt, a "political metaphor for tyranny."[24] The traditional associations of the hunt with war and game are familiar enough, but here the compilers emphasize the rapacity of the sportive tyrant, whose prey included not only beasts but men. Love of the chase was often an attribute of the evil ruler. History reveals the fate of the tyrannous hunter after men: he is in turn hunted, deposed, banished, and often killed, a condign punishment for the transgressor against heaven, earth, and humankind. Except for the ritualistic game in accord with the law of nature or the pursuit of the nation's enemy to restore order, the hunt is a metaphor for the unbound energy of the tyrant in disregard of the ideal political and moral order. This may well be the meaning of the final canto, for upon the ruler depend the survival of society and the maintenance of harmony. Such was the figure of the ideal Confucian prince, whose lasting virtues were vital to the future of the dynasty. Thus a handbook of education was created, a summa of the topics of Confucian humanism.

The tree of dynasty

To close this discussion of *Songs of Flying Dragons*, let us return to an important symbol in the songs – the tree – to explore not only its metaphorical meanings within the context of the Confucian worldview but also how these meanings were brought to bear on the specifically Korean historical

---

[24] Earl W. Wasserman, *The Subtler Language: Critical Readings of Neoclassical and Romantic Poems* (Baltimore: Johns Hopkins University Press, 1959), p. 120.

situation that the poems so adroitly address. Canto 2 invokes tree and water, the static and the dynamic, as emblems of the new dynasty:

> The tree that strikes deep root
> Is firm amidst the winds.
> Its flowers are good,
> Its fruit abundant.

"Rooted in earth and flowering in heaven,"[25] the tree is a symbol of many things to many people. The pine, cypress, chestnut, catalpa, and acacia at the sacred grove or the altar of soil and grain in ancient China – and later in Korea – stood for a ruling dynasty. As a symbol of rule it inspired awe and reverence, reinforcing the correspondence between people and nature. The tree that sprouts from a single seed to many roots, a sturdy trunk, manifold branches, and finally to multitudinous leaves served as a symbol of life for individual, generation, and race. The songs of dynastic legends in the *Book of Songs* (poems 154, 237, 239), for example, show the symbolization of family descent, its unbroken line and future continuity, through spreading young gourd stems and their long vines, thick oak clumps, or extended boughs. Later the symbolism of the tree was tinged by certain Confucian and Daoist virtues such as endurance, fidelity, integrity, order, continuity, freedom, fulfillment, and destiny. Analogies between humanity and tree begin in antiquity: heroic warriors are often compared to stalwart oaks, upright ministers to towering pines, and unsullied recluses to a variety of trees and plants.

Canto 84 elaborates the growth and decay of the tree of a royal house whose members are symbolized by boughs, leaves, and fruits:

> The country had a long history,
> But it was about to lose heaven's mandate.
> Then a withered tree
> Put forth green leaves.

The withered tree in Tŏgwŏn stands for the Wang house of the Koryŏ dynasty. The dead tree symbolizes Koryŏ's loss of mandate. Nature rallies against its destroyer, the last Koryŏ kings whose misrule disrupted cosmic harmony, but equally rallies with a providential sign for its restorer. The miraculous flowering of the dead tree intimates heaven's plan, the imminent re-establishment of cosmic and moral order and the victory of life over death.

---

[25] Howard Nemerov, *The Western Approaches* (Chicago: University of Chicago Press, 1975), p. 88.

The use of the polysemous imagery of the tree is an eloquent reaffirmation of the bond between humans and nature. The Confucian system was based on the correspondence of microcosm and macrocosm: society and nature. The function of the institutions was therefore to bring humankind into harmony with nature, whose pattern people must heed in order to fulfill their own humanity. The requirements for kingship, the concept of the mandate, and moral virtues were all part of political ethics. The ruler is the earthly guardian of universal harmony. The state, whose structure at least is a reflection of that harmony, is a moral and paedeutic institution meant to safeguard the continuity of society. Contemplation of the eternal pattern, the source of human mores, will lead the human community to occupy its cosmic place and perform its proper function, as defined by the concept of the Five Relations. Rebellion against the pattern, by contrast, is a rebellion against one's nature, a rupture of natural relations unleashing division and chaos. "Weird occurrences arise from men," says the *Zuo Commentary;* "It is when men abandon their constant ways that weird things occur."[26] Men cause nature to reflect their hubristic acts. The unnamed hero of *Songs of Flying Dragons,* therefore, is the dynasty, Korea, *res publica,* the first word of the cycle.

KING SEJONG'S BUDDHIST POEMS

The *Wŏrin ch'ŏngang chigok* (*Songs of the Moon's Reflection on a Thousand Rivers*),[27] composed by King Sejong, is another classic written in the new alphabet. Upon the death of Queen Sohŏn on 19 April 1446, the king ordered his second son, Prince Suyang (later Sejo; 1417–1468, r. 1455–1468), to supervise the compilation of a life of the Buddha by combining Sengyou's *Shijia pu* (*KT* 1047) with *Shijia shipu* (*KT* 1049) by Daoxuan (596–667) in a single unified work. King Sejong's own poems in praise of the life of the Buddha – the *Songs of the Moon's Reflection on a Thousand Rivers* – were probably composed before the end of 1446. The *Sŏkpo sangjŏl* (*Detailed Contents of the Life History of Śākyamuni*),[28] published in the new alphabet

---

[26] *Zuozhuan,* Duke Zhuang 14 (Legge, *The Chinese Classics* 5:92b). See also Burton Watson, *Ssu-ma Ch'ien: Grand Historian of China* (New York: Columbia University Press, 1958), p. 15.

[27] I have used by Hŏ Ung and Yi Kangno, *Chuhae Wŏrin ch'ŏngang chigok* (Singu munhwasa, 1999), and *Wŏrin sŏkpo* (Singu munhwasa, 1999).

[28] Yi Tongnim, *Chuhae Sŏkpo sangjŏl* (Tongguk taehakkyo ch'ulp'anbu, 1959), and Kim Yongbae, ed., *Sŏkpo sangjŏl,* 2 vols. (Tongguk taehakkyo pulchŏn kanhaeng wiwŏnhoe, 1986), esp. 1:9–25. Hŏ Ung and Yi Kangno, *Wŏrin sŏkpo,* which combines the *Wŏrin ch'ŏngang chigok* and *Sŏkpo sangjŏl,* has the preface, dated 4 August 1459, by King Sejo. See Sa Chaedong, "*Wŏrin sŏkpo* ŭi kangch'ang munhakchŏk sŏngkyŏk" ("Spoken/sung [prosimetric] Literary Character of *Wŏrin sŏkpo*"), in *Hanguk munhak yut'ongsa ŭi yŏngu* (Chungang inmunsa, 1999), pp. 549–574.

in September 1447, was to provide glosses to the royal composition. The form of this cycle of songs of praise, similar to that of *Songs of Flying Dragons*, evinces a judicious use of parallelism and contrast to reinforce the intended meaning. Each canto generally consists of two songs, and the number of syllables in a song commonly fluctuates between twenty-one and twenty-four. The motive of the *Songs of the Moon's Reflection on a Thousand Rivers* was both literary and devotional: the king's unending desire to experiment and disseminate the new alphabet as well as his strong religious fervor for spreading the Buddha dharma among the people and praying for the repose of his queen's soul. The language is sublime and elegant, commensurate with the theme, and brocaded with rich imagery.

The introductory canto begins:

> How can we relate all
> The immeasurable and limitless
> Merits
> Of the lofty Śākyamuni Buddha?

As in Aśvaghoṣa's *Buddhacarita* (*Acts of the Buddha*), Siddhārtha (563–483 BC or 559–478 BC) is presented as a genuine human being. Memorable events in his career include his birth in the fourth month in the Indian calendar to Śuddhodana and Māyā (cantos 19ff.); his renunciation (cantos 44ff.); his studies under two teachers (cantos 58ff.); his austerities and the temptation by Māra (cantos 68–74); his enlightenment (cantos 79ff.); the two merchants taking refuge in the Buddha and his dharma (cantos 86 and 90); and the conversion of his father, relatives (cantos 128–129), and own son Rāhula (cantos 138–143). Especially moving scenes of contrast include those between his father's wish for him to remain at home and the prince's resolve to leave the household to fulfill his duty to a higher dharma (canto 48), and between the worldly music and song arranged by his father to allure his son and the heavenly music that accompanied his riding out of the palace (canto 51). Śuddhodana's order to close all gates so that his son could not leave home (canto 47) and the sorrow of Yasodhara when her son Rāhula leaves home to follow the Buddha (cantos 140–144) are among the most moving scenes.

The *Detailed Contents of the Life History of Śākyamuni* originally consisted of twenty-four chapters (*kwŏn*), but only volumes 3, 6, 9, 11, 13, 19, 21, 23, and 24 (discovered between 1935 and 1979) are extant. In addition to the biographies compiled by Sengyou and Daoxuan mentioned earlier, the compilers drew extensively from other Buddhist scriptures such as the *Flower Garland Scripture* (*Avataṃsaka*; *KT* 79–80),

Lotus Scripture (*Saddharmapuṇḍarīka*; *KT* 116–117), *Lion's Roar Scripture* (*Śrīmālādevisiṃhanāda*; *KT* 54), *Great Cloud Scripture* (*Mahāmegha*; *KT* 166), and others (108, 177, 402, 765). The first work in vernacular prose after the invention of the Korean alphabet, the *Detailed Contents* is still readable as literary prose. Lives of buddhas and bodhisattvas and other tales quoted in its passages contributed to the formation of classic Korean fictional narrative. The *Songs of the Moon's Reflection on a Thousand Rivers* and its companion volume *Detailed Contents of the Life History of Śākyamuni*, therefore, occupy an important place in the history of Korean vernacular poetry and prose.

CHAPTER 8

Early Chosŏn sijo

Peter H. Lee

FORM AND STRUCTURE

A type of vernacular, short lyric poem/song – known by various names as *sijŏl kajo* (contemporary popular tune), *tanga* (short song), *sinsŏng* or *sinjo* (new tune) – existed long before the term *sijo* began to designate both the poetic form and the accompanying musical tune in the eighteenth century. Contemporary writers such as Sin Kwangsu (1712–1774) and Ch'ae Chegong (1720–1799) credit Yi Sech'un (fl. eighteenth century) with systematizing current musical tunes of the *sijo* song.[1] A musician and singer active in the capital city of Seoul, Yi standardized song tunes current in his day so that the *sijo* could be sung to a uniform musical setting.

The origin of the *sijo* may be traced to such Koryŏ songs as "Spring Overflows the Pavilion," although the "Song of Confucian Scholars" and "The Turkish Bakery" also contain four metric segments in a line. A comparison of stanza 2 of "Spring Overflows the Pavilion" and the regular *sijo* will make this point clear:

2	4	4	3		3/4	4	3/4	4
3	4	3	4		3/4	4	3/4	4
3	4	3	4		3	5	4	3/4

"Spring Overflows the Pavilion"   *sijo*

The third line in the former has not yet acquired the characteristic meter and closure. The *sijo*'s evolution was apparently gradual. Its origins may lie in earlier times, but it only came to be considered an independent genre sometime toward the end of Koryŏ.

Each line of the *sijo* – the most popular, elastic, and mnemonic of Korean poetic forms – consists of four metric segments with a minor pause at the

---

[1] Yi Pyŏnggi, "*Sijo* ŭi palsaeng kwa *kagok* kwaŭi kubun," in *Sijo munhak yŏngu*, ed. Kugŏ kungmunhakhoe (Chŏngŭmsa, 1980), pp. 13–31; and Chin Tonghyŏk, *Kosijo munhak non* (Hyŏngsŏl ch'ulp'ansa, 1982), pp. 12–17.

end of the second segment and a major pause at the end of the fourth. An emphatic syntactic division is usually introduced in the third line in the form of a countertheme, paradox, resolution, judgment, command, or exclamation introduced by characteristic words and phrases: *amado* (perhaps), *nwirasŏ* or *nugusŏ* (who?), *ŏtchit'a* (why?), *chinsillo* (truly), *hamulmyŏ* (much more/less), *tuŏra* (let it be), *ŏjŭbŏ* (alas, ah!), *amuri* (however much), *ch'arari* (I would rather), *munnora* (I ask), *iŭkko* (before long), *ŏdisŏ* (from somewhere), and *ahaeya* (literally boy!). (*Ahaeya, tuŏra*, and *ŏjŭbŏ* are the most popular.)[2]

This division often presents a logical and developmental transition, and a skillful poet can achieve a pattern of thought within strict formal limits and attain unity in variety. The introduction of a deliberate twist in phrasing or meaning is often a test of a poet's originality. The *sijo* was sung and transmitted orally and did not begin to be written down until the early eighteenth century. Even today it is an oral art for the lettered and unlettered alike: even shoeshine boys learn *sijo* texts, though not the melodies.[3] The texts of most songs vary according to the source, and possibly with each performance, and the great number of variants of a given song bespeaks the oral nature of the *sijo*. Variations ranged from changes in verbal endings, particles, or phrases to substitutions of a whole line. Sometimes the contents undergo only minor changes, while minor variations may sometimes alter the contents significantly. Often a single song metamorphoses into two different songs – the more popular one existing in numerous variants, long and short. The lack of fixed texts, especially in the case of anonymous songs, is an insoluble problem: we are not sure which *sijo* are oral compositions created during performances. In any event, the singer was free to alter phrases or lines whenever his memory failed him or his creativity inspired him. Indeed, the spoken word still retained its social and cultural roles. Memory was the thesaurus of poetry, the receptacle of the living word. The frequency of verbal parallels and formulaic expressions, long and short, points to a particular art of creation. The poet's task was to preserve and transmit a living tradition through a new arrangement of old material, thereby imparting added significance to the tradition. The correct sequence of ideas and topics was retained in the poet's memory; he composed by using

---

[2] The interjection preceding a refrain in Koryŏ songs or early Chosŏn eulogies may have developed into the first word in the last line of the *sijo*, where it appears as a form of interjection or address indicating a shift to subjectivity. See Ch'oe Tongwŏn, *Kosijo yŏngu* (Hyŏngsŏl ch'ulp'ansa, 1977), pp. 83–148; and Kim Sangsŏn, "Kosijo ŭi sŏngkyŏk," in *Sijo munhak yŏngu*, ed. Kugŏ kungmunhakhoe (Chŏngŭmsa, 1980), pp. 84–108.

[3] Richard Rutt, trans., *The Bamboo Grove* (Berkeley: University of California Press, 1971), p. 2.

phrases, motifs, and themes, each theme serving as a mnemonic device for himself and his audience. The poet's (or singer's) countless variations on the same theme were a source of pleasure to members of the audience, who were quick to recognize allusions to earlier versions, to see the worth of old material in new contexts, and to savor their own aesthetic responses to the poet's creation. The Korean singer, like the oral poet, served as a memory bank to his society by recalling the past.

Unlike the Silla songs recorded in *hyangch'al* or the *kyŏnggi-ch'e* song recorded in Chinese or *idu*, the *sijo* is preserved mostly in the new Korean alphabet. The *Ch'ŏnggu yŏngŏn (Songs of Green Hills*, 1728), the first collection of *sijo*, and subsequent compilations attribute sixty-one poems to thirty authors dating from the times of Koguryŏ, Paekche, and Silla down to the end of Koryŏ. Examples attributed to persons of the Three Kingdoms period are generally considered spurious, and those attributed to political figures who played an important role in the change of dynasties at the end of the fourteenth century may have been later compositions (such as songs supposedly by Chŏng Mongju, Ch'oe Yŏng, Chŏng Tojŏn, Cho Chun, Yi Pangwŏn).[4] Nevertheless, although the concept of "popular literature" is a romantic construct, these songs, especially those dating from the fourteenth century onward, may have been transmitted orally for a long time because they were easy to sing, recite, and memorize, a good index of their popularity. A concrete confrontation of the singer and listeners constituted a dialogue between the two, and in a culture where the oral and aural coexisted within the written, the lively transmission of *sijo* is easy to imagine. Despite the foregoing caveat, there is no reason to suspect the authenticity of songs attributed to U T'ak (1263–1342), Yi Chonyŏn (1269–1343), Yi Saek (1328–1396), and Yi Chono (1341–1371). Most collections either attribute certain *sijo* to them or list them as anonymous, but seldom do they ascribe the works to other authors. U T'ak, known for his opposition to superstition, was a student of Neo-Confucianism, and his two songs on old age are neither political nor ideological but personal expressions about a topic that provoked his witty response. Yi Chonyŏn, Yi Saek, and Yi Chono, by contrast, lament the troubled times in which they live and their frustration at being powerless to set the world right.

KORYŎ LOYALISTS

Yi Chonyŏn, for instance, outspoken in his loyalty and devoted to his duty as a scholar-official, often admonished King Ch'unghye, the twenty-eighth

---

[4] Kim Suŏp, "*Sijo ŭi palsaeng sigi e taehayŏ*," in *Sijo nŏn*, ed. Cho Kyusŏl and Pak Ch'ŏrhŭi (Ilchogak, 1984), pp. 3–23.

ruler of Koryŏ (r. 1331 and 1340–1344), for his pursuit of sensual pleasures and failure to fulfill his kingly tasks. When his advice was not heeded, Yi resigned in protest and spent the remainder of his days at home. The "awareness" and insomnia referred to in the following *sijo* are caused by his worries about the king and the dynasty:

梨花에 月白하고 銀漢이 三更인제
一枝春心을 子規ㅣ야 아라마는
多情도 病이냥하여 삼못드러 하노라

Ihwa.e / wŏlbaek hago / ŭnhan.i / samgyŏng.inje (3 4 3 4)
Ilchi / ch'unsim.ŭl / chagyu.ya / allya.manŭn (2 3 3 4)
Tajŏng.do / pyŏnginyang.hayŏ / chammot.tŭrŏ / hanora (3 5 4 3)

The moon is white on pear blossoms,
　　　and the Milky Way tells the third watch.
A cuckoo would not know
　　　the intent of a branch of spring.
Too much awareness is a sickness,
　　　it keeps me awake all night.[5]

Here we detect Yi's penchant for four-word Chinese phrases with Korean connectives – a style that combines both learning and lyricism. The first two segments in the first line, "Ihwa.e wŏlbaek hago," can be rendered into pure Korean without changing the meaning or the tone: "paekkoch'e tari palkko." "Ilchi ch'unsim," an allusion to the Liu Song poet,[6] is chosen for its sonority and meter (2/3 or, following syntactic divisions, 3/2 syllables) and Yi Chonyŏn probably could not hit upon Korean equivalents with the same intertextuality. The turns of phrases and diction in the remainder of the song, however, are Korean.

　　The following *sijo* is by Yi Chono:

구룸이 無心단 말이 아마도 虛浪하다
中天에 떠 이셔 任意로 단니며셔
구태야 光明한 날빗츨 따라가며 덥나니

Kurŭm.i / musim.t'an.mari / amado / hŏrang.hada (3 5 3 4)
Chungch'ŏn.e / ttŏ.isyŏ / imŭi.ro / tannimyŏsyŏ (3 3 3 4)
Kut'aeya / kwangmyŏnghan nalbich'ŭl / ttaragamyŏ / tŏmnani! (3 6 4 3)

That clouds have no intent
　　　is perhaps false and unreliable.
Floating in midair

[5] Kim Kwangsun, "Yi Chonyŏn ŭi *sijo* e taehayŏ," in *Sijo nŏn*, ed. Cho Kyusŏl and Pak Ch'ŏrhŭi (Ilchogak, 1984), pp. 179–202.
[6] Hans H. Frankel, "The Plum Tree in Chinese Poetry," *Asiatische Studien* 6 (1952): 88–115.

> freely moving,
> For what reason do they cover
>   the bright light of the day?[7]

The clouds that "cover the bright light of the day" (literally: "intentionally follow the light and cover it") represent an evil one who blinds the intelligence of the ruler. Contextually it refers to the powerful and decadent monk Sin Ton (d. 1371) whom Yi censured but who escaped punishment and retired to his village.

The next *sijo*, by Yi Saek, expresses his agonizing hesitancy before making a decisive move at a crucial point in history:

白雪이 자자진 골에 구루미 머흐래라
반가온 梅花난 어내 곳에 피엇나고
夕陽에 홀로 시이셔 갈 곳 몰라 하노라

Paeksŏr.i / chajajin.kore / kurum.i / mŏhŭrera (3 5 3 4)
Pangaon / maehwa.nŭn / ŏnae.kosae / p'iyŏnnango (3 3 4 4)
Sŏgyang.e / hollo.syŏisyŏ / kalkot molla / hanora (3 5 4 3)

> Rough clouds gather around the valley
>   where the snow lies heavy.
> Where is the welcoming plum,
>   at what place does it bloom?
> I have lost my way, alone,
>   in the setting sun.[8]

The valley where snow and clouds are threatening represents the trials of the speaker's political life. The welcoming plum blossoms, the harbinger of spring, invoke his hope, but the setting sun, which stands for both the twilight of the Koryŏ dynasty and his own political career, poignantly captures the speaker's state of mind. He stands alone and does not know where to turn.

Let us return to Yi Chonyŏn's song to consider its organization: the pear blossoms, white moon, Milky Way, and cuckoo invoked in lines 1 and 2 in the original lead to the speaker's awareness – that is, the nature scene intensifies his anxiety. The function of the images is to reveal the self's state of mind through how they affect the speaker's subjectivity. "[A] branch of spring" (*ilchich'un*), a synonym for "plum," alludes to a poem by the fifth-century Chinese poet Lu Kai who sent a flowering plum branch to his friend with an accompanying poem. The flower in Yi Chonyŏn's song, however,

---

[7] *KYS*, a variorum edition of *sijo* lists 3,335 poems. See *KYS* 293.
[8] *KYS* 1195.

is not the plum but the pear blossom that stands for "spring." The song's organization underscores the gulf between the beautiful dreamlike spring scene and the speaker's inner turmoil. By contrast, it is a parallel between the obscured nature scene and the speaker, searching for "the welcoming plum" but lost in the setting sun, that Yi Saek's song unfolds. In their syntax, diction (especially the forthright, direct, colloquial address), themes, and movement of thought, the *sijo* we have considered are simple and fluent. *Sijo* are generally so plain that, except for certain obsolete or dialect words, they are accessible to the modern reader and offer residual satisfaction. At crucial points the *sijo* employs the rhetoric of questions (For what reason? Why?) aimed at the poet himself, a friend, or the listener; such inquiry is a natural form in which to cast debates and dialogue.[9] It is for this reason that the *sijo* form survives today and challenges poets to test their mastery of it. The *sijo* has proved to be a form well suited to expressing their sense of the world and response to life.

Wŏn Ch'ŏnsŏk (fl. 1401–1410), a Koryŏ loyalist who refused to serve the new dynasty when summoned by King T'aejong, offers a nostalgic comparison of past and present with characteristic imagery:

> Fortune determines rise and fall,
>   Full Moon Terrace is autumn grass.
> A shepherd's pipe echoes
>   the royal works of five hundred years.
> A traveler cannot keep back his tears
>   in the setting sun.[10]

Autumn grass having grown in the palace site, the speaker hears only the shepherd's pipe, which seems to lament the vanquished Wang House. He has become a traveler in the setting sun, shedding tears, because he cannot return to the past.

COURTIER POETS

Maeng Sasŏng (1360–1438) and Hwang Hŭi (1363–1452), by contrast, who served as chief state counselors, sing of a leisurely life in the countryside that is proof of a happy reign they helped to fashion. Maeng's "Kangho sasi ka" ("Four Seasons by the Rivers and Lakes") is the first *sijo* sequence of

---

[9] The frequency of such verbal endings as apperceptive, propositive, rhetorical interrogative exclama-tive, exhortive interrogative, and exclamative doubt – in almost one-third of 3,335 poems in the latest *sijo* collection – is most striking.

[10] *KYS* 3325.

the Chosŏn dynasty. His image of an age of peace and prosperity may be seen in the following summer poem:

> Summer comes to the rivers and lakes,
>   I am idle at the grass hut.
> Friendly waves in the river
>   only send a cool breeze.
> I can keep myself cool
>   because of royal favor.[11]

The idea that the peace the speaker enjoys is a gift of the king recurs in other works. Hwang Hŭi's following *sijo* consists wholly of the vernacular. Its diction is colloquial and close to the daily life of the common people – perhaps to underscore the truth that a state minister and a commoner are one:

> Are chestnuts falling
>   in the valley of red jujubes?
> Are crabs crawling in the stubble
>   after a harvest of rice?
> Wine is ripe, and a sieve seller passes by.
>   What can I do but strain and drink?[12]

The Six Martyred Ministers who plotted to restore the young king Tanjong over his usurper uncle left songs, but a piece universally known to all educated Koreans is this song by Sŏng Sammun (1418–1456):

> Were you to ask me what I'd wish to be
>   after my death,
> I would answer, a pine tree, tall and hardy
>   on the highest peaks of Mount Pongnae,
> And to be green, alone, green,
>   when snow fills heaven and earth.[13]

Sŏng is willing to sacrifice his life for the cause of the dynasty, but after his martyrdom he wishes to be a pine that stands firm and tall, with promises of the continuity and fulfillment that have been denied him. Destiny requires his heroic steadfastness, but he affirms history's inexorable patterns: continuity through change. He wishes to be a living memorial, a guardian of the dynasty, the stalwart pine that accepts suffering, loss, and sacrifice and stands for hope and victory won through death.

---

[11] *KYS* 127.
[12] *KYS* 837; see Cho Tongil, *Hanguk munhak t'ongsa* 2:317.
[13] *KYS* 2323.

Yi Kae (1417–1456) sings of his daily concern for his lord whom he has
been forced to leave:

> The candle burns in the room,
>   from whom has it parted?
> Shedding tears outside,
>   does it know that its inside burns?
> That candle is like me,
>   it does not know its heart burns![14]

Yi's invention lies in his comparison of his inner turmoil with a candle
which does not realize that its inside is burning. It expresses how he is
tormented with anxieties over the exiled king.

Among the poems exchanged between king and courtier, King
Sŏngjong's song to Yu Hoin (1445–1494) and Kim Ku's (1488–1534) to King
Chungjong bear quoting. Yu Hoin, Sŏngjong's favorite courtier, won royal
favor with his poetic gifts. When Yu had to leave the court to care for his
ailing mother, the king wrote him the following song:

> Stay:
>   Will you go? Must you go?
> Is it in weariness you go? From disgust?
>   Who advised you? Who persuaded you?
> Say why you are leaving,
>   you, who are breaking my heart.[15]

The king's diction is kingly: he begins with a command (*isiryŏm*) and
continues with four questions. Only in the first half of the third line does
the king reveal how he really feels, and he concludes the line with the
last request: "Say why you are leaving" (*kanŭn ttŭsŭl nillŏra*). The song
imparts a sense of urgency with dignity and authority, and the depth of
royal affection for a particular courtier.

The occasion for the next *sijo*, it is said, was a surprise nighttime visit to
the Office of Special Advisers by King Chungjong. Kim Ku's immediate
audience was the king himself. Writing to please and even inspire the king,
the speaker registers his affection for the royal personage.

> Until the short legs of the duck
>   grow long as the crane's –
> Until the crow becomes white,
>   as white as the eastern egret –
> Enjoy enduring bliss
>   forever.[16]

[14] *KYS* 1166.   [15] *KYS* 2356.   [16] *KYS* 2126.

The long-legged duck and the white crow are clearly proverbial impossibilities. The crow and the eastern egret are also used allegorically in moral verse – as when the mother of a loyal minister warns her son to avoid the "tearing and cawing crows" that envy the egret's white feathers. The poet's invention lies in his use of the same symbols for epideictic purposes. He works on the association of the duck with the crane, and the crane with the egret, in the mind of the informed listener. The first two lines of the original end with "until" (transposed in translation). The tension thus created is resolved in the final line with a succession of seven spondees that refer the listener to a similar device in the *Book of Songs*. Literally the last line reads: "May you live a billion million years" or "Long may you live!" Phrases denoting perpetuity date back to the poems of blessing and sacrifice in the *Book of Songs*;[17] the pious hope couched here in *adynata*[18] is also expressed in the national anthems of both the Republic of Korea and Japan.[19] The song, originally intended for the king and his entourage, became popular because of its treatment of a subject rich in shared cultural values. In traditional Korean society, which made Confucian decorum and morality its norm and greatly emphasized social virtues, there were many occasions calling for just such a song.

SIJO BY THE YŎNGNAM SCHOOL

Yi Hyŏnbo (1467–1555) is considered to be the founder of the Yŏngnam school that included Chu Sebung (1495–1554), Yi Hwang (1501–1571), and Kwŏn Homun (1532–1587). The texts of the works by Yi Hyŏnbo and Yi Hwang were published in their lifetime: Yi Hyŏnbo's "Five Fisherman's Songs" was printed in a woodblock edition in 1549 with a postface by the poet and Yi Hwang; Yi Hwang's holograph of "Twelve Songs of Tosan" was carved in 1565 on woodblocks that are still perserved in Tosan Academy. The poets of the Yŏngnam school wrote chiefly *sijo* sequences, usually in praise of reclusion with added moralizing. The following song by Yi Hyŏnbo can serve as a declaration of the general mood of *sijo* written by his school:

[17] Arthur Waley, *Book of Songs* (London: Allen and Unwin, 1954), 154, 166, 172, 209, 210, 213, 216, 242, and 262.
[18] Galen A. Rowe, "The Adynaton as a Stylistic Device," *American Journal of Philology* 86 (1965): 392–395.
[19] *Kokinshū* 7:343; Helen C. McCullough, trans., *Kokin Wakashū* (Stanford: Stanford University Press, 1985), p. 83.

Return, return, they say,
    but none has returned.
Fields and gardens are thick with weeds,
    what if I don't return?
Clear breeze and bright moon wait,
    going in and out of my grass hut.[20]

Chu Sebung, the author of "Songs of Five Relations" and nine other pieces consisting mainly of quotations from or allusions to the *Analects*, was didactic. As privileged speakers of the day, Chu Sebung along with Yi Hwang, Song Sun, Pak Illo, Kim Sangyong, and others were intent on indoctrination, and their repetitive and regular speech acts constituted the discursive formation of the Chosŏn-dynasty literati, demonstrating relations of truth, power, and ethics, the central topic of Foucault's archeological analysis.

The first sequence of "Twelve Songs of Tosan" concerns the heart's intent; the second is devoted to learning. The love of nature of "a foolish person" living in the grassy field is ironically called "an incurable disease" (song 1). In his hut made of "smoke and haze," with the wind and the moon as friends, the speaker is reminded of the king's benevolent rule (song 2) to underscore his awareness of the significance of the world of action as a guarantee of simplicity and naturalness. While savoring the fragrant orchids in the valley and white clouds perched on the hills, he avows he cannot forget "the Fair One" (the king; song 4). The speaker also enjoys mountain blossoms in a spring breeze and the autumn moon flooding the loft, but he recalls a passage in the *Doctrine of the Mean*: "The hawk flies up to heaven; the fish leap in the deep [*Book of Songs* 289]. This means that [the Way] is clearly seen above and below."[21] The song concludes: "There is no end to the shadow cast by clouds and heaven's light shining down" (song 6). The description of nature in the first sequence gives way to the speaker's pleasure with books and dispersed meditations on the Confucian and Neo-Confucian way. In diction, however, songs 9 to 12 rely more on the vernacular, engendering a fluent and natural effect, culminating in song 11, which reveals the speaker's desire for a oneness with nature uncontaminated by book learning and dull moralizing:

Why are green hills
    forever green?
Why do flowing waters

[20] *KYS* 347.   [21] Chan, *Source Book*, p. 100.

never stand still day and night?
We too will live without end,
forever green.[22]

Yi Hwang's contribution to the development of *sijo* is his correct understanding of *sijo*'s place in society. In his postface to the sequence, he avers
that he writes *sijo* because only they, not poems in literary Chinese, can be
sung and danced to.[23]

Kwŏn Homun's "Eighteen Songs of Idle Life" (nineteen songs) suffer from excessive abstraction (songs 5–7), diction remote from common
speech (song 14), and words and phrases of Chinese origin. The eleventh
in the sequence, however, depicts the lifestyle of a retired gentleman farmer
with music and books:

> Nature makes clear the windy air,
>   and bright the round moon.
> In the bamboo garden, on the
>   pine fence, not a speck of dust.
> How fresh and fervent my life
>   with a long zither and piled scrolls.[24]

His severance of all ties with the mundane world is reiterated in the concluding lines of song 13: "I have no desire for the world, / Not even a hair's
breadth."

YI I

The poet Yi I (1536–1584), though not a member of the Yŏngnam school,
was a contemporary of Yi Hwang (1501–1571) and shared his profound
understanding of Neo-Confucian philosophy. His sequence, "Nine Songs
of Mount Ko," covers the four seasons and celebrates nine scenes on Mount
Suyang in Haeju. His central design is to establish essential polarities that
lend a polemical force to the structure – an image of harmony and peace
set against the dusty world of humanity. His manner is less obtrusive than
others we have discussed, and on the whole, his songs read fluently in spite
of words of Chinese origin. Each song, except for an introductory piece,
begins with "Where shall we find . . .?" "Kok," as in "ilgok," means song,
bend, or valley. Therefore, "Where is the first bend?" can also be rendered
as "Where shall we find the first song?" Place-names are used as imagery

---

[22] Sim Chaewan, *Sijo ŭi munhŏnjok yŏngu* (Sejong munhwasa, 1972), pp. 80–82.
[23] *KYS* 1248.
[24] *KYS* 1126; Kwŏn Homun, *Songam sŏnsaeng sokchip* (*YMC* 3) 6:4b–5a. For his *sijo* see 4:1a–5b.

for poetic amplifications – as, for example, in "Kwanam," which is at the same time an image, "the crown rock" (song 2).

> Where is the first bend?
> The sun shines on Crown Rock,
> Mist clears above the tall grass,
>   distant hills are a picture!
> I wait for my friends
>   with a green goblet among the pines.[25]

In his hermitage by the water, the speaker studies and teaches as well as makes "poems of moon and breeze" (song 5), plays on his zither (song 8), and contemplates the twilight river along with the fish. In the autumn the speaker is so enraptured he forgets to return home:

> Where is the seventh bend?
>   Autumn tints are lovely at Maple Rock.
> A coat of thin clear frost
>   embroiders the hanging cliffs.
> Alone I sit on the cold stone
>   and forget to return home.[26]

MASTER OF THE FORM

Chŏng Ch'ŏl (1537–1594) is a major poet of the sixteenth century and one of the greatest writers of the Chosŏn dynasty. He is considered a member of the Honam school, which included Song Sun (1493–1583), Kim Inhu (1510–1560), Yu Hŭich'un (1513–1577), Kim Sŏngwŏn (1525–1597), and Im Che (1549–1587), and with some of these men he enjoyed a literary friendship. Born in Seoul on 17 January 1537, he obtained the *chinsa* degree in 1561 and successively filled the following positions: fourth inspector (1562); sixth royal secretary (1578); governor of Kangwŏn province (1580); rector of the national academy (1581); first royal secretary (1582); minister of rites (1583); inspector-general (1584); third and second state counselor (1589); and envoy to Ming China (1593). He died on Kanghwa Island on 7 February 1594 in the midst of the Japanese invasion.

Chŏng is one of the few classic poets in the language for several reasons. His diction is simple and direct, but it carries emotional weight corresponding to the context. His well-integrated imagery arrests the reader for its inventiveness, and his trains of thought generate emotional excitement

---

[25] *KYS* 2424.   [26] *KYS* 3028.

that lead naturally to resolution and closure. Consider the bold, fresh beginnings of the following songs:

> 20
> The juice of bitter herbs has
>   more taste than any meat.

> 48
> How could you leave it to rot,
>   the lumber fit for beams and rafters?

> 51
> Let us strain sour wine and drink
>   until our mouths become sour.

> 60
> Would I envy other's laughter
>   neglecting my troubles?

> 76
> Milky rain on the green hills,
>   can you deceive me?[27]

These beginnings create tension and great expectation, but even the seasoned reader versed in the *sijo* canon would hesitate to supply the remainder
of the songs. The closing lines of each corresponding song are:

> 20
> But my longing for my lord
>   chokes me with grief.

> 48
> O carpenters with ink cup and measure,
>   you rush about to no avail.

> 51
> Let us walk around
>   until the nails in our clogs have worn flat.

> 60
> Would I change my first love,
>   my heart fresh as jade?

> 76
> Yesterday I flung off my silk robe.
>   I have nothing left that will stain me.

Could anyone but an exceptional poet supply middle lines – keeping intact
the progression of poetic idea, imagery, and diction – that would lead

---

[27] *KYS* 1749, 1931, 1748, 584, 2869.

naturally to resolution and closure? This inventiveness represents, surely, the mark of a creative and original poet, a master of the form and the language.

Thus Chŏng Ch'ŏl drew much of his vocabulary from common words and phrases and found his inspiration in Korean sources. He does not hesitate to use colloquial expressions in order to provide the *sijo* with words from the native stock. Skilled in the admirable treatment of obvious themes, his poems are free from recondite figures of speech or obscure allusions. Furthermore, the first seventeen songs of *Songgang kasa* (*Pine River Anthology*), written to teach the people when he was governor of Kangwŏn province, demonstrate his adherence to the cult of moral verse extant in his day: instruction of the common people in Confucian morality.

His bitter resentment of court intrigue and the royal folly of which he was a victim provides his favorite theme. Chŏng was denounced by the opposition for his uncompromising stance in 1581, left his post owing to criticism of his fondness for wine in 1585, remained unemployed until 1589, and provoked the king's ire and was sent into exile in 1591. Following the tradition of "Encountering Sorrow," the poet still longs for his "lord," the king, despite the maltreatment he has suffered at his hands (songs 18–20, 23, 28–30, 32, 34, 71, 74, and 78). His longing to see his king finds expression in his desire for metamorphosis into, successively, a bird (song 28), the rapids of the Han River flowing past the capital (song 29), or the moon (song 30) so that he could shine down upon the king to illuminate and rectify his heart. The speaker also sends the king a snow-covered pine branch standing for constancy (song 71):

> Snow falls on a pine grove;
>   every branch blossoms.
> I wish I could break off a branch
>   to send to my lord.
> No matter if the blossoms fade
>   after he has seen my branch.[28]

Poem 42 is a vigorous work that sternly warns the king not to be influenced by slander:

> When you climb bends of Mount Sumeru,
>   they say, at high noon in midsummer, there is severe frost and
>   heavy snow falls
> On ground rimmed with ice. Have you seen this, my lord, with your own eyes?
>   No matter what everyone else says,
>   please, use your own judgment.[29]

[28] *KYS* 1688.   [29] *KYS* 1798.

The form itself represents a variation in that the second line – the middle of the song – has been extended. In the original, the earnest invocation of the king occurs twice, *nima nima* (O lord, O lord), before the last line to underscore the urgency of his plea. Song 74 verges on hopelessness. Favors once granted are now withheld, the king is out of reach, and the speaker's memory and desire give way to pain.

In song 48, an exercise in veiled vituperation, the movements of syco-phants and flatterers are compared with carpenters running about to no purpose with "ink cup and measure." Flatterers and calumniators disrupt order, turning the structure into "a tumbledown shack" (*hŏlttŭdŏn kiunjip*). "Small men" are "carpenters" who ought to strengthen the royal edifice. The imagery of carpentry traces its pedigree to the Confucian tradition that the acceptance of honest admonition is a requisite of the good ruler. As wood is made straight by use of a plumb line, so the ruler must accept the pattern of former kings as his norm. Broad learning and daily examination of his conduct are therefore often likened to the application of the plumb line, measure, square, and compass. Hence the song's oblique censure of royal folly, and the king's misuse of royal authority that flowed downward to his ministers, culminating in catastrophic disunity in the realm. The king's neglect of his roles untunes the string and foments factiousness at court. "The sick tree" (song 44) on which no bird alights reinforces the message: denied the promise of life, the royal garden has become a bleak, desolate place.

Another group of poems is allegorical. The Old Man of the South Pole (song 33) and the crane (songs 35 and 37), for example, are compared to the speaker's state of mind. The poet is like the polestar or the crane in the sky scorning the dusty world below. His ideal is to remain unstained by the world (song 53):

> A dash of rain upon
>   the lotus leaves. But the leaves
> remain unmarked, no matter
>   how hard the raindrops beat.
> Mind, be like the lotus leaves,
>   unstained by the world.[30]

Therefore, he flings off his silk robe and dons a sedge cape and horsehair hat, the traditional garb of the recluse, declaring "I have nothing left that will stain me" (song 76).

---

[30] *KYS* 1693.

The third group of songs is autobiographical and deals with wine, the black zither, and the poet's life as a recluse. The poet's love of drink is well revealed in songs 21, 22, 24–26, 50, 54, 56, and 58, in which he exchanges imaginary questions and answers with wine. Songs 27, 31, 46, 59, and 63 deal with wine also. Songs 36 and 65 concern Chŏng's understanding of the technique of the black zither; songs 57 and 75 demonstrate his skill with conventional love songs.

The meaning of four songs (60, 66–67, and 78) is indeterminate, mainly because of the ambiguity of the speaker's gender (the pronoun is omitted) and conventional imagery.

60
Would I envy others' laughter,
    neglecting my troubles?
Would I join in another's party,
    leaving a cup of my wine?
Would I change my first love,
    my heart fresh as jade?[31]

The speaker who says "Would I change my first love," however, strikes one as a man, a courtier who is protesting to the king his fidelity to his ideal love. The speaker in songs 66 and 67 might be a deserted woman lamenting her separation from her beloved (*nim*):

66
I know autumn has come:
    the phoenix tree has shed its leaves.
Cool is the night,
    a silken rain falls on the clear river.
My love is a thousand miles away;
    I cannot sleep.[32]

67
I bade you farewell when
    fallen leaves danced in the autumn wind.
Now snow and ice have melted,
    and spring flowers have blossomed.
But you send me no word –
    How sad, my love![33]

The speaker in song 78, however, could be either a man or a woman – the evening sun, cackling geese, burning maples, and feathery reeds prompting in the speaker a renewed desire for reunion:

[31] *KYS* 584.   [32] *KYS* 1015.   [33] *KYS* 448.

78
In the slanting evening sun,
    sky and river are a single color.
O cackling geese flying among
    the burning maples and feathery reeds.
Autumn is almost gone;
    he still keeps silent.[34]

Another song whose meaning is unclear is song 51:

Let us strain sour wine and drink
    until our mouths become sour.
Let us steam bitter herbs and chew them
    until they turn sweet.
Let us walk around
    until the nails in our clogs have worn flat.[35]

It might be about maintaining consistency, carrying something to perfection, or transforming misfortune into happiness.

One of the conventional love songs of Chŏng Ch'ŏl (song 75) goes:

Flowers are bright, bright;
    butterflies fly in pairs.
Willows are green, green;
    orioles sing in pairs.
Birds and beasts love in twos;
    why do I live alone?[36]

In the original, the poet enjoys using reduplicates in Chinese – *chakchak* (bright), *ssangssang* (pairs), *ch'ŏngch'ŏng* (green) – and in order to foreground the speaker's loneliness *ssangssang* is used three times, yielding even a humorous tone. The song, however, lacks intensity and passionate language. Elsewhere I have discussed the faces and phases of love and tried to suggest some reasons for the absence of genuine love lyrics in East Asia. Confucian strictures on passionate desire often resulted in a deemphasis of passion and fulfillment, as was the case with early Chosŏn literati poets. Moving love lyrics occur outside the mainstream. In the early Chosŏn period, they were written and sung by female entertainers (*kisaeng*), such as Hwang Chini, Soch'unp'ung ("Chuckling Spring Breeze"), Maech'ang ("Plum Window"), Hong Nang ("Lady Hong"), and Myŏngok ("Bright Jade").

[34] *KYS* 1561.   [35] *KYS* 1748.   [36] *KYS* 3282.

WOMEN POETS AND IM CHE

In the following song by Hwang Chini (fl. 1506–1544), perhaps the most famous woman poet, the speaker likens her lover to a running stream that will never return and begs him to pause and enjoy the tranquil beauty of the moonlit night:

> Do not boast of your speed,
>   O blue-green stream running by the hills:
> Once you have reached the wide ocean,
>   you can return no more.
> Why not stay here and rest,
>   when moonlight fills the empty hills?[37]

The song's exhortations, based on the impossibility of the stream's return-ing, are rhetorically persuasive. Such a structure, together with the song's situation and imagery, makes the speaker's argument urgent and convinc-ing. Using the metaphorical language characteristic of Hwang's poetry, the speaker successfully transforms amorous passion and reconciles the tension between the tranquility of nature and the turmoil that besets her. Is the speaker herself the moonlight that imbues nature with beauty and stillness? Or is it the full moon that inspires hope in her beloved? Yet the empty hills emphasize the speaker's emotional desolation as well as the illusory nature of the world and the insubstantiality of love. Joy coexists with sorrow – and is all the more poignant because it is so fleeting. Why not prolong that joy, even for a moment?

The speaker in most love songs is a woman, and the singer of such songs was usually a female entertainer who performed at all-male gatherings. It is easy to see how speaker and singer could merge on such occasions. Those members of the audience who were literati had surely had affairs – some-times with the singer who was performing at that very moment. Directly addressed and identified by the speaker/singer as an irreversible stream, each listener would be caught in an inexorable flow of time even while sus-pended in the realm of poetry. Listeners might try to see themselves as not fickle, not irresponsible, and not inconstant like the stream in the song. But because romantic love outside marriage was possible only with someone like the speaker/singer, they knew very well who she was addressing. The speaker/singer refused to recognize the difference in rank that constrained the listeners. The speaker/singer wished to believe that love might triumph; the listeners knew that it could not. The audience brought to the poem

---

[37] *KYS* 2858.

their knowledge of the instability of love, and it was in this complex setting that speaker and audience participated in the recreation of the poem.

A second witty song of Hwang Chini's, again widely known even to the modern reader, goes:

> I will cut in two
> a long November night and
> Place its half under the coverlet,
> sweet-scented as a spring breeze.
> When he comes I shall take it out,
> unroll it inch by inch, to stretch the night.[38]

Sought out by some of the most renowned writers of her day, she befriended some, seduced some, and rebuffed others. Im Che (1549–1587) arrived at her town Kaesŏng after her death and left the following in her memory:

> On a mound where the grass grows long,
> are you sleeping or lying at rest?
> Where is your lovely face?
> Only bones are buried here.
> I have no one to offer a cup,
> and that makes me sad![39]

Another song by Im Che may have been written at Kaesŏng, the old capital city of Koryŏ, and uses the topic of *ubi sunt* ("where are . . .?"), but with characteristic ingenuity:

> Deep among green valley grasses,
> a stream runs crying.
> Where's the terrace of songs,
> where's the hall of dancing?
> Do you know, swallow,
> cutting the sunset water?[40]

Here the speaker has adopted the meditative stance required by the subject and contemplates the ravages of time by the side of a river that is endowed with feeling. The river seems to lament what time and the forces of nature have obliterated: the terrace of songs and the hall of dance, symbols of human glory. The song does not end with the *ubi sunt* formula, however. In the penultimate line, the speaker shows originality by addressing a darting swallow that seems to cut the flow of time, if only for a moment. By addressing not his listeners but the bird, the speaker not only arouses the listener's emotions but asks their cooperation in probing the unanswerable.

---

[38] *KYS* 894.　[39] *KYS* 2900.　[40] *KYS* 2898.

The total rhetorical effect of the song is to awaken the listener's desire to question and explore.

A third song of Im's, addressed to another entertainer called Hanu ("Cold Rain"), was answered by her:

> Some said the northern window was bright,
>   so I started out without rain gear.
> But it snows in the mountain,
>   ·   and cold rain falls in the field.
> Today I am wet with cold rain,
>   so I wish to freeze to sleep.[41]

> Why should you freeze to sleep?
>   for what reason should you be cold?
> A pillow with mandarin-duck design and
>   kingfisher-pattern quilt,
>   how could you freeze tonight?
> Since you came, wet with cold rain,
>   won't you melt to sleep with me?[42]

Hong Nang (fl. 1567–1600), an entertainer of Kyŏngsŏng, wrote the following to Ch'oe Kyŏngch'ang (1539–1583) who was about to leave the north for the capital:

> I send you, my love,
>   select branches of the willow.
> Plant them to be admired
>   outside your bedroom window.
> If a night rain makes them bud,
>   think that it is your girl.[43]

Kyerang ("Laurel Lady", 1513–1550) – real name Yi Hyanggŭm, pen name Maech'ang ("Plum Window") – was an entertainer of Puan who excelled in singing and playing the zither.

> Under a shower of peach blossoms
>   we parted in tears, clinging to each other.
> Now autumn winds scatter leaves,
>   are you too thinking of me?
> A thousand miles away,
>   only my dreams come and go.[44]

Myŏngok, a famous entertainer from Suwŏn of uncertain date, also wrote on the dream motif:

---

[41] *KYS* 1325.   [42] *KYS* 1961.   [43] *KYS* 1047.   [44] *KYS* 2377.

They say dream visits
    are "only a dream."
My longing to see him is destroying me.
Where else do I see him but in dreams?
Darling, come to me even if it be in dreams.
Let me see you time and again.[45]

Comparison of the experience of life with dreams is often a fit metaphor of
the conflict in the lover's mind, where pains of love çoexist with joy, and a
metaphor too of the ephemeral quality of carnal love. Dreams are also an
appropriate metaphor for the lover who strives to seize what is impalpable
and express haunting perturbations and paradoxes. Myŏngok, for example,
entreats her beloved to appear in dreams. If there is no other way to fulfill
my desire, she says, give me an eternal dream. Parting, desertion, separation,
neglect, physical and mental anguish, and internalized seasons – these are
the main themes of love poetry in the early Chosŏn dynasty. Love is indeed
part of people's essential inconstancy, insecurity, and suffering, and Korea's
woman poets have left us memorable works on the subject.

[45] *KYS* 335. See Na Chŏngsun, *Hanguk kojŏn siga munhak ŭi punsŏk kwa t'amsaek* (Yŏngnak, 2000),
pp. 217–250.

CHAPTER 9

Early Chosŏn kasa

Peter H. Lee

FORM AND TECHNIQUE

The origin of *kasa* is traced to popular songs of Koryô, *kyônggi-ch'e* songs, or didactic folk songs. The difference between these forms and *kasa* is one of scale, for the *kasa* allows one to give a lengthier and more sustained treatment. A typical *kasa* line, as in *sijo*, consists of four metric segments. This line is repeated with matched pairings and enumerative development. A poem generally concludes in a line of 3, 5, 4, and 3/4 syllables (again as in *sijo*) in the *kasa* composed by literati and a line of 4, 4, 4, and 4 in the commoner's and women's *kasa*.[1] The simple metric basis of *kasa* invites inventiveness in everything from the development of a theme, narrative techniques, sequences of imagery, and the speaker's ethos to views of life and the world itself. Therefore, the freedom the writer of *kasa* enjoys is considerable.

Although the *kasa* resembles the Chinese *fu* (rhymeprose, or rhapsody) in form and technique, it is neither prose nor rhymed. It is narrative poetry meant to be sung (or chanted in the case of literati *kasa*). Unlike the three-line *sijo*, it tells a story, often adhering to a linear temporal and spatial sequence, though frequently without a plot in the sense of a narrative of events with an emphasis on causality.[2] *Kasa* are organized by certain patterns. Poems built on the seasonal pattern, for example, unfold a series of nature scenes that evoke each season. This pattern works well with poems of reclusion, love, exile, and the country house. If the subject is a single season such as spring, shifting scenes and activities associated with different times of the day provide a structure. Another pattern is based on the rhetoric of argument or complaint: the speaker lists causes of his present state with

---

[1] Kim Kidong, "*Kasa* munhak ŭi hyŏngt'ae koch'al," in *Kasa munhak yŏngu*, ed. Kugŏ kungmunhak hoe (Chŏngŭmsa, 1979), pp. 82–105. For a bibliography of studies on *kasa* see Im Kijung, ed., *Hanguk kasa munhak yŏngusa* (Ihoe munhwasa, 1998).

[2] Ch'oe Kanghyŏn, "*Kasa* ŭi palsaengsajŏk yŏngu," in *Kasa munhak yŏngu* (Chŏngŭmsa, 1979), pp. 13–81.

an enumeration of hardships, as in the poems of exile or unrequited love. Here, too, the seasonal pattern is often used to emphasize aspects of the speaker's tribulations.

Although four extant examples attributed to Monk Naong (Hyegŭn, 1320–1376) are cited as the earliest specimens of *kasa*, they were composed before the invention of the Korean alphabet and recorded long after their composition. There is, however, a possibility that Buddhist monks, like Great Master Kyunyŏ in the tenth century, used vernacular poetry – a form of narrative verse – to proselytize.

It has been suggested that the first Chosŏn writer of *kasa* was Chŏng Kŭgin (1401–1481), whose collected works compiled in the eighteenth century contain two *kyŏnggi-ch'e* songs and the "Sangch'un kok" ("In Praise of Spring"), the latter beginning in a line of 3, 4, 4, and 4 metric segments and ending with a line of 3, 5, 4, and 4. Other early Chosŏn examples written before the emergence of the first master in the form include: "Manbun ka" ("Song of Fury") by Cho Wi (1454–1503), written in exile, protesting the speaker's innocence and loyalty; "Myŏnangjŏng ka" ("Song of Myŏnang Arbor") by Song Sun (1493–1583), a poem in praise of a life of reclusion;[3] "Kwansŏ pyŏlgok" ("Song of the Northwest," 1555) by Paek Kwanghong (1522–1556), a record of the speaker's trip to the northwest region as a government functionary;[4] "Namjŏng ka" ("Song of the Southern Expedition," 1555) by Yang Sajun (fl. 1546), based on the author's participation in the repulse of Japanese pirates in South Chôlla;[5] "Miin pyŏlgok" ("Song of a Beautiful Woman") by Yang Saŏn (1517–1584), a poem in praise of the admirable qualities of a beautiful lady (actually a female entertainer);[6] and five moral and didactic pieces attributed to Yi Hwang (1501–1571) written in learned diction with copious allusions to the Chinese classics.[7]

Because of the form's unlimited length, the *kasa* writer was able to introduce more description and narration, employing such techniques as syntactic and semantic parallelism, contrast, repetition, variation, and the piling up of similes. Chŏng Kŭgin and others often repeat verbal endings, as in *hago . . . hasel hago . . . hase*, to effect synonymous parallelism and contrast in corresponding positions of consecutive lines:

[3] Kim Tonguk, *Hanguk kayŏ ŭi yŏngu sok* (Iu ch'ulp'ansa, 1978), pp. 159–195.
[4] Yi Sangbo, *Hanguk kosiga ŭi yŏngu* (Hyŏngsŏl ch'ulp'ansa, 1982), pp. 145–176.
[5] Kim Tonguk, *Hanguk kayŏ ŭi yŏngu sok*, pp. 225–240; Yi Sangbo, *Hanguk kosiga ŭi yŏngu*, pp. 177–190.
[6] Kim Tonguk, *Hanguk kayŏ ŭi yŏngu sok*, pp. 213–224.
[7] Sŏ Wŏnsŏp, *Kasa munhak yŏngu* (Hyŏngsŏl ch'ulp'ansa, 1983), pp. 279–291.

Today, let's walk on the green grass,
Tomorrow, bathe in the Yi River.
Gather mountain ferns in the morning,
Go angling in the evening.

The four activities listed – walking on the grass, bathing in the river, gathering ferns, and going angling – are associated with the simple pleasures of a retired gentleman. They are synonymous but cumulative, contrasted mainly by the time of day of each activity. In other instances, antonymous contrasts are emphasized by parallel structure as in "Song of Fury":

His bounty great as the sea,
I kept my mind pure as white jade . . .
The south tower in heaven,
The north wind on the earth

The subjects of paired lines may vary while verbs are repeated as in "In Praise of Spring":

Fame and name shun me,   (*kongmyŏng.to nal kkiugo*)
Wealth and rank shun me   (*pugwi.to nal kkiuni*)

Or, inversely, only the verbs may be substituted in otherwise identical consecutive lines for cumulative effect as in "Song of Fury":

The Jade Emperor will decide whether
        this body will dissolve (*nogajŏdo*),
The Jade Emperor will decide whether
        this body will perish (*suiyŏjŏdo*)

Stated comparisons employing the word *tŭt* (as if; like) are one recurrent form of figurative language in *kasa*. "Song of Myŏnang Arbor" contains eleven "as if" constructions; "Song of a Beautiful Woman," eighteen. In describing the stream that flows down from Mounts Okch'ŏn and Yŏngch'ŏn, Song Sun says: "As if two dragons twist their bodies, / As if long silk has been spread, / . . . / As if they are in a hurry, / As if to follow someone." Viewing soaring peaks atop Diamond Terrace, the speaker in "Kwandong pyŏlgok" ("The Wanderings") by Chŏng Ch'ŏl (1537–1594) says:

What abundance of strange forms!
Some fly, some dash –
some stand, some soar –
as if planting lotus,
as if bundling white jade,
as if sifting the Eastern Sea from its bed,
as if heaving up the North Pole!

Chŏng Ch'ŏl (1537–1594) uses ten similes in "The Wanderings," some of them in a literal version to illustrate the point, and eight in the "Sŏngsan pyŏlgok" (Little odes to Mount Star):

> White waves in the blue stream
> rim the arbor,
> as if someone stitched and spread
> the cloud brocade woven by the Weaver Star.

These lines may have been inspired by the similar lines of Song Sun just cited, but a closer examination of the weaving of details into the poetical design of the two works ("Song of Myŏnang Arbor" and "Little Odes on Mount Star") reveals that Chŏng Ch'ŏl is the superior artist.

MASTER OF THE FORM

Chŏng's *kasa* poems were written in the 1580s, the most productive decade of his life. They were very popular in his day, and his contemporaries ranked him first among *kasa* poets of the Chosŏn dynasty.[8] His first *kasa*, "The Wanderings" (1580), is a travel poem in which the poet narrates his journey from Seoul to the entrance of the Inner Diamond Mountains and then describes his joy at observing, contemplating, and depicting the scenes famous for their magnificence. The reader feasts on a continuous unfolding of scenes described from various perspectives, encompassing both the sky and sea, and engaging all the senses. Chŏng's impressive structure and proportion evince his originality, especially when compared with a number of poems on the same subject by a host of writers before him and after. A harmonious blending of scenes and historical reflection drawing on Chinese and Korean tradition confers an added layer of richness. The poem's impelling rhythm comes from a mixture of colloquial and learned diction: a controlled language characterized by balance, parallelism, antithesis, and symmetry.

Chŏng's bold descriptions show great skill in conveying a magnificent scene of nature in simple but carefully chosen words, avoiding the usual similes, as when he transforms waterfalls at the Myriad Falls Grotto (Manp'oktong) into silver rainbows and the furious movements of whales:

> There, silver rainbows,
> dragons with jade tails,
> turning and coiling, spurt cataracts,

---

[8] For Chŏng Ch'ŏl's popularity among his contemporaries see *Songgang pyŏlchip ch'urok* 1–2, in Chŏng Ch'ŏl, *Songgang chŏnjip* (Taedong munhwa yŏngguwon, 1964), pp. 386–441.

rending the hills ten miles away.
Listen to the thunder;
Look, there is snow.

Scrupulous care, the felicitous arrangement of sound, and the repetition of "as if" (*nandŭt*) four times in the original enable the reader to experience nature's intricate and consummate artistry as vividly as possible:

> An extravagant celestial creator!
> What abundance of strange forms!
> Some fly, some dash –
> some stand, some soar –
> as if planting lotus,
> as if bundling white jade,
> as if sifting the Eastern Sea from its bed,
> as if heaving up the North Pole!
> Lofty Height Viewing Terrace
> and lonely Cave Viewing Peak
> shoot into the blue
> and speak to the Maker
> from eons
> constant and unbending.

On Buddha's Head Terrace:

> a cliff hanging in air
> over a thousand fathoms deep.
> The Milky Way
> unrolls its filaments
> showing the warp and woof
> of its hemp cloth.

At the Mirror Cove:

> Behind the old pines rimming like hedges
> I scan a ten-mile long beach
> like ironed and stretched white silk.
> The water is calm and clear,
> I can count the grains of sand.

The poem moves through time and space with subtly alternating visual and auditory imagery:

> Who enraged
> the already angered whale?
> It blows and spews,
> how giddying its tumult!

The silver mountain is leveled;
it crashes in every direction.
What a sight – snow falls
in the boundless sky of the fifth month.

Chŏng combines topographic and didactic motifs to communicate much in little – as, when in Ch'ŏrwŏn, contemplating the past and the violent reversals of fortune, he addresses "magpies chattering / at the palace site of Kungye," the cruel overreacher who proclaimed the short-lived kingdom of Late Koryô at the end of Silla but was murdered during his flight from the government army. Other examples of concision include his punning on the name of the Korean town Hoeyang to refer to the Chinese town Huiyang and Ji Changru, a good official under Emperor Wu of the Han. On seeing cranes nesting on Diamond Terrace, the speaker imagines that they greet Lin Bu (968–1028), "master of the West Lake," the grower of plum trees and the keeper of cranes. Pointed moral reflection occurs atop Vairocana Peak:

Who said the kingdom of Lu
was small?
Who said all under heaven
appeared small to Confucius?
Ah, how could we know
its limits?
Better descend,
if you cannot gain the summit.

While counting 12,000 peaks in clear air, the speaker muses:

If we could gather the air's vitality,
pure yet clean,
clean yet pure,
on every peak
and every crest
and bring it back to create a man!

As a victim of factional strife, he gives voice here to his concern with major public issues. As a practitioner of patience under suffering, lamenting the political disorder caused by small men, Chŏng indulges in an empty dream – if only we had great men at court! Evil courtiers blind the ruler's judgment – hence his prayer, "May the clouds / never cover the sunlight," the sun standing for the king. Such evil, however, does not seem to threaten remote provinces such as Kangwŏn:

Flagpoles for filial sons
adorn the valleys.
Truly the people of Yao and Shun
still seem to linger here.

Chŏng Ch'ŏl also draws on his native tradition, as when he muses on the whereabouts of four knights of Silla, who were thought to have tarried at Three Days Cove, and recalls the romance of Hongjang who was the despair of men of letters.

The poem ends on a festive note. Under the influence of "a cupful of enchanting wine" ("flowing mist") he, like Su Shi (1037–1101) in his rhymeprose *The Red Cliff* 2, is visited by a transcendent who travels on a crane's back. Like Li Bo, the poet is a banished transcendent who can "stride into the great void." When the dream fades, though, "only a jade flute rings in the void." The speaker looks downward to discover only the limitless sea illuminated by the moon. It shines not only on 1,000 hills but on the myriad villages he is about to administer as a public servant.

Both "Sa miin kok" ("Hymn of Constancy") and "Sok miin kok" ("Continued Hymn of Constancy") are allegorical poems in the style of *Encountering Sorrow* (*Li sao*) and the *Nine Declarations* (*Ziuzhang*).[9] They were written around 1585–1587 when the poet was forced by party strife to retire from court and spend several years in the countryside. In both poems, he compares his constancy toward King Sŏnjo with the behavior of a faithful wife longing for her absent husband or beloved.

Poems on the theme of the neglected or forsaken wife are as old as the *Book of Songs*. In the Korean adaptations and imitations of "Encountering Sorrow" and the "Nine Declarations," however – especially *Thinking of a Fair One* (*Simeiren*) among the latter – the unemployed or exiled courtier's longing for the center of power is expressed in terms drawn from the experience of love. Thus the poems derive their artistic detachment from parallels established between his frustrations and the rejected woman's disappointment in love. Decorum declares that the Fair One or Lovely One – the king – cannot be equated with woman, especially in a society where the place of women was humble. Therefore the speaker has to assume the woman's persona. (We must not confuse this convention with the courtly love tradition in the West, where the lady is an agent of the courtier's spiritual development, often presented as a form of feudal service, and her power and fame are accorded her by the poet.)

---

[9] For a translation of these poems see David Hawkes, *Ch'u Tz'u: the Songs of the South* (Oxford: Clarendon, 1959), pp. 21–34, 59–80.

續속義미人인曲곡

뎨가 누며 각시 본 듯 도 호뎌이고 天텬上샹

白빅玉옥京경을 엇디 흐야 離니別별

히고 히 다 티 져믄 날의 눌을 보라 가시난

고 어와 비여이고 내 사셜 드러보오 버얼

굴 이 거동이 님 괴얌즉 흐냐마난 엇딘디

날 보시고 비로 다녀 기실시 나도 님을 미

더 군쯰 디 젼혀 업서 이리야 교티야 어 쥬

러 이 구둣턴 다 반기시난 낫 비치 녜와 엇

다 다루신고 어셩 각 흐고 너러 안자 혜

거 흐니 내 몸의 지은 죄 뫼 フ 티 바혀시니

Example 5.   Chŏng Ch'ŏl (1537–1594), "Continued Hymn of Constancy." *Pine River Anthology* (Sŏngju edn., 1747) 31–33.

하눌히라웬망ᄒᆞ며사ᄅᆞᆷ이라ᄒᆞᆯ랴

셜위풀텨혜니造조物믈들의타시로다글

란셩각마오ᄆᆡ쳔일이이셔이다넘을외

셔이쉬님의일을내알거니믈ᄀᆞ튼얼굴

이편ᄒᆞ실젹멋날일고春춘寒한ᄉᆞᆷ고熱

열은엇디ᄒᆞ야ᄃᆡ내시며秋츄日일冬동

곳뎐은뉘라셔ᄆᆡᆫ엇ᄂᆞ고粥쥭早조飯반

朝됴ᄌᆞ셕ᄆᆡ뵈와ᄌᆞᆺ티셰시ᄂᆞ가기나긴

밤의ᄌᆞᆷ은엇디자시ᄂᆞᆫ고님다히消쇼息

식을아ᄆᆞ려나아자ᄒᆞ니오늘도거의로

다ᄂᆡ일이나사ᄅᆞᆷ올가ᄆᆞ ᄆᆞᆷ들ᄃᆡ업다

"Sa miin kok" is a monologue by a fairy banished from the Moon Palace (literally, the Great Cold Palace). It has six sections: introduction, four sections corresponding to the four seasons, and a conclusion. Every season reminds the speaker of her wretched state: plum blossoms and the dusky moon in spring; the making of warm clothes in summer; wild geese, the moon and stars, and snow in autumn; and a tall bamboo at sunset, the long nights, cold quilt, and harp in winter. Like all calendrical poems, the "Hymn of Constancy" combines similarity and contrasts, variety and continuity. Representing the stages of a woman's life, the four seasons seem to rush by, but there is no possibility for a liberation from the torments of love. Hence her desire for metamorphosis into a butterfly like the transformation of Alcyone and Ceyx into halcyons:[10]

> Better to die
> and become a butterfly.
> Stop at each flower,
> rest upon each branch,
> with scented wings,
> and light upon his cloak.
> He may not remember me:
> yet I will follow him.

The "Sok miin kok" (Continued hymn of constancy) is a dialogue between two fairies. The first starts out in search of her beloved in the hills, then along the river. Exhausted she "sinks into sleep" and has a dream vision. A frivolous rooster wakes her from her slumber, however. At the end, the first fairy wishes to be a setting moon while the second wants to be "a driving rain," like the goddess of Mount Wu, who appeared to King Xiang of Chu in the form of clouds and rain.[11]

The epideictic strategy of the Korean country-house poems, such as Chŏng Ch'ŏl's "Sŏngsan pyŏlgok" ("Little Odes to Mount Star") and Pak Illo's "Tongnaktang" ("Hall of Solitary Bliss") bears similarities to the seventeenth-century English country-house poems – including the ideal landscape reflecting the virtue and character of the subject, like the paradisial setting blessed with soil, air, wood, and water at Penshurst; an absence of display, idealization of the subject by associating him with paragons of virtue in the tradition; emblematic association of plants and animals with

---

[10] Ovid, *Metamorphosis* 11:418; Brooks Otis, *Ovid as an Epic Poet* (Cambridge: Cambridge University Press, 1966), pp. 231–277.
[11] Lois Fusek, " 'The Kao-t'ang Fu,' " *Monumenta Serica* 30 (1972–1973): 412–423.

his virtue; and a combination of the topographical and the didactic. The Korean works, however, omit many characteristics of their English counterparts: description of buildings or their pedigree; the role of the landed aristocracy in the rural community; mention of tenants, retainers, and servants; communal life (public meals and gatherings); the subject's forefathers; and hyperbolic flattery with political implications. The epideictic poet's task is to create an enduring monument of poetry to stimulate emulation; hence the poem dwells on the subject's moral beauties and their lasting impact on society and culture. The praise of moral and spiritual excellence calls for a context of solitude and nature. Often explored are the dialectic patterns of withdrawal and emergence, self and world, the contemplative life as a necessary stage for an active career, moral cultivation as a prerequisite for public service, and the individual's moral sense as the only safeguard for institutions. Thus in the course of describing the subject's moral beauties – be he a Daoist transcendent or a Confucian sage – through praise of landscape the poet reaffirms traditional cultural values and parades his knowledge of history and literature.

Written to praise the elegant life that Kim Sŏngwŏn (1525–1598) had established at the Mist Settling Hall (Sŏhadang) and Resting Shadow Arbor (Sigyŏngjŏng) on Mount Star in South Chŏlla province, Chŏng's "Little Odes to Mount Star" (c. 1585–1587) begins with a question:

> "Listen, Master of the Mist Settling Hall
> and Resting Shadow Arbor,
> despite the many pleasures
> life held,
> why did you prefer to them all
> this mountain, this water?
> What made you choose
> the solitude of hills and streams?"

The poet then catalogues the delights of the four seasons and exclaims that Mount Star exceeds in beauty Tao Qian's Peach Blossom Spring:[12] it is, in fact, "the land of the transcendents." This is a topos of outdoing, but it could also be a reflection of the patriotic theme. The expansive landscape reflects Kim Sŏngwŏn's own liberality, freedom, and unworldliness, and the floating clouds and waterfowl (duck) mentioned elsewhere in the poem symbolize the mind and courtesy of the host. Thus the poet is all the more cautious against the intrusion of cultural barbarians:

[12] James R. Hightower, *The Poetry of T'ao Ch'ien* (Oxford: Clarendon, 1970), pp. 254–258.

Don't boast of
the recluse's riches
lest some find out
this lustrous, hidden world.

The poet then meditates on heaven, men, and fortune. The poem is also a
lament for his own age and all ages:

Alone deep in the mountains,
with the classics, pile on pile,
I think of the men
of all times:
many were sages,
many were heroes.
Heavenly intent goes into the making of men.
Yet fortunes
rise and fall;
chance seems unknowable.
And sadness deep.

At the end the poet, enraptured by the music played by his host on the
black zither, avers that Kim is the true transcendent in harmony with the
workings of the universe, metaphorically flying high on the back of the
crane. The crane is not only a symbol of longevity but a fitting emblem of
unity and harmony. It soars above the world while maintaining an intimate
relation with it, uniting time and space, time and timelessness.

HŎ NANSŎRHŎN

Surviving works by women writers of early Chosŏn are very few except for
two pieces by Hŏ Ch'ohŭi (pen name Nansŏrhŏn, 1563–1589) – an elder
sister of Hŏ Kyun (1569–1618), the putative author of the first vernacular
narrative tale in Korea. Hŏ Nansŏrhŏn enjoyed a reputation similar to that
of Hwang Chini for her poems in literary Chinese, which were published
in China and Japan.[13] At the age of fourteen or fifteen, she was married off
to a mediocre person from Cheju Island and led an unhappy conjugal life
till her death at the age of twenty-six. She is remembered by her two *kasa*:
the "Kyuwŏn ka" ("A Woman's Sorrow") and "Pongsŏnhwa ka" ("Song of
Balsam Flowers").[14]

---

[13] Yi Sukhŭi, *Hŏ Nansŏrhŏn siron* (Saemunsa, 1987).
[14] Also attributed to Chŏngiltang (1772–1822), wife of Yun Kwangyŏn.

"A Woman's Sorrow" is a dramatic narrative. In this poem the introduction of the theme of sorrowful reminiscence is followed by a recollection of her happier past. She was brought up to be "a bride fit for a gentleman," which recalls the first song in the *Book of Songs*: "Lovely is this noble lady / Fit bride for our lord." The "gentleman" brought her by a matchmaker, however, was "a valiant man known as frivolous" who "left home for no fixed place / On a white horse with a gold whip." The remainder of the poem is a moving account of the hazards of such a union. The beauties of spring and autumn and the terrors of summer and winter intensify her agony:

> The plum trees by my window,
> how many times have they fallen?
> The winter night is bitter cold,
> and snow, or some mixture, descends.
> Long, long is a summer's day,
> and a dreary rain comes too.
> And spring with flowers and willows
> have no feeling for me.
> When the autumn moon enters my room
> and crickets chirp on the couch,
> a long sigh and salty tears
> in vain make me recall the past.

Her despair reaches such depths that she even thinks of ending her own life:

> It is hard to bring
> this cruel life to an end.
> But when I examine myself,
> I shouldn't despair so.

The music in which she seeks consolation only echoes in the empty room. She hopes to see her husband in a dream, but fallen leaves rustling in the wind and insects piping among the grasses deny the possibility of a dream vision. Hers is a separation worse than that suffered by the Weaver and Herdboy constellations in the sky, and the water that separated her from her beloved is vaster and more terrifying than the Milky Way.

> Leaning on the balustrade,
> I gaze at the path he took –
> Dewdrops glitter on the grass,
> evening clouds pass by,
> and birds sing sadly
> in the green bamboo grove.

Numberless
are the sorrowful;
but can there be anyone
as wretched as I?
Love, you caused me this grief;
I don't know whether I shall live or die.

We do not know how her poem satisfied the expectations of her first readers, but its affective power is still felt today. Among the many poems built on the motif of the abandoned woman, Hŏ Nansŏrhŏn's succeeds because of her polished style and mastery of conventions.

CHAPTER 10

Late Chosŏn sijo

Peter H. Lee

Several seventeenth-century literati poets wrote *sijo* sequences, including Ko Ŭngch'ŏk (1531–1605), Chang Kyŏngse (1547–1615), Kim Tugyŏn (1555–1637), and Yi Tŏgil (1561–1622). Topics ranged from morality and reclusion to national crisis (especially among those who had fought against the Japanese invaders) and love of the king.

A group of four songs by Cho Chonsŏng (1554–1628), entitled "Calling a Boy," devotes itself to picking herbs, viewing fish, tilling a field, and returning home drunk.

> Boy, lead a cow to the northern village,
>   let's taste new wine.
> My face is rosy with drink,
>   I'll return on cowback in the moonlight.
> Hurrah! I am a Fu Xi tonight,
>   ancient glories at my fingertips.[1]

Wine has made the speaker a Fu Xi, the legendary Chinese cultural hero. Tao Qian (365–427) called wine a "care-dispelling thing"[2] serving to "exorcize all our concerns"[3] and liberating us from life. It is a leveler that makes a sage or an immortal. Wine is associated with the moon, flowers, and friends, as well, as in the following *sijo* by Yi Tŏkhyŏng (1561–1613):

> The moon hangs in the sky, bright, full.
>   Since the dawn,
> It has met wind and frost.
>   Soon it could sink.
> But no, wait, and shine on
>   the gold cup of my drunken guest.[4]

---

[1] *KYS* 1847.
[2] "After Drinking Wine," 7:3; (Hightower, *The Poetry of T'ao Ch'ien*, p. 133).
[3] "The Double Ninth in Retirement," 9 (Hightower, *The Poetry of T'ao Ch'ien*, p. 27).
[4] *KYS* 780.

When the poet asks the moon to "shine on / the gold cup of my drunken guest," he has in mind a famous poem by Li Bo, "Drinking Alone Beneath the Moon," where the revered Chinese poet says: "I raise my cup to invite the moon to join me; / It and my shadow make a party of three."[5]

PAK ILLO

Pak Illo (1561–1643), a commoner who served as a soldier from 1592 to 1605, became an ardent student of Neo-Confucian morality, studied the Confucian classics, and befriended influential scholars and statesmen including Yi Tŏkhyŏng, Chang Hyŏngwang (1554–1637), Cho Hoik (1545–1609), and Chŏng Ku (1543–1620). Pak wrote twenty-nine *sijo* (songs 7–35) describing the scenic spot at Standing Rock (Ibam) in Yŏngil, where Chang Hyŏngwang had a retreat, and two *sijo* when he visited Pepper Well (Ch'ojŏng) in Ulsan with Chŏng Ku. The "Songs of Five Relations" (songs 36–60), comprising twenty-five songs, assign five songs each to the first four relations, two songs to the last, and end with a three-song conclusion. The last eight songs were written around 1636.[6]

Pak's *sijo* songs are didactic – a quality that makes them nearly insufferable today. Standing Rock, for example, inspires the speaker to muse on its firmness and uprightness. Lofty and straight, it soars above the heavens (song 20) and touches the shining bodies in the great universe; it "bears him up" (song 18) and can purify his "base and cluttered mind." He likens it to a "great hero" (song 8) or to a man of virtue unrecognized and unrewarded (song 9). In his dialogue with the rock the speaker hopes that he too will "grow old together" with the rock (song 15), but at the same time the rock reminds him of the relativity of time (the rock can stand for eons, but men cannot: song 16). The arduous ascent to its summit is compared to the stages of self-cultivation (song 11) and the determined effort necessary for advancement in the Way. Hence he enjoins the reader to be "careful [in his behavior] / At a place unseen and unheard of" (song 19), for the practitioner of the Confucian Way must abide in reverence to interiorize moral and spiritual cultivation. Pak then turns his gaze to the stream and sees how it "return[s] to the source / Even when branched off into separate streams" (song 24). That is, we may temporarily go astray, unable to control our own feelings, but in the end we return to our "source" and commit ourselves once more to the attainment of our goals. The speaker

---

[5] Wu-chi Liu and Irving Yucheng Lo, eds., *Sunflower Splendor: Three Thousand Years of Chinese Poetry* (Garden City: Doubleday, 1975), p. 109.
[6] I have used the annotated edition by Yi Sangbo, *Kaego Pak Nogye yŏngu* (Ilchisa, 1962).

is also intent on outdoing his ancient exemplars, as when he has the rock compare him to Yan Guang (song 14). At other points, however, having preserved his equanimity and attained a sense of nondiscrimination, the speaker says he actually envies neither Zeng Xi (song 27) nor Yan Guang (song 30). Having emulated the recluse farmers Changzhu and Jieni mentioned in the *Analects* (18:6), he can declare, "I have nothing to envy" (song 31).

In "Songs of Five Relations," the speaker avows that what distinguishes humans from "birds and beasts" are the Five Relations (song 58). Chŏng Ch'ŏl had already likened men without social virtue to "horse and oxen / Wearing caps and cowls and eating rice" (song 8). The series ends with an impassioned plea to his "juniors" (song 59), probably his intended audience:

> My writing may be clumsy,
>> but it is filled with sincerity and respect.
> Peruse my poems and savor them;
>> then you'll need no other aid.[7]
>
> (song 60)

Although Pak may have been intent on acquiring learning and virtue, he did not fully understand how to make his poetry ethical. He might have thought himself a custodian of morality; but his marked sententiousness, strings of authorities (the Confucian canon), and exempla – homiletic and pedagogic zeal gone awry – make him appear to modern readers a mere mouthpiece for Confucian ideology.

GREAT POET YUN SŎNDO

Yun Sŏndo (1587–1671) was the most accomplished poet writing in the *sijo* form. His lyrics are diverse in mood and technique, and his diction is peerless. Graceful, delicately varied rhythms are natural to him, and every poem exhibits new techniques and a fresh tone. Yet his invention is so subtle that it becomes noticeable only after repeated close readings of his poems. The first group of six songs, entitled "Kyŏnhoe yo" ("Dispelling Gloom," 1618), are the earliest known poems by Yun. They tend to abstraction and a perhaps excessive use of the pathetic fallacy. Nevertheless, these songs sing with an intensity of their own, and the discerning reader can anticipate in them Yun's later poetic genius. In song 4, for example, suspense is created by an emphatic repetition of verbs:

---

[7] *KYS* 2483.

A chain of mountains is long, long;   *Moehŭn kilgo kilgo*
    waters flow far, far.   *murŭn mŏlgo mŏlgo*
Love for parents is endless,   *Ŏbŏi kŭrinttŭdŭn*
    and my heart is heavy.   *mankʾo mankʾo hago hago*
Far off, crying sadly,   *Ŏdŭisyŏ woegirŏginŭn*
    a lone wild goose flies by.   *ulgo ulgo kanŭni.*[8]

The five adjectival verbs in the conjunctive form "*ko*" are among the simplest Korean verbs, but suspense builds as the poem moves steadily from one verb in "*ko*" form to the next. The long vowels in "*kilgo,*" "*mŏlgo,*" and "*mankʾo*" and *l*'s in "*kil,*" "*mŏl,*" and "*ul*" provide a resonant, stately note. In song 6, Yun employs a rhetorical question for emphasis and dramatic contrast:

    Has the dreary rain ceased?   *Kujŭnbi kaedanmalka*
    Have the dark clouds rolled away?   *hŭridŏn kurŭm kŏttanmalka*[9]

Yun was told of a certain court minister who repented and remedied his failings while in exile at Kyŏngwŏn. At that very moment the dreary rain ceased and the clouds rolled away. The poet wrote this song to console himself. Here the "dreary rain" and "dark clouds" are closely bound up with the poet's attitude toward corrupt officials and his political enemies. The "deep swamps" referred to in the song subtly enhance its mood and contrast two different states of affairs. The muddy swamps, perhaps a metaphor for the murk of court life, become "limpid," a place where the poet can wash his cap strings, alluding to the example of Qu Yuan. Similar rhetorical questions appear in song 28 and in a sequence of four didactic songs (29–32).

Yun's masterpiece in the group of songs entitled "New Songs in the Mountain" is the "Ou ka" ("Songs of Five Friends"), written in praise of water, stone, pine, bamboo, and the moon. By naming the five natural objects as his friends, rather than his fickle fellow mortals, the poet has won a new domain for himself and his poetry. Indeed, he has established a relationship with nature that is the preserve of those possessing poetic sensibility. In song 20, tension is achieved by developing the theme with successive contrasts through the fifth line. The tension is resolved only in the sixth line, at the very end of the song:

    They say the color of clouds is fine,   *Kurŭm pitchʾi chotʾahana*
        but they often darken.   *kŏmkirŭl charo handa.*
    They say the sound of winds is clear,   *Paramsorae malktahana*

---

[8] *KYS* 1044.   [9] *KYS* 304.

but they often cease to blow.   *kŭch'il chŏgi hanomaera.*
It is only the *water*, then,   *Chok'odo kŭch'il nwi ŏpkinŭn*
     that is perpetual and good.   *mul ppunin'ga hanora.*[10]

The effect here is achieved by a skillful use of the simple adversative ending *ha-na* (translated as "but") in the first and third lines with the reply given immediately afterward in the second and fourth lines respectively. The adjectives modifying the subjects "cloud" and "wind" are extremely simple, yet they are at once concise and clear, natural and precise. Moreover, they were chosen specifically because their sounds would enhance the rhythmic flow of the song as a whole. In song 23, Yun introduces yet another device:

     You are not a tree,   *Namodo anin kŏsi*
       nor are you a plant.   *p'uldo anin kŏsi.*[11]

First, the omission of a conjunction *ko* between the first and second lines produces a unique intonation and rhythm that quickens the movement of the lines. Second, the ending *i* in this context normally anticipates the interrogative adverb *ŏtchi* or *ŏi*: "You are not a tree; but *why*. . .?" *Oi* appears only in the fourth line, keeping the reader in suspense and heightening the song's dramatic effect. The song moves rapidly through this construction by repetition of *anin* in the first and second lines and the appearance of *nwi* (who) in the third. Furthermore, the song never specifically mentions the bamboo to which it is addressed, but only its characteristics. Thus the six lines comprising the song rush on like a waterfall, keeping the reader's mind ever on the alert.

"At the Beginning of the Feast" and "At the End of the Feast" (songs 29–32) are admonitions to the king, and it is uncertain whether they are indeed impromptu songs composed at a feast. In the first song "house" alludes to the ideal state, while "straight wood" denotes the benevolent government and moral power of the king. "Straight" in the third line alludes to the ways of the ancient sage-kings. In the second song, "wine" and "broth" allude to the virtues of the king, while "yeast," "salt," and "prunes" denote the wise ministers who assist in state affairs. The third song urges moderation in the pursuit of pleasure. Perhaps the poet had in mind poem 114 in the *Book of Songs*. In the first stanza of that poem the monitor says:

     Do not be so riotous
     As to forget your home.
     Amuse yourselves, but no wildness!
     Good men are always on their guard.[12]

---

[10] *KYS* 289.   [11] *KYS* 442.
[12] *Book of Songs* 114; Waley, *The Book of Songs*, p. 199.

"ANGLER'S SONGS"

The image of the fisherman occurs from time to time in both East Asian and Western poetry, but nowhere does it play such an important role as in Korean poetry, particularly in the works of Yun Sŏndo. There the fisherman symbolizes a pure and wise individual who lives aloof from the woes of the day, scorns worldly ambition and personal glory, and devotes himself to the cultivation of sensibility and self. The poet took his inspiration from existing songs, but what he made of them is so original that we must give full credit to his control of the materials and his superior techniques.

The origin of the *Ŏbu sa* (or *ka*), or "Angler's Songs," is obscure. Fishermen's songs were popular from the Koryŏ dynasty on.[13] The earliest reference occurs in a heptasyllabic quatrain, "In Memory of Minister Kim Yŏngdon,"[14] in the *Ikchae chip* ("Collected Works of Yi Chehyŏn"; 4:8b). A note immediately following the poem adds that Minister Kim ordered the female entertainer P'yop'i to sing the angler's songs every time he drank wine. The first reference in Chosŏn-dynasty annals occurs in the *T'aejong sillok* ("T'aejong Annals"; 23:42a). At the banquet held in the Kyŏnghoe Tower in 1412, the former king (Chŏngjong, r. 1398–1400) requested the skilled singer Kim Chasun to sing the angler's songs. Kim's performance so moved Chŏngjong that he rewarded the artist with fine garments. Although the author or compiler of the original twelve songs is unknown, the popularity of the poems during the fifteenth and sixteenth centuries is attested by Yi Hwang who provides the following information. At the banquet given by his uncle Yi U an old female entertainer from Andong sang the "Angler's Songs" so well that he was delighted and jotted them down. During his stay at court he often inquired whether anyone knew the source of these songs, but nobody seemed to have the faintest idea. Then by chance he came across an anthology compiled by Pak Chun (*Words for Songs and Music*) that contained the texts of the songs. Hwang Chullyang (1517–1563) copied them and presented them, together with the texts of ten shorter songs, to Yi Hyŏnbo (1467–1555). Yi Hyŏnbo in turn recompiled the twelve songs into a cycle of nine and compressed the ten shorter songs into a cycle of five.[15] Our source further comments that upon obtaining the texts of the songs, Yi Hyŏnbo devoted himself to their revision and adaptation. The correspondence between Yi Hyŏnbo and Yi Hwang suggests that

[13] Yi Usŏng, "Koryŏ-mal Yijo-ch'o ŭi *ŏbu ga*," *Sŏngdae nonmunjip* 9 (1964):5–27.
[14] Kim served as minister of the left during the reign of the twenty-ninth king of Koryŏ; see *KRS* 104:31a–b.
[15] Yi Hwang, *T'oegye chip* in *T'oegye ch'ŏnsŏ* (Taedong munhwa yŏnguwŏn, 1958) 43:3a–4b; see also Yi Hyŏnbo, *Nongam sŏnsaeng munjip* (*YMC* 3) 3:18a–19b.

the former was careful in his work and submitted his drafts to the latter for comments at various points.

The "Angler's Songs" seems to have been written originally as Chinese heptasyllabic quatrains consisting chiefly of quotations from Chinese poets. The versions preserved in the *Words for Songs and Music* underwent certain modifications: Korean connectives were added to the songs to facilitate recitation or singing; between the second and third lines were inserted a set of Korean verbs, usually connected with the topic of boating, in the imperative mode; between the third and fourth lines were inserted two sets of onomatopoetic expressions (twelve syllables) simulating the movements and sounds of rowing.[16] In his adaptations, Yi Hyŏnbo made the following changes: he did away with Korean connectives, thereby giving his versions a Chinese feeling; his third line invariably consists of nautical Korean verbs in the imperative form, three three-syllable verbs and six four-syllable verbs; his fifth line, invariably consisting of three three-syllable segments, is an onomatopoetic expression simulating the movements and sounds of rowing.[17] Yi's changes served chiefly to improve the third line. In the original version consisting of twelve songs, the verbs in the third lines of the first through the eighth songs are: (1) cast off; (2) hoist anchor; (3) row away; (4) raise sail; (5) row away; (6) stop the boat; (7) lower sail; (8) moor the boat. Thus the first eight songs depict sequentially a boat trip from departure to return. In the ninth song, however, the speaker leaves shore again with a "row away." Thus the verbs in the third lines of songs 9 to 12 are not only redundant but also interrupt the sequence. Furthermore, the fourth line of song 4 reappears in song 9, and line 4 of song 8 reappears in song 12. It is for this reason that songs 9 to 12 are considered to represent later additions to an earlier cycle. Yi's version, however, shows coherence in its sequence: (1) cast off; (2) hoist anchor; (3) row away; (4) lower sail; (5) chant a song; (6) stop the boat; (7) moor the boat; (8) drop anchor; and (9) bring the boat ashore.

Although Yi did away with repetitions and reorganized the envoi (using Korean nautical verbs), his adaptations with their faulty rhythms, heavy Chinese diction, and disunited tone still sound clumsy. In short, they have not yet been made into Korean poetry. The music of Korean, its intrinsic rhythm, is lacking. Indeed, Yun Sŏndo commented that "Yi's sound pattern is faulty, and his diction and meaning leave much to be desired."[18] Yun

---

[16] *ACKS* 15b–17b; for a modern printed version see Kim Hyŏnggyu, *Kogayo chusŏk*, pp. 347–349; and Yi Chaesu, *Yun Kosan yŏngu*, pp. 155–165.

[17] The text is in *Nongam sŏnsaeng munjip* (*YMC* 3) 3:15a–16b.

[18] See Yun Sŏndo, *Kosan yugo* (*YMC* 3) 6B:14b.

therefore set out to create a cycle of angler's songs in the Korean vernacular that would resound with native rhythms. His forty songs depicting the four seasons are products of the poet's leisurely life at a favorite retreat, the Lotus Grotto. They are written in intricate stanzas differing from the conventional *sijo* form. The general pattern is as follows (the numerals indicating the number of syllables in each metric segment):

First line:	3	4	3	4
Envoi:	4	4		
Second line:	3	4	3	4
Envoi:	3	3	3	
Third line:	3	4	3	4

Thus a pair of four-syllable words is added after the first line, and three three-syllable onomatopoetic words after the second line, thus bringing the total number of syllables to fifty-nine. The fortieth song in this series has an unusual form, for in this case the total number of syllables is seventy-two.

The verbs in the first envois of each seasonal set of songs are not only well arranged in narrative sequence but are identical from season to season: (1) cast off; (2) hoist anchor; (3) raise sail; (4) row away; (5) row away; (6) lower the sail; (7) stop the boat; (8) moor the boat; (9) drop anchor; and (10) bring the boat ashore. Together with the intricate organization, the songs are marked by flawless use of the language and a musical quality that depicts images as well as simulates sounds. Indeed, Yun succeeded in casting an authentic depiction of the life of a fisherman into lyrical rhythms.

Throughout the cycle Yun Sŏndo introduces a number of subtle variations in form and organization. The emphatic syntactic division expected in the third line to introduce a deliberate twist in phrasing or meaning is often replaced by a different technique. In the first song of spring, the third line continues the description of a given spring scene (line numbers refer to the original):

line 1   fog lifts, the sun shines
line 2   night tide neaps, high waters rush on
line 3   flowers in the river hamlet, distant views

A similar structure recurs in the first song of winter:

line 1   clouds roll away, the sun is warm
line 2   heaven and earth are frozen, water is clear
line 3   the boundless water is a silk brocade

Here and elsewhere Yun Sŏndo wishes to create an ideal landscape with memorable, fresh particulars – the radiance of spring with visual freshness as in the first example. Aware of the power in the landscape, he attempts to reflect it in his description; at other times, the landscape is designed to harmonize with his mood and superior solitude.

Yun Sŏndo also uses a question and answer form, as in song 7 of spring:

> What have I taken aboard
> On my boat small as a leaf?
> . . .
> Nothing except mist when I set sail,
> When I row back, the moon is my tenant.

In the third variation – as in the fourth song of summer and the eighth of winter – Yun repeats a theme for added significance:

line 2   I wish to go to the Wu River; sad
                are the angry waves of a thousand years.
line 3   Paddle the boat, then, to the Chu River;
                but don't catch the fish of a loyal soul. (Summer 4)

Line 2 refers to the story of Wu Zixu (Wu Yun; d. 484 BC), who was ordered by the king of Wu to commit suicide by drowning for his loyal and prescient admonition and whose corpse was thrown in the Wu River. Line 3 alludes to the wronged upright minister Qu Yuan (c. 343–278 BC), who drowned himself in the Miluo, or Chu, River. Both are known for their integrity and outspoken criticism of their ruler's policy – like Yun Sŏndo himself, perhaps, who is probably comparing his political career to these Chinese paradigms. In song 8 of winter, we find the same method used for emphasis in parallel form. This time the song emphasizes the distance between the lyric speaker and the mundane world:

line 2   Don't scorn the rough clouds –
                They screen the world from us.
line 3   Don't deplore the roaring waves –
                They drown out the clamor of this world.[19]

A variation of the same method, again to emphasize the poem's central concern, occurs in the eighth song of autumn:

---

[19] The same feeling is expressed in spring 8, autumn 2, and autumn 9.

漁⊙父四時詞ᄉ韓外洞時

孤山遺稿

卷之六下   別 六   解 一ᄉ

春
춘

압개예 안개 것고 뒫뫼희 히 비췬다
ᄇㅐ떠라 ᄇㅐ떠라
밤믈은 거의 디고 낟믈이 미러 온다
至국悤 至국悤 於思臥
江村촌 온갓 고지 먼 빗치 더옥 됴타

날이 덥도다 믈 우희 고기 ᄯㅓㄷ다
닫ᄃㅡ러라 단ᄃㅡ러라
ᄀㅕ며기 둘식 세식 오락가락 하ᄂㅡ고야
至국悤 於思臥
낫대ᄂㅡᆫ 쥐ᄋㅕ 잇다 濁酒ᄉ瓶병 시릿ᄂㅕ냐

東동風풍이 건듯 부니 믈결이 고이 닌다 돋ᄃㅏ라라 돋

Example 6.   Yun Sŏndo (1587–1671), *The Angler's Calendar*, Spring 1–5. *Literary Remains of Yun Sŏndo* (1798) 6B:6a–7a.

드라라東동湖호물도라보며西셔湖호로가쟈스라

至지欬국念총至지欬국念총於어思ᄉ臥와압뫼히

디나가고뒨뫼히나아온다

우ᄂ거시버구기가프른거시버들숩가이어라이어

라漁어村촌두어집이닛속의나락들락至지欬국念

총至지欬국念총於어思ᄉ臥와말가호기픈소회온

그믈을주어두랴낙시를노홀일가至지欬국念총至지

고은별티젹안는듸믐결이기름굿다이어라이어리

간고기뛰노ᄂ다

欬국念총於어思ᄉ臥와濯탁纓영歌가의興흥이나

너고기도니즐로다

夕셕陽양이빗겨시니그만흥야도라가쟈돋디여라

돋디여라岸안柳류汀뎡花화눈고비고비새롭고야

孤山遺稿　二／卷之六下　別　七　三篇　七

line 2   Since the west wind's dust can't reach us,
               why fan off the empty air?
line 3   Further, since I have heard no words,
               why should I bother to wash my ears?

Line 2 concerns Wang Dao (276–339) who described his rival Yu Liang (289–340) as being filthy as dust.[20] Line 3 refers to Xu You, a legendary recluse who, when Emperor Yao wished to make him his successor, was so horrified by the suggestion he went to the river to cleanse his ears. The song stresses again the distance between the speaker and the world of politics.[21]

Lastly, what strikes the modern reader is the frequency of four-syllable Chinese phrases (as many as thirty-two instances) – especially when such a sonorous phrase, followed by a Korean marker, begins the third line, occupying the first hemistich (ten instances in the cycle). Here I cite four examples:

This angler's life is how I shall pass my days. (Spring 10)	*ŏbu.saengnae.nŭn*
Northern coves and southern river, does it matter where I go? (Summer 3)	*pukp'o.namgang.i*
Do you hear an oriole calling here and there in the green grove? (Summer 7)	*pyŏksu.aengsŏng.i*
In an empty boat, with straw cape and hat, I sit and my heart beats fast. (Winter 7)	*koju.sarip.e*

Often called in to satisfy metrical requirements and to say much in little to create an echo, these Chinese phrases produce a slow and solemn effect like a succession of spondees. Chosen for orotundity, they stand out amidst the Korean letters calling for an educated response. This dramatic shift in time and diction recalls the use of Latinate elements in English poetry – for example, in "*multitudinous* seas *incarnadine*" (*Macbeth* 2:2:62; emphasis added). The poetics of *sijo* calls for two metric segments in the first hemistich of the third line, but the examples cited offer one five-syllable segment that calls attention to its deliberate irregularity, slowing down the line with a distinct stress on each syllable.

The fourth song in the spring cycle offers an admirable example of the poet's technique:

[20] Richard B. Mather, *Shih-shuo Hsin-yü: A New Account of Tales of the World* (Minneapolis: University of Minnesota Press 1976), p. 429.
[21] Also in spring 8 and autumn 2, 8, and 9.

Is it a cuckoo that cries?	*Unŭn kŏsi pŏkkugiga*
Is it the willow that is blue?	*p'urŭn kŏsi podŭlsupka*
Row away, row away!	*Iŏra iŏra*
Several roofs in a far fishing village	*ŏch'on tuŏ chibi*
swim in the mist.	*naesoge naraktŭrak*
Chigukch'ong chigukch'ong ŏsawa	*chigukch'ong chigukch'ong ŏsawa*
Boy, fetch an old net!	*aheya saegogi orŭnda*
Fishes are climbing against the stream.[22]	*hŏngŭmul naeyŏra*

The song opens with two questions suggesting uncertainty regarding the senses of sound and sight. In the next two lines we actually do see village roofs, however insubstantial they may appear, as they seem to swim in the twilight. The expression *naraktŭrak* suggests that the vision is a splendid one, even if tinged with unreality. The last two lines are brisk and forceful and express a practical and immediate concern with nature. In consequence we proceed from a state of near-illusion to one of magnificence dimly perceived and then, finally, to one of immediate appreciation and delight, with the suggestion that all these follow in sequence. The song therefore presents nature's mystery, beauty, and bounty in terms of illusory loveliness, authentic loveliness, and finally the physical sustenance reaped by those who fish. Thus the song not only imparts the transcendence of vision but reveals as well an awareness of the transience of earthly joy and beauty.

The ten songs in the spring cycle depict a day's activities for a fisherman as he sets sail scanning the river hamlets and distant views. Gulls accompany him and the boy, and he makes sure that a wine flagon has been loaded. Passing hill upon hill, he hears a cuckoo and sees the willow in the distance. He then asks the boy to have an old net ready. Being reminded, however, of "The Fisherman" attributed to Qu Yuan,[23] in which the wise fisherman advises the wronged idealistic courtier on the art of swimming in the sea of life, he asks himself if he should catch fish at all, especially when Qu Yuan's soul might reside in one.

> The sun's fair rays are shining,
>   the water is calm as oil.
> Row away, row away!
> Should we cast a net,
>   or drop a line on such a day?
> *Chigukch'ong chigukch'ong ŏsawa.*
> The Fisherman's Song stirs my fancy;
>   I have forgotten all about fishing.

[22] Another version of lines 7–8 reads: "In the deep and clear stream, / All kinds of fishes are leaping." See *KYS* 2176.

[23] Hawkes, *Ch'u Tz'u*, pp. 90–91.

As twilight approaches, the speaker wishes to return to shore and reaffirms that rank and riches are not what he wants. He then realizes that the moon has occupied the boat, "small as a leaf." The drunken speaker sees peach blossoms floating down the stream, perhaps from Tao Qian's literary utopia, Peach Blossom Spring, an indication that he is far from the world of men. On the boat he wishes to view the moon through a "bamboo awning." Accompanied again by the cuckoo's song, the speaker registers his heart's rapture as he wends his way to his cottage after passing the day as a wise fisherman.

As a seasoned politician who served four kings and spent fourteen years in exile, an allusion to Qu Yuan adds weight to concern for the relative value of loyal admonition and political action. The poet is content to bring in harsher realities – as in the eighth song of summer:

> Let's spread our net out on the sand
> and lie under the thatched awning.
> Moor the boat, moor the boat!
> Fan off mosquitoes,
> no, flies are worse.
> *Chigukch'ong chigukch'ong ŏsawa.*
> Only one worry, even here,
> traitors might eavesdrop.

The literary sources of the "flies" (green flies or bluebottles) is poem 219 in the *Book of Songs* where the flies that buzz about and settle on the fence stand for slanderers.[24] A victim of slander himself, Yun does not banish grim issues from his rural contemplation. "Traitors" in the original is "Minister Sang," Sang Hongyang (152–80 BC) of the Former Han,[25] probably a metonymy for the poet's political foe. Poetry cannot be divorced from reality: it is involved in history and, as the poet says, we cannot dismiss its political and social engagements.

Judging from textual evidence and rhetorical strategy, some might say that Yun failed to fashion his self-image as a fisherman. Yun is not writing an account of his life in his poetry, however, although his biography and other notices in his *Works* testify to his lifestyle. Educated in the classics and literature, Yun wishes to put his ideals into practice but learns painfully that he is born for other things than factional politics. He then accepts

---

[24] Bernhard Karlgren, *The Book of Odes* (Stockholm: Museum of Far Eastern Antiquities, 1960), p. 172: Waley, *The Book of Songs*, p. 322.

[25] Sima Qian, *Shiji*, 10 vols. (Peking: Zhonghua, 1959) 30:1428–1442, and Nancy Lee Swan, *Han Shu 22: Food and Money in Ancient China* (Princeton: Princeton University Press, 1950), pp. 271–272, 317–321.

the heavenly charge of being a guardian of nature ("Heaven appoints me guardian / of peaceful hills and waters") and declares: "Nothing can match my idle pleasures / among trees and springs" ("Random Thoughts" 5). There is no need to separate fact (self) and fiction (role). Who has ever thought that Yun Sŏndo was a simple fisherman-recluse?[26]

Delighting in the manifold richness and beauty of nature, Yun devoted his life to the truth of feeling. Consider spontaneous expressions of his freedom and joy as a fisherman:

> The Fisherman's Song stirs my fancy;
> I have forgotten all about fishing. (Spring 5)
>
> The heart shouts its peak of joy,
> I have lost my way in the dark. (Spring 9)
>
> Rod on my shoulder,
> I can't still my loud heart. (Summer 1)
>
> Whelmed by my exalted mood,
> I had not known my day was ending. (Summer 6)
>
> I'll angle there, of course, but
> my zestful spirit is enough. (Autumn 4)
>
> In an empty boat, with straw cape and hat,
> I sit and my heart beats fast. (Winter 7)

In all these passages, Yun uses the technical term *hŭng*, signifying a surplus of emotion, and its various combinations. Verging on ecstasy – a sensible ecstasy, for he has not thrown decorum overboard – his subjectivity characterizes his poetry, his sense of himself as individual and center. I have stressed Yun Sŏndo's sense of craft, his vocation, his delight in the exercise of linguistic possibilities to convert experience into art. He sounds at ease with himself. No other *sijo* poet wrote like him, and no other *sijo* poet proves more exhilarating and rewarding. Yun Sŏndo is a poet for all seasons.

Yun Sŏndo was summoned to the capital by King Hyojong in 1652, but there the poet's political enemies defamed and reviled him. After a month's stay at court, Yun retired to his retreat. There he wrote "Mongch'ŏn yo" ("The disappointing journey"; literally: "A dream visit to heaven"; songs 73–75), in which the "Jade Emperor" is King Hyojong himself and the "host of spirits" represents his opponents. In its closing song Yun laments the absence of wise ministers who could "raise up" the "White Jade Tower" by delivering the state from the evils of the day.

---

[26] See Longxi Zhang, *The Tao and the Logos: Literary Hermeneutics, East and West* (Durham: Duke University Press, 1992), pp. 110–129, esp. 116–119.

THE TOPIC OF WITHDRAWAL

Poetry about the virtue of withdrawal from active service continued to be a favorite subject of the literati poet. Kim Kwanguk (1579–1656) declares his independence with the symbol of a "bird newly freed,"[27] probably reminded of the lines, "For long I was a prisoner in a cage / And now I have my freedom back again" (Tao Qian, "Returning to the Farm to Dwell," 1:19–20).[28] Such descriptions of a court riven by factional strife and the endorsement of withdrawal constitute criticism of contemporary affairs.

The song of Sin Hŭm (1566–1628) is built on the idea of sufficiency and enjoyment, not ownership, as the criteria of true possession:

> Don't laugh if my roof beams
>   are long or short, the pillars
> tilted or crooked, my grass hut small.
>   Moonlight that pours on the vines,
>   the encircling hills,
>   are mine, and mine alone.[29]

A "grass hut" is a metonymy for the absence of envy and greed, small but self-sufficient as "a snail shell"; but the vines, the hills, and the moon are the speaker's, won by dint of his sensibility and imagination. Those still attached to a world dominated by chaos and absurdity are unable to win the priceless world of nature. Love of nature, its significance known only by the poet who has renounced the world, is the *sine qua non* of the poetic existence. It is proof of the poet's oneness with nature.

Some can register, as Yi Chŏngbo (1693–1766) does here, their bewilderment at those who are still attached to the treacherous court:

> Return, return, they say,
>   but who has bowed out?
> Every man knows – does he? –
>   That name and fame are floating clouds.
> No one's awakened from the dream,
>   and that perturbs me.[30]

The world of politics and power is the world of "dreams" – criticism of a way of life pursued by those who are slaves to worldly ambition. Ignorant of the superiority of solitude over society, they have not discovered nature's intrinsic meanings. Indeed, they have not discovered their own meaning.

---

[27] *KYS* 3232.
[28] Hightower, *The Poetry of T'ao Ch'ien*, p. 50.   [29] *KYS* 3238.
[30] *KYS* 348; Chin Tonghyŏk, *Kosijo munhak non*, pp. 238–275.

The speaker's world is free and spontaneous, a place where he can explore not only the relation between humankind and nature but especially his artistic purpose. It is there that the poet learns the significance of the transformation of self by harmony with nature and the values of the creative independence of poetry.

> Does dawn light the east window?
> Already larks sing in the sky.
> Where is the boy that tends the ox –
> has he not yet roused himself?
> When will he get his plowing done
> in the long field over the hill?[31]

The poet-farmer in this song by Nam Kuman (1629–1711) expresses concern about his agrarian labor, not about obscurity and poverty. The tone is casual and happy, because the speaker has adapted himself to rural felicity.

CHANGES IN *SIJO*

Those who tried to infuse fresh spirit into the *sijo* include Wi Paekkyu (1727–1798), Kwŏn Sŏp (1671–1759), and Yi Sebo (1832–1895). In contrast to the literati poet who struck the pose of an external spectator when he wrote about his subject, Wi Paekkyu assumed the persona of a farmer to express his intimate feelings and concerns. Wi neglected, however, to cultivate the effects of closure – he omitted the third and fourth segments in the third line – mainly because his songs were intended for singing. Kwŏn Sŏp used simple diction to capture the bitterness of disillusion and fragility of the political order. Yi Sebo, the author of 458 songs, touched in simple diction upon, for example, the discomfort of an exile's life on a lonely island. These poets tried to adapt the language of the middle and lower classes to the purpose of poetic pleasure. Together with a few female entertainers, they attempted to effect changes in the repertory of subjects, themes, and imagery as well as to use colloquial diction and fresh turns of phrase.

The rise of professional singers

Singers of *sijo* before the advent of professional singers were female entertainers or servants skilled in singing. Beginning in the eighteenth century, however, a group of professional singers emerged from the lower middle

---

[31] Rutt, trans., *The Bamboo Grove*, no. 156.

class (clerks, soldiers, policemen, messengers, artisans, bow makers, and the like).[32] As demands on them increased, they needed a repertory – which in turn called for a compilation of collections of *sijo*. These include, for example, *Songs of Green Hills* (1728), *Haedong kayo* (*Songs of Korea*, 1755, 1763),[33] and *Kogŭm kagok* (*Ancient and Modern Songs*). Among some sixty singers known to posterity, only a handful left works of their own – for example, Kim Sŏnggi,[34] Kim Samhyŏn, Chu Ŭisik, Kim Ch'ŏnt'aek, Kim Sujang, Kim Chint'ae, Pak Hyogwan, and An Minyŏng. They wrote both regular *sijo* and *sasŏl sijo*, a variant form that flourished from the eighteenth century onward. Let us examine a few of the regular *sijo* they left behind.

> Standing in your lofty tower,
>   don't laugh at this lowly place.
> In the midst of thunder and storm,
>   would you be surprised to slip?
> We sit on level ground;
>   who needs distinctions?[35]

This song by Kim Sujang (1690–1769) opens with an exhortation to those who laugh at the "lowly place." Those who laugh are now subject to the whims of the wheel of fortune ("thunder and storm") that will catch them unawares. In this respect the poem recalls the Western "mirror" literature, whose theme is the fall of princes and other mighty personages from high places (the "lofty tower"). The speaker does not question the causes of these lofty figures' imminent downfall; it is a commonplace assumption that greedy and ambitious people will be brought low sooner or later. The best course is not to climb too high. The tradition emphasizes the virtue of lowliness, as symbolized in Daoism by water. The rhetorical question in the song's last line again calls attention to the advantages of lowliness, while challenging those who still seek fame and insist on making distinctions. One who has renounced worldly ambition and seeks virtue and wisdom, by contrast, is often compared to the pine or the chrysanthemum. In the poetry of praise, the pine repeatedly symbolizes moral integrity and the nobility of fortitude. Although one view holds that height invites misfortune, the towering pine tree that withstands the ravages of time acquired a moral

---

[32] Cho Tongil, *Hanguk munhak t'ongsa* 3:277–283; Ch'oe Tongwŏn, *Kosijo yŏngu*, pp. 222–287 on professional singers. See Hwang Ch'unggi, *Hanguk yŏhang sijo yŏngu* (Kukhak charyowŏn, 1998), pp. 222–428.

[33] See Hwang Ch'unggi, *Haedong kayo e kwanhan yŏngu* (Kukhak charyowŏn, 1996).

[34] Kwŏn Tuhwan, "Kim Sŏnggi non," in *Hanguk siga yŏngu: Paegyŏng Chŏng Pyŏnguk sŏnsaeng hwangap kinyŏm nonch'ong* (Singu munhwasa, 1983), pp. 272–290.

[35] *KYS* 2454; Chin Tonghyŏk, *Kosijo munhak non*, pp. 294–309; Ch'oe Tongwŏn, *Kosijo yŏngu*, pp. 197–221.

significance early in the tradition. It does not represent pride and aspiration but, on the contrary, an awareness that pride and aspiration are ephemeral. In this song by An Minyŏng (1816–1886), the speaker holds an imaginary dialogue with the chrysanthemum, the flower of the retired gentleman that blooms the latest of all flowers.

> Speak, chrysanthemum, why do you shun
>   the orient breezes of the third moon?
> "I had rather freeze in a cruel rain
>   beside the hedge of dried sticks
> Than humble myself to join the parade:
>   Those flowers of fickle spring."[36]

One of the four noble plants – the others are the plum, bamboo, and orchid – the chrysanthemum has long been attributed such special qualities as integrity, nobility, and longevity. Like the pine, it scorns frost; like the retired gentleman, it is steadfast under adverse conditions. The lines of Tao Qian, "Picking chrysanthemums by the eastern hedge / I catch sight of the distant southern hills" ("Twenty Poems After Drinking Wine" 5:5–6),[37] have been among the most beloved and recited of Chinese poetry. Content to freeze rather than compromise its principles, the speaker says, the chrysanthemum does not join the flowers of fickle spring in their gaudy but transient show.

In their own songs, these singers were intent on transmitting what they regarded as the *sijo* tradition. They could not outdo their precursors. Their works are derivative and literary, evoking moods from an accumulation of recognizable topics and allusions. Infiltrated by echoes from prior texts, they valorized high culture and failed to break new ground. One reason may have been that their patrons were mostly literati families whose taste and concerns they had to accommodate.

Rise of sasŏl sijo

Sijo were seldom considered demanding, and matching experience and form had been considered natural for *sijo* writers for several hundred years. The repetition of conventional subjects, images, and diction, however, began to offer little fresh variety. The style and diction once considered appropriate now seemed dated; variations on a given subject, no matter how novel,

---

[36] *KYS* 313; Chin Tonghyŏk, *Kosijo munhak non*, pp. 310–320.
[37] Hightower, *The Poetry of T'ao Ch'ien*, p. 130.

turned out to be jejune; clearly the *sijo* required deliverance by the non-canonical.[38] Above all, it had to respond to the changing actuality of the times if it was to survive as a popular poetic form for high and low alike. What hastened the rise of *sasŏl sijo* was the eighteenth-century rupture of a system of illusory beliefs that were simply a political expedient to perpetuate old social formations and power structures. The contradictions that constituted the social order began to be exposed, and the myth of order and harmony in the form of the Five Relations appeared to be no more than a hollow rhetoric.

The eighteenth century's upward and downward movements in class structure and economic expansion affected all classes and are reflected particularly in the *sasŏl sijo*. Owing to the monopoly of political power by a small number of ruling houses, an increasing number of those excluded from political participation withdrew to the countryside and joined the local gentry. With the distinction between legitimate and illegitimate lines of descent breaking down, men from illegitimate lineages ("middle people"), who had earlier been restricted to posts as technical specialists, interpreters, and government clerks, began to be employed as editor-compilers. The century also witnessed a surge of economic growth as improvements in agricultural technology reduced the amount of labor needed and made large-scale farming common. The commercial production of specialized crops and handicrafts, the development of wholesale commerce, the flourishing of markets in the capital and over a thousand locations throughout the country, the widening use of metal currency – all account for the emergence of landed farmers and wholesale merchants who made fortunes through their control of trade. On the intellectual front, the scholars of practical learning (some of whom were unemployed literati and some from the middle people) conducted research into the social and natural sciences, and made proposals on institutional reforms and land systems as well as on the central, local, and penal administration. As these forces hastened changes in the structure of Chosŏn society, beneath the surface of ruling society a de facto class structure based on economic wealth began to emerge.

Typical authors and popularizers of *sasŏl sijo* came from the middle people. Its audience came from social groups situated between the ruling literati and the commoners, including rich farmers, merchants, moneylenders, interpreters (who amassed wealth from private trade with China), local civil

---

[38] Alastair Fowler, *Kinds of Literature: An Introduction to the Theory of Genres and Modes* (Cambridge, Mass.: Harvard University Press, 1982), p. 158. Russian Formalists held the same view; see René Wellek, *The Attack on Literature and Other Essays* (Chapel Hill: University of North Carolina Press, 1982), p. 131.

functionaries, and clerks. They frequented urban centers of amusement, and the realistic and comic *sasŏl sijo* were sung for amusement on festive occasions. It is no wonder that the eighteenth century was the most productive era for this kind of *sijo*: some 300 examples from this period survive.[39]

Sasŏl sijo is a form in which more than two metric segments in each line, except for the first in the third line, are added. In effect, a three-line song has become a three-stanza song. We do not know the originator of the *sasŏl sijo*, but judging from some 540 extant pieces, mostly by anonymous writers (meaning the common people), the form enjoyed popularity. The form is also called *chang sijo* (long *sijo*); the term *sasŏl* meant "close-stitched" or "closely set."[40] Chŏng Ch'ŏl's "Changjinju sa" ("A Time to Drink") is often cited as a precursor because its opening two lines and final line have the following metrical arrangement:

First line: 2   4/   3   4
Second line: 3   3/   4   4
                        . . .
                        . . .
Last line: 3   4   3/   2   2/   4   3

Chŏng's song is a *kasa*, but the second and last lines can also be considered expanded in a way similar to the *sasŏl sijo*'s development.

In addition to the external structure, the writers introduced innovations in topic, change of scale, voice, diction, point of view, and rhetorical patterns. One notices an increase in the topics of love: disloyalty in love, symptoms of love-sickness, sadness of reminiscence, sleepless longing, and carnal love. (All the same, poems of praise and nature continued to be written even in this new form.)[41] A typical *sasŏl sijo* draws from colloquial speech, including taboo words and puns. A marked feature is enumeration – a list of different windows and hinges in the heart, for example, or a catalogue of a woman's personal ornaments, or a list of different merchant boats from various provinces arriving at the Cho River. One speaker lists as ingredients of a good life an automatic iron kettle, a horse, a cow, and a concubine who weaves. Another list, written in a parody of high style, cites white wine, yellow chicken, a beautiful woman, a noble horse, and a gold cup as essential for a leisurely life. Often these examples are cited to

---

[39]   Ko Misuk, *18-segi esŏ 20-segich'o Hanguk sigasa ŭi kudo* (Somyŏng, 1998), pp. 105–201, 229–250.
[40]   Cho Tongil, *Hanguk munhak t'ongsa* 3:296.
[41]   Ch'oe Tongwŏn, *Kosijo yŏngu*, pp. 151–194; Sŏ Wŏnsŏp, "*Sasŏl sijo* ŭi chuje yŏngu," in *Kasa munhak yŏngu*, pp. 212–259; Pak Nojun, "*Sasŏl sijo* e nat'anan erotisijŭm," in *Sijo munhak yŏngu* (Chŏngŭmsa, 1980), pp. 260–282.

illustrate the hedonistic ethos of *sasŏl sijo*. A desire for a happy mundane life, however, does not necessarily include a willingness to increase production, improve living conditions, or adapt oneself to rapidly changing social circumstances. In this materialist version of the anonymous writers' life, even love can be exchanged for a large house, slaves, paddies, and furniture. The items and objects listed may appear to be in excess of what is required for the occasion, but they convey the author's insatiable appetite for the material world. Indeed, *sasŏl sijo* represents a skillful use of affective and suasive tropes for the purpose of evoking and charging the audience's emotions.

Sasŏl sijo is known as well for its presentation of the texture of ordinary life – especially the explicit presentation of sex, often with exaggeration, grotesquerie, and caricature: faithless wife, lecherous monk, varied experiences of erotic speakers, man and woman, old and young. For example: an old man describes the ecstasy of his first night with a woman; a woman describes her lover the night before as the best she has ever had; another woman expresses her resolve to go and meet her beloved no matter what the obstacles on her way; an old woman dyes her hair hoping to seduce a young man, but on her way to a rendezvous a storm washes her dye away; a woman sees a handsome young man walking by the riverside and hopes to entice him, but if he cannot be hers she hopes that at least he will become her friend's lover, implying that she would simply wait for an opportunity to be near him.

Another group is written from a satiric stance. When a daughter-in-law tells her mother-in-law that she broke a brass rice serving spoon while filling the bowl for her lover, the mother-in-law consoles her by saying that she herself had similar experiences in her youth. Another female speaker lists her sexual adventures with a variety of itinerant vendors and adds, "With this face I can even have a vendor of bamboo strainers!" The farcical portrayal of loose morality in the first example and the speaker's self-absorption in the second draw the reader's laughter. In these and similar examples, the speakers cast a satirical glance at the corrupt, foolish, and lascivious in order to capture various aspects of lowly life.[42] Other *sasŏl sijo* are comic variations on the classic theme of the lovelorn speaker's wish for a metamorphosis to achieve a union: a male speaker wishes to become a piece of his beloved's dress; the ghost of a spinster wishes to become the loincloth of an old monk with missing teeth so that she can feel the warmth of his flesh; a woman

---

[42] Kim Hŭnggyu, "*Sasŏl sijo* ŭi sichŏk sisŏn yuhyŏng kwa kŭ pyŏnmo," *Hanguk hakpo* 68 (1992): 2–30. Kim Hŭnggyu, ed., *Sasŏl Sijo*, Hanguk kojŏn munhak chŏnjip 2 (Koryŏ taehakkyo Minjok munhwa yŏnguso, 1993) contains 429 anonymous examples.

longs for the type of man who "rides on a white horse with a golden saddle" –
a cliché in earlier *kasa* and prose fiction – and frequents a tavern with a
Manchu girl (*hohŭi*), or one who comes only to spend a night but must
leave at dawn.

A favorite rhetorical tactic is to begin the song with a series of similes
and mention the real subject of comparison only at the end. The sorrow of
parting ("To what can I compare my heart / When I parted from him two
days ago?"), for example, is compared to the desperation of a hen pheasant
chased by a hawk on a mountainside without bush or boulder to hide
behind or to a boatman on a battered ship, with a cargo of a thousand bags
of grain, attacked by pirates, in the midst of a sea where there are "white
foamy waves billowing all around."[43] Enumeration, sometimes verging on
mock-*kyŏnggi-ch'e* effusion, gives a sense of plenitude: the sense that the
earth is full of wonders, delights, and torments. Asking his dog ("spotted
with a checkerboard pattern") not to follow him to a fishing beach, the
speaker lists:

> A large-eyed shad fish,
> a long-waisted scabbard fish,
> a winding snake fish,
> a light catfish,
> a thin flatfish,
> a hunchbacked lobster,
> tiny fertile shrimps,
> and cowardly squid lost in fright –
> they all run away mistaking you for a net.[44]

The technique is used to good effect in the following love plaint, where the
speaker wishes to barter the objects a woman prizes for a night of union
"worth thousands of gold pieces":

> Shall I give you money?
> Shall I give you silver?
> A Chinese silk skirt,
> a Korean ritual dress,
> gauze petticoats,
> white satin belt,
> a cloudy wig from the north,
> a jade hairpin,
> a bamboo hairpin,
> a silk knife in an inlaid case,
> a golden knife in an amber case,

[43] *KYS* 440.   [44] *KYS* 1106.

a coral brooch from the far south,
a gold ring set with a blue bell
shaped like a heavenly peach,
sandals with yellow pearl strings,
embroidered hemp sandals?
For a night worth thousands of gold pieces,
give me one chance at your dimples,
lovely and fresh as a flower.
Grant me only one night,
priceless as a swift steed![45]

Next is a definition of love that is utterly characteristic of *sasŏl sijo* in its imagery and diction. What concerns the speaker is the endlessness of love, which is likened to the meshes of a net and the vines of melons, cucumbers, and watermelons:

Love, love,
        strung like meshes of a net
        that covers the wide sea –
        Like the vines of melons,
        of cucumbers and watermelons,
        tangled and strung together,
        climbing and spreading
        in Wangsimni and Tapsimni –
So is his love for me,
I don't know where it ends.[46]

Yet another device is to delay offering the main argument – in the following poem an entreaty to the beloved not to succumb to slander – until one has presented a fantastic tale that consequently serves as an analogy:

Middle- and small-sized needles
        dropped in the middle of the sea.
They say with a foot-long pole
        a dozen boatmen hooked the eye of every needle.
Love, my love,
        don't swallow everything you hear
        when they tell you a hundred tales.[47]

The few examples cited here indicate that the anonymous poets of *sasŏl sijo* not only wrote differently but brought a new dimension to the form.

---

[45] *KYS* 1528.   [46] *KYS* 1398.

[47] *KYS* 834. Cho Kyuik considers *sijo* as song texts based on specific tunes and modes and proposes that the musical tune "Manhoengch'ŏng," used for a group of *sijo* dealing with love between the sexes and riotous fun, should be studied from a fresh perspective. See *Kagok ch'angsa ŭi kungmunhakchŏk ponjil* (Chimmundang, 1994) and *Uriŭi yennorae munhak: Manhoengch'ŏng yu* (Pagijŏng, 1996).

Written in a plain and colloquial diction, with images drawn from daily life, their songs exude worldliness and the capacity for laughter. The sound, color, and feel of words are robust and original, and these are the qualities we associate with the form at its most characteristic. There is no moralistic literati's designs on getting the audience to change their lives: these poets only declare that the experiences they sing are what every feeling person is capable of. They celebrate freedom to live and love and freedom to express that love. Indeed, they affirm the importance of the capacity to thrive, play, and celebrate human values. Passion, so long evaded as a topic by the literati poets, was finally recognized as a legitimate subject of poetry. By writing and performing their songs, these anonymous poets of the eighteenth and early nineteenth centuries celebrated the place of poetry in society and culture.

CHAPTER 11

Late Chosŏn kasa

Peter H. Lee

Kasa poetry of the late Chosŏn period is not only prolific but more varied in subject matter than the early Chosŏn *kasa*. In addition to poems about the Japanese invasions of 1592–1598 and reclusion, there are ones on a diversity of topics: exile; pleasure trips; missions undertaken by envoys to China and Japan; cities such as Seoul; the farmer's works and days; and such unconventional subjects as tobacco[1] and the foibles of foolish men and women.

PAK ILLO

Pak Illo, the author of seven *kasa*, is a major writer in the form.[2] Based on his own experience in late 1598, the "T'aep'yŏng sa" ("Song of Peace") was written at the time of Japanese withdrawal from Korea to encourage the soldiers under his command by predicting the advent of a peaceful era. The poem narrates the sudden onslaught of the Japanese army and the escape of the king, the recapture of P'yŏngyang by the Ming army and ensuing negotiations between China and Japan, another battle, and a return to the barracks and celebration of victory. Then follows a statement of the poet's resolve to brighten the Five Relations and a prayer to heaven that summarizes his recurrent concerns:

> So we pray that you bless our dynasty,
> that the royal house be endless;
> that the sun and moon of the Three Dynasties
> shine on the golden age of Yao and Shun;
> that there be no more war
> for myriad years;

---

[1] For the text of "Namch'o ka" by Pak Sahyŏng (1635–1706), see Kugŏ kungmurhakhoe, ed. *Wŏnmun kasa sŏn* (Taejegak, 1979), pp. 436–439.
[2] I have used Yi Sangbo, *Kaego Pak Nogye yŏngu*. The texts are in Pak Illo, *Nogye sŏnsaeng chip* (*YMC* 3) 3:1a–23a.

that people till the field and dig wells
and sing the praises of peace;
that we always have a holy king above us;
and that he and we share the joy of peace.

The year 1605 brought further signs of Japanese movement off the south-eastern coast, and Pak was named a shipmaster in Pusan. On this occasion he composed "Sŏnsang t'an" ("Lament on the Water"). After an introduction, the poem discusses the origin of ships. The speaker blames the Yellow Emperor for having invented the ship and the First Emperor of the Qin for having dispatched Xu Shi, or Xu Fu, with a company of boys and girls to remote islands to obtain pills or herbs of immortality. He argues that descendants of those boys and girls settled on Japanese islands and became ancestors of the Japanese people. Then, however, the poet reconsiders and admits that, without a ship or boat, a recluse like Zhang Han (c. 258–319) could not have indulged in his noble pursuits south of the river and a fisherman could not "enjoy his life free as duckweed, / a life better than that of three dukes, / among matchless hills and waters." He then notes the difference between such boats and his own ship:

> In olden days
> wine tables crowded ships:
> today,
> only large swords and long spears.
> A ship it is,
> but not as ships once were.

He then vows to repulse the enemy and hopes for their imminent surrender, for only then can he

> sing in a fishing boat
> in autumn moon and spring breeze,
> and laying our heads on high pillows,
> we'll see once more the happy era
> when all the waters sing in unison.

When, in 1611, Yi Tŏkhyŏng (1561–1613) retired to Dragon Ford to spend his last years, Pak Illo used to visit him. Pak had known Yi since 1601 when the latter arrived in Yŏngch'ŏn as inspector of provincial administration. The "Saje kok" ("Song of Sedge Bank") describes scenic spots at Sedge Bank and the idle life and elegant pleasures that Yi enjoyed there. The speaker discovers the beauty of nature alone without a host. Only the enlightened can exclaim that he is "the only host / among these hills and streams / That [he] won't exchange for the titles of three dukes" – the first three state counselors in the Chosŏn government. His cattle are stags and hinds; his companions are monkeys and cranes. His joys surpass those of Zeng Xi, Zhang Han, and Su Shi. It appears that Pak incorporated details from his own biography when he mentions his own mother: "[I will] invite my mother, thus fulfilling / a son's duty till the last." In fact, the poem ends with his determination to serve his ailing mother:

> I'll serve her and age with her
> with the cleansed ears of Xu You,
> with the dresses of Laolaizi,
> until the pines have turned to green iron,
> the pines thick in the stream out front.

Asked by Yi Tŏkhyŏng about his life in the mountains, Pak wrote his most famous *kasa*: "Nuhang sa" ("In Praise of Poverty"). The title itself, literally "Song of the Mean Lane," was inspired by a passage in the *Analects* (6:9) where the master praises his disciple Yan Hui: "Incomparable indeed was Hui! A handful of rice to eat, a gourdful of water to drink, living on a mean street."[3] The poem begins with an admission of the speaker's impracticality and clumsiness (cooking gruel with wet straws), but the tone is self-satirizing in view of a passage in the *Laozi* 45: "The greatest skill is like clumsiness." Strategically placed at the center of the poem is a lament on his need for a farmhand, as well as an ox, without which there can be no plowing. Then comes a wry, humorous episode in which he makes futile efforts to borrow an ox from a rich farmer who was bribed by a peasant with wine. After a sleepless night and a disappointing morning, the speaker resolves to forgo plowing and instead contemplates the green bamboo in the winding waters of the Qi, an allusion to poem 55 in the *Book of Songs*. Then he invokes "the flowery reeds" and "the unsold breeze and unsold moon," intensely polemical symbols, as we shall soon see. Then comes another quotation from the *Analects* (14:11), "To be poor and not resent it is far harder than to be rich yet not presumptuous,"[4] followed by a panegyric to the modest life. The last lines emphasize the fact that poverty cannot bend the noble mind. His only concern is how to delight in the pursuit of the Confucian Way:

> A handful of rice and gourdful of water
> are enough for me.
> To be well fed and well clad
> is not my dream.
> In this world, peaceful and quiet,

[3] Waley, *Analects*, p. 117.   [4] Ibid., p. 182.

let us be loyal and filial,
harmonious with brothers, faithful to friends.
Such a life allows no reproof.
As for other matters,
let them come as they will.

Throughout his poetry Pak Illo emphasizes by constant reference to the classics the importance of the acquisition of knowledge in the Confucian tradition. The overall pattern therefore indicates the interplay of the formal and the informal, the sophisticated and the rustic, the learned and the personal, the *utile* and *dulce*, as the speaker seeks to adopt moderation in life and art. Thus with humor, irony, anecdote, conversations, and a bit of self-satire, Pak has created a convincing picture of a poor but noble poet–farmer's life.

Pak's "Tongnaktang" ("Hall of Solitary Bliss") was written on the occasion of his poetic pilgrimage to the Hall of Solitary Bliss on Mount Purple Jade in Kyŏngju where the remains of Yi Ŏnjŏk (1491–1553) are preserved and Pak paid tribute to the master's memory. Yi Ŏnjŏk passed the civil service examination in 1514 and served as fourth inspector and second censor before he suffered in the 1530 political purge and withdrew to Mount Purple Jade to study Neo-Confucian philosophy. In 1537 he was recalled by royal order and filled the following posts: rector of the national academy; inspector-general; minister of personnel, rites, and punishments and magistrate of Seoul; first adviser in the Office of Special Advisers; and fourth state counselor (1545). The "Hall of Solitary Bliss," however, does not dwell on his political success but on his exemplary virtues. The poet's task is to exalt and perpetuate virtue. Describing the ideal Confucian statesman and philosopher, Pak writes:

He revered the sages of the past
and wrote poems.
In peaceful nature he was so immersed
that he felt at home in all situations.
. . .
He contemplated, sought truth,
and cultivated learning and virtue.

Pak goes on to say that, through study and self-cultivation, he preserved tradition and "opened a bright new path":

His thousand words and myriad sayings
are all wisdoms, each revealing
a long tradition and ways of thought

as bright as the sun and moon –
light
illuminating the dark.

As a statesman he was equal to Houji or Lord Millet, ancestor of the Zhou dynasty, and Jie, a wise minister under the legendary emperor Shun. Caught in a political purge of 1547, however, he was sent into exile to the north where, like the Grand Tutor Jia Yi (201–168 BC) in Changsha,[5] he spent seven years in cold Kanggye. There he transformed the rigors of the political winter into the bliss of a virtuous spring.

The poem utilizes such metaphors of natural harmony as graceful mountain peaks, a winding stream, straight bamboo, a caressing wind, and a dense pine grove and implies that these were spared by heaven and treasured by earth so that their riches could be handed down to their true "owner." The emphasis is on the beauty, purity, and spontaneity of nature, symbolic of the subject's harmonious, enlightened state of mind. The hall itself is a center of moral cultivation; what is praised is a way of life in the ideal setting, a mode of existence vital to the preservation of the enduring norms of the lettered class. Friends there are said to include such emblematic animals as hawks and fishes. These classical images from poem 239 in the *Book of Songs*[6] imply the self-contentedness of even birds and fish – as first, as in the original context, a sign of the extent of moral transformation effected by an ideal ruler (though here fish do not jump into the fishermen's nets in their eagerness to serve the owner)[7] and, second, as emblems of the workings of the Confucian Way seen clearly in heaven and on earth.

Yi's retreat surpasses in beauty and purity the Garden of Solitary Bliss of Sima Guang (1019–1086), Censer Peak on Mount Lu celebrated by Li Bo, the Tiandai Mountains in Zhejiang, or even Peach Blossom Spring, the Chinese Arcadia. When its master is absent, the hall is like an empty hill without a phoenix, yet his fragrance lingers on, for the speaker sees him "in the soup and on the walls."[8] In moral and spiritual stature Yi Ŏnjŏk is compared to Mount Tai or the polestar, supreme emblems of Confucian moral rhetoric. Such hyperbolic description and metonymic representation create the *locus amoenus*: an ideal microcosm that mirrors the ideal state built on the Confucian political–moral philosophy. On another

---

[5] Burton Watson, *Records of the Grand Historian of China. Translated from the "Shih chi" of Ssu-ma Ch'ien*, 2 vols. New York: Columbia University Press, 1961) 1:508–516.
[6] Waley, *The Book of Songs*, p. 213.
[7] Ben Jonson, "To Penshurst," lines 32–33; Thomas Carew, "To Sexham," lines 27–28.
[8] Refers to a tradition that Shun longed for Yao for three years after his death and saw his image on the walls whenever he sat and in the soup whenever he ate.

level, however – since in Confucianism the disrupter of social and moral harmony is humanity itself – the poet has subtly introduced a satirical bite. That is, the images of perfection and hyperbolic praise indirectly deride those ignorant of the pattern of emergence and withdrawal, the art of biding time, and cultivation of the self. A victim of political machination and senseless bloodshed that upset the moral and cosmic harmony, Yi's dream of creating another golden age was shattered and the country became a wasteland. Yet even in exile he "cultivated virtue – the forthright Way" – and history eventually vindicated his name, private academies enshrined him, and he was worshipped in the Confucian Temple, the highest honor accorded a scholar-statesman.

Virtue therefore serves as a bulwark against mutability. The man who dwells in the Hall of Solitary Bliss has conquered time by his paradigmatic acts, and his enduring virtues are bright as the sun and moon and eternal as the "cool wind that blows / over the hall" itself.

> Heaven so high and earth so rich,
> they, too, will dissolve into dust.
> None is eternal but the cool wind that blows
> through the Hall of Solitary Bliss.

"Only the perennial fragrance of my teacher / abides," the poet declares. Virtue, not fame, conquers death. Yi Ŏnjŏk thus becomes an ideal. Side by side the poet sets down the perennial opposing norms of conduct: Confucian and Daoist, world and self, man and nature. The poet, however, affirms those values of history and culture that insist on the correspondence between society and nature. Subtly underlying the poem is the poet's conviction that the return of political–moral harmony depends upon the return of harmony between humankind and nature. The restoration of civil order calls for moral regeneration and such a dream, combining the active and the contemplative, finds expression in the country-house poems. As one's dwelling expresses one's virtue, so should a dynasty. The implication is that only a ruler's bestowal of virtue on people and country can transform chaos into order and reaffirm the values of civilization. The ideal landscape, then, provides a setting in which to contemplate the enduring norms of history and culture.

The "Yŏngnam ka" ("Song of the Southeast," 1635), another praise poem, was written when Yi Kŭnwŏn, governor of the southeast, was about to resign his position in 1635. Moved by his good administration, the people asked him to remain in office. As a model public servant, Yi took "seventy districts as a family":

And with a mother or father's heart,
looking upon motherless people
as infants,
he bestowed love
sweet as raindrops over the grain crops
in time of drought,
fresh as water in a pool
to a fish in a dry rut.

Yi ruled not by laws and decrees but by his personal example: he encouraged agriculture and sericultural production, military preparedness, and education. ("Teaching human relations at school / was the basis of his rule / that serves the Way of Master Kong.") County magistrates emulated his pattern, thus creating an ideal agricultural community in which, as in the days of the sage–emperor Shun, there was no longer litigation. The poem concludes with the speaker's suggestion for hero worship:

Let's buy white silk
and bright colors,
paint his portrait in full figure,
and hang it on the walls
of every house in the southeast,
and when his face flashes through our mind,
we'll see our beloved minister.

Pak wrote his last *kasa*, "Nogye ka" ("Song of the Reedy Stream"), in the spring of 1636, seven years before his death. Reedy Stream is a valley near Taehyŏn village where the poet built himself a grass roof, "leaning on a huge rock" and "fronting the stream with the hills behind." Birds and beasts are his cattle, and he fishes under the moon or plows the "fields among the clouds." His one worry is how to provide for his children:

I can divide among my children
endless hills and waters and idle fields.
But I fear it's hard to allot
a bright moon and a clear breeze.
I'd rather choose him who serves my will,
be he gifted or not,
and leave him all
in a certificate drawn by Li Bo and Tao Qian.
You say my word
is ignorant of the world;
but what else have I
for my children but these?

Even when he tries to fish, he cannot bring himself to "drop a line to cheat" the fishes who know him, although later he does indulge in an imaginary feast of viands and dainties (luscious bracken, scented angelica, pork, venison, fresh-minced perch, *nul* fish, and pheasants). He believes he owes his leisurely lifestyle to royal favor and ends the poem with a prayer:

> May my holy king enjoy long life
> until every hill is made low, and every sea runs dry.
> In the bright, contented world,
> let the sun and moon shine on the peaceful reign,
> let swords be sheathed
> for a thousand and myriad years,
> that people might sing of the blessings of peace
> when they work the fields or dig wells,
> that this body among hills and waters
> might like the winds and moon never age.

Poetry that sings of the happiness of rural retirement and celebrates a discovery of the self and the beauty of nature during the Chosŏn dynasty was also, of course, moral and social criticism. The poet's obsession with the perplexing and insecure world of politics – and fall from power – compelled him to create a counterideology, a "romantic" mythology of a pure countryside, a maternal and beneficent landscape, thus transforming a poetry of reclusion into a poetry of protest. In such poetry, perhaps the most ideological adjective is the recurring word "priceless" (*kabŏpta*). It has two meanings: one is not worth putting a price on, having no value, hence not yet sold; the other having a value beyond all price – as in the following lines from Pak Illo's poems: "the unsold breeze and unsold moon, / they too naturally belong to me"; or "natural [are] the unsold gulls and herons."[9] Corrupt courtiers, for all their power and wealth, could never buy, sell, or become part of the priceless nature that can be won only by the poet's sensibility and imagination. They have rank and riches, but only the poet can find joy in nature. This love of priceless nature, whose significance is comprehended only by the poet who has renounced the world, was the *sine qua non* of the poetic existence.

The state of mind of the alienated literatus who oscillates between nature and society and is desperately in need of a sense of equilibrium is well portrayed in the "Moktong mundap ka" ("Song of the Cowherd") by Im Yuhu (1601–1673). In this poem cast as a dialogue, the literatus speaker addresses a cowherd:

---

[9] From "Song of the Sedge Bank" and "Song of the Reedy Stream" respectively.

Cowherd on the banks
of green willows and fragrant grasses,
do you or don't you know
man's glory and shame?

The speaker comments that a man's life is like a dewdrop on a grassblade
and that he must, like the ancient sages and heroes, aspire to leave a name
behind and never neglect to strive for greatness. The cowherd retorts: "Who
on earth are you / to worry about the affairs of others?" He implies that the
disgruntled speaker is trying to put aside his own concerns and meddle in
others' business. Life, the cowherd continues, is like herding cattle – and
the cow resting under a willow tree is in good circumstances. He even cites
examples of ancients who could not remain constant through adversity.
Name and fame are no concern of his, the cowherd declares; it is best for
him to return to his apricot village to lead an obscure but happy life.[10]

KASA BY EXILES

A mounting political polarity from the late seventeenth century onward
sent many victims of factional struggles into exile. Most were political
offenders, but some were accused of embezzlement of public funds. The
most common places of exile were in Chŏlla province, especially remote
islands off the southern coast, followed by, in descending order of frequency,
Kyŏngsang, Hamgyŏng, P'yŏngan, Ch'ungch'ŏng, Kyŏnggi, Hwanghae,
and Kangwŏn. A typical *kasa* by an exile includes many of the following
motifs: the sorrow of exile and recollection of the past; the causes of exile;
itineraries with a brief description of places, often with allusions to Chinese
places where men of letters had been banished; a description of the place of
exile; the host family's dwelling, diet, and hardships; repentance, longing
for home, and a prayer for a quick recall.[11]

   Both the "Pyŏl samiin kok" ("Separate Hymn of Constancy") by Kim
Ch'unt'aek (1670–1717) and the "Sok samiin kok" ("Continued Hymn of
Constancy") by Yi Chinyu (1669–1730) were inspired by the similarly titled
poems of Chŏng Ch'ŏl. Kim's poem, written about 1708 during his four-
year exile on Cheju Island, is indebted in diction and structure to Chŏng
Ch'ŏl's "Continued Hymn of Constancy," especially its beginning and end.
Kim's "Lady, who goes there, / no more of your sad story" recalls Chŏng's

---

[10] Kim Tonguk, *Hanguk kayo ŭi yŏngu sok*, pp. 281–296; Yi Sangbo, *Hanguk kosiga ŭi yŏngu*,
    pp. 220–267.
[11] Ch'oe Kanghyŏn, *Hanguk kihaeng munhak yŏngu* (Ilchisa, 1982), pp. 70–88.

"Lady, who goes there, / it seems I've seen you before." The speaker wishes for eleven metamorphoses so that she can be near her beloved lord (King Yŏngjo) and concludes:

> What good is it to become
> A cloud or wind?
> Pour a cupful of wine
> And forget your grief.[12]

Yi Chinyu's poem, written about 1725–1727 on Ch'uja Island, is the longest in the group and takes the form of a travel account ending with a fervent hope for prompt forgiveness. Implicated in a succession struggle, Yi was arrested on his return as a vice-envoy from Peking, where he had gone to announce the death of King Kyŏngjong in 1724. Yi was banished first to Naju, then to Ch'uja Island. The poem asserts that when his boat encountered a storm, Yi still thought of the king, recited the classics and histories to console himself, and recalled such Chinese worthies as Qu Yuan and Li Bo. Then comes the description of his "snail shell of a hut," its window unpapered, and infested with vermin (he mentions flies, mosquitoes, gnats, grubs, gadflies, snakes, and centipedes).[13]

For a realistic and moving account, however, of the hardships of exile, tinged with self-mockery and humor, An Chohwan's (fl. 1777–1800) *Manŏn sa* (*An Exile's Life*; literally "Song of Ten Thousand Words") is unsurpassed. Instead of maintaining dignity with a veneer of Confucian ideology, An's poem had a direct appeal even to the court ladies who circulated the manuscript and helped him to be recalled by the king himself. The first problem that an exile encounters is to find a host family willing to put him up. Often, as in An's case, he needed help from the local administration:

> Where will I lodge?
> Whose house shall I seek?
> Tears blind my eyes,
> and I stumble with every step.
> I go to one house for shelter,
> they say they're hard up.
> I go to the next,
> the master makes some excuses.
> Who would like to put up
> an exile as his guest?
> Only because of court pressure,
> they agree to take me in.

---

[12] Sŏ Wŏnsŏp, *Kasa munhak yŏngu*, pp. 185–203.   [13] Ibid., pp. 204–246.

They dare not protest to an official,
but pour out their chagrins to me.
. . .
With only a piece of mat,
I settle down under the
chilly, damp, leaky eaves.
Vermin of all sorts swarm about,
snakes a foot long, green centipedes a span long.
they ring around me –
how terrible, how disgusting!

His next concern is his diet and the dirty clothing he cannot clean, probably
because he has never washed his own clothes before:

After a sleepless night in tears,
I get cooked barley and thin soy sauce.
I push them aside after a spoonful.
Even that is scarce sometimes,
empty stomach on long summer days.
What I call my clothes
only draw a long sigh.
Under a burning sun and sultry air,
my unwashed quilted trousers
wring with sweat and grime –
a straw mat stuffing a chimney!
I wouldn't mind heat or filth,
but what about its stink?

Prodded by the host to contribute to his livelihood, An tries futilely to
catch fish or gather firewood and is finally compelled to go out begging:

I can't fish, being a bad sailor,
Nor am I strong enough to cut trees.
I never wove mats and sandals,
And have nothing to do but go begging.
. . .
Foolish children, big young wives,
snap their fingers at me.
"Here comes a banished fellow!"
Unhappily, shame comes first,
so how can I ask for food?
I bow to a male slave,
use terms of respect to a servant,
and mumble as if talking to myself,
just like a mendicant monk.
One takes the hint and scoops out

a bushel of barley –
"Take it, your lot is bitter.
Exiles often come around."
When I receive it face to face,
I can't help thanking him.
Now that somehow I've got it,
how can I carry it without a slave?

Upon returning to his lodging, he is insulted by the host for behavior
unbecoming a gentleman:

He sneers, laughs in my face:
"What is a gentleman for?
You've gone begging.
How vain to be a noble!
You've a load on your back:
What a disgrace for a plutocrat like you,
you've earned a big supper."

In vain he tries to be productive but cannot make straw sandals without
getting his palms blistered and swollen. He then tries to kill himself by
drowning and starvation:

I'd rather die willingly
to forget my agony.
Slumped in a sandpit,
grieving the whole day,
I try to drown myself
more than once or twice.
I lock myself in,
giving up all lingering regrets,
resolved to perish of hunger.

At the approach of winter, he is at last allowed to come into a room. He
finds, however, that life inside the hut is no better than outdoors:

I obtain a corner in the room,
its walls plastered, but not papered.
Every wall is gaping,
every crack full of insects.
I won't be afraid
of snakes and centipedes.
The host picks up larger ones,
and throws the small ones at me.
I weave a bamboo door

and cover it with an old mat . . .
I rip open a straw sack –
it becomes a satin mattress;
I pull a dog skin over my face –
it becomes a dark red coverlet . . .
Tears that soak my pillow
turn into monuments of ice.

An Chohwan ends the poem with a sophisticated entreaty:

One does not reuse
the calendar which is a year old.
The royal displeasure may be lifted
following a good night's sleep.
Such are the affairs of the world,
my offense a matter of the past.
Please cleanse away my sins
and recall me to your side,
so that our old broken ties
will be bound again, my lord![14]

While the 33-year-old An Chohwan repents his misdeed and prays for a pardon so that he can serve King Chŏngjo and again discharge his filial duties to his parents, Kim Chinhyŏng (1801–1865), exiled in 1854 at the age of 53 to Myŏngch'ŏn in Hamgyŏng, tells not of his hardships but of his romance and pleasant time spent with a female entertainer. Partly because of his family connections and partly because of the fact that local officials in the northeast were mostly military men who wanted to curry favor with a court official like Kim for their future advancement, he was received well by them. Indeed, he was allowed to live in a comfortable house and make an excursion to Mount Ch'ilbo with two female entertainers, Maehong ("Pink Plum") and Kunsanwŏl ("Mountain Moon"). Kim tells of an affair with Kunsanwŏl and, when released, he traveled with her to Wŏnsan where, to her great disappointment, he sent her away. At Anbyŏn he is provided with yet another female entertainer, Pongsŏn, who dressed in male attire and accompanied him to Ch'ŏllyŏng. Thus he ends his "Pukch'ŏn ka" ("Song of a Northern Exile"): "After you [women readers] have read my song, / Be reborn as men in your afterlife / And repeat my wonderful experience!"[15]

---

[14] For the text of quoted passages see Kim Sŏngbae et al., eds., *Chuhae kasa munhak chŏnjip* (Chŏngyŏnsa, 1961), pp. 398, 399, 400, 402–403, 405–407, and 415. See Yu Yŏnsŏk, "An Chowŏn (hwan) ŭi yubae kasa yŏngu," in *Hanguk kihaeng munhak chakp'um yŏngu*, ed. Ch'oe Kanghyŏn (Kukhak charyowŏn, 1996), pp. 515–557.

[15] Kim Sŏngbae et al., eds., *Chuhae kasa munhak chŏnjip*, p. 249.

TRAVEL *KASA*

Travel *kasa* include poems written about famous mountains, lakes, and the like – for example, the eight scenic places in the Diamond Mountains; trips to China and Japan by members of diplomatic missions; and the suffering endured by victims of shipwrecks as they drifted across the sea. Among twenty-five known travel *kasa*, twelve deal with the Diamond Mountains. The first and most famous example is "The Wanderings" (1580) by Chŏng Ch'ŏl. Chŏng's itinerary was: P'yŏnggu Station; Hoeyang; Flower River (Hwach'ŏn); Hundred River Canyon (Paekch'ŏndong); Myriad Falls Grotto (Manp'ok-tong); True Rest Terrace (Chinhyŏltae); Open Mind Terrace (Kaesimdae); All Fragrance Castle (Chunghyangsŏng); Vairocana Peak (Pirobong); Fiery Dragon Pool (Hwaryong-dong); Buddha's Head Terrace (Pulchŏngdae); Twelve Cascade (Sibi p'okp'o); Mountain Glare Tower (Sanyŏngnu); Clustered Rock Arbor (Ch'ongsŏkchŏng); Three-Days Cove (Samilp'o); Ŭisang Terrace (Ŭisangdae); Mirror Cove (Kyŏngp'o); River Gate Bridge (Kangmungyo); West Bamboo Tower (Chuksŏru); and Sea Viewing Arbor (Mangyang-jŏng). Later examples of the genre trace more or less the same places but could not surpass their precursor in diction, scale, and structure. Poems on the northeast include the "Ch'ulsae kok" ("Song of Going out the Pass," c. 1617) by Cho Uin and "Pukchŏng ka" ("A Trip to the North," 1776) by Yi Yong.[16] Poems on the northwest, especially Mount Myohyang, include the "Kwansŏ pyŏlgok" ("Song of the Northeast," 1556) by Paek Kwanghong (1522–1556)[17] and the anonymous "Kisŏng pyŏlgok" ("Song of P'yŏngyang") and "Hyangsan pyŏlgok" ("Song of Mount Myohyang").[18] The topic of the "Tohae ka" ("Song of Crossing the Sea," 1875) by Cho Hŭibaek is a trip to Kanghwa Island.[19]

Among the *kasa* by members of diplomatic missions to Japan, the *Iltong changyu ka* (*Song of a Grand Trip to Japan*, 1764) by Kim Ingyŏm (1707–1772) is the longest (4,122 lines) and most detailed. Kim's view of the Japanese is not favorable. On his way from Seoul to Pusan, for example, he passes through towns and fields and recalls battles and atrocities committed by the Japanese soldiers:

> When I cross the Han River
> and pass by the tombs of two kings,

---

[16] Ch'oe Kanghyŏn, *Hanguk kihaeng munhak yŏngu*, pp. 205–212.
[17] Yi Sangbo, *Hanguk kosiga ŭi yŏngu*, pp. 145–176.
[18] Ch'oe Kanghyŏn, *Hanguk kihaeng munhak yŏngu*, pp. 217–225.
[19] Ibid., pp. 233–239.

> I recall the Black Dragon Year,
> and tears of indignation come into my eyes.[20]

He refers to the Japanese as "island barbarians," as Pak Illo did in his *kasa*, or "dogs and pigs." On the island of Iki, he saw prostitutes who "point to their bared breasts, / . . . / strike their bare buttocks, / and lift garments to show their bottom."[21] He is, however, moved by some learned Japanese who were loath to part with him in Tokyo, "holding his garments, shedding tears."[22] Kim displays his talents at composing poetry in Chinese although the requests by the Japanese are termed "taxing." In Bizen, he harmonized with Japanese until cockcrow and produced one regulated couplet (*pailü*) of one hundred rhymes, another of seventy-two rhymes, penta- and heptasyllabic regulated verse, old-style verse, and cut-off lines, altogether forty pieces. The following is a scene at Osaka (23–24 February 1764):

> On the twenty-second I fell ill,
> lying in the official hostel.
> Our hosts bring me their poems,
> they are heaped like a hill.
> Sickness aside, I answer them;
> how taxing this chore is!
> Regulated verse, cut-off lines,
> old-style verse, regulated couplets –
> some one hundred and thirty pieces.
> Because I dashed them off on draft paper,
> upon revision I've discarded a half.
> If I have to work like this every day,
> it will be too much to bear.
> . . .
> Before dawn on the twenty-third,
> they arrive in streams.
> How hard to talk by means of writing,
> how annoying to cap their verses.
> Braving my illness,
> and mindful of our mission
> to awe them and enhance our prestige,
> I exert myself for dear life,
> wield my brush like wind and rain,
> and harmonize with them.

---

[20] Sim Chaewan, ed., *Iltong changyu ka, Yŏnhaeng ka* (*HKMT* 10), p. 17. See Yu Kwangbong, "*Iltong changyu ka* e nat'anan nori yangsang," in *Hanguk kihaeng munhak chakp'um yŏngu*, ed. Ch'oe Kanghyŏn (Kukhak charyowŏn, 1996), pp. 367–403.

[21] Sim Chaewan, ed. *Iltong changyu ka, Yŏnhaeng ka* (*HKMT* 10), p. 135.   [22] Ibid., p. 229.

When they revise their verses,
they put their heads together –
their writing bid fair to inundate me.
I compose for another round;
they respond with another pile.²³

Kim is struck by moonlit scenery at Akashi ("magnificent view unparalleled under heaven"), by beautiful women in Nagoya, by bustling streets in Osaka ("myriad times more flourishing than Chongno"). Kim also enjoys the Japanese radish and such sweets as rice cakes and candies. His "confused and miscellaneous" *kasa*, he hopes, will help the reader "to while his time away."²⁴

Among travel poems to China, the *Yŏnhaeng ka* (*Song of a Trip to Peking*, 1866) by Hong Sunhak (1842–1892) stands out. Like most works in this group, Hong devotes 772 lines to his itinerary of fifty-eight days, 1,010 lines to his experience and observation in Peking (forty days), and 95 lines to his return trip. What catches Hong's eyes are the Manchu hairdo and "yellow teeth and long fingernails" of the people he met. He touches on their customs (childbearing, for example), historical monuments, entertainments, animals and plants, and Westerners and Catholic churches in Peking. He witnessed at court the eleven-year-old boy emperor carried on a dais and wonders, "Is he the first under heaven, / the one in Manchu attire?" Like all Chosŏn literati, Hong evinces a prejudice against the Manchu – one may recall that King Injo had to surrender to the Manchu emperor Taizong in 1636. Hong laments the circumstances of certain officials descended from Ming times who had to shave their heads and serve the Manchu. Hong's respect is reserved for the Han Chinese, cultured and decorous, not for the Manchu, who are, in his opinion, uncivilized.²⁵

CALENDRICAL *KASA*

Chŏng Hagyu (1786–1855) lived in Yangju as a gentleman farmer most of his life and observed acutely with the informed eye of a farmer. His 518-line poem *Nongga wŏllyŏng ka* ("The Farmer's Works and Days") combines the accumulated experience of a farmer with the description of age-old annual events.²⁶ The lunar calendar was an agricultural system comprising twelve months and twenty-four fortnightly periods (*qi*) – for

---

²³ Ibid., pp. 175–179.   ²⁴ Ibid., pp. 167, 197, 173, 289.
²⁵ Ibid., p. 551; Ch'oe Kanghyŏn, *Hanguk kihaeng munhak yŏngu*, pp. 285–291.
²⁶ The text used is that by Pak Sŏngŭi, ed., *Nongga wŏllyŏng ka, Hanyang ka* (*HKMT* 7, Minjung sŏgwan, 1974), pp. 5–11. See Min Hyŏnsik, "*Nongga wŏllyŏng ka* e taehan text ŏnŏhakchŏk koch'al,"

example, Beginning of Spring, Rainwater, Awakening of Creatures, Spring Equinox, Clear Brightness, and Grain Rain – and Chŏng deftly brings together activities of the farming year and days of folk festivals celebrated each month. Poem 154, "Seventh Month," in the *Book of Songs* and monthly ordinances from the *Record of Rites* stand behind most poems of this type.

Earlier calendrical poems include, for example, "Ode to the Seasons," which compares the stages of a woman's love to the four seasons; "Song of the Lantern Festival," the existing version of which covers only the first five months; and "Monthly Festivals." Activities and observances mentioned in the first month of "The Farmer's Works and Days" include: the king's teachings on agriculture; tilling the patches, keeping farm tools in repair; feeding the draft oxen; spreading manure in the barley field; weaving, thatching, and twisting ropes; roofing the cottage; peeling the bark of fruit trees and planting stones between branches; making wine; watching the moon to divine flood or drought; the New Year's call; boys flying kites and girls playing on a seesaw; the game of *yut*; worship at the ancestral shrine; eating sweet rice on the fifteenth; drinking wine to clear one's ear; chewing chestnuts to keep a boil away; and "selling" the summer heat.[27] In the eleventh month, the speaker asks:

> How much have we stored
>   of our autumn crop?
> We'll sell some, pay the taxes with some,
>   some are for sacrifice,
> some for seed, some to repay a loan,
>   and some for wages.
> Now that we've settled our accounts,
>   not much remains for us farmers.
>   . . .
> No official harasses us,
>   because we are paid up.

Then he continues:

> Under the lamp mind your weaving,
>   see the cloth stretch on the loom.
> Youngsters study the classics,
>   children are at their game.

in *Munhak kwa ŏnŏ ŭi mannam*, ed. Kim Wanjin et al., pp. 320–364; and Yi Sangbo, *Hanguk kosiga ŭi yŏngu*, pp. 300–328.

[27] Pak Sŏngŭi, ed., *Nongga wŏllyŏng ka, Hanyang ka*, pp. 5–11. At dawn on the fifteenth of the first lunar month, the girls shout to each other, asking if any will buy summer heat.

> Some chant, some chatter,
> this is the joy of family life.[28]

The poem represents the experience of a conservative learned farmer who believes in the harmony of humankind and nature as well as in a heaven that intervenes in human affairs. Chŏng's poem can serve as a handbook for the farmer, whose life is depicted as hardworking and frugal but enjoyable – one of peace, contentment, and solidarity.

KASA ON PLACES AND OTHER TOPICS

The 762-line *Hanyang ka* (*Song of Seoul*) by a certain Hansan kŏsa ("Retired Gentleman of Hansan") is written from a commoner's perspective and evinces firsthand knowledge of life on the streets of the capital. The song touches on geographical features of Seoul, palaces, towers, arbors, eunuchs and court ladies, royal guards, institutes and offices, scenic spots, ancient landmarks, clothing, music, *kisaeng* and musicians, markets, shops, merchandise, the civil service examination, royal tombs, and the like. The bustling market is described:

> Crossing the Kwangt'ong Bridge, I find six markets here.
> Those who beckon the customer
> and those shop owners who sell,
> in wide-sleeved tops and horsehair hats,
> narrow-sleeved undergarments with wristlets,
> when they strike a bargain
> they look so impudent.[29]

The author, moreover, often provides valuable information:

> Zither players and singers gather . . .
> For the black zither, Im Chongch'ŏl,
> for singing, Yang Sagil,
> for sad and melancholic tune, Kong Tugi.
> The zither made of the phoenix tree,
> well-tuned and ready . . .
> The decorated butterfly harp with metal strings
> laid there like a departing butterfly.[30]

Im Chongch'ŏl, Yang Sagil, and Kong Tugi were contemporary singers in the late nineteenth century. The author's job is to report and show rather

---

[28] Ibid., pp. 65–69. [29] Ibid., p. 111. [30] Ibid., p. 131.

than criticize social conflicts. He believes that the ruling and the ruled, the literati and merchant, can live together happily. Thus the poem ends:

> Such a capital and such a world,
> was there any like it past and present?
> I prostrate and pray,
> pray to the polestar
> that our country and our king
> may endure a hundred generations without end,
> and that we may age
> together with heaven and earth,
> I pray, I pray.[31]

WOMEN'S *KASA*

Kasa by women in the north of Kyŏngsang province flourished from the eighteenth century. Wives and daughters of literati households not only learned the Korean alphabet and practiced calligraphy but recited, memorized, composed, and circulated *kasa* among kin and friends. Regarded as higher than prose fiction in the generic hierarchy, *kasa* became popular in a most conservative area of Korea. There are at least 6,000 known works, mostly in rolled scrolls, from five to thirty meters long, written in cursive style. A typical family might boast a repertory of more than 100 titles. Lady Yi of Yŏnam, the wife of Yu Sach'un, a descendant of Yu Sŏngnyong, wrote a congratulatory *kasa* on her son's and nephew's passing of the examination (1794) and a travel *kasa* on her visit to her son, the magistrate of Puyŏ (1800). Lady Song of Ŭnjin in Ch'ungch'ŏng wrote of her trip to Kongju (1845). Congratulatory *kasa* include those on successfully passing the examination, a wedding anniversary, the sixtieth birthday of parents, and the like. Amusement *kasa* include those written when women went to the mountain to pick azalea flowers in spring and bake (or fry) them in cake (*hwajŏn*), on boating, and on playing games. Songs lamenting the fate of being born as women compare the relations between man and woman to those between cat and mouse or between falcon and pheasant. A fair number of didactic pieces give instruction, for example, to newlyweds on proper behavior toward their in-laws. Women's *kasa* touch on other topics too, such as work, history, fortune, and religion.[32]

---

[31] Ibid., pp. 179–181.
[32] Kwŏn Yŏngch'ŏl, *Kyubang kasa yŏngu* (lu ch'ulp'ansa, 1980); Na Chŏngsun, *Hanguk kojŏn siga munhak ŭi punsŏk kwa t'amsaek*, pp. 252–278; Yi Chŏngok, *Naebang kasa ŭi hyangyuja yŏngu* (Pagijŏng, 1999); Sŏ Yŏngsuk, *Hanguk yŏsŏng kasa yŏngu* (Kukhak charyowŏn, 1996); Yi Wŏnju,

POPULAR *KASA*: SOCIAL PROTEST

From the end of the seventeenth century, commoners began to produce
kasa, full of social criticism, love, and lament. Commoners comprise both
the "middle people," who could read and write, and the lowborn, most of
whom were illiterate. Poems were often orally composed and transmitted –
mostly chanted or recited – and anonymous except for those by Sin Chaehyo
(1812–1884). The *kasa* sung by male or female lowborn singers, especially
in the vicinity of Seoul, often accompanied by a drum, include the so-
called "Twelve *Kasa*" (such as "Paekkusa" ["Song of the White Gull"]),
some *chapka* (such as "Sipchang ka" ["Song of Ten Strokes"], "Yusan ka"
["Song of a Trip to the Mountain"]), and "Hodu ka" (also called *tanga*; an
introductory piece such as "Kwangdae ka" ["Song of the Singer"]), sung by
the singer before the main *p'ansori* repertory. Authors and composers of the
sung *kasa* are usually unknown. A typical line in the recitation *kasa* consists
of four (sometimes six) metric segments (two to six syllables each), while
the sung *kasa* usually offers fewer fluctuations in the number of syllables in
each of the four segments.[33]

Kasa on social criticism include the "Kammin ka" ("Song of the Kapsan
People"), "Kiŭm norae" ("Song of Weeding"), "Hapkangjŏng ka" ("Song
of Hapkang Arbor"), "Ubu ka" ("Song of Foolish Men"), and "Yongbu
ka" ("Song of a Simple Wife"). These songs expose social contradictions –
especially the heavy imposition of unjust taxes that forced farmers to abandon their land. "Song of the Kapsan People," for example, concerns a
farmer who had to sell everything in order to pay taxes for thirteen men
and, penniless, fled his land with his old mother to avoid being conscripted
for military service. The poem ends with the hope that a magistrate of a
nearby county will set things right. It concludes:

> Were I to tell all my thoughts
> In every detail, this way and that,
> It would take until this time tomorrow,
> To tell even half.[34]

In addition to paying two bolts of cotton cloth per year to defray the
expenses of maintaining the army, farmers were also recruited for military

---

"*Kasa* ŭi tokcha," in *Chosŏn hugi ŭi ŏnŏ wa munhak*, ed. Hanguk ŏmunhakhoe (Hyŏngsŏl
ch'ulp'ansa, 1982), pp. 133–166; Cho Tongil, *Hanguk munhak t'ongsa* 3: 338–346; and Kichung
Kim, *An Introduction to Classical Korean Literature: From Hyangga to P'ansori* (Armonk, N.Y.:
M. E. Sharpe, 1996), pp. 122–136.
[33] Kim Mungi, *Sŏmin kasa yŏngu* (Hyŏngsŏl ch'ulp'ansa, 1983), pp. 14–54.
[34] Ibid., pp. 178–193.

service in times of war or rebellion. When unpaid taxes were collected from neighbors or kinsmen – even exacted from the deceased ("skeleton levies") and from boys registered as adults – farmers were compelled to flee.[35] Oppressive rule and killing of the innocent is the subject of "Chŏngŭp-kun millansi wihang ch'ŏngyo" ("Song Composed at the Time of a Rebellion in Chŏngŭp") in which local petty clerks are likened to "demon soldiers in the underworld." Their extortion and corruption constitute the theme of "Song of Hapkang Arbor." Occasioned by the covetous and cruel governor of Chŏlla province, Chŏng Minsi (1745–1800), who spent large sums of public money for his own pleasure boating, all chickens and dogs in the county are said to have been slaughtered for his party. If farmers thought the governor would relieve their suffering, their hopes were crushed. Although most poems of this genre do not offer a description of a better world, at least they depict how bad society had become.[36]

Satirical kasa

"Song of Foolish Men" enumerates the disreputable behavior of selfish men who challenge the established Confucian norms of conduct. "Song of a Simple Wife" castigates the misdeeds of a wife who, for example, tells lewd stories and runs away with a lover. The fourteen-year-old widow in the "Kwabu ka" ("Song of a Widow") prefers the pleasures of the flesh to chastity, while the speaker in "Noch'ŏnyŏ ka" ("Song of a Spinster") is anxious to find a mate. The subject of "Kyusu sangsa kok" ("Song of a Lovestruck Man") is a bachelor's hopeless love for a married woman. "Tanjang ka (or "sa")" (literally, "Song of Broken Bowels" – that is, Song of heartrending grief) tells of a married man's love for another woman. "Hwajŏn ka" ("Song of the Flower-adorned Cake") bewails the lot of a woman who became a widow five times. "Noin ka" ("Song of an Old Man"), which uses learned diction, laments the sorrows of old age. Another group of songs mocks Buddhist monks and nuns who break their vows and indulge in sex.[37]

We have seen that the literati *kasa* rely on learned diction, especially the orotund Chinese doublets, and allusion. The limited repertory of themes

---

[35] Lee Ki-baik, *A New History of Korea*, trans. by Edward W. Wagner with Edward J. Shultz (Cambridge, Mass.: Harvard University Press, 1984), pp. 225–226.

[36] Kim Mungi, *Sŏmin kasa yŏngu*, p. 200, and Yi Chongch'ul, "Hapkangjŏng 'Sŏnyu ka' ko," in *Hanguk kosiga yŏngu* (T'aehaksa, 1989), pp. 467–487.

[37] For the texts of these songs see Kim Mungi, *Sŏmin kasa yŏngu*, pp. 277–281, 275–276, 292–299 (also called *Ch'ŏngch'un kwabu kok*), 220–232, 209–212, 239–240, 310–339, and 216–219 respectively.

reflects the traditional views of life and the world, and the intertextual affinities arose from the limited number of permissible topics, situations, and feelings. To put it sweepingly, then, the literati *kasa* is a literary discourse of the Confucian literati who uphold and defend their way of life and thought – it draws its strength from high-cultural ideology and is therefore establishment literature. The speaker in most commoner's *kasa*, however, confronts actuality with critical awareness and exposes social contradictions and the hypocrisy of established morality. The commoner's *kasa* resists the dominant ideology of the literati and challenges with humor and satire the value system of the ruling class and their oppression carried out in the name of benevolence. Encouraged by the rise of practical learning, the anonymous writers of the popular *kasa* expanded the matter and manner of the genre with realistic detail, making use especially of onomatopoetic and mimetic words and everyday speech and adapting folk-song meters. They did not have a counterideology, however, or a logic that would subordinate details to the whole. Today the commoner's *kasa* are read more as social documents than literary monuments. In these songs, one senses something of carnival laughter as they give spontaneous expression in an entertaining way to what was in the heart and mind of the common people.

CHAPTER 12

Chosŏn poetry in Chinese

Kim Hŭnggyu

In the Chosŏn dynasty the members of the scholar–official class continued to occupy the dominant ruling position they had held during the Koryŏ period. Based on their Confucian knowledge and refinement, these literati enjoyed cultural superiority. As the civil service examinations emphasized literary talents, they led to a development of literature and produced excellent poets who wrote in literary Chinese. A member of the scholar–official class was a government functionary when in office and a writer when out of service. This lifestyle led to two distinct characteristics in their literary works: one was a courtier literature comprising, for example, diplomatic documents; the other was a literature of retired gentlemen who sang of leisure and joy in nature.[1]

THE POETIC WORLD OF EARLY CHOSŎN

The representative literary figures of early Chosŏn are Chŏng Tojŏn (d. 1398) and Sŏ Kŏjŏng (1420–1488). Chŏng Tojŏn was an influential official who helped Yi Sŏnggye (1392–1398) found the Chosŏn dynasty and was directly involved in formulating its institutions and policies. Chŏng's poetry shows both a critical consciousness of social problems and the determination of a scholar–official who entered the political stage in late Koryŏ with a mission to reform society. We note especially his works that concern the Confucian kingship, the ideology of the scholar–officials, and the solidarity of his Confucian colleagues. The vigorous and progressive spirit of Chŏng's poems derives from his sense of mission. Nature is not merely a place of merrymaking and retirement; his poems reveal the sensibility of a Confucian scholar–statesman who investigates moral principles at work in both people and nature.

---

[1] For an overview of literary figures of early Chosŏn see Im Hyŏngt'aek, "Yijo chŏngi ŭi sadaebu munhak," in *Hanguk munhaksa ŭi sigak* (Ch'angjak kwa pip'yŏngsa, 1984), pp. 359–418.

A century later, Sŏ Kŏjŏng shows a different poetic aspiration. Sŏ's life encompassed the reigns of Sejong (1418–1450) to Sŏngjong (1469–1494) when the Chosŏn institution was firmly grounded and the culture of Chosŏn flourished. Sŏ was a maternal grandson of Kwŏn Kŭn (1352–1409), a famous writer of early Chosŏn. Sŏ headed the Office of Special Advisers for twenty-six years and was himself a representative literary figure during the reign of King Sŏngjong – often said to be the golden age of courtier literature produced by scholar–officials. He left more than 6,000 poems in Chinese, and his poetic style embodies splendor with unassuming beauty. Sŏ's "Ch'unil" ("Spring Day"), for example, deals with an early spring scene when plum blossoms fall and a golden hue surrounds willow branches. It captures the mood of spring by using the vibrant colors of gold and jade that reflect the peace and prosperity of his time.

"Sugi" ("Rising From a Nap") shows the unhurried spiritual world of Sŏ, who enjoyed a life of comfort and wealth:

> The shadow of the bamboo screen falls into the room,
> The fragrance of lotus blossoms drifts in continuously.
> As I rise from a dream during a nap,
> The sound of raindrops upon paulownia leaves.[2]

This pentasyllabic quatrain depicts the feeling that came the instant he was awakened from a summer nap by the sound of raindrops. The speaker realizes that the bamboo screen's shadow has entered deep inside the room as he wakes. While he was napping, time passed and the sun was about to set in the west. When he woke up and took a breath, he felt the strong fragrance of lotus flowers that had filled the room while he was sleeping. The charm of the "activity within tranquility" in this poem lies in the expression of his awakening by the sound of raindrops in an idyllic setting. The aesthetic aspiration of leisure and splendor in Sŏ's poetic world reflects the aristocratic tendencies that prevailed in literature before the rigor of Neo-Confucian moralism came to predominate.

In the late fifteenth century, new writers and scholars appeared from the provincial scholar–official world whose orientation differed sharply from that of the courtier-writers in the capital. Some tried to participate in politics by emphasizing the political realization of Confucian ideals based on moral cultivation; others retired to their home villages to refine their scholarship. Their attitude was to assert the oneness of Confucian learning of the Way and literature. With an emphasis on Neo-Confucian ideals and moderation, they criticized the aesthetic tendency of court literature. In politics,

---

[2] Hŏ Kyun, *Kukcho sisan* (pub. c. 1697; 1980), ch. 1, in *Hŏ Kyun chŏnjip*.

these literary men of Neo-Confucianism stood in opposition to the capital-based aristocrats of renowned lineage. In literature, they opposed ornate poetry and tried to construct a simple and pure poetic world. They recreated thought and emotion based on Neo-Confucianism through appreciation of natural scenery. In their poetic world, nature was the ideal space to experience the principles of the universe and carry on Neo-Confucian inquiry while resisting worldly temptations. Therefore, they often wrote about nature's hidden laws and the spiritual joy of discovery.

Yi Ŏnjŏk (1491–1553) and Yi Hwang (1501–1571) represent the typical poetic world of the Neo-Confucian literati who wrote poems based on philosophy and contemplated philosophy through poems. Yi Ŏnjŏk wrote of the stage of attainment where men become one with nature. His plain style evinces both philosophical depth and literary aesthetics. In his poem "Muwi" ("Doing Nothing"), Yi unifies the workings of the universe with corresponding nonaction and attains a high state of Confucian cultivation that seeks to preserve nature's law and resist personal desires.

Yi Hwang wrote that

> poetry does not wrong people:
> people wrong themselves.
> When one is stirred and feelings well up,
> one cannot stop writing poetry.

Yi defended poetry as an indispensable element of self-cultivation that seeks purity of mind detached from the mundane world. For Yi Hwang, composing poetry was part of the life of scholarly training and the cultivation of mind/heart and human nature. Yi found a vivid principle of nature at work even in the grass growing in his garden and the fishes frolicking in a pond. In his poem about the mountain path from his village to Tosan Academy, Yi captures the harmony of myriad things in nature: flowers, flowing water, and singing birds. Yi's poetic world began to change in his fifties when he resigned from government service and retired to his home village. While at court, Yi often wrote of the "flight to the realm of transcendents"; but when he was studying and teaching at Tosan Academy, he often invoked "moon and plum blossoms." His yearning for the realm of the transcendents was born of the discord between political reality and his inner self – a yearning to be free of the political constraints that fettered him.[3] His recurring image of the moon and plum blossoms was not so much a celebration of their beauty as a pursuit of the elusive world of purity and spiritual freedom.

[3] See Yi Tonghwan, "T'oegye sisegye ŭi han kungmyŏn," *T'oegye hakpo* 25 (1980):73–78.

As the contradictions of the authoritarian regime became more apparent and the internal conflicts of the ruling class intensified in the late fifteenth century, there appeared writers who ignored the moral and social norms. Though antagonistic toward the capital aristocrats, they differed from Neo-Confucian scholars in that they took a sardonic attitude and even preferred ideological heterodoxy. Known as "The Outsiders" (*pangoe in*), their representative figure was Kim Sisŭp (1435–1493), the author of *New Stories from Gold Turtle Mountain*. Kim Sisŭp came from a humble family of military officials. After the usurpation of the throne by King Sejo, Kim roamed the country and concentrated on literary creation. As he continued his spiritual wandering between Buddhism and Daoism, he found that poetry was the only means to assuage the conflicts between self and world, between the ideal and reality. There are two main elements in Kim's poetic world. The first is his criticism of a society that frustrated the ideals of scholar–officials: a strong spirit of resistance, that is, against the tyranny of reality. The second is his compassion for those suffering under the yoke of authoritarian rule. "Yŏng sanga ko" ("Singing about the Suffering of the Mountain Home") deals with the plight of mountain farmers; "Sŏksŏ" ("Big Rat") shows his antipathy toward the corrupt ruling class, which is compared to big rats that eat up the people's grain.

POETRY IN THE REIGN OF KING SŎNJO

The poetic world of early Chosŏn – divided into courtier, Neo-Confucian, and outsider literature – underwent drastic changes around the time of the Japanese invasion of Korea in 1592. The glorious reign of King Sŏnjo (1567–1608) produced many writers and saw a flowering of literature. Among the poets we may single out a group called the "Three Tang-Style Poets": Yi Tal (1539–1612), Ch'oe Kyŏngch'ang (1539–1583), and Paek Kwanghun (1537–1582), all from Chŏlla province and not subject to a strong teaching of the Way. Rejecting the contemporary emphasis on complex rhetorical devices and difficult allusions, they focused instead on composing poems in the Tang style that expressed in simple diction the emotions and feelings of real life.

Yi Tal, the representative poet of the Three Tang-Style Poets, was born of a secondary wife and constructed a poetic world that dealt mainly with the dissatisfaction that ensued from his low social position, which prevented his entry into the normal social order of the time. One of his best poems, "Che ch'ong yo" ("Song of Memorial Service at the Grave"), goes:

A white dog in front and a yellow dog behind,
Clusters of graves amidst grasses in the field.
In a trail through the field, an old man finishes a memorial service
And returns drunk being helped by his small grandson.[4]

The graves – in the field, not on the hills – appear to be recent, perhaps the result of the Japanese invasion. Why are there only an old man and a small grandson present without any other adult? Is the grave that of the old man's son (the little boy's father)? The poet offers no explanation. We can only guess the poem's intent through feelings evoked by the scenery of a farming village.

The works of the Three Tang-Style Poets reveal emotions in an indirect way rather than through logical statement. Their poems parade neither literary skills nor a way of cultivating the mind. In pursuing the faithful expression of emotions and real-life experience, they freed themselves from the constraints of earlier Chinese poetry and the tendency toward argumentation. Instead they espoused the creativity of Tang poetry and emphasized poetic feelings through the suggestive portrayal of scenery. Their works reveal limitations, however, as they skirt the troubling topics of defeat, disappointment, sadness, and worry.[5]

Im Che (1549–1587) from the same period had an unbridled character and disliked the constraints of Confucian ritual. As he was dying, Im forbade his descendants to perform funeral rites by saying: "Many states under heaven pay tribute to the emperor. I was born in a weak state, and there is no reason to be sad about my death." Im's poetic world was based on a brave and indignant rejection of contemporary society. In it one finds a vigorous spirit, an indomitable soul, and an unobstructed realization of human nature. "Muŏbyŏl" ("Farewell Without a Word"), one of Im's typical works, concerns the yearning heart of a beautiful fifteen-year-old girl. A series of poems set in the border region evince on a grand scale the poet's ambition, spirit, and feeling of patriotic fervor.

Kwŏn P'il, who never took office, wrote poems that capture the contemporary social condition with sensitivity and show his condemnation of a depraved society and corrupt power. More skilled at the long old-style poetry than regulated verse, his representative work includes "Ch'ungju sŏk" ("Stone of Ch'ungju"), a poem that satirizes the hypocrisy of those in

---

[4] Yi Tal, *Songok sijip*, in Yŏngin p'yojŏm Hanguk hanmunhak ch'onggan, vol. 61 (Minjok munhwa ch'ujinhoe, 1996), ch. 6.
[5] An Pyŏnghak, "Samdangp'a sisegye yŏngu" (Ph.D. dissertation, Korea University, 1988), pp. 114–116.

power who destroy nature, exploit people, and deceive future generations with misleading language.

NEW TRENDS: THE PRACTICAL LEARNING SCHOLARS

Unlike the early Chosŏn period when the literature of the scholar–official class flourished, the late Chosŏn period saw the development of new literary activities by the "practical learning scholars," the "middle people" (*chungin*), and commoners. Literature written in Chinese of the period is characterized by an influx of writers from other classes, active interchanges with vernacular literature, and a search for new literary styles. In particular, the accomplishments of the literati of practical learning and the middle people reflect the new sensibility that broke away from the entrenched tradition of earlier literature.

Among the practical learning scholars the representative poets are the so-called "Later Four Poets": Pak Chega (1750–1805) whose literary fame increased through his exchanges with Pak Chiwŏn (1737–1805); Yi Tŏngmu (1741–1793); Yu Tŭkkong (1748–1807); and Yi Sŏgu (1754–1825). Not only did they actively absorb new ideas and literary trends from Qing China, but they tried to innovate the poetic style of the time. Under the influence of the Later Four Poets (all secondary sons born of concubines), a group formed to strengthen the unity of their coterie. Rejecting blind imitation and using lively diction, they reproduced the natural scenery, human feelings, and social conditions of contemporary Chosŏn. Taking their subjects from everyday life, these poets created works of exuberant realism through realistic and sensuous descriptions. Along with Pak Chiwŏn's accomplishments in prose, their movement to reform poetry led to a shift in the late eighteenth-century literary scene.

Chŏng Yagyong (pen name Tasan, 1762–1836), who continued the practical learning ideals of Yi Ik (Sŏngho), constitutes the other peak of poetry in Chinese among the practical learning scholars. Chŏng's best works are those produced in his eighteen years of exile. As he experienced the life of the people, Chŏng was able to sharpen his critical consciousness and insistence on political reform, a goal from his younger days. Numerous works protest the bitter reality of people thrown out of their homes into the streets and fields. "As the displaced people fill the streets," he wrote, "it hurts my heart to see their wretched condition, even to the point of losing my own desire to live." One of his representative works goes:

Wolves, wolves,
You have already taken our dogs,
So do not take our chicken.
My sons have been sold,
Who will buy my wife?
Would you skin me
and crush my bones?
Look at our rice paddies and fields –
What a sorry sight!
When even foxtails cannot make it there,
How can mugworts grow?
The murderer has already killed himself;
Who do you intend to harm now?[6]

This is the fifth in a cycle of poems, entitled "Chŏngan kisa" ("Stories from the Farm"), written in 1809. Here Chŏng is describing an incident where a murderer committed suicide for the sake of peace in the community, but local officials used the event as an excuse to exploit people and force them to abandon the place. Wolves stealing cattle and chickens are a metaphor for local functionaries exacting heavy taxes. In the end, farmers could not bear the extortion and left the town to wander from place to place. "Stories from the Farm" portrays the misery of the people and their grievances. This cycle recalls "Big Rat" from the *Book of Songs* (Poem 113) and shows Chŏng's urgent criticism of the times. This fifth poem in the cycle addresses the reader directly. Borrowing the angry voice of a household head who has been displaced by official oppression, the poet exposes the contradictions of society. Chŏng's critical spirit can be seen in all his poems of social criticism such as "Kimin si" ("Poem of Hungry People"), "Ae Chŏryang" ("Alas, the *Musul* Day of the Tenth Month"), "Ch'ungsiksong" ("Pine Caterpillars"), "Hail taeju" ("Drinking on a Summer Day"), and "Yongsan ri" ("Local Clerk of Yongsan").[7]

The abuses that most tormented the people were the grain loan system (*hwangok*) and the military service tax (*kunjŏng*). The grain loan system was originally an institution that lent grain in the spring and collected it in the fall in order to save people from starvation and to control grain prices. In reality, however, the government forced people to take grain loans and punished those who failed to repay with high interest. Some were even

---

[6] Chŏng Yagyong, *Yŏyudang chŏnjip*, 1 chip, ch. 5.
[7] For a comprehensive overview of the Chinese poetry of Chŏng Yagyong see Kim Sanghong, *Tasan Chŏng Yagyong munhak yŏngu* (Tongguk University Press, 1985), and Song Chaeso, *Tasan si yŏngu* (Ch'angjak kwa pip'yŏngsa, 1986).

forced to repay when they did not borrow grain in the first place. Chŏng describes a contrast between destitute farmhouses and the greedy life of officials: "While the people's rice chests do not hold enough to pass the year, winter grains fill the official storehouses."

Chŏng also composed a series of fable poems using animal characters to satirize political and social conditions. "Pine Caterpillars" deals with the discord between the educated men of conscience and the Old Doctrine faction, for example, and "Ojugŏ haeng" ("Cuttlefish") contrasts the poet's integrity and a corrupt official class.

THE CHOSŎN STYLE

The writers of practical learning in late Chosŏn had a deep understanding of Korean national literature and intensified their efforts to introduce everyday language into their work. Pak Chiwŏn observed that "while the graphs are the same as in [China], in writings they are used differently." Pak advocated the Chosŏn style with its originality and independence. Thus he criticized attempts to change *p'ansŏ* to *sangsŏ* (head of six ministries) and "Seoul" to "Changan," comparing them to a woodcutter selling firewood by shouting "Buy salt!" Likewise Chŏng Yagyong advocated writing Chosŏn poetry to overcome the constraints of Chinese prototypes. "I am a man of Chosŏn," Chŏng said, "and I take pleasure in writing Chosŏn poetry." His poems from the years of exile express a vivid local language and show a new aspect of poetry in Chinese. Chŏng depicts the real life of farmers and fishermen by capturing regional details through the use of everyday words such as *poritkogae* (barley hills), *taegam* (minister), *aga* (new bride), *map'aram* (southern wind), and the like. Arising from a new understanding of the people and a realization of Korean uniqueness, there appeared a series of new poems that rejected blind adherence to the rules of classical poetry and focused instead on the natural features, history, and everyday life of Korea. This Chosŏn-style poetry included poems that criticize social ills and comment on everyday life, poems about Korean history and natural features in the *yuefu* style, translations of *sijo* and *kasa* into Chinese, poems in Chinese that show interaction with folk songs, and poems written for amusement by Kim Satkat (1807–1863) and others.[8]

The poems of Yi Ok (1760s–1800s) are clear examples of a practical application of the Chosŏn style. His works depict the life of city dwellers

[8] See Yi Tonghwan, "Chosŏn hugi hansi e issŏsŏ ŭi minyo ch'wihyang ŭi taedu," *Hanguk hanmunhak yŏngu* 3–4 (1979):35–36.

who have cast off the constraints of Confucian custom. Among Yi's works, the most famous is the *Iŏn* (*Women's Songs*), a cycle of sixty-six pentasyllabic quatrains. Divided into four parts, "Ajo," "Yŏmjo," "Amjo," and "Pijo," the cycle concisely portrays in daring manner the vicissitudes of commoner women in the late eighteenth-century cities, characterized as those "of noise and plentiful silks." Yi creates a vivid picture of commoners by using slang and spoken language in his poetry. Aspiring to break away from the Chinese poetic tradition in both content and form, his poems depict scenes of marriage, pleasure quarters, seasonal festivals, and folk religion as well as women's clothing, hair ornaments, food, trinkets, and cosmetics. Thus Yi's works occupy an important place in late-eighteenth-century poetry, especially in the emergence of female emotion and features of folk songs. Here are three examples:

> You are a man,
> I entrusted myself to you.
> You do not pity me,
> But why do you abuse me?[9]

> Become an interpreter's wife,
> Rather than marry a merchant!
> He returned after half a year in the south,
> But is headed south again this morning.[10]

> Sister, sister, my elder cousin sister, how's your married life?
> Sister, don't even mention it. Pepper is hot but not as harsh
>   as married life.
> Sister, sister, my elder cousin sister, how's your married life?
> Sister, don't even mention it. My silk skirts and crimson skirts are all
>   wet from wiping tears.[11]

The first two poems from the *Women's Songs* portray women's sadness and resentment of unhappy marriages. The third is part of a folk song, "Sijipsariyo" ("It's married life"), expressing similar feelings. Using a word like *sanai* (man) from the vernacular, Yi's poems break the rules of Chinese poetry. Although this is not a sudden phenomenon resulting from the efforts of Yi Ok alone, it is nevertheless an innovative effort when seen against the prevailing ideology of the ruling class. With lucid logic Yi Ok defended his motivation for writing *Women's Songs*, and its poetic values. In his critical preface entitled "Samnan" ("Three Difficulties"), Yi criticizes the norms of traditional literature and insists that the focus of true poetry must be the

[9] Yi Ok, *Yerim chapp'ae* (Remarks on poetry by Yi Ok) (Kungnip tosŏgwan, n.d.).
[10] Ibid.   [11] Im Tonggwŏn, *Hanguk minyo chip* (Tongguk munhwasa, 1961) 1:140–141.

authenticity of life "here and now." Yi says: "In investigating myriad things, none is as important as the investigation of men. In investigating men, none is as profound as emotion. In investigating emotion, none is as true as the feeling between men and women."[12] Yi endeavored to give expression to natural desires and to liberate emotion from moral constraints. His *Women's Songs* is a cycle of poems that embodies this daring position.

POETRY OF THE "MIDDLE PEOPLE"

The "middle people" emerged as a new class in the production of literature in late Chosŏn. Comprised of those who occupied a social position between the literati and the commoners, they represented the lower end of the ruling class holding low government positions. Although they met obstacles in upward mobility, they were above the commoners socioeconomically and had considerable learning. They actively engaged in poetry through literary groups and even published selections of their poetry[13] every sixty years.[14]

Hong Set'ae (1653–1725), one of the Four Poets of the Translation Bureau, was a lowly official from a humble middle-people family. His poems often deal with personal misfortune caused by differences in social status:

> Quail in the field,
> You were born and live in the field,
> But built your nest in the midst of reeds.
> Although reeds do not form a lush forest
> They are enough to hide your body.
> When the cold northern wind blows at the end of the year,
> It may feel like the icy stare of a hungry hawk.
> Quail in the field,
> Do not lament that you are small,
> You can solve your hunger in the morning.
> Now I know that things big and small all have their uses,
> Myriad things all contain profound secrets of heaven.[15]

---

[12] Kim Hŭnggyu, *Chosŏn hugi "Sigyŏng" non kwa si ŭi ŭisik* (Koryŏ taehakkyo Minjok munhwa yŏnguso, 1982), pp. 180–184.

[13] Ko Siŏn and Ch'ae P'aengyun, *Sodae p'ungyo* (1737; Asea munhwasa, 1980), Ch'ŏn Sugyŏng et al., *P'ungyo soksŏn* (1797; Asea munhwasa, 1980), and Yu Chaegŏn and Ch'oe Kyŏnghŭm, eds., *P'ungyo samsŏn* (1857; Asea munhwasa, 1980).

[14] For studies on the literary activity of *chungin* literary figures see Yun Chaemin, *Chosŏn hugi chung-inch'ŭng hanmunhak ŭi yŏngu* (Koryŏ taehakkyo Minjok munhwa yŏnguwŏn, 1999), and Kang Myŏnggwan, *Chosŏn hugi yŏhang munhak yŏngu* (Ch'angjak kwa pip'yŏngsa, 1997).

[15] Hong Set'ae, *Yuha chip* (Yŏgang ch'ulp'ansa, 1986) p. 4.

Hong himself declared that "people praise my poetic skills because I use poetry to express my sadness, anger, and feelings of oppression and discontent." Though Hong wishes to become a successful official through scholarship, this ambition is blocked because of his social background. The "quail in the field" expresses the anguish of low social status suffered by all middle people. The quail could not nest in a lush forest but only in a corner of a field – exposed to the winter's rage and hungry hawks. No doubt the quail stands for the poet himself, while the lush forest signifies the scholar–official class he could never dream of entering. The *Yŏmgok ch'ilka* (Seven Songs of Salt Valley), composed late in Hong's life, takes the ancient story of a horse that can travel 1,000 tricents a day and uses it to portray the frustration he encounters because of his low social status.

The representative work of Yi Ŏnjin (1740–1766), another poet from the Translation Bureau who died young, is a cycle of 157 poems, entitled *Tongho kŏsil* (A Couple Living on the Lane). The poems deal mainly with the poet's intense self-awareness. Through use of a unique hexameter line, unconventional metaphor, daring slang expressions, and negation of literary tradition, Yi writes of the painful contradiction between his literary talents and his social standing. His works reveal the individuality of one who wants to throw off the yoke of discrimination.

The middle people – above all the technical officials and clerks in the central government – emerged in late Chosŏn times as a new group of writers with economic power and literary talent who contributed to the demise of the scholar–official's literary monopoly. Although the literati class continued in late Chosŏn, practical learning literature rose from within to form an innovative literary style. When the literary activities of the middle people gained strength and literature expanded to different social classes, late Chosŏn poetry attained even greater accomplishments.

CHAPTER 13

Chosŏn fiction in Chinese

Kim Hŭnggyu

Until the advent of the Korean alphabet (*hangŭl*) in the fifteenth century,
Korean literature relied either on oral transmission or on the universal
written language of East Asia: literary Chinese. The earliest Korean classical
fiction, *Kŭmo sinhwa* (*New Stories from Gold Turtle Mountain*), was written
by Kim Sisŭp (1435–1493) in Chinese. After the alphabet was promulgated, it
remained chiefly the language of expression for men of the lower classes and
upper-class women, while literary Chinese retained its privileged position
as the language of high literature among the literati. Though the use of the
alphabet did gradually percolate through most social strata, the situation
did not change fundamentally until the end of the nineteenth century.
Fiction written in literary Chinese occupies an important place in the
history of premodern Korean fiction. In this chapter we will discover why
the first Korean fiction was written in literary Chinese and why fiction
in the vernacular would have a prevailing influence after the seventeenth
century.

The origins and trajectories of fiction in Chinese have been diverse.
They include *chuanqi* (tales of wonder, romances) along the line of Tang
tales of wonder, biographical fiction incorporating factual biographies with
narrative elements, and unofficial historical fiction written on the basis
of well-known stories in the urban areas. While these stories were brief,
full-length fiction appeared after the *Kuun mong* (*Dream of Nine Clouds*)
at the end of the seventeenth century by Kim Manjung (1637–1692) and
Ch'angsŏn kamŭi rok (*Showing Goodness and Stirred by Righteousness*) by
Cho Sŏnggi (1638–1689), though some suggest they were originally written
in Korean. After the seventeenth century, full-length fiction in Chinese
such as *Illakchŏng ki* (*Record of the Pleasant Pavilion*) by Old Manwa, *Oksu
ki* (*Record of the Jade Tree*) by Sim Nŭngsuk (1782–1857), and *Yungmidang ki*
(*Tale of Six Beauties*) by Sŏ Yuyŏng (1801–1874) followed. Although fiction
in Chinese assumed a sphere of influence in both long and short formats

from an early period, it was simultaneously influenced by fiction written in Korean – resulting in a diverse history of classical Korean fiction.

TALES OF WONDER

Tales of wonder, which originated in China, became in the premodern period the favorite type of narrative prose among the literary elite across East and Southeast Asia – from China and Japan to Vietnam. This genre had been formed through the literary embellishment of folktales while at the same time adopting the biography form. Tales of wonder can be defined generally as fiction written in elegant literary Chinese. The typical plot involves main characters of noble birth but retains a strong propensity toward romance and fantasy. The earliest classical fiction in Korea, *New Stories from Gold Turtle Mountain*, belongs to this category. Considering its high literary quality, however, it must have been influenced by the narrative tradition before the Chosŏn dynasty.

When we glance at the history of previous narrative literature from this perspective, the *Sui chŏn* (*Tales of the Extraordinary*), an anthology of folktales compiled between late Silla and early Koryŏ, draws our attention. This anthology was first compiled by Ch'oe Ch'iwŏn (b. 857) and was supplemented and revised by Pak Illyang (c. 1096) and Kim Ch'ŏngmyŏng of Koryŏ. As no copy of this anthology presently exists, we can at best imagine its original shape by examining the twelve extant stories scattered in various historical and literary sources. We find in this work characters from different social strata as well as a variety of intersecting story lines. Some keep the original folktale form; others can be associated with *New Stories from Gold Turtle Mountain*. Overall the anthology contains both folktales and fiction, some of which can be considered tales of wonder. "The Tale of Ch'oe Ch'iwŏn," for instance, concerns Ch'oe Ch'iwŏn of Silla who, relying on his literary talent, develops a supernatural relationship with remorseful ghosts of Tang China. The plot of the story, the eloquent style, and the narrative technique intensifying the poetic mood persuade us to regard it as a tale of wonder.[1]

Stories in the *Tales of the Extraordinary* retain aspects of the traditional folktale. Tales of wonder, however, gradually drew nearer to fiction by critically minded Confucian literati of early Chosŏn. *New Stories from Gold Turtle Mountain* serves as the best example. The author Kim Sisŭp

---

[1] Im Hyŏngt'aek, "Namal Yŏch'o ŭi chŏngi munhak," in *Hanguk munhaksa ŭi sigak* (Ch'angjak kwa pip'yŏngsa, 1984), pp. 9–25; Frits Vos, "Tales of the Extraordinary: An Inquiry into the Contents, Nature, and Authorship of the Sui chŏn," *KS* 5 (1981): 14–18.

had a life of regret and disappointment due to King Sejo's usurpation of the throne (1455). Hearing this news in his youth, Kim burned all his books and wandered around the country as an unconventional monk. Kim was unable to remain indifferent to behavior that violated Confucian ethical codes. *New Stories* was written during his temporary stay at Gold Turtle Mountain near Kyŏngju. Although Kim Sisŭp's *New Stories* was indebted to *Jiandeng xinhua* (*New Tales Written while Trimming the Wick*) by Qu You (1341–1427), it contains unique features of its own, including the setting and characterization. In this prime example of *chuanqi* fiction, Kim aptly incorporated indigenous Korean elements and Chinese narrative tradition.

Among the five stories, "Manboksa chŏp'o ki" ("Old Bachelor Yang Plays a Chŏp'o Game with a Buddha of Thousand Blessing Temple"), "Yisaeng kujang chŏn" ("Student Yi Peers over the Wall"), and "Ch'wiyu Pubyŏkchŏng ki" ("Student Hong Plays at Floating Emerald Tower") concern love affairs between a young student and the reincarnated spirit of a dead woman. In "Nam yŏmbuju chi" ("Student Pak Visits the Underworld") and "Yonggung puyŏn rok" ("Student Han Visits the Dragon Palace"), the main characters meet with supernatural incarnations and demonstrate their literary talent. As this collection is self-described as the "first series," there may have been a second or even third collection. Even with the surviving five stories, however, the author's broad scope is evident. Among the prominent features of this collection is the image of male characters: young intellectuals with remarkable talents who nonetheless are isolated from social reality. The author resolves their melancholy and anguish either through love affairs with ghosts or through meeting with supernatural characters in their dreams.

In the first story, "Student Yi Peers over the Wall," crises threaten the love between the two main characters. The first crisis concerns a motif common to love stories everywhere: a young man and woman fall in love but encounter objections from their parents. Though they marry, the wife is killed during an invasion – a second crisis that seems to allow no possibility for a realistic escape from their romantic predicament. Only through a supernatural reunion does the couple find a solution. Although this solution is unrealistic, the author elected to resolve the tragic separation through the technique of fantasy.

Stories that tell of loving ghosts or meeting supernatural figures in dreams share the common element of impossibility. Hence the stories in this collection are tinged with tragedy arising from the characters' clash with the world of reality – a feature that becomes the main characteristic of tales of wonder. This point becomes obvious at the conclusion of the story. The main characters, who temporarily solve their problem through unrealistic means, eventually choose either death or seclusion due to irreconcilable reality. In his determination not to compromise with the demands of the real world, despite the certainty of his defeat, the male character becomes tragic.

Apparently the tragic aspect of *New Stories* is connected with the author's life. Unable to compromise with reality, Kim spent most of his life as a vagabond who concluded his wandering at the age of fifty-nine in a small monastery in Kangwŏn province. Indeed, to a considerable degree Kim created his characters in his own image. In fact he hid the manuscript in a cave and hoped that in the future someone might understand him through this book. The author wanted to convey to later generations his deep sense of alienation and the anguish that ensued from his unrealized ambition as a Confucian scholar. In this respect, *New Stories* functions as a fictional confession by an early Chosŏn intellectual who lived as an outsider.[2]

After the *Kijae kii* (*Strange Tales by Kijae*) by Sin Kwanghan (1484–1555),[3] *New Stories* served as the inexhaustible source of seventeenth-century tales of wonder. Representative works include *Chusaeng chŏn* (*Tale of Chu Hoe*)[4] by Kwŏn P'il (1569–1612) describing the love affair between Student Chu and two women, a daughter from a noble family and a *kisaeng*; *Ch'oe Ch'ŏk chŏn* (*Tale of Ch'oe Ch'ŏk*)[5] by Cho Wihan (1558–1649) describing the vicissitudes of the Ch'oe family during the Japanese invasion; and *Unyŏng chŏn* (*Tale of Unyŏng*)[6] portraying a tragic love affair between the court lady Unyŏng and Scholar Kim. These stories show great interest in love between young men and women and depict the resulting tensions between them in realistic terms. Based on this plot structure, seventeenth-century tales of wonder moved from short story to medium-length fiction while broadly reflecting social reality. The supernatural elements

---

[2] Im Hyŏngt'aek, "Hyŏnsil chuŭijŏk segyegwan kwa *Kŭmo sinhwa*" (MA thesis, Seoul National University, 1971); Cho Tongil, *Hanguk sosŏl ŭi iron* (Chisik sanŏpsa, 1977), pp. 224–238; Yi Hyesun, "*Kŭmo sinhwa*," in *Hanguk kojŏn sosŏl chakp'um non* (Chimmundang, 1990), pp. 11–29.

[3] So Chaeyŏng, "*Kijae kii* "yŏngu (Koryŏ taehakkyo Minjok munhwa yŏnguso, 1990).

[4] Pak Illyong, "*Chusaeng chŏn*," in *Hanguk kojŏn sosŏl chakp'um non* (Chimmundang, 1990), pp. 67–82. For the text, see Mun Pŏmdu, *Sŏkchu Kwŏn P'il munhak ŭi yŏngu* (Kukhak cheryowŏn, 1996), pp. 293–305.

[5] Pak Hŭibyŏng, "*Ch'oe Ch'ŏk chŏn*," in *Hanguk kojŏn sosŏl chakp'um non* (Chimmundang, 1990), pp. 83–106; Min Yongdae, *Cho Wihan kwa "Ch'oe Ch'ŏk chŏn"* (Asea munhwasa, 1993).

[6] Pak Illyong, "*Unyŏng chŏn* ŭi pigŭkchŏk sŏngkyŏk kwa kŭ sahoejŏk ŭimi," in *Chosŏn sidae ŭi aejŏng sosŏl* (Chimmundang, 1993), pp. 166–188; Kim Illyŏl, "*Unyŏng chŏn* ŭi sŏngkyok kwa ŭimi," in *Kojŏn sosŏl ŭi ihae* (Munhak kwa pip'yŏngsa, 1991), pp. 136–143.

that characterized the early examples diminished as realistic narrative began to predominate in fiction writing. Although certain formalistic features such as the "dream journey" may be considered major limitations in these works, seventeenth-century *chuanqi* fiction nonetheless constitutes the consummate form of a stylistic tradition that had been gradually developing since late Silla.

The major motifs found in late Chosŏn fiction – the descent of transcendents, for example, or obstacles to marriage – had already been diversely employed in the tales of wonder of the period. Tales of wonder by Confucian literati maintained a relationship of mutual influence with vernacular fiction during the seventeenth century. *The Tale of Unyŏng*, for example, had been translated into Korean during this period – supporting the assertion of a symbiotic relationship between the two modes of writing.

BIOGRAPHICAL FICTION

Biography is the prose genre written with the intent to transmit, under certain ideological restrictions, the life history of an individual. In the Korean context, it can be subdivided into the collected works of a private person or pseudobiography (*kajŏn*). Both genres can be differentiated from fiction, which seeks truth through nonfactual narrative. During late Chosŏn, however, some biographical writings contain strong fictional elements. These works, therefore, may be discussed within the category of fiction in Chinese. Certain works by Hŏ Kyun (1569–1618), Pak Chiwŏn (1737–1805), Yi Ok (c. 1760–1810), and Kim Yŏ (1770–1821) belong to this group. Among biographies (*yŏlchŏn*) in the *Historical Records of the Three Kingdoms* by Kim Pusik (1075–1151), for example, the lives of General Kim Yusin, Tomi, and Ondal contain numerous fictional elements. These fictional elements, however, are mostly due to the fact that either the subject had a fictional propensity or the biographies described characters handed down by oral tradition. These lives must be distinguished from the biographies of late Chosŏn, which represent consciously crafted fictional biographies.

The pseudobiography of late Koryŏ may be considered a transitional form between idealistic allegory and fiction as understood in a modern sense. Pseudobiography was didactic in that it was based on ideological interpretation. At the same time, it took a narrative form because the message was not conveyed as simple knowledge or an idea based on existing fact but was depicted concretely through the life of a character. The mere nonfactuality of the writing, however, does not qualify it as fiction. Its narrative structure and the construction of time and space faithfully follow the typical narrative technique of biography, not fiction. When the personification technique employed in pseudobiography, however, is combined with such narrative technique as that of royal biographies or historical narrative, they begin to approach fiction. Examples include the *Ch'ŏngun chŏn* (*Tale of the Human Mind*) by Kim Uong (1540–1603), *Ch'ŏngun yŏnŭi* (*Romance of the Human Mind*) by Chŏng T'aejae (1612–1669), and *Ch'ŏngun pongi* (*Basic Annals of the Human Mind*) by Chŏng Kihwa (1686–1740).

This fictional aspect in biography can be considered a new literary phenomenon that first became prominent in the seventeenth century. The social atmosphere created by two foreign invasions may explain it. Conflict between the upper and lower classes, the destabilization of values and morals, the inclination toward a profit-oriented society – all were features of this new social atmosphere that influenced the form and content of classical biography. The typical biography, which validated codified norms, gradually drew closer to fiction as it confronted the serious social problems of late Chosŏn. Moreover, the growth of folk art, the rise of fiction as a major narrative genre, and the writer's efforts to describe his environment in a more realistic manner all contributed to the appearance of this new phenomenon.[7]

The major works showing the fictionalization of biography include "Yu Yŏn chŏn" ("Tale of Yu Yŏn," 1607) by Yi Hangbok (1556–1618); "Namgung sŏnsaeng chŏn" ("Tale of Master Namgung") by Hŏ Kyun (1569–1618); "Kim Yongch'ŏl chŏn" ("Tale of Kim Yongch'ŏl")[8] by Hong Set'ae (1653–1725); "Hŏsaeng chŏn" ("Tale of Master Hŏ"), "Hojil" ("A Tiger's Rebuke"), and "Yangban chŏn" ("Tale of a Gentleman") by Pak Chiwŏn (1737–1805); "Yi Hong chŏn" ("Tale of Yi Hong") by Yi Ok (1760–1812); and "Ka sujae chŏn" ("Tale of the Recluse Ka") by Kim Yŏ (1765–1821). "A Tiger's Rebuke," a remarkable work by Pak Chiwŏn, satirizes the hypocrisy of Confucian scholars through Squire Pukkwak's secret affair with Tongnija. Pak claims that he copied this story from a scroll hanging in a small shop in Youtian village in China – a typical disavowal by the writer of fiction – but "A Tiger's Rebuke" must have been transmuted by Pak Chiwŏn's creative spirit. Pak satirizes the Confucian literati of Korea through Squire Pukkwak's self-contradictory behavior. At that time, Korean officials insisted on a northern campaign to punish the Manchu and prove their loyalty to Ming China.

---

[7] Pak Hŭibyŏng, "Chosŏn hugi *chŏn* ŭi sosŏlchŏk sŏnghyang yŏngu" (Ph.D. dissertation, Seoul National University, 1991), pp. 261–293.
[8] Pak Hŭibyŏng, "Sipch'il-segi Tongasia ŭi chŏllan kwa minjung ŭi sam: *Kim Yongch'ŏl chŏn* ŭi punsŏk," in *Hanguk kŭndae munhaksa ŭi chaengchŏm* (Ch'angjak kwa pip'yŏngsa, 1990), pp. 13–51.

What they really wanted, however, was to satisfy their own selfish desires. (The main theme of "Tale of Master Hŏ" may be interpreted along the same lines.) The key episode in "A Tiger's Rebuke" is the last scene where Squire Pukkwak attempts to justify his immoral behavior to a farmer in the field by borrowing words from sages. By contrasting the hypocritical scholar with a diligent farmer, Pak shows whose life is the more noble. A typical example of this emphasis can be found in "Yedŏk sŏnsaeng chŏn" ("Tale of a Nightsoil Man"), which portrays Ŏm Haengsu, a nightsoil collector. Through the image of a commoner who preserves his noble mind despite a dirty appearance, Pak Chiwŏn insists on the recovery of spiritual and moral sanity in the lives of the literati.[9]

Thus biographical fiction expresses concern with lower-class people and brings the individuality of its characters into sharp relief. These elements weakened the essential feature of early biography – its empirical truthfulness – but fictional reality was secured in the process. Formerly dominated by moral solemnity, biography became more dynamic and diverse under the influence of "fictionalization" after the seventeenth century, which consequently expanded the scope of fiction written in literary Chinese during the late Chosŏn period.

UNOFFICIAL HISTORIES

Unofficial history (*yadam*) is the comprehensive term for short literary Chinese narrative works collected in the urban areas during late Chosŏn. The earliest example is *Ŏu yadam* (*Ŏu's Unofficial Histories*) by Yu Mongin (1559–1623). Although conservative Confucian scholars criticized this work because it treated vulgar, nonhistorical matters, *yadam* paved the way for a new artistic stage unprecedented in Korea's literary history. Moreover, because the source of creation was so closely linked with actual life, *yadam* was able to depict human types and social conditions in a more realistic manner. In the eighteenth and nineteenth centuries, *yadam* became more actively written and more widely circulated, leading to the compilation of such works as *Kyesŏ yadam* (*Unofficial Tales from Korea*), *Ch'ŏnggu yadam* (*Unofficial Tales from the Green Hills*), and *Tongya hwijip* (*Assorted Collection from the Eastern Field*).

Tales in these collections took their subject matter from urban life. Characters are common city dwellers, and even though upper-class characters

---

[9] Kim Myŏngho, "Yŏnam ŭi hyŏnsil insik kwa *chŏn* ŭi pyŏnmo yangsang," pp. 55–91; Kim Myŏngho, *Yŏrha ilgi yŏngu* (Ch'angjak kwa pip'yŏngsa, 1990), pp. 184–199.

appear as heroes the narration is strongly tinged with an urban dweller's worldview. Several types of tales appeared: realistic stories conveying an aspect of real character in a plain manner; semi-historical episodes created on the basis of real historical episodes; and general fictional narrative including legends and anecdotes. Since *yadam* encompasses such broad subject matter, it could be taken as a real historical episode or as a well-structured fictional story – and sometimes a mixture of the two. The author or compiler of *yadam* recorded interesting stories without regard to their factuality. Such tales described contemporary reality and social problems critically through their tightly woven structure and the technique of literary realism.

Behind the appearance of *yadam* and Chinese fiction in the *yadam* style lie several historical factors including the development of agricultural technology and the dissolution of authoritarian society during late Chosŏn. As a result, the country's money and commodities were concentrated in urban areas, where numbers of farmers had migrated from the countryside. Indeed, the population of Seoul from the mid sixteenth century almost tripled in 100 years. Others, too, came to the urban areas: officials, relatives and protégés of officials, servants, scamps, impoverished literati, Confucian scholars both inside and outside of town, paupers, merchants, vagabonds, and storytellers. Although the world of *yadam* encompasses this wide variety of characters, the storytellers themselves are impoverished literati or their equivalents who personally experienced the urban atmosphere of late Chosŏn.[10] As they were easily exposed to the real-life experiences of upper and lower classes, the scope of *yadam* fiction was diverse. Moreover, some storytellers appear as professional artists. In the sense that urban vitality produced storytelling as a professional vocation, these characters might be considered the by-products of urban development.

Key figures in the formation of *yadam* were compilers who replaced the content of traditional prose narratives with earthy stories circulating in the cities and towns. In addition to *Tongbi naksŏn* (*A Storytellers' Collection from the East*) by No Myŏnghŭm (1713–1775), An Sŏkkyŏng (1718–1774) compiled *Sapkyo mallok* (*Random Records at Sapkyo*) and Yi Hŭip'yŏng compiled *Kyesŏ yadam* (*Unofficial Tales from Korea*). These writers, despite their knowledge and talent, were intellectuals isolated from the center of power. Thus they had a unique vantage point on people in power and the Confucian order while at the same time staying on good terms with urban

[10] Im Hyŏngt'aek, "Sipp'al-gu segi iyagikkun kwa sosŏl ŭi paltal," *Hangukhak nonjip* 2 (1975):67–86; Yi Kyŏngu, *Hanguk yadam ŭi munhaksŏng yŏngu* (Kukhak charyowŏn, 1997); and Sŏng Kidong, *Chosŏnjo yadam ŭi munhakchŏk t'ŭksŏng* (Minsogwŏn, 1994).

commoners. Because of their position they could interact with various types of people and took interest in contemporary urban life.[11] The formation of Chinese fiction in the style of *yadam*, therefore, was the result of urban development and intellectuals being excluded from political power. The major themes include profound concern with eccentrics, the economic poverty of the literati, the collapse of the status system and ensuing class conflict, the acknowledgment of basic human instincts, and the resistance of the oppressed against the old order.[12] The literary achievements of Pak Chiwŏn, Yi Ok, and Kim Yŏ owe much to the flourishing of the *yadam*.

Chinese fiction in the *yadam* style marks a high point of late Chosŏn literature, though it was bound by certain limitations. Not only did the commentary attached at the end of each story often reflect Confucian morality, but Confucian inclinations sometimes caused alterations in the original content of orally transmitted stories.[13] This phenomenon becomes especially prominent after the mid nineteenth century – due mainly to the fact that *yadam* shifted from a telling/listening format to a writing/reading format. The shortage of dynamic creativity from the urban areas and the conservative temper of the upper-class literati after the nineteenth century influenced this shift as well.

FULL-LENGTH FICTION

While short stories occupied a central position in early Korean fiction, beginning in the seventeenth century some pieces were expanded to full-length works, especially in biographical fiction. Medium-length stories had already appeared in the *Tale of Unyŏng* and the *Tale of Ch'oe Ch'ŏk*. As the short stories could not encompass the complex experiences stemming from the dissolution of Confucian society, these medium-length stories created heroes and other characters in all their complex interrelations. Meanwhile, the life history of an individual was sometimes associated with the vicissitudes of family and court. The extreme form of this tendency can be found in the full-length family stories appearing in the mid seventeenth century. The typical full-length story described the changing fortunes of families connected by marriage over several generations. Kim Manjung's *Dream of*

---

[11] Yi Myŏnghak, "Hanmun tanp'yŏn chakka ŭi yŏngu," in *Yijo hugi hanmunhak ŭi chaejomyŏng* (Ch'angjak kwa pip'yŏngsa, 1983), pp. 262–314.
[12] Pak Hŭibyŏng, "*Ch'ŏnggu yadam* yŏngu" (MA thesis, Seoul National University, 1981), pp. 97–174.
[13] Chin Kyŏnghwan, "Chosŏn hugi *yadam* ŭi sadaebujŏk chihyang kwa kŭ pyŏnmo yangsang" (MA thesis, Korea University, 1983), pp. 39–83.

Nine Clouds, his *Sa-ssi namjŏng ki* (*Record of Lady Sa's Journey South*), and the *Showing Goodness and Stirred by Righteousness* by Cho Sŏnggi (1638–1689) contain elements of early family fiction.

Record of Lady Sa's Journey South was written in Korean; the original language of the other two works is uncertain. Moreover, these three works share a common theme: desire for family prosperity, a value that took hold after the two foreign invasions. This point helps us to understand the background of these works as well as the history of late Chosŏn fiction. Although we will examine this point more closely in Chapter 14, the phenomenon indicates the rise of upper-class women as a major category of readers after the late seventeenth century. Kim Manjung and Cho Sŏnggi, for example, stated that their motivation for writing fiction was to entertain their mothers.[14] The fact that these works were circulated in their Chinese version, however, indicates that they were not read only by women. Indeed, Confucian literati read them with great interest. The creation of fiction in Chinese and its wide readership continued despite upper-class disdain for the genre. In fact, the main target of their criticism was focused on popular fiction written in Korean, which emerged for commercial purposes after the eighteenth century. That there was no criticism of *Record of Lady Sa's Journey South* or *Showing Goodness and Stirred by Righteousness* implies that early full-length fiction written by Confucian literati was recognized as moral writing distinct from popular Korean fiction.

During the eighteenth and nineteenth centuries, a number of works modeled after this fiction began to appear. Not only such full-length fiction as the *Kuun ki* (*Tale of Nine Clouds*), *Ongnin mong* (*A Dream of Ongnin*), and *Illakchŏng ki* (*Record of the Pleasant Arbor*) but family fiction and hero fiction read mainly by the lower classes were also influenced by early full-length fiction in Chinese. As a result, classical fiction came to appear as the principal literary genre in late Chosŏn. Fictionalization of biographies and essays, previously the major genres of Confucian literati, can also be understood along these lines. Fiction in Chinese became the narrative genre satisfying the Confucian literati's appetite for non-factual works.

Nonetheless, one cannot say that fiction in Chinese was accorded the status of orthodox Korean literature in literary Chinese. Like most premodern fiction, the authors and dates of many long pieces of fiction in Chinese are unidentifiable. During the nineteenth century, however, some

---

[14] Im Hyŏngt'aek, "Sipch'il segi kyubang sosŏl kwa *Ch'angsŏn kamŭi rok*," *Tongbang hakchi* 57 (1988): 103–127.

long fiction included not only the authors' names but their motivation. These works include the *Samhan sŭbyu* (*Remains from the Three Han*, 1814) by Kim Sohaeng (1765–1859),[15] *Oksu ki* (*Record of the Jade Tree*) by Sim Nŭngsuk (1782–1840),[16] *Yungmidang ki* (*Record of Six Beauties*, 1863) by Sŏ Yuyŏng (b. 1801),[17] and *Ongnu mong* (*Dream of the Jade Tower*, c. 1835–1840) by Nam Yŏngno (1810–1857). Some were praised by contemporary men of letters such as Kim Maesun (1776–1840) for their literary excellence – which indicates a changed attitude toward fiction.

These writers, mostly living in the vicinity of Seoul, were members of Confucian officialdom. Although they themselves were not situated at the center of authority, they maintained certain links with power. In general, they were politically isolated: their social criticism reflected in fiction seems to have been connected to their social situation in reality. These writers attempted to compensate, through fiction writing, for their lack of praxis. Their criticism fails to penetrate the core of social ills, however, due to their conservative impulse to advocate their own class interest.[18]

Another remarkable feature characterizing nineteenth-century long fiction is the literary portrayal of the upper-class worldview in the form of the hero tale – an example of vernacular fiction asserting a certain influence on the upper-class literati. The hero tales adopted folk elements from vernacular fiction and combined them with realistic aspects inherent in their own tradition. In this respect, long fiction in Chinese has its virtues despite the shortcomings cited here. Certainly, *The Dream of the Jade Tower*, with its high literary quality and wide popularity, serves as a positive example.

FICTION AT THE TURN OF THE CENTURY

At the beginning of the twentieth century when Korea was faced with the dual burden of protecting the country from foreign imperialism and establishing a modern nation-state, Korean literature in literary Chinese became less popular. Meanwhile, the civil service examination was abolished and the position of fiction in Chinese further diminished. Occasionally, however, works such as *Illyŏmhong* (*Love Story between Lady Hong and Bachelor Yi*) and *Sindan kongan* (*Swift Decision on a Public Case*), written in

---

[15] Cho Hyeran, "*Samhan sŭbyu* yŏngu" (Ph.D. dissertation, Eurha Woman's University, 1994).
[16] Kim Chongch'ŏl, "*Oksu ki* yŏngu" (MA thesis, Seoul National University, 1985).
[17] Chang Hyohyŏn, *Sŏ Yuyŏng munhak ŭi yŏngu* (Asea munhwasa, 1988), pp. 228–260.
[18] Kim Chongch'ŏl, "Sipku-segi chungbangi changp'yŏn yŏngung sosŏl ŭi han yangsang," *Hanguk hakpo* 40 (1995):88–108.

vernacular Chinese under the influence of fiction of social exposure during the late Qing, were published serially in newspapers and gained popularity with the general reader. Fiction in Chinese, in its last phase, attempted to transform itself by criticizing the old social order while at the same time accommodating major concerns of the lower classes. Nonetheless, the collapse of the class status system and the abolition of the civil service examination spelled the extinction of fiction in Chinese.

CHAPTER 14

Chosŏn fiction in Korean

Kim Hŭnggyu and Peter H. Lee

Vernacular fiction appeared in the seventeenth century with *Hong Kiltong chŏn* (*Tale of Hong Kiltong*) by Hŏ Kyun (1569–1618) about a century after Kim Sisŭp (1435–1493) had written *New Stories from Gold Turtle Mountain*. Kim Manjung's (1637–1692) *Dream of Nine Clouds* and *Record of Lady Sa's Journey South*, Cho Sŏnggi's (1638–1689) *Showing Goodness and Stirred by Righteousness*, and others followed between the late seventeenth and early eighteenth centuries. It is still unclear whether the first and last of these three were originally written in Chinese or in Korean. One assumes that Kim and Cho wrote in Korean from the fact that they wrote for their mothers, who enjoyed reading vernacular fiction. As Kim's and Cho's works circulated in Chinese and Korean versions immediately upon completion, they acquired a vast readership.

THE FOUNDING OF VERNACULAR FICTION

Why were such works of quality, works that would influence the fiction of later generations, produced at this time? First we may cite the new social reality that obtained after the Japanese and Manchu invasions and a new literary environment: a great number of commoners, the main consumers of vernacular fiction, demanded a literary form corresponding to contemporary reality. Vernacular fiction began as the new literary activity of certain members of the ruling elite who discerned the social contradictions of late Chosŏn society and felt the need to express them. A second reason is the long tradition of writing fiction in literary Chinese and, in turn, literary stimulation through the introduction, translation, and adaptation of popular Chinese fiction. Mentioned in a Koryŏ song dated 1216, the *Taiping guangji* (*Extensive Gleanings of the Reign of Great Tranquillity*, published in 981) – the single most important compendium of early Chinese fiction – had been widely read and partially translated into Korean. From the end of the sixteenth to the beginning of the seventeenth centuries, the four great works of Chinese fiction were imported and widely read by the literati: the *Sanguo[zhi] yanyi* (*Romance of the Three Kingdoms*), *Xiyouji* (*Journey to the West*), *Shuihu zhuan* (*Water Margin*), and *Jinping mei* (*The Plum in the Gold Vase*; or *Jin Ping Mei, Gold Vase Plum*). After the Japanese and Manchu invasions, the *Romance of the Three Kingdoms* was especially popular as more and more literati and middle-level people began to seek fiction. Thus the production of vernacular fiction was stimulated by both internal and external impulses. The final reason is the formation of a wide readership in vernacular fiction and the rise of a commodity economy in which peasants produced items to be sold for cash. With the rise of such an economy, fiction was produced for mass consumption through such commercial institutions as the lending library and the publication of woodblock editions.

Writing vernacular fiction, however, was not something of which the authors could be proud. Indeed, fiction was still despised in the context of a traditional East Asian literary canon that regarded only poetry and prose written in literary Chinese as primary genres. Fiction was still rejected as disrupting customs and corrupting morality. Broadly speaking, there were several reasons for rejection: fiction presents examples of negative human types such as malcontents, dissenters, outlaws, and rebels; it is morally harmful because it depicts passions, fantasies, and dreams that are best suppressed; it presents a distorted version of the real world and depicts at times such improbabilities as traffic between human beings and the dead, ghosts, and other supernatural beings; it exposes people's instinctual behavior, especially sex, and stimulates base desires, a hindrance to moral education; and it creates a world other than that sanctioned by authority and therefore offers an unofficial view of reality. These are the reasons why most authors of vernacular fiction and dates of composition remain unknown. Because of adverse criticism of fiction by the literati, writers hid their identity and readers read in secret. Hŏ Kyun and Kim Manjung – whose works were read by court ladies and were even said to have moved the reigning king, for example – did not openly profess to be writing fiction and seldom referred to their own works. The use of authorial disavowal or anonymity was a convention established to circumvent the Confucian sanction against writing imaginative stories. For these reasons it is difficult to describe the historical development of fiction systematically. Here vernacular fiction is classified by the elements of structure, characters, and themes into the following categories: heroic, dream vision, romance, family, clan, manners, and a few other related types.

TWO TYPES OF HEROIC FICTION

The Japanese and Manchu invasions shook the stable sinocentric East Asian social order. Indeed these two wars created the watershed dividing the Chosŏn dynasty into early and late periods. The many contradictions of early Chosŏn society gradually surfaced, and the literature dealing with human life could not ignore such problems. Hŏ Kyun's *Tale of Hong Kiltong*, considered to have opened an age of vernacular fiction, is a direct product of its time. Born into a distinguished family, Hŏ was on his way to a promising political career by passing the civil service examination with his literary skills. His brother and sister too gained fame as writers. He harbored reformative thought beyond the standard ritualism, however, and rejected the moral canon that represses human instinct and emotion. After experiencing the vicissitudes of honor and disgrace throughout his life, ultimately he was executed on suspicion of treason. The *Tale of Hong Kiltong*, therefore, is a work of fiction as problematic as his own life.[1]

The *Tale of Hong Kiltong* can be divided into three parts. The first part depicts the contradictions of a family system in which Hong Kiltong cannot address his father and brothers as such because he is a secondary son by a concubine of low birth; in the second part he is active as the head of the Save-the-Poor Gang that steals from the rich and helps the poor; the third part presents a utopia of contemporary popular imagination through the construction of the island kingdom Lüdao. The work adopts a structural method of extending the space from family to state and finally beyond the state. The critical consciousness gradually extends, as does the space of the story, from the contradiction inside a family to that of a state system – the result of a family system that discriminated against illegitimate children and a social system that gave peasants no choice but to turn into robbers. Hŏ formulated these social contradictions by making his leading character an actual historical person – an outlaw named Hong Kiltong who was active around Bird Ridge in the early fifteenth century until he was arrested and executed by the government.

Thus the *Tale of Hong Kiltong* depicts a will to resolve the contradictions of contemporary society through a historical figure in a fabulous mode. After undergoing embellishments and adaptations in the process of transmission, the tale was hailed by commoners. In structure the fictional life

---

[1] Kim Illŏyl, "*Hong Kiltong chŏn* ŭi kujojŏk t'ongilsŏng," in *Chosŏn sosŏl ŭi kujo wa ŭimi* (Hyŏngsŏl ch'ulp'ansa, 1984), pp. 34–47; Im Hyŏngt'aek, "*Hong Kiltong chŏn* ŭi sinkoch'al," in *Hanguk munhaksa ŭi sigak*, pp. 113–146; and Chang Yangsu, *Hanguk ŭijŏk sosŏlsa* (Munye ch'ulp'ansa, 1991), pp. 40–68.

of the character Hong Kiltong follows the biography of heroes such as Chumong in the Koguryŏ foundation myth.[2] The tale is not dependent on a mythical atmosphere, however, but is grounded in contemporary social reality in its subject matter and critique. On this point there is a similarity between the *Tale of Hong Kiltong* and a series of historical military romances in which contemporary storytellers depicted the acts of historical figures with romantic techniques as they ruminated over the pain suffered during the two wars: *Imjin nok* (*Record of the Black Dragon Year*), set during the Japanese invasion, and *Pak-ssi chŏn* (*Tale of Lady Pak*) and *Im Kyŏngŏp chŏn* (*Tale of Im Kyŏngŏp*), during the Manchu invasion.[3] Even if the subject and figures of these works were taken from historical reality, their contents are based on fictional narratives circulated among the people after the two invasions. The *Tale of Hong Kiltong* is no exception. They are all fictional histories, reconstructed by popular imagination, rich and simple in their dreams and ideology.

Heroic fiction, also called "created military fiction," is more directly related to the *Tale of Hong Kiltong* via the heroic biographical form. These stories began to be written around the seventeenth century and had become popular by the eighteenth and nineteenth centuries. Published in woodblock editions, they displayed the properties of popular fiction. The early heroic biography represented by the *Tale of Hong Kiltong* can be summarized as follows: a hero of noble birth and extraordinary nature is born under unusual circumstances; he faces unexpected danger; he escapes with the help of a rescuer or foster parent; he finally returns to society after developing strength and intelligence; he wipes out an evil power and gains glory. In addition to *Yu Ch'ungnyŏl chŏn* (*Tale of Yu Ch'ungnyŏl*), the *So Taesŏng chŏn* (*Tale of So Taesŏng*), *Cho Ung chŏn* (*Tale of Cho Ung*), *Chang P'ungun chŏn* (*Tale of Chang P'ungun*), and *Hyŏn Sumun chŏn* (*Tale of Hyŏn Sumun*) are exemplary works of this type.[4]

Stimulated by the prevalence of heroic tales, such works of fiction as *Chŏng Sujŏng chŏn* (*Tale of Chŏng Sujŏng*), *Kim Hŭigyŏng chŏn* (*Tale of Kim Hŭigyŏng*), and *Chŏngbi chŏn* (*Tale of Queen Chŏng*) tried to satisfy the latent desire of women restricted to their inner quarters by establishing them as heroic figures.[5] Unlike the *Tale of Hong Kiltong* or the historical

---

[2] Cho Tongil, "Sosŏl ŭi sŏngnip kwa ch'ogi sosŏl ŭi yuhyŏngjŏk t'ŭkching," in *Hanguk sosŏl ŭi iron*, pp. 197–270.
[3] So Chaeyŏng, *Im-Pyŏng yangnan kwa munhak ŭisik* (Hanguk yŏnguwŏn, 1982), pp. 303–329.
[4] Cho Tongil, "Yŏngung sosŏl chakp'um kujo ŭi sidaejŏk sŏngkyŏk," in *Hanguk sosŏl ŭi iron*, pp. 271–454; Sŏ Taesŏk, *Kundam sosŏl ŭi kujo wa paegyŏng* (Ihwa yŏdae ch'ulp'anbu, 1985), pp. 69–120.
[5] Min Ch'an, "Yŏsong yŏngung sosŏl ŭi ch'urhyŏn kwa hudaejŏk pyŏnmo" (MA thesis, Seoul National University, 1986), pp. 122–127.

military fiction cited earlier, these tales are set in China and their characters and episodes lack a sense of actuality; instead, they abound in coincidences and the fantastic. A sentimental style that exaggerates emotion, a panoramic narrative structure in which conventional and formulaic scenes are repeated, and an ultimate confrontation between good and evil planned in heaven – these are the features of popular fiction that catered to the interests of the reader.

Yet the combination of two different directions – expressed by the rise and fall of heroic characters – can be taken as a fictional sign of the dissolution of the Confucian order. These tales evince on the one hand a worldly direction, the chaos of the Confucian social order, the importance of secular interest, and the pursuit of individual desire; on the other, they reveal a retrospective direction that seeks to revitalize the old order and restore the glory of the individual and the family. Although the method of combining dual impulses differs in each work, nostalgia for the old order and old ideology is generally stronger. It is clear that the heroic tale reflects both the experience and the ideal of traditional society; while upholding Confucian ethics and ideology (such as loyalty and filial piety) on the surface, individual ambition, secular glory, and love between men and women become essential inner motives.

DREAM VISIONS AND ROMANCE FICTION

Soon after the *Tale of Hong Kiltong* and the outbreak of two wars in Korea, Kim Manjung wrote *Dream of Nine Clouds*, considered a masterpiece of classical Korean fiction. By then an uneasiness with Confucian ideology and the moral norm of the Chosŏn dynasty had begun to grow in the consciousness of the upper literati. Kim Manjung, from a prominent family, delineated the state of affairs. *Dream of Nine Clouds* problematizes a man's fundamental attitude and perception as he encounters the generation in which tradition begins to crumble. The main character Xingzhen, who was born in a transcendent world, yearns for a secular life, is reborn in a dream as a new character Yang Shaoyu, then awakes from the dream to comprehend the nature of life and leaves the world.[6]

Certainly the fictional technique – borrowing the dream structure to voice a contemporary complaint or desire – has precedents. In addition to the "Nanke taishou zhuan" ("Prefect of South Branch") by Li Gongzuo

---

[6] Chŏng Kyubok, *Kuun mong yŏngu* (Koryŏdae ch'ulp'anbu, 1974), pp. 247–265; Sa Chaedong, *Pulgyogye kungmun sosŏl ŭi yŏngu* (Chungang ilbosa, 1994), pp. 359–378; and Cho Kwangguk, *Kinyŏdam kinyŏ tŭngjang sosŏl yŏngu* (Wŏrin, 2000), pp. 188–237.

(c. 770–848), the story of Chosin in the *Memorabilia of the Three Kingdoms* possesses such a structure. Several literati critical of mid-Chosŏn society created a unique literary form in which, through the imaginary space of a dream world, they could meet historical persons and express their resentment. Such records of dream journeys include "Taegwanjae mongyu rok" ("Record of a Dream Journey at Great Observation Study") by Sim Ŭi (fl. 1475–1507) and "Talch'ŏn mongyu rok" ("Record of a Dream Journey to Talch'ŏn") by Yun Kyesŏn (1577–1604).[7] *Dream of Nine Clouds* inherited various traditions of dream-journey discourse that skillfully contrast Confucian secularism, which recognizes wealth and honor as the greatest values, with the transient view of Buddhism that denies their worth and pursues the transcendent life.

Thus Kim Manjung demands from both himself and his readers a dialectic understanding of human life through a chain of denial: "reality to dream to reality." This point emerges from the last teaching of the Great Master Liuguan – that the two ways of life represented by Xingzhen and Yang Shaoyu are inseparable. The great master wanted Xingzhen to awake to the fact that the effort to divide them is futile. *Dream of Nine Clouds* is the product of a generation that needed to establish a view of life through a methodical skepticism.[8] Xingzhen would not have seemed mature if he had fallen into a dichotomy in which only the world of Buddhism is true and all that is secular is false. Besides such critical awareness, the work's outstanding fictional accomplishment includes Kim's narrative skill and his vivid depiction of characters and situations. Now let us examine some of Kim's narrative techniques.

The story consists of four narrative movements: descent from the Buddhist paradise to the world of humans; descent to a lower world through dream; ascent from a lower world to the world of humans; and finally ascent to the Buddhist paradise. The cultural values and lifestyle the narrator glamorizes are the qualities of the ideal self which the upper-class literatus aspires to attain. They also pander to the recurrent fantasies of the same class schooled in the romance conventions rich in intertextuality. Characters affirm the cultural values of poetry as shown in the exchange of poems – poetry as the highest accomplishment of the educated. Especially for women characters, reading and writing poems is a means of empowerment and expressing desire. The force of desire motivates and enables them to author their own destiny. Poetry is the only means for them to express their subjectivity.

---

[7] Sin Chaehong, *Hanguk mongyu sosŏl yŏngu* (Kyemyŏng munhwasa, 1944), pp. 98–141.

[8] Chŏng Kyubok et al., *Kim Manjung munhak yŏngu* (Kukhak charyowŏn, 1993), pp. 141–199.

The story explores romance's inward associations with dream. Indeed dreamlike qualities permeate the entire narrative. Dream foreshadows future actions in the plot; functions as an excuse to introduce supernatural and marvelous elements in the narrative; and foregrounds the central theme of the relationship between dream and reality. Upon returning to the foot of the mountain from the Dragon Palace, Shaoyu finds a track that leads to a temple:

Shaoyu went into the temple, burnt some incense and bowed to the Buddha, but as he was coming down the steps afterward he suddenly tripped and awoke with a start to find himself in the camp, sitting with his arms on the table . . . He was very surprised, and asked his aides: "Have any of you been dreaming?" They replied that they had all dreamt they had followed him in a great battle where they defeated a horde of devils and took its commander captive.[9]

On his way home from his Tibetan campaign, Shaoyu has a dream and interprets it to mean that Zheng Qiongbei, his betrothed, has died. It is the empress's trick to deceive him – she tells Qiongbei's mother: "They say that bad omens are lucky. When he comes back, tell him that your daughter has been taken ill and died. In his memorial to the throne, he wrote that he had met her. I want to see whether he recognizes her on the day of wedding."[10] When he returns, Shaoyu has a dream, this time to avenge the cruel trick played on him:

Last night I had a bad dream. Qiongbei came to me and said, "Why have you broken your promise?" She was very angry and gave me a handful of pearls. I took them and swallowed them. It's a terrible omen. When I close my eyes, she presses on me; when I open them she stands in front of me. I shall die.[11]

When Shaoyu pretends to be ill from speaking to the spirit of Qiongbei in his dream, Qiongbei appears in person to convince him that she is alive.

The frequent use of disguise recognizes the inevitable disparity between what is and what shows; how one can easily be deceived by appearances in love; and finally the fictionality of the story. Shaoyu disguises himself as a Daoist nun to gain entry to Minister Zheng's residence in order to get a glimpse of his daughter; Jia Chunyun pretends to be a former lady-in-waiting of the Queen Mother of the West who is now only a ghost; Di Jingfang disguises herself as a boy to get close to Shaoyu; Princess Lanyang pretends to be a commoner to get to know Zheng Qiongbei. Dissolution of the barrier between dream and reality, truth and fiction, plays an important part in smoothing the transition between realms of existence. In

---

[9] Richard Rutt and Kim Chong-un, *Virtuous Women* (Korean National Commission for Unesco, 1974), p. 107.
[10] Ibid., p. 128.   [11] Ibid., p. 140.

addition to various forms of dissimulation including cross-gender disguise, rich oneiric experiences account for the effects of enchantment, mystery, anxiety, and premonition. The story represents a wish fulfillment of the Confucian gentleman in officialdom. Shaoyu wins first place in the civil service examination and is appointed successively as imperial academician, minister of rites, minister of war, marshal of the west, censor-in-chief, grand counselor-in-chief, duke of Wei, and grand preceptor. As a "great hero," he is proficient in both arms and letters. He lives happily with two princesses and six secondary wives and has six sons and two daughters.

Finally, the narrator's deft use of dream and his intrusions questioning whether a given dream or episode is real or fictional "expose the ontological distinctness of the real and fictional world"[12] and unsettle our convictions about the relative status of truth and fiction. As an early example of self-conscious fiction, *Dream of Nine Clouds* is a commentary on the practice of writing fiction that enables us to observe and enjoy the textual and linguistic construction of literary fiction, which is not only meant to move and impress but to enlighten.

Dream of Nine Clouds became the model of classical literary fiction and inspired many imitations, such as *Kuun ki* (*Record of Nine Clouds*), *Oksŏn mong* (*Dream of Hŏ Kŏt'ong*), *Ongnu mong* (*Dream of the Jade Tower*), and *Im Hoŭn chŏn* (*Tale of Im Hoŭn*). Although the nineteenth-century masterpiece *Dream of the Jade Tower* inherited from the *Dream of Nine Clouds* a critical consciousness and dream-vision structure, it takes a more realistic direction and reveals an interest in transient desire and the critical recognition of political reality. Instead of concluding with a Buddhistic awakening, the poor and lowly scholar Yang Ch'anggok is made to confront violently the force that has monopolized power whilst he is in the process of accomplishing wealth, rank, fame, and love, while Kang Namhong, one of his wives and concubines, is developed as a character who improves her lot through lively individuality and action.[13]

Certain elements in the story of secular life correspond to the dream in dream-vision fiction: the descent structure, the colorful military romance of the hero, and the main character. The process of relationships takes on great importance, and the episodes in which Yang Shaoyu has relations with eight beautiful women and enjoys wealth and honor seem to have left a deep impression upon the contemporary reader. The problem of love was a common subject in classical fiction – including, for example, *New Stories*

[12] Patricia Waugh, *Metafiction: The Theory and Practice of Self-Conscious Fiction* (London: Methuen, 1984), p. 32.
[13] Ch'a Yongju, *Ongnu mong yŏngu* (Hyŏngsŏl ch'ulp'ansa, 1981).

from Gold Turtle Mountain, Tale of Chu Hoe, and *Tale of Unyŏng.* Unlike heroic fiction and other types of classical fiction that approach the problem of love by depicting the male protagonist's affairs with women, however, there is a series of works that concentrate on the trials of a young couple before they become husband and wife. These works, which can be termed "love fiction," include *Sukhyang chŏn* (*Tale of Sukhyang*), *Sugyŏng nangja chŏn* (*Tale of Sugyŏng*),[14] *Yun Chigyŏng chŏn* (*Tale of Yun Chigyŏng*), and *Paek Haksŏn chŏn* (*Tale of the White Crane Fan*).

The *Tale of Sukhyang* secured the most readers. The tale of Sukhyang, who wanders begging after she has been overcome by the turmoil of the Japanese invasion but finally marries Yi Sŏn with whom she was matched in heaven, is realistically portrayed. Although Sukhyang experiences physical hardship, her greatest obstacle is the disparity in their social status – underscoring that a difference in social rank was the most serious problem for a man and woman in love.[15] Unlike the tales of wonder that end in tragedy, however, the *Tale of Sukhyang* shows how the couple attains love after overcoming all trials. If the tales of wonder depict the contradictions generated by social status in tragic form, vernacular fiction is an effort to overcome social contradictions in romantic form. A powerful example can be found in *Ch'unhyang chŏn* (*Tale of Ch'unhyang*), the epitome of romance fiction. Thereafter, until the advent of the "new" fiction (*sin sosŏl*), romance fiction continued to be written in the form of new classical fiction – as in *Ch'up'ung kambyŏl kok* (*Song of Longing in the Autumn Wind*), *Puyong sangsa kok* (*Female Entertainer Lotus' Song of Love*), and *Ch'ŏngnyŏn hoesim kok* (*Song of a Youth's Repentance*) in the early twentieth century.

CLAN FICTION AND FAMILY FICTION

Vernacular fiction appears to have repeated various experiments for about a century from the *Tale of Hong Kiltong* to *Dream of Nine Clouds.* Such explorations can be found in the development of *bianwen* (transformation texts) – the transformation of narratives in the Buddhist scriptures.[16] It is difficult to see them as fully developed fiction, however, because they do not qualify in certain regards as works of fiction. Moreover, we need to stress the importance of the influence of Chinese fiction, attested by seventeenth-century records that Ming and Qing works of fiction were bought and

---

[14] Kim Illyŏl, *Sugyŏng nangja chŏn yŏngu* (Yŏngnak, 1999).
[15] Yi Sanggu, "*Sukhyang chŏn* ŭi munhŏnjŏk kyebo wa hyŏnsilchŏk sŏngkyŏk" (Ph.D. dissertation, Korea University, 1993).
[16] Sa, *Pulgyogye kungmun sosŏl ŭi yŏngu.*

enjoyed. Kim Sisŭp and Hŏ Kyun were sufficiently impressed by *Water Margin* and Qu You's (1341–1427) *New Tales Written While Trimming the Wick* (preface dated 1378) to use them as sources of their own fictional creation, and they joined in contemporary debate on controversial Chinese works. Even if the dominant opposition argued that Chinese fiction must be prohibited, its influx did not stop. Translations and adaptations continued.[17] A literatus proficient in classical Chinese was able to enjoy a text strewn with vernacular Chinese, but it had to be translated into Korean for other readers because the demand for new fiction had risen not only among men but among the women of the literati class. Kim Manjung's and Cho Sŏnggi's motive for writing fiction – to satisfy their mothers' desire for reading – seems to support this statement. In the middle of the seventeenth century women's-quarters fiction (*kyubang sosŏl*) was created to enhance the requisite culture for the women of the literati class and as amusement.[18]

Because characters from different clans appear and their tales of discord, honor, and disgrace over several generations are entangled, such works are called long clan fiction or river fiction (*roman-fleuve*). They are also known as Naksŏn Library fiction, because the Naksŏnjae royal library stores a considerable number of them.[19] *Ch'ŏnsusŏk* (*Stones in the Spring Water*), *Nakch'ŏn tŭngun* (*Fall and Rise of General and Statesman Wang*), *Poŭn kiu rok* (*Record of Rare Encounters and Requital of Kindness*), and *Ogwŏn chaehap kiyŏn* (*Rare Reunion of a Couple*) are typical works of this type. They seem to have been read by court ladies or the women of the literati families through book-lending shops in Seoul. These books are long: *Myŏngju powŏlbing* (*Tribulations of the Three Clans*), for example, reaches almost 235 chapters in manuscript form. Such clan fiction had been written since early times: *So Hyŏnsŏng nok* (*Tale of So Hyonsŏng*) and its sequel, *So-ssi samdae rok* (*Three-generation Record of the So Clan*), had already appeared by the middle of the seventeenth century.[20] Long fictional works on clans dating before the eighteenth century include *Han-ssi samdae rok* (*Three-generation Record of the Han Clan*), *Sŏl-ssi samdae rok* (*Three-generation Record of the Sŏl*

---

[17] Pak Chaeyŏn, "Chosŏn sidae Chungguk t'ongsok sosŏl pŏnyŏkpon ŭi yŏngu" (Ph.D. dissertation, Korean University of Foreign Languages, 1993).
[18] Im Hyŏngt'aek, "Sipch'il segi kyubang sosŏl kwa *Ch'angsŏn kamŭi rok*," pp. 103–127.
[19] Yi Subong, *Hanguk kamun sosŏl yŏngu* (Kyŏngin munhwasa, 1992); Ch'a Ch'unghwan, *Sukhyang chŏn yŏngu* (Wŏrin, 1999).
[20] Im Ch'igyun, "Yŏnjakhyŏng samdaerok sosŏl yŏngu" (Ph.D. dissertation, Seoul National University, 1992), pp. 37–76, and *Chosŏnjo taejangp'yŏn sosŏl yŏngu* (T'aehaksa, 1996); Pak Yŏnghŭi, "So Hyŏnsŏng nok yŏnjak yŏngu" (Ph.D. dissertation, Ewha Woman's University, 1994), pp. 34–50; Cho Yongho, *Samdaerok sosŏl yŏngu* (Kyemyŏng munhwasa, 1996).

Clan), and others. The literary horizon of seventeenth-century vernacular fiction was sufficiently broad and colorful to permit the coexistence of short vernacular fiction such as the *Tale of Hong Kiltong* and a long work such as the *Tale of So Hyŏnsŏng*. Kim Manjung's and Cho Sŏnggi's masterpieces from the late seventeenth century did not burst suddenly onto the literary scene after the *Tale of Hong Kiltong* but grew from this fertile ground.[21]

Not only did these clan fictions continue in imitation and derivation throughout the eighteenth and nineteenth centuries. Taking advantage of the popular clan fiction of the seventeenth century, many new and longer works appeared. Such works deal with problems that are as rich and complex as their length. In them one finds the traditional sense of value, the ideal image of the literati, the problem of succession, the role of women in a polygamous system, the problem of princesses marrying below their rank, and monarchic authority. The characters in these works, even if they are of the nobility, are far from the hero types who sacrifice themselves to authoritarian ideology or display superhuman ability. Instead most of them are secular human types who pursue power, wealth, and love. Although their lives are presented on the surface as glorious, a work like *Hyŏn-ssi yangung ssangnin ki* (*Tale of the Hyŏn Brothers*) shows that in fact their private lives are distorted due to an irrational social system and ideology.[22]

Each work presents variations, but long clan fiction views, through the eventful lives of the official class, the contradictions and circumstances of the collapsing authoritarian society. This fact emerges most concretely in the discord between family members. If fiction charting a clan's vicissitudes over many generations is termed long clan fiction, then fiction that deals with the problems in one family can be called family fiction (*kajŏng sosŏl*). Family fiction can be divided into three kinds: a dispute among wives (as, for example, in *Showing Goodness and Stirred by Righteousness*), a dispute between wives and concubines (as in *Record of Lady Sa's Journey South*), and a dispute between stepmother and children from the first marriage (as in *Changhwa Hongnyŏn chŏn* [*Tale of Rose Flower and Pink Lotus*]).[23] The conflict created by the contradictions of a patriarchal and authoritarian family system produces a friction within polygamy, concubinage, or a dispute surrounding estate inheritance. Some works blame family discord on the character flaws of a concubine or the stepmother; others try to

[21] Chang Hyohyŏn, "Kungmun changp'yŏn sosŏl ŭi hyŏngsŏng kwa kamun sosŏl ŭi palchŏn," in *Minjok munhaksa kangjwa* (Ch'angjak kwa pip'yŏngsa, 1995).

[22] Sin Tonghŭn, "*Hyŏnssi yangung ssangnin kie* kŭryŏjin kwijok sahoe ŭi silsang," in *Kossosŏl yŏngu nonch'ong* (Kyŏngin munhwasa, 1994), pp. 479–510.

[23] Kim Chaeyong, *Kyemohyŏng kojŏn sosŏl ŭi sihak* (Chimmundarg, 1996), pp. 71–127.

rationalize the contradictions of the old family system with idealized logic. Since the works portray even the wicked characters realistically, however, they also emerge, despite the author's intent, as victims of the irrational family system. Works such as *Yang Kison chŏn* (*Tale of Yang Kison*) go so far as to explore the contradictions within the concubinage system and present a realistic solution. Many works of the early twentieth century's "new" fiction developed material about the tragedy of the old family system as they shaped the features of twentieth-century fiction.²⁴

P'ANSORI FICTION AND FICTION OF MANNERS

P'ansori fiction (*p'ansorigye sosŏl*) emerged as the *p'ansori* narrative (presumed to be formed around the early eighteenth century), gained strength from its sensational popularity and was gradually converted into reading material. While *Pyŏn kangsoe ka* (or *Katcha sinsŏn t'aryŏng*) among the twelve *p'ansori* titles was not converted into *p'ansori* fiction, *Song of Red Cliff* was made into *p'ansori* from the main episodes of the *Romance of the Three Kingdoms*. It is difficult, therefore, to stipulate a specific relationship between *p'ansori* and *p'ansori* fiction. Nevertheless, it is clear that *p'ansori* narratives generally became *p'ansori* fiction. Beyond this common process of formation, no common structural quality ties them into one type. Yet they are distinguished from the other types cited earlier by the fact that both gained from *p'ansori* a common literary style and rhetorical characteristics, popular character types one might meet in real life, and a popular worldview.²⁵

P'ansori fiction includes *Ch'unhyang chŏn* (*Tale of Ch'unhyang*), *Sim Ch'ŏng chŏn* (*Tale of Sim Ch'ŏng*), *Hŭngbu chŏn* (*Tale of Hŭngbu*), *T'okki chŏn* (*Tale of a Rabbit*), *Pae Pijang chŏn* (*Tale of Subcommander Pae*), *Changkki chŏn* (*Tale of a Pheasant Cock*), and *Ong Kojip chŏn* (*Tale of the Miser Ong Kojip*). Each is considered later in Chapter 15 on *p'ansori*. This group of works deals with the problems a commoner might experience in life. The story is told from a unified view of the world stressing secular reality; the superhuman hero is absent; human experience is emphasized more than ever in the unfolding of episodes. These works present a mixture of verse and prose; of highly refined language and lively colloquialism; of wit and lewdness. Tragedy, together with rich humor or biting satire, broadly

²⁴ Ch'oe Sihan, "Kajŏng sosŏl ŭi kujo wa chŏngae" (Ph.D. dissertation, Sŏgang University, 1989); Yi Wŏnsu, "Kajŏng sosŏl ŭi chakp'um segye wa sidaejŏk pyŏnmo" (Ph.D. dissertation, Kyŏngbuk University, 1991); and Yi Sŏnggwŏn, *Hanguk kajŏng sosŏlsa yŏngu: 17-segi esŏ 20-segich'o sinsosŏl kkaji ŭi yŏksajŏk pyŏnmo wa ŭimi* (Kukhak charyowŏn, 1998).
²⁵ Ch'oe Hyejin, *P'ansorigye sosŏl ŭi mihak* (Yŏngnak, 2000).

shapes the panorama of social life in late Chosŏn times. For these reasons, *p'ansori* fiction gained more popularity than any other type of fiction – as evidenced by the many alternative editions transmitted to the present and their differing contents. Even if *p'ansori* and *p'ansori* fiction were based on the life of commoners, they brought both the upper and lower classes into their sphere in the course of their development.

Thus *p'ansori* fiction had a great impact on many literary forms of late Chosŏn and lent color to late Chosŏn fiction. This effect can be found in its use of concrete expression, in the characteristic literary style, and in the keen depiction of social conditions. Works of fiction on social conditions (*set'ae sosŏl*),[26] such as *Yi Ch'unp'ung chŏn* (*Tale of the Profligate Yi*), *O Yuran chŏn* (*Tale of the Female Entertainer O Yuran*), and *Samsŏn ki* (*Record of Three Transcendents*), depict the life of the common people in a literary style characteristic of *p'ansori* or portray commoners realistically as in *p'ansori* fiction. The *Tale of the Profligate Yi* and the *Tale of the Female Entertainer O Yuran* are two representative works presumed to be influenced by *p'ansori* fiction because they resemble in many aspects *Waltcha t'aryŏng* (*Song of Military Officials*; also called *Musugi t'aryŏng*), and *Kangnŭng Maehwa t'aryŏng* (*Song of Maehwa in Kangnŭng*) among the twelve titles of *p'ansori*.

The influence of *p'ansori* fiction can be found even in a series of fables that deal satirically with human society. Fable fiction developed from short fables circulated among the people long ago. Among them one finds *Tale of a Rabbit* and *Tale of a Pheasant Cock*, works of *p'ansori* fable fiction from *p'ansori*. The first bitingly satirizes, through the figures of a rabbit and turtle, the avarice and concupiscence of a corrupt lord, the Dragon King; the latter allegorizes through a pheasant couple the collapse of a destitute family and its triumph over a nearly insuperable problem. Such fiction is based on the fable's allegorical power to deal with moral teachings and universal human nature from a satiric angle. The animals are configured not as types, however, but as independent entities in order to draw concrete characters and depict the reality of life in late Chosŏn. One finds the same features in *Tukkŏbi chŏn* (*Tale of a Toad*), a novelization of a Buddhist narrative, or in *Sŏ Taeju chŏn* (*Tale of Captain Rat*), a legal narrative. Both deal with rural social conditions in late Chosŏn – conditions that were changing with the shift of economic power – by contrasting the decline of the literati clan and the advance of wealthy commoners.[27] Such fables with their satiric consciousness shine all the more brightly during the patriotic

[26] Yi Sŏngnae, "Hanguk kojŏn p'ungja sosŏl yŏngu" (Ph.D. dissertation, Tanguk University, 1997).
[27] Chŏng Ch'urhŏn, "Chosŏn hugi uhwa sosŏl ŭi sahoejŏk sŏngkyŏk" (Ph.D. dissertation, Korea University, 1992), pp. 30–163; Min Ch'an, "Chosŏn hugi uhwa sosŏl ŭi tach'ŭngjŏk ŭimi kuhyŏn yangsang" (Ph.D. dissertation, Seoul National University, 1990), pp. 13–45.

enlightenment period, and works like "Kŏbu ohae" ("Misunderstanding of Rickshaw Men") and "Kŭmsu hoeŭi rok" ("Proceedings of a Council of Birds and Beasts") became possible.

THE NEW CLASSICAL FICTION

Classical fiction, originally circulated in woodblock editions or manuscripts, was widely read in the twentieth century as a result of the development of movable lead-type print, in so-called "six-cent works of fiction" or *ttaktchi* editions. Chinese graphs were provided alongside the vernacular words, space was provided between words, and their style was corrected to match the new sensibility so that even readers accustomed to the new literary style could understand them easily. Unlike traditional classical fiction, here the story was set not in China but in Korea, and a new transformation was devised with unprecedented content and structure. Before long the "new fiction" reflecting the problems and consciousness of a new generation had become a trend. Of course, classical fiction did not disappear at once with the emergence of the new fiction. Republication of classical fiction (or partial recasting and recreation) continued for some time. Such works can be called "new classical fiction" (*sinjak ku sosŏl*).[28] Among them are works like "Koryŏ Kang sijung chŏn" ("Life of the Koryŏ Minister Kang Kamch'an") and "Hong Kyŏngnae silgi" ("True Record of Hong Kyŏngnae") whose subjects are historical figures. In addition to Kang Kamch'an (948–1031) who repulsed the Khitans, and Hong Kyŏngnae (1780–1812), leader of a major peasant rebellion, the new classical fiction treated historical figures who fought against foreign invaders or opposed the exploitation of the ruling class, such as the Silla general Kim Yusin (595–673), the military commander Nam I (1441–1468), and Kim Tŏngnyŏng (1567–1596), the loyal warrior during the Japanese invasion. Such works were stimulated by the historical biographic fiction created by pioneer intellectuals of the enlightenment period to inspire national independence and a strong patriotic consciousness. These works were therefore intended to overcome the authoritarian system and address the historical problem of foreign incursion. In consciousness of subject and literary quality, however, they lag behind the historical biographic fiction of the enlightenment period. Under Japanese colonial censorship after the annexation in 1910, writers were obliged to dilute patriotic subjects. Thus the new classical

---

[28] Kwŏn Sungŭng, "1910-nyŏndae kuhwalchabon kososŏl yŏngu" (Ph.D. dissertation, Sŏnggyungwan University, 1990) pp. 8–44.

fiction could not deal with topics that might disturb the Japanese colonial government. Their chief subject, therefore, was love. In three representative works – *Song of Longing in the Autumn Wind*, *Female Entertainer Lotus' Song of Love*, and *Song of a Youth's Repentance* – there is a *kasa* song in which the speaker longs for a loved one. Moreover the heroine, separated from the male protagonist of noble status, attains love after conquering all kinds of adversity. These three works deserve attention, because they present the supremacy of love between young couples and expose the constraints and contradictions of the old order.[29]

As commercialism spread, the fiction writer's literary consciousness began to dull and the new classical fiction became ever more conventional. Nevertheless, the new fiction extended the base of readers and created an atmosphere in which a more developed fiction could be accommodated.

---

[29] Ch'oe Wŏnsik, "*Kasa* ŭi sosŏrhwa kyŏnghyang kwa ponggŏn chuŭi ŭi haech'e," in *Minjok munhak ŭi nolli* (Ch'angjak kwa pip'yŏngsa, 1982), pp. 9–36.

CHAPTER 15

P'ansori

Kim Hŭnggyu

P'ansori is an oral narrative that has been cherished by Koreans ever since its inception in the seventeenth century. A highly sophisticated genre that demonstrates diverse Korean musical forms,[1] it is at the same time a form of oral narrative that weaves together an array of characters and events using both verse and prose.[2] Traditionally *p'ansori* was sung by performers known as *kwangdae* in rural villages or marketplaces. Sometimes the *kwangdae* were invited to perform at banquets hosted by the literati and wealthy patrons, too. Their talent was for hire.

P'ansori is deeply rooted in popular art. Unlike mask dance or folk songs, however, it possesses depth and versatility and embraces a much larger and more diverse audience. It includes the use of extreme comic expression, witticisms that make the audience burst into laughter, and the caricature of Confucian ideas and taboos. Furthermore, it uses tragic language that touches the soul and expresses the dark side of life. At the heart of *p'ansori* one finds the vivacious language of the common people combined with a simple grace.

P'ansori performance is remarkably simple. It requires only two performers: a singer (*kwangdae*) and a drummer (*kosu*). The singer stands on a straw mat and the drummer sits two or three meters in front of him facing the singer (or occasionally to the side). As the singer sings, the drummer beats the drum to accompany him. Apart from the singer and the drummer, no other special equipment or assistance is necessary. Consequently, *p'ansori* can be performed anywhere with enough space for a public performance. *P'ansori* performances took place not only on the spacious floors of the rich or in the inner courtyards of the houses of the literati, but in the wide marketplaces and even in the open fields.

[1] Yi Pohyŏng. "*P'ansori* sasŏl ŭi kŭkchŏk sanghwang e ttarŭn changdancho ŭi kusŏng," in *P'ansori ŭi ihae*, ed. Cho Tongil and Kim Hŭnggyu (Ch'angjak kwa pip'yŏngsa, 1978), pp. 180–196.
[2] Kim Hŭnggyu, "*P'ansori* ŭi sŏsajŏk kujo," in *P'ansori ŭi ihae*, ed. Cho Tongil and Kim Hŭnggyu (Ch'angjak kwa pip'yŏngsa, 1978), pp. 103–130.

The singer sang works like *Ch'unhyang ka* (*Song of Ch'unhyang*), *Sim Ch'ŏng ka* (*Song of Sim Ch'ŏng*), *Hŭngbo ka* (*Song of Hŭngbo*), and others comprising the twelve-work repertoire (*madang*). The singer would vary both rhythm and melody in order to reflect changes in circumstance and atmosphere as well as characters' state of mind during various passages of the song. Alternating between sung and spoken passages, the singer would occasionally use colloquial speech to explain the plot and parts of the dialogue. Though *p'ansori* demonstrates versatility – a response to different performative situations – it takes a long time to perform a work. It takes even longer to perform a work that the audience will like because of the colorful and rich content. A full performance of the *Song of Ch'unhyang*, one of the most famous *p'ansori* among the five works still extant, for example, takes seven or eight hours. As *p'ansori* became fixed narratives, circulating as reading materials, they created a readership for *p'ansori* fiction and contributed significantly to the development of realistic depictions of the commoners' social condition in late Chosŏn.

P'ANSORI BEFORE THE EIGHTEENTH CENTURY

Literary documents verifying the early development of *p'ansori* are scarce. As a result, explanations of its origin and formative stages seldom go beyond hypothesis. Among the theories suggested for the origins of *p'ansori,* the most influential is the shamanist narrative song theory. Certainly the songs sung by the shamans in Chŏlla province are in many ways similar to *p'ansori*. First of all, a shaman song is a long oral narrative mixing spoken passages (*aniri*) and singing. Moreover, *p'ansori* and shaman songs from Chŏlla province often are exactly alike or at least similar in rhythmic variations and singing techniques. When one considers, too, that most *p'ansori* singers came from this region, one finds highly persuasive the suggestion that the origin of *p'ansori* is closely related to the songs shamans sing during rituals (*kut*).

Although the shamanist songs and *p'ansori* share similar traits, there is one significant difference. The main character in a shaman song is the shamanist deity, who possesses special power to accomplish things impossible for ordinary people. Therefore the shamanist deity becomes an object of worship. The narrative shaman song, firmly rooted in the worldview of shamanism, fulfills both incantatory and religious functions. It is intrinsically a sacred song. *P'ansori*, however, is an oral narrative that realistically depicts problems arising in the commoners' daily lives. The worldview of *p'ansori* is anti-incantatory and anti-mystical and generally respects the details of everyday life.

Although the origin of *p'ansori* can perhaps be found in the shaman songs, the reason for its establishment as a separate art form can be traced to social changes during the late Chosŏn period. In late-seventeenth-century Chosŏn society, the disruption of the Confucian idea of order and the growth of the commoner class secularized shamanism with great speed. Gradually the belief that the problems of daily life, fortune and misfortune, could be affected by shamanist incantations weakened. Subsequently, shamanist rituals were transformed into occasions to establish a sense of solidarity through celebratory festivals. Originally a ritual performed by a shaman meant a religious ceremony, but it also connoted "a spectacle worth seeing," suggesting a continuous historical transformation. One can naturally assume that the audience's demand for a more realistic and interesting art form lies at the heart of this process. *P'ansori* thus stepped outside the boundaries of shamanist ritual and established itself as narrative song – an artistic form appropriate for the demands of the new era.

When one considers all the evidence to date, it seems that this transformation of *p'ansori* during its incipient stage occurred from the middle to late seventeenth century. In this early stage of *p'ansori*, one conjectures that its content was simple and its expression crude. In order to flourish as secular and professional entertainment, the *p'ansori* singers and their repertoire required constant improvement. In the case of shaman songs, which were a part of shamanist rituals, the religious function was primary and entertainment secondary. For *p'ansori*, however, the entertainment function held primary importance, since providing amusement and leaving an impression on the audience were the means of guaranteeing success. Therefore the *p'ansori* singers, in order to maintain and expand the audience's interest in their art, strove to improve their musical skill and sharpen the colorful content of each work. They chose to embellish, refine, and shape old narratives rather than create new ones. Not only was this practice advantageous in terms of guaranteeing both the intimacy of the performance and its appeal to the public, but it was also an effective method for making a work their very own. An established *p'ansori* repertoire, then, was transmitted from one generation to the next. In the course of continuous improvisation and expansion, the content of the main narrative of a work came to include richer and more colorful episodes. According to an early nineteenth-century source, "Kwan uhŭi" ("On Seeing the Plays of Actors") by Song Manjae (1788–1851),[3] the number of *p'ansori* works eventually reached twelve.

---

[3] Yi Hyegu, "Song Manjae ŭi '*Kwan uhŭi*,'" in *Hanguk ŭmak yŏngu* (1970), pp. 318–364.

Thus one can conclude that the establishment of the twelve *p'ansori* works as a sophisticated musical and literary art form was an eighteenth-century phenomenon. A document strongly supporting this hypothesis is the *Song of Ch'unhyang* in literary Chinese by Yu Chinhan (1711–1791), a sixth-generation descendant of Yu Mongin (1599–1623), the author of *Ŏu yadam* (*Unofficial Stories by Yu Mongin*). Yu Chinhan lived in Mokch'ŏn, Ch'ungch'ŏng province, and was widely known in that region for his poetry. Like many provincial literati, he liked traveling to different provinces and in 1753, at the age of forty-two, he traveled through the southwest region visiting mountains, rivers, and cultural sites. At this time he had the opportunity to hear the *Song of Ch'unhyang* and other *p'ansori* songs which deeply impressed him. The following year, after he returned from his trip, Yu Chinhan wrote the *Song of Ch'unhyang*, a heptasyllabic verse in 200 lines in literary Chinese.[4] Judging from this work, *p'ansori* had reached a highly cultured and refined level and had begun to appeal to the upper class. Even literati who had earlier shown contempt toward the popular art were impressed. The same work also contained a passage that substantiated the existence of the *Paebijang t'aryŏng* (*Ballad of Subcommander Pae*).

Nevertheless, *p'ansori* was still enjoyed predominantly by commoners. Although a small segment of the upper class showed interest, the form had not reached the stage of full support. Furthermore, *p'ansori* was not widely accepted as an entertainment for the literati. This is clear from the fact that Yu Chinhan was criticized by the Confucian scholars of the time for having written the *Song of Ch'unhyang*.[5] Until the eighteenth century, therefore, *p'ansori* reflected the commoners' worldview and their aesthetic values because the *p'ansori* singers themselves were from the lower class and the majority of the audience were commoners as well. The *p'ansori* singers incorporated episodes that mirrored the experiences and interests of the commoners who were not only their main audience but also their financial supporters. By assimilating various elements drawn from folk, shaman, and popular songs current at the time, they gathered together various musical forms and transformed the *p'ansori* narratives into an art form.

Moreover, *p'ansori* developed into a satirical and humorous expressive form by presenting the various aspects of the commoner's everyday life as both sad and ridiculous. While the narrative framework of *p'ansori* derived from old tales and legends, the *p'ansori* singers in the process of embellishing and solidifying the narrative interpolated extraordinary episodes that reflected the social reality of the commoners of the later Chosŏn period and

---

[4] Kim Tonguk, *Ch'unhyang chŏn yŏngu* (Yŏnse taehakkyo ch'ulp'anbu, 1976), pp. 75–77.
[5] Ibid., p. 77.

thus expressed the growing consciousness of the people. A representative example embodying this social aspect is the *Song of Ch'unhyang*, a work that earned fame and attracted large audiences.

Toward the end of the eighteenth century, *p'ansori* met with new challenges. At this time, *p'ansori* was enjoying enormous popularity as a sophisticated form of entertainment, but at the same time it was experiencing significant changes in the composition of its audience. To put it simply, the *p'ansori* performers began to accept the upper-class audiences – the literati, the officials, and the wealthy – as the essential spectators rather than the commoners who had been their traditional audience base. This change did not occur suddenly. Even before these shifts in audience composition became prominent, a gradual transformation had already taken place.

One impetus for this important phenomenon may be attributed to an event known as *yuga* and various other banquets hosted by the literati and the wealthy to celebrate special occasions. During the Chosŏn period, it was the custom for descendants of the literati who had passed the civil service examination to hold banquets. The *Kyŏngdo chapchi* (*Capital Miscellany*) records the following:

> The successful literary licentiate candidate receives his certificate and goes in a celebratory procession accompanied by musicians, singers, and acrobats. The singer is a performer who wears brocade robes and a yellow straw hat pinned with silk flowers. Holding a peacock fan, he dances and plays antics. The acrobat walks the tightrope, tumbles, and performs all kinds of feats.[6]

This passage describes the mid eighteenth-century custom, and it is certain that *p'ansori* was included in the celebratory procession. The *seaksu* were musicians most commonly playing "three strings and six horns"; the acrobats were tight-rope walkers and tumblers; the singers were in charge of songs, farce, and *p'ansori*.

Visiting relatives to celebrate the auspicious event, the successful candidates toured for three days accompanied by musicians, singers, and acrobats.[7] Although this custom is very old, it is apparent that during the

---

[6] Yi Sŏkho, ed., *Tongguk sesigi, Yŏryang sesigi, Kyŏngdo chapchi, Tonggyŏng chapchi* (Taeyang sŏjŏk, 1973), p. 162.

[7] *Yuga* is also called *samil yuga* (a three-day tour). According to *CWS*, during the lean years and major calamities an edict was proclaimed prohibiting this event. "Three strings and six horns," three lines below, consists of two double-reed oboe, one large transverse flute, one two-stringed fiddle, one hourglass drum, and one barrel-shaped drum.

eighteenth century *p'ansori* became an important component in the procession. Singers and acrobats were also summoned to perform at sixtieth-birthday celebrations hosted by the literati and wealthy households, and there they created lively entertainment. Their performances were not always perceived positively by the upper class. Because, however, loud merrymaking was allowed and was even considered necessary, they hired the singers, acrobats, and musicians for large sums of money.

Through these events, *p'ansori* slowly reached upper-class audiences and eventually the singers were able to perform at banquets held in the courtyards of the literati and wealthy families. As a result, the size of the upper-class audience increased. *P'ansori*, unlike other popular arts, needed only one singer and one drummer and so, without much difficulty, the performance could take place in a considerably confined space. Moreover, because of its rich content and musical sophistication, it was suited to upper-class tastes and aesthetic values. In the "Kwagu rok" ("Record of Concern for the Underprivileged") by Yi Ik (1681–1763) and other eighteenth-century documents, one finds frequent mention of the literati being criticized for their excessive indulgence in *kwangdae* performances. Among the folk arts enjoyed by the upper class at this time, it was *p'ansori* that resulted in the new audiences.

Together with this key development came technical sophistication. By the late eighteenth century, a standardized system to evaluate the artistic merit of a *p'ansori* performance had become widely accepted. Audiences had developed the ability to judge which singer was more sophisticated and which excelled in which performative aspects – narrative, musical expression, bodily movements, and acting. More and more audiences were trying to decide, according to the standardized criteria, which singer had the most individuality and artistic accomplishment.

As a result, a clear distinction was made between exceptional singers and mediocre ones. In time, master singers with great skill were recognized by the audience and praised as "great singers" of the time. Such masters received warm and enthusiastic receptions that perhaps compensated for the hardship endured during the long period of training. The masters enjoyed different treatment from the acrobats and other entertainers. Singers who did not reach the status of "great singer," however, simply sang and received a little money. Those who could not even earn such a living had no choice but to become vagabonds – similar to itinerant outcast entertainers. This is why those who aspired to become *p'ansori* singers repeatedly underwent rigorous training in order to become virtuosi. Song Manjae's "On Seeing the Plays of Actors" (1843) presents such a state of affairs:

> *Kwangdae* are mostly from the southeastern region;
> They, too, claim to have come to take the examination . . .
> The successful candidate chooses a singer with excellent skills;
> Singers who scramble for the test resemble Buddhist monks hearing
>   news of special offerings.
> In groups, they come to Seoul where the examination takes place;
> They present various modes of singing groups, pitting their skills
>   against each other.
> In the capital, everyone talks about a master, U Ch'undae;
> Today, who is going to become his protégé?
> With one song, a thousand bolts of silk are granted;
> Kwŏn Samdŭk and Mo Hŭnggap have been well known since their
>   youth.[8]

Here the singers, gathering in Seoul at examination time, speak as if they too had come to take the examination. They have become aware of the significance of the literati as their audience: gaining recognition from them is equivalent to passing the civil service examination. This is the reason for gathering, singing in various modes, and competing against one another: to be recognized and appreciated by the literati.

Candidates who passed the civil service examination would try to choose the most outstanding singer. Choosing the "best" singer was only possible, however, after the candidate's appreciation of *p'ansori* had reached the stage where he had a mature understanding of the general standards. In the early nineteenth century, based on experiences accumulated over a long period of time, appreciation of *p'ansori* expanded even in the upper class. U Ch'undae, whose name is mentioned in "On Seeing the Plays of Actors," was one of the great singers of his time. He performed through the end of the eighteenth century and lived into the early nineteenth century. It is hyperbole to suggest that he received 1,000 bolts of silk for singing one song, of course, but the story reveals that the great singers did receive enthusiastic receptions. In the nineteenth century, appraisal of the great singers was a matter of common knowledge and *p'ansori* lovers argued over who was going to replace the current master singer.[9]

In the first half of the nineteenth century, there were eight great *p'ansori* singers who were considered to be masters. Generally active during the reign of Sunjo (1800–1834), they were called the "P'almyŏngch'ang" ("Eight Master Singers") or "Chŏn p'almyŏngch'ang" ("Former Eight Master Singers"). Among the eight, Kwŏn Samdŭk, Song Hŭngnok, Yŏm Kyedal,

[8] Yun Kwangbong, *Hanguk yuhŭisi yŏngu* (Iu ch'ulp'ansa, 1985).
[9] Kim Hŭnggyu, "*P'ansori* ŭi sahoejk sŏnggyŏk kwa kŭ pyŏnmo," in *Yesul kwa sahoe*, ed. Hanguk sahoe kwahak yŏnguso (Minŭmsa, 1979), p. 66.

Mo Hŭnggap, and Ko Sugwan were exceptional.[10] As *p'ansori* rose to the level of a sophisticated form of art, singers began to regard the upper classes and middle-level people as much more important audiences. After the early nineteenth century, singers adapted the *p'ansori* narratives to suit the tastes of these classes. Although many commoner audiences still existed, they were not in a position to exert much influence on the *p'ansori* singers. Those who won fame as master singers were not only highly regarded but were awarded generous honoraria by the literati, the wealthy, and the officials, whose interests and appraisals exerted a direct influence.[11]

The reduction of the twelve-work canon, which survived until the early nineteenth century, to a five-work repertoire was directly related to the foregoing phenomena. The seven works that were not transmitted represented the worldview and aesthetic sense of commoners and were unlikely to be accepted by the upper class. Opportunities to sing these songs diminished in the nineteenth century as the performances were largely dependent on upper-class audiences. As the transmission of these seven oral traditions weakened, by the mid nineteenth century they had gradually disappeared. Today these works do not exist in the form of *p'ansori* songs – only segments of some works survive in literary sources. This tendency also affected the five remaining works. Depending on the edition, one finds traces of embellishment and partial adaptation catering to the tastes of the literati.

For *p'ansori*, the nineteenth century was an extremely complex but crucial period. Of particular note was the emergence of an intermediary who held a significant position – bridging the gap between the *p'ansori* singers and the upper-class audience – contributing to the refinement of *p'ansori*. One person who played this role was Sin Chaehyo (1812–1884), who not only possessed an extraordinary talent for recognizing excellence in *p'ansori* but also held considerable influence.[12] Sin was from the middle-people class and lived in Koch'ang county in North Chŏlla province. A wealthy patron who enjoyed an elegant and cultured lifestyle, he helped singers and taught them. Sin had great insight into *p'ansori* art and a profound appreciation of it. He refined its vulgar elements and taught singers how to perform sophisticated music and exhibit dramatic acting. As his name was widely

---

[10] Kang Hanyŏng, *P'ansori* (Sejong taewang kinyŏm saŏphoe, 1977), pp. 163–164; Yu Kiyong, "*P'ansori* p'almyŏngch'ang kwa kŭ chongsŭngja tŭl," in *P'ansori ŭi ihae* (Ch'angjak kwa pip'yŏngsa, 1978), pp. 145–162.

[11] Kim Hŭnggyu, "Sipku segi chŏngi *p'ansori* ŭi yŏnhaeng hwangyŏng kwa sahoejŏk kiban," *Ŏmun nonjip* 30 (1991).

[12] Sŏ Chongmun and Chŏng Pyŏnghŏn, eds., *Sin Chaehyo yŏngu* (T'aehaksa, 1997).

known and his assessment of *p'ansori* singers was recognized, there was a saying that without Sin's tutelage a singer could not pass himself off as a master singer.

Sin modified the six *p'ansori* works transmitted to his day, refining the crude elements in an attempt to correct unsuitable materials. These six are the *Song of Ch'unhyang* for male and adolescent singing, the *Song of Sim Ch'ŏng*, the *Song of the Rabbit and the Turtle* (same as the *Song of the Water Palace*), the *Song of Hŭngbo*, the *Song of Red Cliff*, and the *Song of Pyŏn Kangsoe*. In modifying the *p'ansori* narratives and teaching the singers, Sin's aim was not to elevate the aesthetic value of the popular arts. Instead of fully accepting and then improving them, he deleted the life experiences of the lower classes and their way of thinking. As a result, *p'ansori* after Sin Chaehyo, in terms of narrative and music, became strikingly more polished but its distinctive characteristics – humor, satire, and understanding of reality – were somewhat restricted.[13] One cannot, of course, say that Sin's contribution was insignificant in terms of the history of *p'ansori* in the mid nineteenth century. His editorial work marked an end to the process of historical development and continuous transformation of the *p'ansori*. As the first redactor of *p'ansori* texts, Sin played an important role in defining the artistic conventions and standards of *p'ansori* as transmitted to the present day.

In this manner, many great singers were produced and developed their own musical techniques. After the early nineteenth century, *p'ansori* was divided into different schools, each with a different singing technique. Each school developed musical characteristics as well as certain differences in the texts. Singing techniques can be broadly divided into two principal schools: the Eastern school (Tongp'yŏnje) and the Western school (Sŏp'yŏnje). These two schools are further divided into the Central school (Chunggoje) and the River and Mountain school (Kangsanje) respectively. The Eastern school is usually traced back to Song Hŭngnok as its founder, the Western school originated from the school of Pak Yujŏn (c. 1834–1900). Whereas the Eastern school accepted the old singing technique, the Western school stressed a continuous effort to cultivate individual technique, making it more sophisticated and refined. The Central school and the River and Mountain school stressed eclecticism and divergence, respectively. As these schools' techniques were transmitted by various singers, the artistic depth and breadth of *p'ansori* increased extensively.

---

[13] Kim Hŭnggyu, "Sin Chaehyo kaejak *Ch'unhyang ka* ŭi *p'ansorisachŏk* wich'i," *Hanguk hakpo* 10 (1978).

P'ansori encountered a new situation after the establishment of the Wŏngaksa theater in 1903 in Seoul, for one of the most important performing arts presented there was *p'ansori*. In the beginning *p'ansori*, like folk and popular songs, took the traditional form of one person singing. With the influence of Peking opera troupes from China, however, *p'ansori* was transformed into a theatrical performance (*ch'anggŭk*) in which each actor would take on the role of an individual character. *P'ansori*, at this time, was cherished by kings Kojong (1864–1907) and Sunjong (1907–1910). Through these staged performances, singers interacted with the audience and received their enthusiastic support. During the time of the Wŏngaksa, not only did they stage the old transmitted works but, using contemporary experience, they attempted to create a new repertoire. Included in this category is a still-extant work known as the *Ballad of Ch'oe Pyŏngdu*, which was about an incident that took place in Wŏnju, Kangwŏn province. It concerns a corrupt official, Magistrate Chŏng, exploiting innocent citizens and committing atrocities. During the program, however, a relative of the magistrate caused a disturbance and tried to stop the performance. As the actor who played the innocent victim, Kim Ch'anghwan, was being carried off the stage as a corpse, the enthusiastic audience, impressed with his performance, praised him and draped strings of cash around his neck.[14]

The enormous success of modern *p'ansori* lost its vitality, however, when the country lost its independence. In 1905, the Wŏngaksa closed down. With Japanese cultural infiltration, interventions and sanctions were forced on Korean traditional art and music either covertly or overtly. As a result, the singers lost the stage for their activities and dispersed in disappointment. After that, instead of trying to respond to the contemporary situation, *p'ansori* singers simply resorted to preserving the old repertoire.

THE TWELVE WORKS OF *P'ANSORI*

The word *madang* is used to designate a *p'ansori* work that possesses an independent story plot. The *p'ansori* repertoire comprises twelve works or stories. Among the twelve, only five are extant and performed today: the *Song of Ch'unhyang*, the *Song of Sim Ch'ŏng*, the *Song of Hŭngbo*, the *Song of the Rabbit and the Turtle* (or *Song of the Water Palace*), and the *Song of Red Cliff*. Before the nineteenth century, however, all twelve works were

[14] Pak Hwang, *P'ansori sosa* (Singu munhwasa, 1974), pp. 111–114. The *Ballad of Ch'oe Pyŏngdu* was an adaptation from the first half of the "new" fiction entitled *A Silvery World*. See Ch'oe Wŏnsik, "Kaehwagi ŭi *ch'anggŭk* undong kwa *Ŭnsegye*," in *P'ansori ŭi ihae* (Ch'angjak kwa pip'yŏngsa, 1978), and Kim Chongch'ŏl, *P'ansorisa yŏngu* (Yŏksa pip'yŏngsa, 1996), pp. 267–281.

열여 춘향 슈졀가라

슈종 딕왕직위초의 셩덕이너부시사셩자셩

은게ᄉ숭ᄉ흥사금고오족은요슌시졀이요으관문

물은우당의빅금이라좌우보필은츄셔경신이요용

양호위난관셩지장이라조졍의흐르난덕화힝곡

의퍼엿시니사힝구든기슌이원군의어려잇다츙신

은만조흥꼬회자열셔가ᄉ쳐라미셜ᄉ라우슌

풍초흥니함포고보구빅셩덜은쳐ᄉ의겨량가라

잇셔졀난도남원부의월민라하난기싱이잇슈되삼

남의명기로셔일젹퇴기ᄒ야셩가라ᄒ눈양반을

다리고세원을보닉되연잔사순의당하야일결혀류

이업셔일노한이되야장탄슈심의병이되것구나일

일은크게씌쳐예사람으로셩각ᄒ고가군으로쳥입

Example 7. Anon., *Song of a Faithful Wife, Ch'unhyang* (woodblock edn., Chŏnju, n.d.). A copy owned by Kim Sayŏp.

춘향上

흥 야엿자오듸공슌의 훈난마리들르시 셩셩의무샹

은혜갓쳐던지 이셩의 삽부 되야 챵기형 실다바

고 옛모도승샹즁 고여공도 심 슛 것만 무삼죄가컨

즁즁 야일첨 혀륙 업셧스니 육친무죡 우리신

셰션영힝 좌 누라즁 며 사후 감장 어이 하리 명산듸

찰의신공의나즁 야남녀간 낫컨드면 평셩 한을풀

거시니 가군의 뜻 시엇 덩오 셩참판 하는마리일

셩신셰셩 각즁 면자 나 마리당연즁 나비려셔 자식을

나흘진듼 무자할 사람이 잇슬이요즁니 월민닷답

하되 쳔하 셩공부자도 이구산의 비르시고 졍나

라졍자산은 수셩산의 비러나게 셔고 안동 밥 강션을

이를진딘 명산듸 쳔이 업슬손 가 경샹도즁쳔즁

쳔의난누 도록 자녀 업셔 최교봉의 비러 더니

performed. The seven works that were dropped after the nineteenth century include *Pyŏn Kangsoe ka* or *Karujigi t'aryŏng* (*Ballad of Pyŏn Kangsoe*), *Paebijang t'aryŏng* (*Ballad of Subcommander Pae*), *Kangnŭng Maehwa t'aryŏng* (*Ballad of Maehwa of Kangnŭng*), *Changkki t'aryŏng* (*Ballad of the Pheasant Cock*), *Ong Kojip t'aryŏng* (*Ballad of the Miser Ong Kojip*), *Musugi t'aryŏng* (*Ballad of Musugi*), and *Katcha sinsŏn t'aryŏng* (*Ballad of the False Transcendent*).

The singer's tendency to suit aristocratic tastes and the attrition of texts took place during the late nineteenth century as the literati, the middle-level people, and the wealthy became influential audiences. Literary records compiled between 1860 and 1880 already omit works other than the *Song of Pyŏn Kangsoe* and the *Ballad of Maehwa of Kangnŭng*. One cannot conclude that these works all disappeared at once, however, simply because they were excluded from the literary records. Perhaps they were sung infrequently over the years. By the end of the nineteenth century, however, they had disappeared.

The twelve major works are different from the fixed narratives and drama scripts. The *Song of Ch'unhyang* sung by Yi Tongbaek (1867–1950), for example, differs immensely from Im Pangul's (1904–1961) version in terms of music as well as narrative. The same singer singing the same song may also change from performance to performance. Each work allows for the individuality of the singer and, depending on the situation, extensive improvisation is allowed. Even so, each work maintains its fundamental homogeneity. The singer fully digests the text, cultivates his own unique style, tailoring his performance to suit the circumstances, and thus displays his creativity.

The twelve works are products of serial creation: the accumulated efforts and hard work of numerous singers over the years made them possible. They cannot be characterized as the work of an individual, therefore, but are the joint accomplishment of numerous singers. Accordingly, each of the twelve works of *p'ansori* consists of distinct narrative components, especially those that are fixed in the form of fiction. One can recognize these differences in the narratives today, depending on different genealogical lines and the circumstances of the performance.

Among the twelve major works, the *Song of Ch'unhyang* has enjoyed the most popularity and is regarded as the masterpiece. The main theme of the story involves the meeting and parting of two lovers. This story, however, incorporates the realistic dimension of conflict arising out of disparity in social status in the late Chosŏn period. In this work Ch'unhyang, the daughter of a female entertainer, endures unspeakable hardship but does not surrender to the oppression of the new magistrate Pyŏn who summons her to serve him. Ch'unhyang insists on the value of love and chastity. At the end of the story, she is saved by Yi Mongnyong who returns as a secret royal inspector. This simple love story of struggle and salvation questions the social conventions of the later Chosŏn dynasty. The story may accordingly be read as depicting a social change with the dissolution of Confucian values and the emergence of modern consciousness.[15] The *Song of Sim Ch'ŏng*,[16] *Song of Hŭngbo*,[17] *Song of the Rabbit and the Turtle*,[18] and *Song of Red Cliff*[19] were popular too. Given various fictional embellishments and many changes, they were distributed and circulated as reading materials in different editions.

Characters appearing in *p'ansori* are not only colorful but vividly realistic. In the classical fiction popular around the same time, characters lacked realistic qualities. The main characters in these works, portrayed according to the fixed moral code, were stereotyped and one-dimensional. Not only did these works portray stock characters, but they also presented an idealized (fictional) living space and background. Accordingly, the classical fiction was rich in invention but weak in realistic portrayal of daily experience. *P'ansori* stories, by contrast, were set in real-life situations or were reflections of the time. Events in the *p'ansori* narratives are not fabricated tales of talented men and beautiful women but are intimately related to human experience. *P'ansori* characters, good or evil, were not presented as moral archetypes. A positive main character, from time to time, is the object of ridicule; an evil character is not always portrayed as absolutely evil. One of the positive protagonists found in a *p'ansori* work, Blindman Sim in the *Song of Sim Ch'ŏng*, for example, becomes an object of farce in both the earlier and later parts of the work. Yi Mongnyong, in the *Song of Ch'unhyang*, from the outing scene at Kwanghan Tower to the scene of his visit to Ch'unhyang's house, is frequently subjected to vulgarization. Even Ch'unhyang herself, in conversing with Pangja, Yi's male servant, uses vulgar language and,

[15] Sŏl Chunghwan, *Kkumkkunŭn Ch'unhyang: P'ansori yŏsŏt madang ttŭdŏbogi* (Nanam, 2000); and Sŏl Sŏnggyŏng, ed., *Ch'unhyang yesulsa charyo ch'ongsŏ*, 8 vols. (Kukhak charyowŏn, 1998).

[16] Yu Yŏngdae, *Sim Ch'ŏng chŏn yŏngu* (Munhak akademi, 1989); Kim Chinyŏng et al., eds., *Sim Ch'ŏng chŏn chŏnjip*, 11 vols. (Pagijŏng, 1997–2000).

[17] In Kwŏnhan, ed., *Hŭngbu chŏn yŏngu* (Chimmundang, 1991); Kim Chinyŏng and Kim Hyŏnju, trans., *Hŭngbo chŏn* (Pagijŏng, 1997); and Pak Yŏngju, *P'ansori sasŏl ŭi t'ŭksŏng kwa mihak* (Pogosa, 2000), pp. 233–270.

[18] In Kwŏnhan, "*T'okki chŏn* ŭi sŏmin ŭisik kwa p'ungjasŏng," *Ŏmun nonjip* 14–15 (1972):36–53.

[19] Kim Sanghun, "*Chŏkpyŏk ka* ŭi ibon kwa hyŏngsŏng yŏngu" (Ph.D. dissertation, Inha University, 1992).

depending on the situation, exhibits her exceptional skill in everyday human relations. Yet even those negatively portrayed characters who are subjected to satire, criticism, and ridicule may become the object of sympathy and are not always represented as unredeemable evil types. Nolbo in the *Song of Hŭngbo* is one such case. The audience experiences a certain enjoyment watching Nolbo's wicked acts. Even in the depiction of minor characters, *p'ansori* displays an ability to represent commoners by giving them a definite form and shape.

In short, human relationships and moral consciousness were portrayed with a versatile sense of reality in *p'ansori*. The characters in the world of *p'ansori* are neither unequivocally good nor evil but possess multidimensional characteristics. Recognizing all these diverse aspects, the singers perform various events and scenes with a great flexibility that is rooted in a sense of reality found in the lives of the common people. As a result, *p'ansori* was able to endow its various colorful characters with three-dimensional verisimilitude and achieve literary success by depicting the problems of the time either directly or through allegory and farce.

CHAPTER 16

Folk drama

Kim Hŭnggyu

Korean traditional plays include mask dance and puppet plays, as well as the *Tŏtboegi* (mask play) and *Palt'al* ("foot mask") of the roving troupes. All are folk plays transmitted without written scripts by performing troupes of lower-class origin without the help of professional writers. Folk plays did not always belong to the lower-class performers, however.

Although there is not enough evidence to draw definite conclusions, it appears that performing arts similar to theater plays existed from the Three Kingdoms period to the end of Unified Silla. It also appears that such plays were based on ancient agricultural ceremonies and performing arts designed for Buddhist missionary works. According to "Song of Ch'ŏyong" (a Silla song), and the related record of the myth, the struggle between the magical protagonist Ch'ŏyong and the demon of pestilence was performed as a ceremonial play.

In the late Koryŏ period of the thirteenth and fourteenth centuries, as performances at court flourished, song-and-dance plays became one of the main performing arts. One can point to "The Turkish Bakery" as an example with distinct characteristics of a theatrical play. This song, produced during the reign of King Ch'ungnyŏl (1275–1308), tells of a number of women's affairs with a Muslim, a monk, a dragon, and a tavern owner, through song and dance. History records that such song-and-dance plays were popular at court during the late Koryŏ period.[1]

During the Chosŏn period, however, traditional plays declined under the restrictions imposed by Confucian ideology. Neo-Confucian literati looked down on the performing arts and considered them to be deviations from Confucian morality. Therefore plays – except those connected to religious rituals – declined at court and among the ruling elite and gradually disappeared. Folk plays were suppressed as well. As the strict Confucian ideals came to dominate all aspects of Chosŏn society, the development of

[1] *KRS* 71:42a–b.

plays was severely constrained. Even those plays that had been transmitted among the lower classes declined greatly as village society was being transformed according to the Neo-Confucian ideology. Moreover, due to the Confucian prejudice against the performing arts, many performances and plays were never recorded systematically in writing.

As commerce developed and urban culture grew after the seventeenth century, these dire conditions improved somewhat. The ruling class still spurned the plays, but the bustling atmosphere of mercantile centers provided an environment conducive to the growth of all the performing arts. At the same time, some of the wandering people created by the dissolution of the farming villages were absorbed into roving troupes of performers. Various plays developed and spread throughout the country. This is why folk plays are the main legacy of traditional Korean theater arts – and why they reflect the sentiments of the people more than any other art form.

MASK DANCE PLAYS

According to extant records, ancient indigenous Korean plays and performing arts developed on their own while absorbing influence from China and Central Asia. We can see this in names such as "Five Shows" – known to the Chinese as "Korean mask dance and play," "Korean music," and "mask dance plays" – that exerted influence on the formation of Japanese performing culture. "The Five Shows" (*Ogi*) were composed of five plays known as *Kŭmhwan*, *Wŏlchŏn*, *Taemyŏn*, *Soktok*, and *Sanye*, which appear to be related to mask dances. A scene in *Taemyŏn* where a man with a golden mask dances to expel the demon of pestilence with a whip recalls the character Malttugi in Pongsan mask dance play and in the Yangju *pyŏlsandae*. As well, two other dances show a close connection to the development of mask dances. One is the "Hwangch'ang Dance" commemorating the death of fifteen-year-old Hwang Ch'ang who assassinated the king of Paekche. The other is the "Ch'ŏyong Dance," a ceremonial dance to drive out ghosts, which was performed during the reign of Silla's forty-ninth king, Hŏngang, and performed continuously at the courts of Koryŏ and Chosŏn.

Such plays were performed mainly during the Buddhist lantern festival and the "Hundred Plays of Song and Dance" of the Assembly of Eight Prohibitions that sacrificed to the local deities. Various "*sandae* plays" were performed on temporary stages. One can gain insight into these plays through such writings as *Sandae Plays* and *Capital Miscellany* by Yu Tŭkkong (1748–1807). The poem "Namsŏng kwanhŭija" ("Upon Seeing a Play at South Gate") by Kang Ich'ŏn (1769–1801) shows the original form of the mask dances of today. In this poem, which describes the play Kang saw as a ten-year-old boy in 1779 outside the South Gate of the capital city, there are scenes such as the following:

> Old Monk, where do you come from?
> Wearing monk's cloth and holding a staff
> He can't straighten his crooked body,
> Beard and eyebrows are all white.
> A novice follows him
> Continuously saluting as he rubs his hands together.
> He is old and weak;
> How many times did he fall down?
> Here comes a young woman –
> Surprised and happy at meeting her,
> He cannot hide his excitement,
> Breaking his vow, he wants to marry her.[2]

Except for the fact that the modern mask of the old monk has white and red spots on a black face (instead of the white beard and eyebrows depicted here), the overall contents are the same as the "Old Monk scene" of the Yangju *pyŏlsandae* play of today. Other scenes such as "Yŏnnip and Nunkkumjŏgi" ("The Head Monk Lotus Leaf and Blinker, his Attendant"), "Malttugi and Saennim," "Old Man," and "Old Woman" (Miyalhalmi; the old man's wife) show no significant difference from the mask dances that have been transmitted to the present day. Thus mask dances of the "*sandae* play" kind were always being performed more or less the same in the late eighteenth century.

Origin and development

There are differing theories, however, regarding the origin and development of mask dances. One hypothesis that was formulated early on and received substantial support is the theory of "*sandae* play" origin. It asserts that the dance evolved from ancient ceremonies, to Silla plays, to "*sandae* miscellaneous plays" of Koryŏ, to the "*sandae* play" (*sandae togam kŭk*) of Chosŏn. The "*Sandae* play" (*sandae hŭi*) – a performance of songs and dances, acrobatics, and jokes and farce on a stage as big as a mountain (*san*) developed into "*sandae* play" (*sandae kŭk*). When the *sandae* play was abolished as a state-sponsored event after the reign of King Yŏngjo (1724–1776), its performers scattered over the country, marking the beginning of the mask dances of today.[3]

---

[2] Im Hyŏngt'aek, ed., *Yijo sidae sosasi*, 2 vols. (Ch'angjak kwa pip'yŏngsa, 1992) 2:304.
[3] Kim Chaech'ŏl, *Chosŏn yŏngŭk sa* (Hagyesa, 1933), pp. 36–44; Yi Tuhyŏn, *Hanguk ŭi kamyŏngŭk* (Munhwajae kwalliguk, 1969), p. 136.

Others seek the origin of mask dances in foreign influences. One theory proposes that mask dances originated from the mask dance play (*kiak,* J *gigaku*) that Mimaji of Paekche studied in Wu China and later transmitted to Japan (c. 612). This mask dance play is recorded in the Japanese document *Kyōkunshō* (*A Learner's Treatise,* 1233), which explains that it was a morality play and silent drama performed during Buddhist ritual celebrations. Certainly there are similarities in scenes and characters between this mask dance play (*kiak*) and the Yangju *pyŏlsandae* and the Pongsan mask dance play. This theory persuasively explains that *kiak* evolved into folk plays as monks joined roving performers in the aftermath of the early Chosŏn policy of suppressing Buddhism.[4]

Both theories contend that mask dances spread from the upper to the lower classes. Yet it appears that mask dances followed similar developmental stages in both milieus – whether simple dances traditionally performed in farming villages or more developed ones performed in towns and cities after the eighteenth century. Some have traced the origin of mask dances to village shamanist rituals for a good harvest, performed by farmers. One can conjecture that the band members later became musicians for mask dances, that characters following the band became the characters of mask dances, and that regular participants were comparable to audiences for mask dance performances.[5] The *pyŏlsin* ritual of Hahoe village, for example, performs mask dances with music for the village's guardian deities. The band, the audience, and masked characters move around the village and engage in mock fights or sexual play. The masks with human names such as "Imae," "Ch'oraengi," "Yangban," and "Kaksi" originated from masks depicting spirits in the shamanist ritual. Moreover, there is a fight between Summer and Winter praying for fertility and bounty in the village ritual, and we see evidence of a similar story in mask dances as well. In the confrontations between the old monk and Ch'wibari (the old bachelor; also called the prodigal) and between the old woman (Miyalhalmi) and the concubine (Tolmŏrichip), the old characters are driven out and the productive young ones triumph. That a new life begins from the young reflects the ideas behind the rituals performed during agricultural ceremonies.[6]

It is hard to say which of these theories is correct. Perhaps they must be considered as complementing each other. Even if mask dances developed

---

4 Yi Hyegu, "*Sandaegŭk* kwa 'kiak (gigaku),'" in *Hanguk ŭmak yŏngu* (Kungmin ŭmak yŏnguhoe, 1957), pp. 225–236; Ch'oe Chŏngyŏ, "*Sandae togamgŭk* sŏngnip ŭi chemunje," *Hangukhak nonjip* 1 (1973).
5 Cho Tongil, "*T'alch'um* kwa minjung ŭisik ŭi sŏngjang," in *Talch'um ŭi yŏksa wa wŏlli* (Hongsŏngsa, 1979), pp. 45–108.
6 Chŏn Kyŏnguk, *Minsok kŭk* (Hansaem, 1993), pp. 7–48.

on their own from their beginnings as ancient rituals, there must have been various changes and influences from foreign elements over the years – in particular, the influence of the performing arts from the Western Regions and China.

Regional mask dances

Mask dances are also known variously by their traditional names such as *Sandae nori, T'al nori, Pyŏlsin kut nori, Tŏtboegi, Tŭllorŭm,* and *Ogwangdae.* Even the common term *t'alch'um* (mask dance) originally meant mask dances of the Hwanghae region.

Korean mask dances may be divided into three categories according to their developmental stage. The first category includes comparatively simple mask dances that came out of village rituals: the Pukch'ŏng lion dance, the Kangnŭng official slave mask play, and the Hahoe *pyŏlsin* shamanist ritual.[7] The second category contains more developed dances from the coastal areas and the Naktong River delta of South Kyŏngsang. Dances from the region east of the Naktong River (Tongnae, Suyŏng, and Pusanjin) are called *yayu* (outdoor plays), while those from the west of the river (T'ongyŏng, Kosŏng, Chinju, and Kasan) are known as *Ogwangdae* (Five actors play). The third category includes mask dances of substantial content and size such as the Yangju *pyŏlsandae* play and the Songp'a *sandae* play, both from near Seoul, and the Pongsan mask play and Kangnyŏng mask play of Hwanghae province.

While the first category of mask dances has a close affinity with village ritual ceremonies, the outdoor plays and *Ogwangdae* show the urban characteristics of the administrative and economic centers where they developed. Because the *sandae* play and Haesŏ mask dance developed in regions of active commerce, they have more diverse contents and more splendor than the mask dances of farming villages. The rural dances performed during annual celebrations of the first full moon of the year and on the fifth day of the fifth lunar month, have strong characteristics of ritual prayer for bountiful fishing and harvests. Urban dances of the central and Hwanghae regions, by contrast, were performed on other occasions as well. Most of the performers were skilled villagers, but lower-ranking local functionaries might also take the lead in places like Pongsan. The more urbanized the site and the later the period, the more examples we find of performances by somewhat specialized groups.

[7] Sŏ Yŏngho, *Sŏnangkut t'al nori* (Yŏrhwadang, 1991).

Performances do not require any special installation – only a space large enough for a gathering of spectators. Mask dances were performed in a flat space illuminated by torches from dusk to dawn and surrounded by audiences who were either sitting or standing. The masks show greatly exaggerated expressions and were made from wood, gourds, or paper depending on the region. Dance movements, lighting, and viewing angles all produced different expressions.

Overall, mask dances are organized into several loosely connected acts and scenes. Each scene contains characters with distinct dancing styles and movements that are not constrained by time and space as in realist plays. Scenes focus on developing dramatic conflicts clearly and rapidly and are not subject to everyday common sense. The characters not only initiate conversations with audience and musicians, but audience and musicians themselves jump in from time to time – thereby breaking the dramatic illusion and bringing everyone into the performance. Dialogues contain both everyday speeches and songs, but there are also parts where gestures and dance are the main mode of expression as in silent plays.

As the name "mask dance" indicates, dance does have a special significance. Dances are often employed when characters enter and exit and when dramatic confrontations reach their climax. Dancing movements are formulated in a sophisticated way and are sometimes developed to such a degree that they appear to be independent scenes. The "official slave mask play" has no dialogue, and the old monk of the Haesŏ mask play and *sandae* play and the leper of outdoor plays and *Ogwangdae* use only dance and bodily gestures. Dances are closely related to dramatic context and express the psychological states of the characters. These dances all evoke unique aesthetic experiences. The old monk's dances expose psychological confrontation between social norms and everyday desires. Dances of the old monk and Ch'wibari show dramatic confrontation. Dances of the gentleman (*yangban*) and Malttugi reinforce the stupidity of the lettered class. In this way, mask dances heighten dramatic interest as the aesthetic experience of dance is united with the personalities of characters or the themes.

Songs have similar functions. Because mask dances were performed and transmitted by commoners, most were based on everyday speech although some did borrow from conventional Chinese expressions or contain uninhibited vulgarisms and jokes. Here the devices of omission, repetition, and exaggeration provide clear contrasts and heighten dramatic effect. We see the lively power of this popular art form in ideas that take the audience by surprise and in the dynamic body language. Songs are a substantial part of this effect. As various popular folk songs, *sijo*, miscellaneous songs, and *kasa* are brought into the dramatic context of mask dances, these songs create special dramatic effects. Songs such as "Tungdung t'aryŏng" ("Rock-a-bye-baby") and ballads with puns on letters of the Korean alphabet or tetrasyllabic lines from the *Thousand Sinograph Primer* are sung by Ch'wibari to his son, born of a union between him and a young female shaman/entertainer, after he defeats the old monk in the middle scene of the Pongsan mask dance play. Songs such as "Where Have You Gone?" and "How I Miss You!" in the Old Woman scene create heightened interest by expressing bitter longing and the joy of reunion.

Thus mask dances use song and dance to criticize social problems and bring about popular sensations of pleasure. Some scholars use complementary terms like "criticism" and "cheerfulness" to summarize such characteristics.[8] These two characteristics are closely linked and produce both biting satire and festive liveliness – the main reason why commoners of late Chosŏn supported mask dances.

THEMES OF MASK DANCE PLAYS

Although there were regional differences, the main theme of mask dances was a satire attacking social inequity. Old Monk, Little Shaman/ Entertainer, Shoe Peddler, Gentleman, Malttugi, Old Man, Old Woman – such names refer to one's social standing or social group, not one's personal name. Through these names we can see that the main theme of mask dances was not personal problems but friction between social classes. One Old Monk scene, for example, contains a fight between the old monk, who is caught between Buddhist precepts and his own desire, and a street loafer named Ch'wibari. A gentleman scene deals with problems between a gentleman and his servant Malttugi. An Old Woman scene contains a fight over a young concubine between the old man and his wife, who had been separated by poverty and chaos. These three episodes constitute basic motifs to which are added other scenes.

Consider the Old Monk scene. The old monk, who enters the stage with a cantankerous junior monk (*mŏkchung*), breaks his vow at once as he is enchanted by a young female shaman who accompanies the young monk. The old monk is overcome by sexual desire and tries everything to win her. In a scene where the old monk dances for joy after he gains the favor of the female shaman by offering her his rosary, we can see the

---

[8] Kim Hyŏnhyang, "Minjung yŏnhŭi ŭi chŏnt'ong kwa t'alch'um ŭi sŏngjang," in *Minjok munhaksa kangjwa* (Ch'angjak kwa pip'yŏngsa, 1995) 1:329.

Illustration 3.　　Hahoe wooden mask for the "Gentleman" character in Hahoe mask
dance play.

extreme side of a Buddhist monk who had been a captive of empty ideals.
The theme of this scene is not merely to satirize the old monk's breaking of
his vow, however. If that were the theme, the play would recommend that
he abide by the precepts and cultivate the Buddha dharma. Yet there is no
such implication. What the scene shows is that a life which affirms worldly
desires is more valuable than a life of long ascetic cultivation. In other

words: the old monk, through his encounters with worldly characters such as the young shaman and the shoe peddler, got lost between precepts and instincts and was transformed into a person who accepts worldly desires as he escapes from the world of dubious ideals.

The old monk who gives up his precepts and pursues worldly desires gets into a fierce struggle, however, when Ch'wibari tries to take the young shaman away. The old monk loses and is driven out. With money and fighting spirit, Ch'wibari is a character of developed urban dances not to be found in farm-village plays. Through Ch'wibari, mask dance plays tried to emphasize the wholesome side of real-life desire and negate the religious. As we noted earlier, the young man taking a woman away from an old man seems to have originated in the fight between Winter and Summer in agricultural rituals. Based on such a primitive story, mask dances accentuated the positive aspects of life as a new theme. Although the old monk transforms himself by breaking his vow and coupling with the young shaman, his transformation is not complete. With his vestiges of monkhood and old age, he appears weak and languid compared to Ch'wibari – an archetype of the young and lively merchant. Thus the old monk cannot withstand Ch'wibari's fierce snatching of the young shaman.[9]

Although gentlemen characters appear in all mask dance plays, they are not always satirized in the same way. Commonly their masks are distorted and abnormal – thereby insinuating their negative character. Plays also introduce several stupid gentlemen characters who go about flaunting their high social standing and thereby exposing each other's weaknesses. The scene where Monster Yŏngno is about to devour a gentleman also exposes the hypocrisy of the gentleman's power and social status. The most direct satire against the gentleman class, however, is made by Malttugi:

MALTTUGI: Hush, here come some gentlemen. But don't mistake these fellows for retired gentlemen who served in all the top posts of government. These gentlemen are made up of the *"yang"* in *kaejallyang* [dogskin rug] and the *ban* in *kaedari soban* [small dining table].
GENTLEMEN: Hey! What did you just say?
MALTTUGI: Ah, I don't know what you heard. I said here come three brothers of Master Yi who retired after serving in all the high offices of the land.
GENTLEMEN: We are indeed of Master Yi's family.

This is the first segment of the Gentleman scene of the Pongsan mask dance play. Here Malttugi ridicules the empty pretensions of the

---

[9] Cho Tongil, "Nojang kwajang ŭi chuje chaekŏmt'o," in *T'alch'um ŭi yŏksa wa wŏlli* (Hongsŏngsa, 1979), pp. 185–198.

gentlemen by comparing them to a dogskin rug and small dining table. When the gentlemen get angry, he pretends to console them but again laughs at their stupidity. In fact, gentlemen in mask dance plays do nothing but compose poetry, flaunt their high pedigree, or curse at their servant Malttugi. While Malttugi seems to obey them, in reality he turns them into laughing-stocks. As in the foregoing scene, the satire becomes more and more pungent through repetition of Malttugi's ridicule→gentlemen's retort→Malttugi's dissimulation→gentlemen's gullibility. In mask dance plays, Malttugi is a satiric companion of gentlemen. While he belongs to gentlemen as a servant, he has no loyalty toward them and indeed ridicules them. Because he is a servant, he is in a position to expose their faults and malign them as he follows them around. Because he is supposed to perform his duties as a servant, his contrary actions provide a comic confrontational effect.[10]

In the Old Woman scene, the old woman and her husband are the main characters. Although in the *Ogwangdae* play the old man belongs to the gentleman class, they are commoners in all other mask dance plays. Therefore, these plays show the life and hard times of late Chosŏn commoners who drifted from place to place just to survive. The Old Woman scene dramatically depicts people's separation and wandering, problems between wife and concubine, and men's oppression of women. The old woman had to leave her hometown and wander the country because of the chaotic times but finally meets her husband after a series of trying circumstances. Her husband treats her cruelly, however, and their fight escalates when his concubine enters the stage. In the end, the old woman meets a tragic fate. Her difficult life demonstrates the pain of commoners oppressed in the authoritarian age and the sufferings of women as victims of a male-centered society. In the dramatic ending of the old woman's death we see a tragic life crushed by these dual oppressions.

Thus mask dance plays depict the social contradictions of late Chosŏn. Their main themes are satire of the ruling class, a realism that asserts a worldly life while negating empty ideals, and an accusation of oppression by a patriarchal society. These are expressions of popular sentiment against the social ills of late Chosŏn when the Confucian ruling order was slowly dissolving. By using these sentiments, expressed through comic exaggeration and forceful confrontation, mask dance plays show their dynamism more than any other contemporary performing art.

---

[10] Kim Hŭnggyu, "Pangja wa Malttugi: tu chŏnhyŏng ŭi pigyo," *Hangukhak nonjip* 5 (1978): 108–109.

PUPPET PLAYS

Beside mask dance plays, traditional Korean folk plays include the puppet play (*Kkoktu kaksi, Tŏtpoegi*, and *Palt'al*). *Kkoktu kaksi* is a puppet play performed by roving troupes (*namsadangp'ae* or *kutchungp'ae*). Although there were other puppet plays known as *Mansŏkchung* play, Shadow Play, and *Palt'al*, very little has been transmitted to the present. The *Mansŏkchung* play, performed on the Buddha's birthday, the eighth day of the fourth lunar month, used string-controlled puppet characters such as Mansŏkchung, deer, fish, and a dragon. It was said that the play had no dialogue but was accompanied by music. Shadow Play (*kŭrimja inhyŏng nori*) is a play performed with paper cutouts of different animals. *Palt'al*, a play that used masks covering the feet, appears to have been either an alteration of the puppet plays of roving troupes or something spread across the country by traveling bands of performers.[11]

Roving troupes were made up of male performers who used to go from village to village performing six different arts: *P'ungmul* (farmers' music), *Pŏna* (dish spinning), *Salp'an* (acrobatics), *Ŏrŭm* (tightrope walking), *Tŏtpoegi* (mask dance), and *Tŏlmi* (puppet show). Dish spinning, acrobatics, and tightrope walking have theatrical characteristics in that they contain jokes and bodily gestures. Mask dance and puppet shows, however, are bona fide folk plays. Puppet plays were often performed by villagers as well. Perhaps members of roving troupes settled down and became local performers, or the plays may have been transmitted to many localities by wandering troupes.

The oldest written record about puppet plays, Ma Duanlin's *Wenxian tongkao* (*General History of Institutions and Critical Examination of Documents and Studies*, 1224), contains a passage stating that General Li Ji offered to the Tang court the puppet play of Koguryŏ after he had destroyed the kingdom. Later records related to puppet plays include "Kwan nonghwan yujak" ("On Viewing a Puppet Play") by Yi Kyubo (1168–1241), "Kuna haeng" ("On Seeing the Exorcism Rite") by Yi Saek (1328–1396), and "Kwan koeroe chaphŭi si" ("On Seeing Puppet Plays") by Sŏng Hyŏn (1439–1504). Although we are still unsure about the origin of puppet plays in Korea, one finds mutual influences among the puppet plays of Korea, China, and Japan: their stage structure, production methods, and puppet-controlling mechanisms are almost the same and the characters too are similar. Moreover, *kkoktu* in Korean is related to the Gypsy *kuli*, the Mongolian

---

[11] Chŏng Pyŏngho, "*Palt'al*," in *Chungyo muhyŏng munhwajae haesŏl: yŏngŭk p'yŏn* (Munhwajae kwalliguk, 1986), pp. 293–307.

A History of Korean Literature

kodokkochin, the Chinese *guotu*, and the Japanese *kugutsu*. Perhaps roving troupes of Gypsies came to Korea through Central Asia, Mongolia, and China and then to Japan.[12] Considering the Buddhist elements in puppet plays and the connection between Buddhist monasteries and the roving troupes, however, it is possible that skilled monks transformed the religious shows into popular spectacles and transmitted them all over the land after the closing of most Buddhist monasteries in early Chosŏn.[13]

There are no special stage limitations for puppet plays. They only require enough space for audiences in front of the covered stage. There are four columns, each about three meters apart, and all sides are covered except for the front. The main controller (*taejabi*) and his helper (*taejabison*) control puppet movements and deliver the dialogue from inside the stage. Musicians and the interlocutor (*sanbaji*) sit across from the stage and provide accompaniment. As the performances are held at night, torches are lit on both sides of the stage to illuminate the front. Puppets show only their upper bodies and move along the plane facing the audience. The only mobile parts are their two arms, and the puppets move up and down while shaking their upper body. The only exception is the acolyte puppet, which can move its neck, arms, and waist to exhibit interesting gestures and even dances.

Besides the exchanges between puppets themselves, dramatic effects rely on dialogue between puppets and interlocutor. Placing himself in the audience, the interlocutor facilitates the show by talking to puppets as if he were one of the villagers and makes the show three-dimensional by extending the show space into the audience.[14] Of the more than forty characters and animals, the most important is Pak Ch'ŏmji, who provides explanations through his dialogue with the interlocutor and also offers predictions about future events. This is why puppet plays are also known as Pak Ch'ŏmji. While we can find such use of outside elements in mask dance plays, this device is one of the key theatrical aspects of puppet plays.

Puppet plays are organized into two acts (*madang*) and seven scenes (*kŏri*). As in mask dance plays, each scene is more or less independent of the others. In each scene we can find satiric treatment of monks and gentlemen, a protest against patriarchal oppression, and ridiculing of social morality. Even sexual taboos are often broken, not to mention respect for

---

[12] Ch'oe Sangsu, *Hanguk inhyŏnggŭk ŭi yŏngu* (Koryŏ sŏjŏk, 1961), pp. 10–14; Yu Minyŏng, "Hanguk inhyŏnggŭk ŭi yurae," *Yesul nonmunjip* 14 (1975):268–273.
[13] Ch'oe Chŏngyŏ, "*Sandae togamgŭk* sŏngnip ŭi chemunje," pp. 11–24.
[14] Kim Hŭnggyu, "*Kkoktu kaksi norŭm* ŭi yŏngŭkchŏk konggan kwa *sanbaji*," in *Hanguk ŭi minsok yesul* (Munhak kwa chisŏngsa, 1988), pp. 151–165.

gentlemen and the elderly. Composed of four scenes, the Pak Ch'ŏmji act provides several comic confrontations by relatives of Pak Ch'ŏmji. In the Governor of P'yŏngan act, composed of three scenes, the main theme is satire of a cruel and corrupt governor of P'yŏngan province. One of the main characters in these two scenes is Hong Tongji, a nephew of Pak Ch'ŏmji. Hong has a naked body in red and even reveals an erect member. He trounces the corrupt acolyte of the monastery and Monster Isimi and ridicules the governor. Hong Tongji appears to be an amalgam of Malttugi and Ch'wibari from mask dance plays – an archetype of unpretentious high spirits and destructive humor. Finally, the story of Pak Ch'ŏmji's third scene, the *Kkoktu kaksi* scene, is similar to the Old Woman scene in most folk plays.[15]

DECLINE OF FOLK PLAYS

Korean folk plays such as mask dance and puppet plays declined rapidly in the twentieth century. There are several reasons for their failure to transform themselves into modern art forms. First, we can point to changes in commercial urban areas. As river traffic gave way to overland transport and the opening of railways changed the trade routes, traditional centers of folk play performances such as Pammari[16] and Songp'a[17] lost their vitality. Moreover, waves of foreign influence along with colonial invasion into the countryside not only transplanted a new form of entertainment but also destroyed the social foundations necessary for the continued survival of mask dance and puppet plays. Yet the greatest reason for the decline was the Japanese colonial policy of eradicating all forms of Korean culture. As it feared any assembly of the Korean people, the colonial government considered large-scale folk play performances to be dangerous and suppressed them. As opportunities for mask dance and puppet plays began to disappear, even simple transmission of folk plays became difficult and gradually they vanished.

[15] Im Chaehae, *Kkoktu kaksi norŭm ŭi ihae* (Hongsŏngsa, 1977), pp. 55–110; Im Chaehae, "Minsokkŭk ŭi chŏnsŭng chiptan kwa yŏnggam/halmi ŭi ssaum," in *Hanguk ŭi minsok yesul* (Munhak kwa chisŏngsa, 1988), pp. 191–198.
[16] A trading center on the Naktong River, near Hapch'ŏn, South Kyŏngsang province, where the *Ogwangdae* mask play and outdoor play originated.
[17] Southeast of Seoul, on the south shore of the Han River, an important ferry crossing between Seoul and Kwangju and a trading center with some 270 inns and taverns before the twentieth century; currently known as Karaktong Market in the Songp'a district in Seoul, the Songp'a *sandae* play in seven acts and nine scenes originated here.

CHAPTER 17

Literary criticism

Peter H. Lee

With the establishment of the Chosŏn dynasty, which adopted Neo-Confucianism as its official political and moral philosophy, debates on the relative importance of the classics and literature, the classics licentiate (*saengwŏn*) examination and the literary licentiate (*chinsa*) examination, were launched by meritorious officials at court and scholars in retirement. "In engaging men of ability for government service, one should not emphasize only literature or the classics. The civil service examination system recruits all learned men regardless of their predilections," said Chŏng Tojŏn (d. 1398).[1] The debate went on, however, especially regarding the relative merits of classical scholarship and literary composition. At times, the classics licentiate examination was considered more important than the literary licentiate examination. Thus the latter examination was abolished in 1396, restored in 1438, again abolished in 1444, and restored in 1453 to remain until 1894.

The argument of those favoring elucidation of the classics against those favoring literary composition was that students of literature read only selections of poetry and prose in anthologies and neglected the classics. Literaturists retorted that a one-sided emphasis on the classics would produce few writers who could serve as diplomats, write and harmonize with Chinese hosts in China, or entertain Chinese envoys to Korea. Furthermore, they asserted, the candidates in the classics examination faced examiners who might be swayed by their own personal feelings in assessing a candidate's performance. It was also said that such examinations required too much time and thus disrupted agricultural production.

Those who were in charge of drafting state papers and who later controlled the Office of Special Advisors and the Office of Royal Decrees were not only the arbiters of literary taste and style in their day, but were also spokesmen for the dynasty's new politics. These men included Chŏng

[1] Chŏng Tojŏn, *Sambong chip* 7:227–228.

Tojŏn, Kwŏn Kŭn (1352–1409), Pyŏn Kyeryang (1369–1430), Kwŏn Che (1387–1445), Chŏng Inji (1369–1478), Sin Sukchu (1417–1475), Sŏ Kŏjŏng (1420–1488), Sŏng Hyŏn (1439–1504), Nam Kon (1471–1527), and Yi Haeng (1478–1534). As Neo-Confucianism was increasingly understood and applied to statecraft, statesmen–writers began to repeat the moralistic view of literature: literature is a vehicle of the Way. With the appearance of Yi Hwang (1501–1571) and Yi I (1536–1584) in the sixteenth century, literature became the object of censure by Neo-Confucian philosophers.

LITERARY TRENDS OF EARLY CHOSŎN

The literary trends of the early Chosŏn dynasty may be seen in Chŏng Tojŏn's preface to the *Mogŭn munjip* (*Collected Works of Yi Saek*): "Literature is a vehicle of the Way. It means the configurations of men. If one attains the Way, one can illuminate under heaven the teachings of the classics."[2] To illustrate the relationship between the classics and literature, Sŏng Hyŏn said: "The classics are the sayings and deeds of the Sage, and literature is the dregs of the six classics. Not taking the ancients as a model in writing is like facing the wind without wings; not taking the classics as a model is like crossing the waves without an oar."[3] According to Kim Chongjik (1431–1492): "Literature comes from the classics, and the classics are the bases of literature."[4] If one pursues classical scholarship, one cannot help becoming a master of literary art; indeed, such pursuits guarantee that one will attain literary perfection. Yi Hwang, who found Kim Chongjik's writing ornate and shallow,[5] complained elsewhere that "candidates striving to attain verbal beauty only scratch the surface of the classics. Because of the examination system, the talented are thrown into the mire of vulgar learning."[6] Still, Yi himself wrote five volumes of poetry.

That the classics are the gateway to the Way (Yi I)[7] and that literature must embody the Way was repeated by Sŏ Kŏjŏng, Cho Wi (1454–1503), and others. Kim Sisŭp (1453–1493) argued that as a vehicle of the Way, literature cannot be more important than the Way. Yet one cannot ignore poetry, Kim said, because the *Book of Songs* is a Confucian classic that Confucius himself encouraged his pupils to study.[8] The view that the classics are more important than literature led to a view of literature as a "minor skill" or

---

[2] Ibid., 3:92.   [3] Sŏng Hyŏn, *Hŏbaektang chip* (1842 edn.) 12:11a–14b, esp. 11b.
[4] Kim Chongjik, *Chŏmp'ilchae munjip* (1892 edn.) 1:46a–47b, esp. 46a.
[5] Yi Hwang, *T'oegye sŏnsaeng ŏnhaeng nok*, in *T'oegye chŏnsŏ*, II:5:5a–b.   [6] Ibid., 5:11a.
[7] Yi I, *Yulgok chŏnsŏ* (Taedong munhwa yŏnguwŏn, 1958), sibyu, 4:18a.
[8] Kim Sisŭp, *Maewŏltang sijip* (Asea munhwasa, 1973) 4:16b.

a "trifling matter." Because of literature's didactic value, however, it could not be labeled "insignificant."[9] Kim Chongjik said: "Literature is a minor skill, and poetry and rhymeprose are of little importance. But to order personal nature, to attain moral transformation, and to cause the Way to resound in the present day and transmit it to ages without end, poetry and rhymeprose can indeed be relied upon."[10] The poet–critics desired a literature that would be more than a minor skill and that could teach and transform the people.

The view of poetry as an expression of one's personal nature was seconded, but with moralistic overtones. Sŏng Sammun ascribed poetry's ability to effect moral transformation to a belief that it comes from one's personal nature.[11] Because it is an expression of the poet's personal nature, good poetry will move the reader and purify his nature too.[12] A Neo-Confucian writer like Chŏng Yŏch'ang (1450–1504) could assert that one must first mold one's character before undertaking to write poetry, however, whereas Nam Hyoon (1454–1492) stressed that poetry was worth pursuing because it would mold one's character.[13] While thus shielding himself from an attack by moralists, Nam nevertheless declared that "if one's mind is upright, his poetry will be upright; if his mind is depraved, his poetry will reflect this."[14]

Defenders of literature, especially those in positions of power, asserted the importance of literary ability to diplomacy. National crises could be averted by the might of a writer's brush: a petition by Pak Illyang (d. 1096) was sufficiently persuasive to dissuade the Liao emperor from harboring designs on Korea.[15] Korean writers played important roles in China by capping verses and composing poetry jointly with Chinese officials. They also entertained Chinese envoys to Korea with poetry. Thus, if the government failed to nurture talented writers, the country would fare poorly in international relations.[16]

The view of poetry as an expression of *ki* (氣) continued to be held by Chosŏn writers. "Between heaven and earth there is only one vital force," said Pak P'aengnyŏn (1417–1456): "If one obtains it, it stirs and becomes words. Poetry is the finest essence of language. Therefore, one can see in another's poetry the rise and decline of the *ki* in heaven and earth."[17] The *ki* that one receives is part of the vital force that orders nature. Language is the manifestation of the vital force. If someone has received *ki* in abundance,

[9] *TS* 2:45.   [10] Kim Chongjik, *Chŏmp'ilchae munjip* 1:38b.   [11] *TMS* 94:28b.
[12] Sŏ Kojŏng, *Chin Tong munsŏn chŏn* 3a.   [13] *CN* 33:37 (pp. 385–387).   [14] *CN* 37 (p. 387).
[15] *NP* 2B:23; Sŏ Kojŏng, *P'irwŏn chapki* (*CKK*, 1909) 1:13.   [16] *Chungjong sillok* 40:46b.
[17] *TMS* 94:26a–b.

he can express it abundantly. One can determine from his poetry the rise and decline of the *ki* between heaven and earth. Sŏ Kŏjŏng echoed Cao Pi (187–226) when he said, "Poetry issues from the heart and is filled with *ki*. Literature is *ki*."[18] Hence Kim Suon (1409–1481) recommended that one first expand one's *ki* before writing,[19] and Sŏng Hyŏn argued that abundance or paucity of a writer's *ki* would produce a parallel merit in literature.[20] Thus one could determine the relative merits of a literary work according to the amount of *ki* embodied in it. The *ki* manifested in writing would reveal the writer. Depending on the circumstances, however, some believed that a writer could broaden and increase his *ki a posteriori* by dint of conscious effort.

Poetic language was the subject of much practical criticism. A skillful choice and arrangement of words was said to be vital to convey meaning. Diction affected emotion and revealed the writer's character. Indeed, what the diction means is the poem itself. "The marvel of poetry," in Sŏ Kŏjŏng's view, "lies in a single word." He goes on to disparage the use of "obscure and elliptical words that are not clear or fully expressive."[21] Sŏ did favor, however, evocative and significative language; elsewhere he says that all poetry values suggestiveness. Thus he praises Yi Kyubo for having captured "the feeling [or mood] of the scene" by a concise description of the event.[22] Others emphasized concision – the use of as few words as possible to express the meaning in order, for example, to attain "flavor beyond meaning," as Sŏng Hyŏn said of Kim Suon.[23] Some, however, like Nam Hyoon, believed that one's personal style should precede the choice of the right words. As an example, he cites a poem by Yi Chŏngŭn.[24]

Early Chosŏn-dynasty poets continued to read and follow Tang and Song masters. All of them viewed the poetry of their day as a continuation and development of tradition; indeed, the poetry of the past was a living thing to them. Su Shi (1037–1101) and Huang Tingjian (1045–1105) were the most imitated poets until the mid sixteenth century. Sim Sugyŏng (1516–1599), however, noted that in his day writers tended to prefer Li Bo (701–762) and Du Fu (712–770).[25] The general consensus was that imitation was unavoidable and might even be acceptable if it helped the poet achieve a fine effect. Sŏ Kŏjŏng said that even Yi Kyubo, the champion of originality, imitated Du Fu, and even Yi Saek's prose fell short of Su Shi's.[26] Sŏ pointed out that some poets used the technique of reversing the meaning of the

[18] *TS* 2:36. [19] *CN* 9 (p. 375). [20] Sŏng Hyŏn, *Hŏbaektang chip* 6:5b–7a.
[21] *TS* 1:21, 30. [22] *TS* 2:10. [23] *Yongjae ch'onghwa* (CKK, 1909) 9:12.
[24] Nam Hyŏn, *Sau myŏnghaeng nok* 5 (CKK, 1909), p. 392.
[25] Sim Sugyŏng, *Kyŏynhan chamnok* (CKK, 1910), p. 328. [26] *TS* 2:19.

ancients in order to achieve a new effect. To this end he cites Cho Su's (fl. 1401–1431) line, "A polished sickle is like a new moon," which reverses Han Yu's "The new moon is like a polished sickle."[27] Another example is Yi Hon's poem (1252–1312) "Pubyŏk Tower," the first two lines of which read:

> I cannot see a monk in Yŏngmyŏng monastery;
> Only the river flows on in front of the monastery.

This is an allusive variation on two lines in Li Bo's "Climbing Phoenix Terrace at Jinling":

> The phoenix once frolicked in Phoenix Terrace.
> The birds are gone, the terrace empty, and the river flows on.[28]

Often the use of personal, geographical, or historical proper nouns was viewed favorably. The poet-critics usually had in mind Liu Xie's argument in his *Wenxin diaolong* (*The Literary Mind and the Carving of Dragons*; 38):

Factual allusion and textual reference are factors outside the realm of literary composition. In a factual allusion, one adduces a fact to support some generalization; in a textual reference, one cites an ancient text to support a statement . . . When Cui [Yin], Ban [Gu], Zhang [Heng], and Cai [Yung] began to select passages from the Classics and histories, spreading their flowers and fruits far and wide, and established their reputations through writing, they became models who were imitated by later scholars.[29]

Early Chosŏn critics also advised poets to polish their works before publication. Sŏ Kŏjŏng tells how poets in the past showed their works to their teachers and friends for criticism, how certain poets improved on the poems of the ancients by substituting words or phrases, or how suggestions for change were willingly accepted by major poets, as when Yi Saek adopted his son's suggestion for a change of a single word.[30] None of the critics demonstrated how the ancients polished their style and diction, however, perhaps because this was difficult to substantiate.

Comments on individual poets found in the prefaces to their collected works offer unstinting praise, partly because such prefaces were usually written by disciples or friends. Kwŏn Kŭn's praise of his teacher, Yi Saek; Sŏng Hyŏn's praise of Kim Suon; and Sŏ Kŏjŏng's praise of Kim Pusik (1075–1151), Chŏng Chisang (d. 1135), Yi Chono (1341–1371), and Yi Saek – all of these were based on aesthetic principles.[31] Yi Hwang's denunciation

---

[27] *TS* 2:62.   [28] *TS* 1:16.
[29] Vincent Y. Shih, *The Literary Mind and the Carving of Dragons* (Daibei: Zhonghua, 1970), pp. 287–288.
[30] *TS* 1:48.   [31] Kwŏn Kŭn, *Yangch'on chip* 20:20a–b.

of Ch'oe Ch'iwŏn (b. 857), however, may be cited as an exception. Yi took Ch'oe's love of literature and Buddhism as sufficient reason for attacking the latter's work as a whole, an instance of Neo-Confucian bias against all writers who allegedly had neglected the study of the classics and Neo-Confucianism.[32]

Comments on prosody were rare, except those by Sŏ Kŏjŏng (although he did not speak Chinese) and Ŏ Sukkwŏn (fl. 1525–1554), because few Chosŏn-dynasty poets spoke Chinese, relying instead on rhyming dictionaries and Chinese precursors. Equally rare was concrete criticism of imagery, metaphor, or symbolism. Authors of "remarks on poetry" tended toward practical criticism, while writers of literary miscellanies generally focused on the poets themselves, recounting specific episodes from their lives, or giving background information about specific poems.

The foregoing writers, all of whom were practicing poets, agreed that a critic needs scholarship, taste, judgment, and candor. They also attempted to correct or improve current tastes, as when Sŏng Hyŏn complained that students preferred regulated verse to old-style poetry.[33] It is often difficult, though, to see the poet–critics' method at work in their writings. The reason for a critic's choice of certain poems is seldom given, and the comments on the poems cited do not always imply that the writer considered them worth discussing. Seldom do we find a new criticism of prototypical Chinese poems. Perhaps this is because they were too well known, every schoolboy having memorized them for his examinations.

Also lacking is the reason for the ranking of effect, directly or by implication. Yet another difficulty is the critical terminology. Like Chinese writers of *shihua* (Remarks on poetry), early Chosŏn writers also resorted to two-sinograph compounds or four-sinograph phrases to describe their impressions of a poem. They not only repeated the same compounds the Chinese used, but also made up new ones of their own. These vague but evocative phrases were intended to convey the reader's impressions or describe the poem's quality. The range of meaning of such untranslatable phrases, however, is often unclear to the modern reader.

THE MID-CHOSŎN PERIOD

The mid-Chosŏn period covers some 125 years, from the end of the Japanese invasion to the year of Yŏngjo's enthronement (1724). The goal of those who repeated the dictum that literature is a vehicle of the Way was to

---

[32] Yi Hwang, *T'oegye sŏnsaeng ŏnhaeng nok* 5:13b.
[33] Sŏng Hyŏn, *Hŏbaektang chip* 6:7a–9a, esp. 8a.

regulate the family, put the state in order, bring peace to all under heaven, and finally to bring about the way of the Former Kings. The havoc wrought by the literati purges, however, compelled idealistic and doctrinaire Neo-Confucian thinkers to become introspective and to emphasize knowledge. As Yi Hwang said of Cho Kwangjo (1482–1519): "Although Cho's endowment and character were trustworthy and beautiful, his knowledge was not deep enough. Therefore what he wanted to carry into effect could not but run to extremes. Thus he finally failed in his endeavor."[34]

Those who viewed the classics as the models of literature went so far as to say that if one pursued the Way, one's character would become lofty and bright,[35] and one could produce "correct" literature without effort. Literature was viewed not as an autonomous art, but as a by-product of the Human Nature and Principle learning (性理學 *sŏngnihak*). As the scholarship of experts in the study of the Way became more and more abstract and metaphysical and further removed from actuality, it came to be produced purely for the experts themselves, not for the benefit of humankind. Thus the goal of achieving an ideal society and culture existed in name only; it was an empty theory that offered few concrete measures to restore the country after the invasions of the Japanese and the Manchus.

"Our scholars are narrow-minded and restrained, devoid of intent (志 *chi*) and vital force (氣 *ki*)," Chang Yu (1587–1638) remarked; "They say that they study the Cheng brothers and Zhu Xi; in fact, they only mouth the Way and revere appearance."[36] That the probing of *i* (理 principle) and *ki* (氣 material force) could not save the country or the people was pointed out by Hŏ Kyun (1569–1618): "Experts in the study of the Way say that they emulate ancient sages, but so far they have no positive achievements in governing people. Hence they cannot be called true scholars."[37] Turning to literature, Hŏ regretted the fact that in his day literature and the Way were separate and writers indulged themselves in refining technique while ignoring the substance of literature. His Way (*to*) did not refer to the way of the didactic school, however, but to the essence of phenomena. Hŏ and Yi Sugwang (1563–1628) upheld the unity of content and form – a literature that has achieved "vital force" (*ki*), "bones" (inner structure), and technique, as Yi Sugwang said.

Hŏ Kyun and Yi Sugwang valued scholarship, intelligence, and diligence in a poet.[38] They emphasized the difficulty of creating a literary work of

[34] Yi Hwang, *T'oegye sŏnsaeng ŏnhaeng nok* 5:5b.
[35] Kwŏn Ŭngin, *Songgye mallok* (Kyŏnghŭi ch'ulp'ansa, 1969) 2:195a.
[36] *Kyegok manp'il* in *Kyegok chip* (Kyŏngin munhwasa, 1982) 1:24a–b (p. 571).
[37] *SPK* 11:120.   [38] *SPK* 10:118c; *CY* 8:224.

art – a far cry from the commonplace belief that of course one could produce good literature if one studied the Way. Literature was no longer a "petty skill" but an independent art requiring lifelong effort. Hence, not only the classics, which had once been held up as the model of literature, but also all other writings of diverse genres and by different schools were recommended – not as models to imitate but for the sake of whatever might be learned from their style and structure.

"Poetry is where the intent of the heart goes. While lying in the heart, it is 'intent'; when uttered in words, it is 'poetry.' When an emotion stirs one within, one expresses this in words."[39] Poetry as an expression of intent (*chi*) was now interpreted as the "heart's wish" or "emotional purport," thus endowing it with an expressive bent.[40] Hŏ Kyun praised the airs (160 songs) in the *Book of Songs* as embodying personal nature and emotion.[41] In this he echoed Yen Yu (fl. 1180–1235), who said: "Poetry involves a separate kind of talent that is not concerned with books; it involves a separate kind of meaning that is not concerned with principles (*i*)."[42] To Hŏ, the civilizing aspect of manners and customs, hitherto considered to be the primary function of poetry, was a calamity that destroyed poetry.[43]

Indeed, the poet must grasp the mysteries of creation (天機 *ch'ŏngi*) with the ideal of "entering the spirit," "entering into the life of things and capturing their spirit or essence,"[44] as stated, for example, by Yi Haeng (1478–1534).[45] Yi Sugwang's view was that *ki* (氣 individual talent; vital force) gives rise to *chi* (志 heart's wish; will) and that *chi* gives rise to *sin* 神, defined as "incalculable transformations."[46] Both emphasized "miraculous awakening" (妙悟 or intuitive apprehension) as the goal of poetry.

Before the end of the sixteenth century, poets imitated mostly Su Shi and Huang Tingjian and relied on the device of allusion as rhetorical amplification.[47] Hence at least half of the *Tongin sihwa* (*Remarks on Poetry by a Man from the East*, 1474) by Sŏ Kŏjŏng concerns the tracing of allusion. Such poetry, said Hŏ Kyun, lacks the power of reverberation. Meaning should continue even when words end, he said. Those who looked upon allusion as the only way of exhausting meaning, especially the Song and early Chosŏn poets, considered that the function of poetry was to transmit messages, especially about principles. Tang poets, on the other hand, attained inspired gusto (興趣 *hŭngch'wi*), and it is to them that the poet

---

[39] James J. Y. Liu, *Chinese Theories*, p. 69.   [40] Ibid., p. 70.   [41] *SPK* 5:82b.
[42] Liu, *Chinese Theories*, p. 39.   [43] *SPK* 12:128b.
[44] Liu, *Chinese Theories*, p. 37; *SPK* 4:72a; *CY* 9:284.   [45] *SPK* 25:233d.   [46] *CY* 1:223.
[47] *CY* 9:255; Hŏ Kyun, *Haksan ch'odam* (in *Hŏ Kyun chŏnjip*, 1981), 1b.

should turn to learn of their talent or genius (才 chae).[48] The poet should write about what is near to his endowed nature; he should produce a poetry that suits his talents and character. Then one need not worry whether his poetry is closer to that of Tang or of Song.[49]

That poetry is not an instrument to convey the Way but an expression of inspired gusto, or even miraculous awakening, led to a belief that poetry should evoke limitless reverberations in the reader. Thus poets like Hŏ Kyun stressed suggestiveness: meaning beyond words. Equally admired was a poetry that was fresh and permeated with a sense of life as a result of direct observations, inspired gusto, and realistic expression. Hŏ Kyun considered the use by Korean poets of the images of the gibbon, kingfisher, or partridge as mere convention. Like the lion in England, the gibbon is not found in Korea. Similarly, the kingfisher usually represented the Korean "bluebird" while the partridge represented the Korean "magpie."[50] It was felt that a poet must express what he actually observes and hears; otherwise he cannot forcefully convey the essence of things, emotions, and scenes.[51] As for diction, both Hŏ and Yi recommend using everyday, even colloquial, language, and advised against using archaic words.[52] Because the meaning of a word in any language comprises a history of that word, it is impossible to avoid using words used by poets of the past. The poets who stated this proposition were probably referring to words charged with echoes and allusions, since they said elsewhere that poetry must be lucid and easily understood by the educated reader.

Poetry, then, was an expression of personal emotions revealing a miraculous awakening. The poet was viewed as a craftsman, and individuality was indeed considered the hallmark of good poetry. There were certain talented poets who, because they ignored didactic theories, were seldom appreciated; they never held office and led a poor life. Among these were Sŏng Yŏhak (late sixteenth century) and Kwŏn P'il (1569–1612).[53] Still, it was felt that their poetic accomplishments would endure. There was no discussion, however, of how an individual voice, vibrant with immediacy, was to be achieved. Experience, especially the vicissitudes of an exile's life in remote mountains and waters, often helps the poet to capture the spirit of things,[54] although modern writers such as T. S. Eliot might disagree: "The more perfect the artist, the more completely separate in him will be the man who suffers and the mind which creates."[55] Such experiences

---

[48] SPK 4:74a–c; CY 9:251.   [49] CY 8:226.   [50] SPK 25:230c–d.   [51] CY 13:81.
[52] SPK 25:236b.   [53] CY 14:128–129; SPK 4:71b–72b.   [54] SPK 25:237a.
[55] T. S. Eliot, Selected Essays 1917–1932 (New York: Harcourt, Brace, 1932), p. 7.

might have provided motivation and material, as well as time, to perfect the poet's art.

The late Chosŏn period, from the beginning of the eighteenth to the end of the nineteenth centuries, was a period of re-examination and reappraisal of the contribution made by Neo-Confucian thinkers. It also witnessed the rise of practical learning (實學 *sirhak*), which stressed the art of government and the utility and the enhancement of people's livelihood. The aim of such practical learning was to seek truth through the verification of things, and the advocates of such evidential learning encouraged reform in land tenure, the grain relief system, the military service system, the civil service examination, and government organizations. The emphasis may have varied from individual to individual, but adherents of practical learning were one in urging reform to relieve the people. Some even sought knowledge in the West as awareness of Catholicism came to Korea by way of Peking.

Writers in office still advocated the didactic, moralistic view of literature as a petty accomplishment – a vehicle of the Way. In their view, literature merely played a role in reforming society and mores. Now writers who espoused practical learning came to perceive the difference between the Way and literature. As the interpretation of the Way differs from age to age, literature should reflect that change. Literature should not only learn from the past but seek to express contemporary concerns and reality.[56] It is indispensable and deserves to be pursued throughout one's life. A poem has value even if it is a simple popular song, said Hong Sŏkchu (1774–1842): "How could one discard a folk song on the grounds that it is not a poem in the *Book of Songs*?"[57]

Although they were critical of current philosophical trends, the champions of practical learning were still Confucian in philosophical orientation. They advocated a return to the ancient Confucianism of Confucius and Mencius rather than Song Neo-Confucianism. Hence their view of literature did not differ from that of other Neo-Confucian experts on the Way. In fact, they espoused didacticism more positively than courtier writers owing to their conviction that learning must yield knowledge that is useful in governing the state and bringing peace and prosperity to the people. Such views were held by Yi Ik (1681–1763), Pak Chiwŏn (1737–1805), and Chŏng Yagyong (1762–1836), to name but a few. "Not loving the ruler and

---

[56] Nam Kongch'ŏl, *Kŭmnŭng chip* (1815 edn.) 10:17a–b.
[57] Hong Sŏkchu, *Yŏnch'ŏn chŏnsŏ* (Osŏngsa, 1984) 24:660.

not having a concern for the welfare of the country is not poetry," said Chŏng; "Not to praise or criticize, not to promote virtue and reprove vice, is not poetry."[58] Such a view of poetry represents the acme of pragmatism. "Literature is the scholar-official's residue," said Wi Paekkyu (1727–1798); "Yet without literature, one cannot be called a complete man."[59]

Some poets of this period were aware of the importance of national literature. "The Korean alphabet is a great document under heaven. How can it be only an alphabet to record the language of Korea?" asked Chŏng Tongyu (1749–1808).[60] Pak Chiwŏn praised the poetry of Yi Tŏngmu (1739–1793) as revealing the Korean nature and emotions by using the names of native birds, beasts, plants, and trees; he compared Yi's poems to the airs in the *Book of Songs*.[61] This consciousness of national identity was aptly expressed by Chŏng Yagyong – "I am a Korean. I will joyfully write a poetry that reflects the Korean reality" – in an attempt to respond to the pressures of social and historical reality and to capture the spirit of vernacular song in poetry written in Chinese.[62] Some writers in the seventeenth century (Kim Manjung and Hong Manjong, for example) were urging that Korean poetry must be written in the spoken language, citing the *kasa* poems by Chŏng Ch'ŏl and folk songs as models to be studied, while others insisted that Koreans may write in Chinese but should not neglect their own language. "Abandoning our own unique language, we write poetry and prose in a foreign tongue. Even if we approximate the Chinese, it is like parroting another's words," said Kim Manjung (1637–1692) in a similar vein.[63]

This awakening of national consciousness produced sharp criticism of the defects of the literature of the past: weak *ki*; vulgar diction; incomplete expression of principle (*i*); shallowness and carelessness; vulgarity; and overwriting.[64] "In our days there is no poetry. Not that there are no poems written, but there are no good ones,"[65] declared Kim Tŭksin (1604–1684). Poets like Kim clearly pointed out that the chief cause of such defects was the civil service examination, which was viewed by the ruling class as the only means of advancement in life.[66]

---

[58] Chŏng Yagyong, *Yŏyudang chŏnsŏ* 21:9b.
[59] Not in Wi Paekkyu, *Chonjae chŏnsŏ*, 2 vols. (Kyŏngin munhwasa, 1974); cited in Chŏn Hyŏngdae et al., *Hanguk kojŏn sihaksa* (Hongsŏngsa, 1981), p. 342.
[60] Chŏng Tongyu, *Chuyŏng p'yŏn* (Seoul taehakkyo kojŏn kanhaenghoe, 1971) 2:169.
[61] Pak Chiwŏn *Yŏnam chip* (Kyŏnghŭi ch'ulp'ansa, 1966) 7:8a–b.
[62] Chŏng Yagyong, *Yŏyudang chŏnsŏ* 5:34a.
[63] Kim Manjung, *Sŏp'o manp'il* (T'ongmungwan, 1971) B:653.
[64] Chŏn Hyŏngdae et al., eds., *Hanguk kojŏn sihaksa* (Hongsŏngsa, 1981) cites *Myŏnggok chip*; Kim Ch'anghyŏp, *Nongam chip* 22:12b; and Nam Kongch'ŏl, *Kŭmnŭng chip* 11:28b–29a.
[65] *Chongnam ch'ongji*, in Hong Manjong, *Sihwa ch'ongnim* (Asea munhwasa, 1973), p. 381.
[66] *Sŏngho sŏnsaeng chŏnjip* 44:35a; and Chŏng Yagyong, *Yŏyudang chŏnsŏ* 11:22a–23a.

The literary historical situation in the seventeenth and eighteenth centuries induced upper-class writers to turn to a poetry by writers of lower-class origin for aesthetic satisfaction and creative stimulus. Politically repressed, their poetry does not express the ideology of the dominant literati class. Hence their poems manifest natural spontaneity and the mysteries of creation argue, the literati writers who furnished prefaces and postfaces to poetry collections by commoners, the first of which is the *Haedong yuju* (*Remaining Gems of Korea*, 1712) by Hong Set'ae (1653–1725).[67] Living in obscurity and unencumbered by political and moral concerns, their minds were able to create a spontaneous poetry that issued from the heart. Indeed, their intrinsic motives influenced the course of their poetry. Coming from positions of authority and power, the literati's recognition of a difference, if not superiority, in the commoner's poetry is an admission that no amount of theft, revision, or variation of textual antecedents by canonical masters could produce good – and relevant – poetry. Thus the moralistic/pragmatic view and the individualistic view of literature coexisted and at times coalesced: literature as a vehicle of the Way versus literature as distinct from the Way; the educational function of literature versus its affective and expressive function; Chinese classics as models versus poetry of the past and Korean classics as models; literature as a minor skill versus literature as essential to one's humanity; and mannered language versus spontaneous language.

Many believed that Chinese poetry written in Korea had reached its zenith under King Sŏnjo (1567–1608). The main reason for this belief is that poets began to study Tang poetry once they were freed from the influence of Song poetry. The nationalist writers, however, asked: why speak of Tang and Song poetry? Attain the wonder and mystery of poetry itself, and then your poetry too will be good.[68] Literary styles change as human nature and emotions change along with the times and society. New genres will emerge as the content of literature changes because of the writer's involvement in history.[69] Old-style poetry and music bureau (*yuefu*) ballads/songs, hitherto little practiced in Korea, became popular under kings Yŏngjo (1724–1776) and Chŏngjo (1776–1800). Folk songs, too, came to be appreciated, as when Hong Yangho (1724–1802) declared: "One can feel the pulse of Korea in these ballads and folk songs, which, like the airs in the *Book of Songs*, convey moderate, gentle, sincere, and deep feelings."[70] Literature could

---

[67] Yi Kyŏngsu, "Wihang siin ŭi ch'ŏngi non," in *Yijo hugi hanmunhak ŭi chaejomyŏng*, ed. Song Chaeso et al. (Ch'angjak kwa pip'yŏngsa, 1983), pp. 228–242. *Haedong yuju* was succeeded by *Sodae p'ungyo* (1737), edited by Ko Siŏn (1671–1734) and Ch'ae P'aengyun (1669–1731), *P'ungyo soksŏn* (1797), ed. Ch'ŏn Sugyŏng et al., and *P'ungyo samsŏn* (1857), ed. Yu Chaegŏn and Ch'oe Kyŏnghŭm.
[68] Hong Manjong, *Sihwa ch'ongnim*, p. 477.   [69] Chŏng Yagyong, *Yŏyudang chŏnsŏ* 8:35a.
[70] Hong Yangho, *Igye chip* (1893 edn.) 10:22a; Hong Set'ae, *Yuha chip* 9:8b.

still satirize and teach. As Confucius said: "It [the poetry in the *Book of Songs*] can be used to inspire, to observe, to make you fit for company, to express grievances" (*Analects* 17:9).[71] Poetry was generally viewed as an expression of human nature and emotion, but its function was to transform human nature and, ultimately, to civilize society and culture.

Some viewed literature (文 *mun*) as *ki* and the Way as *i* (principle). Literature that expressed vital or primordial force in nature had to be based on *i*. Thus insufficient *ki* would produce vapid writings, while without *ki* there was no need to study poetry, much less write it. Another view was that of the poet as a creator who communicates the mysteries of nature. According to this view, the subtlety of poetry communicates with mountains and rivers. Poetry and nature are mutually imbued with one another's essence, or quintessential spirit (Kim Ch'anghyŏp, 1651–1708). Communion with nature enables the poet to grasp the essence of nature and to concretize it in poetry.[72] The prerequisites of the poet, then, were said to include endowed nature, talent, scholarship, and unremitting effort. Some poets of this period stressed the pictorial element in poetry as promoting verisimilitude;[73] poetry should also be concrete and natural. Thus they rejected imitation and slavish observance of prosody and advocated a return to old-style poetry as the most suitable form.

Criticism, too, was viewed as an independent pursuit. To know the value of literature before criticizing it was deemed most difficult, and understanding poetry was said to require special talent. The poet himself is not necessarily a good judge, and the critic is not necessarily one who knows the secret of poetry. While upholding evaluation, Kim Tŭksin warned against criticizing a literary work in terms of the time of its origin or the social position of its writer.[74] Indeed, works of art should be judged by literary and aesthetic standards. Re-evaluation of earlier compilations and rehabilitation of neglected writers were also undertaken. For example, flaws were detected in the criteria underlying the compilation of the *Tong munsŏn* (*Anthology of Korean Literature in Chinese*).[75] Morever, the works of Yi Kyubo were viewed as falling short of their author's reputation, while Yi Saek (1328–1396) and Pak Ŭn (1479–1504) were said to be too little appreciated.[76] Nam Yongik (1628–1692) and Kim Ch'anghyŏp attempted to classify poetry by mood: Nam listed twenty-five moods for Koryŏ poetry and fifty-four for

[71] James J. Y. Liu, *Chinese Theories*, p. 169; Waley, *Analects*, p. 212.
[72] Kim Ch'anghyŏp, *Nongam chip* 21:16a.
[73] Yi Ik, *Sŏngho saesŏl*, 2 vols. (Kyŏnghŭi ch'ulp'ansa, 1967) 30:42a (p. 512).
[74] *Chongnam ch'ongji*, cited in Chŏn Hyŏngdae et al., eds., *Hanguk kojŏn sihaksa*, p. 420.
[75] Nam Yongik, *Hogok chip* 15, cited in Chŏn Hyŏngdae et al., eds., *Hanguk kojŏn sihaksa*, p. 421.
[76] Kim Ch'anghyŏp, *Nongam chip* 34:8b–9b.

Chosŏn poetry,[77] while Kim discerned twelve moods in Tang poetry.[78] Sin Wi (1769–1845) went a step further and evaluated forty-nine Korean poets in heptasyllabic quatrains, assigning a prevalent mood to each.[79]

Generally, three methods operated in practical criticism: tracing sources (at times with a discussion of the elements of poetry); associating a work with its writer, thereby equating art with life (if the writer was a gentleman, his writing will reflect it); and discerning a mood found in one poem that is found in the writer's other works. The catchwords chosen to describe these impressions of mood were often based on selected lines that were wrenched from context and then applied to other works by the same poet. An absence of analysis, brevity of critical statements, and a lack of organization are defects common to traditional poetry criticism in China and Korea. One exception was the *Sich'ik* (*Principles of Poetry*, 1734), a critical work with five charts. Its author, Sin Kyŏngjun (1712–1781), attempted to synthesize current theories of poetry in a systematic way.[80]

SIJO

Until the compilation of the first anthology of *sijo* – *Ch'ŏnggu yŏngŏn* (*Songs of Green Hills*, 1728) by Kim Ch'ŏnt'aek – there was no anthology of poetry in Chinese or Korean that included the works of all classes of people. Compiled by a professional singer and poet (a commoner) for the purpose of preserving *sijo* as Korean literature, this anthology encompasses authors from kings and princes to *kisaeng* and anonymous writers. The principle that informs the selection of texts in this and subsequent *sijo* collections is mainly literary – that is, a criterion for inclusion is not birth but artistic merit. Thus the compilers stress the fact that literature, at least vernacular literature, is an open system.

Compilers of *sijo* such as Kim Ch'ŏnt'aek, Kim Sujang, Pak Hyogwan, and An Minyŏng wish to state their assumptions about *sijo* in order to justify its importance as vernacular poetry. Another concern was to preserve song lyrics from the onslaught of time. "Like flowering plants in a whirlwind or the pleasant sounds of birds and beasts that pass the ear, songs may be chanted once but become naturally obscure and are subject to oblivion. How regrettable!" says the preface to the *Haedong kayo* (*Songs of Korea*). The fact that all prefaces are written in Chinese seems to mirror a system of power relationships in Chosŏn society. As the first makers of the canon

---

[77] *Hogok sihwa*, in Hong Manjong, *Sihwa ch'ongnim*, pp. 387–388.
[78] Kim Ch'anghyŏp, *Nongam chip* 34:5a.
[79] Cited in Chŏn Hyŏngdae et al., eds., *Hanguk kojŏn sihaksa*, p. 436.
[80] Discussed in ibid., pp. 402–418.

of *sijo*, they point out that *sijo* songs can be compared to the airs (160 songs from fifteen states) in the *Book of Songs*: like them, *sijo* are songs of the common people and have more or less the same functions as the airs. Just as Confucius did not discard the songs from Zheng and Wei, so *sijo* collections comprise songs of all kinds, including the bawdy and indecent, in order to spread virtue and criticize vice. Therefore, Confucius' comment on the "Ospreys" (*Book of Songs*, 1) – that in it "pleasure [is] not carried to the point of debauch, and grief not carried to the point of self-injury" (*Analects* 3:20) – is cited to justify the editorial policy.[81]

"I find the lyrics beautifully elegant and well worth perusing," avers Chŏng Naegyo (1681–1757) in his preface to the *Songs of Green Hills*. Chŏng continues:

Lyrics confined narrowly to one sentiment, be it joy, sorrow, grievance, loneliness, or suffering, are very few. Words seem mild, but alert the reader to further implications, then they turn passionate and prove sharply moving. The finest of them give rise to contemplations of the decline and prosperity of generations and to bearing witness to the beauty and ugliness of customs and mores. The lyrics meet the high standards of poetry [written in literary Chinese] inside and out; there is none that does not fit this. Ah! When one composes lyrics, one does not merely state one's thoughts and announce one's grief but places within them what will captivate, move, excite, and arouse the listener . . . The lyrics may not have exhausted the depths of poetic ability, but the benefits that shall accrue to the world from them are great indeed![82]

Sijo will be able to move the people because they issue from the heart as spontaneous and free expressions of emotion. Indeed, they have captured the creative forces of nature and can move "spirits and ghosts."[83] *Sijo* have attracted the attention of all the Korean people because they are sung or chanted and are easy to transmit orally. This emphasis on the oral and musical aspects of *sijo*, together with their simplicity, distinguishes them from poems written in literary Chinese, making the *sijo* a form universally appealing to the Korean people. The form enables the poet to write candidly about his native experience. The compilers did not forget to add, however, that the *sijo* is "a minor art."[84]

---

[81] Chŏn Hyŏngdae, "*Sijo* chip e nat'anan munhak ŭisik – sŏ pal ŭl chungsim ŭro," in *Hanguk kojŏn pip'yŏng yŏngu* (Ch'aeksesang, 1987), pp. 247–265.

[82] Peter H. Lee, ed., *Sourcebook of Korean Civilization*, 2 vols. (New York: Columbia University Press, 1993–1996), 2:243–244.

[83] Ibid., p. 244.

[84] Yi Kyuho, "Kosijo pip'yŏng kwa siga ilto sasang," in *Hanguk kojŏn sihak non* (Saemunsa, 1985), pp. 211–234, esp. 219; Chŏng Chaeho," Kajip sŏ pal e kwanhan sogo," *Ŏmun nonjip* 12 (1970): 160–190.

As a vernacular poetic form, the *sijo* was at times considered potentially subversive by the ruling class, and compilers chose to justify their activity by imputing didactic function to *sijo* in addition to their aesthetic value. It was an attempt to accommodate the prevalent official view of literature in order to legitimate the autonomy of *sijo* as vernacular poetry.

It is worthwhile looking at two editions of the *Songs of Green Hills* – the O Changhwan copy (called Chinbon) and Ch'oe Namsŏn copy (known variously as Taehakpon, 1930; Chosŏn mungobon, 1939; and T'ongmungwanbon, 1941) – for their methods of compilation and organization. The Chinbon, formerly owned by O Changhwan, chronologically collects *sijo* (1–464) and *sasŏl sijo* (465–580) by 58 known authors along with some anonymous ones. Under Koryŏ it lists Yi Saek (1 song), Chŏng Mongju (1), and Maeng Sasŏng (4). Poets of the Chosŏn dynasty begin with Kim Chongsŏ (2); then come 5 songs by Chosŏn kings (T'aejong, Hyojong, Sukchong); then come 6 commoners – Chang Hyŏn (1), Chu Ŭisik (10), Kim Samhyŏn (6), Kim Sŏnggi (8), Kim Yugi (10), and Kim Ch'ŏnt'aek (30) – with comments by the authors themselves, all dated 1728; then come women – Hwang Chin (3), Sobaekchu (1), Maehwa (1); then come authors with unknown dates, anonymous poems by topic (294–397), and later come *sasŏl sijo*. It has a preface (1728) by Chŏng Naegyo, a postface (1728) by Kim Ch'ŏnt'aek, and a concluding remark by one "Old Woodcutter of Maak" (1727). This copy's features include quotations of critical remarks from an author's individual works or manuscripts or addition of such remarks by the compiler himself (eight occasions). For example, 5 *sijo* by Yi Hyŏnbo are followed by verbatim quotations from Yi's *Works* as well as Yi Hwang's comments from his *Works* (43:3a–4b); 12 *sijo* by Yi Hwang are followed by his own postface (43:23a–24a); 50 poems by Chŏng Ch'ŏl from the Yi Sŏn edition appear with Yi's postface (*Songgang chŏnjip*, pp. 316–317, 415); there are comments by Chŏng Naegyo on 30 lyrics by Kim Ch'ŏnt'aek, in which he compares Kim to Chŏng Ch'ŏl for beauty of expression and mastery of tonal hormony. The Chinbon also provides Chinese translations of certain *sijo* – for example, by Cho Chonsŏng and Sin Hŭm.

The Ch'oe Namsŏn copy (Taehakpon), formerly in the possession of Chu Sigyŏng, includes 999 *sijo* and 16 *kasa* by some 130 known authors arranged by musical mode – hence the principle of organization is not historical. The curious feature of this edition is the inclusion, with no justification, of the works by the Koguryŏ statesman Ŭl P'aso (d. 203), the Paekche loyalist Sŏng Ch'ung (seventh century), and such Koryŏ writers as Ch'oe Ch'ung (984–1068), Kwak Yŏ (1058–1130), Yi Chonyŏn (1269–1343), Yi Chono (1341–1371), Kil Chae (1353–1419), and Wŏn Ch'ŏnsŏk (late fourteenth to early fifteenth century). The text provides brief biographical information for each author at the beginning or end of a text – under U T'ak, for example, "censor under King Ch'ungnyŏl of Koryŏ." Longer notes, such as one under Yi Chonyŏn, consist partly of a verbatim quotation from his official biography (*KRS* 109:12b–13a) – in this case a well-known anecdote that King Ch'unghye could tell Yi's impending visit by his footsteps, straighten himself, and then await him. The *kasa* include part of Chŏng Ch'ŏl's "The Wanderings"; seven out of eight stanzas of *Ŏbu sa* (*The Fisherman's Songs*) with a wrong attribution to Yi Hwang rather than to Yi Hyŏnbo; and "The Return" by Tao Qian with Korean grammatical elements but without identification. The preface, the postface, an introductory poem summing up the contents of the anthology (*che Ch'ŏnggu yŏngŏn hu*, three heptasyllabic *jueju*), and a table of contents are placed at the head of the anthology. Although generally classified under a given musical mode, the arrangement is not systematic and is sometimes lax – as a repetition of a *sijo* attributed to Yi Chonyŏn (36 and 919) may be sung to two different modes.

The intent of the compiler (some latecomer if not Kim Ch'ŏnt'aek himself) is to present a canon comprising as many poets as possible extending over as long a time period as possible. Thus it may have represented an attempt to enlarge the canon through the addition of previously forgotten or unknown texts or perhaps an attempt to rewrite the history of *sijo*, stressing its centrality in Korean culture. This recuperation of a literary past, if it can be proved to be so, may have constituted an effort to construct the *sijo* canon at a crucial historical juncture, involving the awakening of selfhood and national consciousness as well as a zeal for preserving, in as comprehensive a way as possible, the Korean vernacular poetic heritage.

FICTION

An incident that took place in 1790 at a storytelling session in a tobacco shop near Chongno in Seoul caught the attention of the king and the people alike. When the narration reached a point where the protagonist is thrown into despair, one unidentified person from the audience stabbed the storyteller (or reciter) to death.[85] This episode illustrates not only the popularity of storytelling among the common people but also the extent of the audience's emotional identification with the character – how a well-told

---

[85] Yi Tŏngmu, *Ch'ŏngjanggwan chŏnsŏ*, 13 vols. (Minjok munhwa ch'ujinhoe, 1972–1982), 20:8–9. It was a controversial criminal case on which the reigning king himself passed judgment.

work of fiction can capture and hold the attention of the audience. In this episode, the murderer not only identified himself with the character but mistook the storyteller for the author. The storyteller's power to make his audience identify with the character cost him his life. The emergence of the storyteller and the lending library in Seoul from the beginning of the eighteenth century, together with private reading of fiction among upper-class women, indicate a definite change in literary taste among the people. Women in particular were thought to be incapable of discriminating between what is fact and what is fiction (Hong Chikp'il, 1776–1853).[86] Written words are susceptible to misinterpretation, and without the authority's proper guidance, readers and listeners might think that the events in a story actually happened. Indeed, the competence of the general reader was a problem. (Western examples such as Don Quixote and Emma Bovary come to mind.)[87]

It is difficult to imagine how the Korean literati grasped a work as a complex whole. In a cultural milieu antagonistic to such a noncanonical and mixed genre as fiction, their contrary receptions and diverse opinions reflect their expectations and predispositions.[88] (Surely authors of Chinese fiction did not know the horizon of expectations of Korean readers.) Chinese works of fiction appraised in impressionistic terms (referring to the author but not the work itself) include *Water Margin* and *Romance of the Three Kingdoms*. Negative readings of *Water Margin* include those of Hŏ Kyun (1569–1616) – himself a champion of vernacular fiction and the putative author of the *Tale of Hong Kiltong*, which became the target of censure by his peers. Hŏ praises the *The Journey to the West* (*Monkey*; *Xiyou ji*) but condemns *Water Margin*, which he read in a 100- or 120-chapter edition, as "licentious, wily, cunning, and unsuitable for education."[89] Here Hŏ might have wished to deny his indebtedness to the Chinese work. Yi Sik (1584–1647) dismisses the work for its subject matter;[90] and Yi Imyŏng and Yi Ik (1681–1763) conjecture that there is a connection between this

---

[86] In *Maesan chapsik*, cited in Ōtani Morishige, "Richō bunjin no shōsetsu ishiki," *Chōsen gakuhō* 48 (1970):99–100.
[87] Ŏ Sukkwŏn, *P'aegwan chapki* (*CKK*, 1909) 4:39; Peter H. Lee, *A Korean Storyteller's Miscellany*, pp. 24, 41, 225. Earlier uses of the term *xiaoshuo* (*sosŏl*) include, for example, *Zhuangzi* 26 (Watson, *The Complete Works of Chuang Tzu*, p. 296): "If you parade little theories (*xiaoshuo*) and fish for the post of district magistrate, you will be far from the Great Understanding"; and *Analects* 17:12 (Waley, *Analects*, p. 213): "The Master said, To tell in the lane what you have heard on the highroad is to throw merit away." These and other denunciations describe *xiaoshuo/sosŏl* as unfounded fabrication, rumor, or gossip, deceitful and dangerous. For more on this see Sheldon Hsiao-peng Lu, *From Historicity to Fictionality: The Chinese Poetics of Narrative* (Stanford: Stanford University Press, 1994), pp. 37–92.
[88] Yun Sŏnggŭn, "Yuhakcha ŭi sosŏl paegyŏk," *Ŏmunhak* 25 (1971):44–50.
[89] *SPK* 13:137.   [90] Yi Sik, *T'aektang chip* (1764) 15:22b.

work and the rise of banditry and freebooters, especially Li Zicheng (1605–1645), at the end of the Ming period, which hastened the demise of the dynasty.[91] Yi Sik points out the fictionality of the *Romance of the Three Kingdoms* and suggests that it be burnt; Yi Ik regrets its popularity among the literati;[92] Yi Tŏngmu denounces both works as "spinning a vulgar and filthy story and enumerating the mean and weird to delight the eye without a sense of shame."[93] If recorded attacks on *The Plum in the Golden Vase* (published c. 1617) are fewer than those on other works, it is because criticism is an admission of having read the "immoral" work, which was taboo.[94] Yi Sik, Hong Manjong (fl. 1623–1649) (who said that fiction might ruin the state),[95] Yi Tŏngmu,[96] and Chŏng Yagyong (1762–1836) (who likened fiction's calamitous effect to that of a comet, drought, sandstorm, and landslide)[97] all seem to side with the official view: fiction will destabilize the social order and bring about disaster. In 1786, King Chŏngjo finally prohibited the importation of Chinese works of fiction, and the order was repeated in 1787, 1791, and 1793.[98] Inaccessibility, however, increased their prestige. The Korean work of fiction that became the main target of vituperation was the *Tale of Hong Kiltong*. The execution of its author Hŏ Kyun on a charge of treason is, according to Yi Sik, a condign punishment for having written such a lie.[99] Anyone who fabricates such an unethical work – because it did not affirm the value of the Chosŏn society – cannot be an ethical person.

Among a number of apologists and defenders of fiction in the eighteenth century, Kim Ch'unt'aek, Yi Tŏngmu, and his grandson Yi Kyugyŏng (b. 1788) cite the *Record of Lady Sa's Journey South* as offering both pleasure and instruction – images of virtue and vice – and Yi Chae (1680–1748) cites the *Dream of Nine Clouds* for its didactic quality. Yi Yango (1737–1811) recognized fiction's realistic description and beautiful style as a work of art and recommended it for insight into human nature.[100] The comments of Yi Ujun (1801–1867), who himself wrote and sold stories, extended to the *Dream of Nine Clouds*, *Record of Lady Sa's Journey South*, *Showing Goodness and Stirred by Righteousness*, *Ongnin mong* (*Dream of the Jade Unicorn*),

---

[91] Yi Ik, *Sŏngho saesŏl* 9A:39b–40a.
[92] Yi Sik, *T'aektang chip* 15:22b; Yi Ik, *Sŏngho saesŏl* 9A:39b–40a; Yi Tŏngmu, *Sasojŏl* (in *Ch'ŏngjanggwan chŏnsŏ*) 3:7b.
[93] Yi Tŏngmu, *Ch'ŏngjanggwan chŏnsŏ* 5:5b.   [94] Ibid., 53:112a mentions the work.
[95] Hong Manjong, *Sunoji*, in *Wŏnbon Hanguk kojŏn ch'ongsŏ*, vol. 4 (Taejegak, 1975) 4:43b–44a.
[96] Yi Tŏngmu, *Ch'ŏngjanggwan chŏnsŏ* 5:5a. Elsewhere Yi praises *Water Margin* as depicting contemporary social reality and life.
[97] Chŏng Yagyong, *Yŏyudang chŏnsŏ* I:8:36a–b.   [98] *Chŏngjo sillok* 24:34b; 38:32b–33a.
[99] Yun Sŏnggŭn, "Yuhakcha ŭi sosŏl paegyŏk," pp. 45, 50, 65–67.
[100] Cho Tongil, *Hanguk munhak t'ongsa* 3:146.

and the four great Chinese works of fiction: "The intent of each author of these works is deep and far."[101] Yi Isun (1754–1832) is probably the first to recognize the *sosŏl* for what it is: it is fiction, a fictional construct, and cannot be equated with history, a veritable report.[102] Hong Hŭibok (1794–1859), the translator of Li Ruzhen's *Jinghua yuan* (*Flowers in the Mirror*; published 1828), defined fiction as an author's creation whose purport is to give delight, not edification.[103]

From the beginning of the nineteenth century, more and more writers of fiction, either impoverished literati or educated members of the "middle people" class, began to understand the *sosŏl* as a work of invention wherein characters, situations, and actions are constructed to suit an artistic purpose. Indeed, fiction can be compared to "studying the Way and practicing virtue" (Kim Sohaeng).[104] As Sir Philip Sidney (1554–1586) said: "A feigned example hath as much force to teach as a true example." Yi Hŭngmin stressed the harmony of form and content in a work of fiction, adding that fiction is a criticism of actuality.[105]

---

[101] Ibid., 3:148; Cho Tongil, "Hanguk Chungguk Ilbon 'sosŏl' ŭi kaenyŏm" *Sŏnggok nonch'ong* 20 (1989):632. *Ch'angsŏn kamŭi rok*, attributed to Cho Sŏnggi (1638–1689), is a fourteen-chapter story in Chinese and later in Korean translation. *Ongnin mong*, attributed to Yi Chŏngjak (1678–1758), is a story similar in theme to Kim Manjung's *Sa-ssi namjŏng ki* – a jealousy between ladies Yu and Yŏ, but Lady Yu's goodness transforms Lady Yŏ at the end.

[102] Cho Tongil, *Hanguk munhak t'ongsa* 3:149 and Chang Hyohyŏn, "Chosŏn hugi ŭi sosŏllon," *Ŏmun nonjip* 23 (1982):580.

[103] Cho Tongil, "Hanguk Chungguk Ilbon," pp. 632–633.

[104] Chang Hyohyŏn, "Chosŏn hugi ŭi sosŏllon," p. 584.   [105] Ibid., p. 587.

CHAPTER 18

Early twentieth-century poetry

Peter H. Lee

The act of inventing and reinventing literature in East Asia usually required a revaluation of the past.[1] Inventing modern literature, however, required a radical revaluation of the past because its major stimulus came from outside. Never before in the history of East Asian literature had invention been forced by events of such urgency. This called for a rewriting of the past, a deconstruction of the established canon, and a formulation of a new one based on a new ideology to suit nationalist or other motives. The actual forging of modern literature in Korean began with the forced opening of the country to the outside world. It required the shaping of a new language (the vernacular style that corresponds to living speech), new literary genres, and a new theory of literature.

After foreign ships began to appear in numbers in the 1860s, Korea was compelled to open the country, first to Japan in 1876, then to America in 1882. Unlike other cases of invention or reinvention of canons, the invention of modern literature in Korea was prompted by unprecedented historical changes imposed by foreign powers: imposition of unequal treaties, political penetration and economic exploitation, and, finally, seizure of the country itself in 1910. From about 1880 to 1910, progressive officials and reform-minded intellectuals worked frantically on all fronts to learn from the West and Japan. They strove to reform and modernize the country while desperately trying to maintain Korea's independence as a sovereign state; they strove to preserve its cultural and racial identity while adopting Western technology and institutions. From the 1880s they sought, through journalistic activities, to encourage patriotism and political participation. Most editors and writers for the newspapers,[2] as well as advocates of "new" literature, came from the periphery of the ruling literati class – and all were destined to lead the new generation.

---

[1] Frank Kermode, *History and Value* (Oxford: Clarendon, 1989), pp. 108–127.
[2] Lee Kwang-rin, "Newspaper Publication in the Late Yi Dynasty," *KS* 12 (1988):70–71.

LANGUAGE

The 1894 reform abolished the traditional examination system and instituted the Korean language as a subject for the examination for civil servants. Thus the use of Chinese as the official written language began to decline, particularly because of its difficulty and its association with Confucianism and Confucian ideology, which were held responsible for Korea's "feudal" order, class structure, and backwardness. Hence Chinese was viewed as detrimental to the independence of Korea and the Korean people.

Historically, the Korean vernacular had two orthographic styles: a mixed style used in vernacular poetry and prose and a pure Korean used, for example, in traditional narrative fiction.[3] Now Chinese, after 1,000 years of supremacy as the language of the dominant class, was replaced by Korean, written in the phonetic alphabet invented in the mid fifteenth century to record the language actually spoken by the people. Its easy accessibility made it a language of enlightenment. The vernacular had been used by believers of the Tonghak (Eastern learning as opposed to Western learning, that is, Catholicism) and subsequently by Christians: the New Testament was translated into the vernacular and published in 1887.

The transition from Chinese to Korean as the principal written language of the Korean people was slow. In the beginning at least three orthographic styles coexisted: literary Chinese (*hanmun*), a mixed style (*kukhanmun*), and pure Korean (*kungmun*). In 1886 the government publication *Hansŏng chubo* carried a piece in the mixed style, and in 1895 an official gazette published the king's edict on education in the same style. Soon the mixed style was adopted in official documents, and from the 1890s newspapers were printed in Korean (as in the *Independent*) or in mixed style (as in *Korea Daily News*). In 1883, Yu Kilchun, the first Korean to study in Japan and the United States, began to write in the mixed style he used later for his *Sŏyu kyŏnmun* (*Observations on a Journey to the West*, 1895). Space was introduced between words and between metrical segments in poetry, followed by the use of punctuation.[4] Most educated people privileged the use of the vernacular and labeled anyone using Chinese as a stateless nonentity. In this manner, the linguistic aspiration to use the natural language of the Korean people was realized.

---

[3] Yi Kimun, *Kaehwagi ŭi kungmun yŏngu* (Ilchogak, 1970), pp. 13ff.; Cho Tongil, *Hanguk munhak t'ongsa* 4:221–249.
[4] Lee Kwang-rin, "Newspaper Publication in the Late Yi Dynasty," 61–72 esp. pp. 70–71.

REFORM AND ENLIGHTENMENT

Korea's first newspaper, the thrice-monthly *Hansŏng sunbo* (1883–1884), was followed by *Tongnip sinmun* (the *Independent*, 1896–1909), *Hwangsŏng sinmun* (*Capital Gazette*, 1898–1910), *Cheguk sinmun* (*Imperial Post*, 1898–1910), *Taehan maeil sinbo* (*Korea Daily News*, 1905–1910), and others.[5] Most of these carried songs and poems in the vernacular. Patriotic songs were published in the *Independent*, the first of which was dated 11 April 1896, and they were contributed by the readers, made up of Christian converts, students, policemen, soldiers, clerks, and other citizens. Recurrent themes were loyalty to the king, the strengthening of solidarity, the need for enlightenment, and national prosperity and defense.[6] Other songs – one written by Korean Christians to celebrate the birthday of the reigning monarch, for example, and another on the occasion of the groundbreaking ceremony for the Independence Arch – were sung to the tune of Christian hymns or other Western music (such as the British national anthem "God Save the King," military marches, or "Auld Lang Syne"). With the Shimonoseki Treaty marking the end of the Sino-Japanese War, Korea left the orbit of the sinocentric world order. Patriotic songs written at the time evince a buoyant mood, reflecting the optimism following the 1894 reform and China's diminishing influence on Korean politics and diplomacy.

Reform-minded intelligentsia also turned to the *sijo* and *kasa*, two traditional vernacular poetic genres, to register their acute sense of the present. Newspaper editors and contributors alike relied on the *kasa*'s discursive, narrative power and turned the genre into a vehicle for versified editorials. Written in a mixed style, these poems took the form of social criticism and satire, more Juvenalian than Horatian in tone. The objects of censure included contemporary officials, first anonymous but later identified by name (152 Koreans and 17 Japanese). These poems stressed inner cultivation and the need for Koreans to have a strong sense of political and cultural identity. Noteworthy examples are those in the *Korea Daily News*, especially in the column called "Society's Lantern," from December 1908 (634 pieces).[7] These poems, written mostly by the paper's editors, the vanguard

[5] Cho Tongil, *Hanguk munhak t'ongsa* 4:250–299; Lee Kwang-rin, "The Rise of Nationalism in Korea," *KS* 10 (1986):1–12.

[6] Kwŏn Oman, *Kaehwagi siga yŏngu* (Saemunsa, 1989); Pak Ŭlsu, *Hanguk kaehwagi chŏhang siga yŏngu* (Sŏngmungak, 1985); Kim Yunsik et al., *Hanguk hyŏndae munhaksa* (Hyŏndae munhak, 1990), pp. 14–27; Kim Yongjik, *Hanguk kŭndae sisa*, 2 vols. (Saemunsa, 1983) 1:59–97.

[7] Cho Tongil, *Hanguk munhak t'ongsa* 4:409–429; Kim Haktong, *Hanguk kaehwagi siga yŏngu* (Simunhaksa, 1981), pp. 94–180; Kim Yongch'ŏl, *Hanguk kŭndae siron ko* (Hyŏngsŏl ch'ulp'ansa, 1988), pp. 231–254.

of anti-Japanese resistance, introduced to the *kasa* forms such inventions as stanzaic divisions, shortening of length, addition of refrains (nonsense jingles or words with meaning), repetition of interjections, dialogue style, titles in four-word phrases, and occasional citation of Chinese poems to augment the satiric effect of a piece. Diction indicates certain borrowings from oral songs, the *p'ansori* oral narrative, *sijo*, and poetry in Chinese.

Innovations introduced by writers of *sijo* include a formalized three-line metrical scheme, clear marking of each segment in a line, and punctuation to indicate each line. Omission of the fourth metric segment in line 3 was not new, but the cultivation of effects of closure allowed the writer to end a poem with a key word, rather than such expletives as *-hanora* or *-irŏra*, to foreground the poem's central message. At times a folk-song-style refrain was introduced (from 1909). The *sijo* writers expressed more or less the same concerns as the *kasa* writers: the protection of national rights, encouragement of learning, and the importance of national salvation and unity. Most writers of songs, *sijo*, and *kasa* were amateurs, who aimed to express the urgency of social responsibility and moral action to save the country from foreign aggression. These texts convey a strong sense of the contemporary problems unique to Korea in 1890–1910.

NEW-STYLE POETRY

The new-style poetry, composed from 1908 to 1918, was the first significant attempt to break with traditional prosody and diction. "New-style" poetry is not a continuation of *sijo* and *kasa*, nor is it a genuinely new kind of poetry. "New" is not a generic term but simply designates poems other than traditional verse. Examples were written by students who had studied in Japan and who read Western literature in Japanese translation and Japanese experiments in the new-style poetry. Although examples of new verse appeared in newspapers and association journals from 1907 on, "Haeegesŏ sonyŏnege" ("From the Sea to Boys," November 1908) by Ch'oe Namsŏn (1890–1957), published in his own journal *Sonyŏn* (*Boys*), is usually considered to be the first of its kind. Ch'oe himself did not label it a "new-style poem," but simply a "poem." (Later he referred to his own works as "new poems" and also used the term "new-style poem.")

> Thumping, thumping, thunder, roll.
> The sea lashes, smashes, crushes.
> Great mountains like Tai, boulders like houses,
> These flimsy things, what are they to me?

"Do you know my power?" The sea roars,
Lashes, smashes, crushes.
Thumping, thumping, thunder, rumble, boom.

The poem's typographical arrangement on the page – with white space on the upper and lower margins and ninety-eight punctuation marks – must have startled readers. It compels dramatic comprehension by the eye and imposes the poet's intent on the reader: that the poem is meant for both the voice and the eye, that the poet needs the collaboration of the printer, and that his arrangement (and reading) is final. The imposition of the poet's will and interpretation reflects a change in the relationship between the poet and his audience: the poem radically lessens the distance between the two. It breaks with the tradition of generalized and impersonal poetry and presents itself with the immediacy of something distinctive and individual.

The poets of the past seldom used stanzaic forms of unequal length. In Ch'oe's poem, the number of syllables in corresponding lines is the same throughout, and the first and last lines of each stanza are identical. More important, it is not the line, the basic unit of composition in the past, but the stanza that functions as the basic unit here. The first and seventh lines, for example, which consist wholly of onomatopoeia intended to create a musical effect with incantatory overtones, cannot be full sentences. Run-on lines, which discourage pauses, are used to build up the larger unit of rhythmical movement, the stanza. (It is interesting to recall that in *Cathay*, published in London in 1915, Ezra Pound used a line to comprise a full sentence, persuaded by Ernest Fenollosa's plea for the sentence as the natural unit of poetic perception.)[8]

In the past, Korean poems written in the vernacular usually had no titles. Titles were often supplied by the compilers of collections. Shorter poems, such as *sijo*, were usually classified by their musical tunes, subjects, authors, or chronology, again without titles. Formulaic diction and topoi, standard combinations of images, seasonal terms, and inner progression made the subject, occasion, mood, and tone of a poem clear to the reader.

"From the Sea to Boys" is startling for other reasons. Neither the sea nor children were used much in classical East Asian poetry.[9] Even the Japanese, whose pirates infested Korean and Chinese waters, left no memorable verses

---

[8] Donald Davie, *Ezra Pound: Poet as Sculptor* (New York: Oxford University Press, 1964), pp. 41–43. I have used the texts in Ch'oe Namsŏn, *Yuktang Ch'oe Namsŏn chŏnjip*, 15 vols. (Hyŏnamsa, 1973–1975), 5:312–313, 323–326.

[9] As an exception one may cite a rhymeprose by Mu Hua (c. 300), "The Sea"; for an English translation see Burton Watson, *Chinese Lyricism: Shih Poetry from the Second to the Twelfth Century* (New York: Columbia University Press, 1971), p. 162.

about the sea. Likewise, children seldom appeared. Often the speaker in a *sijo* addresses an otherwise unnamed boy: "Boy, lead a cow to the northern village" (Cho Chonsŏng, 1554–1628); or "Boy, fetch your old net!" (Yun Sŏndo, 1587–1671). The "boy" in such cases, however, refers to an unmarried man younger than the speaker, a servant, a friend, or even one who shares the speaker's mood and tastes. He is an ideal companion who sees the world with the eyes of youth, or a youth through whom the speaker relives his own past and thus combats the ravages of time.

The first and last lines of each seven-line stanza consist of what can only be termed an onomatopoetic assault on the reader; four examples of this are found in line 1 above and five in line 7.[10] No classical poem would have begun with four onomatopoetic words. Here these words represent the sound of the sea, and their repetition at the beginning and end of a stanza points to the basic structural principle: the power of these words lies in their sound. Three out of nine such examples are archaic. Worn-out allusions include Mount Tai, and the First Emperor of the Qin ("From the Sea to Boys," stanza 3), the unifier of China and a tyrant who burned books. These, together with a few other allusions in sinographs, appear amid otherwise pure vernacular Korean to produce a grave, orotund, and emphatic effect, like Latinate phrases in English.

The last, but no less significant, innovation is personification. Here the speaker is the sea, and it addresses boys, the focus of adult hopes for the future. As the title of the journal and the poem suggest, "From the Sea to Boys" celebrates the power of young people, those who will undertake the social and literary revolution so desperately needed. The sea is a bridge between nations as well. The sea's majesty, creativity, and power are what the youth of Korea need in their task of forging a modern expression incorporating simple, colloquial language and aspects of modern civilization.

The new features of this poem, then, are the differences in voice, the way in which this new voice is achieved by the poem's subject, diction, figures, and prosody, and the relationship between the poet and his audience. Despite changes in the assumptions concerning poetry, Ch'oe saw its function as traditional and public. Like earlier songwriters, he was primarily concerned with introducing Western civilization, enlightening the people,

---

[10] *T'yŏlssŏk, t'yŏlssŏk, t'yŏk, sswaa* (line 1) and *T'yŏlssŏk, t'yŏlssŏk, t'yŏk t'yururŭng, k'wak* (line 7). In this poem, long and short lines alternate: 1, 3 (4/3/4/5), 5, and 7 are longer; 2 (3/3/5), 4 (3/3/5), and 6 (3/3/5) are shorter. The poem is said to have been inspired by Byron's *Childe Harold's Pilgrimage*, canto 4:182–184. For example: "Thy shores are empires, changed in all save thee – / Assyria, Greece, Rome, Carthage, what are they?" (182:1630–1631), and "And I have loved thee, Ocean! and my joy / Of youthful sports was on thy breast to be / Borne, like thy bubbles, onward: from a boy / I wanton'd with thy breakers – " (184:1648–1651), were cited as evidence. See Samuel C. Chew, ed., *Childe Harold's Pilgrimage*, pp. 202–203.

and arousing the national consciousness; hence his eagerness to draw out the meanings of the sea and boys and moralize upon them.

Ch'oe's experiment in this and other poems – marked by varying line lengths, rejection of traditional meter, use of flexible new rhythms and enjambed lines, recurrence of refrains, and the same syllable count in corresponding lines of each stanza – reflected his desire to break with traditional prosody and introduce more relaxed meter.[11] In this, however, he failed because of his vague understanding of poetic types; he failed to distinguish poetry (*si*) from song (*ka*), for example, and his tripartite division of new poetry (prose poems), songs, and airs (*sijo*) was problematic. Nevertheless, at a time when no professional poets existed and no student abroad majored in literature, his experiment was trailblazing. Ch'oe's poems mix a fixed and a freer meter, tradition-bound elements and West-directed ones, lyricism and eloquence. Finally he thought the prose poem to be a typical form of modern poetry – as shown by his later experiments in a group of poems on T'aebaek Mountain, where only lineation marks them as verse.

THE IMPACT OF SYMBOLISM AND ROMANTICISM

Several months before the costly and ill-fated 1 March 1919 movement for Korean independence, Korean poetry underwent the powerful influence of French symbolism. In late 1918, the *Western Literary Weekly* published translations from Verlaine (1844–1896), Gourmont (1858–1915), and Fyodor Sologub (1863–1927), followed by a description of the French and Western literary scenes. Kim Ŏk (b. 1895), the principal translator, introduced the tenets of symbolism, the art of indirection, and mystical suggestiveness. He proposed that the poet's job was to suggest objects rather than name them (Mallarmé),[12] and he cited Verlaine's dictum "Never the Color, always the Shade, / always the nuance is supreme!" ("Art Poétique," stanza 4, lines 1–2).[13] To Kim, Rimbaud's "Les Voyelles" was the supreme example of musical verse in the symbolist tradition; Baudelaire's "perfumes, sounds, and colors correspond" ("Correspondances," stanza 2, line 4)[14] represented the apex of modern poetry, even though Kim failed to see the correspondences between the material world and spiritual realities and those between the different human senses. Kim concluded that *vers libre*, which he defined

---

[11] For example: "Sin Taehan sonyŏn" ("The New Korean Boy"); "Kkot tugo" ("Flower"); and "P'yŏngyang haeng" ("Journey to P'yŏngyang").

[12] Stéphane Mallarmé, *Oeuvres complètes* (Paris: Gallimard, 1945), p. 869 (from "Réponses à des enquêtes sur l'évolution littéraire").

[13] F. MacIntyre, *French Symbolist Poetry* (Berkeley: University of California Press, 1961), p. 35.

[14] Ibid., p. 13.

as "the music of language to express the poet's inner life," was the supreme creation of the symbolists. He ignored Baudelaire's aspiration toward mysticism or toward art as another cosmos that transforms and humanizes nature.[15]

Kim also gave his own views on translation as an art and, as well, something of his views on poetics.[16] Art, Kim said, is a product of the spirit; a work of art is an expression of the harmony between body and soul. Just as a people has a unique language, so too does the individual. Just as an individual's breathing and heartbeat have their own distinctive rhythms, so too does each poet have his own unique diction, style, and rhythm. Such individual characteristics demand a harmonious and musical form; Kim sought this in free verse or in the characteristic rhythms of the Korean language. He adumbrated the concept of the autonomy of the poet as a conscious artist and craftsman, and later added that the poet must find an adequate medium to express the Korean sensibility. Probably this was a counterpart to the emphasis that Poe, Baudelaire, and Mallarmé placed on the intellect in the creative process. Kim Ŏk and other translators active in the late 1910s and early 1920s reacted against rhetoric, description, didacticism, and political and public themes. They attempted to fuse music and images to create a strange and sad beauty in their work.

Kim's absorption with symbolism culminated, in March 1921, in the publication of his *Onoe ŭi mudo* (*Dance of Anguish*), the first volume of Western poetry in Korean translation. It introduced Verlaine, Gourmont, Samain (1858–1900), Baudelaire (1821–1867), Yeats (1865–1939), and others. Like Ueda Bin's *Kaichōon* (*Sound of the Tide*, 1905) and Nagai Kafū's *Sangoshū* (*Corals*, 1913), the book was at once acclaimed for the beauty of its translations and became a basic text for aspiring poets until the 1940s. Kim translated Japanese, English, French, and Esperanto[17] into soft and

---

[15] René Wellek, *A History of Modern Criticism: The Late Nineteenth Century* (New Haven: Yale University Press, 1965), 4:435, 437, 441. See also David Perkins, *A History of Modern Poetry*, 2 vols. (Cambridge, Mass.: Harvard University Press, 1976–1987), 1:48–52.

[16] Kim Ŏk's works include "Sologub's View of Life" (*T'aesŏ munye sinbo*, November 1918 – January 1919); "The French Poetic World" (*T'aesŏ munye sinbo*, December 1918), which introduced French symbolism; and "Metre and Breadth of Poetic Form" (*Chosŏn munye*, February 1919). In the last paper, Kim said: "We must respect the metre of the individual poet to initiate a new poetic style in modern Korean poetry . . . When poetry is kept to the poet's subjectivity, it is possible to have poetic beauty and metre. That is, metre is based on the poet's respiration and palpitation, and it makes poetry contain the absolute value of the poet's spirit and soul. Metre and respiration in a poetic form, therefore, are always a matter of importance." This translation is from Ho-Byeong Yoon, "French Symbolism and Modern Korean Poetry: A Study of Poetic Language and Its Social Significance in Korea " (Ph.D. dissertation, State University of New York at Stony Brook, 1986), p. 24.

[17] For example, Verlaine's "Chanson d'automne." Kim was an active member of Korea Esperanto-Asocio, founded in September 1920, wrote the first manual, *Esperanto Kurso Ramida* (1931; 2nd

mellifluous Korean, often using colloquial honorific verb forms. Exoticism; a somber, eerie beauty suggestive of the melancholic mood of a dying season; boredom; anguish; abandonment of the self to death – all of these elements appealed to poets who sought models to express their frustration, emptiness, and despair after the collapse of the 1919 independence movement.

In the 1920s, poets took to heart Verlaine's advice "to take eloquence and wring its neck" ("Prends l'éloquence et tors-lui son cou!")[18] and declared that literature is not a medium for enlightenment but has its own objectives. Thus they rejected public poetry in favor of private poetry. The 1920s were also a decade that witnessed a number of important changes favorable to the development of modern Korean poetry. First, while most other forms being experimented with, such as *sijo*, *kasa*, song, and new-style poetry, fell into disuse, free verse was established as the principal form of modern Korean poetry. Another was the flourishing of newspapers, magazines, and literary coterie magazines (little magazines) – such as *P'yehŏ* (*Ruins*, 1920), *Kaebyŏk* (*Beginning*, 1920–1926), *Paekcho* (*White Tide*, 1922), *Kŭmsŏng* (*Venus*, 1923), and *Chosŏn mundan* (*Korean Literary Circle*, 1924–1927), which became the principal media for poetry. Poems must be printed in order to make them public, it was believed. Moreover, with the understanding of the concept of literary property, poets no longer used pseudonyms or pen names as in the past but indicated their own names as if to attach importance to their individuality as poets. The 1920s also saw an increase in the number of writers – most of whom received a modern education abroad in Japan – as well as the number of readers.

Most writers active in this decade came from the middle class. These writers espoused individualism, especially the freedom of individual self-expression, and evinced such traits as thirst for a full life, longing for the absolute, a desire to escape from unpleasant realities, and praise of death. The typical poet craved freedom and believed he could enjoy it only when he could follow his impulses without restraint. Turning his back on tradition and convention, he learned painfully that society, especially under Japanese occupation, was hostile to the artist. His version of the happy life denied, he began to view everyday existence as a river of lies, a process of self-abandonment. The division between individual and society led to a dichotomy between dream and reality, truth and falsehood, freedom and bondage, light and darkness, the subjects of much poetry of the early 1920s.

edn., 1946), and himself translated some Western poems into Esperanto, for which see Kim Yunsik, *Kŭndae Hanguk munhak yŏngu* (Ilchisa, 1973), pp. 112–163.
[18] Translation of "Art Poétique" appeared in *T'aesŏ munye sinbo* 11 (1918).

Poets known for their excess of emotion, sensual description, and escape from reality were usually dubbed "romantic" (Chu Yohan, Hong Sayong, the early Pak Chonghwa and Yi Sanghwa). They introduced in their work terms of a new vocabulary such as dream, tomorrow, passion, tears, beauty, eternity, anguish, boredom, coffin, grave, and vision, most of which came from translations of Western, especially French symbolist, poetry. In their attempts to escape from vulgar reality, poets, especially the *White Tide* group, fondly evoked places that exist on the other side of reality: a secret chamber where one can attain true life and truth (Pak Chonghwa), a hill of light and land of dreams (Pak Yŏnghŭi), the bedroom (Yi Sanghwa), and a village of roses – "site of a fragrant banquet for gods and men" (Hwang Sŏgu). The secret chamber was not a place that would provide answers; it was a place where the poet realizes that nowhere can he find eternal truth. The bedroom of Yi Sanghwa is a place not only of rapture but of death, qualified as one "beyond a one-log bridge of regret and fear" and "an ageless land." His bedroom, the poet continues, is "a cave of resurrection." Death for him is not an end but the beginning of a leap to true life. The romanticization of death, together with an excess of sentimentality and melancholy, was a substitute for an unfulfilled ideal. As members of the middle class, poets of the 1920s embraced individualism and liberalism but had no solution to the problem of colonial oppression. They had to join the colonial system or go under. Deprived of any chance to participate in the political process, they began to deny the value of society and doubted it could understand the anguish of "accursed poets." The vulgar mass, they thought, would probably sneer at their earnest search for enlightenment.[19]

Haep'ari ŭi norae (*Songs of Jellyfish*) by Kim Ŏk, published in June 1923, was the first volume of new verse by a single poet. If the predominant mood of Kim's *Dance of Anguish* was that of autumn, the tenor of *Songs of Jellyfish* was one of autumnal sorrow: a homesick wanderer starts out on an aimless journey in search of a lost spring ("blue, blue May"), a home, or a lost country. The wandering youth blowing a sad old tune on his pipes was a fit metaphor for the state of mind of Korean poets during the 1920s. Kim's sense of form, his frequent use of metaphor and personification, and his emphasis on musicality were all features of the symbolist heritage that furthered the development of modern Korean poetry.[20]

[19] See Kim Hŭnggyu's analysis in *Yi Sanghwa, Pak Chŏnghwa oe* (*HHST* 3), pp. 237–280. For Yi Sanghwa's poetry I have used *Wŏnjŏn taegyo Yi Sanghwa chŏnjip: Ppaeakkin tŭredo pomŭn onŭnga*, ed. Yi Kich'ŏl (Munjangsa, 1982).

[20] Chŏng Hanmo, *Hanguk hyŏndae simunhak sa* (Ilchisa, 1974), pp. 339–393.

Yet such symbolist techniques as the communication of mood, the art of indirection, the creation of symbols, and the fusion of music and images were already present in traditional East Asian poetry. What the new poetry movement helped to advance was the creation of new forms, the view of the poem as an intimate experience of the self (the conscious artist) rather than a rearrangement of traditional imagery, and the emphasis on the intellect in poetic creation (though this was not always practiced). The choice of autumn as the favorite poetic season, with twilight as the most captivating time of day, was nothing new. Autumn had been the favorite poetic season in traditional East Asian poetry, and the deliberate cultivation of the dark and mysterious, the melancholy and enigmatic, and the fleeting and intangible was the highest aesthetic ideal. Hence certain recurring images (scattered stars, a cold moon, white dew, departing swallows, fallen leaves) and the cries of crickets, geese, quail, and snipe were all deployed to symbolize the speaker's state of mind. These insects and birds, however, seldom appeared in Korean imitations of symbolist poetry. A typical symbolist poem was intended to create a world devoid of locality, "dense with specificity but difficult to specify,"[21] an atmosphere or a mood "riddled with nuance," and a poetry of adjectives and adverbs rather than one of verbs. The poet tried to locate his dispossession and entrapment in some outside landscape, but the dim autumnal atmosphere at best reflected his failure to see clearly the nature of his anguish. The poet saw decay and death in the midst of life, but he could find no adequate means to express this dilemma or come to grips with the world.

FOLK-SONG-STYLE POETRY

Chu Yohan (b. 1900), who aspired to approach the folk-song meter as the basis of a new poetry, began to write poems in 1917. *Arŭmdaun saebyŏk* (*Beautiful Dawn*, 1924), a collection of sixty-six poems written between 1917 and 1923, includes such interesting pieces in free verse as "Nun" ("Snow," 1918), "Niyagi" ("A Tale," 1918), and "Pullori" ("Fireworks," 1919). "Snow" describes an early morning scene of snow-covered Seoul as well as an ugly nightlife as symbolic of corruption and moral death. "A Tale" presents the progress of life, life's unattainable goal, in the form of a fairy tale. "Fireworks" is a prose poem of personal feelings couched in a diction that explores emotive connotations. It describes an April day in P'yŏngyang and fireworks on the Taedong River in celebration of the Buddha's birthday.

---

[21] Hugh Kenner, *A Homemade World: The American Modernist Writers* (New York: Knopf, 1975), p. 205.

The speaker declares, "This mind that is alive is dead at the thought of the deceased love...Shall I burn down this heart in that flame? Shall I burn down this sorrow?...To my relief, I would rather [plunge] into the depth of this water tonight...Then would anyone feel pity?" This is a dialogue between the self and the antiself. Some of Chu's poems deal with a vague notion of love or repressed love – often represented by fire standing for liberation and vitality against water, a symbol of traditional Confucian morality. Here, then, the images of fire and water represent a clash between the new and old, the Western and Korean views of life. The poem suffers, however, from a piling up of connectives that results in interminable sentences, exaggeration, dashes, ellipsis marks indicating omission such as the verb "plunge" above, and exclamation – all intended, no doubt, to express the eruption of youthful emotion.[22]

Chu Yohan then turned to the creation of folk-song-style lyrics. In "Pissori" (The sound of rain, 1924), for example, the first stanza goes:

> It rains.
> Night silently spreads its wings,
> And rain whispers in the garden,
> Like chicks talking secretly.

The rain is compared to a mother hen spreading her wings to protect her chicks and then to a loving guest (stanza 3). In the concluding stanza, the rain is coming to bring joyful news to his heart. "The joyful news" is sometimes read as the day Korea "will see a bright new day." According to this symbolic reading, "It rains" or "Rain is coming" is repeated seven times to underscore the suffering of the Korean people under Japanese rule.[23]

In his postface to *Beautiful Dawn* and in "Noraerŭl chiŭryŏnŭn iege (sijakpŏp)" ("To Those Who Would Compose Songs, Poetics," October 1924), Chu Yohan declares that he shunned decadence and tried to bring his poetry close to the people. Chu's notion of poetry for the people included the following guidelines: express the emotion and thought of the Korean people; project the beauty and power of the language; be faithful to your individuality as a Korean; and produce literature that must first be Korean before becoming world literature.[24] The movement for folk-song-style poetry came from the realization that poetic forms inspired by the West cannot express the Korean sensibility. Modern Korean poetry cannot

---

[22] For a complete translation of the poem see Myung-Ho Sym, *The Making of Modern Korean Poetry: Foreign Influences and Native Creativity* (Seoul: Seoul National University Press, 1982), pp. 149–152.
[23] Ibid., pp. 195–196.
[24] See postface to *Beautiful Dawn*, in Myung-ho Sym, *The Making of Modern Korean Poetry*, pp. 196–197, and "To Those Who Would Compose Songs, Poetics" (Sym, p. 197).

be cut off from the past, and imitating Western models will not "modernize" Korean poetry. The establishment of a truly Korean poetic form should come from a study of folk song that evinces the artistic creativity of the people. Folk songs not only reveal the spirit of the Korean people but offer a vision of life that present-day forms (Chu Yohan, Kim Ŏk, Hong Sayong, Kim Tonghwan) cannot. Chu wished to express the vigor of nature and life, as in images of sun, morning, and boulevard, but he held that individuality and music could be achieved by following traditional meter and form.

In his folk-song-style poems, Kim Ŏk too expressed representative feelings (lost love, the sorrow of parting) in conventional rhetoric, stock figures, and metaphors (flowers of joy, fragrance of sorrow). Kim considered music to be the essence of poetry but thought it could be achieved only by fixed meter and form. Seldom did he attain a genuine folk-song rhythm. Unskilled in the choice of words and formation of the poetic line (a stanza consists sometimes of a single sentence spread out to form so many lines), Kim mistook a stringing together of empty modifiers for beautiful diction and was fond of using the literary-style verbal endings (*hanora, irŏra, hanani*). He was also indifferent to history and reality in his pursuit of the dream, as in his stilted, allegorical image of a "wanderer's longing for a star on a dark night."

The practice of folk-song-style poetry fell short of its advocates' aspirations. In the name of popular sentiment, they favored certain topics such as the frustrations of love, sorrow, and vague longing. Obsessed with syllable count rather than meter, they failed to represent the inner experience and to understand that the folk song, unlike a poem by an individual artist, is the expression of a whole singing community. They simplified emotion, suppressed their concern for realism, and favored traditional feelings and local setting as background. Their chief contributions consist in avoiding foreign words in favor of the vernacular by omitting particles or inflections and by incorporating dialect, coined words, and phenomimetic words. Chu Yohan even resorts to quotation marks – as in "brightness" in "Fireworks" – to foreground certain key words in a work. Except for certain poems by Kim Sowŏl, attempts to write modern poems in folk-song style were not successful.

Kim Sowŏl (1902–1934) published his first and only collection of poems, *Chindallaekkot* (*Azaleas*), in 1925, when he was twenty-three. The 127 titles in this book include some of the most popular Korean poems of the twentieth century. Written in simple and haunting rhythms, these lyrics are cited, discussed, and sung by the learned and commoners alike. One source of appeal is a skillful adaptation of folk-song meter. Another has to do with the subject – frustrations of love – spoken by a disappointed woman who evokes the feelings expressed in traditional folk songs, particularly sorrow over the transitoriness of love. The modern poet's adoption of stock diction and meter was to revive the voice of the people at a time when the contemporary trend was an injudicious imitation of Western poetry. Kim Sowŏl also used his regional dialect of the northwest to give his poems a sense of place while incorporating the standard Seoul speech – the medium of literature throughout the twentieth century – of his teacher Kim Ŏk.

Until Kim Sowŏl entered Paejae High School in Seoul in 1922 at the age of twenty, he received his early education in his hometown in North P'yŏngan. As his father was mentally unstable or perhaps epileptic, Kim was brought up by his grandfather who ran a mine. At the age of fourteen he married a girl of seventeen and subsequently had four sons and two daughters, the first born when Kim himself was seventeen. After graduating from high school in March 1923, Kim went to Japan to apply to enter commercial college but failed and returned to Seoul where he spent several months. In 1925 he returned to Namsi in his region as manager of the local office of the *Tonga Daily*. Owing to his business failure, Kim was despondent and, until his suicide by drinking wine mixed with opium, he led an unhappy life in poverty.

Kim began publishing in 1920, and most of his popular poems were written between 1922 and 1925. There are several reasons why the popularity of some of his lyrics has been so lasting. In "Azaleas" (1922) consisting of three four-line stanzas, for example, identical repetitions occur in stanzas 1–4, except in the third line. Three lines in the first, second, and fourth stanzas have the verbal ending -*urida* (deferential volitional marker), and the third line in stanza 3 ends in -*opsosŏ*, an entreaty. In this lyric, the forsaken woman strews an armful of azaleas on the road her beloved will travel. In stanza 4, however, the speaker asks him first to tread on them softly (*sappuni*) and then heavily to beat them down with force and crush them (*chŭryŏ* . . .).[25] The azalea is a symbol of the speaker's self-sacrifice; the abandoned one is first to be plucked, scattered, and finally trampled (no matter how softly he walks on them). The speaker seems to say: "Go on, if you want to leave. Trample upon me, I don't care." In the final stanza where the speaker declares that she will not shed tears even though she dies, the usual word order is broken and *ani*, usually following the verb to negate it, is placed before the noun "tears," in order to stress the act

[25] Yi Kimun, "Sowŏl si ŭi ŏnŏ e tahayŏ," in *Kim Sowŏl*, ed. Kim Hoktong (Sŏgang taehakkyo ch'ulp'anbu, 1995), pp. 165–192.

of not shedding tears. The reaction evoked here is unexpected. She is not willing to die amid the centuries of lament of her own kind. It is therefore hard to accept a reading that the speaker, like the typical Korean woman of the past, is willingly submitting to the situation. Nor is it appropriate to compare "Azaleas" with certain Koryŏ songs, such as "Kasiri" ("Will you Go?"), in which the woman speaker says:

> I could stop you but fear
> You would be annoyed and never return.
> Go, then, I'll let you go,
> But return as soon as you leave.

Nor is it apt to characterize her action as self-torture or containing a threat of vengeance.

The 1922 version of "Mŏn huil" ("Long from Now") shows an improvement over the 1920 version in construction and diction. The first three stanzas have the subjunctive–indicative mood construction (If you would...I would), followed by the indicative. "*Ijŏnnora*" ("I Have Forgotten") is repeated four times to underscore the fact that the speaker cannot forget her beloved; in fact she has never forgotten.[26]

> Long from now, if you should seek me,
> I would tell you I have forgotten.
>
> If you should blame me in your heart,
> I would say "Missing you so, I have forgotten."
>
> And if you should still reprove me,
> "I couldn't believe you, so I have forgotten."
>
> Unable to forget you today, or yesterday,
> but long from now "I have forgotten."[27]

Here we have a paradoxical structure: You forget me; I can never forget you.

"Yejŏnen mich'ŏ mollassŏyo" ("I Didn't Know Before," 1923) is a four-stanza lyric, two lines each, with the same second line: "I didn't know before." The speaker says she did not notice the moon that rises every night, she did not know she would miss her beloved, she did not know how to watch the bright moon, and now the moon is her sorrow.

Such poems have a stock of favorite words and images: sobbing tide, sinking sun, whispering rain, tear-drenched pillow, rainy dunes, sighing or

---

[26] This line is also read as the speaker's admission of her responsibility for the pain of parting; see O Seyŏng, *Hanguk nangman chuŭi si yŏngu* (Ilchisa, 1980), p. 342.

[27] Translated by David McCann, in *SL*, p. 32.

chilling winds, crying ravens, pheasants, grackles, or cuckoos, spring nights, graves, dreams, and sobbing wayfarers, all helping to create a plaintive feeling. There is little specificity of plot, however. Images are commonplace, and they are used to exploit stock responses. The poems offer conventional feelings about the sorrow of love, and this calculated indeterminacy, a characteristic of folk song, contributes to their popularity: the reader can readily identify with the lyric persona. Simple diction, subtle versification, repetition with special effects, economy – all contribute to their charm.

It has been argued that Kim Sowŏl's lyrics are too feminine, that the beloved (*nim*) exists only in the past, that the speaker only laments absence or loss, shuns change, offers no new awareness of the self, tortures herself, renounces rather than resists her lot, and indulges in self-pity. Often Kim is blamed for his platitudes, his lack of historical consciousness, and his penchant for sentimentalism and self-diminishment. Sometimes the sorrow expressed is identified with the traditional notion of *han* – a complex feeling of submission and resistance, frustration and lingering affection, grudge and self-reproach, usually explained as coming from injustice inflicted upon the people by the ruling class or upon women by men. Essentially it describes a feeling of self-pity for one's helpless lot.[28] Another reading has it that the *nim* is hidden because of Japanese colonial oppression, gone with the loss of country; but every reader knows the deep love that abides between the speaker and her beloved. Therefore, like the *nim* in Han Yongun's poems, the *nim* in certain poems by Kim Sowŏl represents the country being stolen, the native tradition being annihilated.

"Ch'ohon" ("Calling Back the Soul," 1925) illustrates how Kim Sowŏl explored to the fullest the multiple meanings of the word *nim*. Here the male speaker makes an impassioned appeal in a sinewy diction begging his lady's soul to return:

> O name broken piecemeal,
> Strewn in the empty void.
> O name without response,
> That suffers me to die as I call it.
>
> The last word carved in my heart
> Was never spoken in the end.
> O you that I love,
> O you that I love.
>
> Crimson sun hangs on the west peak,
> The deer bell and call sadly.

---

[28] Ibid., pp. 333–352.

There on the sheer steep peak
I call your empty name.
I will still call your name
Until sorrow chokes me.
My voice goes aslant, rejected,
Lost between heaven and earth.

Were I to become a stone,
I would still call your name as I died.
O you that I love,
O you that I love.

In this poem, the word *irŭm* (name) is repeated four times in stanza 1 and "O you that I love" is repeated twice in stanzas 2 and 5. In "Were I to become a stone, / I would still call your name as I died," some find a tragic beauty in his resolution.[29] The "name broken piecemeal," "O name without response," and the vocative "you that I love" lend themselves to more than a single reading. Here Kim Sowŏl has shown that he can write a poem whose rhythm and diction are capable of bearing the weight of emotion inherent in the situation, a poem that bears witness to unfathomable sorrow.

Kim's mastery of the medium is best evinced in "Sanyuhwa" ("Mountain Flowers," 1925). Consisting of four four-line stanzas, this poem too exploits simple diction, artful rhythms, and effective repetition. It has an additional quality, however: its subject concerns the perennial question of the relationship between humans and nature. Here are stanzas 1 and 2:

Sanenŭn kkot p'ine	Flowers in the mountain bloom,
kkotch'i p'ine	the flowers bloom.
kal pom yŏrŭm ŏpsi	Fall, spring, and summer through,
kkoch'i p'ine	the flowers bloom.
sane	On the mountain,
sane	the mountain,
p'inŭn kkoch'ŭn	the flowers blooming
ch'ŏmanch'i honjasŏ p'iŏ inne	are so far, so far away.[30]

---

[29] Sin Tonguk, for example, thinks so. See Kim Yŏlgyu and Sin Tonguk, eds., *Kim Sowŏl yŏngu* (Saemunsa, 1986), 3:11. (This book has peculiar pagination: each of four parts begins with p. 1.) Although Kim sang the feeling of destitution during the colonial period, he sought a solution in the past. Relying on memory, he was wont to escape into his childhood, nature, or dream. Because his *nim* existed in the past, he was denied any possibility of meeting the beloved in the present or future, except in the shamanist ritual of summoning the *nim*'s soul. The mode of existence of Kim's *nim* is very different from that of Han Yongun.

[30] David McCann in *SL*, p. 37. I have consulted Kim Sowŏl, *Kim Sowŏl chŏnjip*, ed. Kim Yongjik (Seoul Taehakkyo ch'ulp'anbu, 1996).

In stanza 2, the repetition of *san* (mountain) in *sane sane* implies all the mountains. The key word that makes this poem the most challenging of his works is the first word in the fourth line: *chŏmanch'i* (that much, to that extent). Does it point to the discontinuity between humankind and nature? Nature is cyclical, but we are not. "*Ch'ŏmanch'i*" also means that nature exists on its own accord, is sufficient unto itself, transcending human values and standards, and its freedom, freshness, innocence, and purity are its mode of existence. As a modern man the speaker cannot commit himself to nature without committing himself to the finality of death and the terror of discontinuity. This poem, intricately and subtly wrought, shows the mark of the poet's art – how Kim was able to transfigure what appeared to be commonplace.

After his move to the northwest close to his birthplace in 1925, Kim Sowŏl published dozens of poems in journals. Recently a holograph copy of his manuscript was discovered. These poems, now in print, show considerable change in subject, prosody, and mood – more positive, forward-looking – and a range of emotions arising from contemporary life in the late 1920s and early 1930s. Kim, however, seldom took firm hold of contemporary life. Living in a remote country town, burdened with family responsibilities, cut off from the literary world in Seoul, he felt both cultural and personal isolation. Finally, on 24 December 1934, Kim took his life. Despite a few bright poems he left behind, Kim failed to pluck laughter from despair; hence many of his less successful poems read like a whimper. Some of his lyrics, however, such as the ones discussed here,[31] will survive because of their masterful use of language and prosody.

HAN YONGUN: THE PLIGHT OF COLONIAL RULE

The first authentic Korean interpreter of the country's plight was Han Yongun. Han adopted colloquial language and free verse to reveal how people could transcend such obstacles as enslavement, tyranny, and censorship as they penetrated their own sense of self. When the Japanization of Korean history and culture was under-way and Korean cultural identity was being erased by the thought-crime law (1923) and peace preservation law (1925), Han not only reflected his culture's crisis but went beyond suffering to find an awareness that was at once old and new.

Han Yongun, poet, patriot, and Buddhist monk, was born on 29 September 1879 in Hongsŏng, South Ch'ungch'ŏng. He studied Chinese classics

---

[31] And such other poems as "Kŭmjandi" ("The Golden Meadow"); "Kanŭn Kil" ("The Road Away"); and "Chŏptongsae" ("The Cuckoo").

at a village school and was married at thirteen. He then entered a hermitage on Mount Sŏrak, where he studied Buddhism and became a monk
in 1905. In 1908, he went to Japan to observe the modernization process of
the Buddhist church. In his essay "On the Revival of Korean Buddhism"
(1910), he denounced the traditional ills of Korean Buddhism, preached
that Buddhist reform could not be brought about without the regeneration of the human heart, and strove to revive the faith. He also fought
against the Japanese infiltration of the Korean Buddhist church and in
1914 published a digest of Buddhist doctrine in the vernacular. At the time
of the 1919 Independence Movement, he helped draft the "Declaration of
Independence" and was one of the thirty-three patriots who signed the
document. In prison he wrote another essay expounding the importance of
Korean independence in the preservation of peace in East Asia. Released in
March 1922, he continued his patriotic activities through public speaking
and writing until his death of palsy on 29 June 1944 in the eastern suburbs of
Seoul.

In May 1926 Han published his single volume of poetry, *Nim ŭi ch'immuk*
(*The Silence of Love*), comprising eighty-eight poems plus a foreword and
a note to the reader. *Nim* is a complex word in Korean: in love poetry it is
the beloved; in allegorical poetry, the king; in religious verse, the god. In
Han's poetry, *nim* is both the object and subject of love, be it the nation,
life, the Buddha, or enlightenment. His poems are built upon dialectic:
engagement and withdrawal, motion and stillness, action and nonaction,
life and death, nirvana and saṃsāra, enlightenment and illusion. He forged
a poetics of absence based on the paradoxical reciprocity of presence and
absence. Truth exists only as absence, Han says, and this Buddhist approach
to reality is expressed through the language of love. The speaker in most of
Han's poems is a woman who talks Ch'ungch'ŏng dialect,[32] and addresses
her beloved *nim*. In the foreword Han says that "the loved one is not only
the beloved but everything yearned for." The beloved for Śākyamuni is
living beings, for Kant it is philosophy, for the rose a spring rain, and for
Mazzini Italy: "The beloved is not only one that I love, but who loves me."
The title poem, "The Silence of Love," goes:

> Love is gone. Ah, my love is gone.
> Sundering the mountain's green color, severing our ties, love is gone
>   down a path leading to a maple grove.
> The old vows, firm and glowing like a gold blossom, have turned to
>   cold dust and flown away in the breeze of a sigh.

---

[32] The speaker mentions a mirror stand (poem 35), sewing (poem 55), and needlework (poem 72).

The memory of a keen first kiss reversed the compass needle of my
fate, then retreated and vanished.
I am deafened by love's fragrant words and blinded by love's
blossoming face.
Love, too, is a man's affair. We feared parting at meeting, warned
against it, but parting came unawares and the startled heart bursts
with new sorrow.
Yet I know that to make parting the source of vain tears is to sunder
myself my love, so I transformed the unruly power of sorrow and
poured it over the vertex of new hope.
As we fear parting when we meet, so we believe we will meet again
when we part.
Ah, love is gone, but I have not sent my love away.
My song of love that cannot endure itself curls around the silence of
love.

The poem's situation, as well as the identities of the speaker and addressee, signal to the reader that more is intended here than just love talk.
Semantically, the poem's controlled indeterminacy allows the reader to explore other interpretive horizons – for example, the range of meaning and
connotation of the word *nim* in a given context, in the literary tradition,
and in the Korean collective experience. Syntactic changes, repetition of
key words (*ploce*),[33] and special connotations imparted to certain words
help the reader experience the multiple significance of the narrative situation. The absent lover is addressed as if he were present. His *nim* is
boundless. It is with him – one who is truly nonexistent but also mysteri-
ously existent and who represents a state that is permanent and existent –
that the speaker seeks reunion. To link the lines, Han employs the rhetorical device of *ploce*: *nim* (seven times), "to go" (four times), "to part" (five
times), and the related verb "to fly away" (once). The repetition of key
words reinforces the rhythmic pattern and enables the poet to dispense with
punctuation.

The beloved's defining characteristic is that he is not here. Despite this
imposing absence, he is capable of being addressed. Parting is a form of
love between the speaker and *nim*, the time to discover *nim*'s visage: "*Nim*'s
face is more lovely at parting" ("The Beloved's Face at Parting," 66). The
more absent he is, the more present he is. Absence is the mode of existence
of *nim*, and his absence is direct proof of his true existence. To measure the
amount of love, the speaker says, we can measure the distance between us.

[33] A. C. Partridge, *The Language of Modern Poetry: Yeats, Eliot, Auden* (London: Deutsch, 1976),
p. 148.

If the distance is great, the amount of love will be great; if it is small, the amount of love will be small ("The Measure of Love," 20). That is: *nim* exists as absence, but this absence is achieved only through the poet's power of negation. Our sorrow comes from the fact that we must live in the age of negation.

The only right path for the speaker is to accept suffering and await the return of *nim* – but vigorous hard work is required to meet *nim* ("Waking Dream," 18). "I'll take off even the clothes of life"; indeed, "Sorrowing for you is my life itself" ("Please Don't Doubt Me," 23). "Do as you will with me, give me life or death," declares the speaker ("If Not For You," 17). The more hardships there are in the path of waiting, the stronger is the desire for love ("Obedience," 38). "Lest the rope of your love be weak I doubled the rope of my love for you" ("The Meditation Master's Sermon," 43). Sometimes, however, the speaker realizes that "her *nim* becomes a smile hiding in [her] heart" ("Everywhere," 65). The duality of existence and absence, parting and meeting, being and nonbeing, is presented in the form of a paradox – a paradox of love:

> Others say that they think of their loves; but I want to forget you.
>
> ("I Want to Forget," line 4)
>
> Love, come, if you don't intend to come, I'd rather you'd go.
>
> ("I'd Rather," line 15)

Aware that the language of love is the language of paradox, the speaker is able to embrace the contradictions between existence and absence. She must overcome the darkness of her age with the dialectical Middle Way. Absence is the lack of presence, but presence must transcend absence. That which transcends the conditional and unconditional is true emptiness. Thus Han Yongun can make his speaker say: parting is not an end but a beginning of true love. Through parting *nim* enables me to discover myself; through absence he proves my existence; through silence he speaks to me. *Nim* is an absolute existence, but he exists through me. He is the sole meaning of my being and the guarantor of the possibility for my existence. Yearning for *nim* enables me to continue to live; to deny the existence of *nim* is to deny my existence. The process of waiting takes the form of struggle for the actualization of *nim*.

Although Han Yongun attributes power to language ("I am deafened by love's fragrant words"), he is also aware of its inadequacy, because "words do not exhaust meaning." Han declares, however, that "beauty is parting's creation" – namely, he endeavors to create an aesthetic object, a poem.

His song is different from the vulgar songs ("My Song," 16), however, and as in "Double Seventh" (81) the speaker avers that "True love cannot be described . . . They [the Herdboy and Weaver constellations] can't see my love," for "the sanctity of love is not in expression but in secrecy." Indeed, "love's secret is known only by the poet's imagination" ("The Existence of Love," 29).

An impassioned eulogy to *nim* ("Praise," 51) conveys the speaker's fervent hope for light:

> O beloved, you're gold tempered a hundred times over.
> Receive the love of the Heavenly Kingdom until the mulberry roots
>   turn to coral.
> O beloved, my love, first steps of the morning sun!
> . . .
> O beloved, you love spring, light, and peace.
> Become a merciful bodhisattva who sprinkles tears on the heart of
>   the weak.
> O beloved, my love, spring breeze over the sea of ice!

The beloved is the morning light, spring, peace, a compassionate bodhisattva. *Nim* will enable the speaker to resist darkness with light, to overcome oppression by melting it with a spring breeze, to bring about peace and harmony: a poetics of hope.

Three characters are mentioned by name in Han's work. Nongae and Kyewŏrhyang are female entertainers who died for Korea during the Japanese invasions of 1592–1598. At the banquet in the Ch'oksŏk Tower, Nongae (d. 1592) jumped into the South River with a Japanese general in her arms. Kyewŏrhyang, another female entertainer who helped a Korean general to kill a drunken Japanese warrior in P'yŏngyang, is a heroine in the *Imjin nok* (*Record of the Black Dragon Year*), a popular narrative story about the invasion. In "Pledging Love at Nongae's Shrine" (52), the male speaker (who is the poet himself) declares that Korea is like a grave upon which a flower blossoms. The corpse in the grave decays, but the flower does not. Nongae's dancing sleeves create a wind, awesome and cold. There is a flower grove in the land of shades and the sun sets beyond it. The wind freezes the sun – that is, Nongae's determination to die for her people has the power to stop the sun from sinking further. The poet refuses to plant a flower on the grave, not only because the shrine is not Nongae's abode, but also because planting flowers accepts that she is dead and gone. The poem ends as the speaker struggles to utter the truth in terms of paradox:

Nongae, who will not die for a thousand autumns,
Nongae, who cannot live even a day.
How glad and how sad that my heart loves you.
My laughter turns to tears, my tears turn to laughter.

In "Upon Reading Tagore's 'Gardenisto,'" Han chides the Bengali poet (1861–1941) for espousing a view that love ends in parting and in death. Tagore, he says, lacks historical consciousness:

Peace, my heart, let the time for the parting be sweet,
Let it be a death but completeness.[34]

[Tagore]

Friend, my friend,
No matter how good the fragrance of death, you cannot kiss the lips
    of the white bones,
Don't enmesh that grave with golden song; place a blood-stained
    banner on the grave!

[Han]

Known in Korea from 1917 mainly as a prophet for a people suffering under British colonial rule and, too, as the voice of freedom and independence, Tagore was read for his call to patriotic self-sacrifice and his belief in poetry as a vital expression of life. Tagore's subject matter, diction, tone, and poetic devices inspired a number of poets, including Han Yongun.[35] Han, however, finds Tagore lacking in awareness of society, history, and revolution, both spiritual and moral. Han's firm grasp of time and place is the subject of "I Saw You" (36):

I am homeless, and for other reasons as well, I've no family register.
"A woman who has no register has no civil rights. What has chastity
    to do with you who has no civil rights?" a general once said and
    tried to violate me.
After resisting him, the moment my rage toward others was turning
    into sorrow, I saw you.
Ah, I realized that all ethics, morals, and laws are nothing but
    incense burnt for the sword and gold.
Should I accept eternal love, should I ink-blot the first pages of
    history, should I take wine – At that moment I saw you.

---

[34] Rabindranath Tagore, *Collected Poems and Plays of Rabindranath Tagore* (New York: Macmillan, 1965), p. 104.

[35] Beongcheon Yu, *Han Yong-un and Yi Kwang-su: Two Pioneers of Modern Korean Literature* (Detroit: Wayne State University Press, 1992), pp. 57–59; Kim Haktong, *Hanguk kŭndae siin yŏngu* (Ilchogak, 1974), pp. 47–85.

What happens to one who has no nation? In a colonized society, there is no such thing as a truly free person. The loss of sovereignty and the absence of *nim* bring humiliation. It is the problem not only of the speaker but of all Koreans. Should one withdraw from history into some transcendence, deny history as false, or accept an inauthentic life of pleasure? To ingratiate oneself with oppressors and lead a wanton life is no solution. *Nim* will come to those who resist by silence and long for the day oppression is finally overcome. No wonder that Nongae and Kyewŏrhyang, who wrestled for the survival of the people, are presented as paragons of patriotism. In such poems as "Please Don't Go" (5), by contrast, the addressees are those who might impulsively succumb to temptation (the enemy's banners, the devil's glare, the sword's laughter) and accept momentary comfort that brings pleasure to the self but death to the people. Some are deceived by such high-sounding words as "freedom," some are enticed by "their own shadows" (" Foreword"), and some mistake bondage in love for freedom ("Meditation on Sorrow," 22). It is the poet's duty to warn the deluded away from destroying themselves and their country.

Poets writing through the mid-1920s all wished to reflect in various ways the profound changes that were taking place in Korean daily life. Some imported romanticism, decadence, and a *fin-de-siècle* mood. Their experiments with new forms and new subjects, however, couched in imprecise language, reflected at best their own frustrations. They struggled to establish a distinct identity, echoing the romantic glorification of the poet, but their self-expression, couched as it was in past conventions, resulted ironically in the abandonment of the self. Unable to define their function in a society in flux – a society that was indifferent and often antagonistic to the poet – they were content to devote themselves to suffering and self-examination. Seldom did Korean poets assume any role other than that of estranged, lonely, and melancholy artists inhabiting the twilight world of dreams.

Han Yongun, however, forged a distinctive voice through the use of the past and the creation of the new. Drawing on the epistemology of Buddhism, the religion most firmly rooted in the people, he enriched his works with the common store of Buddhist references. Unlike past Buddhist meditations on the merits and virtues of buddhas and bodhisattvas, Han's poetry, couched in the language of love, is a spiritual exploration of the relationship between self and others, the one and the many. Like seventeenth-century English devotional verse, Han's poetry is a spiritual exercise that contemplates the origin and end of his beloved, the Buddha, and his country. According to Han, the self cannot exist apart from society. A man cannot be rootless; nor can he deny the claims of the flesh. Han's rhythmic language, specific and sensuous in its abundant detail, belongs to the convictions, hopes, and anxieties of all Koreans.[36] Han Yongun is the first great poet of modern Korea to expound the actuality of colonial rule and sing of the reality to come.

FROM PURE POETRY TO POETRY FOR LIFE

The 1930s was an eventful decade for the history of modern Korean poetry. It saw the appearance of pure poetry, imagism, modernism, surrealism, and the poetry for life school, to name a few. With Japan's invasion of Manchuria in September 1931 and the establishment of the puppet state of Manchukuo, Korea became an important part of Japan's expanding war industry. With the education policy of 1934, forced Japanese-language use, and the ban on the Korean language in schools and even on the streets, writers responded with a deeper exploration of the inherent beauties of the Korean language in their works. The Korean Language Society (formerly the Society for the Study of the Korean Language) standardized the *hangŭl* orthography, worked to popularize the use of the Korean alphabet, and began to compile a dictionary of the language. All these efforts were undertaken when Minami Jirō as governor-general inaugurated a rule of terror from 1936 and Japan's war with China began in 1937. The wartime assimilation policy was enforced; war mobilization began; and all aspects of Korean life were under stringent control by the Japanese.

The pure poetry movement

At the time of the emergence of the pure poetry movement, centered on the poetry journal *Simunhak* (*Poetic Literature*, 1930) with its theme of anti-ideological purity and love for the Korean language, the literary world was dominated by leftist writers who viewed literature as a tool for class struggle. "Pure" in this case designates a literature that upholds its purity against such "impure" literature (also called purpose literature) as nationalist literature that attempts to arouse national consciousness or leftist literature that attempts to incite a proletarian revolution. Therefore, "pure" meant a liberation from ideological content and moral didacticism. "Pure" is also opposed to popular literature – serial full-length fiction in the newspapers, historical fiction, and mass-circulation monthly entertainment magazines,

---

[36] See Kim Chaehong, *Han Yongun munhak yŏngu* (Ilchisa, 1982); Kim Yŏlgyu and Sin Tonguk, eds., *Han Yongun yŏngu* (Saemunsa, 1987), a collection of twenty essays.

all to meet the popular taste of the readership. Literature, the *Poetic Literature* group upheld, is art rather than pastime and the group devoted its energies to the problems of the individual rather than those of sociopolitical reality. Pak Yongch'ŏl, for example, defined pure poetry as an "assault on philistinism, politicization, and vulgar art." More important, the emergence of pure literature was a response to the global political situation: the rise of fascism in Europe and militarism in Japan. As the pressure of Japanese censorship and colonial policies intensified, writers turned to the aesthetic world of literature to consecrate life to the truth of feeling.

The founding members of this group, Pak Yongch'ŏl (1904–1938) and Kim Yŏngnang (1903–1950), were both from Chŏlla province in the southwest. Built on a binary opposition of inside/outside, Pak's speaker looks out from inside his room ("Even to my narrow sky / Birds come . . ."); only in his imagination does he dream of going outside: "[His] mind dashes out to a hill in the plain, / And under a round sky as roof, / Strokes a boulder" ("A Patch of Sky"). Locked in a dark night he gazes up at the sky. His path ahead is remote; he has a long way to go. Sometimes he tells himself that life is an empty shadow, that he cannot believe a new sun will ever rise again in the east, or that he will leave for a land of peace and rest. His dark night is made of such negative images as wind (often malignant), black clouds, mist, dreary rain (the most recurrent image perhaps from his experience in his hometown Songjŏng, near Kwangju), snow, and dew. Among these only snow seems to be positive, for he likes to fly up lightly like snowflakes and pray, with head lowered, before the white snow that falls with hidden sounds. His beloved who can bestow hope resides in the sky, far from the speaker, and he wishes to set sail "lest [he] spend [his] youth in tears" ("A Departing Ship," 1930). He has not, however, overcome the dichotomy between light and darkness, inside and outside, for his favorite time is twilight when contradictions seem to blur and the earth withdraws.[37]

In Pak's poetics, a poem is written not by technique alone but by refinement of emotion and depth of experience. As an objective being, a poem has aesthetic value, and the search for a lyrical beauty is likened to standing in "an ancient castle perched on a storm-beaten rock." The danger and loneliness inherent in the project notwithstanding, Pak's speaker seeks such a goal because modern Korean poetry has failed to attain the stage of pure lyricism that approaches the essence of poetry. Absorbed in the creation of beauty, his poetry excludes ideology and content but stresses individuality

---

[37] See Kim Hyŏn's reading of Pak's poetry in *Kim Yŏngnang, Pak Yongch'ŏl oe, HHST* 7 (1982), pp. 176–183.

and technique. Pak believed in inspiration that "impregnates the poet," who must patiently wait until the maturity and parturition of a newborn poem. That a poem requires patience, that it cannot be made intentionally, leads him to an inseparability of poetic experience and expression. A fire that burns toward the Muse in the poet's heart (Pak declared that poets must nurture a bright flame in their heart) is the spirit of purity. What makes a poet is his ability to transfigure himself, steeped in the depth of experience, into a blossom or a bird, another existence. The question of language and expression is related to that of technique (*kisul*) as a path to attaining a poetic goal. Like a string stretched taut that makes a sound just by being grazed, this impulse must be intense and true. Such an impulse, the beginning of creation, requires expression; hence technique, inseparable from experience, should be understood as part of the creative process.[38] Pak was not successful, however, in putting his theory into practice.

A strong sense of music ("De la musique avant toute chose;... De la musique encore et toujours"; "Art Poétique") in Kim Yŏngnang's poetry comes from an introduction of prose rhythm – a variation of long and short rhythms – and Chŏlla dialect. The semantic oddity of these words compels a rereading until the reader is able to scan the text. Verlaine is the only Western poet mentioned by name in Kim's work ("Today I call Paul Verlaine with my hands in empty pockets"), and what Kim wishes to accomplish is to create nuance ("Never the Color, always the Shade, / always the nuance is supreme!" "Art Poétique," stanza 4). To approximate such an effect in his work, Kim resorts to inversion, the use of adverbs, and creation of emotional resonance ("stillness in motion"): dim (*arŭmp'ŭt'an*) twilight, a vanishing echo, slightly tinged pastel, the smell of flesh – all these are recalled but found elusive. Kim's favorite word is "heart/mind" (*maŭm*; used more than fifty times in his total output of some seventy poems) and "I/mine"(more than sixty times). Kim's search for beauty – as epigraph to his first volume of poetry he used Keats' "A thing of beauty is a joy forever" – is accomplished by escape and alienation; he wishes to maintain

[38] Pak translated Housman's *The Name and Nature of Poetry* in 1933, which had an influence on his theory: for example, "Poetry is not the thing said but a way of saying it"; "If I were obliged, not to define poetry, but to name the class of things to which it belongs, I should call it a secretion; whether a natural secretion, like turpentine in the fir, or a morbid secretion, like the pearl in the oyster." See A. E. Housman, *The Name and Nature of Poetry* (New York: Macmillan, 1933), pp. 35 and 47–48. Pak was also influenced by Rilke's *The Notebooks of Malte Laurids Brigge*, trans. Stephen Mitchell (New York: Vintage Books, 1985), pp. 19, 20 ("poems are not simply emotions but are experiences"), and Rilke's *Letters to a Young Poet*, trans. Stephen Mitchell (New York: Vintage Books, 1986), pp. 9, 23–25 ("Being an artist means: not numbering and counting, but ripening like a tree, which doesn't force its sap, and stands confidently in the storms of spring"). See also Han Kyejŏn et al., *Hanguk hyŏndae sironsa yŏngu* (Munhak kwa chisŏngsa, 1999), pp. 155–165, 210–213.

his unsullied and aesthetic self without admitting change. His poetic world is fashioned to produce sweet sensations by exploring the inherent beauty and folk flavor in the language, but at times he complains that he cannot find anyone to share it (for example, in "Ch'allanhan sŭlp'um" ["Gorgeous Sorrow"]). In his later works, Kim confronts reality and death. His zeal to preserve his integrity despite a strong sense of loss (loss of country) finds expression in "With Poison" (1939) – poison as a weapon to confront oppression. In another poem, "Ch'unhyang" (1940), the speaker repeats the refrain "O sincere heart" (literally "a piece of crimson heart"). In Kim's poem Ch'unhyang dies for her conviction; she accepts death for the sake of love, and only by death does she fulfill her love. Kim is an "undialectic man" forever cut off from society.[39]

Another poet who wrote with more sentiment than intelligence is Sin Sŏkchŏng (1907–1974). The subject of his poetry is rural experience close to nature, and some of his works show an affinity to Gourmont (especially *Simone: Poème Champêtre*, 1898), Tagore, and Han Yongun. In his first collection, *Ch'otppul* (*Candlelight*, 1939), he often uses inversion and repetition. Longing is represented in a group of poems on dreams, such as "Naŭi kkumŭl yŏtposigessŭmnikka" ("What if you Look into my Dream?" 1932). He evokes the world of the child and likens himself to a mountain bird. "Ajik ch'otppul ŭl k'yŏlttae ka animnida" ("Not Yet Time to Light a Candle," 1933) and "Kŭ mŏn nara rŭl arŭsimnikka" ("Do you Know of that Far-off Land?"), addressed to "Mother," are attempts to overcome the dark hours of the present suffocating reality. In another poem, "Nalgae ka toch'ŏtamyŏn" ("If I Had Wings"), again addressed to "Mother," he says he wishes to be a gardener in the field of stars. Dawn, however, does not arrive, and he affirms his resolution to keep on lighting the candle throughout the night. In later poems he continues to sing of transience, longing, hope, and transcendence, but he avoids the complexity of life.[40] The poetry of Pak, Kim, and Sin is neither deep nor particularly wise. Romantics devoted to symbolist techniques, they are remembered chiefly for their effort to refine lyricism in modern Korean poetry.

Imagism

To rescue poetry from "a flood of sentimental romanticism," some advocated that the poet must be a conscious artist who, without tears and

---

[39] For Kim Hyŏn's reading of Kim's poetry see Kim *Yŏngnang, Pak Yongch'ŏl oe*, pp. 183–193; and Kim Yongjik et al., *Hanguk hyŏndae sisa yŏngu*, pp. 257–279.

[40] For Kim Ujŏng's Daoist reading see Sin Sŏkchŏng, *Sin Sŏkchŏng* (*HHST* 11 [1985]), pp. 163–195.

anger, can produce a poetry of the intellect, bright and healthy, that reflects the complexity of modern civilization. Bidding farewell to the music and nuance so valued in a poetry of personal self-expression, this new poetry should be written in a language that achieves a unity of emotion and intellect. It rejects the vague sentimental verbiage of the 1920s and attempts to present imagery that is concrete, sharp, and precise. Advocates of this kind of poetry accepted Pound's definition of an image as "that which presents an intellectual and emotional complex in an instant of time."[41] The foremost advocate of this modernist poetry with imagist principles was Kim Kirim (b. 1909), who studied English literature at Tōhoku Imperial University. He introduced the critical writings of T. E. Hulme, I. A. Richards, T. S. Eliot, and Ezra Pound. In his two collections – *Kisangdo* (*The Weather Chart*, 1936), inspired by Eliot's *The Waste Land* (1922),[42] and *T'aeyang ŭi p'ungsok* (*The Custom of the Sun*, 1939) – Kim denounced sentimental verse as "the etiquette of afternoon" and praised the virtues of the sun and morning, a "poetry of the forenoon." The use of shocking images for novelty's sake and violent (or altogether missing) transitions between the parts in *The Weather Chart*, despite its satirical intent, make it a minor work today. Kim's earlier experiments indicate that direct application of modernist poetic techniques from the West to Korean soil does not necessarily produce good poetry.

The aim of Kim Kwanggyun (1914–1993) was to write a poetry that was a conscious product of the modern intellect and spirit. He chose the language of the city (factory, hotel, express train, cellophane paper) and preferred pictorial quality to musicality: "Atop a telegraph pole / Standing blankly on a ridge fronting the sea, / A speck of passing cloud is drenched with an evening glow" ("Oeinch'on" ["The Foreigners' Village"], 1935, lines 4– 6). In this poem, Kim Kwanggyun paints a picture of a sunset from the external world for direct apprehension by the reader but does not "refuse to implicate the poem's effect in extended abstract meaning."[43] The "speck of passing cloud . . . drenched with an evening glow" easily lends itself to multiple readings because of its previous associations with sorrow, nostalgia, anticipation, and the like.

---

[41] *Poetry*, March 1913.

[42] Jong Gil Kim, "T. S. Eliot's Influence on Modern Korean Poetry." See also Kim Haktong, *Kim Kirim yŏngu* (Simunhaksa, 1991), and Kim Kirim, *Kim Kirim chŏnjip*, 6 vols. (Simsŏltang, 1988) 2: *siron*.

[43] In Alex Preminger, ed., *Encyclopedia of Poetry and Poetics*, p. 377b, imagism is defined as "a belief in the short poem, structured by the single image or metaphor and a rhythm of cadences presenting for direct apprehension by the reader an object or scene from the external world, and refusing to implicate the poem's effect in extended abstract meaning." See Alex Preminger and T. V. F. Brogan, eds., *The New Princeton Encyclopedia of Poetry and Poetic*, pp. 574a–b. For imagism see also Perkins, *A History of Modern Poetry* 1:329–347.

Poets such as Kim Kwanggyun, Chang Manyŏng (1914–1977), and to some extent Sin Sŏkchŏng all tended in their practice to stress the pictorial characteristics of poetry ("paint poetry"), for which they are labeled imagists and therefore modernists. A direct presentation of concrete images alone, however, does not make a poem modern: in addition to being written in the modern colloquial language and with modern poetic technique, a poem truly "modern" must issue from the modern sensibility and a modern manner of looking at experience. Indeed, an imagist and modernist poem had been published as early as 1926 by Chŏng Chiyong.[44]

Surrealism

Yi Sang (born Kim Haegyŏng, 1910–1937), Chŏng Chiyong's protégé, was probably the most westernized poet in the early 1930s in Korea. He made a literary debut with a story, "December the Twelfth" (1930), and a group of visually startling and enigmatic poems in Japanese in the journal *Chōsen to kenchiku* (*Korea and Architecture*, 1931). How he came to Dada and sur-realism is not clear, but Chŏng Chiyong had already written three poems with varying sizes of letters and visual devices. Yi Sang's use of letters of varying sizes, diagrams, parentheses, placing dots on the side of words and sentences for emphasis (equivalent to italics), arabic numbers, letters of the English alphabet, English and French words, heavy Chinese dic-tion, together with the absence of space between words and punctuation, and intentional subversion of linguistic stability – these devices show not only his determination to break with the past but his kinship with an essential strain in surrealism. Kim Kirim called Yi Sang "the best reader of surrealism."[45] He may have wished to assert artistic freedom; question accepted taste; taunt the public; explore the unconscious, dream, and hal-lucinatory states; redefine reality; or change consciousness. His dazzling images, startling comparisons, and conjunction of apparently unrelated objects and words, and willful dislocation of objects and context[46] seem to follow Mallarmé's teaching that there is no such thing as immediate poetry.

Yi Sang's father, who earned his living as a laborer, gave Yi Sang to his elder brother (d. 1932), an engineer in the service of the colonial government. After graduating from the College of Engineering in 1929, he was employed

---

[44] The poem, entitled "Café France," was published in *Hakcho* (June 1926). Chŏng's other poems published in the same journal also have an imagist quality.
[45] Kim Yunsik, *Yi Sang yŏngu* (Munhak sasangsa, 1988), p. 158.
[46] C. W. E. Bigsby, *Dada and Surrealism* (London: Methuen, 1972), p. 60.

as a civil engineer to supervise the construction of a building in downtown Seoul. In April 1930 he began to cough blood and in 1933 he was compelled to resign his position and go to Paekch'ŏn spa for recuperation. There he met Kŭmhong (or Yŏnsim), a tavern woman of twenty-one, with whom he tried to run a tearoom, "The Swallow," near Chongno, Seoul, until September 1935. His dissolute life, financial hardships (he scorned all pragmatism), worsening illness, and last glimpse of hope took him in late 1936 to Tokyo where he died on 17 April 1937.

When a series of fifteen poems entitled "Ogamdo" ("A Crow's-Eye View") began to appear in the *Chosŏn Chungang Daily* (24 July – 8 August 1934), with material never before used in literature and obtrusive and often amusing devices, they at once invited accusations of irrelevance and impertinence. One cannot tell how many readers understood them. Whether Yi Sang attached importance to chance in poetic creation or practiced automatic writing is uncertain, but most of his extant poems show careful planning. The first poem, for example, depicts thirteen children running at full speed (*chilchu*). Each says he is frightened. But it is all right that one or two of them are frightening children, or frightened children. It is also fine that thirteen children do not run at full speed. And a street can be a dead-end or a through street. (These statements appear in parentheses.) In the title poem, the speaker compares himself to a crow (by omitting a horizontal stroke from the graph for the bird): a bird of ill omen and death perched high on a treetop from which vantage point it observes the scene below. Written matter-of-factly with an abstract quality (concrete nouns are few), its diction is archaic (for example, *ahae*, *chilchu*) because it is not the contemporary spoken language. The repetition of *che* and *kŭ* in the beginning and *o* and *so* at the end of sentences makes it read like a spell.

The poem does not distinguish between frightened children and frightening children. They experience fright but no reason is given why. Why are their minds troubled? Do they feel an existential anguish? The poem is built on antithesis and parataxis (lines 3–15, for example): children run at full speed – children do not run at full speed; the street is a dead-end alley – it is also a through street. The speaker presents both the positive and negative sides of the experience, trying to make us aware of the true meaning of things. Not identity but the identity of opposites – contradiction – is a potential source of truth. The number 13, hitherto only a mathematical sign, becomes a symbol at the end, pointing to the frightening existential agony. The children are in constant fear of oppression, impending wars, conscription for labor, cold and hunger. To their fear, however, we should add one additional fear: the fear of consumption and death that stalked our poet.[47]

Yi Sang's first poems in Korean were "Kkonnamu" ("A Flowering Tree") and "Kŏul" ("The Mirror"). Published in *Catholic Youth* in July and October 1933 respectively, they illustrate the recurrent themes in his literary effort.

A flowering tree stands in the middle of the field. No other tree is nearby. As if deeply thinking of another flowering tree, it stands, eagerly opening its blossoms. The flowering tree cannot go to the tree it longs for. I ran away. As if for the sake of a flowering tree, I ran away, a truly strange mimicry.

A recurrent theme in his poems and stories concerns the relation between man and woman; indeed, a number of parallel passages are usually cited to support it. Generally the speaker in his works cannot trust a woman. Although she is the mirror in which his desire is reflected, she is portrayed as inaccessible and unknowable. Yi Sang's love is not a liberating or transforming force, as in Eluard, but fraught with fear of betrayal and anxiety of abandonment. (Yi's live-in companion Kŭmhong left him at least four times.)[48] Although he valiantly resists the lure of suicide, he contemplates it as a last resort – so frightened is he by a lung hemorrhage. Is death not a magical substitution of life?

> There is no sound in the mirror,
> No other world so still.
>
> In the mirror I do have ears,
> Two pitiful ears that don't grasp my words!
>
> The I in the mirror is left-handed,
> Who can neither accept nor know my handshake.
>
> I can't touch the I in the mirror because of the mirror,
> But without the mirror, how could we have met?
>
> Now I've no mirror, but the I in the mirror is always there.
> He must be absorbed in some sinister venture.
>
> The I in the mirror – my other self – looks like me.
> Regretfully I can't worry about him or examine him.

The mirror provides the occasion to be aware of the self's division into two. Ironically the two selves are alike but reverse. The everyday self wishes to know the essence of the other self; but because of the mirror the former

[47] Kim Yunsik, *Yi Sang yŏngu*, p. 68.
[48] J. H. Matthews, *Surrealist Poetry in France* (Syracuse: University of Syracuse Press, 1969), pp. 110–113.

can neither examine nor touch the latter. Plato's myth expounded in the *Symposium* (that is, the original division of one being into two parts and the subsequent search for reunion), Rimbaud's "Je est un autre" (I is another self),[49] and Lacan's notion of split subject may be cited as distant parallels.

In "A Flowering Tree," we recall, by putting forth its blossoms the tree shows its yearning for a union with another tree, but this desire is frustrated – a true meeting of one thing with another is denied. The "I" runs away because he reads in the field the impossibility of a union of two flowering trees. He runs away because of fear: a fear of not being able to achieve reunion with his other, or true, self, or his beloved. We recall, too, that the world of consciousness which controls the life of thirteen children in "A Crow's-Eye View" (poem 1) is described as frightening. Yi Sang vainly sought some form of reconciliation, communion, or concord, but no such possibility is suggested in his poetry. In his life, in fact, he seems to have intensified his alienation. The alienated man in solitude, trying to commune with himself, Yi Sang was obsessed with his own problems but could not transcend them. Although he keenly felt the difficulty of communication in the modern world, was aware of the anguish of loneliness, he does not, however, reflect the Korean actuality of the 1930s; there is little sense of place and time in his work. Unwilling to assume responsibility for his lifestyle, he courted and hastened his own death.[50]

The poetry of resistance

The poetry of resistance, voicing sorrow and anger at the ruination of the land, illustrates a keen awareness of time and place and a modern awareness of history. Yi Sanghwa (1900–1943), Sim Hun (1904–1937), Yi Yuksa (1905–1944), and Yun Tongju (1917–1945) knew how to express in poetry their encounter with history and to expand the poet's consciousness and establish his authority. The speaker in Yi Sanghwa's "Does Spring Come to Stolen Fields?" (1926) wishes to return to the earth as a child might return to

---

[49] Wallace Fowlie, *Age of Surrealism* (Bloomington: Indiana University Press, 1960), pp. 49–50 (Rimbaud) and p. 199 (Plato).

[50] For Yi Sang's life and work I have consulted Kim Yunsik, *Yi Sang yŏngu* (Munhak sasangsa, 1988); Yi Sŭnghun, *Yi Sang si yŏngu* (Koryŏwŏn, 1987); and *Yi Sang munhak chŏnjip*, and *Yi Sang* (*HHST* 9, 1988); and Kim Sŭnghŭi, *Yi Sang si yŏngu* (Pogosa, 1998). Kim Sŭnghŭi's reading of Yi's poems is informed by the theories of Lacan (1901–1981) and Kristeva (b. 1941): the former's theory of the "mirror stage" in the development of a child's sense of self and the symbolic, imaginary, and real registers of human experience, and the latter's differentiation between the "semiotic" (*le sémiotique* and the "symbolic," two heterogeneous elements in signification. For Kim's detailed study of the structure and symbolism of Yi Sang's recurrent image of the mirror, see pp. 331–449.

his mother. Yet the mother as the land, or land as the mother, are both unattainable.[51]

Sim Hun, in "Kŭnari omyŏn" ("When that Day Comes"), reveals his aspirations to independence in impassioned language. The speaker says he will "soar like a crow at night / and pound the Chongno bell with [his] head," and "skin [his] body and make a drum and march with it in the vanguard." Couched in *adynata*, the trope of impossibilities, the poem is an affirmation of the speaker's unshakeable belief in liberation. He looks forward to the day when the Chongno bell, traditionally struck on festive days, will resound and "the thundering shout" of his people will greet the restoration. In his claim that "nature will share his joy and rise and dance with him," Sim uses the ancient trope of a moment so rapturous, a joy so extreme, that the speaker will burst the confines of his body.[52]

Yi Yuksa, the first nationalist poet to die at the hands of the Japanese, had been imprisoned seventeen times. Born in Andong, North Kyŏngsang, on 18 May 1904, Yi Yuksa (also called Wŏllok, Wŏnsa, or Hwal) was the fourteenth-generation descendant of Yi Hwang (1501–1571), a great Neo-Confucian philosopher of the Chosŏn dynasty, and received the traditional Confucian education. In 1925 he joined the Ŭiyŏltan, a secret anti-Japanese society organized in 1919, and in 1926 enrolled in the Peking Military Academy. Upon his return to Korea in 1927, he was implicated in the bombing of a branch office of the Korea Bank in Taegu and served a three-year term. His cell number was 264, pronounced "*iyuksa*" in Korean, so he adopted "Sixty-Four" (*yuksa*) as his pen name. In 1930 he went back to China, where he is said to have studied sociology at Peking University. Upon his return in 1933 he began his literary career and published poems, essays, and translations from modern Chinese verse and prose, including Lu Xun's story *Guxiang* (*The Old Home*, 1921). He was most productive from 1936 to 1941. In 1943, upon his return from another visit to China, he was arrested by Japanese police in June and sent to Peking prison, where he perished on 16 January 1944.

Yi made his literary debut in 1933 with "Hwanghon" ("Twilight") and, before his death in 1944, produced some thirty poems. They show a strong sense of form, rhythm, and imaginative space. The reader is struck by his expansive spatial imagery: a wide plain, mountain range, plateau, forest, lake, river, sea. He also mentions the Caucasus plain, a coral island, the Southern Cross, the Gobi Desert, Indra's Realm, and the tundra – all

---

[51] For a translation of Yi's poem see Peter H. Lee, ed., *Sourcebook of Korean Civilization* 2:491–492.
[52] For Sim's poem see ibid., 2:492–493, and Maurice Bowra, *Poetry and Politics 1900–1960* (Cambridge: Cambridge University Press, 1966), pp. 92–93.

contributing to the expansion of poetic space in modern Korean poetry. His poetic space, however, also encompasses a back room, a shelter for the persecuted self. Two poles in his time frame are represented by childhood days of the past and myriad years in the future. Such images of time as twilight, night, and winter show his awareness of the present dark days of Korea. In his early poems he compares his youth to "a smuggler's junk in the western sea," that

> Bleached by salt, swollen by the tide,
> No sooner clears a reef
> Than fights a typhoon.
> ("Nojŏng ki" ["Travelogue"])

In such poems as "Tokpaek" ("Monologue") and "Naŭi myuŭjŭ" ("My Muse"), he is less skillful in making poetry out of common everyday experience. Indeed his reputation rests on a handful of strong poems – "Chŏlchŏng" ("Summit," 1940), "Ch'ŏngp'odo" ("Deep-Purple Grapes," 1939), "Kwangya" ("The Wide Plain"), "Kyomok" ("Tall Tree," 1940), and "Kkot" ("Flower") – in which we hear his mighty voice reverberating with seasoned character and strong faith. His is the voice of a Confucian scholar, as his birth and education seem to support, who courageously utters his lofty vision in adversity[53] (a high plateau, a rainbow, the fragrance of plum blossoms, a white horse, a superman).

"The Wide Plain" opens with a story of the foundation of Korean history and goes on to deal with its beginnings, stressing the inviolability of the land and its continuity:

> On a distant day
> When heaven first opened,
> Somewhere a cock must have crowed.
>
> No mountain ranges
> Rushing to the longed-for sea
> Could have dared to invade this land.
>
> While busy seasons gust and fade
> With endless time,
> A great river first opens the way.
>
> Now snow falls,
> The fragrance of plum blossoms is far off.
> I'll sow the seeds of my sad song here.

---

[53] This is Kim Chongchŏ'l's view in *Yi Yuksa, Yun Tongju* (*HHST* 8, 1984), p. 120. Kim Yongjik, ed., *Yi Yuksa* (Sŏgang taehakkyo ch'ulp'anbu, 1995) contains critical essays on Yi's poetry.

When a superman comes
On a white horse down the myriad years,
Let him sing aloud my song on the wide plain.

"Here" is modern Korea. "Now" is the winter of trial, the dark period of Japanese rule. The plum blossoms are a symbol of integrity – for they, as in China, are the first to blossom even before winter is over. Who is the "superman," though, and what is his relationship to the speaker? It is perhaps the same as that between the lyric persona and "the traveler" in another of his poems, "Deep-Purple Grapes." Here the speaker is a prophet of the future: a myriad years, a hundred years, or a moment.

In "The Summit," the self stands alone on a precipitous brink:

Beaten by the bitter season's whip,
I am driven at last to this north.

I stand upon the sword-blade frost,
Where numb sky and plateau merge.

I do not know where to bend my knees,
Nor where to place my vexed steps.

I cannot but close my eyes and think –
Winter;
Winter is a steel rainbow.

Homeless, fugitive, the poet does not shrink from the terror and absurdity of history. Not by a shrill scream, but by a plunge into the depths of the self, he recreates an existence in extremity and makes us contemplate our ultimate destiny. All the lines in the poem have four stresses and are metrically self-contained. The poem's power comes from the use of personification ("season's whip"), metaphor ("vexed steps"; "sword-blade frost"), metonymy ("bend my knees"), and oxymoron ("steel rainbow"), as well as a combination of strong, harsh, aspirated affricates and fricatives. The fusion of sound and sense evokes the encroachment of the harsh winter, as the speaker struggles to "outface / The winds and persecutions of the sky." The speaker is modern in that he reveals a vision of a moment of time: a new way of viewing human existence. He posits a frightening discontinuity, a nothingness, the modern "I" on the summit where he makes his last stand. There are no certainties, only an authentic response. Like some of Hemingway's heroes, the speaker makes no pretense of sentiment or self-pity; he is faithful to his own experience, which is universally valid.

The recurrent concerns of Yun Tongju (1917–1945), who perished in Fukuoka prison on 16 February 1945, are the sorrows of the oppressed, the reality of death, and the problem of the sensitive individual beset by existential despair and spiritual desolation. At times he feels a nostalgic dismay at the image of his divided and displaced self, which the age besieges and obliterates. In "Chahwasang" ("Self-portrait," 1939), for example, the speaker finds his present image falling short of his ideal. Although he stands up and walks away, he still longs for the young man who stands there like a memory. In "Tto tarŭn kohyang" ("Another Home," 1941), his three divided selves – white bones (his older self, white referring probably to the white garments worn by Koreans), I (present self), and beautiful soul (ideal self) – confront one another. The home of the ideal self (another beautiful home) is probably on the opposite side of his dark room. "Faithful" in "the faithful dog," refers to a patriot, a witness to darkness, or another stupidly honest person who makes the sound of darkness but does not know the voice of heaven or the world of a beautiful soul.[54]

In "Sŏsi" ("Prologue," 1941), Yun says:

> I must love all death-bound things.
> With a heart that sings to the stars
> I must follow the path given me.
> The wind grazes the stars again tonight.

The wind grazing the stars reminds him of dark reality, but it is a call to reaffirm his faith. Even in darkness he reiterates his resolve to overcome the obstacles in his path: a continuous self-reflection. Elsewhere he compares his self to a mirror ("Ch'amhoe rok" ["Confessions," 1942]) – he must polish his consciousness so that it can reflect his ideal potential. Only then will the mirror reflect a greater self, "walking alone below a meteorite." Indeed, he compares his fate to a falling meteorite looking for a proper place to land. If the age denies your self-fulfillment, he says, destroy the status quo. Yun's poetry is a record of his rigorous progress toward the realization of his aesthetic, existential, and ethical self.

Dispassionately viewing an immense void, he realizes in "Musŏun sigan" ("Awful Hour," 1941) that it is futile to seek an illusive peace:

> Who is calling me?
>
> I still breathe
> In the shade of a budding tree.
>
> I've never raised my hand,
> I've no heaven to mark.

---

[54] For Kim Uch'ang's reading of "the faithful dog" see *Yi Yuksa, Yun Tongju*, p. 142. I have consulted Wang Sinyŏng et al., eds., *Yun Tongju chap'il sigo chŏnjip* (Minŭmsa, 1999).

I have no place under any heaven.
Why are you calling me?
The morning I die after my task's done,
Heartless leaves will fall –
Don't call me.

To be a poet is "a sad mandate," but Yun accepts his terrible fate and finds new ways of identifying his inner anguish with Korea's national crisis. His poems reflect the crisis of his culture, and his short life embodied his people's troubles.

Han Yongun and the later poets of resistance were ever aware of Korea's loss of sovereignty. Seeking insights into his personal fate and that of his fellow men, Han found a lyrical correlate in Buddhist contemplative poetry. By using a single word with myriad connotations, he communicated the full measure of his anxieties, questions, and final illumination. These poets were witnesses to national humiliation, especially the banishment of Koreans from the public realm. "Action" as interaction with others, the basis of political life, was denied Koreans, leaving only "labor" and "work."[55] Tormented by exile and unfulfillment, these poets opted for brief but meaningful lives. Their pessimism was finally balanced by affirmation, the celebration of a triumph of the self that was purchased with suffering.

CHŎNG CHIYONG: A MODERN MASTER

Poets through the 1930s continued the exploration of new diction and prosody made necessary by "a new conception of the self."[56] Chŏng Chiyong, Korea's first truly successful modern poet, was a master of his medium and is still a continuing presence. If younger poets wish to surpass him, it is like children wishing to slay a father whose mastery of language and form is breathtaking. Chŏng's some 120 poems, written from 1925 to 1941, deal mainly with the sea, the mountains, the city, the country, and religion. Wishing to recall the virtues of classical strength and lucidity, he rendered particulars exactly and explored the unlimited implication of words. He scorned belated romanticism. In astringent remarks he made his views on poetry clear: "The mystery of poetry is the mystery of language"; "only the poet can infuse blood and breath into language"; "if a poem weeps

---

[55] Hannah Arendt, *The Human Condition* (Chicago: University of Chicago Press, 1958), p. 221.
[56] Richard Ellman, *The New Oxford Book of English Verse* (New York: Oxford University Press, 1976), p. xxiii.

first, the reader will not have time to contemplate the tears"; "the poet must indefatigably explore his spirit."

Chŏng Chiyong was born in Okch'ŏn, North Ch'ungch'ŏng, on 15 May 1903. He graduated from Dōshisha University in Kyoto with a thesis on Blake and introduced the works of Blake and Whitman to Korea. He taught English at Hwimun High School (1929–1945) and later at Ewha Woman's University, where he was dean of the School of Letters. He also lectured on the *Book of Songs* at Seoul National University. Beginning his poetic career in the early 1920s, Chŏng was active as a member of *Poetic Literature*. A consummate artist, he produced poems marked by grace, precision of sensuous detail, and masterful craftsmanship. As poetry editor first of *Catholic Youth* (1933–1936) and later of *Munjang* (*Literature*, 1939–1941), he was responsible for introducing talented younger poets such as Yi Sang and the Green Deer group. His prose poems in *Paengnoktam* (*White Deer Lake*, 1941) also exerted a great influence on the development of modern Korean poetry, especially on poets like Yun Tongju and Pak Tujin. Chŏng also wrote, often under his baptismal name Francis, religious poetry as a convert to Catholicism (from which he was later estranged). After the liberation of 1945, he leaned toward the left but was unproductive as a poet. He is presumed to have been killed during the Korean War.

His "Yurich'ang" ("Window," 1930) deals with the death of his child. It is the first of two poems on the subject.

> Something cold and sad haunts the window.
> I dim the pane with my feverless breath;
> It flaps its frozen wings, as if tamed.
> I wipe the glass, wipe again,
> Only black night ebbs, then dashes against it,
> Moist stars etched like glittering jewels.
> Polishing the window at night
> Is a lonely, spellbinding affair.
> With the lovely veins in your lung broken,
> You flew away like a mountain bird!

No other poet had written a poem so arrestingly modern in its sensibility. Although Chŏng found the material for the poem in his own life, he deepens the meaning of his experience by letting his powerful descriptions speak for themselves. From the first line, which begins matter-of-factly, to the last exclamation, Chŏng makes us see and feel the objects evoked in a fresh, surprising, and inventive way.

The poem begins with the speaker at the window that separates inside from outside, the speaker from the dead. That the death is not visible is related to the fact that the glass is transparent – nothing is more transparent than the invisible. The adjective "sad" (*sŭlp'un*), rarely used elsewhere in Chŏng's work, is preceded by "cold," cooling the warmth and moisture of sadness. The combination of "cold" and "sad" demonstrates the speaker's degree of restraint. Generally, however, an adult does not dim the window-pane with the steam of breath. Is writing a poem akin to dimming the pane with steam? It is words that flow out like vapor that dim the windowpane, and the speaker's breath is a conversation with the dead. His warm, moist breath thaws the frozen wings and enables them to flutter. To infuse life into the dead, the wings endow the dead with flesh so that the living can see it. They make us see what is invisible.

Breath that stands for nostalgia, monologue, conversation with the other-world, is akin to language – between this and other worlds there is language. Night is kinetic, and what makes it so is the poet's sensibility. The moist stars (*mulmŏgŭn pyŏl*) are related not only to the dimmed windowpane but also to the speaker's eyes filled with tears. In the original, the adverb *pantchak* (line 6), which modifies both the "moist stars" and "jewel," is preceded and followed by a comma in order to foreground the word so that it glitters: moist stars glitter like a jewel, come to the speaker, embed them-selves in his pupils. Also *kohŭn* (lovely) is more mellow in sound and color than *koŭn* with the same meaning; so is *nŭi* (you) more intimate than *nŏ*, meaning the same. The epenthetic *s* ㅅ in *sanssae ch'ŏrŏm* (like a mountain bird), inserted between *san* (mountain) and *sae* (bird), resembles pictorially a bird perched on a branch of a tree. The last two lines, together with the traditional association of the soul with a bird, set the speaker's experience at a distance – magnificently tempering his sorrow. Thus the whole poem evinces how the poet's educated sensibility selects and organizes the material in an original way.[57]

Chŏng's first collection (1935) was followed by *White Deer Lake*, which transports the reader into the harmonious world of nature. The title poem, published in 1939 and comprising nine sections in prose, presents the poet's experience in a vivid colloquial style. The theme may be conventional, but the poet's use of the right words in the right context produces an effect that is totally modern. Compact phrasing and a very distinctive blending of Sino-Korean and native words suggest the speaker's "discovery of his thought in the process of saying it."[58] Upon seeing a motherless calf, the speaker thinks of having to "entrust his children to a strange mother"

---

[57] These two paragraphs summarize a sensitive reading of the poem by Chŏng Hyŏnjong in "Kamgak, imiji, haengdong," in *Saengmyŏng ŭi hwanghol* (Segyesa, 1989), pp. 205–215.
[58] Perkins, *History of Modern Poetry* 1:593.

(section 6). He also contemplates his ultimate homecoming: "I don't mind turning white as a birch after death" (section 3). The audacious listing of alpine plants, included for their sounds, may be unpoetical in themselves, at least in the hands of a lesser poet, but they are given new life (section 8):

Flowering ferns, bracken, bellflowers, wild asters, umbrella plants, bamboo, manna lichens, alpine plants with starlike bells – I digest them, and drunk on them, fall into a doze. Yearning for the crystalline water of White Deer Lake, their procession on the range is more solemn than clouds. Beaten by showers, dried by rainbows, dyed by flowers, I put on fat.

Section 9 reads: "The sky rolls in the blue of White Deer Lake. Not even a crayfish stirs. A cow skirts around my feet, disabled by fatigue. A wisp of chased cloud dims the lake. The lake, on whose mirror I float daylong, is lonesome. Waking and sleeping, I forget even my prayers." The lake is a symbol of stillness and purity. The speaker describes "a condition of the spirit where the self is completely dissolved in the lucid apprehension of nature."[59] Self and nature reflect one another; waking and sleeping become one. The collection represents the symbolic progress of the spirit to a state of lucidity, a fusion of man and nature, as in classical Chinese mountain poetry. The arduous ascent to the summit of Mount Halla, where White Deer Lake is located, represents the stages of a spiritual pilgrimage in the archetypal themes of journey, quest, and initiation.

POETRY FOR LIFE

Among those who found the poetry of the previous decades to lack a relentless inquiry into the quality of Korean life were Sŏ Chŏngju and Yu Ch'ihwan. Known as the poetry for life school (*saengmyŏngp'a* or *in-saengp'a*), their group was not a homogeneous body with similar poetic taste. Their recurrent concerns included a defense of emotion and intu-ition, a strong sense of awe and respect for life, a defiance of logic and reason, and an emphasis on the candid voice issuing from within. At the end of their search for the existential meaning of life, they often confronted absolute nothingness; but rather than seeking salvation from some almighty being, they accepted death as the end of biological life. Their defense of the purity of their work may have been an attempt to rationalize their escape from actuality at the end of Japanese rule. Their inquiry may originate in

---

[59] Uch'ang Kim, "Sorrow and Stillness: A View of Modern Korean Poetry," *Literature East and West* 13 (1969): 154.

repentance for having chosen, not the path of resistance, but that of escape or self-exile. Their poetry is not deeply touched by historical and social forces despite their self-torturing anger and will to life. "Poetry is written not by theory but by crying like an animal,"[60] said Yu Ch'ihwan. Their lack of form, intricate organization of material, and refined technique was compensated by their frank voice and celebration of the primordial energy of life.

Early poems of Sŏ Chŏngju (1915–2000), often called the Korean Baudelaire, were characterized by sensuality and diabolism in a specifically Korean setting: "A lovely snake that lies on the path thick with musk and mint" and "breathless as if drunk kerosene, drunk kerosene" ("Hwasa" ["Flower Snake"], 1936), or "the path winding like the yellow back / of an opium-stunned snake / my love runs, calling me after" ("Taenat" ["Midday"], 1936), or

> Saddened by the sun
> and blue of the sky
>
> the leper ate a child
> at moonrise by the barley fields
>
> and through the night cried out
> his sorrow red as a flower.[61]
> ("Mundungi" ["Leper"], 1936)

Although these images were new to Korean poetry, we note a combination of Korean folk life and modern sensibility. About "Chahwasang" ("Self-portrait," 1935) – which begins "Father was a serf" and ends with "I've come, tongue hanging out, / Panting through sun and shade like a sick dog" – Sŏ Chŏngju remarked later that his father was not in fact a serf but was fictionalized for symbolic purposes. And "Midday," he says, was written at Haein Monastery to "overcome such trifles as tragedy and with strong will to come alive with the sun." Sŏ is known for his many masks and roles in his earlier work.[62] His later work shows him delving into native shamanism and Buddhism to transform intractably unpoetic elements into works of art. He is credited with exploring the hidden resources of the language – from haunting mysticism to colloquial earthiness.

---

[60] Quoted in O Seyŏng, *Isip segi Hanguk si yŏngu* (Saemunsa, 1990), p. 228.
[61] David R. McCann, trans., *Selected Poems of Sŏ Chŏngju* (New York: Columbia University Press, 1989), pp. 5, 4, and 3. I have consulted *Midang si chŏnjip*, 3 vols. (Minŭmsa, 1994). Sŏ's poems discussed here are translated by McCann.
[62] This is Hwang Tonggyu's view in *Sŏ Chŏngju, HHST* 16 (1981), pp. 226–227.

A year after the publication of his first volume of poetry in 1939, Yu Ch'ihwan (1908–1967) went to Manchuria to spend five years until liberation. There he encountered primitive violence and appalling hardship. Contemplating the heads of bandits exposed on stakes, the speaker resolves to be strong:

> Now as I pace along this wind-swept thoroughfare,
> I am resolved afresh of the dogged ferocity of life.
> You who housed your uncontrollable souls of treachery,
> Close your eyes in peace! May merciful heaven
> Cover this landscape of waste thoughts with deep, deep snow![63]

Some of his poems offer a relentless investigation of our place in the non-human world of nature and the meaning of existence:

> When I stand all alone in a wind-flapped garment
> In the midst of soul-cleansing solitude,
> I shall be brought to face myself, as if my fate.
> If I do not thus regain
> The primal state of my being, my life,
> I shall not rue my bones bleaching on the sand.[64]
>
> ("Saengmyŏng ŭi sŏ ilchang"
> ["The Chapter of Life"], stanza 3)

His existential despair, however, led him to a passion for life. His god, however, is "not one who bestows or can bestow grace on him beyond what he is now, but one who allows time and space and all living things to exist. His god is without form, ineffably vague, an obscure power," similar to the East Asian concept of heaven or providence.[65]

Although some of his poems suffer from literary diction (with Sino-Korean words) and stiff (at times oratorical) syntax, in his mature work Yu shows a quiet control of method and matter. Like the sunflower that defies the tyranny of the sun ("Haebaragi pat' ŭro karyŏo" ["I Will Go to the Field of Sunflowers"]) or the rock that ignores storm and wind ("Pawi" ["Rock"], 1941), Yu writes of a life of quiet integrity. So long as he has the sun and moon above him, he is content to die at any moment; yet on his enemy and those who flatter his enemy, he asks the sun and moon to avenge

---

[63] Korean Poets Association, ed., *Poems from Modern Korea* (1970), p. 36. Pak Seyŏng (b. 1902), in such poems as "The Last News" (1936), and Yi Yongak (1914–1971) in such poems as "A Girl Like a Swallow," describe the hardships of Korean immigrants in Manchuria.

[64] Sung-Il Lee, trans., *The Wind and The Waves: Four Modern Korean Poets* (Berkeley: Asian Humanities Press, 1989), p. 87.

[65] Kim Yongjik et al., *Hanguk hyŏndae sisa yŏngu* (Ilchisa, 1987), pp. 379–389; Pak Ch'ŏlsŏk, ed., *Yu Ch'ihwan*, pp. 209–302.

him ("Irwŏl" ["Sun and Moon"]). He succeeds in giving a philosophical cast to genuine feeling – an overtone typically Confucian in its refusal to be fettered by the tribulations of life or to be marred by the pursuit of name and fame.

THE 1940S: DECADE OF SILENCE

Owing to the Japanese suppression of all writing in the Korean language, the early 1940s were a dark period in all branches of Korean literature. In February 1940 Koreans were ordered to adopt Japanese names, and those who spoke Korean in public were seized and imprisoned. Two Korean newspapers were suspended on 10 August 1940, and the two literary journals *Literature* (1939–1941) and *Inmun p'yŏngnon* (*Criticism of Culture*, 1939–1941) were discontinued in the following year. When in 1941 the Sino-Japanese War developed into the Pacific War, the Japanese army ceased relying on volunteers, as it had since 1938, and began conscription. A massive mobilization resulted in the drafting of nearly 4 million Korean workers, sent as far as Sakhalin and Southeast Asia. Scholars of the Korean language were sent to prison (1942), and the Chindan Society, a scholarly association of Korean history and literature organized in 1934, was dissolved.

The prohibition of the official use of the Korean language drove Korean literature underground. Indeed the Japanese denied the existence of Korean literature as an independent entity and treated it as a literature of a province in their empire. Government-patronized associations were formed to mobilize writers to support Japan's military policy, and they were asked to justify the inevitability of the war, stress the importance of Korean volunteers, and create an image of the war dead as Japanese heroes. In fact, the aim of mobilization literature was to transform Koreans into Japanese subjects. In the only literary journal sponsored by the government, *Kungmin munhak* (*National Literature*, 1941–1945), which published only in Japanese from 1942, a few Korean contributors managed to write about personal feelings, but others poured out unctuous rhetoric in extolling the military cause. Some Korean writers went to improve the morale of the soldiers in China; some took part in the meetings of the Greater East Asia Writers Congress (1941–1942 in Tokyo; 1943 in Nanking).[66] Those who kept silent would emerge only after the liberation. These writers included poets in the Green Deer group (Pak Mogwŏl, Pak Tujin, and Cho Chihun), whose work is discussed in Chapter 21.

[66] O Seyŏng, *Isip segi Hanguk si yŏngu*, pp. 232–272; Song Minho, *Ilchemal amhŭkki munhak yŏngu* (Saemunsa, 1991).

LEFTIST POETRY

Upon his return from Tokyo in May 1923, Kim Kijin (1903–1985) began to publish a series of polemical essays denouncing the current literary scene. He posited a dichotomy between bourgeois and proletarian literature: the former, he said, was decadent and fin-de-siècle; the latter was socially conscious and sympathetic to the working masses. Kim went to Tokyo in 1920, and in 1921 he enrolled in the English Department of Rikkyō University. Instead of studying, however, he befriended the Japanese socialist Aso Hisashi (1891–1940), who advised him to go back to Korea and sow the seeds of socialism. Upon his return in May 1923, Kim translated the debate between Henri Barbusse (1874–1935), author of the war novel *Clarté* (1919), and Romain Rolland (1866–1944), endorsing the former's call for dedication to social reform and emphasizing the social obligation of art. The new tendency became leftist literature advocating class consciousness when, on 23 August 1925, the Chosŏn P'ŭrollet'aria Yesul Tongmaeng (Korea artista proleta federatio = KAPF) was formed by nineteen members.

As a leftist literary critic following the Marxist theory of the superstructure of society being dependent on the economic base, Kim believed that life shapes ideas. Influenced by the Russian Marxist Georgy Plekhanov (1856–1918), Kim held that literature could not be a direct weapon for revolution and hence should not be used as a vehicle of politics. He discussed three major topics: form and content; the creation of short narrative verse as a proletarian verse form; and the popularization of fiction. Kim believed in the harmony of form and content – as evinced in his debate with Pak Yŏnghŭi, who argued that form depends on the content – and in the need for a new form of proletarian literature. According to Kim, a short narrative verse form is best suited to proletarian poetry. As an example he cited "Uri oppa wa hwaro" ("My Older Brother and a Brazier") by Im Hwa.[67]

As a poet, however, Kim's works during the period were crude and flat. The speaker in "Kodaehanŭn maŭm" ("The Mind that eagerly Awaits," 1926) waits for a radical change in society; the speaker in "Hwagangsŏk" ("Granite," 1924) compares the silent masses to granite and prophesies that the masses rather than politicians and poets will be the final judges of history. Sympathizers such as Yi Sanghwa, who later rejected the subordination of poetry to ideology and politics, chose his subjects from the world of the impoverished farmer or laborer, as in "Pinch'on ŭi pam" ("Night

[67] Kim Kijin, *Kim P'albong munhak chŏnjip*, ed. Hong Chŏngsŏng, 6 vols. (Munhak kwa chisŏngsa, 1988–1989), 1:99–197; Kim Yunsik, *Hanguk kŭndae munhak sasangsa* (Hangilsa, 1984), pp. 141–179; Im Kyuch'an and Han Kiyŏng, eds., *KAPF pip'yŏng charyo ch'ongsŏ* (T'aehaksa, 1990); Pak Sangjun, *Hanguk kŭndae munhak ŭi hyŏngsŏng kwa sinkyŏnghyangp'a* (Somyŏng, 2000).

in an Impoverished Village") and "Kurumakkun" ("A Carter," 1925). Kim Tonghwan (b. 1901), who made his debut with "Chŏksŏng ŭl sonkkarakchil hamyŏ" ("Pointing to the Red Star," 1924) about hardship in the border area, produced "Pukch'ŏng ŭi mulchangsa" ("A Water-seller in Pukch'ŏng"), "Tchokkyŏganŭn muri" ("The Chased Group"), "P'aŏp" ("Strike"), and a long narrative verse, "Kukkyŏng ŭi pam" ("Night on the Border," 1924), with a sixteen-year-old girl, the daughter of a married Buddhist priest, as the protagonist.[68] These poets thought their works, imbued with youthful idealism for the future, could bring about a revolution in sensibility. Although they wished to side with the masses, the key members of the new-tendency school came from the middle class and had no experience of labor. Obsessed with an urge to create a new literature modeled on Russian examples, they had little time to polish their art. So long as they believed that literary technique and artistic design were bourgeois – as, for example, Kim Kijin did – their works remained crude and too often propagandistic. Often their diction betrayed their ignorance of the daily language of the working people.

In 1931 a group of young leftists in their twenties, all educated in Tokyo with bourgeois or petit-bourgeois backgrounds, emerged with an indictment of older members of the league. They opened doors to the masses and advocated that members work side by side with farmers and laborers. The leader of this young group was Im Hwa (real name Im Insik, 1908–1953), who joined KAPF in December 1926, went to Tokyo to study cinema in 1929, and returned in the second half of 1931. Im seized the leadership at the age of twenty-three. During the first arrest of KAPF members in August 1931 he was imprisoned for three months; during his second arrest in May–October 1934 as the league's secretary, he escaped imprisonment because of ill health. Im's group held fast to ideology: the inculcation of class consciousness was the sole objective of literature, they insisted, at the expense of artistic quality. Im Hwa published a series of narrative poems beginning with "Negŏri ŭi Suni" ("Suni at the Square," 1929), "Uri oppa wa hwaro" ("My Older Brother and a Brazier," 1929), "Usanssŭn Yokohama ŭi pudu" ("Holding an Umbrella at Yokohama Pier," 1929), "Yangmal sogŭi p'yŏnji" ("A Letter inside the Sock," 1930), and "Hyŏnhaet'an" ("Hyŏnhae Strait," 1936; the title later changed to "Romanticism in the Strait"). In "Suni at the Square," the young men and women are represented as "laborers"; the mother of Suni, the speaker's young sister to whom the poem is addressed, is said to have died of poverty. Suni's friend, "that cherished young man you

---

[68] For Kim Tonghwan see Kim Yongjik, *Hanguk kŭndae sisa* 2:81–84; and Ch'oe Manmuk, ed., *Hanguk hyŏndaesi taegye*, 3 vols. (Hanguk munhwasa, 1996) 1:311–357 for poems.

love and the beloved of all working women," disappeared – that is, he is in prison. ("Today your valuable youth, brave man / with his emaciated fingers with which he labored diligently in his young days, / is now drawing a calendar on the brick wall.") The poem ends by asking Suni at Chongno Square to "hold hands with him and enter an alley for the sake of tomorrow, [her] young man, and the beloved of all working women."[69] As in other pieces, Im's diction and syntax are awkward and some lines do not scan well.

"My Older Brother and a Brazier," we recall, was praised by Kim Kijin as the best proletarian poem – a new poetic form suited to popularization for the masses. The poem depicts three proletarian siblings – the oldest working at a printing house; his younger sister at a silkworm factory; and the youngest Yongnam at a cigarette factory. One day the oldest comes back home from work and smokes three cigarettes in silence, staring at the ceiling. Then Japanese police break in, come up to the veranda in boots, and drag him away. The reason for his arrest is not given, but we know he has been taken for interrogation and imprisonment. The first section begins with the breaking of a brazier with a turtle pattern; the second concerns the brother's anguish prior to his arrest; the third concerns the young sister's resolution to withstand the hardships brought about by his absence:

> Don't worry, however, older brother,
> I'm a girl of the same blood as you, a brave youth of this country.
> Am I not your younger sister who bought the turtle-patterned iron
>   brazier that you and Yongnam always praised?
> By the way, older brother, your other young friends visited and left
>   here a while ago
> With the tearful news about you.
> They were lovely youths and brave,
> The most courageous young men in the world.
> The brazier broke, but the fire tongs remain like a flagpole.
> Though you left, your lovely "pioneer" Yongnam is with me,
> And the warm bosom of a sister of all young "pioneers,"[70]
> My heart is still warm.

---

[69] Kim Yunsik, *Hanguk kŭndae munhak sasangsa*, pp. 327–349; Kim Yongjik, *Hanguk kŭndae sisa* 2:172–187, 327–349; Kim Yongjik, *Im Hwa munhak yŏngu* (Segyesa, 1991), pp. 37–57, 58–94; Im Hwa, *Im Hwa chŏnjip*, ed. Sin Sungyŏp (P'ulppit, 1988); and Im Hwa, *Im Hwa p'yŏngnon chip: munhak ŭi nolli* (Sŏŭm ch'ulp'ansa, 1989).

[70] From the Russian term "pioner" (pioneer): a young people's group for those between the ages of ten and fifteen years, founded as an auxiliary to the Komsomol (All-Union Leninist Communist Union of Youth) in 1922. The aim of the movement is to "make its members convinced fighters for the communist party cause, inculcate in them a love of labor and knowledge, and assist the formation of the younger generation in the spirit of communist consciousness and morality." See John Paxton, *Encyclopedia of Russian History: From the Christianisation of Kiev to the Break-up of the USSR* (Santa Barbara: ABL-CLIO, 1993), pp. 315 and 213.

Older brother,
Am I the only sister who lost her loving brother and Yongnam the
    only one who lost his strong brother?
I am neither sad nor lonely.
The world has considerate youth – your countless great friends –
And cherished friends of countless girls and younger brothers who
    lost their elder brothers . . .

Im Hwa posits a symbolic hero juxtaposed against his younger sister who
endeavors to overcome her emotion. Thus the poem transforms personal
tragedy into collective heroism. "The creation of the unyielding proletarian
girl," Kim Kijin comments, "is a realistic portrayal, not a vague psychological one." Nevertheless, he cites Im's defects – repetition, crude explanation,
and vague impressions – and goes on to suggest his own views on short
narrative verse: it should deal with an event in narrative form, be written
in simple, clear language, describe the life conditions and social situations
of the masses, and popularize proletarian art. That is, it must have popular
appeal and be easy for the workers to recite – the creation of the proletarian
rhythm.

The subtext of "Holding an Umbrella at Yokohama Pier" (September)
is "Shinagawa Station in the Rain" (February 1929) by the Japanese Marxist poet Nakano Shigeharu (1902–1979).[71] In Im's poem, the speaker is a
colonized male factory worker in Japan about to be deported; his beloved
is a fellow Japanese woman worker. Thus they belong to the same class
but must part because of their class solidarity. The place is Yokohama pier,
where countless meetings and partings take place. It is a rainy, windy day,
and the umbrella, meant for the deported Korean, must serve as a shield
to protect his colleagues released from prison. The deported man vows he
will return to Yokohama after Japanese imperialism has been destroyed. By
that time, he will have passed through Pusan and Tokyo and will arrive in
Yokohama with comrades:

O woman at the port,
Don't come running on the dock.
Rain falls on your frail back
And the wind blows your umbrella.

In both poems, the deportees are Koreans. In one, the speaker asks the
deported workers to pass through Kobe and Nagoya, enter Tokyo, and kill

---

[71] See Miriam Silverberg, *Changing Song: The Marxist Manifestos of Nakano Shigeharu* (Princeton:
Princeton University Press, 1990), on pp. 160–162, for a translation of the poem.

the emperor; in the other, the speaker asks the Japanese woman to hurl her anger at the emperor's face and head. KAPF was dissolved on 20 May 1935. Im Hwa himself carried the notification to the police. Im's works after the failure of the Marxist literary movement include "Hyŏnhaet'an" ("Hyŏnhae Strait"), in which the speaker is a young man whose sharp eye watches poor Korean workers shipped to factories or mines or picked to work in Japan:

> Below the third class cabin in a deep corner,
> Dirtied beds wet with mothers' tears,
> Dim light steamed up with fathers' sighs.
> The painful tingling cry
> Of children who lost their fathers –
> What crimes have they committed?
> I still recall clearly a foreign language
> That brutally silenced their tearful voice.

The image of Koreans here is not confined to the dislocated laborers but extends to the Korean people as a whole under the colonizers' yoke. With this poem Im Hwa showed that he could write with tight structure and flowing rhythm based on Korean reality. Note the use of anaphora: the word "some" (*ŏttŏn saram*) repeated at the beginning of four lines:

> Some crossed the strait and did not return,
> Some died as soon as they returned,
> Some we don't know whether they're dead or alive,
> Some grieve over a painful defeat,
> – If some shamelessly betrayed our hope, resolve, and pride,
> I don't wish to recall that now.[72]

The failure of leftist literature in the 1920s and 1930s can be traced to the failure of leftist writers to reconcile Marxist theory and Korea's reality. A recent reassessment, however, views the leftist literature movement as part of the nationalist movement. It is credited with sharpening the awareness of colonial reality and providing concrete literary expressions of anti-imperialist and anticolonial resistance. It also emphasized the historical mission of the proletariat as vanguards in the revolution. Leftist literature attempted to show, directly or indirectly, the results of class struggle so that readers would be able to see their image in literary works. The movement also proclaimed the ideological function of literature, the significance of logical argument in critical discourse, and the importance of organization

---

[72] Kim Yongjik, *Hanguk kŭndae sisa* 2:58–94; Kim Yunsik, *Hanguk kŭndae munhak sasangsa*, pp. 334–347, esp. p. 342.

in a literary movement. It stimulated debates on agrarian literature, as well, which produced works dealing with farm and labor problems.[73]

WOMEN'S POETRY

In the 1920s several pioneering women challenged the gendered sexual hierarchy of male aggression and female passivity and insisted instead on expressing their own views on Korean women, society, literature, and the arts. (Some ignored the traditional feminine virtues such as chastity and monogamy.) These pioneers include Kim Myŏngsun (1896–1951?), a writer of short stories, poems, and essays; Na Hyesŏk (1896–1946), the first Korean woman to study Western oil painting with a degree from Tokyo Women's College of Arts in 1918 and later in Paris; and Kim Wŏnju (1896–1971), the organizer of a women's group called Ch'ŏngdaphoe (Bluestockings, 1919) – perhaps inspired by the founding of the Seitōsha (Bluestocking Society) and launching of the journal *Seitō* (*Bluestocking Magazine*, September 1911) by Hiratsuka Raichō. Kim Wŏnju was in fact the founder of her own journal, *Sinyŏja* (*New Women*, March 1920), the first magazine published by a Korean woman with a feminist agenda.

Kim Myŏngsun published her first story, "Ŭisim ŭi ch'ŏnyŏ" ("A Girl under Suspicion") in 1917; Na published her first story, "Kyŏnghŭi" (1918) in the *Yŏjagye* (*Women's World*), published by the Association of Korean Women Students in Japan; and Kim Wŏnju published a series of articles to improve women's status. As most aspiring writers have done to date, all three also wrote poems. In the dozen poems left by Kim Myŏngsun, one notes her propensity for Sino-Korean diction; the title of the poem, "Ch'oro ŭi hwamong" ("Dream of Flowers with Morning Dew") has four graphs, for example, and the poem itself has some thirty such compounds. Her poems cover such topics as longing, dreams, consolation, solitude, the road, and the southern country.[74]

"Nora" (1921) is among three poems left by Na Hyesŏk:

> Even as I am happy
> playing with a doll,
> a doll to my father as his daughter,
> a doll to my husband as his wife –
> an object of comfort am I,
> giving them joy.
> (refrain)

---

[73] Kwŏn Yŏngmin, *Hanguk kyegŭp munhak undongsa* (Munye ch'ulp'ansa, 1988), pp. 349–355.
[74] Ch'oe Manmuk, ed., *Hanguk hyŏndaesi taegye* 1:132–143.

> Let Nora go,
> pray let her go,
> finally but gently
> let her out from walls
> firmly blocked,
> opening up gates
> tightly closed.
>
> (stanza 1)[75]

In addition to her early poems (1926), Kim Wŏnju's religious poems appeared in the magazine *Pulgyo* (*Buddhism*) when she served as its literary editor.

Among the women poets active in subsequent decades, Mo Yunsuk and No Ch'ŏnmyŏng stand out. Poet, politician, and publisher of the monthly literary magazine *Munye* (*Literary Arts*, 1949–1954), Mo Yunsuk (1910–1990) was born in Wŏnsan, South Hamgyŏng, and graduated from Ewha Woman's University in English literature. She is known for her exuberance and eloquence and habitual use of apostrophe and exclamation. Two poems in her first collection, *Pinnanŭn chiyŏk* (*The Glorious Region*, 1933), caught the Japanese censor's eye and she was imprisoned (1940). The first stanza of the first poem, "I saengmyŏng ŭl" ("This life," 1933) goes:

> If you call, I'll come running,
> Though I've no skirt adorned with gold sash,
> Nor necklace of pearls,
> If you call, I'll come.

"Chosŏn ŭi ttal" ("A Daughter of Korea," 1933) reads:

> When my mind is not still with waves,
> His trustworthy voice flies to me
> And shakes the soul's ears,
> "What are you thinking now?"
>
> When I lament my torn skirt,
> From somewhere his face appears
> And whispers through a chink in the window,
> "Aren't you a daughter of Korea?"
>
> (stanzas 1 and 3)

After 1948 Mo served as a member of the Korean delegation to the United Nations, as national assemblywoman, and later as secretary-general of the

---

[75] Translated by Yung-Hee Kim.

Korean Center of the International PEN. When war broke out in June 1950, she could not evacuate Seoul in time and had a hard life in hiding. "Oeyangkan ŭi haruppam" ("A Night in the Cowshed"), written in August 1950, conveys what it was like to live under communist rule:

> This is compassionate heaven –
> On straws as a bed
> I and a cow journey in the path of dreams.
> When people have to be so careful,
> O cow, you're faithful to your friend.
> Your eyes are a kingdom of fortitude
> On a night when distant sorrow rustles.
> I wish to lean on
> The walls of your heart deep as a lake.
> Friend, your master must have been driven out
> To a distant land tonight,
> Where crimes flourish like flowers.
> Let's close our eyes and rest,
> Tonight I will drink your tears.

Her sentences fail to seduce the contemporary reader, however, and no single poem evokes her mind/heart – the strength of mind and energy.[76]

In "Chahwasang" ("Self-portrait"), the first poem in her first collection *Sanhorim* (*A coral forest*, 1938), No Ch'ŏnmyŏng (1913–1957) portrays herself as a short woman with a thin face, thick eyebrows and big eyes, a cold look, and thick hair: a woman who loses sleep even over a tiny impediment, a woman with tightly shut mouth that swallows troubles rather than spouting them, a woman who snaps like bamboo rather than bending like copper. Unlike Mo Yunsuk, No was praised for her self-control, her conscious efforts to refine her emotions, her poetic art which was compared to that of the British poet Alice Meynell (1847–1922). Others, however, fault her for unclear subject matter, essay-like rambling, and an autobiographical strain.[77]

No Ch'ŏnmyŏng was born in Changyŏn, Hwanghae province, and graduated from Ewha Woman's University in English literature (1934). She served as a reporter, school-teacher, and lecturer at a private university. "Sasŭm" ("Deer"), the title of the following poem, together with "rose" and "solitude" are among her favorite words:

[76] On Mo see Mo Yunsuk, *P'ungt'o* (Munwŏnsa, 1970), and Ch'oe Manmuk, ed., *Hanguk hyŏndaesi taegye* 2:163–177.

[77] On No see No Ch'onmyŏng, *Sasŭm: No Ch'ŏnmyŏng chŏnjip*, vol. 1 (Sol, 1997), pp. 295–317, and *Nabi: No Ch'ŏnmyŏng chŏnjip*, vol. 2 (Sol, 1997), 461–482, for biographical and critical comments.

With a long neck, you're a sad animal!
Always dignified, you are quiet.
With a fragrant crown,
You must be from a noble tribe.
Watching your own image in the water,
You recall bygone legends, and
Lost in irresistible nostalgia,
Scan faroff hills with a sad neck.

This poem reveals a penchant for solitude and longing, a sense of resignation, a refusal to compromise with reality, and a wish to return to nature. In "Naegasam e changmirŭl" ("The Rose in my Heart"), the speaker is "clumsy as the deer"; like a deer she wishes to run free leaving behind those who know her sorrow ("The Song of the Deer"); "seeking a beautiful legend, / chewing on a gorgeous sorrow, / the deer runs through an elixir-like afternoon thought" ("Song of May"). Another of her favorite expressions is "to scan the sky far away" when, for example, solitude rushes in like a tide ("Blue May"); when she is depressed, she looks at the hill ("Hill"); longing for the sea, she consoles herself with "departing clouds" ("Longing for the Sea"), clouds being likened elsewhere to ephemeral life ("Like the Cloud"); or "Scanning the mountain of another town, / my mind follows the clouds in the western sky" ("Nostalgia") – all represent her longing for release from the pain of life. She enjoys asparagus ("Sad Picture") and juxtaposes the rose (a Western flower) with Korean edible greens (*sannamul*) – her way of representing modernity as a colonized woman of the intelligentsia. She could delight equally in asparagus and mountain greens. She discovered the self through the absence of the beloved, the loss of home; and her relentless self-scrutiny maintains a distance between the self and the world.

For her collaboration with the Communist Literature League during the Korean War, she was tried and imprisoned (1950–1951), and several poems, such as "Myŏnhoe" ("Visit"), deal with her prison life. In "Kkotkil ŭl kŏrŏsŏ" ("Walking the Flower Road"), the subject is a man in military uniform who left for the front but has not returned. The last stanza goes:

Lord,
please bring reunification this spring
and let him who has won return
walking down the road full of azalea blossoms.

On 24 April 1951, she was baptized as "Veronica" in the Catholic church. (Her parents were Catholic.) She might have felt at home in the bucolic setting she evokes in "Irŭm ŏmnŭn yŏini toeŏ" ("Becoming a Nameless Woman"):

> I want to enter a small mountain
> and become a woman with no name.
> Grow pumpkin vines on the grass roof,
> plant cucumber and squash in the field,
> weave a fence with wild roses,
> eagerly bring the sky into the yard,
> and embrace the stars to my heart's content.

All her life she longed for her hometown in the country. Veronica Ch'ŏnmyŏng No, the poet of the deer, died of acute anemia; she was single.

CHAPTER 19

Early twentieth-century fiction by men

Kwŏn Yŏngmin

Modern Korean fiction was formed in the historical context of the new Western world order and the heightened sense of national independence that followed the breakup of the traditional Chosŏn society. The enlightenment and education movements were quite active during the first stage (mid-nineteenth to early twentieth centuries) of modern Korean literary history. Literary works of this period show dramatic change. The central characteristic was the formation of a vernacular literature influenced by the new movements. As Chinese literary influence declined, various literary forms using the Korean language expanded to the masses through newspapers such as the *Independent* (*Tongnip shinmun*), *Capital Gazette* (*Hwangsŏng sinmum*), *Korea Daily News* (*Taehan maeil sinbo*), *Imperial Post* (*Cheguk shinmun*), *Independence News* (*Mansebo*), and *Korea People's Press* (*Taehan minbo*). Another new movement urged writers to criticize contemporary reality and express enlightenment consciousness.

BIOGRAPHIES OF HEROES

Before any other narrative form of the enlightenment and education movements, we must discuss biography. Above all biography reflected a strong social consciousness that resisted foreign influence and sought independence. Biographies of the time offered the ideal heroic types that contemporary Korean society hungered for.

Aeguk puinjŏn (*Life of a Patriotic Woman*, 1907) by Chang Chiyŏn (1864–1921) depicted the life of Joan of Arc. Although the protagonist was the daughter of a poor peasant family, she participated in the struggle against foreign invaders. The main motivation for writing this work was to present a model of a heroine that appealed to patriotic feeling among Korean women. To provide such examples in a time of national crisis, Sin Ch'aeho (1880–1936) wrote biographies of Korean heroes such as *Ŭlchi Mundŏk* (1908), *Sugun cheil wiin Yi Sunsin chŏn* (*Life of Yi Sunsin, the Greatest Admiral*,

1908), and *Tongguk kŏgŏl Ch'oe tot'ong chŏn* (*Life of Commander-in-Chief Ch'oe Yŏng, Korea's Great Hero*, 1909). Sin Ch'aeho believed that the heroic actions of Korean patriots offered stirring examples in the struggle to recover national sovereignty.

Once Korea became a Japanese colony, these biographies were banned. The Government-General of Korea did not tolerate works that urged national independence. Thus we find no further examples of the narrative form of biography during the colonial period.

FABLES AND SATIRES

Fables of the enlightenment period focused on human activity or moral positions that created social problems. Writers used the didactic function of fables to alert people to the dangers of foreign invasion, to criticize corrupt officials, and to warn against the collapse of morality. "Tigusyŏng miraemong" ("Dream of the Earth's Future"; anonymous, 1909), "Monggyŏn Chegal Yang" ("Dreaming of Zhuge Liang"; Yu Wŏnp'yo, 1908), and "Mongbae Kŭm T'aejo" ("Dreaming of the Founder of the Jin"; Pak Ŭnsik, 1911) all used a framework of dreams or imaginary space as opposed to real life. In "Dreaming of Zhuge Liang," the narrator dreams that he meets with Zhuge Liang (181–234), debates contemporary problems, and then criticizes the political situation. "Dream of the Earth's Future," set in an imaginary space, talks about the reality of Chosŏn under foreign domination and finally presents a view of a future world. Some stories used animals to satirize the human world. "Kŭmsu hoeŭirok" ("Proceedings of the Council of Birds and Beasts"; An Kuksŏn, 1908), "Kyŏngsejong" ("A Bell Warning the Public; Kim P'ilsu, 1908), and "Kŭmsu chaep'an" ("Trial of Birds and Beasts"; Hŭmhŭmja, 1910) all used animal characters to criticize the human world and present a new way of life.

Along with fable stories, another important narrative genre of the period was satire. Representative works include "Sogyŏng kwa anjŭmbangi mundap" ("Questions and Answers between a Blind Man and a Cripple"), "Kŏbu ohae" ("Misunderstanding of Rickshaw Men") from the *Korea Daily News*, and "Chŏryŏng sinhwa" ("New Funny Story that Loosens the Hat String") from *Korea People's Press*. Apparently the writers of these stories worked in the newspaper business. Instead of action, these works present conversation and debate. Our interest in these stories arises from the confrontation with opposing themes, values, and ideas. The main characters in "Questions and Answers Between a Blind Man and a Cripple" are a blind person practicing divination and a cripple who makes Korean headbands

for a living. Their conversations are mostly about the corruption of government officials, perfunctory reforms, and foreign threats. The story brings
out paradoxical effects because these conversations occur between a man
who cannot see and a man who cannot move. "Misunderstanding of Rickshaw Men" involves conversations between rickshaw pullers who cannot
understand such new developments as the institutional reforms and establishment of the Residency-General. Their misunderstanding is presented
through linguistic play using the pretence of ignorance and in turn becomes
an attack on political change and social transformation. "New Funny Story
that Loosens the Hat String," based on conversations between a scholar
going to market and a scatterbrain going to Seoul, ridicules the changing
social situations of the enlightenment period. Neither the scholar nor the
commoner can do anything, but they both criticize the times and expose
corruption.

The satire form is further expanded in "Pyŏngin kanch'inhoe rok"
("Record of a Reunion of the Sick," 1910) and *Chayujong* (*Liberty Bell*;
Yi Haejo, 1910). In *Liberty Bell*, women gathered for a birthday party spend
the night discussing such pressing issues as women's rights and education,
national independence, and social reform. "Record of a Reunion of the
Sick" involves disabled people who fight social discrimination by forming
an organization called "Reunion of the Sick" to show their united will and
determination. While the speakers in this work recognize their physical
handicaps, they also point out that the handicaps of moral failings and
corruption are far more serious.

NEW FICTION AND THE LIMITS OF MODERNITY

The new fiction came in the 1900s. As traditional fiction gradually declined
with changes in the Confucian social structure, new fictional works reflecting the life and consciousness of the new era emerged. In the early days, such
works of fiction were serialized in newspapers and later published in single
volumes and thus gained a large readership. With the emergence of such
professional writers as Yi Injik (1862–1919), Yi Haejo (1869–1927), Ch'oe
Ch'ansik (1881–1951), and Kim Kyoje (fl. 1911–1923), new fiction gained
a mass following. Yi Injik published *Hyŏl ŭi nu* (*Tears of Blood*, 1906),
Ch'iaksan (*Mount Pheasant*, 1908), and *Ŭnsegye* (*A Silvery World*, 1908).
Yi Haejo published *Pinsangsŏl* (*Snow on the Temple Hair*, 1908), *Kumagŏm*
(*The Sword that Drives away Demons*, 1908), *Liberty Bell* (1910), and *Hwa
ŭi hyŏl* (*Tears of Flowers*, 1912). Ch'oe Ch'ansik's *Ch'uwŏlsaek* (*Color of the
Autumn Moon*, 1912) is another well-known work. Through its use of the

vernacular, the new fiction became the mass literature. It also, however, established its own unique characteristics in story construction and narrative styles.

Tears of Blood concerns a P'yŏngyang family that suffered during the Sino-Japanese War in the late Chosŏn period. The main part of the story deals with a family splintered by war. The story, however, also leads the main character, Ongnyŏn, who had become separated from her family, to the path of enlightenment. Thus the war provides an occasion for Ongnyŏn to find a new life. Yet the war that enabled Ongnyŏn to find enlightenment was won by Japan, and the biggest loser was not Qing China but Chosŏn Korea as Japan was able to extend its influence over the peninsula as a result of its victory. Although Ongnyŏn is led toward enlightenment, the enlightenment movement itself ended with the Japanese colonial rule.

Tears of Blood is continued in *Moranbong* (*Peony Peak*), which deals with Ongnyŏn's reunion with her family and her marriage negotiations with Ku Wansŏ. While *Peony Peak* deals with Ongnyŏn's return to Korea, it is totally different from *Tears of Blood*. Ongnyŏn's parents try to marry her off to a wealthy idler and as Ku Wansŏ's return becomes imminent, trickery visits Ku's parents. Basically this story adopts the typical pattern of a series of obstacles to marriage. No longer is there any talk of enlightenment; instead the work addresses the breakdown of social morality. *A Silvery World*, set around the time of the reform of 1894, reflects dissatisfaction with the corrupt times and urges reform of the political system – especially the oppressive administration of corrupt officials.

Snow on the Temple Hair by Yi Haejo treats the troubles between wife and concubine using the moral frame of rewarding good and punishing evil. The story reflects changes in a life that had been secularized and individualized. There is a strong theme of shattering superstition in *The Sword That Drives Away Demons*, but beneath the story there is another theme of secular desire and its problems. Materialism lurks in *Manwŏltae* (*Full Moon Terrace*, 1910), which concerns a family that prospered through commercial activity and overcame unhappiness through an unlikely windfall. While *Ssangokchŏk* (*Two Jade Flutes*, 1911) has the exaggerated style of a detective story, it is nevertheless an interesting tale. *Morangpyŏng* (*Peony Screen*, 1911) illustrates a depraved life of human desire through the story of selling a daughter to a swindler and delivering the female protagonist from prostitution.

After Yi Haejo, more works of new fiction were produced by authors like Ch'oe Ch'ansik and Kim Kyoje, but these works were transformed into popular stories appealing to a general readership. This attachment to popular amusement shown by the authors of the new fiction weakened its social educational aspect but at the same time shifted its direction toward individual tastes.

FICTION UNDER JAPANESE COLONIAL RULE

Korean literature faced a historical ordeal as the peninsula came under Japanese colonial rule. Japan forced Korea to sign the Annexation Treaty of 1910, established the Government-General, and began its militaristic rule. Because of the severe press censorship, there was no longer any expression of desire for national sovereignty.

Discovery of the individual

Around this time, Yi Kwangsu (b. 1892) advanced his ideas on literature based on the Western theory he had acquired in his studies in Japan. In his essay "Munhak ŭi kach'i" ("Value of Literature," 1910), Yi defined literature as an "art that expresses elements of human feeling using words." Yi became a leading figure after he published "Sonyŏn ŭi piae" ("Sorrow of a Youth," 1917), a short story about personal anguish, and the full-length work of fiction *Mujŏng* (*Heartless*, 1917). While *Heartless* did not evince a thorough perception of colonial reality, we recognize its modernity as the story weaves together the life of an individual and the historical context. The most striking point in *Heartless* is the aspect of fate embodied in the life of two individuals, Yi Hyŏngsik and Pak Yŏngch'ae. Yi Hyŏngsik is an orphan who later becomes a teacher who resists the Confucian order and articulates new values based on enlightenment and education. This life of Yi Hyŏngsik goes hand in hand with the social changes of the time. The life of Pak Yŏngch'ae also manifests social change during the enlightenment period, which saw the collapse of traditional family structure and individual morality. This work stresses the value of enlightenment and new education as the best of all social conditions. Above all the work promotes the supremacy of enlightenment, which offers an opportunity of new life. Although Pak Yŏngch'ae must endure personal sacrifice during the collapse of the old order, she gains an opportunity for rebirth by seizing the ideology of civilized enlightenment.

In Korean literary history, the work of Yi Kwangsu signaled a rediscovery of the self. It is remarkable that most writers of the period advocated liberation of the self even though they themselves were under a colonial rule that made national identity impossible. While Yi Kwangsu focused on problems of self-awakening and love in *Heartless*, he failed to express an objective awareness of the context in which the self is rooted. With its positive assessment of the modern society yet to come, this work is clearly situated at the end of the enlightenment period.

The birth of modern fiction

Based on the national self-awakening touched off by the March First movement, the literary world began to express the themes of self-discovery and individuality. Apart from a number of coterie magazines such as *Ch'angjo* (*Creation*, 1919), *P'yehŏ* (*Ruins*, 1920), and *Paekcho* (*White Tide*, 1922), creative activity flourished in such general magazines as *Kaebyŏk* (The Beginning, 1920). Moreover, Korean newspapers such as *Tonga Daily* and *Chosŏn Daily* provided wider ground for literary activity.

Slowly the main concerns of modern Korean fiction began to shift from didacticism to the creation of new characters and subjectivity. The establishment of a prose style based on the spoken language, in particular, marked a turning point. Now one finds portrayals of the anguish of restless intellectuals in the dark reality of colonial life and the terrible state of life among laborers and farmers. Furthermore, the modern short story was established by works of fiction in this period. Indeed, the mainstream of fiction was represented by short stories offering detailed portrayals and elaborate construction of slices of life.

Kim Tongin (1900–1951) assumed leadership of the magazine *Creation* when he was studying in Tokyo and became a pioneer in establishing the modern short story through his publication of "Yakhanja ŭi sŭlp'ŭm" ("Sorrow of the Weak," 1919), "Paettaragi" ("The Seaman's Chant," 1920), and "Kamja" ("Potato," 1925). "The Seaman's Chant" is one of the best short stories written in the early period of modern Korean literature. This is a frame story (a tale within a tale) of two brothers' downfall caused by an inferiority complex and misunderstanding. "Potato" portrays the tragic death of the main character Pongnyŏ, living in utter poverty, who prostitutes herself after losing her sense of morality. The work is written in a concise clinical style that tells the reader only the course of events.

Hyŏn Chingŏn (1900–1943) began his literary career by participating in the White Tide group. His representative works are "Pinch'ŏ" ("Poor Wife," 1921), "Sul kwŏnhanŭn sahoe" ("A Society to Promote Wine," 1921), and "T'arakcha" ("A Fallen Man," 1922), which portray the failures and anguish of colonial intellectuals, and "Unsu choŭn nal" ("A Lucky Day," 1924), which presents a slice of the life of poor laborers. The main character of "Poor Wife" is an unknown writer whose pursuit of spiritual value is shaken by everyday desires but ultimately recovers. This work achieves realistic effects by juxtaposing episodes of everyday life with the anguish of a petit bourgeois who is immersed in reading and writing without recompense and the psychological changes in a wife who relies only on her husband. "A Lucky Day" is the first work in which Hyŏn shifts his attention from the life of petit-bourgeois intellectuals to the world of workers – an indication that both Hyŏn and Korean literature were facing a new social situation. This work shows the painful life of people suffering in abject poverty through its ironic construction of a story in which the lucky day for the rickshaw puller is also the day his wife dies of hunger.

Na Tohyang (1902–1927), another member of the White Tide group, published "Pŏngŏri Samnyong" ("Samnyong the Mute," 1925), "Mulle-banga" ("Water Mill," 1925), and "Ppong" ("Mulberry," 1925). "Samnyong the Mute" portrays overcoming a physical handicap through self-sacrifice. The death of the main character and the arson at the end of the story are characteristic of the works of the New Trend school. It also brings out the intense effect of the main theme, however, by presenting anger, resistance, and the fever of love in the symbolism of fire. "Water Mill" and "Mulberry" deal with the problems of poverty and desire. While these stories portray the confrontation of the haves and have-nots, they also show the corruption of human nature arising from sexual and material desires.

Yŏm Sangsŏp (1897–1963) began his literary activity by joining the Ruins group of writers. His status as a writer was secured with his publishing of the trilogy "P'yobonsil ŭi ch'ŏnggaegori" ("The Green Frog in the Specimen Gallery," 1921), "Amya" ("Dark Night," 1922), and "Cheya" ("New Year's Eve," 1922). These works portray the personal anguish of young intellectuals during the colonial period. "The Green Frog in the Specimen Gallery" is a first-person story that foregrounds the character of a madman in order to expose the dark side of life. This work lacks a tight structure and concrete description, however, and advances crude ideals. The work that overcame this ideological limitation was *Mansejŏn* (*Before the March First Movement*, 1924). This medium-length story offers a realistic description of everyday life as witnessed by a Korean studying in Tokyo who must return home when he learns of his wife's critical condition. The author compares colonial Korea to "a cemetery full of maggots" – a concrete portrayal of colonial reality that cannot be found prior to this work. It is only when we get to *Before the March First Movement* that we find modern fiction which presents personal problems and social situations in a synthesized fashion.

Class movements and ideology

Beginning in the mid-1920s, Korean literature split into two opposing ideological centers: national literature and class literature. As people gained class consciousness and began to recognize the contradictions of colonial modernity, a New Trend school was born. In this new school, which focused on the problems of real life and pursued the political ends of class struggle, works of fiction are deeply involved in contemporary problems. Fictional texts show the features of the "literature of poverty" and the "literature of resistance." Such fiction also depicts with careful fidelity its political objectives: an interest in class divisions, a dialectical historical view, and the prospect of class revolution.

Ch'oe Sŏhae (1901–1937) published "Koguk" ("Homeland," 1924), "T'alch'ul gi" ("Record of an Escape," 1925), and "Kia wa sallyuk" ("Starvation and Murder," 1925), which can be called realizations of a creative project of the New Trend school. Ch'oe's subject matter includes Korean refugees in southern Manchuria and the terrible poverty of peasants. His portrayal of murder, arson, and destruction is quite persuasive because such acts were the last resort for people confronting an oppressive reality, miserable poverty, and pain inflicted on family members. These works describe the class consciousness that grew naturally in the social context of utter poverty.

Cho Myŏnghŭi (1894–1942) published the play *Kim Yŏngil ŭi sa* (*Death of Kim Yŏngil*, 1921) and a collection of poems entitled *Pom chandibat wie* (*On Spring Grass*, 1924). When Cho joined the Chosŏn P'ŭrollet'aria Yesul Tongmaeng (Korea artista proleta federatio=KAPF) in 1925, however, his creative activity turned to the writing of fiction. His "Nongch'on saramdŭl" ("Farm-village people," 1927) depicts a person who is killed resisting the agents of Japanese imperialism who destroyed his family. "Naktonggang" ("Naktong River," 1927) draws attention to the process of overcoming the self. Through class organization, with the help and leadership of young intellectuals, peasants manage to stop Japanese imperialism. Although this work's major theme is the liberation of the oppressed class, its real importance lies in its account of Japanese brutality. Thus the story focuses more on national confrontation between imperial Japan and colonial Korea than on socialist ideology.

Yi Kiyŏng (1895–1984), the representative writer of the class literature movement, published two full-length works of fiction *Hongsu* (*Flood*, 1930) and *Sŏhwa* (*Rat Fire*, 1933), that dealt with the life of peasants. *Flood* tells of peasants suffering a vicious cycle of poverty who fight landlords with the help of education and persuasion by the main character. The schematic story line's separation from reality can be traced to the political objectives demanded by the class literature movement. *Rat Fire* exposes the collapse of farming communities via two symbolic events: the rise of gambling and decline of traditional fire play. *Kohyang* (*Hometown*, 1933–1934), one of the best peasant fictions of the colonial period, gained the applause of contemporary critics by creating lively descriptions of events in the real life of farmers. *Hometown* describes the pain of peasants suffering from abject poverty and the exploitation of oppressive landlords. With the appearance of the main character, a young intellectual, the peasants gradually become aware of their own existence and develop class consciousness. United they fight the landlord class to gain control of their own future. This work not only shows the reality of a farming village and the gradual growth of peasants' self-awareness but also recreates their life and their customs convincingly.

Han Sŏrya (1901–1963) focused on the social formation of the working class and the changes in their consciousness through such works as "Kwadogi" ("Age of Transition," 1929), "Ssirŭm" ("Wrestling," 1929), and "Sabang kongsa" ("Erosion Work," 1932). His efforts are considered a major contribution to the establishment of working-class fiction. "Age of Transition" and "Wrestling" describe how members of the working class, transformed from farmers into urban laborers, arrive at class consciousness instead of falling into despair and self-pity. Han's interest in class consciousness is greatly intensified in his long work of fiction entitled *Hwanghon* (*Twilight*, 1936). The first half of the story deals with the life of a textile factory owner who belongs to the capitalist class subordinated to colonial power. The second half depicts the fight of the working class against these colonial capitalists. The story develops naturally by tracing the life of the main female character and is notable in that the author recognizes the growth of working-class organizations during the expansion of Japanese militarism.

Song Yŏng (1903–1979) portrays a worker's life in his "Yonggwangno" ("Melting Furnace," 1926) and "Sŏkkong chohap taep'yo" ("Representative of the Stonemasons' Union," 1927). "Melting Furnace" emphasizes the struggle of workers against the exploitation of a factory owner; "Representative of the Stonemasons Union" points out the hard life of stonemasons. In contrast to couples indulging in unrestrained merrymaking on the Taedong River, workers in the stonemasonry resolve never to forget the despicable ruling class that commissions the stone monuments of everlasting remembrance.

Given the political objectives of the class literature movement, the fiction on class conflict during the colonial period focused mostly on the organized struggle and mass resistance of the working class. Thus it is impossible to find a literary work of this period that embodies the positive meaning of labor or the true value of a worker's life. Because most writers were obsessed with class struggle, inevitably the organization of fiction took on a fixed pattern with stereotyped main characters.

Colonial conditions and the expansion of fiction

Korean fiction faced an important change with the strengthening of Japanese militarism and the oppression of literary ideals after the mid-1930s. In particular, we see the emergence of fiction dealing with various aspects of personal lives rather than the pursuit of mass ideology that had formed the mainstream of Korean literature after the 1920s. The newspaper companies published monthly magazines such as *Sindonga* (*New East Asia*), *Chogwang* (*Korea's Light*), and *Chungang* (*Center*) that expanded the arena of literary activity, and general literary magazines such as *Munjang* (*Literature*) and *Inmun p'yŏngnon* (*Criticism of Culture*) produced new writers.

The main issue facing the literary world during the mid-1930s, when the KAPF was disbanded, was how to portray real life in fiction. This new issue began with the debate on the realism of fiction and then expanded to other questions such as the writer's creative attitude and worldview, the creation of model characters, and the balanced pursuit of character and environment. Along with this interest came an expansion of full-length fiction dealing with various themes. Not only were writers now able to present the full aspect of life but the times demanded new views on society and history.

Among the full-length works of fiction of the time, one especially captures our attention: *Samdae* (*Three Generations*, 1931) by Yŏm Sangsŏp. This work depicts the full dimension of Korean society from the late nineteenth century to the colonial period by following a family's history spanning three generations. Although the story's main focus is on changes in the history of a big landowning family, Yŏm also pays attention to changes in Korean society such as the sense of class solidarity that developed over these three generations. The work's main themes are changes in the value system and intergenerational confrontation in the Cho family. By writing from the viewpoint of the main character, a moderate reformist, Yŏm manifests his own worldview as he explores the confrontation of value systems and intergenerational contradictions.

T'angnyu (*Muddy Currents*, 1937) by Ch'ae Mansik (1902–1950) is essentially the tragic story of a woman's life, yet it is not simply a sad tale. The true meaning of the main character Ch'obong's life is in the ordeals she must endure as tradition clashes with the new culture. In this work, all the characters surrounding the protagonist lack direction. They are motivated only by money and the satisfaction of mundane desires. Thus while they are sited at the periphery of the main character's life, they have no sense of their own situation or awareness of contemporary problems. Prisoners of material desire, they are swept into the muddy waters of reality. *T'aep'yŏng ch'ŏnha* (*Peace under Heaven*, 1938), another example of Ch'ae Mansik's full-length fiction, depicts the moral collapse of the landlord class that maintained its social position by collaborating with the colonial power. While *Three Generations* by Yŏm Sangsŏp chronicles a family's history, *Peace under Heaven* presents slices of everyday life to illuminate the relationships among family members and their attitudes to life. This work is quite successful in exploring the dramatic effects of conversation and satirical expression.

Ch'ŏnbyŏn p'unggyŏng (*Scenes on the Riverside*, 1936) by Pak T'aewŏn (1909–1986) recreates everyday space in various episodes involving individualized characters. This work does not follow the structural principle that plot must be consistent in actions and events; instead various episodes are presented one after another like vignettes. What the author discovers in the life of an urban marketplace is the individualized appearance of people – a turning point in the methodology of perception.

In the late 1930s historical fiction begins to appear. Works based on historical materials include *Im Kkŏkchŏng* (1940, 1948) by Hong Myŏnghŭi (1888–1968), *Maŭi t'aeja* (*Prince in Hemp Cloth*, 1928) by Yi Kwangsu, *Unhyŏn-gung ŭi pom* (*Spring of Unhyŏn Palace*, 1948) by Kim Tongin, *Muyŏngt'ap* (*Shadowless Stupa*, 1938–1939) by Hyŏn Chingŏn, and *Kŭmsam ŭi p'i* (*Blood on the Embroidered Hem*, 1938) by Pak Chonghwa (1901–1981). If the writer's interest is focused mainly on the material itself, then historical fiction based on real events and personalities becomes nothing more than popular stories of history. Historical fiction demands that the writer create new characters by reinterpreting history using his abundant imagination even if the plot itself is based on historical fact. *Im Kkŏkchŏng* recreates a new human model, Im Kkŏkchŏng, as a popular hero. Moreover, the work depicts in detail the social world and customs of late Chosŏn and portrays the life of the lower classes. *Spring of Unhyŏn Palace* concerns the human side of the historical figure Taewŏngun (Prince of the Great Court, 1820–1898) and details the fall of the Chosŏn dynasty through this single character.

In addition to the foregoing works, *Chŏkto* (*The Equator*, 1939) by Hyŏn Chingŏn describes a life dominated by materialism and pleasure-seeking with this story of complications in a love affair. *Sangnoksu* (*Evergreen*, 1936) by Sim Hun points out the implications of the rural education movement. Other notable works of fiction of the period include *Hŭk* (*Soil*, 1932–1933) by Yi Kwangsu, *Taeha* (*Great River*, 1939) by Kim Namch'ŏn (b. 1911), *Pom* (*Spring*, 1940–1941) by Yi Kiyŏng, and *T'ap* (*Stupa*, 1940–1941) by Han Sŏrya.

STYLE AND THE SPIRIT OF MODERNISM

One of the most important changes in 1930s fiction is the modernistic inclination of literary style and spirit. Among the writers of this period, the works of Pak T'aewŏn (1904–1986), Yi T'aejun, Yi Hyosŏk (1907–1942), Yi Sang (1912–1939), Ch'oe Myŏngik (b. 1903), Hŏ Chun (b. 1910), and An Hoenam (1910–1966) are closely related to the tendencies of modernism in a larger sense. Their works reveal such attributes of modernism as the portrayal of characters trapped in an urban landscape, a psychological approach, and a symbolic technique that exposes the inner life of the self and the true nature of desire hidden there. Other characteristics often seen in the works of this period are a fascination with sexual hunger, the search for meaning in everyday life, and a new interpretation of time and space.

Pak T'aewŏn's work represents key tendencies of modernist fiction as he focuses on the reconstruction of meaning in everyday life. Unlike the fiction prior to this period, which valued the importance of theme or the problems of subject matter, this acceptance of everyday life and space as the main subject signifies an epistemological change. Pak's representative works are *Sosŏlga Kubossi ŭi iril* (*A Day in the Life of Kubo the Writer*, 1934), *Sŏngt'anje* (*Christmas*, 1937), and *Scenes on the Riverside*. In *A Day in the Life of Kubo the Writer*, the main character is not a social figure who represents the masses in class ideology and social consciousness. Indeed he wanders through the urban space without connecting with the people around him. For such an individualized human being divorced from social reality, the only way to reconfirm the meaning of existence is self-awareness. Thus we find here the emergence of the techniques of modern psychological fiction, especially stream of consciousness.

Yi T'aejun laid the technical foundation of modern Korean fiction through his introspective portrayal of characters and his elaborate organization. "Talpam" ("Moonlit Night," 1933), "Kamagwi" ("Crow," 1936), and "Yŏngwŏl yŏnggam" ("Old Man Yŏngwŏl," 1939), his main works, strongly appeal to the zeitgeist in a world of emptiness. "Moonlit Night" brings out tender human feelings that persist despite a changing world. The story is like a painting depicting the mood of a warm night, the people within it, and the lives of those who retain their humanity even in times of failure. "Crow" turns a compassionate gaze upon a dying person. Especially notable here is Yi's ability to create atmosphere through his verbal painting of a timeworn villa and his aural description of the cry of crows.

The literary activities of Yi Hyosŏk can be divided into two major periods. The early period saw such works as "Tosi wa yuryŏng" ("City and Ghost," 1928) and "Noryŏng kŭnhae" ("The Russian Coast," 1930); the later period includes "Ton" ("Pig," 1933), "San" ("Mountain," 1936), and "Memilkkot p'il muryŏp" ("When the Buckwheat Blooms," 1936). The works of Yi Hyosŏk focus on sex. In particular, by repeatedly juxtaposing animal copulation and the sexual desire of his characters, Yi explores basic human impulses. The animals in Yi's works – the pig in "Punnyŏ" (1936), the boar in "Tokpaek" ("Monologue"), and other animals such as a dog, a donkey, a chicken, and birds – are all used to evoke the sexual hunger of his main characters. In "Pig," for example, the sexual desire of the main character is revealed through the description of a boar's attack on a brood sow. In "When the Buckwheat Blooms," perhaps Yi's best story, the main character is illuminated through the separation of time into night and day and the separation of space into marketplace and mountain trail. These divisions of time and space enable the reader to see both sides of Yi's characters. The main themes in this work – the affinity with nature, the essence of human life, and primitive love – appear repeatedly in Yi's other works. Yi Hyosŏk's unique literary style is a lyrical search for an intimate harmony between setting, characters, and events.

Yi Sang portrays desire and the crisis of the self confronting reality in his "Chijuhoesi" ("Spiders meet a Pig," 1936), "Nalgae" ("Wings," 1936), and "Tonghae" ("A Boy's Bones," 1937). "Spiders and Pigs" tells of a parasitic protagonist living off his wife who in turn makes a living cheating customers in their café. One of the story's striking features is the author's unique perception of human relations. This story understands the relation between individuals as capitalistic and exploitative; its objective is to condemn the loss of solidarity among individuals and the phenomenon of materialism. Using the technique of spatialization, "Wings" is a work that explores formation of the self, skepticism about a way of life, and the desire to escape from an abnormal life represented by a small room occupied by a prostitute wife and a spiritless protagonist. This desire to escape, symbolized as wings, is not a positive omen for the future, however. Rather it represents a confession of desperate inner hunger that cannot be translated into action. In "A Boy's Bones," the writer captures alienation by alternating events of real life and interior descriptions of the narrator's mind. Here the narrator's interiority is linked to the suicide motif. The notion of regret over a wasted life appears elsewhere as keenly felt self-torment in "Chongsaenggi" ("End of my Life," 1937).

Ch'oe Myŏngik published "P'yeŏin" ("Lungfish Man," 1939), "Simmun" ("Ripples in the Heart," 1939), and "Changsam isa" ("The Common Crowd," 1941). The special feature of Ch'oe's literary world is his faithful description of the anxiety of the intelligentsia set in everyday space. "Ripples in the Heart" shows the poor adjustment of depressed and self-conscious intellectuals to real life, as well as their boredom and depravity. In "The Common Crowd," the speaker rides a third-class train and draws pictures of ordinary but diverse groups of commoners. He brings to our attention the meaning of ordinariness by depicting the routine life of unknown people. Hŏ Chun explores the inner world of the intelligentsia in his short story "T'angnyu" ("Muddy Stream," 1936). Elsewhere he depicts the inner life of intellectuals who have shut themselves in the nihilism of the time in his "Yahan ki" ("Night's Cold," 1938) and "Sŭpchaksil esŏ" ("From a Study," 1941). An Hoenam (1910–1966) published "Yŏngi" ("Smoke," 1933) and "Myŏngsang" ("Meditation," 1937), which deal mainly with psychological quests in a history of self and family. In "T'ugye" ("Cockfight," 1939), he presents the social conditions in a tavern. Even though his description of events and characters is often convincing, An's works are sometimes judged to have been preoccupied with triviality.

SATIRE AND FOLK CUSTOMS

In 1930s fiction, Ch'ae Mansik was the one who gave shape to the method of satirizing reality and viewing life from a critical standpoint. His "Redimeidŭ insaeng" ("Ready-made Life," 1934) presents sarcastic portraits of intellectuals alienated from society. When the unemployed protagonist cannot find work, he ridicules himself as a "ready-made life" waiting to be sold. Ultimately he finds a job for his nine-year-old son in a printing shop instead of sending him to school so that his son does not become yet another "ready-made life." "Ch'isuk" ("My Idiot Uncle," 1938) depicts the inane life of an uncle from the perspective of the speaker who makes a living by ingratiating himself to a Japanese shopkeeper. This story presents a positive human type by focusing on a negative human model. It criticizes the contradictions of materialism through piercing satire. In works like "Kim kangsa wa T'kyosu"

("Lecturer Kim and Professor T," 1935), Yu Chino (1906–1987) describes the inner life of intellectuals by taking up such themes as their compromise with reality and the agonizing contradictions of their worldview.

The stories of Kim Yujŏng (1908–1937) are based on a sense of humor. Kim's humor is constructed through such devices as the tactless frankness and impudence of his characters, unexpected behavior in the conclusion, the refractory view of the writer, obscene talk carried to the point of anti-aestheticism, and colloquial expressions. Kim shows us the dark side of contemporary village life and the lifestyle of peasants through his sense of caricature. "Pombom" ("Spring, Spring," 1935) is a fine example of this sense of humor. Here Kim depicts the actions of a sly father-in-law and a shrewd Chŏmsun through the eyes of a naïve speaker. "Tongbaekkot" ("Camellias," 1936) is mainly a love story between a young boy and girl in a farming village. A problem arises when the male protagonist fails to understand the amorous pursuit of Chŏmsun who has just awakened to love. By juxtaposing the assertive Chŏmsun who understands carnal love and a foolish "I" who is still blind to relations between men and women, Kim presents the innocence of love between rural youths in a humorous way.

The literary world of Kim Tongni (1913–1995) is rooted mainly in folk customs – as in his "Munyŏdo" ("Portrait of a Shaman," 1936), which can be considered the starting point of Kim's creative career. Kim expanded and repeated the themes of "Portrait of a Shaman" in his later works and indeed revised the story many times. In 1978 this work was developed into a full-length work of fiction called *Ŭrhwa*, and here the writer depicts in even greater detail the world of shamanism that was only the background in the original short story. The main theme of "Portrait of a Shaman" is the spiritual clash between traditional folk belief and Christianity. The world occupied by the shaman Mohwa is the traditional realm of spirits. The intruder into this world is her own son Uk, who has returned home a Christian. The collision between traditional and foreign worldviews has great significance in modern Korean history. Although "Portrait of a Shaman" approaches this problem, it is hard to find a truly spiritual contest here because Mohwa's belief is set in a primitive world of shamans. Instead the story develops into a clash between spirit and man and comes to a destructive end with the brandishing of a sword. We find the mythical world of folk and popular customs in Kim's "Hwangt'o ki" ("Loess Village Story," 1939) as well. This work tenaciously inquires into a nihilistic sense of fate through meaningless fights between two characters, Oksoe and Tŭkpo, whose actions involve the pursuit of primitive impulses such as drinking, fighting, and lust. This world is recreated in his other stories as well, such as "Pawi" ("The Rock," 1936).

In the 1930s, Chu Yosŏp (1902–1972) turned away from the New Trend school and began to show an interest in depicting interiority and the problems of love. His representative works of the period include "Sarang sonnim kwa ŏmŏni" ("Mama and the Boarder," 1935) and "Anemone ŭi madam" ("Madame in the Anemone Tearoom", 1936). "Mama and the Boarder" explores in a subtle way an adult's attitude toward love by using the young daughter as the narrator; "Madame in the Anemone Tearoom" deals with the world of love as well.

CHAPTER 20

Early twentieth-century fiction by women

Carolyn So

MODERN WOMEN WRITERS

The public act of publishing women's texts enables a concrete and viable point of departure for a historical interpretation of women's entrance into the modern history of Korean literature. Prior to the twentieth century, a woman writer composed her works largely within the space of her home. In the early twentieth century, however, Korean women writers began to appear in literary journals and women at large began making their appearance in social and public domains by taking advantage of the impetus for women's participation provided by the movements engaged in the enlightenment, modernization, and, ultimately, liberation of Korea.

Women's public participation, therefore, was initially spurred at the end of the nineteenth century by Korea's urgent need to maintain its independence, as it was caught in the web of becoming a colony of another nation. Enlightenment thinkers and, later, nationalists during the colonial period (1910–1945) sought to educate women in an effort to modernize Korea. In this sense, the fate of women writers was intrinsically tied to central social and national issues. Furthermore, the traditional framework of Confucian patriarchy transformed to a new form of patriarchy[1] that demanded women be modern while still remaining within the strictures of the Confucian gender role. The modern gender role for women, then, meant continuing to carry out the duties of wise mother and good wife, maintaining some form of womanly virtues, while absorbing modern values. Women's texts portray the issues pertaining to social, cultural, and historical conflicts and dilemmas.

Despite the overwhelming need of the time which demanded that Korean leaders, whether men or women, address Korea's political and social predicaments as a colony of Japan, women writers remained committed

---

[1] Partha Chatterjee, *The Nation and its Fragments* (Princeton: Princeton University Press, 1933) , p. 127.

to women's preoccupations during the modern period. Since they were women, they took the stuff from their everyday lives as literary topics: love and marriage, family, motherhood, and other social changes that directly affected them such as jobs and literary trends. Female protagonists dominate their creative space, and the figure of a woman intellectual struggling between morality, love, marriage, and career appears frequently. Although the woman writer's preferences and tendencies determined the content of the textual narratives, each text reflects the issues the writer dealt with in her complex and rapidly changing world. She engaged in both hegemonic and marginalized discourses, displaying a wide variety of themes and styles, ranging from ideology-oriented works to confessional fiction, exhibiting the richness of the time and literary history. During the colonial period, there were only about a dozen active women writers of fiction, illustrating the significant historical and literary space each occupied. Their small number shows the relative scarcity of public women and women writers. Nevertheless, these privileged women were remarkable people, who braved their precarious position, visible and possibly vulnerable, to enter the patriarchal space of Korean literature. Their few numbers meant, however, that the public was enthralled more by the events of their lives than by their works, shown by controversies surrounding some of the women writers.

In the ensuing sections we discuss three phases of works by women writers by considering the time of their debut and also when their works gained prominence. The three phases in no way imply a fixed set of criteria, of course, but rather suggest a negotiable one established to outline salient features. Prominence, in particular, reflects the most pressing issues or general tendencies of the time, as well as the relationship between texts and literary issues. Canonization and the critique of women's texts, in particular, surface as recurring issues that continued to haunt women writers throughout the colonial period. We will therefore focus also on the relevant extraliterary events that affected the canonization of women's texts.

During the early phase of modern Korean women writing, the most persistent theme is the exploration of women's issues. Although the motif of lovers and mothers may overlap in the second phase, motherhood figures appear rarely in the early phase. By the late 1930s, well into the third phase, works that focused on the interiorization of the feminine space became prominent. Here, this interiorization refers to the investigation of woman's selfhood, her subjectivity, and the freedom to express her femaleness divorced from social expectations. Thus the earlier exploration of women's issues became one of women's identity, existence, and selfhood as independent individuals. The text of a woman writer in the third phase, then, becomes much more significant than her life as she seeks to establish an independent feminine space. Thus we concentrate on literary themes in this section.

The first phase – 1910s – consists of writers like Kim Myŏngsun (1896–1951?), Na Hyesŏk (1896–1946), and Kim Wŏnju (1896–1971). The second phase – from the 1920s to the early 1930s – includes Pak Hwasŏng (1904–1988), Kang Kyŏngae (1907–1943), and Paek Sinae (1910–1939). The third phase—from the early 1930s until the liberation of Korea in 1945 – involves the writers Kim Malbong (1901–1962), Yi Sŏnhŭi (1911–1949?), Chi Haryŏn (1912–1960), Ch'oe Chŏnghŭi (1912–1990), Chang Tŏkcho (b. 1914), and Im Ogin (1915–1995). Although Chang Tŏkcho and Ch'oe Chŏnghŭi were active throughout the second phase, socialist themes were prominent during this phase. Thus, as their works largely deal with womanhood, their works gain prominence in the late 1930s. Kim Malbong and Im Ogin wrote few works prior to 1945: the majority appeared after the liberation. A few continued to be productive after 1945 in South Korea. They are Pak Hwasŏng, Kim Malbong, Ch'oe Chŏnghŭi, and Im Ogin. Chi Haryŏn, married to a leftist intellectual Im Hwa (1908–1953), left for North Korea with her husband in 1947. Her oeuvre in North Korea needs further research.

THE FIRST PHASE: FROM THE PRIVATE SPACE TO THE PUBLIC

By a strange coincidence, the three pioneering women writers Kim Myŏngsun, Na Hyesŏk, and Kim Wŏnju were all born in 1896 – Na Hyesŏk and Kim Wŏnju in the same month. They were born the year after the Sino-Japanese War (1894–1895), when China suffered a surprising loss to Japan, into a time of rapid change as Korea attempted to transform itself into a modern nation. During this phase, rather than their literary output, the women writers' appearance in the public eye and their personae gain prominence. Following the modernizing zeal of the time, all studied in Japan and led a flamboyant and eccentric lifestyle, living the lives they wrote. Both Kim Myŏngsun and Na Hyesŏk debuted in the late 1910s with "Ŭisim ŭi sonyŏ" ("Suspicious Girl," 1917) and "Kyŏnghŭi" (1918), respectively. Kim Wŏnju followed in 1920 with "Kyesi" ("Revelation").

Symbolic of their celebrated positions, the three had eventful lives corresponding to the multifarious intellectual and literary activities present in colonial Korea. An examination of literary criticism published during the early 1920s shows topics ranging from romanticism and realism to expressionism and Dada. This was a time when disparate literary discourses from the West, along with China and Japan, influenced the newly tilled soil of modern Korean literature. It was common to encounter Dostoevsky, Tolstoy, and Ibsen in the same literary space as Tagore, Dante, and Walt Whitman.[2] There was freedom and a wealth of ideas – from the hegemonic trends of the main literary groups to subversive ones on women's issues, especially set forth by the Swedish thinker Ellen Key (1849–1926). Key's views on motherhood in her essay "Love and Marriage" (1911) outlined the sacred task of raising children, regardless of the legality of marriage between the mother and the father. Key's ideas were introduced into Korea during the early 1920s. Although these thoughts were revolutionary at the time, both men and women embraced her ideas because of the modern belief in the freedom of love, having the right to choose, one of the core ideas during the modernization process in Korea.

In this rich atmosphere of ideas and radical sexual morality, the three women unfurled their ambitions as modern women writers and pioneering intellectuals. A comparison of "Kyŏnghŭi" and "Suspicious Girl" reveals some of the issues that concerned women writers as well as the diversity of current trends. In the tradition of the ideological novel, a dominant pole in the modern literary scene, "Kyŏnghŭi" has an obviously didactic message: a woman must get an education if she wishes to depart from a life bound to the evils of the traditional gender role assigned to a woman. A clear didactic goal is absent, however, in "Suspicious Girl." Instead, it exhibits a wealth of literary styles and motifs by focusing on the identity of the suspicious girl in the literary tradition of domestic intrigues in Korean literature. "Suspicious Girl" explores linguistic and stylistic issues – another dominant literary force concerning pure art. Together, "Kyŏnghŭi" and "Suspicious Girl" reveal the incipient journey into woman's independence and selfhood. Although Na Hyesŏk and Kim Wŏnju wrote fictional narratives, their output is relatively minor. Na Hyesŏk is better known as the first Korean woman practitioner of the Western style of painting. She wrote five short stories in her lifetime, and the bulk of her writings consist of essays. Her best-known work is "Inhyŏng ŭi chip" ("Doll's House," 1921), a verse that celebrates Nora in Henrik Ibsen's play *The Doll's House*. Following the scandal surrounding her affair and subsequent divorce, her essay "Ihon kobaek sŏ" ("Confession of a Divorce"), published 1934 in the literary journal *Samch'ŏlli* (*Three Thousand Tricents*), caused a public stir.

Remaining true to the ideas of Key and Alexandra M. Kollontai (1872–1952), Kim Wŏnju, well known as a controversial feminist and activist,

---

[2] See Kwŏn Yŏngmin, ed., *Hanguk hyŏndae munhak chakp'um yŏnp'yo 1:1894–1975* (Seoul taehakkyo ch'ulp'anbu, 1998).

sought freedom of love and liberation of women in the 1920s. Kollontai extended Key's radical ideas on free love and free marriage by espousing a new sexual morality for new women, especially revealed in her fiction "Vasilisa Malygina," translated as *Free Love* or *Red Love*.[3] Korean women who practiced such freedom were branded as a new woman (*sin yŏsŏng*) by the late 1920s, a term that originally lacked negative connotations. Kim Wŏnju served as the editor of *Sinyŏja* (*New Women*),[4] one of the earliest journals for women, and, like Na Hyesŏk, she gained notoriety with her essay "Na ŭi chŏngjo kwan" ("My Beliefs on Chastity," 8 January 1927). In this particular essay, published in *Chosŏn Daily*, she argued for the spiritual rather than physical chastity of a woman. That she believed in her pioneering status as a woman writer is revealed in her pen name, Iryŏp, from the Korean pronunciation of the name of Higuchi Ichiyō (1872–1896), a celebrated Meiji woman writer.[5]

Unlike Na Hyesŏk and Kim Wŏnju, Kim Myŏngsun concentrated on creating fictional narratives as well as poetry. Her first work of fiction, "Suspicious Girl," has been heralded as the first modern Korean work of fiction by a woman writer. Kim Myŏngsun's texts converge elements of romanticism, expressionism, and mysticism – displayed in her sole anthology *Saengmyŏng ŭi kwasil* (*Fruits of Life*, 1925), which consists of poetry, fiction, and essays. She translated Edgar Allan Poe's "The Assignation" as "Sangbong" ("The Meeting") and three stanzas of "The Raven" as "Taea" ("The Giant Jackdaw") in 1922.[6] In fact, she is the only woman writer who translated Western works into Korean during the colonial period. Her fictional narratives often take on aspects of autobiography, confession, and reflections.

The tortuous course taken by her initially celebrated "Suspicious Girl" parallels her own life. Although Yi Kwangsu (b. 1892), a towering figure in modern Korean literature, praised "Suspicious Girl" in 1917 as one of the few works that succeeded in departing from the old style of didacticism,[7] he recanted his earlier view during a conversation with Chu Yohan (1900–1979) in 1942. Yi Kwangsu commented during their exchange that "Suspicious Girl" is in fact a pirated work of Japanese fiction.[8] Although he refrained

---

[3] For more on the connection between Key and Kollontai and Korean women writers see Pak Yŏnghye and Sŏ Chŏngja, "Kŭndae yŏsŏng ŭi munhak hwaltong," in Pak Yŏnghye, ed., *Hanguk kŭndae yŏsŏng yŏngu* (Sungmyŏng yŏja taehakkyo, 1987), pp. 185–217.

[4] See Yung-Hee Kim, "From Subservience to Autonomy: Kim Wŏnju's 'Awakening,'" *KS* 21 (1997): 1–30.

[5] Hong Hyomin, *Hanguk mundan inyŏmsa* (Kip'ŭn saem, 1983), p. 11.

[6] See Kim Pyŏngch'ŏl, *Hanguk kŭndae pŏnyŏk munhaksa yŏngu* (Ŭryu, 1988), pp. 429–430.

[7] Yi Kwangsu, *Yi Kwangsu chŏnjip*, 20 vols. (Samjungdang, 1962), 20:374.   [8] Ibid., 20:256.

from elaborating, this view has colored much of the negative assessment of Kim Myŏngsun's life and work even in the post-1945 period. Corroborating evidence that may support Yi Kwangsu's claim is absent from ensuing scholarship. Certainly plagiarizing was common during the colonial period. And certainly other writers – such as Chŏn Yŏngt'aek (1894–1967), who did actually plagiarize – did not suffer from similarly disparaging assessments. Furthermore, since "Suspicious Girl" contains elements that recur in her later works, such as double meanings, autobiographical symbols, and repeated dialogue motifs, this evidence actually contradicts the suggestion that Kim Myŏngsun plagiarized. Kim Myŏngsun essentially stopped publishing fiction after 1929 and continued only intermittently with poetry until 1938. Her personal life deteriorated during the 1930s due to destitution following the death of her mother and Kim's eventual madness. Lacking any means of support, she had to beg for her livelihood – living with acquaintances and peddling toothbrushes, socks, and sweets in the streets of Tokyo.[9] She stopped publishing entirely after 1939 and disappeared from public view. Although the three pioneering writers in this phase continued to pursue issues concerning women and literature in the ensuing decades, their fame gradually turned into notoriety before finally fading away. All three women met with tragic and ignoble ends to their once-glorious lives. The public shunned them for their flagrantly unconventional lifestyles. Both Kim Myŏngsun and Na Hyesŏk died alone in an asylum. Kim Wŏnju became a Buddhist nun in 1933.

THE SECOND PHASE: SOCIAL COMMITMENT AND MOTHERHOOD

Pak Hwasŏng, Kang Kyŏngae, and Paek Sinae, three women writers who became visible in this phase, were born in the early 1900s and debuted between the 1920s and early 1930s. During this second phase, the once-popular discourse on new women begins to disintegrate and committed literature becomes prominent as leftist/socialist thoughts blossom in East Asia following the success of the Russian Revolution. The discourse on motherhood, following the influential essay by Ellen Key, also becomes prominent in works by women writers. With the failure of the peaceful March First movement in 1919, socially conscious Korean intellectuals turned their attention to Russia; the formation of leftist groups in Korea, including literary circles, was a result of the Russian Revolution. The Chosŏn P'ŭrollet'aria Yesul Tongmaeng (KAPF, 1925–1935), headed by prominent

[9] See *Samch'ŏlli* 5:9 (1933):548–549.

leftists Kim Kijin (1903–1985) and Pak Yŏnghŭi (b. 1901), for example, was part of a larger communist movement in East Asia. Women writers too participated in leftist issues by portraying the plight of underprivileged laborers and tenant farmers.

Although they did not belong to KAPF, Pak Hwasŏng and Kang Kyŏngae surfaced as prominent women writers who focused on leftist/socialist issues. Kang Kyŏngae, in particular, is often singled out by literary critics in both South and North Korea, as well as in China, as an exceptional woman writer of the colonial period. Kang Kyŏngae's representative works include the serialized works of fiction *Ŏmŏni wa ttal* (*Mothers and Daughters*, 1931–1932) and *Ingan munje* (*Human Problems*, 1934). Her short story "Chiha ch'on" ("Underground Village," 1936) is often cited by critics as one of the best examples of proletarian literature of the marginalized. Since Kang Kyŏngae wrote the bulk of her work in Manchuria, the diaspora community of Chosŏnjok (Koreans in China) also claims her as one of its own. Chosŏnjok scholars and writers praise her "Sogom" ("Salt," 1934), for example, as a representative work of literature that deals with Jiandao, Manchuria.[10] The canonization of her works presents an interesting variation in the canonization of women's texts. Scholars during and following the colonial period have readily accepted her into the literary canon. The reason for their positive assessment of Kang Kyŏngae seems to be located in her alliance with the leftist socialist issues – one of the hegemonic movements of the 1930s along with cultural nationalism (*minjok chuŭi*).

Kang Kyŏngae's work concentrates on the plight of the impoverished peasant farmers and factory workers. Her first story, "P'agŭm" (Broken Zither, 1931), explores socialist issues through the evolution of the consciousness of the protagonists. Kang Kyŏngae also excels in the realistic prose that at times verges on the grotesque, especially revealed in her "Underground Village," effecting an Aristotelian catharsis. The desperate misery and despair in her works begs the question: why must there be such misery? This is the question textualized in *Human Problems*, and she explores it by portraying people placed in the most depressing situations imaginable. Then, through an exposition of family relationships, Kang Kyŏngae reveals the reality women faced in colonial Korea and the tragedy of family-centered lives. Her texts represent a kind of anti-love or anti-family discourse. Heroines who do attain independence and freedom sever ties with their loveless and hopeless relationships. Only a woman socially conscious and

---

[10] Chŏn Sŏngho, "Kang Kyŏngae ŭi changp'yŏn *Sogŭm* yŏngu," unpublished conference paper, Chaeoe uri minjok munhak ssimp'ojium, Yanbian, 8 August 1998.

unafraid of standing alone becomes truly free, as does the protagonist Ogi in "Mothers and Daughters."

Pak Hwasŏng first appeared on the literary scene in 1924 with her short story "Ch'usŏk chŏnya" ("Evening Before the Harvest Moon Festival"). Her next work, however, appeared in 1932, and she remained active throughout the 1930s. Her representative works include the historical fiction *Paekhwa* (*White Flower*, 1932), "Hongsu chŏnhu" ("Before and After the Flood," 1934), and "Kohyang ŏmnŭn saramdŭl" ("People without a Native Land," 1936). She engaged in direct criticism of the Japanese colonial government by portraying the lives of laborers and peasants. Her "People Without a Native Land," for example, concerns poor peasant farmers who leave their hometown for a northern part of Korea in search of a better place to live. She remained conscious of being labeled a woman writer and sought to find literary devices to overcome her gender restriction, such as portraying male heroes (unlike a majority of other women writers).

Along with the socialist theme of labor, the portrayal of motherhood became prominent in the late 1920s. Although she was initially actively involved with socialist groups, perhaps even guerrilla activities, Paek Sinae later concentrated on drawing a paradigm of Korean motherhood. Paek began her career as a primary-school teacher in the early 1920s. Soon expelled due to her involvement in socialist organizations, she traveled to Vladivostok, Japan, and Shanghai. Her international vision can be seen in works such as "Kkŏraei" ("Koreans," 1934), which concerns Koreans in Russia. Beginning in the late 1920s, perhaps unable to sustain her seditious public activities, she turned to literature – a road followed by many Korean intellectuals.

In "Chŏkpin" ("Destitution," 1934), she draws a portrait of a persevering, silent, but strong mother who will sacrifice herself for her family. Old One, the matriarch of "Destitution," struggles heroically to save her family despite hardships. She even delays relieving herself because she believes that her body filled with excrement will give her the strength to live. Like Ch'ae Mansik (1902–1950), the great writer of satire during the colonial period, Paek Sinae often resorts to irony and taps into the tradition of satire in Korean literature.

Although the writers from the first phase continued to write, they produced very few fictional narratives during this second phase. A comparison of Paek Sinae's "Destitution" and Kim Wŏnju's "Chagak" ("Awakening," 1926) reveals a variation of the strong and persistent motherhood image. Unlike the dedicated mother of "Destitution," who abandons her needs and desires for her family, the mother of "Awakening" leaves her child behind and opts, instead, to achieve personal success. The protagonist's position is particularly striking considering the *a priori* status of motherhood in Korea, subverting and challenging the existence of hegemony even within the texts of women writers.

Despite Kang Kyŏngae's success in negotiating a public space for herself, women writers continued to be rejected by the canonizers – including Paek Sinae, whose passion, according to Paek Ch'ŏl, cripples her ability to create stable, balanced works.[11] Even in cases of grudging acceptance, men sought to limit women's participation in literature by arguing for a distinction between literary topics for men and for women. Pak Hwasŏng, for example, was criticized as a writer who wrote "like a man." She was also accused of publishing another man's work as her work of fiction *White Flower*, since a woman "could not have written a historical novel."[12] The canonization and exclusion of women writers, therefore, continued to provide insights into literature, society, and gender.

THE THIRD PHASE: A ROOM OF ONE'S OWN

During this third phase, nonideological issues received increasing attention. The overall pattern of Korean literature in the late 1930s, in fact, required such interiorization, due to suppression and censorship by the increasingly militaristic colonial government. Writers had to limit themselves to nonpolitical/nonideological issues, ironically opening up a way for women writers to disengage themselves from the hegemonic in order to concentrate on women's issues. Some writers, consequently, turned to historical fiction. Chang Tŏkcho, for example, wrote "Hanya wŏl" ("Moon on a Leisurely Evening," 1938), focusing on the husband/wife relationship between Prince Yŏnsan (1476–1506, r. 1494–1506) and his consort Sin. Most of the women writers in this phase were born in the 1910s and debuted well into the 1930s and 1940s. Chi Haryŏn, for example, began to publish in 1940 with "Kyŏlbyŏl" ("The Farewell").

Morever, the family-bound and family-oriented women of the second phase began to question their inheritance. Women writers, therefore, began to textualize their new insights into love, marriage, family, motherhood, and career. They investigated woman's selfhood, as in Yi Sŏnhŭi's "T'angja" ("Prodigal Child," 1940) and Chi Haryŏn's "The Farewell" – establishing the interiorization of the feminine space as lovers, mothers, and wives.

---

[11] Paek Ch'ŏl, *Sinmunhak sajosa* (Singu munhwasa 1982), p. 409.
[12] See Carolyn So, Chapter 4 in "Modern Korean Fiction under Colonialism: Structure and Dynamic in the Works of Four Women Writers," Ph.D. dissertation, UCLA, 1995.

Women possessing a much bolder and more independent spirit appear in the texts of women writers, who moved from a position of dependence to a deliberate separation from traditional mores.

Radically departing from previous works, women as unconventional lovers begin to appear as a prominent literary theme. These lovers have abandoned the traditional norms in the sense that they are not legitimate wives. As bona fide family-oriented women of questionable repute, they reveal a change in the writer's perception of traditional morality. No longer suffocated by the moral strictures imposed on women, they simply stand their own ground, based on new ideas, without feeling obliged to justify themselves. These women protagonists take charge of their situation – often without men. Although women had stood alone in the past as the head of the family – as in much of the work by writers from the second phase – the women in the late 1930s do not complain about being without husbands. Instead, they choose to be without men. Love, in some form, any form, continues to be an obsession for these women.

A representative example of the new lover appears in the series on relationships (*maek*)[13] by Ch'oe Chŏnghŭi, *Chimaek* (*Earthly Ties*, 1939), *Inmaek* (*Human Ties*, 1940), and *Ch'ŏnmaek* (*Heavenly Ties*, 1941). Ch'oe Chŏnghŭi entered the literary scene in 1931 with "Chŏngdanghan sŭp'ai" ("Justified Spy"). The portrayal of a single mother and intellectual struggling to support her family in "Hyungga" ("Haunted House," 1937) continues in the *maek* series as the heroines of *Earthly Ties* and *Heavenly Ties*. In the first two parts of the *maek* series, the heroine has an illegitimate child and a lover who is dead and gone. In each case, the protagonist finds her path on her own. She rejects the possibility of establishing a comfortable home for herself and opts to survive alone. Her unconventional, romantic interest – the object of her desire is often a married man – suggests that she has stepped outside of the traditional moral bounds. She is essentially "a woman with the lamp of her heart always lit" (*maŭm ŭi tŭngpul ŭl hangsang palk'i go innŭn yŏja*). This phrase, from Ch'oe Chŏnghŭi's post-1945 work *Yŏja ŭi p'unggyŏng* (*Scenery of a Woman*, 1966), encapsulates the essence of the lovers and the tirelessly flirtatious heroine of that later work.

The figure of the woman with the lamp of her heart always lit continues in Yi Sŏnhŭi's "Yŏnji" ("Lipstick," 1938), where the newly wed wife considers beginning her life afresh with a lover. She opts for an independent life instead, however, because she fears that her new lover would hate her baby. In her "Prodigal Child," the heroine already has a fiancé but develops

[13] *Maek* refers, variously, to a network of relationships and paths.

a romantic interest in a suicidal lighthouse keeper. Yi Sŏnhŭi, active in the late 1930s, originally debuted in 1934 with *Purya yŏin* (*Woman without Evenings*). Her other representative works include "Maesobu" ("Prostitute," 1938), where she depicts the parasitical relationships between a prostitute, her family, and her customers. In another example, the battle between the sexes is taken to extremes in Yi Sŏnhŭi's "Yŏin to" ("City of Women," 1937),[14] where Amazonian women go out in search of a world inhabited by men in order to enslave them.

As evinced in works by Ch'oe Chŏnghŭi and Yi Sŏnhŭi, motherhood continues to be the main preoccupation for women writers. In much of their work it is motherhood – women as mothers – that allows them to conquer hardship and suffering to achieve financial and emotional independence. They choose their children over their lovers. In *Earthly Ties* and "Lipstick," the mothers leave their prospective lovers and future husbands, believing that their choice will ultimately be best for their children. Even legitimate wives choose unconventional lives, based on personal choice and freedom, while managing to escape irreparable personal ruin as a consequence. The wife in Ch'oe Chŏnghŭi's *Human Ties*, for example, leaves her husband temporarily for a lover after being rejected by her friend's husband. She eventually returns, following the profession of love by her friend's husband, and rejoins her husband. The newly wed wife in Yi Sŏnhŭi's "Lipstick" also leaves her husband for another man. The views of the prostitute Ch'aegŭm in Yi Sŏnhŭi's "Prostitute," however, provide an ironic contradiction to what it means to be someone's wife. Ch'aegŭm observes that the most fortunate life for a woman is becoming a legitimate wife.

Such a view illustrates the conflict between women's roles and duties during this period. Im Ogin's "Huch'ŏ ki" ("Record of a Second Wife," 1940) and "Chŏnch'ŏ ki" ("Record of the First Wife," 1941) explore the issue of being a proper wife. In "Record of a Second Wife," the protagonist has to raise someone else's children as a result of the first wife's death. She, however, readily bears the criticism of her nonconformist actions that show little respect for the previous wife. Then, in "Record of the First Wife," the abandoned first wife questions the validity of her husband's original love for her, since he left when she failed to produce heirs for him.

Implicit in this theme of unconventional women is a direct or indirect criticism of patriarchy and traditional gender roles that began in the first phase – regardless of whether one is a wife, a mother, or a lover. The texts

---

[14] Although a work of fiction, this is included in a volume of essays, revealing the unclear genre division during the colonial period. See Pang Ŭngmo, ed., *Hyŏndae Chosŏn munhak chŏnjip* (Chosŏn ilbo ch'ulp'anbu, 1936), 4.

of women writers remain critical of the double standard of patriarchy – men are free to have affairs, but women are all too readily chastised. Chi Haryŏn's "The Farewell" presents a psychological drama that unfolds as a result of the wife's direct criticism of her husband. After confronting her husband emotionally and intellectually, she finally recognizes his inferiority and servility. She bids farewell to him emotionally and stands completely alone. In "San kil" ("Mountain Path," 1942), Chi Haryŏn focuses on the hypocritical logic of patriarchy in the portrayal of a husband who casually explains away his affair as a temporary mistake. Kim Malbong's works, however, are much more conservative in their gender outlook. Although her first work "Sijip sari" ("Married Life with the In-laws") appeared in 1925, her next work "Mangmyŏng nyŏ" ("A Woman Refugee"), appeared some seven years later in 1932. In the later work, unconditional love reigns supreme over all else.

By this time the writers of the first phase had all but disappeared from the literary scene. Kim Myŏngsun had published a few poems, Kim Wŏnju had become a Buddhist nun, and Na Hyesŏk had written essays almost exclusively since the second half of the 1920s. Even socially committed writers such as Kang Kyŏngae, Pak Hwasŏng, and Paek Sinae were focusing largely on personal relationships and love during this phase. Pak Hwasŏng, for example, portrayed the plight of a young woman sold to an old man in "Onch'ŏnjang ŭi pom" ("Spring at the Spa," 1936). By the early 1940s, very few of these writers remained active. Even Chi Haryŏn, who debuted in December 1940 with "The Farewell," published nothing from April 1942 to August 1946. Indeed very few works by Korean writers were produced between 1942 and 1945, as the Japanese colonial government enforced the changing of Korean surnames in 1940 and the publication of all works in Japanese in 1941. In 1944, "comfort women" began to be recruited. In 1945, only three fictional works were published before Korea's liberation on 15 August.

THE LEGACY

During the colonial period, women writers moved textually from a position of being bound to the past to independence. Their works reveal the suppressive value systems of society as well as shifting gender roles. Women's responses changed, too, from struggling with the constraints of the past to standing on their own. In the early phase of modern literary activity, women writers attempting to establish a foothold in the male-centered field of literature met with enormous challenges. When a woman writer entered the public arena through publication, she became the target of public scrutiny. Her appearance, however, did not mean that the male-dominated literary circle suddenly saw her as an equal. Her text had to continue the negotiation within the boundary set forth by the dominant discourse, and she herself was often a token figure whose life and work were judged by others more powerful. The following poem, "Yuŏn" ("Will"), published in Kim Myŏngsun's *Fruits of Life*, reveals the frustrated voice of an early woman writer:

> Oh, Korea! When I part from you forever,
> Whether fallen headlong in a ditch
> Or blood splattered on a field,
> Abuse even my dead body.
> If that is still not enough for you,
> When someone like me is born the next time,
> Abuse her again as much as you can.
> Then we, despising each other,
> Will forever and ever part.
> You vicious place!
> You vicious place![15]

To justify her place in the literary world, then, the woman writer had to deal not only with literary issues but with the question of gender, as well, and her writings reveal that she participated alongside male writers while continuing the tradition of women writers. Certain conventions and traits found in the new fiction, for example, can also be found in works by pioneering women writers. Often a victim of bias and moral condemnation, she was acutely aware of her role and her legacy. The modern woman writer, nevertheless, differed from her predecessors. In premodern works by women, society did not offer any solutions for the woman's lot. She could only accept her fate and grieve silently. The newly emerging modern woman, however, had other options – at least theoretically – and she sought to deal with her situation in a new, seemingly modern, context. The woman writer was also more privileged than her female contemporaries, who remained largely illiterate and silent.[16] The woman writer was given a voice via her works and her reader became her audience. Since the woman writer endeavored to understand herself and her surroundings as a woman, most of her protagonists are women and her narrators take on

---

[15] Kim Myŏngsun, "Yuŏn," in *Saengmyŏng ŭi kwasil* (Hansŏng tosŏ chusik hoesa, 1925), p. 36.
[16] Even in the 1930s, for example, about 90% of women were illiterate. See Pak Yŏnghye and Sŏ Chŏngja, eds., *Hanguk kŭndae yŏsŏng yŏngu* (Sungmyŏng yŏja taehakkyo, 1987), p. 191.

a female perspective. Her environment, at times confusing and oppressive, is manifested through the voice of her heroines.

In the post-liberation period, quite a few women writers of the colonial period continued to engage actively in literature. Pak Hwasŏng, in particular, abandoned her intense concern with ideological issues to concentrate on the feminine space. The most prolific, probably, is Ch'oe Chŏnghŭi, who briefly explored socialist issues between 1945 and 1950 before returning to her thematic interest in women. The legacy of the early twentieth-century women writers continues in these women as well as in the exploration of femininity, gender roles, and criticism of patriarchal society.

CHAPTER 21

Late twentieth-century poetry by men

Peter H. Lee

Korea was liberated from Japanese rule on 15 August 1945. On the poetic front, the controversy between left and right that had raged in the
late 1920s and early 1930s revived in full force amid frantic groupings and
regroupings. Pressing concerns for the writers included a purging of the
vestiges of Japanese colonialism, self-criticism of pro-Japanese activities
by certain writers, either coerced or voluntary, and the recovery of the
mother tongue and establishment of a national literature. While the left
emphasized strong class consciousness and Marxist literature, the right
called for a defense of humanity and an emphasis on individuality. Before
hard-core leftists went north prior to the establishment of the Republic
of Korea (15 August 1948), the literary scene in Seoul was vibrant and
dynamic: poetry readings, open debates on literary and political issues, celebration of the publication of individual volumes of poetry or occasional
music appreciation sessions in coffee shops such as Dolce and Flower.
In short, two movements came into being: one advocating the restoration of Korean tradition and the other insisting on class literature for the
masses.

A separation of poetry and politics was the only means to preserve the
Korean language and literature during the colonial period – an inevitable
result of Korea's historical situation – and symbolism was a means of veiled
expression of political or national concerns. Fervor for political possibilities
and patriotic ardor prevented writers from objectively understanding the
true meaning of liberation and social formation. Subjective emotion found
expression in political verse of the time, devoid of aesthetic device, and the
absence of a leading theory led to the mechanical production of ideological
verse. Chŏng Chiyong declared that "if the poet's sensitivity is a biological
condition, why try to deny it?" In other words, the poet has an instinct to
go along with the prevailing ideology of the time, and Chŏng often spoke
of the "people's front" (*inmin chŏnsŏn*). Leftists proposed the liquidation
of the remaining vestiges of Japanese imperialism and feudalism and the

rejection of extreme right-wingers. Leadership, they insisted, must come from the working class – a return of political power to the masses.

The liberation, however, ushered in a wave of poetry of all kinds – beginning with such collections as *Haebang kinyŏm sijip* (*Collection in Celebration of Liberation*, 1945), including poets of both left and right (twenty-four pieces), and *Samil kinyŏm sijip* (*Collection in Commemoration of the March First Movement*, 1946) celebrating the return of patriots from abroad and praying for the repose of martyred nationalists. Some poets were determined to record events of their time; others sought to deepen their identification with traditional Korean values; still others drew variously on Western modernist verse in the hope of elevating their art beyond local concerns and restrictions. What united poets of all persuasions was the desire to voice their own authentic testimony regarding the moments of history.

GREEN DEER GROUP

Comprising the poems of Pak Tujin (1916–1998), Pak Mogwŏl (1917–1978), and Cho Chihun (1920–1968), *Ch'ŏngnok chip* (*Green Deer Anthology*, 1946) represents the work of three poets who had no blemish on their records during the colonial period. This anthology is often read as the foundation of a national poetry (*minjok si*). These three poets, each with a distinct individual voice, made their debut in 1939 but refused to publish after 1941 in protest against the Japanese ban on the use of the Korean language in literary works.

Pak Tujin

Pak Tujin's early poems are allegorical pieces masking his patriotic fervor or his vision of prelapsarian life. Often they build on a tension between innocence and experience, light and dark. By using such nature imagery as mountain, sea, sky, star, and river, he summons hope for a new life and a cosmos of perfect harmony: "Mountain, mountain, mountain, you have kept a long tedious silence for myriad years. Mountain, could I wait for the flame to leap out of your soaring peaks and prostrate ridges? Could I hope to see the day when foxes and wolves leap in joy with deer and rabbits to find bush clover and arrowroot?" ("Hyanghyŏn" ["Fragrant hills"], 1939). Pak relies for his effect on incantatory techniques – alliteration, consonance, assonance, and onomatopoeia – together with balanced structure, the rhythm and sonority produced by recurring sibilants, liquids, nasals, and trilled consonants, and, as well, word associations and rhetorical questions. The same devices recur in the later poem "Hae" ("Sun," 1949): "Rising sun, sun uprising, clean washed face of the comely rising sun; across the mountains, over the mountains consumed the dark, nightlong over the mountains ate up the dark, you comely uprising sun with ruddy unfledged face." Inversion of normal word order and repetition help the speaker express his mood. The poem transcends the world of logic, while its forceful rhythm creates a world full of energy and zest.

As political corruption and repression increased in South Korea, Pak's moral consciousness came to the fore and his poems from the mid-1960s reveal a strong historical and cultural consciousness that bears testimony to contemporary reality. This group of poems includes "Nŏksŭl p'ara" ("Soul-sellers," 1968) and "Sawŏl" ("April" 1969).[1] "Eighty percent servile spirit and the rest is gall" – so begins "Soul-sellers." The speaker registers indignation at what his nation has been as opposed to what it might be. "Gold, silver, ginseng . . . virgins" were traditional tributes sent to China by annual Korean missions. Indeed, Koreans sold themselves, their kin and ancestors. Devoid of self-awareness, integrity, and decency, they indulged in monetary appeasement and easy solutions to national and international affairs. As a poet, however, Pak will not be silenced by the organized brutality of soulless bureaucrats as they attempted to silence censors, remonstrators, scholars, and writers of the past. The literati in the Chosŏn dynasty used culture as an instrument of class domination and social mystification. Modern toadies, however, are outdoing their forebears and maintain their hegemony in the name of modernization and industrialization:

> A dagger pointed at me,
> A cup of poison to be drained,
> I must embrace you.

The poet's world in "Sawŏl" ("April") is the place of his origins where he examines his plight as it reflects that of every thinking Korean caught up in the reality of the time. His strong moral passion and nobility of mind are revealed in the interior landscape, and his total awareness communicates the measure of his faith and belief. There is hope of regeneration, a spiritual rebirth, for contemporary Korea. Flowers will blossom again in the poet – and in Koreans as well – when they have achieved a victory beyond suffering and sacrifice.

In other poems, the crane or deer represents the speaker, conscious of being a select disciple of one who will come. Indeed, after a vigorous

---

[1] For the four poems cited see *SL*, pp. 137, 143 (tr. Sammy E. Solberg), 151 and 153.

progress toward his aim he waits on a high mountain where the orchid blooms. The imagery of ascent, symbolic of the speaker's progress, stands for fulfillment following hardship. On the summit the speaker welcomes a bright dawn and the ocean – both mountain and sea representing the space of transcendence. Flowers (sometimes the rose) will open only for one who rejects the earth's darkness and waits for a miracle. Later Pak withdrew to the world of nature to discover its power in water-washed stones – the topic of some 200 poems, Pak's homage to nature as a creative force.[2]

In his essay on the spirit of poetry, Pak quotes Aristotle's *Poetics* and avers that poetry represents the world of imagination, that it is more philosophical and serious than history, that it deals with the universal, and that it cares not for what has happened but for what may happen.[3] Poetry prefers impossible probabilities, and poetic imitation is an imitation of inner human action. Pak Tujin finds distinctions between verse and prose meaningless. He stresses rhythm, regularity of recurrence, devised or intrinsic, and the power to endow images with meaning and secure their suggestiveness.

Pak Mogwŏl

The earlier poems of Pak Mogwŏl written in folk-song rhythm reproduce the local color of southeastern Korea with effortless grace and control, as in "Ch'ŏng noru" ("Green Deer").[4] Unlike traditional spring poems, "Green Deer" does not evoke feelings of melancholy, loneliness, or the passage of time through nostalgic recollection of bygone springs. Spring is full of life – snow melts, the birds are healthy, elms sprout, and a green deer watches. As in the classical *sijo*, the phrasing is clear, swift, and uncluttered, but still evocative, while the fragmented syntax facilitates rapid transitions. The poem evokes a quiet warm spring day veiled in mist, but only the poet can observe the rolling cloud in the deer's eyes. The poem progresses from things far away (distant hills) and an unperturbed state, symbolized by the color blue in "Blue Cloud Monastery," to a close-up. Moreover, as the view becomes closer, the poem uses fewer words: the last stanza in the original consists of just two syllables per line – *tonŭn / kurŭm* (A cloud / rolls). The landscape, the subject, and the sensibility are Korean, and the poem presents its images in a fresh, new way.

---

[2] Pak Tujin, *Susŏk yŏlchŏn* (Ilchisa, 1974) and *Sok susŏk yŏlchŏn* (Ilchisa, 1976).
[3] W. K. Wimsatt, Jr., and Cleanth Brooks, *Literary Criticism: A Short History* (New York: Vintage Books, 1957), pp. 25–27.
[4] *SL*, p. 164.

From the late 1950s Pak Mogwŏl abandoned the quiet hills to find material for his poetry in the urban experience of ordinary citizens. His later works, which tend to prefer open forms and looser measures, are marked by a plain, natural, often powerful diction. Pak was preoccupied with the plight of modern man, his entrapment, and the search for meaning in an inhuman world. Pak's view of life is that one should not judge right and wrong – an enlightened Daoist view. He defines "pure" (*sunsu*) as that which transcends social and utilitarian value and yields a sense of life, infinity, interiority, and fresh relationships. Poetry and life, Pak feels, are inseparable. As all art concerns how to live, no opposition exists between the poet and the ordinary person. Quoting Rilke's dictum, Pak contends that poetry comes from experience and the poet must wait until it comes into being. Agreeing with Frost that poetry "begins in delight and ends in wisdom,"[5] Pak stresses introspection, self-reflection, and subjectivity as opposed to science's emphasis on knowledge of the external world.

Pak has an angle of vision that seeks to discover the material for poetry in the commonest experience of quotidian life in Seoul and turn it into sudden flashes of knowledge. In "Tarŭn ipku" ("Another Entrance"), descending the steps to an underground walk, he muses: "They don't know the chill fatal loneliness / of the underground." In "Somyo" ("Sketch"): "People walk toward the tunnel, / Each holding a plastic umbrella / he cannot see." In "Changmat" ("Taste of Soy Sauce"), a staple seasoning in Korean food, the speaker declares:

> We live out a given life,
> Getting along somehow or other,
> But year after year soy sauce
> Tastes sweeter than honey.

In another group of poems the speaker contemplates aging and impending death as in "Hagwan" ("Lowering the Coffin") at a brother's funeral:

> I hear you call me;
> My voice does not reach you.
> This is a world where I hear the thud
> If a fruit falls.

In "Kyŏul sŏnja" ("Winter Fan"), he realizes: "Between the pink flower that adorned your lapel / And the white flower pinned at the same place, / A moment" – between a wedding and a funeral is only a moment. In

---

[5] Robert Frost, "The Figure a Poem Makes," in *Complete Poems of Robert Frost* (New York: Holt, 1962), p. vi.

"P'yŏngil sich'o" ("Selections on an Ordinary Day"), the speaker avers: "Poet or farmer, / One who polishes the stone / For his own grave grows wise." "Everyman gives one ear," the speaker says in "Sawŏl sangsun" ("Early April"), "to the other world." Pak compares his own poems to "a burnt meteorite," clean and light.[6] Like most people in East Asia, the poet accepts finality with serene resignation.

Cho Chihun

In a return to Buddhist and court life, Cho Chihun proposes that there are specific poetic words separated from everyday language and resorts to archaic word endings – *nora*, *ora*, and *soida*, as, for example, in "Sŭngmu" ("Monk Dance," 1939), "Kop'ung ŭisang" ("Ancient-style Garment," 1939), and "Nakhwa" ("Falling Flowers," 1946). His adjectives and adverbs suggest only a vague emotion, mostly in similes (*-ch'ŏrŏm*, *kat'i*, *tŭsi*, *inyang*), and cannot project the interior. Cho uses Buddhism for its poetic beauty and seldom develops it into a state of concentration as in the school of meditation. In "Monk Dance," his sound pattern overpowers the senses, and he inserts unnecessary particles (*-iya*, *-ira*). A stanza of two lines characterizes eight of his twelve poems in the *Green Deer Anthology*, and when translated into English these poems read like imitations of classic Chinese verse. He attempted to deal with contemporary events – in "Tabuwŏn esŏ" ("At Tabuwŏn"), for example, that concerns the Korean War – but his social poems were not successful.[7]

As a critic Cho defended pure poetry as poetry that will arouse a response from all humanity, and he associated it with a humanism that denies utility. Instead he stressed subjectivity, independence, and autonomy (although his own poems do not always achieve these qualities). Cho emphasized tradition, the exploration of the national soul, and completion of a national language, and he advocated pure poetry as national (*minjok*) poetry. Literature, he believed, purifies ideology and society.[8]

SŎ CHŎNGJU

Sŏ, the author of *Hwasa* (*Flower Snake*, 1938), published his second collection, *Kwich'okto* (*The Cuckoo*, 1948), with poems that are unmistakably his

---

[6] Pak's poems discussed here may be found in *SL*, pp. 168–187; for the original I have consulted *Pak Mogwŏl si chŏnjip* (Sŏmundang, 1984).
[7] For the original I have consulted Cho Chihun, *Cho Chihun chŏnjip*, 9 vols. (Nanam, 1996), I.
[8] Ibid. 2 contains his views on poetry.

in theme, diction, imagery, and symbolism. In "Kukhwa yŏp'esŏ" ("Beside a Chrysanthemum," 1948),[9] the speaker says that to bring a chrysanthemum (likened to his sister) to flower, the cuckoo has cried since spring, thunder has boomed, frost has fallen, and he has gone without sleep. The creation of a poem demands the same arduous preparation. It also demands the cooperation of animals, nature, and the poet. Like the image of a flower, especially the rose, in Pak Tujin's poems, the chrysanthemum is a symbol of life's long trials – opening only for those who reject darkness and expect a miracle. As one of the emblematic flowers of East Asia, the chrysanthemum is usually portrayed as being content to freeze rather than compromise its principles – it does not join the flowers of a fickle spring in their gaudy but transient show. If the subject matter is common, Sŏ's language and way of expression make the poem inimitable.

In "Sudaedong si" ("Poems of Sudaedong"), where a home built of earth stands, and in "Kolmok" ("Alleyway")[10] "where P'alman the beggar and Poktong live," we find poems of nostalgia for Sŏ's home village – as in earlier poems such as "Mirŏ" ("A Whispered Secret"), where he addresses "Suni, Yongi, and Nam gone to rest! / Open your firmly closed ash-hued gates and come out / See the flowerbeds lingering at the edges of spring sky,"[11] and in "Puhwal" ("Resurrection") where he sees the dead Suna among the young girls coming toward him at Chongno Square and asks her spirit to descend and appear before him.[12] His hometown is where "poor, broken-off / people watched the ground,"[13] and his abode is a hut. The speaker asks: "Let's rest before we go, friends, let's rest, then go."

Sŏ's quest for native tradition, Silla Buddhism and shamanism, and heroes and heroines of folktales and legends introduces us to the Bodhisattva Who Observes the Sounds of the World in Stone Grotto Cloister (Sŏkkuram) near Kyŏngju (the ancient Silla capital), the seventh-century Silla queen Sŏndŏk, and the chaste wife Ch'unhyang, all of whom speak in monologue. The first three lines in "Hanguk sŏngsa yak" ("Brief History of Stars in Korea") recall "Song of the Comet" (594) by Master Yungch'ŏn (see Chapter 3): "Fifteen hundred to a thousand years ago, / A star came down to help knights climbing Diamond Mountains and swept the path before

[9] *SL*, pp. 122 and 129.   [10] *SL*, pp. 129 and 125.
[11] Brother Anthony of Taizé, trans., *The Early Lyrics of Sŏ Chŏng Ju* (London: Forrest Books, 1993), p. 28.
[12] Ibid., p. 125.
[13] For Brother Anthony of Taizé's selections from *The Essence of Silla* (1960) see ibid., pp. 76–115; McCann, trans., *Selected Poems of Sŏ Chŏngju*, pp. 25–29, and Kevin O'Rourke, trans., *Poems of a Wanderer: Midang So Chong-ju* (Dublin: Daedalus, 1995), pp. 36–46. For the original I have consulted *Sŏ Chŏngju si chŏnjip*, 3 vols. (Minŭmsa, 1994).

their feet." The historical intervention of Neo-Confucianism and Japanese imperialism, inimical to the native tradition, banished the comet to the high heavens where only the speaker/poet can retrieve it. Saso, mother of King Pak Hyŏkkŏse; Paekkyŏl; an old cowherd (c. 702–737) who dedicated an azalea flower to Lady Suro, wife of Lord Sunjŏng – these stories illustrate how nature and human beings are one, as nature took part in human affairs in olden days.

Chilmajae sinhwa (*Tales of Chilmajae*, 1972) contains poems about the poet's hometown, where as a storyteller he narrates tales he has heard. *Ttŏdori ŭi si* (*Poems of a Wanderer*, 1975) offers the wisdom the poet has acquired over the course of seventy years. *Hagi ulgo kannal tŭre si* (*Poems after the Crane Left*, 1982)[14] contains versions of stories narrated by a traditional storyteller as in the literary miscellany on historical persons – such as the story of the female entertainer Hwang Chini; of the unconventional writer Kim Sisŭp (1435–1493); of the scholar-general Kwak Chaeu (1552–1617) who distinguished himself during the Japanese invasion; and of the painter and calligrapher Kim Chŏnghŭi (1786–1856). Some are entertaining, some are didactic – just like the prose portraits in the literary miscellany. In addition, Sŏ tells *pourquoi* stories – for example, why Koreans love to wear white garments. Sŏ is credited with exploring the hidden resources of the language, from sensual ecstasy to spiritual quest, from haunting lyricism to colloquial earthiness. Some consider Sŏ the most "Korean" of contemporary poets. Yet he appears to have been untouched by historical forces (even though he attempted suicide during the Korean War).

MODERNIST POETRY

Hubangi group

A slim volume entitled *Saeroun tosi wa simin ŭi hapch'ang* (*The New City and the Chorus of Citizens*, 1949) includes poems by Kim Kyŏngnin (b. 1919), Pak Inhwan (1926–1956), Kim Suyŏng (1921–1968), and others. They are poets with an urban sensibility – conscious of cities overcrowded with people and new commodities – and a sense of the fleeting and contingent, both exhilarating and dangerous.[15] Characterized by experiments with language and a longing for the West, their poems show a sense of anxiety about the impact of material civilization and a pessimistic worldview. They wished

---

[14] For translations from *Tales of Chilmajae* and *Poems of a Wanderer*, see O'Rourke, trans., *Poems of a Wanderer*, pp. 74–135.
[15] Peter Nicholls, *Modernisms: A Literary Guide* (Berkeley: University of California Press, 1995), p. 17.

to create a climate for new poetry, stimulated by the influx of Western literature, and to learn the current trends and future of world literature. When their activities were disrupted by war, they moved to Pusan, the temporary capital, and organized a coterie called the Hubangi Tonginhoe. They aimed to confront not only the modern war, with its terrifying power of destruction, but also modern civilization.

Kim Kyŏngnin and Kim Kyudong (b. 1925) articulated their notion of modernism. To the first, language is a means of experimentation with imagery drawn from real life and a vague idea of time. He upheld the use of intellectual imagery, the reception of existentialism, and positive confrontation with actuality. Kim Kyŏngnin defined poetry as a progressive thought and emphasized pictorial imagery, especially its plastic quality. Kim Kyudong defined poetry in modernist terms evoking Pound's logopoeia – "dance of the intellect among words," the role of the mind in art – as opposed to Kim Kirim's phanopoeia, the making of the bright image. Pak Inhwan, by contrast, cited spiritual anguish and awareness of history as his concerns. The uncertainty of the times was blamed for the dissociation of sensibility – an age of anxiety without hope. This group, however, was often criticized for their inability to digest the war, their uncritical acceptance of the West, and their lack of a viable method to explain their practice (as well as their failure to analyze society).[16] Technique alone, without the reform of consciousness, can achieve little. Pak's "Mongma wa sungnyŏ" ("A Rocking Horse and a Lady"), for example, mentions Virginia Woolf and the English word "pessimism"; "Sarainnŭn kŏsi ittamyŏn" ("If there are Living Things") quotes the first three lines from Eliot's "Burnt Norton" as the epigraph, but its significance is muted. "Ŏrin ttal ege" ("To my Young Daughter"), written in Pusan, is sentimental and resorts to such clichés as "your eyes are blue as the lake."[17]

Most of the new generation in the 1950s experienced the horror of war as students and later as soldiers (Kim Suyŏng, for example). Far from being able to enjoy the fruits of liberation, Korea faced a more formidable problem than ever before: division of the country. The armistice, in failing to bring about unification, simply added a new set of problems. Conscious of the political, social, and moral chaos caused by the war and its aftermath, a cluster of young writers arose to reject this chaotic world and challenge the ruling literary conventions. The war made the traditional lyric, especially the Green Deer tradition, look out-of-date. For the war was the first modern

---

[16] Han Kyejŏn et al., *Hanguk hyŏndae sironsa yŏngu*, pp. 252–282.
[17] Pak Inhwan, *Pak Inhwan sijip: mongma wa sungnyŏ*, pp. 8–10, 41–46, and 126–128.

conflict fought in Korea: a war for everyone, soldiers and schoolboys alike. The dilemma of young writers in the early 1950s is reflected in the poets of the Hubangi group. This group and later ones, more successful, repudiated the matter and manner of prewar verse that no longer reflected the contemporary state of society or the disintegration of values. Some began with a dire criticism of postwar Korea, scathingly analyzing the emptiness of modern life and illuminating their works with bitter irony. Others intended to shock the reader into awareness of contemporary idiocy and injustice. The modernist movement they launched was a revolt, in both form and content, that relentlessly pursued variety and individuality. Poverty of thought or shallowness of vision, however, cannot be cloaked by a manipulation of texture. Often experiments in form and language resulted in nothing more than flat prose, the writing of which has been likened by Frost to playing tennis without a net. Postwar poets who contributed to the modernization of the Korean language and poetry include Kim Suyŏng (1921–1968), Kim Ch'unsu (b. 1922), and their successors like Hwang Tonggyu (b. 1938), Chŏng Hyŏnjong (b. 1939), and others.

Kim Suyŏng

Although Kim's poetic career is usually divided into works written before the student revolution of April 1960 and those written after, his second published poem, "Kongja ŭi saenghwallan" ("Hard Life of Confucius," 1946), hints at his characteristic theme and technique:

> Friends, I'll now look steadily at
> The physiologies of matter and matter,
> Their number and limit,
> Their stupidity and lucidity
> And then I'll die.

"I will now look steadily at . . . matter . . . and die" recalls Confucius' remark: "In the morning hear the Way, in the evening die content" (*Analects* 4:8). The poet will confront reality and understand it; he wants to look at things steadily, not in a commonsensical but in an uncommon way, by recourse to an uncommon use of a common language. All established language and fixed usage are dishonest, Kim says. Hence he seeks to exercise freedom through an unconventional perception of objects in a new diction. He views established facts as his enemy – his ideal language is one that flees from facts. Beginning with a need for the integrity of self, he rejects customary feelings that demand alienation and refuses to debase human values.

One of his earlier poems, "Tallara ŭi changnan" ("The Game on the Moon," 1953), expresses the sorrow of the disenfranchised urban petit-bourgeois as he watches a child at play. A child spinning a top in a wealthy family that looks like "another world" is likened to a game on the moon. Spinning is miraculous, but the poet's survival in a metropolitan city is miraculous too. He sees his own image in a top – an image that has somehow survived:

> When I think about it, the top is sad –
> For the power that propels you and me to spin,
> For some common cause, I must stifle my sobs.

In "Ha kŭrimja ka ŏpta" ("Ha, There is No Shadow," 1960), written a month before the April 1960 revolution, Kim declares that

> our battle fills heaven and earth.
> A democratic battle must be fought democratically.
> As there is no shadow in heaven,
> There is no shadow in a democratic battle.

In "P'urŭn hanŭl ŭl" ("Blue Sky"), he screams for freedom – political freedom:

> One who has ever soared
> For the sake of freedom
> Knows
> Why the lark sings
> Why freedom reeks blood
> Why a revolution is lonely
>
> Why revolution
> Has to be lonely.

The poet is a born revolutionary, but revolution cannot be had simply by envying the lark or thinking about it. The poet fights against a modern society that curbs free action, freedom of speech, to prevent him from indicting the status quo and the reigning political machine. Kim's longing for freedom is absolute with no room for compromise.

The central images in his last poem, "P'ul" ("Grass," 1968), are grass and wind. A first reading may identify grass with people and winds with outside forces, but such a reading cannot withstand close analysis. In stanza 1, grass is passive and the winds active: the grass lies down, weeps, lies down again, perhaps representing the existential conditions of despair and sorrow. In stanza 2, the grass is active: it lies down, rises, and weeps more quickly than the wind, implying that despair and sorrow are not controlled by outside forces. Stanza 3 synthesizes the previous two stanzas: the grass lies down later than the wind, but rises before the wind. It rises before the wind but weeps later than the wind and laughs before the wind. This paradox seems to transcend every theory of life. The last line, "Cloudy – the root lies down," suggests liberation from duality. Here the grass is released from the dialectic of lying down / rising and weeping / laughing.[18]

In his essay "Siyŏ ch'imŭl paet'ŏra" ("Poetry, Spit it out!", 1968), Kim remarks that the poet is one who writes, not criticizes, poetry. Poetry must have a dialectical unity of form and content. One writes a poem not with the brain or heart, but with one's whole body. Rejecting the limits of 1930s modernism, with its suppression of ideology, its solitude of the lyric speaker, and its sentimentalism, Kim espouses both reality and artistic quality and divests himself of prejudice and established ideas. Fierce honesty is the poet's responsibility, and he accepts the "immature" state of Korean society – immaturity arising from lack of freedom. "You must push it forward, with your whole body and with all your strength," he says, referring to the inseparable unity of form and content. Alluding to Heidegger's "Origin of the Work of Art," Kim says an adventure in poetry means a "disclosure of the world." In Heidegger's words:

The art work opens up in its own way the Being of beings. This opening up, i.e., this disconcealing, i.e., the truth of beings, happens in the work. In the art work, the truth of what is has set itself to work. Art is truth setting itself to work. What is truth itself, that it sometimes comes to pass as art? What is this setting-itself-to-work?[19]

If poetry is an adventure, its nature lies in a tension between disclosure and concealment, world and earth.

Kim understood modernism not as the mere exposure of sensational avant-gardism, but as the spirit's attitude as it makes sense of reality. He condemned frivolous modernism as the worship of cheap fashion. He also scorned experiment for experiment's sake, which he labeled as fraud. Technique must be accompanied by conscience, and Kim advises poets to confront the problem that is immediate to them. It is the poet's conscience that becomes the ground for a pursuit of modernity. Art, Kim avows, is a pursuit of the impossible, hence it is disquieting. His poetry is a record of

---

[18] For a comparative reading of literary *Zhuangzi* and Kim's poems, see Kim Hyesun, "Munhakchŏk Changjia wa Kim Suyŏng ŭi sidamnon pigyo yŏngu," pp. 151–193; esp. 186–193 for a discussion of "Grass."

[19] Martin Heidegger, *Poetry, Language, Thought*, trans. Albert Hofstadter (New York: Harper & Row, 1971), p. 39.

that struggle. Moreover, his gift of irony and commitment to the creative power of language often turn his frustration into startling revelations.[20]

Kim Ch'unsu

Kim Ch'unsu (b. 1922) is one of the most original and prolific of modern poets. Making his debut in 1947, he had already published five volumes of verse by 1960 and two volumes of critical essays on poetry. Realizing in his earlier works that a poetic idea could only be expressed in a concrete image, he was on the side of the image, not the world, and tried to find a name for it. In "Kurŭm kwa changmi" ("The Cloud and the Rose"), he tries to harmonize the traditional and the Western in the rose that one of Kim's favorite Western poets, Rilke, called "pure contradiction" (*reiner Widerspruch*).[21] Kim realized that his interior had been cracked, he says, when the cloud came to him through his senses; but the rose arrived as an idea, a present from a guest, a taste for the exotic, as the poets in the 1920s sought inspiration in a faraway West. In "Kkot" ("Flower"), the flower must be seen as a flower, nothing else. Kim called this the "poetry of perception" (*insik*):

Until I spoke his name,
he had been
no more than a mere gesture.

When I spoke his name,
he came to me,
and became a flower.[22]

Kim attempts, not to introduce emotion or will, but to describe the object's existence by describing its form. In "Kkot ŭi somyo" ("Sketches of a Flower 1"), however, the festival of ideas comes to him "as a remote remembrance."[23] A certain idea can be conveyed through an image, but what lies beyond language? Remove meaning, and a word collapses. Sometimes Kim gave words a meaning – although he struggled not to – and sometimes not. Then he learned to delete ideas from words, because a metaphorical image

[20] Kim Suyŏng, *Kim Suyŏng chŏnjip*, 2:253, where the poet cites a remark attributed to Robert Graves (1895–1985), "As long as the world maintains freedom, confusion that goes with it should be allowed." Kim Chuno thinks that remark has inspired the poet's notion about it (*Tosisi wa haech'esi*, p. 57). For a collection of critical essays on Kim Suyŏng see Hwang Tonggyu, ed., *Kim Suyŏng ŭi munhak* (Minŭmsa, 1983). For translations of Kim's poems discussed, see *SL*, pp. 191–212.
[21] Rainer Maria Rilke, *Sämtliche Werke* (Wiesbaden: Insel, 1957) 2:185.
[22] Jong-Gil Kim, trans., *The Snow Falling on Chagall's Village: Selected Poems by Kim Ch'un-su* (Ithaca: Cornell East Asia Program, 1998), p. 26.
[23] Ibid., p. 30.

is only a means for an idea. What he desires is an image for its own sake. Description, Kim says, does not mean drawing a scene itself as it is but selecting elements of a scene and letting logic and association creep in. Then the object's form crumbles and the object itself disappears – the birth of a "poem of no meaning." The essence of such poetry should be sought not in the figurative image but in the descriptive. His "formal beauty" means the exclusion of meaning.[24]

In "Ch'ŏyong tanjang" ("Fragments on Ch'ŏyong"), which presents a dream and fantasy filled with childhood, Kim again avoids worldly images; instead he points to purity and objectivity. He wishes to show, he says, an impressionist's sketch, a Cézanne-like abstraction, the action painting of Jackson Pollock: "a poetry that has no logic, a display of free associations or momentary fantasies." He wishes to see the color of nothingness – for him there is no image, only nothingness. Kim rejects the human point of view. Instead he seeks a stage akin to that of nonaction in the Daoist philosophy of Laozi and Zhuangzi. Above all Kim is intent on formulating a poetics for a type of poetry – another form of pure poetry – that opposes committed poetry. A critic has observed: "What stands out throughout his search is his determination to get down to the concrete, to that which lies at the bottom of our experience of self and the world."[25] One feels an exhilarating freshness in Kim's poetry not just from his new technique – including a number of exotic Western terms and names such as Archaeopteryx, Gethsemane, Cana, Shestov, Unamuno, Medea – but because it asks us to open our heart, destroy the rational frame of understanding, and experience paradox beyond the obvious and figurative.

Hwang Tonggyu

The early poems of Hwang Tonggyu (b. 1938) reflect his interior journey with its struggles and humiliations. In these poems one finds recurrent motifs such as waiting, loneliness, wandering, and the journey:

> Every night a dream of shipwreck
> Shook me awake at midnight. I drank
> Young wine and went back to sleep.
> Every morning I remembered the blinding sunlight.
>   ("Four Twilight," stanza 3)

---

[24] See Kim Ch'unsu, *Kim Ch'unsu si chŏnjip*, 2 vols. (Minŭmsa, 1994) 2:499–531 for his thoughts on poetry.
[25] *SL*, pp. 214–215.

His scope then expands to include the state of South Korea in the late 1960s and 1970s. The country Hwang knows is a land ruled by whim and decree where existence is marginal and extinction stalks every man. In "Samnam e naerinŭn nun" ("Snow Falls in the South," 1967), Hwang contemplates the defeat of Chŏn Pongjun (1854–1895), a leader of the Tonghak peasant uprising:

> Pongjun is weeping, illiterate, illiterate,
> Utterly illiterate.
> If only he knew how to read the classics,
> If only he knew how to cry softly!

If Chŏn had remained a farmer without demanding social or political reform in the interests of the people, he would not have been beheaded. Had he received a classical education, however, like a member of the ruling class, would he have dared to attempt reforms that were destined to fail? His failure was the epitome of the Korean tragedy, a tragedy that included the collapse of the old order, the subjugation of the nation, and finally its division. Hwang therefore views history at a distance, with a sense of irony, for the situation has not changed after some eighty years. His country is still ruled by whim and decree, by power and terror. Bearing testimony to the corruption of justice, he will live on to express his compassion for humanity. In his later poems, images range from the barbed wire besieging his consciousness to snowflakes that fall from the sky. The snowflakes symbolize consciousness, purification, and the power of the imagination:

> Ah, those are sick words.
> My soles shiver.
> I'm determined to become a simple man!
> When dry winds,
> Daylong,
> Chase snow here and there,
> In the evening
> Every snowflake is muddy –
> When the sun-shaped sun suddenly sets,
> My dream shattered,
> Prostrate on the ground,
> I wipe my eyes, nose, and mouth.
> Terrifying even to myself,
> Am I turned into
> Muddy snow
> Driven about and trampled again?

"I'm determined to become a simple man," says the speaker in "Kyeŏmnyŏng ha ŭi nun" ("Snow under Martial Law"); but can a poet afford to do this, even if he knows he will turn into "Muddy snow / Driven about and trampled again"? There is nothing idealistic in the poem. Its conversational tone, disjunctive progressions, rapid transitions, and reliance on symbol and a sequence of emotions for meaning – all serve to arouse analogous emotions in the reader. The speaker shows no feeling of piety toward history; it is merely terrifying, and these "sick words" make one's "soles shiver."²⁶

In the cycle titled *P'ungjang* (*Wind Burial*, 1982–1995), consisting of seventy poems, Hwang confronts death in order to explore the meaning of life with fresh diction and striking imagery. Wind burial is a traditional practice in the western and southern parts of Korea. The corpse is carried to a small uninhabited island and placed under a makeshift roof. When it has dried sufficiently, it is buried with ceremony. (The practice is prohibited now for sanitary reasons.) Hwang says he wishes to tame death slowly and make it his own. He therefore stages his own death: by performing a symbolic death, he postpones a real death. As if he were leaving for a trip, he asks in Poem 1:

> When I leave the world, let me have a wind burial,
> Dressed in plain clothes, lest I should feel uneasy,
> With an electronic watch still running on my wrist.
> Put me in a leather bag
> So that I won't feel too cold.

He then reaches an island – a connecting point between heaven and earth viewed as a cosmic womb, a place where a passage from death to rebirth takes place. A vessel that carries the speaker is a boat (*pae*), a homophone for stomach (*pae*). Removing all his accessories, including clothes and shoes, represents a process of purification so that the speaker can return to the original state:

> Let me cover my body with wind like a blanket,
> Without makeup or promise of redemption,
> Let me be tucked in with the wind.
> And let me play with the wind
> Until my blood dries up.²⁷

---

²⁶ For a translation of Hwang's poems see *SL*, pp. 265–285. I have consulted the original in Hwang Tonggyu, *Hwang Tonggyu si chŏnjip*, 2 vols. (Munhak kwa chisŏngsa, 1998).
²⁷ Hwang Tonggyu, *P'ungjang: Hwang Tonggyu yŏnjak sijip* (Munhak kwa chisŏngsa, 1995); Grace Loving Gibson and Hwang Tong-gyu, trans., *Wind Burial: Poetry by Tong-gyu Hwang* (Laurinburg,

This is a rite of evaporation – of ascension. Through contrastive images of heaven and earth, past and present, fire and water, the poet implies extinction and the rebirth of existence. With the sound of self-destruction, existence is freed from all attachment and restraint (Poem 26). Outside and inside abolished, the distinction between Self and Other disappears (Poem 40). The ecstasy attained when he throws himself open is likened to the image of a maple tree reflected in the snow (Poem 36). Gradually the speaker experiences annihilation of the self. He then attains a state with no bulk or weight, lightness itself (Poem 59), a peaceful rest (Poems 22 and 49). To die, as the Korean expression goes, is to leave (*ttŭda*) the world. *Ttŭda*, however, also means to "float."

Chŏng Hyŏnjong

The recurrent concerns in the early work of Chŏng Hyŏnjong (b. 1939) include the question of death, life's emptiness, inescapable boredom, and frustration. If death is the only absolute truth, how should one live? His favorite images – wind, fire, sand, and desert – possess both the destructive force to turn life into sand and the productive force to blow vitality into life: wind blows inside to evoke fear of our finitude and blows outside to awaken our dormant consciousness. The poet's positive wonder at life's emptiness is expressed in "waterdrops of the rainbow land" – in his engagement with life, he can transform pain into a festival.[28] Life is compared to the wind frolicking in the void, a gratuitous movement that is aptly likened to dance – and to dance fervently is to live well in rapture. The will to live is proportional to the intensity of existence. Chŏng wishes to affirm the possibility of a world other than the one he inhabits: "When I move toward something outside myself, I always move toward myself . . . My life is a writhing desire to be born repeatedly in the womb we call the external world. Likewise, the objective world fears to be born endlessly within my womb. (Let us call this the imagination.)"[29]

From "Nanŭn pyŏl ajŏssi" ("I am a Star Uncle," 1978) and "Han kkot-songi" ("A Single Blossom," 1992), Chŏng's matter and manner change from modernist opaque diction imbued with philosophical gloom to a more relaxed and natural approach. Everything in nature offers occasion for sensual pleasure if you but open your body. In "A Single Blossom,"

N.C.: St. Andrews Press, 1990), p. 24. For his comments on his own poetry see Hwang Tonggyu, *Naŭi siŭi pit kwa kŭnŭl* (Chungang ilbosa, 1994).
28 *SL*, pp. 288–289.
29 Chŏng Hyŏnjong, *Chŏng Hyŏnjong chŏnjip*, 2 vols. (Munhak kwa chisŏngsa, 1999) 1:106.

flesh is a window through which we glimpse the primordial: our home. The throbbing movement of impulse is a blossom of flesh rooted in the uncontrollable urge and the promise of sensual joy:

> We live in the scintillating flesh,
> the ambling window through which
> we view the primordial,
> the vortex of energy that
> swells with the heave of a bellows,
> and makes the flesh bloom.
> I feel a poem coming on! I have a blossom.[30]

Fondly he describes the naked man's ecstasy in sensual pleasure as he delights in the resilience he feels when he walks on a dirt road or when he wishes to become a fish ("Pabo Manbogi" ["Idiot Manbok"]). Now the breath of life and cosmos are one: wind becomes the breath of life. He expresses the unity of self and things, their complex structure, their mysterious world. We must be humble, he says, before the sacredness of all creation. The art of seeing things with playful laughter is captured well in his diction – indeed, he starts a rebellion against everyday language with his wit, parody, and irony in order to overturn customary usage.[31]

In spring he too burns with the flaming red of azaleas ("Pome" ["In Spring"]).[32] By peering into the eyes of a goat, "I revert / to my own nature" ("Na ŭi chayŏn ŭro" ["Natureward"]).[33] Through the throbbing pain of a bee sting, his body merges with "nature in its abyss / of vastness" ("Pyŏl e ssoigo" ["The bee sting"]).[34] Trees are a source of life: when he sees a fallen tree he too falls ("Namu yŏ" ["O Tree"]),[35] because we breathe with the leaves and sink our roots into the ground with theirs. In "Hwanhamnida" ("Dayshine"), his mind runs to a persimmon-laden tree and ripens brilliantly.[36] Holding a fresh-laid egg, he says:

> The hallowed stirrings of life,
> I who hold the universe in my hand –
> I am made glorious!
> Never before has the earth
> Buoyed up my footsteps.[37]

---

[30] Wolhee Choe and Peter Fusco, trans., *Day-Shine: Poems by Chong Hyon-jong* (Ithaca: Cornell East Asia Program, 1998), p. 76.
[31] Yi Kwangho, ed., *Chŏng Hyŏnjong kip'i ilkki* (Munhak kwa chisŏngsa, 1999), pp. 91–330.
[32] Chŏng Hyŏnjong, *Chŏng Hyŏnjong chŏnjip* 2:41.   [33] Choe and Fusco, trans., *Day-Shine*, p. 26.
[34] Ibid., p. 99.   [35] Chŏng Hyŏnjong, *Chŏng Hyŏnjong chŏnjip* 2:51–52.
[36] Choe and Fusco, trans., *Day-Shine*, p. 33.   [37] Ibid., p. 65.

By looking into grass he discovers universe, nirvana, and salvation ("P'ul ŭl tŭryŏdabonŭn il iyŏ ["Looking into the Grass"]). He builds his nest in the birds' wings and declares:

> When the total self is in motion,
> it alleviates burden and wound.
> What, then, can be better than flight
> that moves with the mind?
> ("Sae hant'e kidaeŏ" ["Leaning on Birds"])[38]

"As poetry breathes into us," he declares, "our spirit leaps and soars, also released from our heaviness." He breaks the quotidian links between things to view the world in a fresh light. Unlike Frost, who is intent on building fences and mending walls, Chŏng rejoices when he sees a hole in a wall.

> Through this hole,
> the toil of squirrels or children – does it matter? –
> flows an ecstasy akin to finding salvation;
> flows an atmosphere which renders divine sanctions inane.
> Oh ho!
> I shall generate holes in every wall
> with the squirrels
> with the children.
> ("Tame ttullin kumŏng ŭl pomyŏn" ["When I See a Hole in a Wall"])[39]

His latest volume, _Kalchŭng imyŏ saemmul in_ (_Thirst and Spring_, 1999), explores the mutual functions of thirst and spring, like the link between the festival and pain cited earlier, and shows an existential thread between the two. Both thirst and spring are related to water, the origin of life. Here the speaker often addresses "you" (_nŏ_), a dual sign of lack and sufficiency – you are the source and condition of my lack and sufficiency, my ecological condition. I too, however, am your condition: you, my existential condition, are within me. Discovery of correspondence forms the center of his poetic project – the expansion of a dialogic space. "You," such as sunlight, are absent as form but enable things to appear ("Ach'im haetppit" ["Morning Sunlight"]). Your voice is that of life – the signs of small existences in the universe ("Nŏ ŭi moksori" ["In Your Voice"]). His intent is to establish a cosmic rapport, to open himself to others, to merge the self into cosmos through transformation and participation.

Time figures as another important topic. Released from historical time, he experiences cosmic time: the moment as a space of dancing infinity. The time a particular flower blooms is the first time and the time a particular cock crows is also the first: called "green, green [new] time" (_p'ŭrŭrŭn putsigan_),

[38] Ibid., pp. 90, 106, 93.   [39] Ibid., p. 87.

it is the primordial time reborn whenever it returns to the beginning of the world. On seeing a calf, for example,

> a calf
> just a month old
> frolics about.
> Because of you
> this world first spun
> a month ago.[40]

Infinity of cosmic time also means infinity of space. The cosmos is conceived, not in terms of center and periphery, but as a large space enveloping continually smaller spaces or a connected structure of many centers. From the perspective of the cosmos, time and space are born anew always. The words "The letters [of the alphabet] I am writing now are a fossil I have discovered" ("Sigan ŭn turyŏum e ssayŏitta" ["Time Enveloped by Fear"]) lead Chŏng to the comprehension of time as vast and primordial. He then compares the speed of a snail with that of a machine to show that speed, after all, is relative. Throughout, his fresh diction captures the resilience of life – moments of ecstatic movement of living things large and small. "We are truly alive when our awareness and receptivity are fresh and keen," Chŏng remarks in his credo ("Sum kwa kkum" ["Breath and Dream"] 1).[41]

DISSIDENT POETRY

In the 1980s there emerged a group of postmodern poets who confronted socioeconomic reality and tried to depict it objectively. Indicting the dehumanization of the industrial age brought about by the influx of multinational capitalism, they wish to reflect pluralistic worldviews and the complexity of postmodern experience. Skeptical of conventional belief in truth and good and evil – there is little to trust – they refrain from judgment and merely report. Their technique is to plagiarize, quote, gather, reassemble, and display – from newspaper and journal articles, captions of pictures, charts, diagrams, advertisements, musical scores, comics, arabic numerals. As ironic critics, they propose that what they have assembled is a work of art consisting of heterogeneous material compiled playfully. Hence they do not separate life from art. Fragments of experience are connected randomly – a subversion of poetic conventions such as the hierarchy of genres, the cult

---

[40] Ibid., p. 16.
[41] See Yi Kwangho, ed., *Chŏng Hyŏnjong kip'i ilkki*, pp. 363–370 for the original; for the translation see Choe and Fusco, trans., *Day-Shine*, pp. 111–115.

of authorship and originality, and the capacity of language to render truths about the world. In "Hanguk saengmyŏng pohŏm hoesa Song Irhwan ssi ŭi ŏnŭnal" ("One Day in the Life of Mr. Song Irhwan of the Korean Life Insurance Company"), Hwang Chiu (b. 1952) begins with the date, the temperature, what Song has bought on that day, comics, his belongings, and does not present the speaker's voice until the last line. "O Beirut, O Beirut" consists mostly of newspaper articles, as does "Simin" ("Missing Persons"):[42]

> Kim Chongsu: left home in May 1980,
> not heard from since; call-up papers arrived November 3;
> return awaited; anyone knowing him please contact his sister
> Tel. 829-1551

After two more such items, the poem concludes: "I squat down / and shit." This brand of postmodern poetry practiced by Hwang and others is called *haech'e si*, literally, the poetry of deconstruction. A poetry of open form, it resorts to pastiche, collage, and the schizoid experience of urban dwellers.

Urban poetry – sometimes considered together with the poetry of open form as a kindred type – has overcome the poetry of labor and politics and is practiced by a group belonging to a "new practical learning school" (*sin sirhak p'a*). They value the smallest detail: concreteness won back from the fiction of false consciousness that prevents people from recognizing their true alienation and exploitation. These poets try to feel actuality with their skin, a recovery of individuality against a collective body. Sometimes they wish to show freedom from all oppressive structures, a lightness of existence unencumbered by the pious and serious. The repetitive mechanism of life in the city, however, anonymous and uniform, leaves only a feeling of transience – as the image of a dayfly seems to indicate. The world is a husk. Is there anything more ordinary than ugliness? one asks. The city is the site of ordinariness and modernity, as Pak Mogwŏl and Kim Suyŏng discovered earlier. Oppressed by the tyranny of modern life in a world of bewildering complexity, everything seems transient and ruined, everything is disposable, invoking a strong sense of alienation, dissolution, and absurdity. Although their observation is not always accurate, they seek to expose the impoverished ethos behind the façade of city life.

The juxtaposition of heterogeneous elements from different times produces both simple and complex effects – as in Chang Kyŏngnin's "Ch'ŏnggyech'ŏn yukka" ("Ch'ŏnggye Sixth Street"), where four martyred

---

[42] Brother Anthony of Taizé, trans., "Hwang Ji-u," *Korean Literature Today* 4:3 (1999):38.

Confucian ministers from the fifteenth century are portrayed as taking a walk, heads lowered, through the pleasure quarters in the back alleys of Sixth Street. In "Kanjŏp p'uri k'ik" ("Indirect Free Kick"), a description of a soccer match between the Korean and Brazilian teams (on a TV screen) is juxtaposed against four key historical dates for Koreans: the independence movement of 1 March 1919; the liberation of 15 August 1945; the beginning of the Korean War on 25 June 1950; and the military coup of 16 May 1961. A frivolous and ironic spirit is found, for example, in Pak Namch'ŏl's "Chu kido mun" ("Lord's Prayer") with its tension between sublime language and the degraded world of human beings. The city is viewed as ugly, disorderly, corrupt, a place where history is "a condom discarded after an unconditional use" (Yi Yunt'aek). Some write about themselves with candor; sometimes their characters are monuments to maladjustment. Some works are comic, playful, impromptu, even blasphemous, obsessed with surface, novelty, style for style's sake. Their language is allusive, parodic, wrangling. The distance between high and low literature seems to dissolve here, engendering a kind of paraliterature.[43]

POETRY OF ENGAGEMENT

Some of the poets who came of age after the liberation attempted to assimilate elements of Korean history, both its high and its low points, as well as the contemporary scene. Their imagination was fired by the events and issues of their time – especially the vicious repetition of history represented by the division of the country and its attendant wave of repression and censorship.

Sin Tongyŏp

Sin Tongyŏp (1930–1969), who made his debut in 1959, regrets the significant loss of the innocence of earlier times, as the harmonious life of Korean agrarian society was crushed by imperialist powers, as in "Hyang a" ("To Hyang," 1959):

> Keep life simple as wild asters,
> as when you weeded bean rows, barefooted.
> Let us go back to our primitive land,
> to the village dance of legend-rich past,
> danced under the moon with swirling skirts,
> to the fresh earliness of the rippling stream,
> to the land of our heart.[44]

---

[43] For a discussion on this section see Kim Chuno, *Tosisi wa haech'esi*, pp. 11–215.
[44] *SL*, p. 233.

Sin fondly evokes rural plants such as the day lily ("Wŏnch'uri" ["Day Lily"], 1963), in which he hears the voice of his ancestors in an age of innocence unsullied by modern civilization, as in the Adamic myth in American literature:

> I hear the tap
> echoing down the ages
> and sense the dancers of old,
> the smell of bean soup.[45]

In "Kkŏpttegi nŭn kara" ("Husk, Go Away," 1967), he likens the oppressed to the grain of the country and the oppressors to empty husks. Sin oscillates, however, between utopian nostalgia and a concern with contemporary events. The use of past events and figures, especially folk heroes who mirror the mind of a historical period, is a recurrent device in modern poetry. In his narrative poem of some 4,800 lines, *Kŭmgang* (*The Kŭm River*, 1967), Sin identifies himself with the courage and conviction, devotion and toil, and ultimate martyrdom of the heroes of the Tonghak peasant uprising. Sinhanŭi from Ch'ungch'ŏng province is his alter ego, and he meets Chŏn Pongjun, two years his senior, in a Seoul inn and the two swear to be brothers. Sin's special use of historical events questions the idea of society and the justifications for power. Korea's plight is seen as arising from the misuse of power by those in authority. Sin incorporates the Tonghak teaching in section 4:

> Man is Heaven,
> Slaves, peasants, untouchables,
> All men are Heaven.
> Heaven lives in us.
> When Heaven is outside us,
> it is wind, it is water.
> We realize Heaven in us
> but we cannot give it to others.
> All living beings,
> serve your neighbors
> as you serve Heaven.[46]

In Epilogue 2, Sin links the Tonghak peasant uprising with the 1919 independence movement and the 16 April 1960 student revolution that toppled the Syngman Rhee regime. He affirms:

[45] *SL*, p. 238.   [46] *SL*, p. 245.

I believe the day of peace will come
bloodless, won by our long-suffering wisdom
and our long-growing compassion,
not to be lost again to blood-suckers.[47]

Sin Kyŏngnim

After his literary debut in 1956 with routine lyric verse, Sin Kyŏngnim (b. 1936) returned to his hometown Chungwŏn in South Ch'ungch'ŏng and kept silent until 1965. In the debate on existentialism, then in fashion in literary circles, he found the recurrence of such words as "god," "being," "existence," and other terms of Western origin distasteful and uninteresting. From 1956 to 1965 he worked as a farmer, miner, or laborer. He then realized that the realistic portrayal of farming villages and the gloomy life of farmers should be his task – directly related to his own historical consciousness. His first collection, *Nongmu* (*The Farmer's Dance*, 1975), deals with those whose lives are rooted in the soil but who have been pushed to the margins of society by industrialization:

> We fools are pleased enough
> just seeing each other's faces.
> Carving a melon by the barber shop,
> gulping *makkŏlli* at a wine stall,
> we all have old friends' faces
> . . .
> Talk of drought in the southwest,
> of debts to the co-op.
> ("P'ajang" ["Market's Closing"])

– a slice of the farmer's life depicted realistically. Or in "Farmer's Dance":

> The full moon shines as one fellow
> bellows like a bandit, another
> sneers like Sorim the outlaw.
> But what use is this commotion,
> kicking the heels, crushed
> into a hole in the mountains?
> . . .
> Past the cow dealers, turning
> by the slaughterhouse
> comes the spell, and I
> lift one foot and blow the brass horn,
> shaking my head, twisting my shoulders.[48]

[47] *SL*, p. 247.   [48] *SL*, pp. 255 and 258.

These early poems are replete with self-scorning resignation, described by Sin as "the powerless people's sigh." Although Sin has returned to the farm, he has not truly grasped agrarian reality. Here and in later works he combines scenery sketches, narration, and lyricism, as in "Kaltae" ("Reed"): "To live is to weep / silently and inwardly." He presents not conflict but harmony.

As a poet of the farmer, his focus turns to the poetry of the people (*minjung*) in *Nam Hangang* (*South Han River*, 1987), a long narrative verse of over 4,000 lines, which traces a history of the Korean people's tribulations from shortly after the fall of Chosŏn to some years after the liberation. Part 1, "Saejae Hill," tells the story from 1910 to 1913 from the point of view of Tolbae, who serves as witness and spokesman of the downtrodden. As a member of the Righteous Army against the Japanese and a chivalrous outlaw, Tolbae joins the farmers' revolt, attacks a rich man's granary, and beats the Japanese engineer who fondled a Korean woman's breasts. Tolbae and his group are active in North Kyŏngsang and Ch'ungch'ŏng provinces, but his comrades are killed one by one, and he too is wounded, captured, and decapitated, his head displayed as a warning to the people. Here Tolbae represents "us" and his exclusive anger is directed at "them," landowners and oppressors. This simplistic dichotomy and the monotonous narration, however, create little aesthetic appeal. Inside the "we" there is not complexity but emotional unity. Although Sin's poetry is meant to console the downtrodden, he tends to lionize the farmers and overloads the texture with folk songs and shamanist chants, a heteroglossic communal voice, to win the reader's sympathy. The lyrical passages come not from the speaker, however, but from the poet.

Part 2, "South Han River," covering 1919–1923, concerns the independence movement of March 1919 and modernization under Japanese rule. Here Yŏnŭi, Tolbae's former sweetheart, is the central character. Instead of avenging Tolbae's death, she opens a tavern and falls in love with a fiddle player – Tolbae's later self – and satisfies her carnal desire. This section is usually commended for its realistic description vibrant with life. Part 3, "Soemuji Field," covering the post-liberation years, concerns war victims, Koreans returning from abroad (some 4 million lived outside Korea's borders until 1945), pro-Japanese landowners, the conflict between left and right, the presence of American soldiers, and the US Army's handling of land reform. Here the protagonist is a whole social group: the people. According to the farmers' view, the nation is composed of the rich and powerful, power is law, and power comes from money. In "Hwaeppul" ("Torch") the speaker asks:

Nation and law are on their side,
What they build, they discard,
But above them is heaven,
And beneath them the earth.
Heaven and earth know the earth is ours.
We recovered our nation,
And it is our day, this is our world:
But they don't find the stolen land,
Who will find it, if we don't?

These lines are not in themselves remarkable as poetry, but they do evoke an atmosphere and demonstrate a mastery of the rhythms of language. Sin's language is seldom private or decorous, but it evinces honesty and a warmth of mind and heart. His steadfast dedication to his vocation, coupled with an indifference to poetic fashion, has often been cited.[49] In late collections such as *Kil* (*Road*, 1990) and *Ssŭrŏjin cha ŭi kkum* (*Dream of the Fallen*, 1993), Sin has proved himself to be a successful lyric poet as well, one who gives voice to the dreams of commoners and their everyday life.

MINJUNG POETRY

Poetry stressing political and social issues came into being in the 1920s. In the 1960s, the relevance of engagement literature was again discussed. Then in the mid-1970s, a debate on *minjung* (the people, the masses) literature began, and most literary circles and the press helped to disseminate it. To understand *minjung* poetry we need to know a little about the political and economic background of the 1970s and 1980s. In October 1972, a number of factors, domestic and international, led the Park Chung Hee regime to proclaim martial law, followed by a series of revitalization (*yusin*) reforms. A *yusin* constitution was ratified and a number of emergency measures followed, especially Measure 9, which made criticism of the president a criminal act. Then came the assassination of President Pak in 1979, a coup d'état led by Chun Doo Hwan, the Kwangju massacre of May 1980, Chun Doo Hwan's abrupt suspension of debate on constitutional reform in 1987, and the subsequent June uprising. Economically, export-oriented industrialization brought about alienation and inequality; in 1970 a garment worker named Chŏn T'aeil immolated himself in protest against labor exploitation and became a symbol for future workers' struggles. Militant labor disputes

---

[49] Sin Kyŏngnim, *Nam Hangang* (Ch'angjak kwa pip'yŏngsa, 1987). For a collection of critical essays on Sin's poetry see Ku Chungsŏ, Paek Nakch'ŏng, and Yŏm Muung, eds., *Sin Kyŏngnim munhak segye* (Ch'angjak kwa pip'yŏngsa, 1995).

ensued, and union membership increased. The gulf between rich and poor led to a class struggle, as industrialization transformed lifestyles and class structures. Workers stepped up their strikes in the teeth of government attempts to silence all sources of opposition.

To resolve the country's political and economic contradictions, student and labor groups sought solutions in the ideas of Gramsci, Marx, Fanon, dependency literature, and even Kim Ilsung's *juche* (*chuch'e*: self-reliance) ideology. Radical factions organized indoctrination groups to discuss relevant texts by dividing literature into required reading and taboo reading. Banned books included the so-called "pure" literature – defined as literature without social and political criticism – and anything that did not deal with *minjung* issues. In the 1980s, several thousand students were expelled from school for their antigovernment activities, or dropped out and entered factories to help raise workers' consciousness. In 1987, the torture-killing of a university student drove students and workers, religious groups, and the urban middle class into active protest. In the late 1980s, labor organizations began publishing their own newspapers. Theorized by activists familiar with liberation theology, *minjung* ideology is a consciousness-arousing movement that aims to change society.[50]

What is *minjung* poetry? In the 1920s, leftist writers used such terms as trend, class, proletarian, agrarian, labor, and *minjung* literature. They also advocated short narrative verse and folk-song-style poetry as means to appeal to the working class. All these ideas were revived in the 1970s with a different awareness of the times. The advocates of *minjung* insisted on a democratic society; its goals were independence, freedom, and equality. While the leftist literature of the 1920s, produced under Japanese rule, was related to the restoration of Korea's sovereignty, *minjung* literature in the 1970s and 1980s was created under a military dictatorship and urged the restoration of civil rights. Advocates of *minjung* literature avoided such terms as *kungmin* (nation, people) and *minjok* (race, people, nation) and opted instead for *minjung*.

Originally the term included the urban petite-bourgeoisie, workers, the progressive intelligentsia, farmers, the self-employed, the salaried, and poor citizens at the periphery of urban centers. Generally, however, the term refers to alienated people, oppressed politically and exploited economically. Thus the meaning of *minjung* varies from group to group and depends on their

[50] Kenneth M. Wells, ed., *South Korea's Minjung Movement: The Culture and Politics of Dissidence* (Honolulu: University of Hawaii Press, 1995), esp. pp. 87–118, 167–219. See also Kwŏn Yŏngmin, *Hanguk hyŏndae munhaksa 1945–1990* (Minŭmsa, 1993), pp. 213–252.

ideology. *Minjung* literature is purposeful literature – a means for realizing political objectives. Its content is political and social problems. Its aim is not only to reflect political reality but to lead to direct action: exposure, criticism, agitation. In order to harness culture, restore Korean identity, and revive nationalist sentiment, advocates promoted traditional culture and beliefs to revive nationalist sentiment and returned to various forms of oral literature from the past, often in parody or burlesque. Each decade from the 1960s has produced a group of *minjung* poets, each with different emphasis, subject matter, and technique. All, however, seem to espouse the priority of content over form.

This was also an age of some forty "mooks" (a word coined by combining "magazine" and "book") run by alienated and unemployed intellectuals, advocates of the practical literature movement, anticonservatives and experimentalists in a new kind of writing. Advocating a movement to abolish genres and destroy the poetic grammar, their campaigns were concerned with farmers and agrarian issues, labor and workplace, social contradictions and absurdity, the environment and pollution, nuclear proliferation and foreign powers, and the possibility of unification.

VOICES OF THE 1970S AND 1980S

We have already discussed Sin Tongyŏp and Sin Kyŏngnim. Here we consider two well-known voices of the 1970s and 1980s: Kim Chiha and Ko Ŭn.

Kim Chiha

Born in Mokp'o, South Chŏlla, a region known for its spirit of revolt ("The hot south is a land of revolt," Kim said) from the Tonghak peasant uprising and the November 1929 Kwangju student movement, Kim Chiha (b. 1941) wrote about Chŏn Pongjun, a leader of the Tonghak uprising: "Under the gleaming bayonets, the sneers, / you must live. Live, though they cut / the head from my lifeless body."[51] When the Korean War ended in July 1953, Kim was beginning Mokp'o middle school, but the devastation of war and senseless slaughter must have left indelible scars – as we see, for example, in "Songjadong ŏndŏk ŭi nun" ("Snow on Songjadong Hills") or "Hwangt'o kkil" ("Yellow Earth Road"):

---

[51] David McCann, trans., *The Middle Hour: Selected Poems of Kim Chi Ha* (Standfordville, N.Y.: Human Rights, 1980), p. 22.

Down the road through the yellow earth
I follow the fallen drops
of blood, Father.
Where you died
now blackened
only the sun burns.[52]

In 1954 Kim's family moved to Wŏnju, Kangwŏn province, and as a student at Wŏnju high school he began to attend the Catholic church where later he met Bishop Chi Haksin and worked closely with him. In 1956 Kim moved to Seoul, graduated from high school, and enrolled in the department of aesthetics at Seoul National University (1959). He then took part in the 19 April student revolution. As one of the students targeted by the authorities, he had to leave Seoul and begin a life of hiding. In "Yongdangni esŏ" ("At Yongdangni") we read:

My death at Yongdangni,
will it come with phlegm spilling over?
In the salt wind,
in the midst of stone
it sways nearer,
while at the waterfront
a workman is dying.
But my death, where
is my death?[53]

In "Ttangkkŭt" ("Land's End"):

Graceful, clear
sulphur flames sink down,
and while my eyes stare
through the long, long night,
across my forehead wander ceaselessly
the soft screams of the falsely accused,
to sink into the sea.[54]

In March he returned to Seoul but was arrested for opposing the Korea–Japan normalization talks. "P'urŭn ot" ("Blue Clothes"), the Korean prison uniform, says:

Red tag, square and stiff:
to be free of you
I might gladly die,
gladly become scattered ash.[55]

---

[52] *SL*, p. 317.	[53] McCann, trans. *Middle Hour*, p. 20.	[54] Ibid., p. 21.	[55] Ibid., p. 25.

Although referring to 1960, his lines "Burn! Burn away / the long tyranny of silence / rising up in blackness"[56] seem to express his firm resolution. In 1970 he published "Ojŏk" ("Five Outlaws"), his first satirical verse, in the monthly omnibus journal *Sasanggye* (*World of Thought*, 1953–1970), which at once aroused the sympathy of readers. The journal with a circulation of 40,000 was immediately seized and banned. Kim had provoked the ire of the authorities once again. He then published his first volume, *Hwangt'o* (*Yellow Earth*, 1970), dedicated to his mother. Now he began to work closely with Bishop Chi for the cause of democracy and human rights and was baptized. In 1971 he was designated as subversive and a warrant was issued against him. He then went underground and wrote a play, "Kŭmgwan ŭi Yesu" "The Gold-Crowned Jesus". "Pulgwi" ("No Return") summarizes his agony:

> No one returns
> Once [they] set foot in that white room and fall
> down into the drowsiness settling deep in the flesh,
> the fathomless vertigo.[57]

In 1972, Kim published another long satirical verse: "Piŏ" ("Rumors"). In November 1973 he took part in the democracy movement, and in January 1974 the emergency measures outlawing all criticism of military rule were issued. Again Kim was blacklisted, and again he tried to hide. "1974-nyŏn irwŏl" ("January 1974") and "Pada esŏ" ("By the Sea") were probably written while he was fleeing. He was arrested on Taehŭksan Island (25 April), tried, and sentenced to death (13 July), but his sentence was commuted to life imprisonment. Released in February 1975, he vowed: "I will fight as long as I am alive." In August Kim's "Declaration of Conscience" was published in the United States to counter the government fabrication that Kim was a communist.[58] From 1961 to 1975 his life was a succession of arrests, bail, hiding, and battling tuberculosis. "What is absolutely necessary now is truth," Kim declared, "and my passion for suffering is because I love that truth."

Written to satirize injustice and the corruption of the privileged minority, "Ojŏk" ("Five Outlaws") concerns a tycoon, assemblyman, government official, general, and minister. Some rare Chinese graphs, seven with the "dog" radical, are chosen for their homophone. For example: the tycoon is homophonic with "mad dogs"; the assemblyman with "hunchbacked crafty angry dogs snarling at apes"; the government official with "crouching

[56] Ibid., p. 18.   [57] Ibid., p. 61.
[58] Ibid., pp. 78–87; Chong Sun Kim and Shelley Killen, *The Gold-Crowned Jesus and Other Writings* (Maryknoll, N.Y.: Orbis Books, 1978), pp. 13–38.

meritless three-legged ox"; the general with "long gorillas"; and the minister with "goggling cataract-eyed mad dogs." "Piŏ" ("Rumors") comprises three parts: "Sori naeryŏk" ("The Story of a Sound") concerns farmers who lost their farms, and the gulf between rich and poor; "Kogwan" ("View from the Buttocks") deals with the inverted awareness and perverted life of high-ranking officials against the background of the Taeyŏnggak Hotel fire; and "Yukhyŏlp'o sungbae" ("Adoration of a Six-shooter") involves the self-destruction of those in power and the conflict between politics and religion. "Aengjŏk ka" ("Song of Cherry Bandits") concerns opportunists who do not want to lose their position, and "Ttong pada" ("Sea of Excrement," 1974) satirizes Japanese economic plunder and sex tourism.[59]

The function of such poetry is to pose a frontal challenge to political reality by means of indictment and exposure: a "superb cultural bomb." This is a voice, issuing from an unknown source and directed at an unknown place, that can shake the government. According to Kim, the violence of actuality calls forth sorrow in the poet, and his sorrow gives rise to artistic violence – satire consisting of sorrow, grievance (*han*), and humor. Directed at the people, humor is at the center and satire on the periphery; directed at the people's oppressors, however, satire is primary and humor secondary. True courageous nonviolence and disobedience will lead to what Kim calls the "violence of love" (*tan*). Modeling voice and gestures on the singer of *p'ansori*, his satirical verse usually begins with a statement, "I am going to tell you this story," and ends with "such a story is being told" – similar to the typical narrator of traditional popular fiction. The persona who dominates his verse, highly rhetorical and not always aesthetically moving, is that of the moralist living in a world of injustice and corruption. Repetition, enumeration, transposition, and summary are used to achieve a desired poetic effect: to distort the object of ridicule and elicit laughter. "The Story of a Sound," for example, describes Ando:

> One foot down, the other up,
> one foot up, the other down,
> if this one is up, that one down,
> if that one is up, this one down,
> veering this way, lurching that,
> hop, hop, jump, jump,
> at this frantic pace he sets out.[60]

---

[59] Kim Chiha, *Kim Chiha si chŏnjip: Ojŏk, Kim Chiha tamsi chŏnjip* (Sol, 1993). For a translation of "Five Outlaws" see Chi Ha Kim, *Cry of the People and Other Poems* (Hayama: Autumn Press, 1974), pp. 39–59; for "Rumors" see pp. 60–89.

[60] The first four lines present a literal version to show the technique. See McCann, trans., *Middle Hour*, p. 37.

Taesŏl nam (*Big Story South*, begun in 1982) consists of three parts (*p'an*), each composed of three scenes (*madang*), and each scene consists of three subsections (*taemok*). This is, according to Kim, a simple story, a big long story, a story that will enable the people to make their own story. In terms of space it focuses on everything from the universe to the Korean peninsula and ranges from time immemorial to the present. A "big lie" – including odds and ends, the noble and the base, songs and poems, curses, idle talk – it can be called the professional singer's story (*kwangdae sŏl*), or simply a big story (*taesŏl*). The theme is that although people are living under oppression and pain, their resistance brings even harsher oppression and tragedy.

Ko Ŭn

Poet, former monk of the meditation school, political activist, writer of fiction, essayist, Ko Ŭn (b. 1933) is generally regarded as Korea's foremost contemporary poet. Known for his breadth and depth of imagination and skillful use of language, he is also the most prolific. In 1952, during the Korean War, he joined the Buddhist order and practiced meditation for ten years. Ko had published two earlier volumes of poetry in the romantic lyrical mode, showing a monk's spiritual thirst on a pilgrimage for illumination. *Munŭi maŭl e wasŏ* (*At Munŭi Village*, 1974) established him as a poet. Here the images of path, traveler, separation, and hometown recur. In this volume the poet meets the world and tries to explore life among the people. The speaker finds that the villagers have abandoned their homes and land in search of a better life elsewhere; but "holding my arms I stand and endure [pain]" – this is as far as he can go: he can only endure.

In the 1970s, Ko was in the vanguard of the struggle for human rights and democracy, fighting the military regime, and spent several years in prison. With "Imjong" ("At the Deathbed," 1977) and "Hwasal" ("Arrows," 1978), he proclaims an end to fixed ideas, worldly fantasy, and lingering affection for illusory tradition – a new departure:

> I won't go to the Pure Land across a billion leagues,
> Love, but will remain in my country after death.
> My body will become dirt, water, and wind,
> A gentle breeze over this land.
> No, I'll burst from the region between this life and next,
> Linger and get drunk on our strong brew.
> An heir of wanderers through the aeons,
> I'll bid apricot trees blossom everywhere, . . .
> I will sing when the birds sing,

> To be the song of my country, . . .
> Why should I go to the dissolute Pure Land?
> There's no death; my country is my death.
> Love, I won't go to the Pure Land.[61]

A manifesto – a pledge to offer himself to a new era – "Arrows" is shot at oppressive power:

> Transformed into arrows
> Let's all go, body and soul!
> . . .
> In dark daylight the target is rushing toward us,
> Finally, as the target topples in a shower of blood,
> Let's all just once as arrows bleed.[62]

In "Kil" ("Road") he says:

> I am part of this nation that has spent
> its whole history on a rugged road –
> . . .
> I must travel along every road
> in North and South, from end to end.
> For come what may there is a road
> that leads to one united land.[63]

Some of his poems in the 1980s are requiems for the victims of the Kwangju massacre in May 1980. In stanza 2 of "Chajak namu sup ŭro kasŏ" ("Visit to a Birch Grove"), included in *Choguk ŭi pyŏl* (*Homeland Stars*, 1984), the speaker is weeping. The poet, he says, is one who weeps for others and weeps their weeping (stanza 4):

> The time is coming when people will realize
> that they are each one part of a multitude.
> When I was a child, I was already old.
> Arriving here, now I have to be born again.
> So in this moment, one with the white birch's
> quiet natural winter,
> I return to a state of charm and prettiness,
> growing up as another person's only child.[64]

He had already grown old as a child because of his hard life under colonial rule, his wanderings, and his political activism. Here he returns to a state

---

[61] Peter H. Lee, ed., *Modern Korean Literature: An Anthology* (Honolulu: University of Hawaii Press, 1990), pp. 291–292.
[62] Brother Anthony of Taizé and Young-Moo Kim, trans., *The Sound of My Waves: Selected Poems by Ko Ŭn* (Ithaca: Cornell East Asia Program, 1993), p. 39.
[63] Ibid., p. 48.   [64] Ibid., p. 55.

of innocence. Through a dialectic of self-criticism, he has attained a stage where, an awakened monk, he affirms life and is ready to lead his people to freedom and equality.

Ko married in 1983, settled down in Ansŏng, near Seoul, and began a prolific phase of his career. One of his massive projects is *Manin po* (*Ten Thousand Lives*, 1986–1997, 15 vols.) about 3,000 people he has met – an exploration of the whole of life with a steady gaze on the concrete truth of everyday affairs. Beginning with his immediate family (grandparents, father and mother, maternal uncle), and his neighbors, the list expands to those he has met in society as well as historical figures from ancient times to the present – expanding, that is, from what is better known to what is less familiar. His hometown neighbors and those who live some distance from Kunsan, as far north as Taech'ŏn in South Ch'ungch'ŏng, include the liar, the miser, the idler, the gambler, the slanderer, the prostitute, the virtuous, and the immoral. A typical entry recounts a human situation, often with vivid images. The poem's organization is not uniform: some entries are in dialogue or monologue form and some have quoted speeches. In "Pongt'ae" ("You and I Vied for First Place in Grade School"),[65] for example, the poet speaks through a lyric persona. "Chongdu's mother," the magistrate's wife, is praised for her unassuming lifestyle, and "Chaeryongi," the first gong player in a village band, for his love affair. Wit, slang, dialect, proverbs, swear words, nicknames, scenes and manners, exclamations, apostrophes to names of plants, places, native objects – all adorn *Ten Thousand Lives.*

Ko's art of narration is much the same as one finds in the prose portraits in the literary miscellany of the past, but generally his entries are longer and less concentrated. His method is least successful with historical personages, and he has been criticized for "ideological schema and tedious expository narration." The list of characters written about includes, for example, Chu-mong, the mythical founder of Korugyŏ (37–19 BC); King Kwanggaet'o, the nineteenth ruler of Koguryŏ (391–413); Kim Yusin (595–673) who helped unify the Three Kingdoms; Kwŏn Yul (1537–1599), the general who repulsed the Japanese invaders at Haengju in 1593; the rebel Chŏng Yŏrip (d. 1589); and Yi Hwang (1501–1571), the most famous Neo-Confucian philosopher; down to such twentieth-century patriots as Kim Ku (1876–1949) and Kim Kyusik (1881–1950). Some entries are didactic, some entertaining, some graphic with a sharp eye for the homely, some moving in their emotional directness. Such facility, however, can create problems: some portraits are loose in form, some lack tension and focus, some lack careful craftsmanship. Moreover, the events described often overpower the subjects.[66]

---

[65] Ibid., p. 91.   [66] So far fifteen volumes have been published.

Ko's narrative verse in seven volumes, *Paektusan* (*Mount Paektu*, 1987–1994), covers the period from the 1900s to 1940 and traces the activities of, among others, Korea's Righteous Army and the independence army active in Manchuria.[67] The story, however, centers on Cho Hwayŏn – the only daughter of Cho *kamsa* (deputy director of the office of state records) – who elopes with the manservant Ch'u (later Kim T'uman or Kim Pau) and is condemned to death. Together they escape the Japanese assassins employed by Deputy Director Cho. Finally they settle down near Heavenly Lake on Mount Paektu, a sacred mountain, cradle of Korean history, and symbol of the life force. Lady Cho becomes an anti-Japanese fighter and is portrayed as the embodiment of the Korean people's struggles, resolution, solidarity, peace, forgiveness, and sharing – indeed, she is a symbol of the ideal Korean woman.

Since the early 1970s, Ko Ŭn has continued a popular literary tradition that has as its objective the elevation of the nation and its people. He has vigorously opposed the view that modern Korean literature is only a clone of Western literature. In the preface to *Ten Thousand Lives*, he declares: "Now I have freed myself from foreign literary influence." He upholds a national literature of hope in order to achieve what Koreans desire universally – democracy and unification.

Other poets

Yi Sŏngbu (b. 1942), the author of "Paekche haeng" ("Journey to Paekche," 1977), and Ch'oe Harim (b. 1939) both wrote internalized *minjung* poems. Although they have been criticized as "poems that have not developed a strong faith in history," their works have attained some literary value. Other poets have written about a healthy vibrant life of the people, a life where love binds community; still others have aimed at criticism of actuality, or liberation of workers, by exposing their wretched condition and the contradictions of capitalistic society. Worker-poets such as Pak Nohae have based their works directly on Marxist ideology.

EPILOGUE

If the language of the poetry of engagement is strong, it is because the poet draws not only from the self but also on the common predicament

---

[67] Seven volumes. For a collection of critical essays on Ko's poetry see Sin Kyŏngnim and Paek Nakch'ŏng, eds., *Ko Ŭn munhak ŭi segye* (Ch'angjak kwa pip'yŏngsa, 1993).

of the people. The poet's singular voice expresses what others know but cannot say. The poem's structure, diction, and feel reflect the modernist or popular tradition, producing a bold, plain language that highlights the contrast between personal and social realities on the one hand and the poet's dreams on the other. Poets know there is no easy affirmation, but they must define, as best as they can, their own role in relation to both the flux of events and the audience. This is not protest for novelty's sake but a passionate concern for the survival of the poet's culture – poets cannot abdicate their role as artists of their time. Indeed, a poem is written by somebody, it comes from somewhere, it relates to others, and it must have meaning.

Twentieth-century Korean poetry came into existence with "From the Sea to Boys" almost a century ago. The primary concerns of Korean poets have been: can the self be free in an enslaved society? How can one create a national literature and a national consciousness when there is no nation? How can poetry be consonant with the times and with the Korean reality? Finally, how can poetry that takes its material from the sufferings of a specific time and place be at once local and perennial? The struggle against tradition meant a struggle with the language – a search for new ways to express political and spiritual dilemmas. Cultural and moral crisis fostered experiments and stimulated the modernization of the language of poetry through the adoption of colloquialisms, distinction of tenses and numbers, identification of the subject, use of free verse, and broadening of the subject matter. Early in the development of modern Korean poetry, however, poets learned that technical innovation alone could not create a new poetry for a new self. They learned, too, that poets must take their place in society and culture if they are to be heard. Poets of consequence have delved into the resources of the language to contact the audience and produce the effects they desired. Knowing that the meaning of words constitutes their history and making use of the intertextual capacity of words, poets have fulfilled their role by adding new dimensions to the Korean language.

Deviations from standard Korean – anomalies of syntax and linguistic structure, together with elliptical associations and elusive metaphors – also reflect the pressure of difficult circumstances. Even so, poets of consequence have entered readers' lives by identifying their inner anguish with our common human plight. Poets of their time reflect the contemporary realities of their culture; they are advocates for the values by which their fellow men and women must live. The poetry of engagement and relevance is the product of a fierce honesty that scorns the threat of annihilation and affirms.

Whatever their concerns and techniques, postwar Korean poets have refused to avert their gaze from disagreeable facts of history or to simplify life's complexity. In their search for order, for what Frost called "a momentary stay against confusion," and in their illumination of the problem of Korean conscience in our time, Korean poets affirm their situatedness by bald articulation of their way of being in the world. Like their predecessors, they do not jettison the cognitive claims or social functions of poetry. Instead they give us that sense of purpose and coherence that only poetry can afford. The major poets of modern Korea have perfected the art of being themselves: Korean voices issuing from Korean themes and the Korean soil. Informed by a powerful moral vision, they sing of life without deception or illusion. They have delved into tradition to redeem the past and to verify the new world they have created, a poetry of validity and appeal. As Laozi said, the longest journey is the return home.

CHAPTER 22

Late twentieth-century poetry by women

Kim Chŏngnan

Today, more than ever before, Korean women poets are cultivating a determined voice all their own. Their works are diverse and their ability is impressive. Indeed, their literary achievement surpasses that of "men's poetry" in quantity and quality to such an extent that classifying "women's poetry" as a separate genre seems embarrassing.

Although the problem of establishing exactly when Korean women's poetry originated leaves room for discussion, scholars generally view women poets who became active around the 1920s as the pioneers. This was when Korean society was transformed from authoritarianism to enlightenment and Koreans experienced a radical change of consciousness. Yet the change in women was even more radical than in men – it was a case of vertigo. Women poets who initiated a certain "realistic" revolution not only in their work but also in their lives can be regarded as its extreme manifestation.

THE FIRST WAVE

If we divide modern Korean women's poetry into periods for the sake of discussion, the first wave of poets would include Kim Myŏngsun (1896–1951?), Kim Wŏnju (1896–1971), and Na Hyesŏk (1896–1946). These poets are celebrated more for their lives, however, than for their work: Kim Myŏngsun is said to have suffered from delirium; Kim Wŏnju and Na Hyesŏk turned to religion after scandalous extramarital affairs. Judging from the attitudes of Korean society, where adultery is still a crime, one can easily imagine how deviant their behavior must have seemed at the time. In light of today's literary sensibility, this first period of women's poetry seems naïve and not very prolific. Still, keeping in mind the tenor of society at the time, these women's thirst for independence and recognition of repression is extraordinary.

Women poets active during the 1930s left a richer body of work than the first wave, but they suffered from the criticism leveled at their predecessors.

Unlike the pioneers, who were independently active, they began their writing careers under the "guidance and care" of male writers. Thus, although they secured a position in the literary world, they were hindered in expressing their female identity. This circumstance prevailed almost until the 1960s. Nevertheless, during this period Korean women poets were able to polish their technique and develop their literary skills. If there was no great progress toward the recognition of female identity, women's poetry did attain independence from the liberation (1945) to the 1960s as women poets began to proliferate and their work grew in both quantity and quality. This period also saw the emergence of women poets who succeeded publicly, such as Kim Namjo (b. 1927), Hong Yunsuk (b. 1925), Hŏ Yŏngja (b. 1938), and others who are still active. Although the women poets of this period made great progress in technical sophistication, however, surpassing the rough work of earlier poets, the self-conscious female identity in their work lags behind that of their predecessors. The principal emotion pervading their poetic world is a sentimentalism that emphasizes "feminine passivity." Despite these limitations and considering the inferior position of women in Korean society, their achievements are brilliant.

THE INVASION OF "FLESH"

The 1970s saw for the first time women's poetry in the genuine sense that secures both artistic achievement and an independent female identity. Kang Ŭngyo (b. 1945) and Mun Chŏnghŭi (b. 1947) had already mastered the technical sophistication of the poets of the 1960s. In addition, they were the first women poets to recognize the meaning of "being women" in ontological and social terms. The peculiar separatist label of "female" (*yŏryu*) that contemptuously followed women of letters began to disappear around this time – due largely to the activity of these two poets.

The literary changes, however, were not limited to women's poetry. In the 1970s Korean literature experienced a radical change in quantity and quality. There were several reasons for this. First was the emergence of the *hangŭl* generation, who had received a proper education in the pure vernacular and were trained to write – unlike the previous generation, who had been educated under Japanese colonialism. Second was the expansion of modernization. This was the period when Koreans secured, above all, a citizen's consciousness. After liberation, despite unprecedented political chaos, slowly they began to acquire an outlook that enabled them to participate as subjects in historical development. The revolution of 19 April 1960 represented a decisive point in the formation of this consciousness.

Third was the burst of publishing activity. Sudden economic expansion not only provided the crux of Korea's stability but also mass-produced numerous contradictions. This state of affairs stirred an urgent resistance in the intellectuals, and it created the media: *Munhak kwa chisŏng* (*Literature and Intellect*), *Ch'angjak kwa pip'yŏng* (*Creation and Criticism*), and other journals were founded. Literature became a key cultural and social strategic point of the intellectuals' resistance. Moreover, as the volume of publication increased, the opportunity to publish was extended to women poets.

These changes exerted a direct influence on Korean women's poetry. The formation of a citizen's consciousness spurred the growth of self-identity even in women. The themes and images that appear in the early work of Kang Ŭngyo and Mun Chŏnghŭi, who became active during the 1970s, are surprisingly similar despite the clear differences in their dispositions. The common points that link the early poems of these two women converge on the word "flesh" (*sal*). From this word alone it can be seen that they pursued a female identity clearly distinct from the previous generation of women poets. Even as late as the 1960s, a woman evoking her own body in poetry, not conceptually but existentially, was unimaginable. Indeed we cannot forget our shock, for example, when we first read the word "flesh" in Kang Ŭngyo's poems – the word "flesh," not "body," flesh that exults and grieves, flesh that emits fragrance and stench, flesh that is born and decays. Flesh that civilization has decreed as women's lot, that has been sent to the hell of the other, together with women, in order to maintain the predominance of mind. It is difficult to believe that Kang Ŭngyo and Mun Chŏnghŭi were consciously aware of the meaning of this word when they were writing. They moved intuitively, recognizing anew what the metaphysics of men repressed most in women: their bodies.

We can give a more immediate meaning to the word "flesh." Although these two poets reveal a self-consciousness concerning the female condition in a universal sense, in the context of Korean society the word has a far more active meaning. The 1970s were a time when political oppression represented by *yusin* was rampant.[1] All the critical voices denouncing the development of a dictatorship were silenced. Korean society was crushed under a heavy atmosphere of death and oppression. The "flesh" of Kang Ŭngyo and Mun Chŏnghŭi can be analyzed as a strategic code confronting this political oppression: flesh pulsating as the liveliest and most immediate proof of innocence as opposed to political lies and pervasive death. While

---

[1] A series of "revitalizing reforms" announced by President Park Chung Hee in 1972. See Carter J. Eckert et al., *Korea Old and New: A History*, (Ichogak, 1990), p. 365.

the male poets were pursuing modernism and ideology, Kang Ŭngyo and Mun Chŏnghŭi were celebrating "flesh." They overcame the lie of the time by depending on flesh.

FROM PEOPLE TO WOMEN

Korean women's poetry felt the pulse of positive change throughout the 1970s – from vague sentimentalism to philosophical subjects, from abstract diction to concrete discourse. The flow of this change becomes clear after the Kwangju Uprising at the beginning of the 1980s. Korean literature, oppressed throughout the 1970s, was now thrust into an even darker tunnel. As the political situation grew worse, poets were forced to respond. To confront a corrupt reality, one must possess the power to analyze actuality meticulously. The poets, therefore, armed themselves with an intense historical consciousness. Throughout the 1970s the currents of literary change had been integrated with the flow of realism. Beneath the main current, however, were smaller tributaries soon to become major streams.

Ko Chŏnghŭi (1948–1991) was active in the mid-1980s, before other poets, for precisely these reasons. She was clearly distinguished from other women poets because of her consciousness of reality. Before turning to literature, she had studied theology. In her early poems Christianity is associated with liberation. In one sense, her literature can be seen as a means to practice her faith: working for the liberation of the people. Certainly her literary efforts were always faithful to the major goal of integrating life and literature. After the first half of the 1980s, Ko Chŏnghŭi's poetic activity moved toward integrating *minjung* (people) liberation and women's liberation. This change related to her insight that social alienation is exemplified in the problem of women. Recognizing that even within their socioeconomic "class" women are alienated – and recognizing too that if female alienation is not solved, even *minjung* liberation will become a fabricated ideology – made her a combative women's rights activist. She published a women's newspaper on her own, organized the feminist association Another Culture, and plunged into publication, among other activities. In June 1991 she met her death while climbing Mount Chiri – a profoundly symbolic and meaningful end.

DEATH AND STRONG INDICTMENT OF OTHERNESS

The political corruption of the 1980s that began with the Kwangju Uprising continued with the unprecedented abolition of free speech. Intellectual journals encountered heavy frost. Despite their differences of tone and literary aim, the liberal camp, represented by the journal *Literature and Intellect*, and the realist camp, represented by *Creation and Criticism*, formed a united front. The liberals took part in this combat with "deconstructionist poetry," an exceptional formal aestheticism. Among women poets, Ch'oe Sŭngja (b. 1952) was the frontrunner.

Ch'oe Sŭngja attacked corrupt society with corrupt language. In her work there is no trace of the gentility and elegance once considered "feminine." Instead there is rough and urgent breathing, vulgarity, and curses – a far cry from the pretty "female poetry" of the 1960s. This rough language itself, however, has no intrinsic meaning. The poet's shrewd spirit of denial has methodically mobilized it; in order to attack duplicity, she has chosen these words strategically. Her poems aroused interest from the time of her debut and were loved by many; and not only because women were able to experience catharsis through them. In her poems women discovered the possibility of a new, independent feminism different from anything that had preceded it: that of a sorceress on her own; a woman stranded in dignity; a powerful, subjective, unfortunate woman – not a pretty princess who is the object of men.

That same spirit of denial drove Yi Yŏnju (1953–1992) to suicide. Yi began to publish in the late 1980s. After publishing her first volume of poetry in 1991, she took her life. Although she can be seen as a poet of the 1990s in terms of chronology, we must discuss her together with Ch'oe Sŭngja because their poetic spirits seem to touch. Also, after Ch'oe Sŭngja's tragedy and Yi Yŏnju's suicide, women poets of the late 1980s and the 1990s were able to construct a rich and self-sufficient female poetic world. Yi Yŏnju's first collection is entitled *Maeŭmnyŏ ka innŭn pamŭi sijang* (*Night Market with Prostitutes*). The choice of the word "prostitute" is itself profound: it indicates that the poet's self-identity was suffering from a confusion sufficiently violent for her to choose the ultimate solution.

In order to understand Yi Yŏnju's breakdown, one must understand the crux of her problem: the city and a patriarchal civilization. The "city" is not only the pinnacle of patriarchal cultural glory but also an evil setting. Yi Yŏnju exposes its contradiction; she identifies with the prostitute – an unfortunate woman, at the city's periphery, who cannot be incorporated into the system. The prostitute is a product of urbanization and one of the most brazen contradictions of a patriarchal civilization whose double standard of monogamy is only a façade. Yi Yŏnju's poems, centered on the prostitute's life, are full of the vocabulary of self-abasement. It seems that she attempts to incorporate into her identity what Sandra Lee Bartky calls a "horrible message of inferiority"[2] that is internalized in certain women with an evil intensity: the perfection of self-torture.

This indictment of women's otherness is not the result of passively accepting the colonization accorded women in a patriarchal society. It involves pain that must be overcome if women are to construct a true identity – to borrow Ch'oe Sŭngja's words, "in order to be born again." It urges women to recognize their condition, to stand on their own, and to rage against oppression. Indeed, the "liberation of rage" is a major stage of women's consciousness-raising. In the case of Yi Yŏnju, rage devoured a poet.

INSIGHTFUL MOTHERS

Kim Sŭnghŭi (b. 1952) and Kim Hyesun (b. 1955), however, conquered women's otherness with a definite social consciousness and blissful maternity. The beginning of Kim Sŭnghŭi's poetic career in the early 1970s was distinguished by her pursuit of a mythological world. Her early poems – like those of many young poets – are idealistic but display undeniable talent. She quickly overcame her early idealism and turned to cultural criticism in the late 1980s. Her early mythological imagination is not allowed free rein because of the strong wind of realism that rushed in immediately afterward. This gifted poet, however, did not break down; even in her despair, she developed her poetic world. By the end of the 1980s, that world had become the subject of widespread attention, and she enjoyed the rare good fortune of winning a literary award.

From her debut, Kim Hyesun indiscriminately attacked men's dark rigor with her lively imagination. Even in her later work, her imagination is still novel and fresh. She possesses a sharp female poetic consciousness that cuts through the political meaning of the "act of discourse." This keen perception links Kim Sŭnghŭi and Kim Hyesun and is confirmed by the fact that they are among the first women poets to steadily publish exceptional prose on poetry.

Kim Hyesun is a contemporary of Ch'oe Sŭngja and began her literary career in the 1980s, but because of her diction she has more in common with new generations of poets than with her colleagues. She does not so much present the content of her poem as convey its expression. Thus she exploits a sophisticated technique of making the "act of discourse" itself an internally meaningful poetic strategy. From the first, her poems grasp

---

[2] Sandra Lee Bartky, *Femininity and Domination: Studies in the Phenomenology of Oppression* (New York: Routledge, 1990).

the conspiracy of patriarchy. This insight does not allow her to settle for monotonous diction. She hits and runs. Unlike Ch'oe Sŭngja and Kim Sŭnghŭi, who criticize in a singular and direct way the male value system that oppresses them, Kim Hyesun uses diverse methods – parody, black humor, material image, and dialogical technique – to express the existence of the other: the other that is introduced into the domain of the self to criticize the absoluteness of the subject, the basis of male metaphysics. She moves freely in all directions. Her diversity, however, sometimes has the effect of blurring her poetic intent by blinding the reader with exquisite technique.

Kim Sŭnghŭi and Kim Hyesun have a definite consciousness insofar as the question of identity is concerned. Beginning with Kang Ŭngyo and Mun Chŏnghŭi, and continuing through Ko Chŏnghŭi and Ch'oe Sŭngja, one can say that the meaning of "being a woman" was revealed. Kim Sŭnghŭi and Kim Hyesun, however – conscious of their own substantial, affirmative, and independent maternity – leaped over the dimension of Kang's and Mun's inclusive meaning of "flesh," Ko's ideological democratic feminism, and Ch'oe's indictment of female rage through the recognition of otherness based on lack. In the background was the feminist activity that began in Korean society in the 1980s.

LOVELY WOMEN FOR MEN

Essentially the 1980s ended with the president's declaration of 29 June 1987 and the Seoul Olympics.[3] A change began to accelerate in Korean literature. Lightness rather than heaviness, individuality rather than totality, became its center. In women's poetry, a change occurred also. Due to the successes of the first half of the 1980s, almost all the taboos of women's poetry, taboos of poetic diction and the body, disappeared. Female poets in the latter half of the 1980s were able to use freely uninhibited expressions and exhibit their own bodies. Even their own sexual desire was talked about naturally. The "woman as sexual subject," whom even Mun Chŏnghŭi – who did not hide the bodily functions – perceived with a guilty conscience, has now become an everyday theme in Korean women's poetry. Women poets no longer consider their sex as an obstacle. In a certain sense, it can even be said that being a woman is advantageous for writing. (In fiction this is definitely true.)

---

[3] A bold eight-point program of reform was announced by President Roh Tae Woo. See Eckert et al., *Korea Old and New*, p. 382.

Examining the issue more closely, however, we find that almost nothing has changed. After a meticulous analysis of the 1980s reactionary movement, literary authorities have driven women's poetry into a corner with a very subtle formula. The deconstructionists (dissident postmodernists using open forms) active during the 1980s swept up most of the literary awards and entered the pantheon of stars. The conservative literary authorities, however, were consistently critical. Their main complaint was that "deconstructionist poetry" was ruining traditional lyricism. Although popular support and the serious evaluation of young critics helped to quiet this criticism, it was the male poets who were seizing the literary awards. The literary authorities, however, denied recognition of Ch'oe Sŭngja, who was among the "deconstructionist poets," until the end.

One can guess why literary men cheered the reactionary women's poetry that came out during the latter half of the 1980s. This restoration, or reaction, was a phenomenon not only in women's poetry but also in men's, and it is very significant in that it regained some of the lyricism that poetry lost when it was mobilized as an instrument of combat against social corruption in the 1980s. "Ah, we are exhausted from fighting. Poetry, console us. You especially, women poets, console us men." Men abandoned their battlefield colleagues and returned to find their women. The female identity revealed by the poetry of Hŏ Sugyŏng (b. 1964) and Pak Nayŏn (b. 1951), two women poets who were praised by literary men in the late 1980s, seems to play this role. The title of the volume that made Pak Nayŏn famous is suggestive: *Sŏul e sanŭn P'yŏnggang kongju* (*Princess P'yŏnggang who Lives in Seoul*). The legendary Princess P'yŏnggang, who married the idiot Ondal and transformed him into a great warrior with absolute devotion, represents the traditional female (see Chapter 6). Hŏ Sugyŏng displays a charming femininity and presents herself as a consoler of the menfolk returning from the violent battles of the 1980s.

Two other women who started publishing poems at the same time present a feminine self that is agreeable to men. Hwang Insuk's poetry has images of the "girl" and Yi Chinmyŏng's offers those of the "chaste wife." Compared to their earlier work, however, their current poems do not show much development. It appears they could not muster the courage to smash the female image that is comfortable to men – an image that was, to a degree, the cause of these poets' success. Hwang Insuk (b. 1958) failed to mature, and Yi Chinmyŏng (b. 1955) could not pull herself from the depths of the interior and repeatedly shows a tendency to cling to dogma. (In her poetry it appears in the image of Scripture. The problem is that she does not show what is in the Scripture, just the external image.) Her poetry stretches and lengthens but fails to gain density. She loiters at one spot, unable to leave, and to justify her loitering she becomes talkative.

One cannot deny the literary accomplishment of these four women. Their poems are indeed well written. Hŏ Sugyŏng's work displays deft diction and shapes a decadent beauty in the indigenous tones of the Korean language. Hwang Insuk's fresh poetry constructs a sophisticated urban aestheticism. Yi Chinmyŏng, with severely decorous and virtuous language, steps toward a religious speculation that is rare in Korean literature. Yet they do have their limitations. Unless female poets can resist aesthetic accommodation, true women's literature is impossible.

TODAY'S GENERATION: THE 1990S

A number of "middle-aged women poets" have secured their position. Given the Korean literary world's practices, however, their chances of survival are slim. They are the "destitute of language" who lack the customary links to elite Korean society: having attended certain schools; a specific regional background; knowing the right people. They all made their literary debut at a very late age, experienced acute psychological distress during their youth, and are groping for deliverance through literature. (One suspects that this distress was the result of the forcible repression of their literary talent. For, despite their late start, their talent is prodigious.)

Their appearance can be explained not only in terms of their personal history but also in terms of Korean literary history. They entered the scene in the postmodernist 1990s, when self-narrative that could not be expressed in the 1980s rose to the surface as resourcefulness was being restored to literature. Given these circumstances it seems almost a miracle that these poets were read with interest. That women who embark upon a literary career after a certain age are labeled "middle-aged women poets" is the reality of the Korean literary world.

Three of these women are publishing works at an astonishing rate. Concentrated by the urgency of life they have repressed, and by their thirst for a language that was alienated by patriarchal values, their poems explode from their interiors. Indeed, their poetry is fresher and more energetic than that of most young poets. Male poets of the same age, by contrast, simply repeat the same matter and manner. Yi Kyŏngnim (b. 1947) exploits a language that is a mix of Ch'oe Sŭngja's and Hŏ Sugyŏng's, with inborn talent and a powerful sense of female identity. She writes almost in gasps – so repressed that, having gained an outlet, sometimes she tries to speak too urgently. In her latest poems, she manipulates a more diverse breathing technique, as if she has acquired confidence. Pak Sŏwŏn (b. 1960) is another poet with a seething interior. Her poems offer striking images and an intense and confessional narrative that recalls the poetry of Sylvia Plath (1932–1963) or Anne Sexton (1928–1974). With its gorgeous yet ferocious images and primitive religious sentiment, her work exudes an odd sacrilegious air. Yi Hyangji (b. 1942), the oldest of the three, exploits a language that is severe in self-censorship and concealed under layer after layer. In fact, however, her "tied tongue" is a poetically meaningful device. Among the three, she writes the most daring and successful poems.

We turn now to Kim Chŏngnan (b. 1953), who made her debut in the 1970s, and Chŏng Hwajin (b. 1959), who published her first poetry collection in the 1980s. Poets of the 1990s, their poetic world has a distinct character. Although they accept the achievements of 1980s women's poetry, they diverge from it. The pivotal point of this change is present in Kim Hyesun's work. If Kim Hyesun is looking for "you" to dissolve the old self and construct a new one, exploring the true identity of this "you" is the main thrust of Korean women's poetry in the 1990s.

The women of this generation seem to grasp the contemporary mission of women's poetry as constructing a new ontology instead of indicting feminine otherness or rejecting social constraints. The ontology that invites "you" is ultimately the ontology that restores the other, whom the philosophy of male self-identity has shoved into oblivion. Consequently, if this generation of women poets wants to talk about "love," it is appropriate. This love is far from the "love" in poems mass-produced by Korean women poets of the 1960s. It is not the romantic love so despised by feminists nor is it the passive love that tries to make up for social inferiority by offering a self-sacrifice for men. It is, rather, an act of searching for a new identity constructed by demolishing the old frame of existence. It is an act of being united with the flow of life in the flux of the universe. These poets no longer feel pain being women. Their feminine identity is now a beacon of their pride: a mark of conviction that they did not side with power or serve power. In order to practice this ontology, the current generation of Korean women poets is slowly entering the deep recesses of the soul, still an unexplored realm. Already they have conquered new territory. While men agonize over the surface world's aridity, Korean women are pushing open the door of the unconscious and calmly walking barefoot the waterway that Rimbaud had left unfinished at the end of the nineteenth century.

Their poetic world reveals the possibility of a new metaphysics we might call "self-religion." From deep within they are quietly resurrecting a spiritual immediacy that religion lost when it began to lean on reason and institutions. It has nothing to do with this or that doctrine; it is not a matter of religion but a problem of religiosity. These poets seem to know where their ontology is headed. They seem prepared to accept the postmodernist "pursuit of religiosity" as theirs. The reason why this summons came not to novelists but to poets – especially women poets – is paradoxically because poetry, especially women's poetry, is the most powerless literary genre in Korean society. Consequently, it has the least exchange value, is least corrupted by commercialism, and is the farthest removed from the grand symbolic framework of postmodern society. This point is crucial. After all, the problem of writing poetry in modern society is that of securing a pure language that can withstand all the symbolic manipulation. Korean women poets, especially the current generation, are all sensitive to the problem of language and clearly understand the political meaning of the "act of discourse."

CHAPTER 23

Late twentieth-century fiction by men

Kwŏn Yŏngmin

Although Korea was liberated from Japanese colonial rule in 1945, the country faced national division due to its inability to overcome ideological contention and conflict. The tragic experience of colonialism was relived through fiction that critically examined the humiliating circumstances of the time. Fiction also established a new direction for life within the "liberation space" (*haebang konggan*) – the space between colonial liberation and the beginning of the Korean War. During the post-liberation period, creative practices centered on assigning meaning to the new life and understanding the social conditions and demands that accompanied the new freedom from colonialism. Most fictional works focused on realism by problematizing the notion of understanding reality.

FICTION DURING THE "LIBERATION SPACE"

Among the works published during the post-liberation period that hold significant historical weight are those that appropriated the colonial experience into the fictional realm and examined it critically. In Pak Chonghwa's *Ch'ŏngch'un sŭngni* (*Youth's Victory*, 1949), Pak Nogap's *Sasimnyŏn* (*Forty Years*, 1948), and An Hoenam's "P'okp'ung ŭi yŏksa" ("Tumultuous History," 1947), the authors describe colonial experience with a critical eye. Realistic portrayals in fictional works within the space of liberation are embodied in Kye Yongmuk's "Pyŏl ŭl henda" ("Counting the Stars," 1946), Chi Haryŏn's "Tojŏng" ("Journey," 1946), Hŏ Chun's *Chandŭng* (*Lamplight*, 1948), Yi Kŭngyŏng's "T'angnyusogŭl kanŭn Pak kyosu" ("Professor Pak who Walks the Muddy Stream," 1948), Yŏm Sangsŏp's "Ihap" ("Meeting and Parting," 1948), Hwang Sunwŏn's "Sul iyagi" ("Liquor Story," 1946), Ch'oe Chŏnghŭi's "P'ungnyu chap'inŭn maŭl" ("Landowner Sŏ's Birthday Celebration," 1947), and Pak Yŏngjun's "Kohyang ŏmnŭn saram" ("People without Hometowns," 1947). In these works, characters returning home after liberation appear frequently as a motif signaling a path to new life.

Writers whose creative practices were closely tied to political ideology include Ch'ae Mansik (1902–1950), Yi T'aejun (b. 1904), and Kim Tongni (1913–1995). Ch'ae Mansik, standing in the middle ground, enthusiastically critiqued the situation of the time, while Yi T'aejun and Kim Tongni represented the leftist and rightist literary tendencies, respectively. Ch'ae Mansik, the first writer to attempt self-criticism, courageously revealed his own humiliating experiences of the colonial period. His "Minjok ŭi choein" ("A Sinner before his People," 1948–1949) depicts intellectuals who engaged in pro-Japanese activities endeavoring to acquire a new moral consciousness by introspection and repenting past misdeeds. In this story Ch'ae describes intellectuals who voluntarily stopped writing, those who collaborated with the Japanese, and those who remained as newspaper reporters in order to maintain their livelihood. By describing each through the character's self-criticism, Ch'ae emphasizes the attainment of a national moral consciousness. Rather than stressing the euphoria of liberation, Ch'ae criticizes the extension of the colonial chaos and deception into the post-liberation era. In short, Ch'ae uses satire to criticize reality. His short story "Maeng sunsa" ("Officer Maeng," 1946) condemns the present-day fraud that allows a colonial-era police officer to become a liberation-era police officer. Moreover, he examines the possibility that a colonial criminal may become a police officer. By equating the police officer and the criminal, Ch'ae censures the absence of ethics. "Mist'ŏ Pang" ("Mr. Pang") comically portrays parasitic people who attach themselves to the newly arrived American soldiers.

Yi T'aejun's "Haebang chŏnhu" ("Before and after Liberation," 1946) portrays two contrasting characters who hold different views of life. One is a young urban man who goes to the countryside at the end of the colonial period and gives up writing; the other is an old man who maintains a local Confucian school. The young man, who has been colluding with the Japanese under pressure, disconnects himself from everything and follows a progressive ideology by taking the lead in the leftist literary movement. Contrary to the old man's inability to sever ties with the traditional way of thinking, the protagonist buries the past and steps forward into a new phase of history. One reason why the protagonist is portrayed as if he has overcome a weak, colonial mental state by choosing a new ideology is to illustrate an aspect of the intelligentsia's psychology at the time. Using the North Korean land reform as a backdrop, Yi's full-length work of fiction entitled *Nongt'o* (*Farmland*, 1948) describes a protagonist who, having been a destitute tenant farmer, finally becomes a landowner. The story is about one who rightfully acquires land following the reform – signifying that at this new historical juncture the farmers have become the true owners of the land. This theme incorporates the author's intent to explain what liberation meant for Korea in parallel with the ideology of class revolution.

When the literary world divided into two ideological camps immediately after liberation, Kim Tongni, while advocating individual freedom and human dignity, became a literary spokesman for the nationalist camp. Although Kim claimed that literature is "life's ultimate form," his method and way of life are notable in that they go beyond understanding reality objectively. *Yŏngma* (*The Post-horse Curse*, 1948) describes the tragic fate of a man who falls in love with his half-sister. The core of the story lies in the protagonist's ultimate abandonment of his love and acceptance of moral principle. Instead of challenging his fate, he wanders aimlessly. In this sense the story fails to address current social problems and merely delineates one person's life that is bounded by certain conditions of reality.

FICTION AND THE KOREAN WAR

The Korean War was a national historical tragedy in which the people keenly felt the country's division and their separation from family members. Ideological blindness was one of the elements that prevented the development of a national consciousness. When the division became permanent, literature sought a way to deal with the ongoing reality of the war, the refugee experience, and the recovery of Seoul from the North Korean army. After the mid-1950s, literature regained some stability in viewpoint and methodology as the nation slowly recovered from the cataclysm of the war and social confusion.

Awakening to reality

An important aspect of postwar Korean literature is the process of transformation experienced by older writers who began their career during the colonial period. Writers such as Pak Chonghwa, Yŏm Sangsŏp, Chŏng Pisŏk, Kim Tongni, Hwang Sunwŏn, and An Sugil are representative of the older generation. Among these writers, the most notable are Kim Tongni, Hwang Sunwŏn, and An Sugil.

Kim Tongni's critical stance on the war and its chaos are embodied in works of "war fiction" such as "Kwihwan changjŏng" ("Returning Soldier,"

1950) and "Hŭngnam ch'ŏlsu" ("The Retreat from Hŭngnam," 1955). In later years, Kim concentrates on searching for human destiny in such works as *Tŭngsinbul* (*Life-sized Statue of Buddha*, 1963) and "Kkach'i sori" ("Cry of Magpies," 1966). *Life-Sized Statue of Buddha* deals with the theme of original sin and religious salvation. In "Cry of Magpies," Kim depicts a protagonist who has returned from the war by describing in detail an amalgam of complex psychological states such as fear of death, wishing for life, fury against the enemy, and guilty feelings toward fellow soldiers. *Saban ŭi sipchaga* (*The Cross of Shapan*, 1955–1957) discusses original sin, seeking a road to salvation within Catholicism. In contrast to *The Cross of Shapan*, Kim fictionalizes shamanism in *Ŭrhwa* (*Ŭrhwa the Shaman*, 1978).

Hwang Sunwŏn (1915–2000), expanding his literary horizons after liberation, contributed many important postwar works. The transformation of his literary world is marked by his departure from the established boundaries of the short story genre. His short stories "Tokchinnŭn nŭlgŭni" ("The Old Potter," 1950), "Kogyesa" ("Clowns," 1952), and "Hak" ("Cranes," 1953) are rough sketches of reality. Starting with his full-length work of fiction entitled *K'ain ŭi huye* (*The Descendants of Cain*, 1954), Hwang concentrates on shaping the consciousness of life in novelistic form. *The Descendants of Cain* is about the savage terrorism that took place in post-liberation North Korea. In this work Hwang criticizes the tyranny of ideological blindness that crushes an individual's free will. In both *Ingan chŏmmok* (*Human Grafting*, 1957) and *Namudŭl pit'are sŏda* (*Trees on a Slope*, 1960), he addresses the process of overcoming the wretched aftermath of the war and its wounds. These two works are significant in that they represent the writer's ability to examine the postwar situation from a comprehensive humanistic point of view. Apart from these works, Hwang contributed to the development of narrative technique and a deepening of literary sensibility in works such as *Irwŏl* (*The Sun and the Moon*, 1965) and *Umjiginŭn sŏng* (*The Moving Castle*, 1973).

An Sugil (1911–1977) accurately depicts the postwar reality and shows how the war distorted the values and consciousness of the petite bourgeoisie in "Chesam inganhyŏng" ("A Third Kind of Man," 1953) and "Paesin" ("Betrayal," 1955). His long work of fiction *Pukkando* (*North Jiandao*, 1959), centering on a family that has migrated to North Jiandao in China, describes the vicissitudes of historical change the nation undergoes from the end of the Chosŏn dynasty to the colonial period. This work describes the Korean farmer's attachment to the land and relates the undercurrent of national consciousness in the form of a *roman-fleuve*.

A new moral consciousness

After the Korean War, a new tendency surfaced in postwar literature. Writers who had experienced the war expressed resistance against current social values – rejecting the moral consciousness established by the older generation when the prospect for a new life in the postwar ruins became uncertain. Writers like Chang Yonghak (b. 1921), Kim Sŏnghan (b. 1919), and Sŏnu Hwi (1922–1998), with their critical attitude toward historical consciousness and reality, occupied important positions in the realm of postwar fiction.

Chang Yonghak attempted to escape from the current framework of fiction while appropriating the dark postwar reality as a fictional background. "Yohan sijip" ("Poetry Book of St. John," 1955) critically describes how the meaning of existence is damaged by such abstract and meaningless concepts as ideology, people, and class during and after the war. His full-length work of fiction titled *Wŏnhyŏng ŭi chŏnsŏl* (*Legend of the Circular Fate*, 1962) probes the meaning of original sin and equates the distorted reality of national division to the idea of life and death.

Kim Sŏnghan's works draw attention by excluding passive and submissive characters and creating human figures with quintessential human dignity and justice. "Obungan" ("For Five Minutes," 1955) and "Pabido" ("Pabido," 1956) delineate the people's determination to protest an absurd reality. Due to his unprecedented literary technique and intellectual sensibility, Kim has gained recognition. With the publication of the three-part historical fiction *Yi Sŏnggye* in 1966, his interest has shifted toward fictional re-evaluation of historical events and characters.

Sŏnu Hwi stresses the significance of active participation and firm decisions through short stories such as "T'erorist'u" ("The Terrorist," 1956), "Pulkkot" ("Flowers of Fire," 1957), and "Ori wa kyegŭpchang" ("A Duck and an Insignia," 1958). In "Flowers of Fire," the time from the colonial period until the Korean War is compressed into the lifetime of a protagonist who evinces a strong will to confront his times. "A Duck and an Insignia" critically examines the prevalent exercise of abusive power in Korean society by staging a relationship between ruler and ruled. To establish such a hierarchical relationship, one always needs a leader. With the power that comes with being the leader, problems are solved. Thus Sŏnu elucidates a contradiction in the contemporary situation. Prior to the mid-1960s, he had stressed the significance of an intellectual's responsibility and the need for active participation in the present reality, but now his attitude shifts toward passivity, showing greater interest in the interior life. "Sipchaga" ("The Cross," 1965) and "Muksi" ("The Revelation," 1971) are stories that represent this latter attitude. Instead of criticizing history and reality, these stories concentrate on the inner life and human sincerity.

Postwar fiction gains attention as it criticizes the irrational conditions of the time with intensity: the so-called "indictment literature" (*kobal munhak*). This new tendency indicates a different way of examining postwar reality – in this case, a fierce critical spirit of the absurd is the principal axis. This psychological tendency – a directional shift from outer reality to inner – manifests a self-awareness that resolves the situation.

Son Ch'angsŏp (b. 1922) presents the dark aspects of people at the bottom of the social scale in such works as "Hyŏlsŏ" ("Written in Blood," 1955), "Mihaegyŏl ŭi chang" ("An Unsettled Chapter," 1955), "Yusilmong" ("Lost Dream," 1956), and "Ingyŏ ingan" ("Superfluous men," 1958). Most characters in his works are either abnormal or physically handicapped. Their deficiency comes not from the characters themselves, however, but from the situation created by postwar reality. Son emphasizes distorted human beings created by the split between individual and society.

Yi Pŏmsŏn's "Hangmaŭl saramdŭl" ("People of Crane Village," 1957) focuses on the meaning of history and the nation's true character. In "Obalt'an" ("A Stray Bullet," 1959) and "Naenghyŏl tongmul" ("A Cold-blooded Animal," 1959), however, Yi stresses the absurdity of reality. "A Stray Bullet" explores the impact of the war by depicting the psychological destruction and material destitution people faced afterwards and indicting the sentiments of frustration and defeatism prevalent in postwar Korea.

Ch'oe Inhun (b. 1936), using a unique literary structure, captures the intellectual's postwar anguish and disorientation in such works of fiction as *Kwangjang* (*The Square*, 1961), *Kuunmong* (*A Nine-cloud Dream*, 1962), *Hoesaegin* (*A Gray Man*, 1963), and *Ch'ongdok ŭi sori* (*The Governor-General's Messages*, 1967–1968). *The Square*, in particular, portrays the national division and ideological split by critiquing North Korea's forced group mentality and isolation from the outside world while criticizing the South's social inequality and unrestrained individualism.

Chŏn Kwangyong (1919–1988) criticizes a hypocritical human type by depicting a shrewd opportunist sidestepping the violent historical juncture in "Kkŏp'it'an Ri" ("Kapitan Ri," 1962). In "Tarajinŭn saldŭl" ("Wearing Flesh," 1962), Yi Hoch'ŏl (b. 1932) describes the wretched void in people's lives. In *Sosimin* (*The petite bourgeoisie*, 1964–1965) Yi critically approaches the problem of reality – the national division. "I sŏngsuk han pam ŭi p'oong" ("An Embrace on this Mature Night," 1960) by Sŏ Kiwŏn (b. 1930) portrays the postwar generation's destitution and aimlessness through the character of an army deserter who suffers from a guilty conscience. O

Yŏngsu (1914–1979) seeks innocence and kindness within the painful post-war situation in "Hwasanttaek" ("The Woman from Hwasan," 1952) and "Kaenmaul" ("Seaside Village," 1953). "Sunan sidae" ("Two Generations of Suffering," 1957) by Ha Kŭnch'an (b. 1931) is about a father and son who endure pain and anguish from the colonial period to the Korean War. "Wangnŭng kwa chudungun" ("A Royal Tomb and Occupation Forces," 1963) centers on the social changes following the stationing of the American military in South Korea.

FICTION IN AN AGE OF INDUSTRIALIZATION

After the mid-1960s, Korean society crossed the threshold of industrialization. As economic development drove forward and industrial policy was realized, the countryside began to disintegrate in the wake of rapid urban expansion. Waves of industrialization further exacerbated social hierarchy and provoked regional conflict. Moreover, social tensions continued to intensify as political unrest persisted. Korean fiction around this time began to portray the sensibilities of the petite bourgeoisie and their daily lives, while at the same time criticizing the contradictions of the social structure by describing the decay of the rural community. Such fiction also depicts the extension of mass culture, the changing values of the younger generation, and the plight of the workers. Such critical issues as debates on national literature and literary realism are reflected in the creative process, as well, and a new critical understanding of the division of the country began to be embodied in fiction. This tendency brought about an expansion of the modes of fiction, and an increase of medium- and full-length fiction may be said to reflect the writers' changing views of the world and life.

Advent of the hangŭl generation

At the threshold of the 1960s, a new generation of writers emerged who had not received a colonial education: the "*hangŭl* generation." The appearance of Kim Sŭngok (b. 1941) marks the beginning of their literary activity. His story "Mujin kihaeng" ("A Journey to Mujin," 1964) evinces his early literary world and his personal ambition to overcome that realm. In this work, a "returning home" motif is used – shifting to the protagonist's everyday consciousness and reality, describing an internal conflict arising from that reality. Kim's sensibility is fully manifested in such works as "Seoul 1964 nyŏn kyŏul" ("Seoul: 1964, Winter," 1965) and "60 nyŏndae sik" ("The Sixties Style," 1968) wherein Kim details lower-middle-class consciousness and everyday lives bounded by the individual's existence. In this manner, the problems of reality are depicted in minute detail through his unique style and sensibility.

Yi Ch'ŏngjun (b. 1939) has a distinct writing style as well. If Kim Sŭngok is a writer of "sensibility" (*kamsŏng*), Yi may be called a writer of "concept" (*kwallyŏm*). Yi writes fiction, not with the language of sensibility, but with the intellect. He grapples with the meaning of structure in "Pyŏngsin kwa mŏjŏri" ("The Idiot and the Fool," 1966); and in "Maejabi" ("The Falconer," 1968) he explores the corresponding relationship between reality and the ideal, void and will, in a constructed framework. He has a strong tendency toward illustrating experience both intellectually and symbolically. Yi wrote such distinguished works as "Somun ŭi pyŏk" ("Walls of Rumor," 1971), "Ttŏdonŭn maldŭl" ("Floating Words," 1973), and *Tangsindŭl ŭi ch'ŏnguk* (*Your Paradise*, 1976) at the height of the political oppression in the 1970s. In these works he explores the tyrannical relationship between sociopolitical mechanisms and the people's will to confront oppression. Furthermore, in "Chaninhan tosi" ("Cruel City," 1978) he details the closed society and the significance of gaining freedom from it. In both "Sigan ŭi mun" ("Time's Gate," 1982) and "Pihwa milgyo" ("The Fire Worshippers," 1985) Yi concentrates on the theme of time and the realization of human existence. Pursuing this new theme through an artistic mode elucidates Yi's firm belief in the power of art.

Fiction by Ch'oe Inho (b. 1945) can be divided into two categories. First, in the midst of rapid urbanization Ch'oe uses various narrative techniques to describe the modality of personal existence in an urban living space. His interest lies in exploring true character as one faces the problems arising out of the urban space and the loss of personal identity in the age of industrialization. In "Sulkkun" ("The Boozer," 1970), "T'ain ŭi pang" ("Another Man's Room," 1971), "Tol ŭi ch'osang" ("Portrait of a Stone," 1978), and "Kipko p'urŭn pam" ("Deep Blue Night," 1982), he heightens his literary style and vitality and treats the serious problems of consciousness generated by an industrial society. By way of contrast, *Pyŏldŭl ŭi kohyang* (*Hometown of Stars*, 1973), "Pabodŭl ŭi haengjin" ("Parade of Fools," 1973), "Korae sanyang" ("Whale Hunting," 1982), and "Kyŏul nagŭnae" ("Winter Traveler," 1983) represent another aspect of his work that has expanded his readership and indeed the realm of fiction. Centered on the urban space, with refined psychological description, these works are endowed with dramatic elements.

Fiction by Yi Munyŏl (b. 1948) can be classified into three tendencies by considering the writer's intent and narrative technique. First, exemplified in the legends and history in "Saram ŭi adŭl" ("Sons of Human Beings," 1979) and *Hwangje rŭl wihayŏ* (*For the Emperor*, 1980), are the so-called "substitute history" or works written in allegorical mode. In these works, inner reality itself criticizes the present situation in an allegorical manner. Second, in *Yŏngung sidae* (*The Age of Heroes*, 1984), *Pyŏngyŏng* (*Frontier*, 1989), and "Uridŭl ŭi ilgŭrŏjin yŏngung" ("Our Distorted Hero," 1987), Yi presents the reality of the national division. *The Age of Heroes* cultivates a new literary dimension by dealing with the confrontation arising out of ideological conflict and ultimately choosing the socialist ideology. In *Frontier* Yi brings historical events into the literary realm. These two works are representative in evaluating his literary depth and breadth. Third, the writer's self-experience and his faith in art are fictionalized in *Chŏlmŭnnal ŭi ch'osang* (*Portrait of a Youth*, 1981), *Kŭdae tasinŭn kohyang e kaji mot'ari* (*You Can Never Return to your Hometown*, 1980), and "Kŭmsijo" ("Phoenix," 1983). These works deal with such ideological subjects as life and art, which might be termed "romantic," rather than reality itself. Yi's elegant prose style and minute descriptions give expression to these themes.

Agrarian and labor fiction

In post-1970 Korea, one of the major problems that surfaced in the age of industrialization was the plight of rural communities. The agrarian population decreased dramatically after the massive rural exodus to the city, where industries prospered. Moreover, the disparity between city and country – in terms of both community structure and living style – became more apparent with the rapid deterioration of rural areas.

Yi Mungu (1941–2003) has dealt extensively with the contradictions of rural society and the farmers' suffering. Starting with "Amso" ("A Cow," 1970), *Kwanch'on sup'il* (*Kwanch'on Miscellany*, 1977), and *Uri tongnae* (*Our Village*, 1981), Yi's works illuminate various aspects of farmers' lives and rural reality. In particular, *Kwanch'on Miscellany*, published in the linked-story format (*yŏnjak sosŏl*), describes the rapid changes and consequent collapse of the traditional order in the countryside. Inevitable rural transformations that must be endured are narrated in the form of recollection in an elastic literary style.

The rural reality in the industrial age is often discussed in parallel with the lives of the suburban lower class. The majority of the lower class is made up of farmers who left the countryside to become day laborers in the city – yet another social problem that confronted Korean society after the

1970s. Hwang Sŏgyŏng (b. 1943) grapples with the problems arising out of the laborers' workplace and their struggle for existence through "Kaekchi" ("Strange Land," 1974) and "Samp'o kanŭn kil" ("The Road to Samp'o," 1973). The literary significance of "Strange Land" is that it illustrates the dilemma of social relationships through wandering laborers. This story dramatizes their struggles and defeat and develops the story through the mediation of a protagonist. "The Road to Samp'o" symbolically depicts a landscape of urban reality and the pronounced character of the 1970s era of industrialization. Following these efforts, Hwang worked on such pieces of long fiction as *Chang Kilsan* (1984) and *Mugi ŭi kŭnŭl* (*The Shadow of Arms*, 1987). *Chang Kilsan* describes the Chosŏn dynasty's vitality and within that framework illustrates a utopia in the form of the Maitreya religion. *The Shadow of Arms* delineates the contradictions of national division and the ideological problems of the Vietnam War from an objective position.

Nanjaengi ka ssoaollin chagŭn kong (*A Little Ball Launched by a Dwarf*, 1978) by Cho Sehŭi (b. 1942) is written in the linked-story format. The dwarf family represents the oppressed class who are trampled on and whose livelihood is fundamentally destroyed by the wave of urban changes, anxiety stemming from unstable moral standards, and social jealousy and alienation. This story is considered one of the most important works of 1970s fiction. Here the shifting of the narrators' viewpoints and situations is in harmony with the linked-story format describing present-day reality and antireality using a unique sentence style.

Yun Hŭnggil acutely revealed through the industrialization process the problem of working-class life and the formation of fiction. Using the linked-story format, the two stories "Ahop k'yŏlle ŭi kuduro namŭn sanae" ("The Man who was Left as Nine Pairs of Shoes," 1977) and "Chiksŏn kwa koksŏn" ("Straight Lines and Curves," 1977) capture the social contradictions born out of distortions in the age of industrialization. In these works, Yun describes a psychological symptom of the time by illustrating a protagonist who escapes from self-awareness, sacrifices himself in the workplace, and experiences a new self-awakening.

Fiction's awareness of the divided reality

In the 1970s, an effort to unfold the tragedy of the Korean War through fiction provided yet another approach to fiction regarding the problems arising out of industrialization. A distinct feature in these works is the divided nation and the painful experience of the war.

Kim Wŏnil (b. 1942) embodies the national division and its historical tragedy in "Ŏdum ŭi hon" ("Soul of Darkness," 1973), *Noŭl* (*Sunset,*
1978), *Hwanmyŏl ŭl ch'ajasŏ* (*In Search of Disillusionment,* 1983), and *Kyŏul
koltchagi* (*Winter Valley,* 1987). *Sunset* is a celebrated work that deals with
the confusion of the post-liberation period and its continuation into the
Korean War. This work stresses the ongoing contradiction of the underlying conservative social structure and the national division. *Winter Valley*
recreates the violent times from the post-liberation period to the Korean
War within a confined space. By dealing directly with ideological conflicts
and the division that led to the war, Kim explains the ongoing historical
tragedy as originating in the colonial period's societal conflict and its social
structure.

As in Kim Wŏnil's writings, one of the frequent themes in works by
Chŏn Sangguk (b. 1940) is the Korean War and its aftermath. His *Sanullim*
(*Echo,* 1978) and *Angae ŭi nun* (*Misty Snow,* 1978), in particular, probe the
hardships of the refugees. *Abe ŭi kajok* (*Abe's Family,* 1979), notable in its
treatment of the fundamental problem of the division, presents the wound
that will not heal through a woman's life – a woman who lived through
the war and the postwar situation. Abe the victim symbolizes the tragedy
of the war and the widespread suffering endured. By the logic of this story,
all Koreans are Abe's family.

"Pullori" ("Playing with Fire," 1983), by Cho Chŏngnae (b. 1943), together with "Yuhyŏng ŭi ttang" ("Land of Exile," 1981), dramatizes the
reality of the division. Using the war as a backdrop, Cho's works illustrate
how the firmly established class differences and conflicts arising out of traditional Korean society unfold. Cho understands the outbreak of the Korean
War and the division as contradictions inherent in Korea's class structure
and shows how this structure is being dismantled by ideology.

Rise of the roman-fleuve

One of the most distinguished literary trends in the industrial age has been
the rise of the *roman-fleuve*. Pak Kyŏngni's *T'oji* (*Land,* 1969–1994) extends
the author's concerns from the historical framework to present-day life. Yi
Pyŏngju's *Chirisan* (*Mount Chiri,* 1972–1978), Hwang Sŏgyŏng's *Chang
Kilsan* (1984), and Kim Chuyŏng's *Kaekchu* (*The Inn,* 1981) were published
serially throughout the 1970s. Cho Chŏngnae's *T'aebaek sanmaek* (*T'aebaek
Mountains,* 1986) and Yi Munyŏl's *Frontier* became the focus of attention
after the mid-1980s. In terms of scope, these works possess characteristics

unprecedented in the history of Korean literature. Considering the significant themes, they attest to the fact that the Korean literary realm has expanded to the point of encompassing works with great breadth and different viewpoints.

Pak Kyŏngni's *Land* describes, in thirteen volumes, the historical changes and transformations of a fallen gentry family whose lives cover a century from the end of the Chosŏn dynasty to the colonial period. The core of the narrative is the characterization of four generations whose lives and relationships are arranged vertically according to different historical times, described from different class backgrounds, and illustrated through each person's life. By elucidating the shift of the family's blood relations and its historical expansion, *Land* is successful in creating lives of ordinary people living on the threshold of modernization at the end of the Chosŏn dynasty (see Chapter 24).

In Hwang Sŏgyŏng's *Chang Kilsan*, the people's will and determination to live are embodied in the figure of Chang Kilsan. Although the overall plot is based on the life of this character, he is not portrayed as a heroic figure. Through the lives of Chang and his followers, this work reveals the suffering of the lower class who, during the Chosŏn dynasty, lost the foundation of their livelihood due to a greedy and oppressive ruling class. The book reveals their resistance as well as their dreams of a new life.

Unlike *Chang Kilsan*, Kim Chuyŏng's *The Inn* takes on a slightly different subject. The story describes a particular social group that emerged toward the end of the Chosŏn dynasty: the wandering merchants. Thus importance is attached not to an individual character's fate but to the merchants' lives, the public's moral concerns and attitudes toward life and customs at the time.

Among the *romans-fleuves* published in the 1980s, Cho Chŏngnae's *T'aebaek Mountains*, in particular, gained considerable attention. Portraying the unceasingly violent times from liberation to national division and civil war, this work begins by exploring the origin of the partisan movement on Mount Chiri and linking it with the communist guerrilla movement in the Yŏsu-Sunch'ŏn area (1948). *T'aebaek Mountains*, however, is not intended to explain the process of transition and its correlation to the Yŏsu-Sunch'ŏn rebellion. Rather, Cho attempts to verify the historical meaning of national division by unfolding the situation through a series of events. To accomplish this, he juxtaposes both real and fictional characters, describing their socioeconomic status. In this way, Cho broadens our understanding of national division and questions the ideological conflict.

The plot of the work extends from the end of the Chosŏn dynasty to liberation. Through the extension of historical space to the interior aspects, it discloses the dramatic effects of the division. *T'aebaek Mountains* demands a fresh understanding of ideology in the oppressive space of the 1980s. Furthermore, this work demonstrates that the tragedy of national division and the Korean War originated in the contradictions of the nation and the people.

CHAPTER 24

Late twentieth-century fiction by women

Ch'oe Yun

It has been said that liberation crept up on the Korean people like a thief.[1] Then the Korean War hit before the nation had time to establish itself. Ideologies completely filled the interval of liberation, and before political discourse could achieve much depth, Korea moved into a divided era. Accordingly, there was no other choice but a division into North and South Korean literature. Out of the chaotic circumstances of the postwar days that followed the short space of liberation, women's fiction nourished itself on the barren postwar landscape and the destitution bequeathed by the period of colonization. It was the women who, amidst the harsh reality of a Korea divided and reduced to ruins, were charged with the duty to live on, both in the home and in society, at a time when men had either been wounded or simply disappeared.

LIBERATION AND THE KOREAN WAR: FICTION OF THE 1950S AND 1960S

For Korean women writers, the ideological struggles that arose after the liberation, as well as the complex political situation that surrounded the struggle to establish the nation, emerged as sensitive subjects. Mainly active before the liberation, writers like Pak Hwasŏng (1904–1988), Ch'oe Chŏnghŭi (1912–1990), Kim Malbong (1901–1961), and Chi Haryŏn began to write about the social problems of a transformed reality. One example is Kim Malbong's *Hwaryŏhan chiok* (*A Splendid Hell*), which was published serially in *Puin sinbo* (*Women's News*) starting in 1946–the first work to deal directly with women's movements. *A Splendid Hell*, Kim's first fictional treatment, showed a concern for gender issues. Indeed Kim led efforts to abolish licensed prostitution after the liberation and contributed to the resulting changes in legislation.

---

[1] Ham Sŏkhŏn, *Sŏngsŏjŏk ipchangesŏ bon Chosŏn yŏksa* (Sŏnggwang ch'ulp'ansa, 1954), p. 280.

The women writers discussed in this section made their initial appearance in the 1950s and 1960s.[2] Those who first came on the literary scene included Han Musuk (1918–1993), Kang Sinjae (b. 1924), and Son Sohŭi (1917–1987), who published in literary journals such as *Yesul Chosŏn* (*Korean Art*), *Paengmin* (*The White-clad People*), *Sinch'ŏnji* (*New World*), and *Munye* (*Literary Art*). After the Korean War, Pak Kyŏngni (b. 1927), Han Malsuk (b. 1931), Chŏng Yŏnhŭi (b. 1935), and others made their appearance through journals such as *Sasanggye* (*World of Thought*), *Munhak yesul* (*Literature and Art*), and *Hyŏndae munhak* (*Contemporary Literature*). Despite the harsh circumstances in which they lived, these writers presented detailed observations of reality. Nevertheless, their works must be considered examples of the fiction of manners. Starting with early works like "Hŭkhŭk paekpaek" ("Black is Black, White is White," 1956) and *Pulsin sidae* (*The Age of Distrust*, 1957),[3] Pak Kyŏngni introduced the figure of the defiant woman who confronts both social violence and traditional ideas that destroy the individual and embitter women's lives. Especially in her full-length fiction, *Sijang kwa chŏnjang* (*Marketplace and Battlefield*, 1964), Pak compares women's everyday battleground – the marketplace – and their ideological battleground – war. It has been suggested that Pak's particular reading of reality, which connects family history with history proper, constitutes not a narrow vision,[4] but an effort to articulate a point of view that only women writers who have struggled on the everyday battleground can have – an effort that acquires significance precisely as a search for truth.

Rather than constituting a lightning assault on the social issues of South Korea, the works of women writers of this period are more likely to express the historical or social atmosphere of the 1950s and depict the prevailing social conditions. Indeed, the distinguishing characteristics of these women writers lay elsewhere. On the one hand, there were works that could be termed the fictional representation of women's inner reality. Other works, on the other hand, called attention to the wounds suffered by a newly formed society.[5] In the course of the historic reforms after liberation, the

---

[2] The periodization of the writers dealt with here is based on a distinction between two principles: the moment when they first made their appearance, and their period of greatest activity.

[3] The works referenced reflect the year(s) in which the work or the most sections of a work were published. Hence, the years following a work indicate the dates of publication or of serial publication.

[4] In Hong Sajung's view; cited in Kim Chuhyŏn and Kang Insuk, "Hanguk hyŏndae yŏryu chakka non," *Hyŏndae munhak* 14 (1968):351–359.

[5] The general ideas presented here are derived from the concept of *l'écriture* as used by Roland Barthes. One kind of linguistic expression concerns the connections one has with society. Another kind concerns a disillusionment with literature itself. The general idea designates aspects of works that become visible through these two kinds of essential understanding. The foregoing significance is suggested whenever *l'écriture* is henceforth alluded to. See Barthes, "Qu'est-ce que l'écriture?" in *Le degré zéro de l'écriture* (Paris: Gallimard, 1953).

burden was on women to return once more to the confines of the home. A free sensibility was expressed more delicately, however, by women than by men at the time – a phenomenon that can be observed in the works of the period. If the new sensibility embodied in works like Han Malsuk's *Sinhwa ŭi tanae* (*The Precipice of Myth*, 1957) and Kang Sinjae's *P'omal* (*Bubble*, 1955) and "Chŏlmŭn nŭt'inamu" ("The Young Zelkova," 1960) is labeled "postwar" or "Western," it is because these works embody the thematic and stylistic rupture of the fictional tradition. That these accomplishments can be attributed to Korean women is of profound significance.

The social dimension of writings by Pak Sunnyŏ (b. 1928) is evident in works that deal with Japanese imperialism, the Korean War, evacuation, and national division, including "Kodokhan panggwanja" ("The Solitary Bystander," 1966), and "Ŏttŏn p'ari" ("A Fly," 1970). By turning her gaze on unique characters presented with fresh dialogue and level-headed depictions, her works reveal the dignity achieved by Korean women writers. Having survived the most difficult of circumstances, the quiet determination of her characters to preserve their humanity recalls Pak Kyŏngni's heroines. Pak Sunnyŏ's works, however, which investigate the impulse toward solidarity in human relations in an enjoyable language, exhibit a different kind of allure specific to women's fiction.

Through the serial publication of full-length fiction, this era bore witness to growing signs of the importance of Korean women writers. Certainly the crumbling of South Korea's traditional value system contributed to the birth of these works. Here we discover women characters who, freeing themselves from family and Confucian ethics, recognized freedom as a new value and confronted the modern space. A transitional freedom such as this, however, combined with an unfamiliar modernity, cannot help but be confusing. In response to this situation, writers have foregrounded such topics as the emotional quest of individuals or the depths of despair presented romantically – often resulting in the pursuit of escapist love.

The characters in Son Sohŭi's *T'aeyang ŭi kyegok* (*Valley of the Sun*, 1957–1958), Han Malsuk's *Hayan tojŏng* (*White Path*, 1960–1961), Chŏn Pyŏngsun's "Chŏlmang twie onŭn kŏt" ("What Comes after Despair," 1962), and Yi Sŏkpong's "Pich'i ssahinŭn haegu" ("The Illuminated Inlet," 1963) are often visionary and pursue a blind, reckless love. These women characters, unlike their precursors, wander the streets outside the home and begin their initiation journey at the site of the traditional home's disintegration. Son Changsun's early heroines, who attempted to realize a free individuality within the space of women's fiction, can be said to walk the same streets. For the most part, however, the unmarked terrain delineated during this era was unstable and desolate. It is worth asking whether these works in the 1960s express the history of the decade and social emptiness from the woman's point of view. The addiction to love, a topic that pervades many of these works, can be read as one of these forms of expression. Rather than focusing on literary achievements, however, their social significance must be reassessed from a historical point of view specific to Korean women's fiction.

The excitement and frustration fueled by 19 April 1960 and 16 May 1961 effected a generational shift in South Korean literature.[6] The women's fiction that emerged from this complex situation, judged by the number of writers or the quantity of works produced, may be characterized as part of "an era of conscious awakening and the cultivation of talent."[7] It was not until the end of the 1960s, however, that women's fiction began to extricate itself from the notion that it represented an exceptional or discriminatory label: "female." This era actually began with the succession of writers, representing a new generation, who began to write actively at the start of the 1970s.

UNOFFICIAL HISTORIES: FICTION OF THE 1970S

Spirited debates over history, realism, literary theory, the literature of national division, and national literature, which gained momentum during the 1970s, took place under the *yusin* reforms, despotism, and the spur of industrialization. It was out of this whirlpool that women writers began to find their voice.

Paradoxically, Korean women began to flourish within conditions of breathless modernization. In the brutal conditions following the Korean War, women, through their will to survive, began to appear as donors of cheap labor offered in the course of modernization. Women who single-handedly took it upon themselves to look after the burdens of progress began to exist (not as in the West but in smaller ways) as modern women

---

[6] Here 19 April 1960 marks the date of the climax of the April student revolution, in which some 30,000 university and high school students demonstrated in Seoul against the Syngman Rhee regime. The students were fired on, and about 130 students were killed and 1,000 wounded. The date 16 May 1961 is that of the military coup that installed Pak Chŏnghŭi as president of South Korea.

[7] Pak Hwasŏng, "Hanguk chakka ŭi sahoejŏk chiwi ŭi pyŏnch'ŏn: yŏsŏng chakka ŭi ipchang esŏbon," *Yŏryu munhak* 2 (1968):204–215. In the same piece, Pak refers to the place of Korean women writers of the period as follows: "The notion that what we call woman is a different and inferior being, who exists apart from man, is expressed most plainly in the Korean literary world, which should, by all accounts, be more progressive and creative. This kind of customary discrimination according to one's social standing is a remnant of the feudal era and is rooted deeply in a popular Korean society that fancies itself a democracy; it goes so far as the literary world, which, needless to say, should be the most progressive segment of society."

for the first time. This process resembles that of nineteenth-century Western industrialization. For women of non-Western nations, however, modernity often carries both liberating and oppressive aspects at the same time. The features of just such a duality are illuminated in a variety of ways in women's fiction of the 1970s.

Writers like Kim Chiyŏn, Kim Chiwŏn, Sŏ Yŏngŭn, O Chŏnghŭi (b. 1947), Pak Sijŏng, Ku Hyeyŏng, and Pak Wansŏ (b. 1931), who first made their appearance in the latter half of the 1960s, began brisk activity as they entered the 1970s. Along with those who came on the scene later – Yi Kyŏngja, Kang Sŏkkyŏng (b. 1951), Kim Ch'aewŏn (b. 1965), Yun Chŏngmo (b. 1946), Yang Kwija (b. 1955), and others – these writers helped Korean women's fiction of the 1970s to take shape both quantitatively and qualitatively. Until the 1970s, however, neither women's issues nor women's fiction seem to have shaped the predominant course of Korean literature. Women's fiction of the 1970s, for the most part, was seen as part of an "exceptional minority" by the prevailing masculine system of values or standards of appraisal more appropriate to a masculine literary tradition. At a time when all writers were being caught up by urgent political and social issues rather than women's specific realities, the issues became the preferred topics of investigation. Women writers strove to develop unique styles of their own, to indict the harsh reality of women's lives, and to affect the shape of popular dissent. Rather than grant these issues their distinctive importance, however, the literary world tended to read women writers' work in terms of the social function of literature or in a dimension of criticism that emphasized the "inherent, universal problems of Korean society."

We have already noted Pak Kyŏngni's earlier work. The lightning speed with which her *roman-fleuve T'oji* (*Land*, 1969–1994)[8] began to be published in the 1970s reflected the rapid pace at which South Korean postliberation fiction sought to problematize modernity and historical understanding. Pak interprets history through her female characters: a departure of profound significance.[9] *Land* has been acclaimed as a woman writer's

---

[8] The years and sources in which *Land* was published are as follows: part 1, *Hyŏndae munhak* (September 1969–September 1972); part 2, *Munhak sasang* (October 1972–October 1975); part 3, *Toksŏ saenghwal* (January–May 1977); *Hanguk munhak* (June 1977–January 1978); *Chubu saenghwal* (January–December 1979); part 4, *Chŏnggyŏng munhwa* (July–December 1983); *Wŏlgan kyŏnghyang* (August 1987–May 1988); part 5, *Munhwa ilbo* (September 1992–August 1994).

[9] In fact, the historical romances that deal with the stories behind the past dynasties sought to reinterpret reality differently. These works of historical fiction appeared in modern Korean literature as a very important subgenre of fiction. One can presume that, as Western modernity was imported, one of the greatest effects on Korean literature was most likely the development of historical consciousness. History, however, was always the province of men.

historical fiction that has expanded the possibilities of historical fiction in general. The reader can decipher Pak's effort to construct a fundamental feminine strength, a powerful life force, through diverse heroines spanning several generations. On the surface, problems are related to the disappearing class structure through relations of love in the course of Korean society's modernization. It is not hard to see how certain narratives have developed out of a writer's fascination with strong female personalities like Madame Yun or Sŏhŭi – women who had the audacity to slap men's cheeks, both literally and figuratively. In light of the strength shown by the women in *Land*, their attachment to the land, their bitterness related to the Confucian patriarchal society and colonial experience (*han*), and their family consciousness are read as the values of a masculine world. The achievement this massive work represents in the history of women's fiction, however, cannot be underestimated. In truth, historical fiction after Pak Kyŏngni is no longer the exclusive province of male writers.

In works such as *Honppul* (*Soul Fire*, 1983–1996) by Ch'oe Myŏnghŭi (1945–1998), the interpretation of a time period that encompasses both past and present gives birth to a unique work that is faithful to the imperatives of historical fiction written in a poetic style. In the transitional period of modernization, subject to sudden changes, the principles of existence exhibited by a feminine strength were subtly brought into relief. At the same time, rarely in the history of Korean literature does one encounter works like *Soul Fire* that manage to convey aesthetically the everyday life of a Confucian culture.

Still, women writers of the 1970s occupy a unique position in Korean literature. In the works of writers active in this period, including Pak Wansŏ, Sŏ Yŏngŭn, O Chŏnghŭi, and Kim Ch'aewŏn, diverse facets of women's reality emerge as a significant literary subject. Perhaps for the first time in modern Korean literature, awareness of issues concerning a feminine identity becomes an inducement for writing. Women's fiction of this era reveals the process by which heroines who are situated at the threshold of childhood, youth, or adulthood arrive at a genuine consciousness of a feminine economy – a revelation with aspects of the *Bildungsroman* (fiction with an emphasis on the development of a young person). This maturity may be connected to the absence of the father, a common theme in the works of the central women writers of the 1970s. The father's absence not only represents a rupture but is necessary in the process of creating a new feminine economy in a fractured time – a search for identity.

The change in understanding women's reality called for a new literary sensibility. As more writers worked to draw out the realities of women – either through a suitably rhythmic literary style, a vision that focuses directly on these realities, or narrative structure – the history of modern Korean fiction could no longer fail to notice the distinguishing characteristics of women's lives. Thus women writers contributed to the formation of an expanded and distinctive literary space. If inner monologues, garrulity, the magnification of sensation, and the depiction of everyday life can be said to be responsible for a new literary style, it follows that a linear narrative structure – the logic of cause and effect that usually connects events – becomes less important in women's fiction. In their place, through eventless associations, the unfolding of events through dialogue, or the use of an open structure without conclusion, issues concerning the reality of a uniquely feminine literary style came to the fore.

The works of Pak Wansŏ, for example, could only have been written by a woman. Extending her reach until she touches the most personal aspects of feminine reality – such is the way she finds the material of her writing. In this respect, Pak Wansŏ can clearly be distinguished from Pak Kyŏngni. As such, her works open another chapter in Korean women's fiction. Certainly Pak's works can be distinguished from popular love fiction written by women in former times when serious women's fiction was suppressed. It is not that subjects commonly treated by male writers, such as history delimited by questions of politics, power, or the "big issues," have been diluted in women's writing. Rather, as the assessments of Pak in the 1970s demonstrate, her success rests in having clung tenaciously to two kinds of topics: criticism of the vulgar values of the growing middle class in a fetishized industrial society and the personal experience of national division.

Whatever the field of issues on which her works rest, Pak's literary sensibility understands the questions as they are in various ways connected to a specifically feminine reality. Pak's long works *Namok* (*The Bare Tree*, 1970) and *Hwich'ŏnggŏrinŭn ohu* (*Staggering Afternoon*, 1976), as well as the short stories collected in *Pukkŭrŏum ŭl karŭch'imnida* (*I'll Teach You Shame*, 1976) and *Paeban ŭi yŏrŭm* (*Treacherous Summer*, 1978), explore issues connected to the Korean War, the industrialization that followed, the material structures of the foreign oppression of capitalism, and patriarchal oppression within the family. In each case her works depict with startling accuracy a reality that can only be perceived by women – women who have taken care of everything with enthusiasm but in the end are alienated. As a writer known for showing early on in her work that men's realities are not universal, Pak represents a key turning point in Korean literature. Although these are not the only reasons for the importance of Pak's work, her influence on writers who have taken pains to represent a feminine reality is considerable.

O Chŏnghŭi's works reveal another new side of Korean women's writing – one that contributes to the representation of women's inner reality. Inasmuch as O's language, commonly described as poetic, opens our eyes to women's sense of foreboding concerning the world and a recognition of its barrenness, her poetic style has a paradoxical function. Whether her topics are perverted sex, an obsession with death and unrest as in "Pulgŭn kang" ("Fire River," 1977) and "Yunyŏn ŭi ttŭl" ("Childhood Garden," 1980), a troubled woman who tries to escape from her husband as in "Paramŭi nŏk" ("Spirit of the Wind," 1982), a madness that takes root in unexceptional normality, or simply the creation of a grotesque atmosphere, O expresses a unique femininity that cannot be approached through the language of masculine fiction.

It is not simply that the patterns of masculine language that Lacan has called the "symbolic order" are rejected in the works of O. Rather, due to her desire to expose a certain foundation of impossibility that governs most people, the place where the symbolic might enter into her work does not in a strict sense exist. This can most likely be attributed to her effort to realize and fulfill in a world of language an impossibility pertaining to a logical, regulated, and institutional "law." This is the world of imagination: the foundational world where Self and Other, mother and daughter, earth and water, are united. This is why O's heroines cannot possess men. Concretely this amounts to a restoration of motherhood. The countless cripples and murderers, the encroaching old age that resembles death, the soul that is always prepared for the event of death – these are the characteristics of works that do not cease to dream of an order of imagination in which the Self and Other once overflowed their boundaries. It is at these sites that a poetics of absence is born. O's language is a refined language, but a language of madness. It stops before a reality that cannot be apprehended by a rational, logical structure and plumbs its depths.

In various ways, women's fiction of the 1970s expresses disharmony with society. Society is depicted as oppressive to women, and the possibility of a spatial and temporal feminine economy begins to open up to the extent that an escape is sought from this oppression. The modern, reformed space and time of an industrial society offer women the latitude to come face to face with themselves, but inevitably they collide head on with an everyday reality that is supported by an endlessly oppressive value system.

Apart from the expression of social disharmony, or an ontological form of expression, several writers deny the Other and devote themselves to creating their own worlds. Sŏ Yŏngŭn, for example, uses the phrase "the movement of everyday resistance" to describe the struggle with the Other that takes place within the purview of an everyday law that puts authenticity (purity) in shackles.[10] In her works "Samak ŭl kŏnnŏnŭn pŏp" ("How to Cross the Desert," 1975) and "Hwangŭm kitt'ŏl" ("A Gold Feather," 1979), the way to authenticity is through magnifying self-awareness and peering into one's desires. Although the sacrifice and aesthetics of Sŏ's "Mŏn kŭdae" ("Dear Distant Love," 1983) can be said to open a new door, what ultimately brings out Sŏ's uniqueness as a writer is her emphasis on the suffering caused by the laws of a masculine modernity in the course of Korean modernization.

From a certain perspective, the literary space of the works by these new women, whose self-awareness has grown stronger, exhibits a feature of self-sufficiency. Another way to live in this space is to possess an extremely private, personal sphere – a possession through the senses. It is true that this self-sufficiency may be due to the fact that women's realities survived for a time as exceptional realities. In Kim Ch'aewŏn's writing, however, they are expressed in different ways. Kim's vision of reality is very minute and sensuous. It is as though the joy of understanding might help people live luxuriously. Hence various mundane objects in the surrounding world might not illuminate my reality, but my reality can be explained as depending on these very objects or their atmosphere – as, for example, in "Paminsa" ("Night Greeting," 1975) and "Ch'orokpit moja" ("The Green Hat," 1979). The sensory impression of objects therefore reflects the omnipresence of the self. This is different from the impressionistic depictions of reality that began with Kang Sinjae. Kim's is a sensuousness that is captured by a clear vision behind a phenomenon. Often the boundary between fantasy and reality grows dim in her work – an inner feminine realm within which the conflict between rational will and desire becomes meaningless. While a certain narcissism is ensconced in her world, Kim does not mean to valorize self-satisfaction but stresses the significance of what can be called the possibility of a self-respecting language. She shows us works that exist without a thread of connection.

The various qualities shown by women's fiction of the 1970s are meaningful insofar as they anticipate the directions that develop thereafter. Particularly from the 1980s to the 1990s, when feminist discourse came to the fore as a major issue in the South Korean literary world, these qualities, together with the advances of women writers, played a role in the formation

---

[10] Cho Yŏngbok, "Chuch'e tŭrŏnagi wa t'aja paeje hagi," in *Hanguk sosŏl munhak taegye* (Tonga ch'ulp'ansa, 1995), pp. 585–595.

of the feminist agenda. Moreover, a sensitive reader can observe these very qualities in themes and topics that are consistently revisited and developed in the works of future generations.

THE RISE OF FEMINISM: FICTION OF THE 1980S AND AFTER

Women's fiction cannot exist in isolation from the complexities of the transformation of Korean society. The indices in the historical changes in Korean society apply as well to the developmental process of women's fiction. Events that determined such a tremendous transformation in Korean literature at large – the *yusin* reforms of the 1970s, the Kwangju massacre of 1980, the various stages of South Korea's definitive democratization in the aftermath of the resistance of June 1987 – may well help explain the corresponding stages of development in women's fiction. From the point of view of women's fiction, however, these historical divisions only acquire significance when they are considered together with the qualities present in women's works.

There is a measurable difference between the qualities of women's fiction that began to take shape in the late 1970s and those that came later. The latter can be distinguished by the intensity of a natural process of progressive expansion. Until then women's fiction had been produced by a minority of writers. Not until the start of the 1980s did a realistic appreciation of women writers from several angles become readily apparent. It was then that the movement for women's liberation began to emerge and gain strength in women's circles. Because they were generally excluded from official historiography, discussions of popular (*minjung*) movements, people's literature of the 1980s, and activist literature are more likely to be found in historical studies of women's realities – particularly investigations of women's realities before the liberation.[11]

Moreover, factors directly connected to Korean women's realities had a profound influence on the development of Korean women's fiction. The establishment of women's studies at universities in the 1970s, the equalization of educational opportunity, the explosive increase in these opportunities in the 1980s – all represented prime moments for an awakening to the potential of female agency. For the most part, the women writers active in the early 1980s received their education at roughly the same time – that is,

---

[11] Hanguk yŏsŏng yŏnguhoe, Yosŏngsa bunkwa (Society for the study of Korean women), "Hanguk yŏsŏngsa ŭi yŏngu tonghyang kwa kwaje," *Yŏsŏng kwa sahoe* 5 (1994):297–327.

in the new environment just described. These women were compelled to raise new questions about their own economy from within the participatory whirlwind that seemed to engulf the entire public at the time. Whether they emerged from the general population or from a particular activist group, these women came to seek answers from the hotly debated topics of feminism. In truth, the young writers of the mid-1980s were influenced, consciously or not, by these new and complex movements.

Another important stage was the appearance of women workers in the process of industrialization as well as the emergence of middle-class women who had acquired material comfort. Moreover, journals on women's studies of the mid-1980s – along with cultural activities that were designed to magnify the importance of feminism, which was now emerging as an alternative value system – opened themselves to these popular movements after the democratization of 1987. This kind of transformation represented a quantitative gain for women writers, one among several broad trends that improved their social situation. The fact that it was these self-same female troops who helped form the class of female readers was an irreducible factor in the expansion of women's fiction.

Women's fiction extricated itself from minority status in the 1980s. The general expansion of education extended to women as well. Despite such expansion, however, it seemed that in the course of the fight for democratization in the 1980s Korea's patriarchal structure was paradoxically growing stronger. If the 1980s were devoted to the fight for justice, it was indeed ironic that the traditional meaning of the heroic term "to fight" was, after all, masculine. Hence women were obliged to lay their concerns once again on a dead ground of meaning. It was toward the end of the 1980s that women writers began to touch on this problem.

Still, it appears that social justice emerged as a more pressing issue in women's fiction at the time. The trend of reporting women's concerns from a popular, national point of view could also be observed in the treatment of the problems of prostitution or the exploitation of women living near military bases – as in *Koppi* (*Reins*, 1988) by Yun Chŏngmo (b. 1946). In Pak Wansŏ's *Ŏmma ŭi malttuk 2, 3* (*Mother's Stake 2 & 3*; 1981, 1982), the problems of national division are viewed from a similar angle. Through selected works that took the lead in investigating the psychology of the middle class, the conflicts of families whose children were involved in popular movements, and the organizations of working women, the works of Kim Hyangsuk, collected in *Surebak'wi sogesŏ* (*Within the Wagon Wheel*, 1988), faithfully evoke the atmosphere of the period.

So too do the works of Kang Sŏkkyŏng. In "Supsoge bang" ("A Room in the Woods," 1985) she draws a catastrophic portrait of a young woman who fails to find a place in the student movements and activism of the era. In "Nat kwa kkum" ("Days and Dreams," 1983) she treats the daily existence of Korean women living in military towns. The works of Yang Kwija, collected in *Wŏnmidong saramdŭl* (*The People of Wŏnmi-dong*, 1987), depict the isolation and alienated existence of small towns that bear every characteristic of modernization. These works too belong in the category of fiction that apprehends from a feminine perspective the awakened social consciousness of the 1980s.

This era, however, may also have been the first to exhibit, with unprecedented force, the masculine power of Korean literature. This is a central experience in the history of Korean literature – antithetical to the development of women's literature. It resulted in a kind of provisional period that helped awaken the uniquely liberating side of women's fiction that was to emerge. The class of young writers linked to feminism could not be indifferent to the feminist discourse that has spread so widely through the influence of women scholars educated in the West as well as the wholesale influence of popular movements.

In the context of the popular movements of the 1980s, works of fiction treating women's issues began to appear in large numbers. Among them Yun Chŏngmo's *Reins*, written for the purpose of "scientifically explaining women's relations with outside forces and with kin," illuminated the early form of this kind of fiction. In this work a young woman who had once prostituted herself cuts the reins of her past and takes leave of her fanatically pro-American younger brother when offered a new life provided by a husband who had been implicated in an anti-imperialist incident. As a work which concludes that "prostitution and ruin have a deep functional relation to outside influences," *Reins* has become known as a vehemently "anti-American fiction." For several writers, the enormous task of grafting women's issues onto a Korean reality dominated by outside influences (America) has become an urgent critical issue. But a structure that shows only the writer's awareness of issues as essential points, the lack of necessary connections between events, and the lack of justification in human actions – these are defects found not only in *Reins*.

The work of Yi Kyŏngja – such as "Chŏnban ŭi silp'ae" ("The Failure of a Half," 1983) – deals with the patriarchal family structure from multiple viewpoints: the complex relations between mothers-in-law and daughters-in-law, the exhausting lot of working wives who do double-duty at home and the office, husbands' abusive behavior, prostitution, and issues related to divorce. Yi's treatment of the patriarchal family from a multiple point of view is characteristic of 1980s fiction; previously the complications of family life were treated as dyadic. Because the organization of female victims and male abusers is depicted from a perspective that thoroughly supports the woman's side, Yi is often charged with establishing a narrow interpretation of feminine reality. Nevertheless she has secured many readers.[12]

On the whole, women's movements, women's discourse, and the introduction of countless Western theories helped inscribe the concerns of feminism onto the landscape of Korean literature. These concerns are further reinforced by the appearance of the standard narratives that followed. Beginning in the 1990s, women's works felt the popular reverberations of these influences. We may cite, for example, Kong Chiyŏng's *Muso ŭi ppul ch'ŏrŏm honjasŏ kara* (*Go Alone like a Rhino's Horn*, 1993), which gained the immediate applause of popular movements and feminism alike. We may also cite Kim Hyŏngyŏng, a writer of the same generation, whose "Sewŏl" ("Time and Tide," 1995) autobiographically depicts the process by which a feminine economy was formed. These works took the struggles of single women trying to survive in Korean society as a basic plot and secured a huge response from female readers – a necessary stage in a South Korean reality that continued to lag behind that in the West, particularly with regard to women's social status.

Having deepened theoretically, the tides of the times already gave the ineluctable impression of having entered a new domain before the various investigations of reality could deliver their conclusions and the political phases of Korean society could come to pass. In the 1990s, the tendency to misinterpret the open structure of discourse in the self-respecting female economy as something that was already in women's possession trivialized these writers' deepened awareness of women's realities. Throughout this process, feminist discourse universally occupied literary debates to the extent of giving birth to works that caricature feminism to an extreme – as in Yang Kwija's "Nanŭn somanghanda naege kŭmjidoen kŏsŭl" ("I Desire What is Forbidden Me," 1992), which introduced a "feminine warrior" tale of revenge that includes kidnappings and the imprisonment of men, aimed at overthrowing "the history of women's subjugation."[13]

The fruits of feminism include the historical yet literary reillumination of works in the 1980s and 1990s. Such reilluminations were vigorously

---

[12] Kim Yŏnghye, "Yŏsŏng munje ŭi sosŏlchŏk hyŏngsanghwa," *Ch'angjak kwa pip'yŏng* 75 (1989):55–74.

[13] Yi Sohŭi, "P'eminijŭm munhak e taehan myŏtkaji saengkaktŭl," *Tto hana ŭi munhwa* 9 (1993):200–217.

produced by women writers in the late 1980s and early 1990s and often included considerations of women writing earlier, such as Na Hyesŏk, Kang Kyŏngae, Paek Sinae, Ch'oe Chŏnghŭi, and Kim Malbong, as well as the more recent works of those who were important in the 1960s and 1970s. Departing from the general estimation of the literary world and relying on feminist theoretical frameworks developed in the West, women writers took a fresh look at these earlier writers' work. These reilluminations are the product of not only literary critics but women scholars in general.[14] This understanding of the past has influenced writers of the new era. Women's fiction thereafter, especially in their self-expression, is less cautious and freer. Women's fiction of this new era is entrusted with a larger role in Korean literature and is making progress in winning popularity and discussion of the intrinsic value of works themselves. It is an era when women writers are being inscribed with great diligence into the history of Korean literature.

The struggles for democratization in 1987 and the collapse of socialist authority in Eastern Europe influenced trends in South Korean literature. In the period that followed, literature in the South became to some extent freed from the demands of social participation visited on literature in the early 1990s, as well as from the grave debt of critical consciousness with respect to an undemocratic history. Beyond this, the example of German unification, which claimed significance as a worldwide event, has been used by South Koreans living in a comparable situation to predict a difficult and exciting Korean reunification.

On the one hand, women's fiction during this period filled the gaps left as these exhaustive discussions were ebbing. On the other hand, adopting an introspective stance with regard to the literature of former times, they also began to examine the areas overlooked by South Korean literature. Women's fiction began to create distinctive social views and to explore the origins of existence, the secrets of being, and the tribulations of eking out a living as a woman in a new setting. Since the investigation of a new reality calls for a new language, the women writers of this period devised multiple variations of literary style and aesthetics.

The work of Ch'oe Yun (b. 1953) – in particular, *Chŏgi soriŏpssi hanjŏm kkonnip'i chigo* (*There a Petal Silently Falls*, 1988), "Hoesaek nunsaram" ("Gray Snowman," 1991), and "Soksagim, soksagim" ("Whispers," 1993) – depicts personal experiences related to the history of the Kwangju massacre,

---

[14] Examples are the work of the literary researchers who participated in the making of "Olbarŭn yŏsŏng munhak ŭi chŏngnip ŭl wihayŏ," which was serially published in the yearly *Yŏsŏng*, founded in 1987, and the work in the special issue (spring 1991) on the world of Pak Wansŏ, in which Pak Hyeran and Cho Hyejŏng participated.

popular movements, and national division and attempts a deeper reinterpretation of a continuously problematic reality. Ch'oe's works, which radically express discomfort with the controlling modern value systems of authority, men, and collective ideology, adhere to the distanced perspective of outcasts in order to capture changing and alternative realities. What distinguishes Ch'oe is her concern for an escape from modernity – a concern that translates in her writing into a manner of fictionally examining her own view of the world. Because this form of writing is new and unfamiliar in South Korean literature, it is sometimes characterized as "an aesthetic model that aptly unites politics and the individual."[15]

Fundamental questions that could not be dealt with seriously in the period following liberation are confronted in the works of Sin Kyŏngsuk – for example, in "P'unggŭmi ittŏn chari" ("Where the Organ Once Stood," 1993) and "Oraejŏn chibŭl ttŏna ttae" ("When I Left Home Long Ago," 1996). Sin's works, written in a poetic language and a hesitating, tremulous literary style,[16] reconstruct memories of family that elicit a nearly mythic fragrance and become wellsprings of sorrow and testaments to endurance. Sin's feminine writing is revealed in the power of memory and in the poetry of the body, evident in nearly every work, rather than in her subject matter which is more or less traditional. Yet it is possible to detect a trace of narcissism in the rhythm of the writing that advances the story in "Oettan pang" ("An Isolated Room," 1995) – particularly in its attempt to draw forth a distinctive self through feminine writing. This self-sufficient view of language may help explain her wish that women's speech must steadfastly remain an anti-authoritarian and marginal language.

The language and realistic situations in the works of Kong Sŏnok – collected in *P'iŏra susŏnhwa* (*Bloom, Jonquil*, 1994), especially in the title piece or "Uri saengae ŭi kkot" ("The Flowering of our Lives," 1994) – differ sharply from the impression given in works by Sin Kyŏngsuk. In Kong's writing, an untroubled zone of sensibility is realized where speech may become free. Her work makes readers infer a previous experience of the extremities of life such as the Kwangju massacre. The strength of a tenacious existence saturates the language and actions of characters who unflinchingly brave harsh conditions. (In Kong's work we meet the newly armed Kang Kyŏngae, who reveals her subjectivity through writing.)

---

[15] Paek Chiyŏn, "Chubyŏnin ŭi sasaek, mangmyŏngja ŭi sam," *Hanguk munhak* (Autumn 1997): 64–79.

[16] Pak Hyegyŏng, "Ch'uŏk, kkŭtŏpssi pasŭrajinŭn munwi ŭi sam," in *Sin Kyŏngsuk sosŏl chip: P'unggŭm i ittŏn chari* (Munhak kwa chisŏngsa, 1993), p. 290.

In a manner different from Kong's stark language, the works of Ŭn Hŭigyŏng (b. 1959), having shrewdly hidden their true character, draw out the unpleasant and minor details of everyday oppression through an untroubled, voluble, and derisive language. These works are noteworthy as a form of retrograde feminine opposition before a state of affairs so completely distorted as to be nearly insurmountable.

Korean women's fiction of the 1990s, based on the respective characteristics of the different authors, has achieved a form of writing that can be called an authentic literature. In the years to come, it is sure to become more firmly established. Owing to the bubbling economy that followed the 1988 Olympics held in Seoul as well as the new liberalism and consumer culture then in full bloom, the 1990s may be regarded as the era when literature became commercialized in an unprecedented way. Works appearing on the literary scene expressed reaction to social and weighty topics of former times or exhibited, through other means, lightness, the meaninglessness of reality, or an abandonment to the senses. On the one hand, these works, positioned somewhere between popular and serious literature, appear to advocate a technical freedom to expose the cramped quality of traditional writing. On the other hand, given the commercialized postmodernism cited by Lash, these works reflect an ambivalence of Korean society that, in the 1990s, shows both modern and postmodern tendencies.[17]

Ham Chŏngim (b. 1964) came on the scene stressing the Western experimental consciousness of fiction. Pae Sua (b. 1965) offers works of imagination that seek to approximate the fictionalization of simple caricatures that first appeared in a thriving era of popular literature. The works of Song Kyŏnga (b. 1971) rest, in a writerly way, on the unique power to invent a suitable imaginary reality in the electronic space of the information age. These works form one stream of women's fiction in the 1990s.

In the South Korean literary world, the future of literature will depend on the universal movements of globalization. Today the diagnosis of globalization resides with those writers who show the distinguishing characteristics of the information age. However informationalization might affect literature, one characteristic is clear: the significance of literature is diminished, and its expression tends to expand without censorship.

---

[17] Scott Lash, *The Sociology of Postmodernism* (London: Routledge, 1990), p. 48.

CHAPTER 25

Literature of North Korea

Kwŏn Yŏngmin

As the division between North and South Korea hardened in the period following the country's liberation from Japan's colonial rule in 1945, North Korea set forth a number of objectives designed to ensure the establishment of a socialist polity in the North. The construction of socialist culture was one such objective – and literature, as an integral part of this culture, was to play a prominent role in the concerted effort to pursue class-based socialist ideology. The term "literature of North Korea" refers to literature based on such an objective since 1945. The development of North Korean literature, therefore, reflects changes that were taking place in North Korean society and politics. The period from the liberation to the early 1960s was marked by an emphasis on the duty of literature, as the artistic realization of socialist ideology, to serve party and people. For the North Korean government, the paramount goal that emerged through a sequence of experiences – the liberation, the Korean War, and the division of the Korean peninsula – was the establishment of a socialist order. For the accomplishment of this goal, literature became the central tool in rallying support for this aim and in the consolidation of socialist ideology in North Korean society.

From the mid-1960s, however, North Korean literature came increasingly to focus on the *chuch'e* (self-reliance, autonomy) thought of Kim Ilsŏng as the ideological basis for literary production. As the system of government in which the party provides the sole leadership became firmly entrenched and the *chuch'e* thought of Kim Ilsŏng was subsequently expounded in North Korea, a new emphasis was placed on literature resting on the ideology of self-reliance. This theory of literary creation valorized Kim Ilsŏng's theory and practice of revolution as providing both the literary canon and the standards by which literature is to be evaluated. Literary works paying tribute to Kim's theory of revolution – the ideological basis of the party – were hailed as the literature of *chuch'e*.

Thus North Korean literature sought to realize socialist ideology from immediately after the liberation to the early 1960s. From the mid-1960s, literature was conceptually defined and its value assessed anew according to the *chuch'e* thought of Kim Ilsŏng. With the appearance of *chuch'e* ideology, therefore, the emphasis shifted from aesthetic principles of socialist realism to revolutionary ideology based on *chuch'e* thought.

FOUNDATIONS

From 1945, North Korean literature took a leading role in educating the masses ideologically in order to establish a socialist political order. In March 1946, for example, a literary organization called the North Korean Artists' Federation was founded for the express purpose of realizing a socialist vision through the arts. In October of the same year, this organization was restructured as a federation of various groups in different areas of the arts and renamed the Federation for North Korean Literature and Arts. In a climate of growing polarization between North and South, the Federation for North Korean Literature and Arts separated from the Korean Writers' Federation, which was established in Seoul in February 1946, and emerged as an independent organization overseeing literary activities centered on P'yŏngyang in the North. The principal members of this organization – Yi Kiyŏng (1896–1988), Han Sŏrya (1901–1963), An Hamgwang (1910–1982), Song Yŏng (1903–1979), Pak Seyŏng (1902–1989), Yi Tonggyu (1913–1951) – gave up their literary activities in Seoul and crossed over to the North in order to engage in the production of literary works firmly rooted in socialist ideology. Calling for "the establishment of national culture based on progressive democracy, the obliteration of feudalistic and antinationalistic influence in the arts, and the critical inheritance of national cultural legacy," these writers ultimately dominated the literary scene in North Korea.

With the aesthetics of socialist realism as its principle, the federation subordinated the direction of literary movement to communist political ideology, which was actively promoted through the Central Arts Operative, founded in May 1946. Writers, for example, stood at the vanguard of the campaign known as "the movement to promote the ideology of nation building," which sought to galvanize the people of North Korea and reshape their consciousness according to communist ideology. This course of development in literature was further secured within the party through a rearticulation of the theory of literary production and consolidation of the political platform. A resolution regarding "the construction of nationalist culture in North Korea," adopted in March 1947 at the twenty-ninth meeting of the party's Central Committee, provided detailed regulations regarding literary activities. The resolution, premised on the belief that cultural and artistic activities must serve the homeland and the people, stipulated that literature, under the absolute rule of the proletariat, must aim at developing a socialist mindset among the masses. This stipulation was, in turn, forced directly upon all North Korean artists. As a result, North Korean literature in this period expressed ardent support for the construction of a new socialist nation and revealed an optimistic outlook upon social revolution. This trend is commonly referred to as revolutionary romanticism.

Active in the initial stages were Pak Seyŏng (1902–1989), Pak P'aryang (b. 1905), Yi Ch'an (b. 1910), Kim Chogyu (b. 1914), Ch'oe Sŏktu (1917–1951), Yi Chŏnggu, Im Hwa (1908–1953), and O Changhwan (1918–1951). Subsequently, Cho Kich'ŏn (1913–1951), a second-generation Korean-Russian who appeared in P'yŏngyang's literary scene immediately after the liberation, and Kang Sŭnghan (1918–1950), who first began writing at this time, entered the spotlight. In particular, Cho Kich'ŏn, with the publication of poems entitled "Tumangang" ("Tumen River") and "Ttang ŭi norae" ("Song of Land"), as well as the lengthy narrative poem *Paektusan* (*Mount Paektu*, 1947), came to occupy the central position in the world of North Korean poetry. *Mount Paektu* is a celebration of Kim Ilsŏng's revolutionary achievements in his armed struggle against the Japanese during the colonial period in northern Manchuria. In this work Kim Ilsŏng's revolutionary struggles are described as heroic feats and portrayed as receiving the energetic support and affirmation of the Korean people. Through a description of how Kim Ilsŏng overcomes Japanese colonial oppression and emerges victorious, the poet emphatically asserts that Kim Ilsŏng's revolutionary struggle represents a crucial victory in the liberation of his people. The subject matter of these poems clearly presages how North Korean poetry will continue to utilize Kim Ilsŏng's anti-Japanese struggles in order to fashion him as a national hero. Kang Sŭnghan, by contrast, who appeared for the first time in North Korea's literary world, began to gain notice with the publication of *Hallasan* (*Mount Halla*, 1948), a narrative poem dealing with the communist rebellion of Cheju Island in 1948, known as the April Third Incident. Unlike *Mount Paektu*, Kang's work does not describe a specific individual as a hero but takes as its subject the class solidarity of common people and depicts their struggle. Though these works, in their exaggeration of reality to achieve a specifically ideological agenda, fail to present an objective understanding of historical reality, one can see in them an attempt to realize certain narrative possibilities in the poetic form that emerged immediately after liberation.

In fiction, North Korean literature was dominated by writers who had insisted on proletarian literature from the colonial period – such as Yi Kiyŏng, Han Sŏrya, Yi Pungmyŏng (b. 1910), and Yi Tonggyu – and newly emerging writers such as Hwang Kŏn (1918–1991) and Ch'ŏn Sebong (1915–1986). Among the works by these writers, Yi Pungmyŏng's *Nodong ilga* (*A Family of Laborers*, 1947) represents a continuation of a motif that had appeared frequently in preliberation proletarian literature: labor. With the Hŭngnam Fertilizer Plant in the period immediately following liberation as the setting and the struggles of the laborers as the plot, the author shows the process by which people overcome self-interest and establish class consciousness as the first step to building a new socialist nation. Often read as lending enthusiastic support to the creative working lives of the proletariat, the work reveals the author's intent to promote a socialist vision of society in which the working class is master. Yi Tonggyu's *Kŭ chŏnnal pam* (*On That Eve*, 1948) presents a critique of contemporary South Korean politics at the time of the 1948 elections by focusing on the political struggles of the working class against the establishment of a separate government in the South. In *Ttang* (*Land*, 1949), Yi Kiyŏng interprets the growth of the proletariat and the establishment of the socialist system of government as historical inevitabilities in the narrative of a life of a peasant set against the backdrop of North Korea's land reforms after liberation. The protagonist, an exploited farmhand on the estate of a vicious landowner during the colonial period, becomes a genuine owner of the land after the land reforms who then devotes himself unselfishly to revitalization of the countryside. Despite the work's schematic structure, the portrait of peasants suffering under the exploitation of landowners presents an extreme contrast to the image of the peasant enjoying freedom as the rightful owner of the land he tills in the post-liberation socialist state. For this reason, *Land* is seen as a work that successfully creates a new character type suited to the period of democratic nation building in North Korea.

POSTWAR LITERATURE

After the bitter experience of the Korean War and then the demise of the Communist Party in the South, North Korea conducted a large-scale purge of writers. Under the party's directive, a significant portion of southern writers who had crossed over to the North, including Im Hwa, Kim Namch'ŏn (1911–1953), Sŏl Chŏngsik (1912–1953), and Yi T'aejun (b. 1914), were expunged from literary circles. According to the party literature, this purge, which preceded the postwar reconstruction efforts, was conducted to reject the factional and disruptive activities of writers and to pulverize bourgeois literary thought that paralyzes the revolutionary consciousness and the militant mindset of the masses. After completing the purge and securing control of thought, the North Korean government once again systematically mobilized writers in the postwar reconstruction efforts and economic campaigns. These reconstruction efforts, sometimes referred to as "Ch'ŏllima Undong" (Gallant Steed Campaign), enabled the establishment of the socialist order and the enactment of thought control against the masses.

Literary works eulogizing the revolutionary character of Kim Ilsŏng's anti-Japanese struggles during the colonial period and seeking to promote his leadership qualities during the Korean War began to appear with great frequency in North Korea following the war's conclusion. Such works, in fact, have since become the staple of mainstream North Korean poetry and fiction. Also worthy of note is a critique of the United States, especially the US military, and criticism of the social reality in South Korea has become an important theme in North Korean literature.

The poem "P'ibal sŏn saehae" ("Bloodshot New Year"), by Yi Yongak (1914–1971) published during the Korean War, justifies the war effort as a historical necessity for the liberation of the homeland. Paek Injun, in "Ŏlgurŭl pulk'ira, Amerik'a yŏ" ("Blush in Shame, America"), offers a bitter condemnation of US participation in the Korean War. Cho Kich'ŏn's long poem, "Chosŏn ŭn ssaunda" ("Korea Fights," 1951) is a work that pledges the victory of the war effort as a stage in the revolutionary struggle. Min Pyŏnggyun's narrative poem "Ŏrŏri pŏl" ("The Plains of Ŏrŏri," 1952) relates the story of an ordinary peasant woman who joins a guerrilla unit on Mount Kuwŏl after losing her husband and children at the hands of the enemy.

This tendency in poetry continued in the postwar period, as Cho Pyŏgam (b. 1908) sang of a victory in the war for the liberation of the homeland and the leadership of Kim Ilsŏng in "Kwangjang esŏ" ("In the Square," 1953). In "Samgaksan i poinda" ("I Can See Mount Samgak," 1956), Cho sang of reunification with the poet's eyes gazing at the southern sky. The poem "Saedŭrŭn sup'ŭro kanda" ("Birds Fly to the Forest," 1954) by Chŏng Munhyang (b. 1919) celebrates the firm resolve of workers being mobilized in the postwar reconstruction campaign. This work, through the metaphor of birds that fly up in surprise when they hear the alarm sounding the changing factory shift, exalts the collective resolve of workers.

In the case of fiction, many works appeared in the postwar period that sought to mobilize workers in the reconstruction effort and to advertise the results of the campaign. Among the works depicting scenes from the work sites of the Gallant Steed Campaign, Hwang Kŏn's *Kaema kowŏn* (*Kaema Plateau*, 1956), Siryŏn sok esŏ (*Amidst Hardship*, 1957) by Yun Sejung (1912–1965), and Ch'ŏn Sebong's *Sŏkkaeul ŭi saebom* (*A New Spring by Sŏk Stream*, 1958) received the most critical attention. These works all treat success stories in the campaign and seek to exalt communal consciousness and class solidarity through the abandonment of self-interest. Set in the mountain regions of the North, *Kaema Plateau* depicts activities promoting socialist class ideology and the struggle in a mountain village in the period from liberation to war. The subject of *Amidst Hardship* is the collective will of factory workers taking part in postwar reconstruction efforts. Together the workers overcome great hardships as they labor to restore an ironworks destroyed by US bombing during the war. Reconstruction of the countryside is depicted in *A New Spring by Sŏk Stream*. This work narrates the story of peasants who abandon their individual self-interest and establish a cooperative in order to reconstruct a farming village decimated during the war.

The two works of fiction that have received the most critical attention among those produced during this period are *Sŏsan taesa* (*Great Master Sŏsan*, 1956) by Ch'oe Myŏngik (b. 1908) and Yi Kiyŏng's *Tumangang* (*Tumen River*, 1961). *Great Master Sŏsan*, which takes as its setting the battle of P'yŏngyang fortress during the Japanese invasions of 1592–1598, emphasizes the heroic spirit of the Righteous Army and monk soldiers led by the Great Master as they struggle against foreign aggression. Though this work borrows its subject from a historical event and contrasts the brutality of the Japanese army with the Korean people's spirit of valiant struggle, the work simultaneously provides an allegorical critique of the UN army's storming of P'yŏngyang during the Korean War. Yi Kiyŏng's fiction of epic dimensions, *Tumen River*, was published in three parts from shortly after the war to 1961. The work may be seen as picking up where the author's previous work, *Pom* (*Spring*, 1941), published during the colonial period, left off. Against the backdrop of turbulent history from the breakdown of authoritarian Chosŏn society at the end of the nineteenth century to colonization by the Japanese, the author keeps his eye on the process by which peasants form a class. In order to present a portrait of peasants struggling to demolish a feudalistic social structure, the author remains faithful to the ideological tenets of socialist realism. Yi Kiyŏng further emphasizes the historical inevitability of their victory by interweaving Kim Ilsŏng's revolutionary campaign and the struggles of the peasants.

LITERATURE IN THE PERIOD OF *CHUCH'E*

Literature in the North after 1960 reveals a shift toward simultaneous exaltation of the ideals of *chuch'e* and revolution as the aesthetics of socialist realism were redefined according to Kim Ilsŏng's ideology. If the literature before 1960 placed great importance on socialist ideology, class, and the need for solidarity among common people while stressing the creation of the communal and the representative, the literature after 1960 emphasized the spirit of revolutionary struggle and the characteristics of *chuch'e*, thereby enhancing the ideological character of the works.

The reestablishment of revolutionary ideology in North Korean literature in accordance with the demands of *chuch'e* ideology has an intimate relationship with the Communist Party's policy of consolidating its position as the sole political party. The theory of literary production based on the idea of *chuch'e* that emerged after 1970 provides a clear articulation of the overall framework and character of this phenomenon. A prominent aspect of this theory is the effort to combine the particular and the universal: reinterpretation of national forms of literature by way of the ideology of socialist revolution sought simultaneously to propound the national uniqueness of the art forms and the universal character of socialist ideology. In actuality, however, we can see little conceptual change in the *chuch'e* theory of literature or the works it produced. What the *chuch'e* theory of literature emphasizes as "national forms" is far from a modern reappraisal of traditional aesthetic forms particular to Korea. The model of national literature is in fact the kind of literature that expresses revolutionary ideology based on Kim Ilsŏng's theory of revolution rather than aesthetic principles of socialist realism. In this way, the "form reflecting revolutionary creation of literature" refers specifically to anti-Japanese revolutionary literature which is said to have been produced during the colonial period under the leadership of Kim Ilsŏng. Seen as an artistic expression of Marxist-Leninist revolution under the leadership of the proletariat, anti-Japanese revolutionary literature is said to provide an imperishable model that socialist literature must imitate. This literature is also seen as enabling the masses to arrive at class consciousness, contributing actively to the formation of the revolutionary worldview, and articulating the demands and participation of the masses. Similarly the requisite content of socialist ideology propounded in this theory also became fixed as it was equated to Kim Ilsŏng's theory of revolution. Perhaps it is only to be expected that this theory, the only ideology of leadership within the party, would provide the content of literary works written, after all, for the victory of the revolutionary struggle and effectiveness of construction efforts.

Two important aspects of literary production in North Korea are the concepts of the seed and the stress on speed. The seed (*chongja*) is defined as the nucleus of a work. Literary theorists of North Korea consider the seed as providing the basic criterion for evaluating the work's value as a whole. In creating a literary work, one must first capture the seed properly in order to convey one's ideological-aesthetic intent and secure the philosophical basis of the work. For this reason, all works of literature must reveal the author's unique and original seed and aesthetic formalization must arise from the seed. Thus we can see that the seed of a work is simultaneously the aesthetic and ideological element of greatest importance, since it contains both the central subject the author wishes to discuss and the basic element of ideology. Hence the subject matter and the ideological content of a work, as well as the aesthetic form, are determined by the seed.

The ideological character, of course, is of paramount importance in the seed theory. By "ideological character" is meant accurate reflection of the party's policies and the ability to suggest an ideologically correct answer to contemporary sociopolitical tasks based on the party's projected plans and stated policies. Before all else, the working masses must have an ideological character that can be nurtured through the spirit of communist revolution. Therefore, a work's ideological character becomes the most appropriate criterion for judging its value as literature, which in turn results from correctly attaining the essence of the seed. In other words, capturing the seed is the act of correctly combining the ideological and the aesthetic character in the creative process of the aesthetic formalization, as well as the method by which literary art is transformed into an expression of genuine communist humanism.

Artists of North Korea, in order to act upon these guiding principles, must nurture their own artistic talents through ideological aestheticism. Literature becomes possible, not through independent experimentation with aspects of one's unique creativity, but through enthusiastic support and deep understanding of Kim Ilsŏng's teachings and their reflection in the party's policies. Writers must directly experience revolutionary zeal and taste social reality where the party's policies are being implemented. Only within their active participation in this ideological project can they discover their unique seed. Moreover, they must undertake a creative process after they have undergone the preparation of directed ideological aestheticism. Socialist literature must at all times conform to the aesthetic demands of the working masses, who stand at the vanguard of revolutionary struggle, and present a vision of historical progress.

The second aspect worthy of note in the North Korean theory of literary production is the concept of speed (*soktojŏn*). According to this concept, a high level of productivity must be sustained immediately after the seed is captured in order to ensure the quality and ideological integrity of the work. The principle of speed seeks to guarantee a greater number of high-quality works in a shorter period of time by calling on writers to tackle their duties actively in accordance with the reality of revolutionary struggle and to maintain a state of creative tension free of stagnation or slumps. The central goal of this method is the simultaneous acceleration of literary production and enhancement of the ideological aestheticism of the output. With this method, writers experience a high degree of political zeal and creative speculation. When the writer, swept up in a single burst of creative fervor, overcomes all personal and narrow-minded thoughts and concentrates on the revolutionary ideology of the leader as the sole provider of party ideology, he is then able to heighten the quality of his work. To carry out this principle of speed effectively, North Korean writers often engage in "communal creation" or collective writing. Competition for speedier production of literary output is itself considered an instance of the battle mindset put to use in the arena of artistic creativity.

Literature written in the 1970s, during which the *chuch'e* theory of creative writing became generally accepted and widely practiced, can be divided broadly into three categories: the first praises accomplishments of Kim Ilsŏng in his anti-Japanese military struggles; the second propounds the greatness of the socialist state established in North Korea; and the third emphasizes the task of revolutionary reunification with the South. The task of praising Kim Ilsŏng's revolutionary struggles was considered the most important of the three, and the activities of Kim's entire family became a subject of literary hero formation. The entire series of *Pulmyŏl ŭi yŏksa* (*Imperishable History*), conceptualized as a grand tribute to Kim Ilsŏng's revolutionary struggles, was published over a period of several years from the mid-1970s to the 1980s. It contains over fifteen works chronologically detailing Kim Ilsŏng's life and revolutionary struggles: *Tat ŭn ollatta* (*The Sail is Raised*, 1982) by Kim Chŏng; *Ŭnhasu* (*Milky Way*, 1982) by Ch'ŏn Sebong; *Kŭngŏji ŭi pom* (*Spring at the Base*, 1981) by Ri Chongnyŏl; *Konan ŭi haenggun* (*The March of Suffering*, 1976) by Sŏk Yungi; *Paektusan kisŭk* (*At the Foot of Mount Paektu*, 1978) by Hyŏng Sŏnggŏl and Ch'oe Haksu; and others. In addition to extolling Kim Ilsŏng, these works incorporate mythic elements in order to present Kim Ilsŏng's achievements as sacred. Two works cast Kim Ilsŏng's parents as protagonists in the presentation of his heritage as imbued with the revolutionary spirit: *Yŏksa ŭi saebyŏk kil* (*The Road at the Dawn of History*, 1972) by Yi Kiyŏng and *Chosŏn ŭi ŏmŏni* (*Mother of Korea*, 1970) by Nam Hyojae. Works fictionalizing the life of Kim Chŏngsuk, Kim Ilsŏng's wife, can be grouped under the series title of *Ch'ungsŏng ŭi han kil esŏ* (*On the Road of Loyal Devotion*) and include five related works of substantial length: *Yugyŏkku ŭi kisu* (*Standard-bearer of a Commando*, 1975) and *Saryŏngbu ro kanŭn kil* (*The Road to Headquarters*, 1979) by Ch'ŏn Sebong, as well as *Kwangbok ŭi haebal* (*Sunbeams of Liberation*, 1982) and *Kŭrinŭn choguk sanch'ŏn* (*The Homeland I Long to See*, 1985) by Pak Yuhak and *Chindallae* (*Azaleas*, 1985) by Ri Chongnyŏl. After the 1980s a significant number of works praising Kim Chŏngil emerged.

Works of tribute to the Kim family are prominent in poetry as well. Poems written in the 1960s include Yi Yongak's "Uri tang ŭi haenggun no" ("The Marching Path of our Party," 1961), which sings of the party's history as being built upon the spiritual base of Kim Ilsŏng's revolutionary struggles, Pak Seyŏng's "Millim ŭi yŏksa" ("History of a Dense Forest," 1962), which presents a written pilgrimage of the sites associated with Kim Ilsŏng's revolutionary struggles, and the collectively written "Inmin ŭn norae handa" ("The People Sing," 1962). Since the 1970s, poems praising Kim Ilsŏng have become so numerous that they are grouped as a separate genre of *songga* (hymns).

A significant portion of the literature from this period advertises the greatness of socialist nation building. In the case of fiction, such works include Kwŏn Chŏngung's *Paegilhong* (*Crape Myrtle*, 1961), Sŏk Yungi's *Haengbok* (*Happiness*, 1963) and *Sidae ŭi t'ansaeng* (*Birth of an Era*, 1966), Ch'oe Haksu's *P'yŏngyang sigan* (*P'yŏngyang Time*, 1976) and *Saengmyŏng su* (*Water of Life*, 1978), and Kim Kyuyŏp's *Sae pom* (*New Spring*, 1978). *Crape Myrtle*, read as a portrait of humanism associated with the Gallant Steed period, casts a railroad guard in a valley of Mount Nangnim as the main character. Though his wife is dissatisfied with his occupation and wants to move to a city, she is ultimately won over by the spirit of voluntarism and service among her husband's fellow watchmen and comes to assist her husband actively. *Birth of an Era* presents scenes from the Korean War. The story of a miner who manages to capture an American divisional commander in the battle at Taejŏn out of his determination to carry out revolutionary struggle, the work emphasizes the author's feelings of hostility toward America in the preface. *P'yŏngyang Time* fictionalizes the process of restoring the devastated urban center of postwar P'yŏngyang through the experience of one laborer. *Water of Life* relates the stories of a successful irrigation project in a country village. *New Spring* describes the process by which the People's Party came to power through the prism of class conflict, which is ultimately resolved by the ideology of revolution. In the case of poetry, Paek Injun's "Taedonggang e hŭrŭnŭn iyagi" ("A Story Flowing in Taedong River," 1962), a celebration of postwar reconstruction and factory building under the great guidance of Kim Ilsŏng, shares similar thematic concerns with Chŏng Munhyang's "Sidae e taehan saenggak" ("Thoughts on the Era," 1961) and O Yŏngjae's "Choguk i sarang hanŭn ch'ŏnyŏ" ("A Young Woman the Homeland Loves," 1963). "Thoughts on the Era" shows the changing reality of life under the progress of the Gallant Steed Campaign; "A Young Woman the Homeland Loves" depicts, through the unpretentious eyes of a peasant girl, a portrait of a countryside developing under the same campaign.

Pak T'aewŏn's *Kabo nongmin chŏnjaeng* (*Peasant Revolution of the Year Kabo*, 1977–1980) and Hong Sŏkchung's *Nopssae param* (*Northeastern Wind*, 1983) have received much attention as works of historical fiction dealing with the Tonghak peasant uprising (1894): the former work revolves around the person of Chŏn Pongjun (1854–1895); the second concerns the repulsion of Japanese marauders at three southern ports in 1510. Collective efforts to recreate literary works dealing with anti-Japanese rebellions were also conducted on an epic scale during this period. "Kkot p'anŭn ch'ŏnyŏ" ("Flower Girl"), "P'i pada" ("Sea of Blood"), and "Han chawidan ŭi unmyŏng" ("Fate of a Self-defense Force") were recast and promoted widely under the heading of revolutionary theater, revolutionary fiction, and revolutionary cinema, respectively. These efforts confirm that the tradition of anti-Japanese revolutionary literature became entrenched as the primary ideological requisite in the literature of North Korea.

Two characteristics distinguish North Korean literature written after 1980 in terms of their overall direction. The first is the establishment of orthodoxy in order to complete the objective of building a socialist culture based on *chuch'e* ideology. In particular, the depiction of Kim Chŏngil as a hero becomes more prominent in preparation of his succession to *chuch'e* thought. The second characteristic is a vigorous critique of South Korean reality. Literary works in North Korea sought to present a critique of South Korean literature and sociopolitical reality – especially the conflicts surrounding the Kwangju democratic movement – and propound the greatness of socialist culture by contrast and to establish its historical justification.

These developments in North Korean literature are linked to the passing of the baton to Kim Chŏngil and, as well, to class conflict and social division in South Korea. Among the works that portray Kim Chŏngil as the new leader are Pak Hyŏn's "Akkisinŭn maŭm" ("The Heart that Cares For Us," 1984), Ri Taesang's "Tasi ssŭn nonmun" ("A Rewritten Essay," 1984), Hyŏn Sŭnggŏl's "Taeji" ("The Great Earth," 1985), Kim Yŏnggŭn's "Yŏngsaeng" ("Eternal Life," 1985), Kim Sŏnggwan's "Annyŏng" ("Hello," 1987), Paek Ŭnp'al's "Sarang ŭi saem" ("Spring of Love," 1988), and Ch'oe Haksu's "Nun pusida" ("Dazzling," 1988). In these works, the portrait of Kim Chŏngil that generally emerges is not one of a revolutionary warrior but of a gentle humanist. Kim Chŏngil's actions in these texts highlight his leadership and painstaking care over various problems occurring all over North Korean society. For this reason, Kim Chŏngil in these works often figures, not as the main character, but as the resolver of difficult conflicts and a personification of human love. He is a kind leader with a deep sympathy for a manager facing termination from his job ("The Heart that Cares for Us"); a gentle leader who praises a soldier for thinking of a new military strategy ("A Rewritten Essay"); and a humane leader who takes interest even in small personal details while watching a graduation ceremony ("Eternal Life"). In "Spring of Love," as well, Kim Chŏngil is a thoughtful and caring leader: while watching a movie with a major writer of the party, he makes a mental connection between the scenes in the movie and the writer's personal life and realizes that the writer is concerned about his wife's illness. By depicting Kim Chŏngil as a leader who displays kind thoughtfulness in having an owl caught so that it can be used as medicine for the writer's sick wife, the work presents a view of Kim as a warm personage capable of extending love even to people in their everyday lives. Such depictions helped to promote the image of Kim as a leader who possesses "love toward his people."

The critique of South Korea's social reality found in many works of North Korean literature written after 1980 focuses on the political contradictions in the South that erupted in the Kwangju democratic movement (May 1980). Fictional works such as "Pom uroe" ("Spring Thunder," 1984) by Sŏk Yugyun and "Haengjin kok" ("A March," 1988) by Ri Kyŏngsuk are two examples. "Ryangsim ŭi kil" ("The Path of Conscience," 1988) by Ri Myŏnghun deals with the labor movement led by college students. In "Spring Thunder," the central character is a man injured in the Kwangju struggles. After his injury, he resolves to leave the barricades of social struggle altogether and devote himself to science in order to serve his society as a technician. Then he comes face to face with a passionate woman who, though born into a wealthy doctor's family, stands at the vanguard of struggle and ultimately changes his mind. The work ends with these two figures standing side by side at the van of a new struggle. In "The Path of Conscience," the main character is a college student studying science who suffers economic hardship. He subsists on the money his wife gets by selling her blood, but ultimately he faces expulsion for being unable to pay the tuition. As masses of college students are imprisoned for their involvement in the democratization movement, the main character finally finds a company job. He too, however, comes to stand at the center of the labor movement when he opposes the company's decision to fire factory workers. These works, because they portray a single aspect of South Korean society in an exaggerated manner, distort factual reality and present artificial characters. The exaggeration of South Korean poverty, the critique of the United States, the emphasis on struggle – all arise from policy considerations designed to stress the superiority of socialist culture in North Korea.

Even more blunt critiques can be seen in poetry. Of particular prominence are works that criticize the process of the Fifth Republic's formation in South Korea and the brutalities committed in Kwangju: Cho Sŏnggwan's "Chŏju" ("A Curse," 1981), Ri Tonghu's "Tanjoe handa maeguk yŏkchŏk ŭl" ("Nation's Traitors, We Proclaim your Guilt," 1984), Cho Pyŏngsŏk's "P'i ŭi purŭm" ("The Call of Blood," 1985), Chu Hich'ŏl's "P'i hŭllin ttang e chayu nŭn ori" ("Freedom Lands where Blood has been Shed," 1985), and An Chŏnggi's "Chŏnghaejin unmyŏng" ("Fate Decided," 1989).

LITERATURE AND IDEOLOGY

Since Korea's liberation from Japan in 1945, the literature of North Korea has consistently emphasized the general requisites of socialist culture such as the party, the masses, and class, as well as the ideological value of revolutionary character. The task of socialist culture building, which charts the direction of North Korean policy on literary creation, is itself explained through the concept of socialist revolution. Social transformation through *chuch'e* thought is proclaimed as the central task facing North Korean society. Literature, in this context, is a weapon of socialism to be used in line with the party's policies. In particular, the ideology of revolution receives special attention – for the revolution must continue, not only in North Korea, but until South Korea is liberated as well.

The issue of revolutionary character began to appear in North Korean literature in the early 1960s. In a speech entitled "Hyŏngmyŏngjŏk munhakyesul ŭl ch'angjakhalte taehayŏ" ("On the Creation of Revolutionary Literature") – delivered in November 1964 against the backdrop of crises in foreign affairs such as the expansion of American supremacy and the outbreak of the Vietnam War, the solidification of a military regime in South Korea, the conflict between China and the Soviet Union, and the alienation of North Korea – Kim Ilsŏng stressed the importance of revolutionary ideology not only in building a socialist nation in North Korea but also in revolutionizing South Korea as the first step toward ultimate reunification. To achieve this goal, North Koreans must, first, strengthen socialist nation building in North Korea and establish the base for revolution in politics, the economy, the military, and culture; second, consider the task of South Korean revolution as a duty on which their own lives depend; and, third, establish solidarity with international revolutionary capacity and oppose US imperialism in order to isolate the United States. In compliance with Kim Ilsŏng's views, North Korean writers since the 1960s have spent most of their energy in the production of revolutionary literature. In the process, North Korea has formed a theory of literary production based upon Kim Ilsŏng's *chuch'e* thought, established anti-Japanese revolution literature said to have been produced in the 1930s under Kim Ilsŏng's influence as the "national" form of literature, rewritten literary history according to the requisites of this ideology, and proposed a method of literary creation in keeping with it. In short, the ideology of revolution emphasized in North Korean literature may be seen as the nucleus of Kim Ilsŏng's *chuch'e* thought as well. Kim Ilsŏng, in the process of postwar reconstruction and with Lenin's argument regarding the national mission of the working class as his basis, argued that a nation's socialist revolution must occur for the benefit of the masses, in accordance with the national realities, and with the masses as the subject. Such a position was officially publicized as a new Marxist-Leninist ideology of leadership elevating the autonomy and creativity of the masses. In the 1960s, it was accepted as the great ideology of revolution that elucidates both the fundamental position of socialist revolution and the method by which it can be achieved. Later, Kim Ilsŏng's position was proclaimed as the sole ideology of the North Korean Labor Party. *Chuch'e* thought, which advocates the principle of autonomy in the realms of thought, politics, economy, and defense, has become North Korea's ruling ideology. In this regard, we might say that the people of North Korea are living in the era of *chuch'e*.

Literature exists in North Korea in order to find appropriate expressions of the leader's system of thought, the sole ideology of the party. By arming the working class with the ideology of revolution and establishing within them a revolutionary worldview, literature executes its revolutionary mission. According to North Korean theorists of literature, the revolutionary and class-based content of socialist realism, through its expression in national literary forms that resonate with the spirit of the people of a particular nation, can nurture them into fervent revolutionaries and genuine communists. Socialist realism may unfold in different ways in different nations according to their specific conditions of history. *Chuch'e* literature finds its theoretical moorings precisely in this ideological reinterpretation of socialist realism. Kim Ilsŏng's definition of socialist realism as "pouring the socialist content into a national form" represents a creative re-working of concepts of socialist realism according to the sociohistorical conditions specific to North Korea.

In this way, the *chuch'e* theory of literature pursues artistic realization through national forms well suited to the national spirit evidenced in artistic talent, creative wisdom, and everyday sentiments of the people. To heighten the aesthetic realization of literature, a writer must struggle to safeguard a high level of ideological aestheticism by truthfully reflecting the realities of life through national literary forms. The *chuch'e* theory of literature, however, does not value aesthetic realization in and of itself. Harmony between a work's form and content can only be achieved through a faithful presentation of the revolutionary ideology of the working class by means of national forms of literature. The socialist content, in turn, is only possible when the artist faithfully reflects the reality of life seen from the position of the party, the proletariat, the people. The *chuch'e* theory of literature is thus a unique synthesis that seeks to combine the universality of socialist content and the formal specificity of the national form. That this theory is advanced in North Korea as the pinnacle of achievement in literary studies attests to the importance of the theoretical synthesis it seeks.

In the end, the national form propounded in the *chuch'e* theory of literature is the literary form of revolution attributed to Kim Ilsŏng. The content of socialist ideology that must unite with the national literary form is also that of Kim Ilsŏng and has become the sole ideology of the party. The *chuch'e* theory of literature is premised on the belief that only the accurate reflection of the revolutionary ideology of the Great Leader and the party represents the path of progress for socialist literature. In the final analysis, the revolutionary ideology of Kim Ilsŏng has provided the doctrinal cage in which the literature of North Korea has been imprisoned since the mid twentieth century.

Bibliography

EAST ASIAN SOURCES

(All Korean-language texts were published in Seoul unless indicated otherwise.)

Akamatsu Chijō and Akiba Takashi. *Chōsen fuzoku no kenkyū* (Studies in Korean shamanism). Tokyo: Osakayagō shoten, 1937–1938.

Akchang kasa (Words for songs and music). In Wŏnbon Hanguk kojŏn ch'ongsŏ (Korean classics series in the original). Taejegak, 1972.

An Ch'uk. *Kunjae chip. KMC* 2; 1973.

An Pyŏnghak. "Samdangp'a sisegye yŏngu" (Study of the poetic world of Three Tang-Style poets). Ph.D. dissertation, Korea University, 1988.

Ch'a Chunghwan. "*Sukhyang chŏn" yŏngu* (Study of the *Tale of Sukhyang*). Wŏrin, 1999.

Ch'a Yongju. "*Ongnu mong" yŏngu* (Study of the *Dream of the Jade Tower*). Hyŏngsŏl ch'ulp'ansa, 1981.

Chang Hyohyŏn. "Chosŏn hugi ŭi sosŏllon" (Theory of fiction in late Chosŏn). *Ŏmun nonjip* 23 (1982):575–596.

Sŏ Yuyŏng munhak ŭi yŏngu (Study of Sŏ Yuyŏng's works). Asea munhwasa, 1988.

"Kungmun changp'yŏn sosŏl ŭi hyŏngsŏng kwa kamun sosŏl ŭi palchŏn" (Formation of long fiction in Korean and the development of clan fiction). In *Minjok munhaksa kangjwa* (Lectures on a history of national literature). Ch'angjak kwa pip'yŏngsa, 1995, 1:268–282.

Chang Tŏksun. *Hanguk sŏrhwa munhak yŏngu* (Studies in Korean narrative literature). Seoul taehakkyo ch'ulp'anbu, 1970.

Chang Yangsu. *Hanguk ŭijŏk sosŏlsa* (History of fiction about the righteous robber). Munye ch'ulp'ansa, 1991.

Chang Yu. *Kyegok manp'il* (Random jottings of Chang Yu). In *Kyegok chip* (Collected works of Chang Yu). Kyŏngin munhwasa, 1982.

Chen Shou. *Sanguozhi* (History of the Three Kingdoms). 5 vols. Peking: Zhonghua, 1962.

Chin Kyŏnghwan. "Chosŏn hugi *yadam* ŭi sadaebujŏk chihyang kwa kŭ pyŏnmo yangsang" (Confucian orientation of late Chosŏn unofficial stories and its transformation). MA thesis, Korea University, 1983.

Chin Tonghyŏk. *Kosijo munhak non* (Study of classic *sijo* literature). Hyŏngsŏl ch'ulp'ansa, 1982.

Cho Chihun. *Cho Chihun chŏnjip* (Collected works of Cho Chihun). 9 vols. Nanam, 1996.

Cho Hyeran. "*Samhan sŭbyu* yŏngu" (Study of *The Tale of Heroism from the Three Kingdoms*). Ph.D. dissertation, Ewha Woman's University, 1994.

Cho Kwangguk. *Kinyŏdam kinyŏ tŭngjang sosŏl yŏngu* (Study of fiction with female entertainers as characters). Wŏrin, 2000.

Cho Kyuik. *Kagok ch'angsa ŭi kungmunhakchŏk ponjil* (The literary essence of *kagok* song texts). Chimmundang, 1994.

Uriŭi yennorae munhak: Manhoengch'ŏng yu (Our old song literature: the *Manhoengch'ŏng* genre). Pagijŏng, 1996.

Cho Tongil. "Kamyŏngŭk ŭi hŭigŭkchŏk kaltŭng" (Comic conflicts in the mask play). *Kungmunhak yŏngu* 5 (1968):1–226.

Hanguk sosŏl ŭi iron (Theory of Korean fiction). Chisik sanŏpsa, 1977.

"*T'alch'um* kwa minjung ŭisik ŭi sŏngjang" (Mask plays and the growth of popular consciousness). In *Talch'um ŭi yŏksa wa wŏlli* (History and theory of mask dance plays). Hongsŏngsa, 1979.

"Nojang kwajang ŭi chuje chaekŏmt'o" (Re-examination of the theme of the Old Monk scene). In *T'alch'um ŭi yŏksa wa wŏlli* (History and theory of mask dance plays). Hongsŏngsa, 1979.

"Hanguk Chungguk Ilbon 'sosŏl' ŭi kaenyŏm" (The concept of fiction in Korea, China, and Japan). *Sŏnggok nonch'ong* 20 (1989):621–655.

Hanguk munhak t'ongsa (General history of Korean literature). 5 vols, with a separate index. 2nd edn. Chisik sanŏpsa, 1989.

Cho Tongil et al. *Hanguk sŏrhwa yuhyŏng pullyu chip* (Type and motif index of Korean narratives). Supplementary volume. Sŏngnam: Hanguk chŏngsin munhwa yŏnguwŏn, 1989.

Cho Yŏngbok. "Chuch'e tŭrŏnagi wa t'aja paeje hagi" (Displaying subjectivity, eliminating the other). In Hanguk sosŏl munhak taegye (Works of Koren fiction series). Tonga ch'ulp'ansa, 1995.

Cho Yongho. *Samdaerok sosŏl yŏngu* (Study of fiction covering three-generation records). Kyemyŏng munhwasa, 1996.

Ch'oe Cha. *Pohan chip* (*KMC* 2), 1973.

Ch'oe Ch'iwŏn. *Kyewŏn p'ilgyŏng chip* (Collection of plowing a cassia grove with a writing brush). Sibu congkan.

Ch'oe Chŏngyŏ. "*Sandae togamgŭk* sŏngnip ŭi chemunje" (Problems in the formation of *sandae* plays). *Hangukhak nonjip* 1 (1973):6–24.

Ch'oe Hyejin. *P'ansorigye sosŏl ŭi mihak* (Aesthetics of *p'ansori* fiction). Yŏngnak, 2000.

Ch'oe Inhak et al. *Hanguk minsok yŏngusa* (History of studies on Korean folk customs). Chisik sanŏpsa, 1994.

Ch'oe Kanghyŏn. "*Kasa* ŭi palsaengsajŏk yŏngu" (Study of the rise of *kasa*). In *Kasa munhak yŏngu* (Studies in the *Kasa*). Chŏngŭmsa, 1979.

Hanguk kihaeng munhak yŏngu (Studies in Korean travel literature). Ilchisa, 1982.

ed. *Hanguk kihaeng munhak chakp'um yŏngu* (Studies in Korean accounts of travels). Kukhak charyowŏn, 1996.

Ch'oe Manmuk, ed. *Hanguk hyŏndaesi taegye* (Outline of modern Korean poetry). 3 vols. Hanguk munhwasa, 1996.

Ch'oe Namsŏn. *Yuktang Ch'oe Namsŏn chŏnjip* (Collected works of Ch'oe Namsŏn). 15 vols. Hyŏnamsa, 1973–1975.

Ch'oe Sangsu. *Hanguk inhyŏnggŭk ŭi yŏngu* (Study of Korean puppet plays). Koryŏ sŏjŏk, 1961.

Ch'oe Sihan. "Kajŏng sosŏl ŭi kujo wa chŏngae" (Structure and development of family fiction). Ph. D. dissertation, Sŏgang University, 1989.

Ch'oe Tonghyŏn and Yu Yŏngdae, eds. *"Sim Ch'ŏng chŏn" yŏngu* (Studies in the *Tale of Sim Ch'ŏng*). T'aehaksa, 1999.

Ch'oe Tongwŏn. *Kosijo yŏngu* (Studies in classic *sijo*). Hyŏngsŏl ch'ulp'ansa, 1977.

Ch'oe Wŏnsik. "Kaehwagi ŭi *ch'anggŭk* undong kwa *Ŭnsegye*" (The enlightenment period's *ch'anggŭk* movement and *A Silvery World*). In *P'ansori ŭi ihae* (Understanding *p'ansori*), ed. Cho Tongil and Kim Hŭnggyu. Ch'angjak kwa pip'yŏngsa, 1978.

"*Kasa* ŭi sosŏrhwa kyŏnghyang kwa ponggŏn chuŭi ŭi haech'e" (*Kasa*'s tendency to become fiction and the dissolution of feudalism). In *Minjok munhak ŭi nolli* (Logic of national literature). Ch'angjak kwa pip'yŏngsa, 1982.

Ch'oe Yŏngmu, ed. *Chuhae sasan pimyŏng* (Inscriptions to the monuments at four mountains annotated). Asea munhwasa, 1987.

Chŏn Hyŏngdae. "Yi Kyubo ŭi si yŏngu" (Study of Yi Kyubo's poetry). In *Hanguk kojŏn munhak yŏngu: Paegyŏng Chŏng Pyŏnguk sŏnsaeng hwangap kinyŏm nonch'ong* (Studies in classic Korean literature: Festschrift for Professor Chŏng Pyŏnguk on his sixtieth birthday). Singu munhwasa, 1983, 3:241–249.

"*Sijo* chip e nat'anan munhak ŭisik – sŏ pal ŭl chungsim ŭro" (Literary consciousness in *sijo* collections, especially in prefaces and postfaces). In *Hanguk kojŏn pip'yŏng yŏngu* (Critical study of Korean classics). Ch'aeksesang, 1987.

Chŏn Hyŏngdae et al., eds. *Hanguk kojŏn sihaksa* (History of literary thoughts on classic poetry in Chinese). Hongsŏngsa, 1981.

Chŏn Kyŏnguk. *Minsok kŭk* (Folk plays). Hansaem, 1993.

Chŏn Sŏngho. "Kang Kyŏngae ŭi changp'yŏn *Sogŭm* yŏngu" (Study of Kang Kyŏngae's full-length work of fiction *Salt*). Unpublished conference paper. Chaeoe uri minjok munhak ssimp'ojium. Yanbian, 8 August 1998.

Ch'ŏn Sugyŏng et al. *P'ungyo soksŏn* (Sequel to a collection of poetry in literary Chinese by [members of] the middle people). Asea munhwasa, 1980.

Chŏn Sut'ae and Ch'oe Hoch'ŏl. *NambukHan ŏnŏ pigyo* (Linguistic comparison between South and North Korea). Nokchin, 1989.

Chŏng Chaeho. "Kajip sŏ pal e kwanhan sogo" (Study of prefaces and postfaces in song collections). *Ŏmun nonjip* 12 (1970):160–190.

Chŏng Chiyong. *Chŏng Chiyong chŏnjip* (Collected works of Chong Chiyong). 2 vols. Minŭmsa, 1995.

Chŏng Ch'ŏl. *Songgang chŏnjip* (Collected works of Chŏng Ch'ŏl). Taedong munhwa yŏngguwŏn, 1964.

Chŏng Ch'urhŏn. "Chosŏn hugi uhwa sosŏl ŭi sahoejŏk songkyŏk" (Social nature of fable fiction in late Chosŏn). Ph.D. dissertation, Korea University, 1992.

Chŏng Hanmo. *Hanguk hyŏndae simunhaksa* (History of modern Korean poetry). Ilchisa, 1974.

Chŏng Hyŏnjong. *Saengmyŏng ŭi hwanghol* (Ecstasy of life). Segyesa, 1989.

Chŏng Hyŏnjong chŏnjip (Collected poetry of Chŏng Hyŏnjong). 2 vols. Munhak kwa chisŏngsa, 1999.

Chŏng Inji and Hwangbo In, eds. *Sejong sillok* (*CWS* 2–6).

Chŏng Inji et al. eds. *Koryŏ sa* (History of Koryŏ). 3 vols. Tongbanghak yŏnguso, 1955–1961.

Chŏng Kyubok. *Kuun mong yŏngu* (Study of the *Dream of Nine Clouds*). Koryŏdae ch'ulp'anbu, 1974.

Chŏng Kyubok. et al. *Kim Manjung munhak yŏngu* (Studies of Kim Manjung's literary works). Kukhak charyowŏn, 1993.

Chŏng Pyŏngho. "*Palt'al*" (foot mask). In *Chungyo muhyŏng munhwajae haesŏl: yŏnghŭk p'yŏn* (Important intangible cultural assets: plays). Munhwajae kwalliguk, 1986.

Chŏng Pyŏnguk. *Sijo munhak sajŏn* (Dictionary of *sijo* literature). Singu munhwasa, 1966.

Chŭngbop'an Hanguk kojŏn siganon (Augmented Studies in classic Korean poetry and songs). Singu munhwasa, 1999.

Chŏng Tojŏn. *Sambong chip* (Collected works of Chŏng Tojŏn). Kuksa p'yŏnch'an wiwŏnhoe, 1961.

Chŏng Tongyu. *Chuyŏng p'yŏn* (Random jottings of Chŏng Tongyu). Seoul taehakkyo kojŏn kanhaenghoe, 1971.

Chŏng Yagyong. *Yŏyudang chŏnsŏ* (Collected works of Chŏng Yagyong). 6 vols. Kyŏngin munhwasa, 1982.

Chŏng Yŏngho. "Chungwŏn Koryŏ pi ŭi palgyŏn chosa wa yŏngu chŏnmang" (Discovery of a Koryŏ monument at Chungwŏn and an outlook for its investigation). *Sahakchi* 13 (1979):1–19.

Chōsen sōtokufu, ed. *Chōsen kinseki sōran* (Compendium of Korean epigraphy). 2 vols. Chōsen sōtokufu, 1919.

Chosŏn chakka tongmaeng, ed. *Chŏnjin hanŭn Chosŏn munhak* (The progress of Korean literature). P'yŏngyang: Chosŏn chakka tongmaeng ch'ulp'ansa, 1960.

Chosŏn munhak (Korean literature). P'yŏngyang: Chosŏn chakka tongmaeng ch'ulp'ansa, 1980–1989.

Chosŏn chakka tongmaeng chungang wiwŏnhoe, 4.15 ch'angjaktan. *Pulmyŏl ŭi yŏksa* (Imperishable history). P'yŏngyang: Munye ch'ulp'ansa, 1980.

Chosŏn inmin konghwaguk Sahoe kwahagwŏn, ed. *Sahoe chuŭijŏk munhak yesul esŏ saenghwal myosa* (Description of life in socialist literature). P'yŏngyang: Kwahak paekkwa sajŏn ch'ulp'ansa, 1979.

Chosŏn rodongdang, ed. *Uri tang ŭi munye chŏngch'aek* (Party policies on literature). P'yŏngyang: Sahoe kwahak ch'ulp'ansa, 1973.

Chu Yohan. *Arŭmdaun saebyŏk* (Beautiful dawn). Chosŏn mundansa, 1924.

Fan Ye et al. *Hou Hanshu* (History of the Later Han). 12 vols. Peking: Zhonghua, 1963.

Guo Maoqian. *Yuefu shiji* (Collection of music bureau poems). Peking: Zhonghua, 1979.

Ha Yun and Pyŏn Kyeryang, eds. *T'aejo sillok* (*CWS* 1).

Ham Sŏkhŏn. *Sŏngsŏjŏk ipchangesŏ bon Chosŏn yŏksa* (Korean history viewed from a biblical standpoint). Sŏnggwang ch'ulp'ansa, 1954.

Han Chungmo and Chŏng Sŏngmu. *Chuch'e ŭi munye riron yŏngu* (Study in literature of *chuch'e*). P'yŏngyang: Sahoe kwahak ch'ulp'ansa, 1983.

Han Kyejŏn et al. *Hanguk hyŏndae sironsa yŏngu* (Studies in modern Korean poetic theory). Munhak kwa chisŏngsa, 1999.

Han Yongun. *Han Yongun chŏnjip* (Collected works of Han Yongun). 6 vols. Singu munhwasa, 1973.

Hanguk yŏsŏng yŏnguhoe, Yosŏngsa punkwa. "Hanguk yŏsŏngsa ŭi yŏngu tonghyang kwa kwaje" (Research trends and issues in the history of Korean women). *Yŏsŏng kwa sahoe* 5 (1994):297–327.

Hisaki, Yukio. *Daigakuryō to kodai jukyō* (The academy and ancient Confucianism). Tokyo: Saimaru, 1968.

Hŏ Hŭngsik. *Hanguk kŭmsŏk chŏnmun* (Complete Korean epigraphy). Asea munhwasa, 1984.

Hŏ Kyun. *Sŏngso pokpu ko*. Taedong munhwa yŏnguwŏn, 1972.

Hŏ Kyun chŏnjip (Collected works of Hŏ Kyun). Taedong munhwa yŏnguwŏn, 1981.

Hŏ Ung and Yi Kangno. *Chuhae "Wŏrin ch'ŏngang chigok"* (Annotated *Songs of the Moon's Reflections on a Thousand Rivers*). Singu munhwasa, 1999.

Wŏrin sŏkpo (Songs of the moon's reflection on a thousand rivers and the *Life history of Śākyamuni combined*). Singu munhwasa, 1999.

Hong Hyomin. *Hanguk mundan inyŏmsa* (History of Korean literary world's ideology). Kip'ŭn saem, 1983.

Hong Manjong. *Sihwa ch'ongnim* (Anthology of remarks on poetry). Asea munhwasa, 1973.

Sunoji (Essays written in fifteen days). In Wŏnbon Hanguk kojŏn ch'ongsŏ (Korean classics series in the original), vol. 4. Taejegak, 1975.

Hong Set'ae. *Yuha chip* (Works of Hong Set'ae). Yŏgang ch'ulp'ansa, 1986.

Hong Sŏkchu. *Yŏnch'ŏn chŏnsŏ* (Collected works of Hong Sŏkchu). Osŏngsa, 1984.

Hong Yangho. *Igye chip* (Works of Hong Yangho). 1893.

Hwang Ch'unggi. *Haedong Kayo e kwanhan yŏngu*. Kukhak charyowon, 1996.

Hanguk yŏhang sijo yŏngu (Study of the commoner *sijo*). Kukhak charyowŏn, 1998.

Hwang Chiu. *Saedŭl to sesang ŭl ttŭnŭnguna* (Even the birds are leaving the world). *Munhak* kwa chisŏngsa, 1983.

Kenunsok ŭi yŏnkkot (A lotus blossom inside a crab's eye). Munhak kwa chisŏngsa, 1990.

Hwang P'aegang et al., eds. *Hanguk munhak yŏngu immun* (Introduction to studies on Korean literature). Chisik sanŏpsa, 1982.

Hwang Suyŏng, ed. *Chŭngbo Hanguk kŭmsŏk yumun* (Augmented epigraphic remains of Korea). Ilchisa, 1978.

Hwang Tonggyu. *Naŭi siŭi pit kwa kŭnŭl* (Light and shadow of my poetry). Chungang ilbosa, 1994.

P'ungjang: Hwang Tonggyu yŏnjak sijip (Wind burial: Hwang Tonggyu's poem sequence). Munhak kwa chisŏngsa, 1995.

Hwang Tonggyu si chŏnjip (Collected Poetry of Hwang Tonggyu*)*. 2 vols. Munhak kwa chisŏngsa, 1998.

ed. *Kim Suyŏng ŭi munhak* (Essays on Kim Suyŏng's poetry). Minŭmsa, 1983.

Im Chaehae. *Kkoktu kaksi norŭm ŭi ihae* (Understanding the puppet play). Hongsŏngsa, 1977.

"*Siyong hyangak po* sojae mugaryu siga yŏngu" (Study of shamanist songs in *Notations for Korean Music in Contemporary Use*). *Yŏngnam ŏmunhak* 9 (1982): 155–182.

"Minsokkŭk ŭi chŏnsŭng chiptan kwa yŏnggam/halmi ŭi ssaum" (Groups that transmitted folk plays and conflicts between the Old Man / Old Woman). In *Hanguk ŭi minsok yesul* (Korean folk arts). Munhak kwa chisŏngsa, 1988.

Im Ch'igyun. "Yŏnjakhyŏng samdaerok sosŏl yŏngu" (Study of the serial fiction covering three generations). Ph.D. dissertation, Seoul National University, 1992.

Chosŏnjo taejangp'yŏn sosŏl yŏngu (Study of long works of fiction during the Chosŏn dynasty). T'aehaksa, 1996.

Im Hwa. *Im Hwa chŏnjip* (Collected works of Im Hwa), ed. Sin Sungyŏp. P'ulppit, 1988.

Im Hwa p'yŏngnon chip: munhak ŭi nolli (Collection of Im Hwa's critical essays: Theory of literature). Sŏŭm ch'ulp'ansa, 1989.

Im Hyŏngt'aek. "Hyŏnsil chuŭijŏk segyegwan kwa *Kŭmo sinhwa*" (Realistic worldview and *New Stories from Gold Turtle Mountain*). MA thesis, Seoul National University, 1971.

"Sipp'al-gu segi iyagikkun kwa sosŏl ŭi paltal" (Eighteenth- and nineteenth-century storytellers and the development of fiction). *Hangukhak nonjip* 2 (1975):67–86.

Hanguk munhaksa ŭi sigak (A perspective on Korean literary history). Ch'angjak kwa pip'yŏngsa, 1984.

"Namal Yŏch'o ŭi chŏngi munhak" ("Tales of wonder" in late Silla and early Koryŏ). In *Hanguk munhaksa ŭi sigak*.

"Yijo chŏngi ŭi sadaebu munhak" (Literature of the literati in the early Yi period). In *Hanguk munhaksa ŭi sigak*.

"*Hong Kiltong chŏn* ŭi singoch'al" (New study of *Tale of Hong Kiltong*). In *Hanguk munhaksa ŭi sigak*.

"Sipch'il segi kyubang sosŏl kwa *Ch'angsŏn kamŭi rok*" (Seventeenth-century boudoir fiction and *Showing Goodness and Stirred by Righteousness*). *Tongbang hakchi* 57 (1988):103–127.

ed. *Yijo sidae sŏsasi* (Narrative poetry of the Yi dynasty). 2 vols. Ch'angjak kwa pip'yŏngsa, 1992.

Im Kijung, ed. *Hanguk kasa munhak yŏngusa* (Bibliography of studies on the *kasa*).
Ihoe munhwasa, 1998.

Im Kyuch'an and Han Kiyŏng, eds. *KAPF pip'yŏng charyo ch'ongsŏ* (Collection of
critical essays by KAPF members). T'aehaksa, 1990.

Im Tonggwŏn. *Hanguk minyo chip* (Collecion of Korean folk songs). Tongguk
munhwasa, 1961.

In Kwŏnhan. "*T'okki chŏn* ŭi sŏmin ŭisik kwa p'ungjasŏng" (Commoners' consciousness and satirical nature of *Tale of the Rabbit*). *Ŏmun nonjip* 14–15
(1972):36–53.

—— ed. *Hŭngbu chŏn yŏngu* (Studies in the *Tale of Hŭngbu*). Chimmundang, 1991.

Iryŏn. *Samguk yusa* (Memorabilia of the Three Kingdoms), ed. Ch'oe Namsŏn.
Minjung sŏgwan, 1954.

Jeon Jae-Ho. *Kugŏ ŏhwisa yŏngu* (Study of the history of the Korean lexicon). Taegu:
Kyŏngbuk University Press, 1992.

Kang Hanyŏng. *P'ansori*. Sejong taewang kinyŏm saŏphoe, 1977.

Kang Myŏnggwan. *Chosŏn hugi yŏhang munhak yŏngu* (Studies in commoners'
literature in late Chosŏn). Ch'angjak kwa pip'yŏngsa, 1997.

Kim Chaech'ŏl. *Chosŏn yŏnŭk sa* (History of Korean drama). Hagyesa, 1933.

Kim Chaehong. *Han Yongun munhak yŏngu* (Studies in Han Yongun's works).
Ilchisa, 1982.

Kim Chaeyong. *Kyemohyŏng kojŏn sosŏl ŭi sihak* (Poetics of traditional fiction about
the stepmother type). Chimmundang, 1996.

Kim Ch'anghyŏp. *Nongam chip* (Works of Kim Ch'anghyŏp*). Kyŏngmunsa,
1980.

Kim Ch'angnyong. *Hanguk kajŏn munhaksŏn* (Selections of Korean pseudobiography). Chŏngŭmsa, 1985.

Kim Chiha. *Kim Chiha si chŏnjip: Ojŏk, Kim Chiha tamsi chŏnjip* (Collected works
of Kim Chiha. "Five Outlaws," collected narrative poems). Sol, 1993.

Taesŏl Nam (Big Story South). 5 vols. Ch'angjak kwa pip' yŏngsa, 1982–1985 (vols.
1–3) and Sol, 1994 (vols. 4–5).

Kim Chinyŏng and Kim Hyŏnju, trans. *Hŭngbo chŏn (Tale of Hŭngbo*). Pagijŏng,
1997.

Kim Chinyŏng et al., eds. *Sim Ch'ŏng chŏn chŏnjip* (Collectd editions of the *Tale
of Sim Ch'ŏng*). 11 vols. Pagijŏng, 1997–2000.

Kim Chongch'ŏl. "*Oksu ki* yŏngu" (Study of the *Record of the Jade Tree*). MA thesis,
Seoul National University, 1985.

"*Ongnu mong* ŭi taejungsŏng kwa chinjisŏng" (Popularity and sincerity of the
Dream of the Jade Tower). *Hanguk hakpo* 1 (1990):22–46.

"Sipku-segi chungbangi changp'yŏn yŏngung sosŏl ŭi han yangsang" (An aspect
of full-length hero fiction during the mid nineteenth century). *Hanguk hakpo*
40 (1995):88–108.

P'ansorisa yŏngu (Study of the history of *p'ansori*). Yŏksa pip'yŏngsa, 1996.

Kim Chongjik. *Chŏmp'ilchae munjip* (Collected works of Kim Chongjik). 1892.
Also in *YMC* 2.

Kim Chong-taek. *Kugŏ ŏhwi ron* (Korean lexicography). Tower, 1993.

Kim Chuhyŏn and Kang Insuk. "Hanguk hyŏndae yŏryu chakka non" (Comments on modern Korean women writers). *Hyŏndae munhak* 14 (1968):351–359.

Kim Chuno. *Tosisi wa haech'esi* (Poetry of the city and poetry of open form). Munhak kwa pip'yŏngsa, 1992.

Kim Ch'unsu. *Kim Ch'unsu si chŏnjip* (Collected works of Kim Ch'unsu). 2 vols. Minŭmsa, 1994.

Kim Haktong. *Hanguk kŭndae siin yŏngu* (Studies in modern Korean poets). Ilchogak, 1974.

Hanguk kaehwagi siga yŏngu (Studies in the poetry and songs of Korea's enlightenment period). Simunhaksa, 1981.

Kim Kirim yŏngu (Study of Kim Kirim). Simunhaksa, 1991.

Kim Hamyŏng. *Munhak yesul chakp'um ŭi chongja e kwanhan riron* (Regarding the seed theory of literature). P'yŏngyang: Sahoe kwahak ch'ulp'ansa, 1977.

Kim Hŭnggyu. "Pangja wa Malttugi: tu chŏnhyŏng ŭi pigyo" (Pangja and Malttugi: comparison of two human types). *Hangukhak nonjip* 5 (1978):103–113.

"Sin Chaehyo kaejak *Ch'unhyang ka* ŭi *p'ansori*sachŏk wich'i" (Sin Chaehyo's adaptation of *Song of Spring Fragrance*: its position in the history of *p'ansori*). *Hanguk hakpo* 10 (1978):2–40.

"*P'ansori* ŭi sŏsajŏk kujo" (Narrative structure of *p'ansori*). In *P'ansori ŭi ihae* (Understanding *p'ansori*). Ch'angjak kwa pip'yŏnysa, 1978.

"*P'ansori* ŭi sahoejŏk sŏngkyŏk kwa kŭ pyŏnmo" (*P'ansori*'s social characteristics and their transformation). In *Yesul kwa sahoe* (Arts and society), ed. Hanguk sahoe kwahak yŏnguso. Minŭmsa, 1979.

Chosŏn hugi "Sigyŏng" non kwa si ŭi ŭisik (Late Chosŏn theories on the *Book of Songs* and poetic consciousness). Koryŏ taehakkyo Minjok munhwa yŏnguso, 1982.

"*Kkoktu kaksi norŭm* ŭi yŏngŭkchŏk konggan kwa *sanbaji*" (Dramatic space of puppet plays and the musician-interlocutor). In *Hanguk ŭi minsok yesul* (Korean folk arts). Munhak kwa chisŏngsa, 1988.

"Sipku segi chŏngi *p'ansori* ŭi yŏnhaeng hwangyŏng kwa sahoejŏk kiban" (Early nineteenth-century *p'ansori* performative situation and social foundation). *Ŏmun nonjip* 30 (1991):1–42.

"*Sasŏl sijo* ŭi sichŏk sisŏn yuhyŏng kwa kŭ pyŏnmo" (Types of poetic perspective and their change in *sasŏl sijo*). *Hanguk hakpo* 68 (1992):2–30.

ed. *Sasŏl sijo*. In Hanguk kojŏn munhak chŏnjip (Complete collection of classical Korean literature), vol. 2. Koryŏ taehakkyo Minjok munhwa yŏnguso, 1993.

Kim Hyesun. "Munhakchŏk Changja wa Kim Suyŏng ui sidamnon pigyo yŏngu" (A comparative study of literary *Zhuangzi* and Kim Suyŏng's poetic discourse). In *Kim Suyŏng tasi ilkki* (Rereading Kim Suyŏng). P'resŭ 21, 2000.

Kim Hyŏnggyu. *Hanguk pangŏn yŏngu* (Study of Korean dialects). Ilchogak, 1982.

Kogayo chusŏk (Annotated ancient songs). Ilchogak, 1983.

Kim Hyŏnhyang. "Minjung yŏnhŭi ŭi chŏnt'ong kwa *t'alch'um* ŭi sŏngjang" (Tradition of popular plays and the growth of mask plays). In *Minjok munhaksa kangjwa* (Lectures on national literary history), vol. 1. Ch'angjak kwa pip'yŏngsa, 1995.

Kim Illyŏl. "*Hong Kiltong chŏn* ŭi kujojŏk t'ongilsŏng" (Structural unity of the *Tale of Hong Kiltong*). In *Chosŏn sosŏl ŭi kujo wa ŭimi* (Structure and meaning of Chosŏn fiction). Hyŏngsŏl ch'ulp'ansa, 1984.
"*Unyŏng chŏn* ŭi sŏngkyŏk kwa ŭimi" (Nature and meaning of the *Tale of Unyŏng*). In *Kojŏn sosŏl ŭi ihae* (Understanding classic Korean fiction). Munhak kwa pip'yŏngsa, 1991.
Sugyŏng nangja chŏn yŏngu (Study of the *Tale of Sugyŏng*). Yŏngnak, 1999.
Kim Ilsŏng. *Uri hyŏngmyŏng esŏ ŭi munhak yesul ŭi immu* (The role of literature in our revolution). P'yŏngyang: Chosŏn rodongdang ch'ulp'ansa, 1965.
Hyŏngmyŏngjŏk munhak yesul ŭl ch'angjak halte taehayŏ (The creation of revolutionary literature). P'yŏngyang: Chosŏn rodongdang ch'ulp'ansa, 1978.
Kim Kidong. "*Kasa* munhak ŭi hyŏngt'ae koch'al" (Study of the form of *kasa*). In *Kasa munhak yŏngu* (Studies in *kasa* literature), ed. Kugŏ kungmunhak hoe. Chŏngŭmsa, 1979.
Kim Kijin. *Kim P'albong munhak chŏnjip* (Collected works of Kim Kijin). Edited by Hong Chŏngsŏng. 6 vols. Munhak kwa chisŏngsa, 1988–1989.
Kim Kirim. *Kim Kirim chŏnjip* (Collected works of Kim Kirim). 6 vols. Simsŏltang, 1988.
Kim Kwanggyun. *Kim Kwanggyun chŏnjip* (Collected works of Kim Kwanggyun), ed. Kim Haktong. Kukhak charyowŏn, 2002.
Kim Kwangsun. "Yi Chonyŏn ŭi *sijo* e taehayŏ" (On the *sijo* of Yi Chonyŏn). In *Sijo non* (Essay on the *sijo*), ed. Cho Kyusŏl and Pak Ch'ŏrhŭi. Ilchogak, 1984.
Kim Kyŏngsu. *Yi Kyubo simunhak yŏngu* (Studies in the poetry and prose of Yi Kyubo). Asea munhwasa, 1986.
Kim Manjung. *Sŏp'o manp'il* (Random jottings of Kim Manjung). T'ongmungwan, 1971.
Kim Mungi. *Sŏmin kasa yŏngu* (Studies in the commoner *kasa*). Hyŏngsŏl ch'ulp'ansa, 1983.
Kim Myŏngho. "Yŏnam ŭi hyŏnsil insik kwa *chŏn* ŭi pyŏnmo yangsang" (Pak Chiwŏn's awareness of historical time and transformation of biography). In *Chŏnhwangi Tongasia munhak* (East Asian literature in the transitional period). Ch'angjak kwa pip'yŏngsa, 1990.
Yŏrha ilgi yŏngu (Study of *Jehol Diary*). Ch'angjak kwa pip'yŏngsa, 1990.
Kim Myŏngsun. *Saengmyŏng ŭi kwasil* (Fruits of life). Hansŏng tosŏ chusik hoesa, 1925.
Kim Ŏk. *Ansŏ Kim Ŏk chŏnjip* (Collected works of Kim Ŏk). 9 vols. Hanguk munhwasa, 1990.
Kim Pusik. *Samguk sagi* (Historical records of the Three Kingdoms). Edited by Yi Pyŏngdo. Ŭryu, 1977.
Kim Pyŏngch'ŏl. *Hanguk kŭndae pŏnyŏk munhaksa yŏngu* (Study of the history of translated literature in modern Korea). Ŭryu, 1988.
Kim Sanghong. *Tasan Chŏng Yagyong munhak yŏngu* (Study of Chŏng Yagyong's literary works). Tongguk University Press, 1985.
Kim Sanghun. "*Chŏkpyŏk ka* ŭi ibon kwa hyŏngsŏng yŏngu" (Study of different editions and formation of *Song of Red Cliff*). Ph.D. dissertation, Inha University, 1992.

Kim Sangsŏn. "Ko *sijo* ŭi sŏngkyŏk" (The nature of classic *sijo*). In *Sijo munhak yŏngu* (Studies in the *sijo*). ed. Kugŏ kungmunhakkoe. Chŏngŭmsa, 1980.

Kim Sisŭp. *Maewŏltang sijip* (Collected poetry of Kim Sisŭp). Asea munhwasa, 1973.

Kim Sŏngbae et al., eds. *Chuhae kasa munhak chŏnjip* (Annotated collection of *kasa* literature). Chŏngyŏnsa, 1961.

Kim Sowŏl. *Kim Sowŏl chŏnjip* (Collected works of Kim Sowŏl), ed. Kim Yongjik. Seoul taehakkyo ch'ulp'anbu, 1996.

Kim Sŭnghŭi. *Yi Sang si yŏngu* (Study of Yi Sang's poetry). Pogosa, 1998.

ed. *Kim Suyŏng tasi ilkki* (Rereading Kim Suyŏng). Pŭresŭ 21, 2000.

Kim Suŏp. "*Sijo* ŭi palsaeng sigi e taehayŏ" (On the time of birth of *sijo*). In *Sijo non*, ed. Cho Kyusŏl and Pak Ch'ŏrhŭi. Ilchogak, 1984, pp. 3–23.

Kim Suyŏng. *Kim Suyŏng chŏnjip* (Collected works of Kim Suyŏng). 2 vols. Minŭmsa, 1981.

Kim T'aegyŏng. *Kim T'aegyŏng chŏnjip* (Collected works of Kim T'aegyŏng). Asea munhwasa, 1978.

Kim Tonguk. *Ch'unhyang chŏn yŏngu* (Study of the *Tale of Ch'unhyang*). Yŏnse taehakkyo ch'ulp'anbu, 1976.

Hanguk kayo ŭi yŏngu sok (Continued studies in Korean songs). Iu ch'ulp'ansa, 1978.

"'To ijang ka' ŭi munhŏn minsokhakchŏk koch'al" (A bibliographical and folk-loristic study of "Dirge for Two Generals"). In *Koryŏ sidae ŭi kayo munhak* (Song literature of Koryŏ), ed. Kim Yŏlgyu and Sin Tonguk. Saemunsa, 1982.

Kim Wanjin. *Hyangga haedokpŏp yŏngu* (Studies in the reading of Silla songs). Seoul taehakkyo ch'ulp'anbu, 1980.

Kim Wanjin et al., eds. *Munhak kwa ŏnŏ ŭi mannam* (Meeting of literature and language). Singu munhwasa, 1996.

Kim Yŏlgyu and Sin Tonguk, eds. *Kim Sowŏl yŏngu* (Studies in Kim Sowŏl). Saemunsa, 1986.

Han Yongun yŏngu (Studies in Han Yongun). Saemunsa, 1987.

Kim Yŏngbae, ed. *Sŏkpo sangjŏl* (Detailed contents of the life history of Śākyamuni). 2 vols. Tongguk taehakkyo pulchŏn kanhaeng wiwŏnhoe, 1986.

Kim Yongch'ŏl. *Hanguk kŭndae siron ko* (Studies in the theory of modern Korean poetry). Hyŏngsŏl ch'ulp'ansa, 1988.

Kim Yŏnghye. "Yŏsŏng munje ŭi sosŏlchŏk hyŏngsanghwa" (Fictional presentation of women's issues). *Ch'angjak kwa pip'yŏng* 75 (1989):55–74.

Kim Yongjik. *Hanguk kŭndae sisa* (History of modern Korean poetry). 2 vols. Saemunsa, 1983.

Im Hwa munhak yŏngu (Study of Im Hwa's works). Segyesa, 1991.

ed. *Yi Yuksa*. Sŏgang taehakkyo ch'ulp'anbu, 1995.

Kim Yongjik et al. *Hanguk hyŏndae sisa yŏngu* (Studies in the history of modern Korean poetry). Ilchisa, 1987.

Kim Yŏngnang. *Kim Yŏngnang, Pak Yongch'ŏl oe* (*HHST* 7), 1982.

Kim Yunsik. *Unyang chip* (Collected works of Kim Yunsik). 2 vols. Asea munhwasa, 1980.

Kim Yunsik. *Kŭndae Hanguk munhak yŏngu* (Studies in modern Korean literature). Ilchisa, 1973.

Hanguk kŭndae munhak sasangsa (History of literary thoughts on modern Korean literature). Hangilsa, 1984.

Yi Sang yŏngu (Study of Yi Sang). Munhak sasangsa, 1988.

Kim Yunsik et al. *Hanguk hyŏndae munhaksa* (History of modern Korean literature). Hyŏndae munhak, 1990.

Ko Misuk. *18-segi esŏ 20-segich'o Hanguk sigasa ŭi kudo* (Sketch for a history of Korean songs from the eighteenth to the twentieth centuries). Somyŏng, 1998.

Ko Siŏn and Ch'ae P'aengyun. *Sodae p'ungyo* (Poetry from the bright era). Asea munhwasa, 1980.

Ko Ŭn. *Paektusan* (*Mount Paektu*). 7 vols. Ch'angjak kwa pip'yŏngsa, 1987–1994.

Manin po (*Ten Thousand Lives*). 15 vols. Ch'angjak kwa pip'yŏngsa, 1986–1997.

Ku Chungsŏ, Paek Nakch'ong, and Yŏm Muung, eds. *Sin Kyŏngnim munhak segye* (The literary world of Sin Kyŏngnim). Ch'angjak kwa pip'yŏngsa, 1995.

Kugŏ kungmunhakhoe, ed. *Wŏnmun kasa sŏn* (Selections of the original *kasa* texts). Taejegak, 1979.

Kuksa p'yŏnch'an wiwŏnhoe, ed. *Hanguk sa* 13 (1993) and 23 (1994).

Kwŏn Homun. *Songam sŏnsaeng chip* (Collected works of Kwŏn Homun) (*YMC* 3).

Kwŏn Kŭn. *Yangch'on chip* (Collected works of Kwŏn Kŭn). Asea munhwasa, 1974.

Kwŏn Oman. *Kaehwagi siga yŏngu* (Study of poetry and songs during the enlightenment period). Saemunsa, 1989.

Kwŏn Sungŭng. "1910-nyŏndae kuhwalchabon kososŏl yŏngu" (Study of the 1910s fiction in old movable type). Ph.D. dissertation, Sŏnggyungwan University, 1990.

Kwŏn Tuhwan. "Kim Sŏnggi non" (Study of Kim Sŏnggi). In *Hanguk siga yŏngu: Paegyŏng Chŏng Pyŏnguk sŏnsaeng hwangap kinyŏm nonch'ong* (Studies in Korean poetry and songs: Festschrift for Professor Chŏng Pyŏnguk on his sixtieth birthday). Singu munhwasa, 1983.

Kwŏn Ŭngin. *Songgye mallok* (Random jottings of Kwŏn Ŭngin). Kyŏnghŭi ch'ulp'ansa, 1969.

Kwŏn Yongch'ŏl. *Kyubang kasa yŏngu* (Studies in women's *kasa*). Iu ch'ulp'ansa, 1980.

Kwŏn Yŏngmin. *Pukhan ŭi munhak* (Literature of North Korea). Ŭryu, 1989.

Hanguk kyegŭp munhak undongsa (History of the Korean class literature movement). Munye ch'ulp'ansa, 1998.

Sŏsa yangsik kwa tamnon ŭi kŭndaesŏng (Narrative forms and the modernity of discourse). Seoul taehakkyo ch'ulp'anbu, 1999.

Hanguk hyŏndae munhaksa (History of modern Korean literature), vol. 1: 1896–1945; vol. 2: 1945–2000. Minŭmsa, 2002.

ed. *Yi Sang munhak yŏngu yuksip-nyŏn* (Study of Yi Sang in the past sixty years). Munhak sasangsa, 1998.

Hanguk hyŏndae munhak chakp'um yŏnp'yo 1: 1894–1975 (Chronology of modern Korean literary works 1894–1975). Seoul taehakkyo ch'ulp'anbu, 1998.

Lingfu Defen, ed. *Zhoushu*. 3 vols. Peking: Zhonghua, 1971.

Liu Xu, ed. *Jiu Tangshu*. 16 vols. Peking: Zhonghua, 1975.

Min Ch'an. "Yŏsŏng yŏngung sosŏl ŭi ch'urhyŏn kwa hudaejŏk pyŏnmo" (The appearance of the fiction on women heroes and its later transformation). MA thesis, Seoul National University, 1986.

"Chosŏn hugi uhwa sosŏl ŭi tach'ŭngjŏk ŭimi kuhyŏn yangsang" (Aspects of multilayered meaning in fable fiction in late Chosŏn). Ph.D. dissertation, Seoul National University, 1990.

Min Hyŏnsik. "*Nongga wŏllyŏng ka* e taehan text ŏnŏhakchŏk koch'al" (Textlinguistic study of *The Farmer's Works and Days*). In *Munhak kwa ŏnŏ ŭi mannam* (Meeting of literature and language), ed. Kim Wanjin et al. Pp. 320–364.

Min Pyŏngsu. *Hanguk hansi sa* (History of Korean poetry in literary Chinese). T'aehaksa, 1996.

Min Yŏngdae. *Cho Wihan kwa "Ch'oe Ch'ŏk chŏn"* (Cho Wihan and the *Tale of Ch'oe Ch'ŏk*). Asea munhwasa, 1993.

Minjok Munhaksa Yŏnguso. ed. *Minjok munhaksa kangjwa* (Leatures on national literary history). 2 vols. Ch'angjak kwa pip'yŏngsa, 1995–1997.

Mo Yunsuk. *P'ungt'o*. Munwŏnsa, 1970.

Mun Pŏmdu. *Sŏkchu Kwŏn P'il munhak ŭi yŏngu* (Study of Kwŏn P'il's works). Kukhak charyowŏn, 1996.

Na Chŏngsun. *Hanguk kojŏn siga munhak ŭi punsŏk kwa t'amsaek* (Analysis and investigation of classical song literature). Yŏngnak, 2000.

Nam Hyoon. *Ch'ugang naenghwa* (Literary miscellany of Nam Hyoon). (*CKK*, 1909).

Sau myŏnghaeng nok (Sayings and conducts of teachers and friends) (*CKK*, 1909).

Nam Kongch'ŏl. *Kŭmnŭng chip* (Collected works of Nam Kongch'ŏl). 1815.

Nam Yongik. *Hogok chip* (Collected works of Nam Yongik) (*Kia* in ch. 15). Asea munhwasa 1980.

No Ch'ŏnmyŏng. *Sasŭm: No Ch'ŏnmyŏng chŏnjip*, vol. 1 (The deer: Collected works of No Ch'ŏnmyŏng). Sol, 1997.

Nabi: No Ch'ŏnmyŏng chŏnjip, vol. 2 (The butterfly: Collected works of No Ch'ŏnmyŏng). Sol, 1997.

No Susin et al. *Sinjŭng Tongguk yŏji sŭngnam* (Revised and augmented Korean gazetteer). Kojŏn kanhaenghoe, 1958.

O Seyŏng. *Hanguk nangman chuŭi si yŏngu* (Studies in Korean romantic poetry). Ilchisa, 1980.

Isip segi Hanguk si yŏngu (Studies in twentieth-century Korean poetry). Saemunsa, 1990.

Ŏ Sukkwŏn. *P'aegwan chapki* (A Korean storyteller's miscellany) (*CKK*, 1909).

Ōtani Morishige. "Richō bunjin no shōsetsu ishiki" (Yi-dynasty literati views of narrative fiction). *Chōsen gakuhō* 48 (1970):93–106.

Ouyang Xiu and Song Qi. *Xin Tangshu* (New History of the Tang). 20 vols. Peking: Zhonghua, 1975.

Paek Chiyŏn. "Chubyŏnin ŭi sasaek, mangmyŏngja ŭi sam" (Thoughts of the marginalized: the life of an exile). *Hanguk munhak* (Autumn 1997):64–79.

Paek Ch'ŏl. *Sinmunhak sajosa* (History of trends in new literature). Singu munhwasa 1982.

Pak Chaeyŏn. "Chosŏn sidae Chungguk t'ongsok sosŏl pŏnyŏkpon ŭi yŏngu" (Study of translations of popular Chinese fiction during the Chosŏn dynasty). Ph.D. dissertation, Korean University of Foreign Languages, 1993.

Pak Chiwŏn. *Yŏnam chip* (Collected works of Pak Chiwŏn). Kyŏnghŭi ch'ulp'ansa, 1966.

Pak Ch'ŏlsŏk, ed. *Yu Ch'ihwan*. Munhak segyesa, 1999.

Pak Hŭibyŏng. "*Ch'ŏnggu yadam* yŏngu" (Study of *Unofficial Stories from the Green Hills*). MA thesis, Seoul National University, 1981.

"Sipch'il-segi Tongasia ŭi chŏllan kwa minjung ŭi sam: *Kim Yongch'ŏl chŏn* ŭi punsŏk" (Wars and people's lives in seventeenth-century East Asia: analysis of the *Tale of Kim Yongch'ŏl*). In *Hanguk kŭndae munhaksa ŭi chaengchŏm* (Critical issues in modern Korean literary history). Ch'angjak kwa pip'yŏngsa, 1990.

"*Ch'oe Ch'ŏk chŏn*" (Tale of Ch'oe Ch'ŏk). In *Hanguk kojŏn sosŏl chakp'um non* (Studies in classic Korean works of fiction). Chimmundang, 1990.

"Chosŏn hugi *chŏn* ŭi sosŏlchŏk sŏnghyang yŏngu" (Study on fictional qualities in late Chosŏn biographies). Ph.D. dissertation, Seoul National University, 1991.

Hanguk kojŏn inmul chŏn yŏngu (Study of classical Korean biography). Hangilsa, 1992.

Pak Hwang. *P'ansori sosa* (Short history of *p'ansori*). Singu munhwasa, 1974.

Pak Hwasŏng. "Hanguk chakka ŭi sahoejŏk chiwi ŭi pyŏnch'ŏn: yŏsŏng chakka ŭi ipchang esŏbon" (Changes in Korean writers' social status as seen from the standpoint of a woman writer). *Yŏryu munhak* 2 (1968):204–215.

Pak Hyegyŏng. "Ch'uŏk, kkŭtŏpssi pasŭrajinŭn munwi ŭi sam" (Memory: the pattern that ceaselessly dissolves). In *Sin Kyŏngsuk sosŏl chip: P'unggŭm i ittŏn chari* (*Collection of Sin Kyŏngsuk's fiction: Where the organ once stood*). Munhak kwa chisŏngsa, 1993.

Pak Illo. *Nogye sŏnsaeng chip* (Works of Pak Illo) (*YMC* 3).

Pak Illyong. "*Chusaeng chŏn*" (Tale of Chu Hoe). In *Hanguk kojŏn sosŏl chakp'um non* (Studies in classic Korean works of fiction). Chimmundang, 1990.

"*Unyŏng chŏn* ŭi pigŭkchŏk sŏngkyok kwa kŭ sahoejŏk ŭimi" (Tragic aspects of the *Tale of Unyŏng* and their social significance). In *Chosŏn sidae ŭi aejŏng sosŏl* (Love stories of the Chosŏn dynasty). Chimmundang, 1993.

Pak Inhwan. *Pak Inhwan sijip: Mongma wa sungnyŏ* (Collected poems of Pak Inhwan: A rocking horse and a lady). Kŭnyŏk sŏjae, 1982.

Pak Kyŏngju. *Kyŏnggi-ch'e ka yŏngu* (Study of *kyŏnggi-ch'e* songs). Ihoe munhwasa, 1996.

Pak Kyŏngsin. " 'Taeguk' ŭi chaengchŏm kwa chakp'um ihae ŭi kibon panghyang" (Basic direction of understanding and critical issues in "The Large Country"). In *Hanguk kojŏn siga chakp'um non* (Studies in classic Korean poetic works), vol. 1. Chimmundang, 1992.

Pak Mogwŏl. *Pak Mogwŏl si chŏnjip* (Collected poetry of Pak Mogwŏl). Sŏmundang, 1984.

Pak Nojun. "*Sasŏl sijo* e nat'anan erotisijŭm" (Eroticism in *sasŏl sijo*). In *Sijo munhak yŏngu* (Studies in the *Sijo*). Chŏngŭmsa, 1980.

Koryŏ kayo ŭi yŏngu (Study of Koryŏ songs). Saemunsa, 1990.

Pak Pyŏngch'ae. *Koryŏ kayo ŭi ŏsŏk yŏngu* (Study on the vocabulary of Koryŏ songs). Iu ch'ulp'ansa, n.d.

Pak Sangjun. *Hanguk kŭndae munhak ŭi hyŏngsŏng kwa sinkyŏnghyangp'a* (The formation of modern Korean literature and the New Tendency school). Somyŏng, 2000.

Pak Sŏngŭi, ed. *Nongga wŏllyŏng ka, Hanyang ka* (*HKMT* 7). Minjung sŏgwan, 1974.

Pak Tujin. *Susŏk yŏlchŏn* (Connected traditions of water-washed stones). Ilchisa, 1974.

Sok susŏk yŏlchŏn (Connected traditions of water-washed stones continued). Ilchisa, 1976.

Yeremiya ŭi norae (Song of Jeremiah). Ch'angjak kwa pip'yŏngsa, 1982.

Pak Tujin munhak chŏngsin (The literary mind of Pak Tujin). 7 vols. Sinwŏn munhwasa, 1996.

Pak Ŭlsu. *Hanguk kaehwagi chŏhang siga yŏngu* (Studies in resistance poetry during Korea's enlightenment period). Sŏngmungak, 1985.

Pak Yŏnghŭi. "*So Hyŏnsŏng nok* yŏnjak yŏngu" (Study of serial composition of the *Tale of So Hyŏnsŏng*). Ph. D. dissertation, Ewha Woman's University, 1994.

Pak Yŏnghye and Sŏ Chŏngja, eds. *Hanguk kŭndae yŏsŏng yŏngu* (Studies in modern Korean women). Sungmyŏng yŏja taehakkyo, 1987.

Pak Yŏngju. *P'ansori sosŏl ŭi t'ŭksŏng kwa mihak* (Features and aesthetics of *p'ansori* fiction). Pogosa, 2000.

Pak Yongun. *Koryŏ sidae sa* (History of the Koryŏ dynasty). 2 vols. Ilchisa, 1989.

Koryŏ sidae ŭmsŏje wa kwagŏje yŏngu (The protected appointment system and civil service examination system in Koryŏ). Ilchisa, 1990.

Pang Ŭngmo, ed. *Hyŏndae Chosŏn munhak chŏnjip* (Collection of modern Korean literature). Chosŏn ilbo ch'ulp'anbu, 1936.

Sa Chaedong. *Pulgyogye kungmun sosŏl ŭi hyŏngsŏng kwajŏng yŏngu* (Study of the formation of Buddhist fiction in Korean). Chungang ilbosa, 1994.

Hanguk munhak yut'ongsa ŭi yŏngu (Study of the circulation of Korean literature). Chungang inmunsa, 1999.

Sahoe kwahagwŏn munhak yŏnguso. *Chuch'e sasang e kich'ohan munye riron* (Literary theory founded on *chuch'e* thought). P'yŏngyang: Sahoe kwahagwŏn ch'ulp'ansa, 1975.

Chosŏn munhaksa (History of Korean literature). 5 vols. P'yŏngyang: Kwahak paekkwa sajŏn ch'ulp'ansa, 1981.

Shiratori Kurakichi. "Chōsen-go to Ural-Altai go tono hikaku kenkyū" (Comparative Study of Korean and Ural-Altaic languages). In *Shiratori Kurakichi zenshū* (Collected works of Shiratori Kurakichi), vol. 3. Tokyo: Iwanami, 1972.

Sim Chaegi. *Kugŏ ŏhwi non* (Korean lexicography). Chimmundang, 1983.

Sim Chaewan. *Sijo ŭi munhŏnjŏk yŏngu* (Bibliographic study of *sijo*). Sejong munhwasa, 1972.

ed. *Iltong changyu ka, Yŏnhaeng ka* (Song of a Grand Trip to Japan, Song of Seoul) (*HKMT* 10). Kyomunsa, 1984.

Kyobon yŏktae sijo chŏnsŏ (Variorum edition of the complete *sijo* canon). Sejong munhwasa, 1972.

Sim Hun. *Sim Hun munhak chŏnjip* (Collected works of Sim Hun). 3 vols. T'amgudang 1966.

Sim Sugyŏng. *Kyŏnhan chamnok* (Essays in idleness) (*CKK*, 1910).

Sima Qian. *Shiji* (Historical records). 10 vols. Peking: Zhonghua, 1959.

Sin Chaehong. *Hanguk mongyu sosŏl yŏngu* (Study of Korean records of dream journey). Kyemyŏng munhwasa, 1994.

Sin Kyŏngnim. *Nongmu* (Farmer's dance). Ch'angjak kwa pip'yŏngsa, 1975.

Nam Hangang (South Han River). Ch'angjak kwa pip'yŏngsa, 1987.

Kaltae (Reed). Sol. 1996.

Sin Kyŏngnim and Paek Nakch'ŏng, eds. *Ko Ŭn munhak ŭi segye* (The literary world of Ko Ŭn). Ch'angjak kwa pip'yŏngsa, 1993.

Sin Sŏkchŏng. *Sin Sŏkchŏng* (*HHST* 11), 1985.

Sin Sukchu et al. *Sejo sillok* (*CWS* 7–8).

Sin Sungsŏn et al. *Sŏngjong sillok* (*CWS* 8–12).

Sin Tonghŭn. "*Hyŏnssi yangung ssangnin ki* e kŭryŏjin kwijok sahoe ŭi silsang" (Aristocratic life depicted in the *Three Generation Record of the Sŏl Clan*). In *Kososŏl yŏngu nonch'ong* (Collected essays on classic fiction). Kyŏngin munhwasa, 1994.

Sin Tongyŏp. *Sin Tongyŏp chŏnjip* (Collected works of Sin Tongyŏp). Ch'angjak kwa pip'yŏngsa, 1975.

Sin Wan, ed. *P'yŏngsan Sin-ssi sebo* (Genealogy of Sin clan of P'yŏngsan). 4 vols. 1702.

Siyong hyangak po (Notations for Korean music in contemporary use). In *Wŏnbon Hanguk kojŏn ch'ongsŏ* (Korean classics series in the original). Taejegak, 1972.

So Chaeyŏng. *Im-Pyŏng yangnan kwa munhak ŭisik* (Japanese and Manchu invasions and literary consciousness). Hanguk yŏnguwŏn, 1982.

"*Kijae kii" yŏngu* (Study of "Kijae kii"). Koryŏ taehakkyo Minjok munhwa yŏnguso, 1990.

Sŏ Chŏngju. *Midang si chŏnjip* (Collected poetry of Sŏ Chŏngju). 3 vols. Minŭmsa, 1994.

Sŏ Chongmun and Chŏng Pyŏnghŏn, eds. *Sin Chaehyo yŏngu* (Studies in Sin Chaehyo). T'aehaksa, 1997.

Sŏ Kŏjŏng. *P'irwŏn chapki* (Writing brush garden miscellany) (*CKK*, 1909).

Tong munsŏn (Anthology of Korean literature in Chinese). 3 vols. Kyŏnghŭi ch'ulp'ansa, 1966–1967.

Tongin sihwa (Remarks on poetry by a man from the East). Hagusa, 1980.

Sŏ Taesŏk. *Kundam sosŏl ŭi kujo wa paegyŏng* (Structure and background of the war tale). Ihwa yŏdae ch'ulp'anbu, 1985.

Sŏ Wŏnsŏp. "*Sasŏl sijo* ŭi chuje yŏngu" (Study of the themes of *sasŏl sijo*). In *Sijo munhak yŏngu*, ed. Kugo kungmunhakhoe. Chŏngŭmsa, 1980.

Kasa munhak yŏngu (Studies in *kasa* literature). Hyŏngsŏl ch'ulp'ansa, 1983.

Sŏ Yŏnhŏ. *Sŏnangkut t'al nori* (Sŏnang rites and mask plays). Yŏrhwadang, 1991.

Sŏ Yŏngsuk. *Hanguk yŏsŏng kasa yŏngu* (Study of Korean woman's *kasa*). Kukhak charyowŏn, 1996.

Sŏl Chunghwan. *Kkumkkunŭn Ch'unhyang: P'ansori yŏsŏt madang ttŭdŏbogi* (Dreaming Ch'unhyang: Examining the repertory of six *p'ansori*). Nanam, 2000.

Sŏl Sŏnggyŏng, ed. *Ch'unhyang yesulsa charyo ch'ongso* (Collection of source materials for the art of Ch'unhyang). 8 vols. Kukhak charyowŏn, 1998.

Song Chaeso. *Tasan si yŏngu* (Study of Chŏng Yagyong's poetry). Ch'angjak kwa pip'yŏngsa, 1986.

Song Chaeso et al., eds. *Yijo hugi hanmunhak ŭi chaejomyŏng* (Reillumination of late Yi literature in Chinese). Ch'angjak kwa pip'yŏngsa, 1983.

Song Chunho. "Chosŏn hugi ŭi kwagŏ chedo" (The examination system in late Chosŏn). *Kuksagwan nonch'ong* 63 (1995):37–47.

Sŏng Hyŏn. *Hŏbaektang chip* (Collected works of Sŏng Hyŏn). 1842.

Yongjae ch'onghwa (Literary miscellany of Sŏng Hyŏn) (*CKK*, 1909).

Akhak kwebŏm (Canon of music). Yŏnse taehakkyo Inmun kwahak yŏnguso, 1968.

Sŏng Kidong. *Chosŏnjo yadam ŭi munhakchŏk t'uksŏng* (Literary characteristics of Chosŏn unofficial anecdotes). Minsogwŏn, 1994.

Song Minho. *Ilchemal amhŭkki munhak yŏngu* (Study of literature in the dark period of Japanese occupation). Saemunsa, 1991.

Sŏnggyungwan taehakkyo Inmun kwahak yŏnguso, ed. *Koryŏ kayo yŏngu ŭi hyŏnhwang kwa chŏnmang* (The present situation and prospects of studies for Koryŏ songs). Chimmundang, 1996.

Suh Cheong-soo. *Kugŏ munpŏp* (Korean grammar). Hanyang taehakkyo ch'ulp'anbu, 1996.

Sugano no Mamichi. *Shoku Nihongi* (Chronicles of Japan continued), ed. Aoki Kazuo et al. 6 vols. Tokyo: Iwanami, 1989–2000.

Takakusu Junjirō and Watanabe Kaigyoku, eds. *Taishō shinshū daizōkyō* (Taishō Tripiṭaka [The Buddhist canon, new compilation of the Taishō era]). 85 vols. Tokyo: Taishō issaikyō kankōkai, 1924–1934.

Wang Sinyong et al., eds. *Yun Tongju chap'il sigo chŏnjip* (Collected works of Yun Tongju in holograph). Minŭmsa, 1999.

Wei Shou. *Weishu*. 7 vols. Peking: Zhonghua, 1974.

Wi Paekkyu. *Chonjae chŏnsŏ* (Collected works of Wi Paekkyu). 2 vols. Kyŏngin munhwasa, 1974.

Yagisawa Hajime. *Mindai gekisakka kenkyū* (Studies in Ming playwrights). Tokyo: Kodansha, 1959.

Xun Qing. *Xunzi*. Sibu congkan.

Yi Chaesu. *Yun Kosan yŏngu* (Studies in Yun Sŏndo). Hagusa, 1955.

Yi Chehyŏn. *Ikchae chip* (Collected works of Yi Chehyŏn) (*KMC* 2).

Nagong pisŏl (or *Yŏgong p'aesŏl*) (Lowly Jottings by Old Man "Oak") (*KMC* 2).
Yi Chongch'ul. "Hapkangjŏng 'Sŏnyu ka' ko" (Study of the "Boating song" in
    Hapkang arbor). In *Hanguk kosiga yŏngu* (Studies in old Korean poetry and
    songs). T'aehaksa, 1989.
Yi Chŏngok. *Naebang kasa ŭi hyangyuja yŏngu* (Study of the audience of woman's
    kasa). Pagijŏng, 1990.
Yi Chongt'ak. *Hanguk uhwa munhak yŏngu* (Studies in Korean fables). Iu
    ch'ulp'ansa, 1982.
Yi Hwang. *T'oegye chŏnsŏ* (Collected works of Yi Hwang). 2 vols. Taedong munhwa
    yŏnguwŏn, 1958.
Yi Hyegu. "*Sandaegŭk* kwa 'kiak (gigaku)'" (Sandae plays and "ancient masked
    dance drama"). In *Hanguk ŭmak yŏngu* (Studies in Korean music). Kungmin
    ŭmak yŏnguhoe, 1957.
"Song Manjae ŭi 'Kwan uhŭi.'" (Song Manjae's "On seeing the plays of actors").
    In *Hanguk ŭmak yŏngu*. 1957.
Yi Hyesun. "*Kŭmo sinhwa*" (New Tales from Gold Turtle Mountain). In *Hanguk
    kojŏn sosŏl chakp'um non* (Studies in classic Korean works of fiction).
    Chimmundang, 1990.
Yi Hyŏnbo. *Nongam sŏnsaeng munjip* (Collected works of Yi Hyŏnbo) (*YMC* 3).
Yi I. *Yulgok chŏnsŏ* (Collected works of Yi I). Taedong munhwa yŏnguwŏn, 1958.
Yi Ik. *Sŏngho saesŏl* (Literary miscellany of Yi Ik). 2 vols. Kyŏnghŭi ch'ulp'ansa,
    1967.
Yi Illo. *P'ahan chip* (Jottings to break up idleness) (*KMC* 2).
Yi Ki et al. *Chungjong sillok* (*CWS* 14–19).
Yi Kidong. *Silla kolp'umje sahoe wa hwarangdo* (Silla's bone rank society and the
    way of *hwarang*). Ilchogak, 1984.
Yi Kimun. *Kaehwagi ŭi kungmun yŏngu* (Studies in the Korean language during
    the enlightenment period). Ilchogak, 1970.
    Kaejŏng kugŏsa kaesŏl (Revised introduction to the history of Korean). Minjung
    sŏgwan, 1976.
    "Sowŏl si ŭi ŏnŏ e tahayŏ" (Kim Sowŏl's diction). In *Kim Sowŏl*, ed. Kim
    Haktong. Sŏgang taehakkyo ch'ulp'anbu, 1995.
Yi Kwangho, ed. *Chŏng Hyŏnjong kip'i ilkki* (To read deeply Chŏng Hyŏnjong's
    works). Munhak kwa chisŏngsa, 1999.
Yi Kwangsu. *Yi Kwangsu chŏnjip* (Collected works of Yi Kwangsu). 20 vols.
    Samjungdang, 1962.
Yi Kyŏngsu. "Wihang siin ŭi ch'ŏngi non" (Theory on the "natural spontaneity"
    revealed by commoner poets). In *Yijo hugi hanmunhak ŭi chaejomyŏng* (Reil-
    lumination of late Yi literature in Chinese), ed. Song Chaeso et al. Ch'angjak
    kwa pip'yŏngsa, 1983.
Yi Kyŏngu. *Hanguk yadam ŭi munhaksŏng yŏngu* (Study of the literary quality of
    Korean unofficial anecdotes). Kukhak charyowŏn, 1997.
Yi Kyubo. *Paegun sosŏl* (Jottings by the Retired Gentleman White Cloud)
    (*KMC* 1).
    Tongguk Yi-sangguk chip (Collected works of minister Yi of Korea). Tongguk
    munhwasa, 1958.

Yi Kyuho. "Ko *sijo* pip'yŏng kwa siga ilto sasang" (Criticism of classic *sijo* and oneness of poetry in Chinese and vernacular songs). In *Hanguk kojŏn sihak non* (Thoughts on classic poetry in Korea). Saemunsa, 1985.

Yi Myŏnggu. *Koryŏ kayo ŭi yŏngu* (Study of Koryŏ songs). Sinasa, 1980.

Yi Myŏnghak. "Hanmun tanp'yŏn chakka ŭi yŏngu" (Study of short-story writers in literary Chinese). In *Yijo hugi hanmunhak ŭi chaejomyŏng* (Reillumination of late Yi literature in Chinese). Ch'angjak kwa pip'yŏngsa, 1983.

Yi Ok. *Yerim chapp'ae*. (Remarks on poetry by Yi Ok). Kungnip tosŏgwan, n.d.

Yi Pohyŏng. "*P'ansori* sasŏl ŭi kŭkchŏk sanghwang e ttarŭn changdancho ŭi kusŏng" (Change in construction of rhythm and melody in dramatic situation in *p'ansori* narratives). In *P'ansori ŭi ihae* (Understanding *p'ansori*), ed. Cho Tongil and Kim Hŭnggyu. Ch'angjak kwa pip'yŏngsa, 1978.

Yi Pyŏngdo. "Chungwŏn Koryŏ pi ŭi taehayŏ" (On the Koryŏ monument in Chungwŏn), *Sahakchi* 13 (1979):21–32.

Yi Pyŏnggi. "*Sijo* ŭi palsaeng kwa *kagok* kwaŭi kubun" (The rise of *sijo* and its difference from *kagok*). In *Sijo munhak yŏngu* (Studies in *sijo* literature), ed. Kugŏ kungmunhakhoe. Chŏngŭmsa, 1980.

Yi Saek. *Mogŭn mungo* (Works of Yi Saek). In *Yŏgye myŏnghyŏn chip* (Collection of works by renowned worthies of late Koryŏ). Taedong munhwa yŏnguwŏn, 1959.

Yi Sang. *Yi Sang* (*HHST* 9, 1988).

Yi Sang munhak chŏnjip (Collected works of Yi Sang). 4 vols. Munhak sasangsa, 1994.

Yi Sangbo. *Kaego Pak Nogye yŏngu* (Revised study of Pak Illo's poetry). Ilchisa, 1962.

Hanguk kosiga ŭi yŏngu (Studies in classic Korean songs). Hyŏngsŏl ch'ulp'ansa, 1982.

Yi Sanggu. "*Sukhyang chŏn* ŭi munhŏnjŏk kyebo wa hyŏnsilchŏk sŏngkyŏk" (Literary lineage and realistic character in the *Tale of Sukhyang*). Ph.D. dissertation, Korea University, 1993.

Yi Sanggyu. "*Siyong hyangak po* sojae 'Kunma taewang' ŭi kuŭmpŏp" (Oral sounds in "Great King of Warhorse" in *Notations for Korean Music in Contemporary Use*). *Onji nonch'ong* 2 (1996):37–53.

Yi Sanghwa. *Wŏnjŏn taegyo Yi Sanghwa chŏnjip: Ppaeakkin tŭredo pomŭn onŭnga* (Collected works of Yi Sanghwa collated and edited: "Does Spring Come to Stolen Fields?"). Edited by Yi Kich'ŏl. Munjangsa, 1982.

Yi Sik. *T'aektang chip* (Works of Yi Sik). 1764.

Yi Sohŭi. "P'eminijŭm munhak e taehan myŏtkkaji saengkaktŭl" (Several thoughts on feminist literature). *Tto hana ŭi munhwa* 9 (1993):200–217.

Yi Sŏkho, ed. *Tongguk sesigi, Yŏryang sesigi, Kyŏngdo chapchi, Tonggyŏng chapchi*. Taeyang sŏjŏk, 1973.

Yi Sŏnggwŏn. *Hanguk kajŏng sosŏlsa yŏngu: 17-segi esŏ 20-segich'o sinsosŏl kkaji ŭi yŏksajŏk pyŏnmo wa ŭimi* (Study of Korean family fiction – historical change and significance of fiction from the seventeenth to twentieth centuries including "New Fiction"). Kukhak charyowŏn, 1998.

Yi Sŏngmu. *Kaejŏng chŭngbo Hanguk ŭi kwagŏ chedo* (The civil service examination system in Korea, revised and augmented). Chimmundang, 1994.

Yi Sŏngnae. "Hanguk kojŏn p'ungja sosŏl yŏngu" (Study of classic Korean satirical fiction). Ph.D. dissertation, Tanguk University, 1997.

Yi Subong. *Hanguk kamun sosŏl yŏngu* (Study of Korean clan fiction). Kyŏngin munhwasa, 1992.

Yi Sugwang. *Chibong yusŏl* (Literary miscellany of Yi Sugwang) (*CKK*, 1915).

Yi Sukhŭi. *Hŏ Nansŏrhŏn siron* (Study of Hŏ Nansŏrhŏn's poetry). Saemunsa, 1987.

Yi Sŭnghun. *Yi Sang si yŏngu* (Study of Yi Sang's poetry). Koryŏwŏn, 1987.

Yi Sungin. *Toŭn (mun)jip* (Works of Yi Sungin). In *Yŏgye myŏnghyŏn chip* (Collection of works by renowned worthies of late Koryŏ), ed. Sŏnggyungwan taehakkyo Taedong munhwa yŏnguwŏn, 1959.

Yi T'aemun. "Mugagye Koryŏ sogyo ŭi yŏksasŏng kwa sahoesŏng" (Sociohistorical nature of shamanist Koryŏ songs). In *Koryŏ kayo ŭi munhak sahoehaksŏng* (Socioliterary study of Koryŏ songs), ed. Im Kijung. Kyŏngun ch'ulp'ansa, 1993.

Yi Tal. *Songok sijip* (Poetry of Yi Tal). In Yŏngin p'yojŏm Hanguk hanmunhak ch'onggan (Collectanea of Korean literature in Chinese, photolithographed and punctuated), vol. 61. Minjok munhwa ch'ujinhoe, 1996.

Yi Tonghwan. "Chosŏn hugi hansi e issŏsŏ minyo ch'wihyang ŭi taedu" (Rise of a device to include folk-song diction in late Chosŏn poetry written in literary Chinese). *Hanguk hanmunhak yŏngu* 3–4 (1979):29–71.

"T'oegye sisegye ŭi han kungmyŏn" (An aspect of Yi Hwang's poetic world). *T'oegye hakpo* 25 (1980):73–78.

Yi Tŏngmu. *Ch'ŏngjanggwan chŏnsŏ* (Collected works of Yi Tŏngmu). 13 vols. Minjok munhwa ch'ujinhoe, 1972–1982.

Yi Tongnim. *Chuhae "Sŏkpo sangjŏl"* (*Detailed Contents of the Life History of Śākyamuni* annotated). Tongguk taehakkyo ch'ulp'anbu, 1959.

Yi Tongyŏng. *Hanguk munhak yŏngusa* (History of histories of Korean literature). Pusan: Pusan taehakkyo ch'ulp'anbu, 1999.

Yi Tuhyŏn. *Hanguk ŭi kamyŏngŭk* (Korean mask plays). Munhwajae kwalliguk, 1969.

Yi Usŏng. "Koryŏ-mal Yijo-ch'o ŭi ŏbu ka" ("The fisherman's songs" at the end of Koryŏ and beginning of Chosŏn). *Sŏngdae nonmunjip* 9 (1964):5–27.

Yi Wŏnju. "*Kasa* ŭi tokcha – Kyŏngbuk pukpu chibang ŭl chungsim ŭro" (The readership of *kasa*, especially in the northern part of North Kyŏngsang). In *Chosŏn hugi ŭi ŏnŏ wa munhak* (Language and literature of late Chosŏn), ed. Hanguk ŏmunhakhoe. Hyŏngsŏl ch'ulp'ansa, 1982.

Yi Wŏnsu. "Kajŏng sosŏl ŭi chakp'um segye wa sidaejŏk pyŏnmo" (The world of family fiction and generational change). Ph.D. dissertation, Kyŏngbuk University, 1991.

Yi Yuksa. *Yi Yuksa, Yun Tongju* (*HHST* 8), 1984.

Yŏ Chŭngdong. "Ssanghwajŏm norae yŏngu" (A study of "The Turkish Bakery"). In *Koryŏ sidae ŭi kayo munhak* (Song literature of Koryŏ), ed. Kim Yŏlgyu and Sin Tonguk. Saemunsa, 1982.

Yŏ Unp'il. *Yi Saek ŭi simunhak yŏngu* (Studies in Yi Saek's poetry). T'aehaksa, 1995.

Yu Chaegŏn and Ch'oe Kyŏnghŭm, eds. *P'ungyo samsŏn* (Third collection of poetry in Chinese by the middle people). Asea munhwasa, 1980.

Yu Chaeyŏng, trans. *Paegun sosŏl yŏngu* (Study of *Jottings by the Retired Gentleman White Cloud*). Iri: Wŏngwang taehakkyo ch'ulp'anguk, 1979.

Yu Ch'ihwan. *Yu Ch'ihwan chŏnjip* (Collected works of Yu Ch'ihwan). 3 vols. Chŏngŭmsa, 1985.

Yu Kiyong. *"P'ansori* p'almyŏngch'ang kwa kŭ chongsŭngja tŭl"* (Eight master singers of *p'ansori* and their disciples). In *P'ansori ŭi ihae* (Understanding *P'ansori*), ed. Cho Tongil and Kim Hŭnggyu. Ch'angjak kwa pip'yŏngsa, 1978.

Yu Kwangbong. *"Iltong changyu ka* e nat'anan nori yangsang" (Forms of spectacles mentioned in *A Grand Trip to Japan*). In *Hanguk kihaeng munhak chakp'um yŏngu* (Studies in Korean accounts of travels), ed. Ch'oe Kanghyŏn. Kukhak charyowŏn, 1996.

Yu Minyŏng. "Hanguk inhyŏnggŭk ŭi yurae" (The origins of Korean puppet plays). *Yesul nonmunjip* 14 (1975):268–273.

Yu Sŏngjun. *"Chŏn Tangsi* sojae Sillain si" (Poetry written by Silla nationals in *Complete T'ang Poems*). *Hanguk hanmunhak yŏngu* 3–4 (1979):101–119.

Yu Yongdae. *Sim Ch'ŏng chŏn yŏngu* (Study of the *Tale of Sim Ch'ŏng*). Munhak akademi, 1989.

Yu Yŏnsŏk. "An Chowan (hwan) ŭi yubae kasa yŏngu" (Study of exile *kasa* by An Chohwan). In *Hanguk kihaeng munhak chakp'um yŏngu* (Studies in Korean accounts of travels), ed. Ch'oe Kanghyŏn. Kukhak charyowŏn, 1996.

Yun Chaemin. *Chosŏn hugi chunginch'ŭng hanmunhak ŭi yŏngu* (Studies in literature in Chinese by the middle people class in late Chosŏn). Koryŏ taehakkyo Minjok munhwa yŏnguwŏn, 1999.

Yun Kwangbong. *Hanguk yuhŭisi yŏngu* (Study of Korean entertainment poetry). Iu ch'ulp'ansa, 1985.

Yun Sŏndo. *Kosan yugo* (Literary remains of Yun Sŏndo) (*YMC* 3).

Yun Sŏnggŭn. "Yuhakcha ŭi sosŏl paegyŏk" (Confucianists' denunciation of fiction). *Ŏmunhak* 25 (1971):43–76.

Yun Tongju. *Hanŭl kwa param kwa pyŏl kwa si* (Sky, wind, stars, and poetry), ed. Kwŏn Yŏngnin. In *Yun Tongju chŏnjip* (Collected works of Yun Tongju). vol. 1. Munhak sasangsa, 1995.

WESTERN SOURCES

Andresen, Martha. "Ripeness is All: Sententiae and Commonplace in King Lear." In *Some Facets of King Lear: Essays in Prismatic Criticism*, ed. Rosalie Colie and F. T. Flahiff. Toronto: University of Toronto Press, 1974.

Anon. *Histoire de Dame Pak*, trans. Mark Orange. Paris: Asiatheque, 1982.

Anthony of Taizé, Brother. "Hwang Ji-u." *Korean Literature Today* 4:3 (1999):33–39.

Arendt, Hannah. *The Human Condition*. Chicago: University of Chicago Press, 1958.

Bakhtin, M. M. *The Dialogic Imagination*, ed. Michael Holquist. Austin: University of Texas Press, 1981.

——. *Rabelais and His World*, trans. Helene Isowolsky. Bloomington: Indiana University Press, 1984.

Barthes, Roland. *Le degré zéro de l'écriture*. Paris: Gallimard, 1953.

Bartky, Sandra Lee. *Femininity and Domination: Studies in the Phenomenology of Oppression*. New York: Routledge, 1990.

Bercovitch, Sacvan, and Myra Jehlen, eds. *Ideology and Classic American Literature*. Cambridge: Cambridge University Press, 1986.

Bigsby, C. W. E. *Dada and Surrealism*. London: Methuen, 1972.

Bodde, Derk. *Festivals in Classical China*. Princeton: Princeton University Press, 1975.

Boin-Webb, Sara. trans. *Śūraṃgamasamādhisūtra*. London: Curzon Press, 1998.

Borgen, Robert. *Sugawara no Michizane and the Early Heian Court*. Cambridge, Mass.: Harvard University Press, 1986.

Bowra, Maurice. *Heroic Poetry*. London: Macmillan, 1961.

——. *Poetry and Politics 1900–1960*. Cambridge: Cambridge University Press, 1966.

Buzo, Adrian, and Tony Prince. *Kyunyo-jon: The Life, Times and Songs of a Tenth Century Korean Monk*. University of Sydney East Asian Series 6. Broadway, NSW: Wild Peony, 1993.

Chan, Wing-tsit. *Source Book in Chinese Philosophy*. Princeton: Princeton University Press, 1963.

Chang, Suk-Jin. *Korean*. Amsterdam: Benjamins, 1996.

Chatterjee, Partha. *The Nation and Its Fragments*. Princeton: Princeton University Press, 1993.

Chew, Samuel C. *The Virtues Reconciled*. Toronto: University of Toronto Press, 1947.

——. ed. *Childe Harold's Pilgrimage*. New York: Odyssey Press, 1936.

Cho Chŏngnae. *Playing with Fire*, trans. Chun Kyung-ja. Ithaca: Cornell East Asia Program, 1997.

Cho, Choon-hak. *A Study of Korean Pragmatics: Deixis and Politeness*. Seoul: Hanshin, 1982.

Cho, Dong-il. *Korean Literature in Cultural Context and Comparative Perspective*. Seoul: Jipmoondang, 1997.

Cho, Oh-kon. *Traditional Korean Theatre*. Berkeley: Asian Humanities Press, 1988.

Ch'oe, Hae-ch'un, trans. *Sandae: Korea's Intangible Cultural Asset No. 2*. Pusan: Jeail Publishing Company, 1988.

Ch'oe Inhun. *The Square*, trans. Kevin O'Rourke. Devon: Spindlewood, 1985.

Ch'oe Inhun. *A Grey Man*, trans. Kyung-ja Chun. Seoul: Si-sa-young-o-sa, 1988.

Ch'oe Mansik. *Peace Under Heaven*, trans. Chun Kyung-ja. Armonk, N.Y.: M. E. Sharpe, 1993.

Ch'oe, Yŏng-ho. *The Civil Examination and the Social Structure in Early Yi Dynasty Korea 1392–1600*. Seoul: Korea Research Center, 1987.

Choi, Won-shik (Ch'oe Wŏnsik). "Rethinking Korean Literary Modernity." *KJ* 35:4 (1995):5–25.

"Seoul, Tokyo, New York: Modern Korean Literature Seen Through Yi Sang's 'Lost Flowers.'" *KJ* 39:4 (2001):118–143.

Chŏng Chi yong. *Distant Valleys: Poems of Chong Chi-yong*, trans. Daniel A. Kister. Berkeley: Asian Humanities Press, 1994.

Chŏng, Hyŏnjong. *Day-Shine: Poems by Chong Hyon-jong*, trans. Wolhee Choe and Peter Fusco. Ithaca: Cornell East Asia Program, 1998.

Chou, Ying-hsiung. "Lord, Do Not Cross the River: Literature as a Mediating Process." In *China and the West: Comparative Literature Studies*, ed. William Tay et al. Hong Kong: Chinese University Press, 1980.

Chung, Chong-wha. *Modern Korean Literature: An Anthology 1908–65*. London: Kegan Paul International, 1995.

——— ed. *Korean Classical Literature*. London: Kegan Paul International, 1989.

Chung, Jae-young (Chŏng Chaeyŏng). "Sŏkdokkugyŏl in the Koryŏ Period." *SJK* 12 (1999):29–45.

Chung, Ok Young Kim, trans. *Encounter: A Novel of Nineteenth-Century Korea*. Berkeley: University of California Press, 1992.

Clippinger, M. E. "Korean and Dravidian: Lexical Evidence for an Old Theory." *Korean Studies* 8 (1984):1–57.

Conze, Edward. *Buddhist Wisdom Books Containing the Diamond Sutra and Heart Sutra*. London: Allen & Unwin, 1958.

Davie, Donald. *Ezra Pound: Poet as Sculptor*. New York: Oxford University Press, 1964.

Eckert, Carter J. et al. *Korea Old and New: A History*. Seoul: Ilchogak, 1990.

Eliot, T. S. *Selected Essays 1917–1932*. New York: Harcourt, Brace, 1932.

Ellman, Richard. *The New Oxford Book of English Verse*. New York: Oxford University Press, 1976.

Epstein, Stephen J. "Elusive Narrators in Hwang Sun-wŏn." *KS* 19 (1995):104–111.

——— "The Meaning of Meaningless in Kim Sŭng-ok's 'Seoul: Winter 1964.'" *KJ* 37:1 (1997):98–107.

Evon, Gregory N. "Eroticism and Buddhism in Han Yongun's *Your Silence*." *KS* 24 (2000):25–52.

Fowler, Alastair. *Kinds of Literature: An Introduction to the Theory of Genres and Modes*. Cambridge, Mass.: Harvard University Press, 1982.

Fowlie, Wallace. *Age of Surrealism*. Bloomington: Indiana University Press, 1960.

Frankel, Hans H. "The Plum Tree in Chinese Poetry." *Asiatische Studien* 6 (1952):88–115.

Frodsham, J. D. *The Murmuring Stream: The Life and Works of Chinese Nature Poet Hsieh Ling-yun, Duke of K'ang-lo*. 2 vols. Kuala Lumpur: University of Malaya Press, 1967.

Frost, Robert. *Complete Poems of Robert Frost*. New York: Holt, 1962.

Fulton, Bruce and Ju-chan Fulton, trans. *Words of Farewell: Stories by Korean Women Writers*. Seattle: Seal Press, 1989.

——— *Wayfarer: New Fiction by Korean Women*. Seattle: Women in Translation, 1997.

Fusek, Lois. "The Kao-t'ang Fu." *Monumenta Serica* 30 (1972–1973):412–423.

Gadamer, Hans-Georg. *Wahrheit und Methode: Grundzüge einer philosophischen Hermeneutik.* Tübingen: Mohr, 1965.

Graham, A. C. *Poems from the Late T'ang.* Harmondsworth: Penguin, 1965.

Haboush, JaHyun Kim, trans. *The Memoirs of Lady Hyegyŏng: The Autobiographical Writings of a Crown Princess of Eighteenth-Century Korea.* Berkeley: University of California Press, 1996.

Hambis, Louis. "Notes sur l'histoire de Corée a l'époque mongole." *T'oung Pao* 45 (1957):178–193.

Hawkes, David. *Ch'u Tz'u: The Songs of the South.* Oxford: Clarendon, 1959.

Heidegger, Martin. *Poetry, Language, Thought,* trans. Albert Hofstadter. New York: Harper & Row, 1971.

Hightower, James R. *The Poetry of T'ao Ch'ien.* Oxford: Clarendon, 1970.

"Han Yü as Humorist." *Harvard Journal of Asiatic Studies* 44 (1984):5–27.

Hŏ Nansŏrhŏn. *Visions of a Phoenix: The Poems of Hŏ Nansŏrhŏn,* trans. Yanghi Choe-Wall. Ithaca: Cornell East Asia Program, 2001.

Holzman, Donald. "Literary Criticism in China in the Early Third Century AD." *Asiatische Studien* 28 (1974):113–149.

Housman, A. E. *The Name and Nature of Poetry.* New York: Macmillan, 1933.

Hoyt, James, trans. *Songs of the Dragons Flying to Heaven: A Korean Epic.* Seoul: Korean National Commission for Unesco and Royal Asiatic Society, Korea Branch, 1971.

Hulbert, H. B. *A Comparative Grammar of the Korean Language and the Dravidian Languages of India.* Seoul: Methodist Publishing House, 1905.

Hurvitz, Leon. *Scripture of the Lotus Blossom of the Fine Dharma.* New York: Columbia University Press, 1976.

Hwang, Juck-Ryoon. "Role of Sociolinguistics in Foreign Language Education with Reference to Korean and English Terms of Address and Levels of Deference." Ph.D. dissertation, University of Texas at Austin, 1975.

Hwang, Sŏgyŏng. *The Shadow of Arms,* trans. Kyung-ja Chun. Ithaca: Cornell East Asia Program, 1994.

Hwang, Sunwŏn. *The Stars and Other Korean Stories,* trans. Edward W. Poitras. Hong Kong: Heinemann Asia, 1980.

The Moving Castle, trans. Bruce Fulton and Ju-chan Fulton. Seoul: Si-sa-yong-o-sa, 1985.

Sunlight, Moonlight, trans. Sŏl Sun-bong. Seoul: Si-sa-yong-o-sa, 1985.

Shadows of a Sound: Stories by Hwang Sun-wŏn, trans. J. Martin Holman. San Francisco: Mercury House, 1990.

The Descendants of Cain, trans. Ji-moon Suh and Julie Pickering, Armonk, N.Y.: M. E. Sharpe, 1997.

Hwang, Tonggyu. *Wind Burial: Poetry by Tong-gyu Hwang,* trans. Grace Loving Gibson and Hwang Tong-gyu. Laurinburg, N.C.: St. Andrews Press, 1990.

Strong Winds at Mishi Pass, trans. Seong-Kon Kim and Dennis Maloney. Buffalo: White Pine Press, 2001.

Jameson, Fredric. *The Political Unconscious: Narrative as a Socially Symbolic Act.* Ithaca: Cornell University Press, 1981.

Kang, Sinjae. *The Waves*, trans. Tina L. Sallee. London: Kegan Paul International, 1989.

The Dandelion on the Imjin River, trans. Sŏl Sun-bong. Seoul: Dongsuh munhaksa, 1990.

Kang, Sŏkkyŏng. *The Valley Nearby*, trans. Choi Kyong-do. Portsmouth, N.H.: Heinemann, 1997.

Kang, Young-zu. "Hong Myŏng-hŭi: Korea's Finest Historical Novelist." *KJ* 39:4 (1999):36–60.

Karlgren, Bernhard. *The Book of Odes*. Stockholm: Museum of Far Eastern Antiquities, 1960.

Kenner, Hugh. *A Homemade World: The American Modernist Writers*. New York: Knopf, 1975.

Kermode, Frank. *History and Value*. Oxford: Clarendon, 1989.

Kim, Chewon. "Han Dynasty Mythology and the Korean Legend of Tangun." *Archives of Chinese Art Society of America* 3 (1948–1949):43–48.

Kim, Chi Ha. *Cry of the People and Other Poems*. Hayama: Autumn Press, 1974.

The Middle Hour: Selected Poems of Kim Chi Ha, trans. David R. McCann. Standfordville, N.Y.: Human Rights, 1980.

Heart's Agony: Selected Poems of Chiha Kim, trans. Won-Chung Kim and James Han. Fredonia, N.Y.: White Pine Press, 1995.

Kim, Chong Sun, and Shelley Killen. *The Gold-Crowned Jesus and Other Writings*. Maryknoll, N.Y.: Orbis Books, 1978.

Kim, Chong-un. "Images of Man in Postwar Korean Fiction." *KS* 2 (1978):1–27.

Kim, Chong-un, and Bruce Fulton, trans. *A Ready-Made Life: Early Masters of Modern Korean Fiction*. Honolulu: University of Hawaii Press, 1998.

Kim, Ch'unsu. *The Snow Falling on Chagall's Village: Selected Poems by Kim Ch'unsu*, trans. Jong Gil Kim. Ithaca: Cornell East Asia Program, 1998.

Kim, Hŭnggyu. *Understanding Korean Literature*, trans. Robet J. Feuser. Armonk, N.Y.: M. E. Sharpe, 1997.

Kim, Jong Gil. "T. S. Eliot's Influence on Modern Korean Poetry." *Literature East and West* 13 (1969):359–376.

trans. *Slow Chrysanthemums: Classical Korean Poems in Chinese*. London: Anvil Press, 1987.

Kim, Kichung. *An Introduction to Classical Korean Literature: From Hyangga to P'ansori*. Armonk, N.Y.: M. E. Sharpe, 1996.

Kim, Suyŏng. *Variations: Three Korean Poets*, trans. Brother Anthony of Taizé and Young-Moo Kim. Ithaca: Cornell East Asia Program, 2001.

Kim, T'aegil. "A Study of Values as Presented in Contemporary Korean Novels." *KJ* 21:5 (1981):4–20.

Kim, Tongni. *The Cross of Shaphan*, trans. Sol Sun-bong. Seoul: Si-sa-yong-o-sa, 1983.

The Shaman Sorceress, trans. Hyun-song Shin and Eugene Chung. London: Kegan Paul International, 1989.

Kim, Uch'ang. "Sorrow and Stillness: A View of Modern Korean Poetry." *Literature East and West* 13 (1969):141–166.

Bibliography

"The Agony of Cultural Construction: Politics and Culture in Modern Korea." In *State and Society in Contemporary Korea*, ed. Hagen Koo. Ithaca: Cornell University Press, 1993.

"Extravagance and Authenticity: Romantic Love and the Self in Early Modern Korean Literature." *KJ* 39:4 (1999):61–89.

trans. *Selected Poems of Pak Mogwol*. Berkeley: Asian Humanities Press, 1990.

Kim, Yoon-shik (Kim Yunsik). *Understanding Modern Korean Literature*, trans. Jang Gyung-ryul. Seoul: Jipmoondang, 1998.

Kim, Yung-Hee. "From Subservience to Autonomy: Kim Wŏnju's 'Awakening.'" *KS* 21 (1997):1–30.

"A Critique on Traditional Korean Family Institutions: Kim Wŏnju's 'Death of a Girl.'" *KS* 23 (1999):24–33; translation of the story on 34–42.

Kim-Cho, Sek Yen, *The Korean Alphabet of 1446*. Seoul: Asia Culture Press, and Amherst, N.Y.: Humanity Books, 2002.

Kim-Renaud, Young-Key, ed. *The Korean Alphabet: Its History and Structure*. Honolulu: University of Hawaii Press, 1997.

Ko, Ŭn. *The Sound of My Waves: Selected Poems by Ko Ŭn*, trans. Brother Anthony of Taizé and Young-Moo Kim. Ithaca: Cornell East Asia Program, 1993.

Kolb, Harold H., Jr. "Defining the Canon." In *Redefining American Literary History*, ed. A. La Vonne Brown Ruoff and Jerry W. Ward, Jr. New York: Modern Language Association, 1990.

Konishi, Jin'ichi. *A History of Japanese Literature*, trans. Aileen Gatten and Nicholas Teele; ed. Earl Miner, vols. 1–2. Princeton: Princeton University Press, 1984–1986.

Korean Poets Association, ed. *Poems from Modern Korea*. Seoul: Korean Poets Association, 1970.

Kwŏn, Youngmin (Kwŏn Yŏngmin). "Literature and Art in North Korea: Theory and Policy." *KJ* 31:2 (1991):56–70

"The Logic and Practice of Literary Nationalism." *KS* 16 (1992):61–81.

"Enlightenment Period Fiction and the Formation of a Writer Class." *KS* 18 (1994):23–29.

Lash, Scott. *The Sociology of Postmodernism*. London: Routledge, 1990.

Lau, D. C. *Tao Te Ching*. Harmondsworth: Penguin, 1963.

Mencius. Harmondsworth: Penguin, 1970.

Ledyard, Gari. "The Korean Language Reform of 1446: The Origin, Background, and Early History of the Korean Alphabet." Ph.D. dissertation, University of California, Berkeley, 1966. Published as *The Korean Language Reform of 1446*. Seoul: Singu munhwasa, 1998.

"Korean Travelers in China over Four Hundred Years 1488–1887." *Occasional Papers on Korea* 2 (1974):1–42.

Lee, Ann. "Yi Kwangsu and Korean Literature: The Novel *Mujŏng* (1917)." *JKS* 8 (1992):81–137.

"The Kwangju Uprising and Poetry of Ko Chong-hui, a Writer of South Cholla." *Bulletin of Concerned Asian Scholars* 29:4 (1997):23–32.

Lee, Ann Sung-hi. "Korean Peasant Literature during the Japanese Colonial Occupation: The Novel *Kohyang* [Hometown] by Yi Ki-yŏng." *SJK* 9 (1996):41–52.

Lee, Cheong-Ho. *Haesŏl yŏkchu Hunmin chŏngŭm. Translated and Annotated Hunmin Chŏngŭm.* Seoul: Korean Library Science Research Institute, 1972.

Lee, Hyun Bok. *Korean Grammar.* Oxford: Oxford University Press, 1989.

Lee, Ki-baik. *A New History of Korea,* trans. Edward W. Wagner with Edward J. Shultz. Cambridge, Mass.: Harvard University Press, 1984.

Lee, Kwang-rin. "The Rise of Nationalism in Korea." *KS* 10 (1986):1–12.

"Newspaper Publication in the Late Yi Dynasty." *KS* 12 (1988):62–72.

Lee, Peter H. *Lives of Eminent Korean Monks.* Cambridge, Mass.: Harvard University Press, 1969.

Songs of Flying Dragons: A Critical Reading. Cambridge, Mass.: Harvard University Press, 1975.

Celebration of Continuity: Themes in Classic East Asian Poetry. Cambridge, Mass.: Harvard University Press, 1979.

A Korean Storyteller's Miscellany. Princeton: Princeton University Press, 1989.

The Record of the Black Dragon Year. Seoul: Korea University Institute of Korean Culture, and Honolulu: Center for Korean Studies, University of Hawaii, 2000.

ed. *The Silence of Love: Twentieth-Century Korean Poetry.* Honolulu: University Press of Hawaii, 1980.

ed. *Anthology of Korean Literature: From Early Times to the Nineteenth Century.* Rev. edn. Honolulu: University of Hawaii Press, 1990.

Modern Korean Literature: An Anthology. Honolulu: University of Hawaii Press, 1990.

Sourcebook of Korean Civilization. 2 vols. New York: Columbia University Press, 1993–1996.

Sources of Korean Tradition. 2 vols. New York: Columbia University Press, 1997–2000.

Myths of Korea. Somerset, N.J.: Jimoondang International, 2000.

The Columbia Anthology of Traditional Korean Poetry. New York: Columbia University Press, 2002.

trans. *Pine River and Lone Peak: An Anthology of Three Chosŏn Dynasty Poets.* Honolulu: University of Hawaii Press, 1991.

Lee, Sang-taik (Yi Sangt'aek). "Myŏngju Bowŏl-bing (*Myŏngju powŏlbing*)." *SJK* 6 (1993):35–74.

Lee, Sung-il, trans. *The Wind and the Waves: Four Modern Korean Poets.* Berkeley: Asian Humanities Press, 1989.

The Moonlit Pond. Seattle: Copper Canyon Press, 1998.

Lee, Woo-kyu. "Honorifics and Politeness in Korean." Ph.D. dissertation, University of Wisconsin, Madison, 1991.

Legge, James. *The Chinese Classics.* 5 vols. Hong Kong: Hong Kong University Press, 1960.

Levin, Harry. "The Title as a Literary Genre." *Modern Language Review* 72 (1977):xxiii–xxvi.

Lin, Tai-yi, trans. *Flowers in the Mirror.* Berkeley: University of California Press, 1965.

Liu, James J. Y. *Chinese Theories of Literature*. Chicago: University of Chicago Press, 1975.

Liu, Wu-chi, and Irving Yucheng Lo, eds. *Sunflower Splendor: Three Thousand Years of Chinese Poetry*. Garden City: Doubleday, 1975.

Lu, Sheldon Hsiao-peng. *From Historicity to Fictionality: The Chinese Poetics of Narrative*. Stanford: Stanford University Press, 1994.

Mallarmé, Stéphane. *Oeuvres complètes*. Paris: Gallimard, 1945.

McCann, David R. *Form and Freedom in Korean Poetry*. Leiden: E. J. Brill: 1988.

———. "The Meaning and Significance of Sowŏl's 'Azaleas.'" *JKS* 6 (1988–1989):211–228.

———. *Early Korean Literature: Selections and Introductions*. New York: Columbia University Press, 2000.

McCullough, Helen C., trans. *Kokin Wakashū*. Stanford: Stanford University Press, 1985.

MacIntyre, F. *French Symbolist Poetry*. Berkeley: University of California Press, 1961.

Martin, Samuel E. "Lexical Evidence Relating Korean to Japanese." *Language* 42 (1966):185–251.

———. *A Reference Grammar of Korean*. Rutland: Tuttle, 1992.

Mather, Richard B. *Shih-shuo Hsin-yü: A New Account of Tales of the World*. Minneapolis: University of Minnesota Press, 1976.

Matthews, J. H. *Surrealist Poetry in France*. Syracuse: University of Syracuse Press, 1969.

Miller, Edwin H. *The Professional Writer in Elizabethan England*. Cambridge, Mass.: Harvard University Press, 1959.

Miller, Roy A. *The Japanese Language*. Chicago: University of Chicago Press, 1967.

Miner, Earl. "The Collective and the Individual: Literary Practice and Its Social Implications." In *Principles of Classical Japanese Literature*, ed. Earl Miner. Princeton: Princeton University Press, 1985.

Miyazaki, Ichisada. *China's Examination Hell*, trans. Conrad Shirokauer. New Haven: Yale University Press, 1981.

Murayama, Shichiro. "The Malayo-Polynesian Component in the Japanese Language." *Journal of Japanese Studies* 2:2 (1976):413–436.

Myers, Brian. "Mother Russia: Soviet Characters in North Korean Fiction." *KS* 16 (1992):82–93.

———. *Han Sŏrya and North Korean Literature: The Failure of Socialist Realism in the DPRK*. Ithaca: Cornell East Asia Program, 1994.

Nelson, Sarah M. *The Archaeology of Korea*. Cambridge: Cambridge University Press, 1993.

Nemerov, Howard. *The Western Approaches*. Chicago: University of Chicago Press, 1975.

Nicholls, Peter. *Modernisms: A Literary Guide*. Berkeley: University of California Press, 1995.

Nienhauser, William H., Jr., ed. *Indiana Companion to Traditional Chinese Literature*. Bloomington: Indiana University Press, 1986.

Nylan, Michael. *The Five"Confucian" Classics.* New Haven: Yale University Press, 2001.

O, Yŏngsu. *The Good People*, trans. Marshall R. Pihl. Hong Kong: Heinemann, 1984.

Ohno, Susumu. *The Origin of the Japanese Language.* Tokyo: Kokusai bunka shinkōkai, 1970.

Olof, Allard M. "The Story of Prince Allakkuk: *Wŏrin Sŏkpo* vol. 8." *KJ* 23:1 (1983):13–20

O'Rourke, Kevin. "The Philosophy of Life of Cho Pyŏnghwa." *KS* 5 (1981):93–107.

The Book of Korean Shijo. Cambridge, Mass.: Harvard University Asia Center, 2002.

Otis, Brooks. *Ovid as an Epic Poet.* Cambridge: Cambridge University Press, 1966.

Owen, Stephen. *Readings in Chinese Literary Thought.* Cambridge, Mass.: Harvard University Press, 1992.

Paik, Nak-chung (Paek Nakch'ŏng). "The Poetry of Kim Su-yŏng: The Living Kim Su-yŏng." *KJ* 39:4 (1999):144–163.

Pak, Kyŏngni. *Land*, trans. Agnita Tennant. London: Kegan Paul International, 1996.

Pak, Wansŏ. *The Naked Tree*, trans. Yong-an Yu. Ithaca: Cornell East Asia Program, 1995.

My Very Last Possessions and Other Stories, trans. Kyung-ja Chun. Armonk, N.Y.: M. E. Sharpe, 1999.

A Sketch of the Fading Sun, trans. Hyun-jae Yee. Buffalo: White Pine Press, 1999.

Park, Chan E. "Playful Reconstruction of Gender in *P'ansori* Storytelling." *KS* 22 (1998):62–81.

Partridge, A. C. *The Language of Modern Poetry: Yeats, Eliot, Auden.* London: Deutsch, 1976.

Paxton, John. *Encyclopedia of Russian History: From the Christianization of Kiev to the Break-up of the USSR.* Santa Barbara: ABL-CLIO, 1993.

Perkins, David. *A History of Modern Poetry.* 2 vols. Cambridge, Mass.: Harvard University Press, 1976–1987.

ed. *Theoretical Issues in Literary History.* Cambridge, Mass.: Harvard University Press, 1991.

Pihl, Marshall R. "Engineers of the Human Soul: North Korean Literature Today." *KS* 1 (1977):63–110.

The Korean Singer of Tales. Cambridge, Mass.: Harvard University Press, 1994.

"Koryŏ Sŏn Buddhism and Korean Literature." *KS* 19 (1995):62–82.

Pihl, Marshall R., Bruce Fulton, and Ju-chan Fulton, trans. *Land of Exile: Contemporary Korean Fiction.* Armonk, N.Y: M. E. Sharpe, 1993.

Preminger, Alex, ed. *Enydepedia of Poetry and Poeties.* Princeton: Princeton University Press, 1965.

Preminger, Alex, and T. V. F. Brogan, eds. *The New Princeton Encyclopedia of Poetry and Poetics.* Princeton: Princeton University Press, 1993.

Ramstedt, G. J. *Studies in Korean Etymology.* Helsinki: Suomalis-Ugrilanen Seura, 1949.

Redfield, James. *Nature and Culture in the Iliad*. Chicago: University of Chicago Press, 1975.

Rilke, Rainer Maria. *Sämtliche Werke*, 7 vols. Wiesbaden: Insel, 1955–97.

The Notebooks of Malte Laurids Brigge, trans. Stephen Mitchell. New York: Vintage Books, 1985.

Letters to a Young Poet, trans. Stephen Mitchell. New York: Vintage Books, 1986.

Roberts, Moss, trans. *The Three Kingdoms: A Historical Novel, Attributed to Luo Guan-zhong*. Berkeley: University of California Press, and Peking: Foreign Language Press, 1991.

Rowe, Galen A. "The Adynaton as a Stylistic Device." *American Journal of Philology* 86 (1965):392–395.

Roy, David T., trans. *The Plum in the Golden Vase, or Chin P'ing Mei*. Princeton: Princeton University Press, 1991.

Rutt, Richard, trans. *The Bamboo Grove*. Berkeley: University of California Press, 1971.

"Traditional Korean Poetry Criticism." *Transactions of the Korea Branch of the Royal Asiatic Society* 47 (1972):105–143.

Rutt, Richard, and Kim Chong-un, trans. *Virtuous Women*. Seoul: Korean National Commission for Unesco, 1974.

Sallee, Hyun-jae Yee, trans. *The Snowy Road and Other Stories: An Anthology of Korean Fiction*. Fredonia, N.Y.: White Plain Press, 1993.

Saunders, J. W. *The Profession of English Letters*. London: Routledge, 1964.

Seo, Dae-seok (Sŏ Taesŏk). "The Theory of Heroic Novels." *SJK* 4 (1991):33–57.

Shapiro, Sidney, trans. *Outlaws of the Marsh*. 3 vols. Peking: Foreign Language Press, 1980.

Sheavyn, Phoebe. *The Literary Profession in the Elizabethan Age*. Manchester: Manchester University Press, 1967.

Shih, Vincent Y. *The Literary Mind and the Carving of Dragons*. Daibei: Zhonghua, 1970.

Shin, Gi-wook, and Michael Robinson, eds. *Colonial Modernity in Korea*. Cambridge, Mass.: Harvard University Asia Center, 1999.

Silverberg, Miriam. *Changing Song: The Marxist Manifestos of Nakano Shigeharu*. Princeton: Princeton University Press, 1990.

Sin, Kyŏngnim. *Variations: Three Korean Poets*, trans. Brother Anthony of Taizé and Young-Moo Kim. Ithaca: Cornell East Asia Program, 2001.

Skillend, W. E. *Kodae Sosŏl: A Survey of Korean Traditional Style Popular Novels*. London: School of Oriental and African Studies, University of London, 1968.

"The Texts of the First New Novel in Korean." *Asia Major* n.s. 14:1 (1968):21–62.

So, Carolyn. "Modern Korean Fiction under Colonialism: Structure and Dynamic in the Works of Four Women Writers." Ph.D. dissertation, UCLA, 1995.

Sŏ Chŏngju. *Selected Poems of Sŏ Chŏngju*, trans. David R. McCann. New York: Columbia University Press, 1989.

The Early Lyrics of Sŏ Chŏng Ju, trans. Brother Anthony of Taizé. London: Forrest Books, 1993.

Poems of a Wanderer: Midang So Chong-ju, trans. Kevin O'Rourke. Dublin: Daedalus, 1995.

Sohn, Ho-Min. *Linguistic Expeditions*. Seoul: Hanshin, 1986.

"Orthographic Divergence in South and North Korea: Toward a Unified Spelling System." In *The Korean Alphabet: Its History and Structure*, ed. Young-key Kim Renaud. Honolulu: University of Hawaii Press, 1997.

The Korean Language. Cambridge: Cambridge University Press, 1999.

Song, Ki Joong (Song Kijung). "The Writing Systems of Northeast Asia and the Origin of the Korean Alphabet, *Han'gŭl*." *SJK* 11 (1998):3–50.

Suh, Ji-moon, trans. *The Rainy Spell and Other Korean Stories*. Armonk, N.Y.: M. E. Sharpe, 1997.

Sung, Baeg-in. "The Present State and Problems of Genealogical Studies of Korean." *KJ* 37 (1997):166–225.

Swan, Nancy Lee. *Han Shu 22: Food and Money in Ancient China*. Princeton: Princeton University Press, 1950.

Sym, Myung-ho. *The Making of Modern Korean Poetry: Foreign Influences and Native Creativity*. Seoul: Seoul National University Press, 1982.

Tagore, Rabindranath. *Collected Poems and Plays of Rabindranath Tagore*. New York: Macmillan, 1965.

Takakusu, Junjirō. *Amitāyurdhayāna sūtra*. Sacred Books of the East 49. Oxford: Clarendon, 1894.

Thomas, Patrick M. "The Troubadour, the Shaman, and the Palace Lady: The Crosscurrents of Desire." *Comparative Criticism* 18 (Cambridge, 1996):127–153.

Vos, Frits. "Tales of the Extraordinary: An Inquiry into the Contents, Nature, and Authorship of the *Sui chŏn*." *KS* 5 (1981):1–25.

Waley, Arthur. *The Analects of Confucius*. London: Allen and Unwin, 1949.

The Book of Songs. London: Allen and Unwin, 1954.

Wasserman, Earl W. *The Subtler Language: Critical Readings of Neoclassical and Romantic Poems*. Baltimore: Johns Hopkins University Press, 1959.

Watson, Burton. *Ssu-ma Ch'ien: Grand Historian of China*. New York: Columbia University Press, 1958.

Chinese Lyricism: Shih Poetry from the Second to the Twelfth Century. New York: Columbia University Press, 1971.

trans. *Records of the Grand Historian of China. Translated from the "Shih chi" of Ssu-ma Ch'ien*. 2 vols. New York: Columbia University Press, 1961. Revised and enlarged edn. in 3 vols., Hong Kong and New York: *Renditions* – Columbia University Press, 1993.

Hsün Tzu: Basic Writings. New York: Columbia University Press, 1963.

Su Tung-p'o: Selections from a Sung Dynasty Poet. New York: Columbia University Press, 1965.

The Complete Works of Chuang Tzu. New York: Columbia University Press, 1968.

The "Tso chuan": Selections from China's Oldest Narrative History. New York: Columbia University Press, 1989.

Waugh, Patricia. *Metafiction: The Theory and Practice of Self-Conscious Fiction.* London: Methuen, 1984.

Wellek, René. *A History of Modern Criticism: The Late Nineteenth Century.* New Haven: Yale University Press, 1965.

The Attack on Literature and Other Essays. Chapel Hill: University of North Carolina Press, 1982.

Wells, Kenneth M., ed. *South Korea's Minjung Movement: The Culture and Politics of Dissidence.* Honolulu: University of Hawaii Press, 1995.

Whitman, J. B. "The Phonological Basis for the Comparison of Japanese and Korean." Ph.D. dissertation, Harvard University, 1985.

Wilhelm, Richard. *The I Ching or Book of Changes,* trans. Cary F. Baynes. 2 vols. New York: Pantheon Books, 1950.

Wimsatt, W. K., Jr., and Cleanth Brooks. *Literary Criticism: A Short History.* New York: Vintage Books, 1957.

Yeh, Michelle. "Metaphor and *Bi*: Western and Chinese Poetics." *Comparative Literature* 39:3 (1987):237–254.

Yi, Ch'ŏngjun. *The Prophet and Other Stories,* trans. Julie Pickering. Ithaca: Cornell East Asia Program, 1999.

Yi, Kyu-bo *Singing Like a Cricket, Hooting Like an Owl: Selected Poems of Yi Kyu-bo,* trans. Kevin O'Rourke. Ithaca: Cornell East Asia Program, 1995.

Yi Munyŏl. *The Poet,* trans. Chong-wha Chung and Brother Anthony of Taizé. London: Harvill Press, 1995.

Our Twisted Hero, trans. Kevin O'Rourke. New York: Hyperion East, 2001.

Yoon, Ho-byeong. "French Symbolism and Modern Korean Poetry: A Study of Poetic Language and Its Social Significance in Korea." Ph.D. dissertation, State University of New York at Stony Brook, 1986.

Yu, Anthony. *The Journey to the West.* 4 vols. Chicago: University of Chicago Press, 1977–1983.

Yu, Beongcheon. *Han Yong-un and Yi Kwang-su: Two Pioneers of Modern Korean Literature.* Detroit: Wayne State University Press, 1992.

Yu, Jong-ho (Yu Chongho). "Shin Tong-yŏp: A Retrospective Prophet." *KJ* 39:4 (1999):164–186.

Yu, Pauline. "Metaphor and Chinese Poetry." *CLEAR* 3:2 (1981):205–224.

Yun, Chang-sik. "The Structure of the *Kuun mong* (Dream of Nine Clouds)." *KS* 5 (1981):27–41.

Zhang, Longxi. *The Tao and the Logos: Literary Hermeneutics, East and West.* Durham: Duke University Press, 1992.

Suggestions for further reading

1. LANGUAGE, FORMS, PROSODY, AND THEMES

Kim, Hŭnggyu. "Language, Style, and Meter" and "Genres of Korean Literature."
In Hŭnggyu Kim, *Understanding Korean Literature*, trans. Robert J. Fouser.
Armonk, N.Y.: M. E. Sharpe, 1997. pp. 22–50, 51–78.

Ledyard, Gari K. *The Korean Language Reform of 1446*. Seoul: Singu munhwasa,
1998.

Song, Ki Joong (Song Kijung). "The Writing Systems of Northeast Asia and the
Origin of the Korean Alphabet, *Han'gŭl*." *SJK* 11 (1998):3–50.

2. FROM ORAL TO WRITTEN LITERATURE

Cho, Dong-il. "Oral Literature and Popular Consciousness." In *Korean Literature
in Cultural Context and Comparative Perspective*, pp. 31–47.

Kim, Hŭnggyu. "The Extent of Korean Literature." In Hŭnggyu Kim, *Understanding Korean Literature*, pp. 7–21.

3. HYANGGA

Kim, Kichung. "The Mystery and Loveliness of the Hyangga." In *An Introduction
to Classical Korean Literature: from Hyangga to P'ansori*. Armonk, N.Y.: M. E.
Sharpe, 1996, pp. 11–23.

McCann, David. "Ch'ŏyong and Manghae Temple: A Parable of Literary Negotiation." In *Early Korean Literature: Selections and Introductions*. New York:
Columbia University Press, 2000, pp. 101–122.

4. SILLA WRITINGS IN CHINESE

Chung, Jae-young (Chŏng Chaeyŏng). "Sŏkdokkugyŏl in the Koryŏ Period." *SJK*
12 (1999):29–45.

5. KORYŎ SONGS

Kim, Kichung. "The Incomparable Lyricism of Koryŏ Songs." *Introduction*,
pp. 25–47.

6. KORYŎ WRITINGS IN CHINESE

Lee, Peter H. "Prose Essays." In Lee, ed., *Anthology of Korean Literature: From Early Times to the Nineteenth Century*. Rev. edn. Honolulu; University of Hawaii Press, 1990, pp. 51–57.

trans. *Lives of Eminent Korean Monks*. Cambridge, Mass.: Harvard University Press, 1969.

Pihl, Marshall R. "Koryŏ Sŏn Buddhism and Korean Literature." *KS* 19 (1995):62–82.

Vos, Frits. "Tales of the Extraordinary: An Inquiry into the Contents, Nature, and Authorship of the *Sui chŏn*." *KS* 5 (1981):1–25.

Yi Kyu-bo. *Singing Like a Cricket, Hooting Like an Owl: Selected Poems of Yi Kyu-bo*, trans. Kevin O'Rourke. Ithaca: Cornell East Asia Program, 1995.

7. EARLY CHOSŎN EULOGIES

Hoyt, James, trans. *Songs of the Dragons Flying to Heaven: A Korean Epic*. Seoul: Korean National Commission for Unesco and Royal Asiatic Society, Korea Branch, 1971.

Olof, Allard M. "The Story of Prince Allakkuk: *Wŏrin Sŏkpo* vol. 8." *KJ* 23:1 (1983):13–20.

8. EARLY CHOSŎN *SIJO*

McCann, David. "The Sijo." In *Form and Freedom in Korean Poetry*. Leiden: E. J. Brill, 1988, pp. 1–23.

9. EARLY CHOSŎN *KASA*

McCann, David. "The Kasa." In *Form and Freedom in Korean Poetry*, pp. 24–46.

10. LATE CHOSŎN *SIJO*

Kim, Kichung. "Notes on Shijo." In *Introduction*, pp. 75–93.

Lee, Peter H., trans. *Pine River and Lone Peak: An Anthology of Three Chosŏn-Dynasty Poets*. Honolulu: University of Hawaii Press, 1991, pp. 66–86, 122–140, 143–168.

McCann, David. "Performance of Korean *Sijo* Verse: Negotiating Difference." In *Early Korean Literature*, pp. 139–158.

O'Rourke, Kevin, trans. *The Book of Korean Shijo*. Cambridge, Mass.: Harvard University Asia Center, 2002.

11. LATE CHOSŎN *KASA*

Kim, Kichung. "The Literature of Chosŏn Dynasty Women." In *Introduction*, pp. 122–139.

Lee, Peter H., trans. *Pine River and Lone Peak*, pp. 45–65, 88–121.

12. CHOSŎN POETRY IN CHINESE

Hŏ, Nansŏrhŏn. *Visions of a Phoenix: The Poems of Hŏ Nancŏrhŏn*, trans. Yanghi Choe-Wall. Ithaca: Cornell East Asia Program, 2001.

Lee, Sung-il, trans. *The Moonlit Pond*. Seattle: Copper Canyon Press, 1998.

13. CHOSŎN FICTION IN CHINESE

Kim, Kichung. "The Literature of Shirhak: Yŏnam, Pak Chi-wŏn." In *Introduction*, pp. 171–195.

Ledyard, Gari. "Korean Travelers in China over Four Hundred Years 1488–1887." *Occasional Papers on Korea* 2 (1974):1–42.

Lee, Peter H., "Biographies," "Early Yi Romance," and "Satirical Stories." In Lee, ed. *Anthology of Korean Literature*, pp. 22–36, 79–91, 212–236.

Skillend, W. E. "The Stork Decides a Case." In *Korean Classical Literature*, pp. 44–53.

14. CHOSŎN FICTION IN KOREAN

Anon. *Histoire de Dame Pak*, trans. Mark Orange. Paris: Asiatheque, 1982. *Histoire de Suk Hyang*, trans. Kim Su-chung.

Cho, Dong-il. "The Sublime in Korean Literature and the Tragic in Western Literature." In *Korean Literature in Cultural Context and Comparative Perspective*. Seoul: Jipmoondang, 1997, pp. 185–206.

Haboush, JaHyun Kim, trans. *The Memoirs of Lady Hyegyŏng: The Autobiographical Writings of a Crown Princess of Eighteenth-century Korea*. Berkeley: University of California Press, 1996.

Kim, Hŭnggyu. "The Trade in Literary Works." In Kim, *Understanding Korean Literature*, pp. 176–192.

Kim, Kichung. "The Literature of Chosŏn Dynasty Women," "Hŏ Kyun: *Hong Kiltong chŏn* and the Hanmun Lives," and "*Kuun mong* and 'Unyŏng chŏn.'" In *Introduction*, pp. 95–111, 141–157, 159–170.

Kim, Manjung. *A Nine Cloud Dream*, trans. Richart Rutt. In Richard Rutt and Kim Chong-Un, trans., *Virtuous Women*. Seoul: Korean National Commission for Unesco, 1974.

Lee, Peter H. *The Record of the Black Dragon Year*. Seoul: Korea University Institute of Korean Culture, and Honolulu: Center for Korean Studies, University of Hawaii, 2000.

Lee, Sang-taik (Yi Sangt'aek). "Myŏngju Bowŏl-bing (*Myŏngju powŏlbing*)." *SJK* 6 (1993):35–74.

Seo, Dae-seok. "The Theory of Heroic Novels." *SJK* 4 (1991):33–57.

Skillend, W. E. *Kodae Sosŏl: A Survey of Korean Traditional Style Popular Novels*. London: School of Oriental and African Studies, University of London, 1968. trans. "The Story of Sim Chung." In *Korean Classical Literature*, pp. 114–155.

Yun, Chang-sik. "The Structure of the *Kuun mong* (Dream of Nine Clouds)." *KS* 5 (1981):27–41.

15. P'ANSORI

Anon. *The Song of a Faithful Wife*, trans. Richard Rutt. In *Virtuous Women*.
Cho, Dong–il. "Performance and Text of *P'ansori*." In *Korean Literature*, pp. 61–83.
Kim, Kichung. "Notes on P'ansori." In *Introduction*, pp. 197–208.
Park, Chan E. "Playful Reconstruction of Gender in *P'ansori* Storytelling." *KS* 22 (1998):62–81.
Pihl, Marshall R. *The Korean Singer of Tales*. Cambridge, Mass.: Harvard University Press, 1994.

16. FOLK DRAMA

Cho, Oh-kon. *Traditional Korean Theatre*. Berkeley: Asian Humanities Press, 1988. [To be used with caution.]
Ch'oe, Hae-ch'un, trans. *Sandae: Korea's Intangible Cultural Asset No. 2*. Pusan: Jeail Publishing Company, 1988.

17. LITERARY CRITICISM

Rutt, Richard. "Traditional Korean Poetry Criticism." *Transactions of the Korea Branch of the Royal Asiatic Society* 47 (1972):105–143.

18. EARLY TWENTIETH-CENTURY POETRY

Chŏng Chiyong. *Distant Valleys: Poems of Chong Chi-yong*, trans. Daniel A Kister. Berkeley: Asian Humanities Press, 1994.
Evon, Gregory N. "Eroticism and Buddhism in Han Yongun's *Your Silence*." *KS* 24 (2000):25–52.
McCann, David. "The Meaning and Significance of Sowŏl's 'Azaleas.'" *JKS* 6 (1988–1989):211–228.
Yu, Beongcheon. *Han Yong-un and Yi Kwang-su: Two Pioneers of Modern Korean Literature*. Detroit: Wayne State University Press, 1992, pp. 37–83, 161–177.

19. EARLY TWENTIETH-CENTURY FICTION BY MEN

Ch'ae Mansik. *Peace Under Heaven*, trans. Chun Kyung-ja. Armonk, N.Y.: M. E. Sharpe, 1993.
Cho, Dong-il. "The Two-Stage Transitional Period to Modern Literature," and "Traditional Forms of the Narrative and the Modern Novel." *Korean Literature*, pp. 103–117, 177–183.
Choi, Won-shik (Ch'oe Wŏnsik). "Rethinking Korean Literary Modernity." *KJ* 35:4 (1995):5–25.
"Seoul, Tokyo, New York: Modern Korean Literature Seen Through Yi Sang's 'Lost Flowers.'" *KJ* 39:4 (2001):118–143.

Kang, Young-zu. "Hong Myŏng-hŭi: Korea's Finest Historical Novelist." *KJ* 39:4 (1999):36–60.

Kim, Chong-un, and Bruce Fulton, trans. *A Ready-Made Life: Early Master of Modern Korean Fiction.* Honolulu: University of Hawaii Press, 1998.

Kim, Kichung. "*Ŭnsegye*: Art versus Ideology." *KS* 5 (1981):63–77.

"*Mujŏng*: An Introduction to Yi Kwangsu's Fiction." *KS* 6 (1982):25–39.

"The Question of the Betrayal." *KJ* 31:4 (1991):40–53.

Kim, Uchang. "The Narrative Tense in the Korean Novel: A Speculative Observation." *KS* 5 (1981):79–91.

"Extravagance and Authenticity: Romantic Love and the Self in Early Modern Korean Literature." *KJ* 39:4 (1999):61–89.

Kwŏn Youngmin (Kwŏn Yŏngmin). "The Logic and Practice of Literary Nationalism." *KS* 16 (1992):61–81.

Lee, Ann. "Yi Kwangsu and Korean Literature: The Novel *Mujŏng* (1917)." *JKS* 8 (1992):81–137.

Lee, Ann Sung-hi. "Korean Peasant Literature during the Japanese Colonial Occupation: The Novel *Kohyang* [Hometown] by Yi Ki-yŏng." *SJK* 9 (1996):41–52.

Shin, Michael D. "Interior Landscapes: Yi Kwangsu's *The Heartless* and the Origins of Modern Literature." In Gi-wook Shin and Michael Robinson, eds., *Colonial Modernity in Korea.* Cambridge, Mass.: Harvard University Asia Center, 1999, pp. 248–287.

Skillend, W. E. "The Texts of the First New Novel in Korean." *Asia Major* n.s. 14:1 (1968):21–62.

Yi Injik. "Tears of Blood" trans. W. E. Skillend. In *Korean Classical Literature*, pp. 159–221.

Yu, Beongcheon. *Han Yong-un and Yi Kwang-su*, pp. 87–160, 161–177.

20. EARLY TWENTIETH-CENTURY FICTION BY WOMEN

Kim, Yung-Hee. "From Subservience to Autonomy: Kim Wŏnju's 'Awakening.'" *KS* 21 (1997):1–30.

"A Critique on Traditional Korean Family Institutions: Kim Wŏnju's 'Death of a Girl.'" *KS* 23 (1999):24–42.

Suh, Ji-moon, trans. *The Rainy Spell and Other Korean Stories.* Armonk, N.Y.: M. E. Sharpe, 1997.

21. LATE TWENTIETH-CENTURY POETRY BY MEN

Chŏng, Hyŏnjong. *Day-Shine: Poems by Chong Hyon-jong*, trans. Wolhee Choe and Peter Fusco. Ithaca: Cornell East Asia Program, 1998.

Hwang, Tonggyu. *Wind Burial: Poetry by Tong-gyu Hwang*, trans. Grace Loving Gibson and Hwang Tong-gyu. Laurinburg, N.C.: St. Andrews Press, 1990.

Strong Winds at Mishi Pass, trans. Seong-Kon Kim and Dennis Maloney. Buffalo: White Pine Press, 2001.

Kim, Chiha. *The Middle Hour: Selected Poems of Kim Chi Ha*, trans. David R. McCann. Standfordville, N.Y.: Human Rights, 1980.
Heart's Agony: Selected Poems of Chiha Kim, trans. Kim Won-Chung and James Han. Fredonia, N.Y.: White Pine Press, 1995.
Kim, Ch'unsu. *The Snow Falling on Chagall's Village: Selected Poems by Kim Ch'unsu*, trans. Kim Jong Gil. Ithaca: Cornell East Asia Program, 1998.
Kim, Suyŏng. *Variations: Three Korean Poets*, trans. Brother Anthony of Taizé and Young-Moo Kim. Ithaca: Cornell East Asia Program, 2001.
Kim, Yoon-shik (Kim Yunsik). "On Poetry." In Kim, *Understanding Modern Korean Literature*, trans. Jang Gyung-ryul. Seoul: Jipmoondang, 1998, pp. 43–70.
Ko, Ŭn. *The Sound of My Waves: Selected Poems by Ko Ŭn*, trans. Brother Anthony of Taizé and Young-Moo Kim. Ithaca: Cornell East Asia Program, 1993.
O'Rourke, Kevin. "The Philosophy of Life of Cho Pyŏnghwa." *KS* 5 (1981):93–107.
Paik, Nak-chung (Paek Nakch'ŏng). "The Poetry of Kim Su-yŏng: The Living Kim Su-yŏng." *KJ* 39:4 (1999):144–163.
Sin, Kyŏngnim. *Variations*, trans. Brother Anthony of Taizé and Young-Moo Kim.
Sŏ, Chŏngju. *Selected Poems of Sŏ Chŏngju*, trans. David R. McCann. New York: Columbia University Press, 1989.
The Early Lyrics of Sŏ Chŏng Ju, trans. Brother Anthony of Taizé. London: Forrest Books, 1993.
Poems of A Wanderer: Midang So Chong-ju, trans. Kevin O'Rourke. Dublin: Daedalus, 1995.
Yu, Jong-ho (Yu Chongho). "Shin Tong-yŏp: A Retrospective Prophet." *KJ* 39:4 (1999):164–186.

22. LATE TWENTIETH-CENTURY POETRY BY WOMEN

Lee, Ann. "The Kwangju Uprising and Poetry by Ko Chong-hui, a Writer of South Cholla." *Bulletin of Concerned Asian Scholars* 29:4 (1997):23–32.

23. LATE TWENTIETH-CENTURY FICTION BY MEN

Cho Chŏngnae. *Playing with Fire*, trans. Chun Kyung-ja. Ithaca: Cornell East Asia Program, 1997.
Ch'oe, Inhun. *The Square*, trans. Kevin O'Rourke. Devon: Spindlewood, 1985.
A Grey Man, trans. Chun Kyung-ja. Seoul: Si-sa-young-o-sa, 1988.
Epstein, Stephen J. "The Meaning of Meaningless in Kim Sŭng-ok's 'Seoul: Winter 1964.'" *KJ* 37:1 (1997):98–107.
Hwang, Sŏgyŏng. *The Shadow of Arms*, trans. Chun Kyung-ja. Ithaca: Cornell East Asia Program, 1994.
Hwang, Sunwŏn. *The Stars and Other Korean Stories*, trans. Edward W. Poitras. Hong Kong: Heineman Asia, 1980.
The Moving Castle, trans. Bruce Fulton and Ju-chan Fulton. Seoul: Si-sa-yong-o-sa, 1985.

Sunlight, Moonlight, trans. Sŏl Sun-bong. Seoul: Si-sa-yong-o-sa, 1985.

Shadows of a Sound: Stories by Hwang Sun-Wŏn, ed. J. Martin Holman. San Francisco: Mercury House, 1990.

The Descendants of Cain, trans. Suh Ji-moon and Julie Pickering. Armonk, N.Y.: M. E. Sharpe, 1997.

Kim, Chong-un. "Images of Man in Postwar Korean Fiction." *KS* 2 (1978): 1–27.

Kim, T'ae-gil. "A Study of Values as Presented in Contemporary Korean Novels." *KJ* 21:5 (1981):4–20.

Kim, Tongni. *The Cross of Shaphan*, trans. Sŏl Sun-bong. Seoul: Si-sa-yong-o-sa, 1983.

The Shaman Sorceress, trans. Shin Hyun-song and Eugene Chung. London: Kegan Paul International, 1989.

Kim, Uchang. "The Agony of Cultural Construction: Politics and Culture in Modern Korea." In *State and Society in Contemporary Korea*, ed. Hagen Koo. Ithaca: Cornell University Press, 1993, pp. 163–195.

Kim, Yoon-shik (Kim Yunsik). "Historical Overview," "On [the] Novel," and "Issues of Korean Liteature." In Kim, *Understanding Modern Korean Literature*, pp. 3–40, 73–102, 105–172.

O, Yŏngsu. *The Good People*, trans. Marshall Pihl. Hong Kong: Heineman, 1984.

Yi, Ch'ŏngjun. *The Prophet and Other Stories*, trans. Julie Pickering. Ithaca: Cornell East Asia Program, 1999.

Yi, Munyŏl. *The Poet*, trans. Chong-wha Chung and Brother Anthony of Taizé. London: Harvill Press, 1995.

Our Twisted Hero, trans. Kevin O'Rourke. New York: Hyperion East, 2001.

24. LATE TWENTIETH-CENTURY FICTION BY WOMEN

Choi, Kyeong-Hee. "Neither Colonial Nor National: The Making of the 'New Woman' in Pak Wansŏ's 'Mother's Stake 1.'" In Shin and Robinson, eds., *Colonial Modernity in Korea*, pp. 221–247.

Fulton, Bruce, and Ju-chan, Fulton, trans. *Words of Farewell: Stories by Korean Women Writers*. Seattle: Seal Press, 1989.

Wayfarer: New Fiction by Korean Women. Seattle: Women in Translation, 1997.

Kang, Sinjae. *The Waves*, trans. Tina L. Sallee. London: Kegan Paul International, 1989.

The Dandelion on the Imjin River, trans. Sŏl Sun-bong. Seoul: Dongsuh munhaksa, 1990.

Kang, Sŏkkyŏng. *The Valley Nearby*, trans. Choi Kyong-do. Portsmouth, N.H.: Heineman, 1997.

Pak, Kyŏngni. *Land*, trans. Agnita Tennant. London: Kegan Paul International, 1996.

Pak, Wansŏ. *A Sketch of the Fading Sun*, trans. Hyun-jae Yee Sallee. Buffalo: White Pine Press, 1993.

The Naked Tree, trans. Yu Yong-nan. Ithaca: Cornell East Asia Program, 1995.
My Very Last Possessions and Other Stories, trans. Chun Kyung-ja. Armonk, N.Y.:
M. E. Sharpe, 1999.

25. LITERATURE OF NORTH KOREA

Kwŏn, Youngmin (Kwŏn, Yŏngmin). "Literature and Art in North Korea: Theory
and Policy." *KJ* 31:2 (1991):56–70.
Myers, Brian. "Mother Russia: Soviet Characters in North Korean Fiction." *KS* 16
(1992):82–93.
*Han Sŏrya and North Korean Literature: The Failure of Socialist Realism in the
DPRK*. Ithaca: Cornell East Asia Program, 1994.
Pihl, Marshall R. "Engineers of the Human Soul: North Korean Literature Today."
KS 1 (1977):63–110.

Index